Controversial Issues in Adventure Programming

Bruce Martin and Mark Wagstaff

EDITORS

Human Kinetics

Library of Congress Cataloging-in-Publication Data

Controversial issues in adventure programming / Bruce Martin and Mark Wagstaff, editors.

   p. cm.

Includes bibliographical references.

  ISBN 978-1-4504-1091-5 (hardcover) -- ISBN 1-4504-1091-X (hardcover) 1. Adventure education. I. Martin, Bruce, 1969- II. Wagstaff, Mark, Dr.

  LC1038.C66 2012

  371.3'84--dc23

                     2011048021

ISBN-10: 1-4504-1091-X (print)

ISBN-13: 978-1-4504-1091-5 (print)

The web addresses cited in this text were current as of February 2012, unless otherwise noted.

Acquisitions Editor: Gayle Kassing, PhD; **Developmental Editor:** Ray Vallese; **Assistant Editor:** Derek Campbell; **Copyeditor:** Amanda M. Eastin-Allen; **Permissions Manager:** Martha Gullo; **Graphic Designer:** Nancy Rasmus; **Graphic Artist:** Kathleen Boudreau-Fuoss; **Cover Designer:** Keith Blomberg; **Photographer (cover):** © Robert Postma/First Light/age fotostock; **Photographer (interior):** Courtesy of Mark Wagstaff (pp. 3, 17, 29, 197, 273, and 317 [bottom]); © Greg Epperson/fotolia.com (p. 47); © tiero - Fotolia.com (p. 63); courtesy of the American Motorcyclist Association (p. 79); © Julien Leblay/fotolia.com (p. 95); © iStockphoto/Mark Rose (p. 111); © Photodisc/Getty Images (p. 127); © Human Kinetics (p. 145); courtesy of Steve Ahrens (p. 149); courtesy of Alaska Resources Library and Information Services (ARLIS) (p. 150); courtesy of Scott Eggers (p. 151); © Joggie Botma/fotolia.com (p. 165); © Oleg Kozlov/fotolia.com (p. 183); © iStockphoto/Galyna Andrushko (p. 211); © Studioli - Fotolia.com (p. 227); © iStockphoto/Robert Churchill (p. 241); courtesy of Ron Berger, photo by Ken Lindsay (p. 255); © Monkey Business - Fotolia.com (p. 287); © Maxim Petrichuk - Fotolia.com (p. 301); courtesy of Bruce Martin (p. 317 [top]); **Photo Asset Manager:** Laura Fitch; **Visual Production Assistant:** Joyce Brumfield; **Photo Production Manager:** Jason Allen; **Art Manager:** Kelly Hendren; **Associate Art Manager:** Alan L. Wilborn; **Illustrations:** © Human Kinetics, unless otherwise noted; **Printer:** Sheridan Books

Printed in the United States of America   10 9 8 7 6 5 4 3 2 1

The paper in this book is certified under a sustainable forestry program.

Human Kinetics

Website: www.HumanKinetics.com

United States: Human Kinetics
P.O. Box 5076
Champaign, IL 61825-5076
800-747-4457
e-mail: humank@hkusa.com

Canada: Human Kinetics
475 Devonshire Road Unit 100
Windsor, ON N8Y 2L5
800-465-7301 (in Canada only)
e-mail: info@hkcanada.com

Europe: Human Kinetics
107 Bradford Road
Stanningley
Leeds LS28 6AT, United Kingdom
+44 (0) 113 255 5665
e-mail: hk@hkeurope.com

Australia: Human Kinetics
57A Price Avenue
Lower Mitcham, South Australia 5062
08 8372 0999
e-mail: info@hkaustralia.com

New Zealand: Human Kinetics
P.O. Box 80
Torrens Park, South Australia 5062
0800 222 062
e-mail: info@hknewzealand.com

E5462

Contents

Part II Contemporary and Emerging Issues in Adventure Programming

Preface

More than 10 years have passed since the publication of the last text devoted to examining controversial issues in the field of adventure programming. The last such book, *Controversial Issues in Adventure Education: A Critical Examination* (Wurdinger and Potter, 1999), has been a valuable resource to teachers, students, and practitioners in the field. However, much has changed within the industry and around the world since its publication.

Terrorism has emerged as a primary threat to global stability and security. America and its allies have embarked on prolonged wars in Afghanistan and Iraq in response to terrorist threats during this period. China, India, Brazil, and other developing countries have emerged as significant economic competitors to the United States and Western Europe. Global climate change has been recognized as a significant threat to global stability and security. Nations around the world have experienced severe economic turmoil due to the recession that began in 2008. The national treasury of the United States has been depleted during the past 10 years, and the nation now faces historic budget deficits and soaring national debt. Europe currently faces dire economic challenges due to the potential for national defaults in Greece, Italy, Spain, and Portugal. An epidemic of obesity and related health concerns continues to grow in the United States. Illegal immigration has continued to exert political, economic, and environmental stresses on the United States, nations within the European Union, and other developed nations around the world. Technological developments have continued to revolutionize the way that humans live and interact, and new terms such as Google, Twitter, and Facebook have entered the English lexicon.

The field of adventure programming has experienced a number of changes and developments during this time as well, many related to broader societal changes and many related to the natural maturation of the field. The body of knowledge on which the industry is based has continued to expand as scholars and practitioners work to promote evidence-based practice within the field. Professional standards and mechanisms for regulating practice within the industry have continued to evolve during the past decade. The outdoor industry has become more involved in education reform through the growth of organizations and initiatives such as Expeditionary Learning in the United States, Learning Outside the Classroom in Great Britain, and other alternatives to traditional schooling around the world. The economic turmoil of recent years has diminished enrollments in summer camps, wilderness therapy programs, and traditional wilderness programs such as Outward Bound and the National Outdoor Leadership School. Changing rules and regulations related to use of parks and protected areas have influenced the accessibility of public lands and waterways for adventure programming. The development of new instructional technologies has led to the creation of online outdoor education programs and curricula.

These broad political, economic, social, cultural, technological, and environmental changes as well as changes within the adventure programming industry itself call for a critical reassessment of the field of adventure programming. In what ways have broad societal changes affected the adventure programming profession during the past decade? In what ways has the industry positioned itself to respond to these broad changes? And, absent industry adaptation to these changes, how should the industry position itself to address anticipated developments in the decades to come? In addition, how has the adventure programming industry changed internally during the past 10 years? To what extent has the industry grown and changed over the past 10 years due to natural maturation? What has contributed to these changes?

Controversial Issues in Adventure Programming is intended to fill the need for a contemporary account of such considerations in the field of adventure programming. Many of the issues addressed in this book relate to the theoretical foundations of the discipline. These issues provide an opportunity to reassess the underlying assumptions on which the practice of adventure programming is based. Many of the issues relate to new developments within the industry and provide an opportunity to critically examine implications of these developments for emerging practice. Many of the issues relate to broader social, cultural, political, economic, technological, and environmental changes in society. These issues provide an opportunity to consider how best to position the field of adventure programming in addressing broader societal concerns (e.g., health care, global climate change, school reform, and so on). The adventure programming industry is only as relevant as the social concerns that it tackles.

This book is divided into two parts. Part I addresses issues of ongoing concern in the adventure programming industry. Many of the issues in this section have been topics of discussion for decades. That the discussions are still ongoing shows that they merit inclusion in this text. Examples include the certification debate, motorized versus nonmotorized forms of outdoor recreation, and program accreditation. Part II addresses issues that have become prominent in recent years. For example, with the rise of the Internet and new instructional technologies, online educational programming is beginning to emerge in the field of adventure programming. Many in the industry would consider such programming to be contradictory to the very nature of adventure programming. How do we reconcile the juxtaposition of educational goals and processes inherent in the delivery of online educational programs in adventure programming?

Each issue addressed in *Controversial Issues in Adventure Programming* is considered within the framework of a debate. Each debate is prefaced with a brief discussion of the historical background of the issue and its significance in light of broader social and industry concerns. Authors assume opposing points of view or ethical stances regarding each issue and argue in favor of their particular point of view. Some arguments are based on deeply held beliefs about the merits of the author's stance and are laden with emotional intensity. Other authors accepted the challenge of arguing in favor of perspectives that do not represent their true beliefs. They agreed to play devil's advocate for the sake of ensuring that important issues are addressed. We compelled these authors to refrain from qualifying their positions with disclaimers and apologies in order to avoid softening their stances. We offer those disclaimers and apologies here, and we thank those authors for having the courage to argue on behalf of unpopular stances. We thank all of the authors for contributing to the lively debates that follow in this text.

The purpose of *Controversial Issues in Adventure Programming* is to help frame critical classroom discussions around selected dilemmas and help students explore a wide range of issues to broaden their understanding of the field. It is intended to help students critically question many of the underlying assumptions on which the practice of adventure programming is based. The book encourages students to participate in some of the central debates that occur in the field of adventure programming by introducing them to these debates in the classroom.

This approach is rooted in the dialogical method described by Paulo Freire (1970) in which teachers and students engage in a coconstruction of meaning within the context of their discourse. Freire (1970) also refers to this approach as "problem-posing" education, in which "people develop their power to perceive critically *the way they exist* in the world *with which* and *in which* they find themselves; they come to see the world not as a static reality, but as a reality in process, in transformation" (p. 83). This approach can help students in professional preparation programs to become critical participants in the profession. It can help prepare students to contribute not only to the regeneration and reproduction of the profession but also to its evolution and transformation. By helping students learn to critically question underlying assumptions and conventional practices within the profession, we can help to prepare them to work to continually improve the profession. This book provides an opportunity for students and teachers to engage in this dialogical approach to education.

Controversial Issues in Adventure Programming is intended primarily for college and university students (whether in online classrooms, backcountry classrooms, or traditional on-campus classrooms) in upper-division undergraduate and graduate-level courses related to adventure programming. However, it is useful to other audiences as well. It provides current practitioners with up-to-date information on enduring and emerging issues in the field and offers a synthesis of the most recent scholarly literature available on each of these issues. The book also provides governmental policy makers with an understanding of how the adventure programming industry can contribute to addressing issues of broad concern in society. It serves as a useful source of information in framing decisions on issues of school reform, stewardship of public lands and waterways, health care, and other prevalent social concerns.

In short, the book should be useful to anyone interested in understanding the value of adventure programming in addressing a broad range of societal and industry-specific concerns. As noted earlier, the debates that follow provide an opportunity to consider how best to position the field of adventure programming to address broader societal concerns. This book asks readers to become critical participants in this discourse. The adventure programming profession is only as meaningful as the broader societal issues that it attempts to address. Unless we all work collectively to position the profession to effectively address these larger concerns, the profession will continue to be perceived as an esoteric pursuit and relegated to the margins of key public policy arenas.

References

Freire, P. (1970). *Pedagogy of the oppressed*. New York: Continuum.

Wurdinger, S.D., & Potter, T.G. (1999). *Controversial issues in adventure education: A critical examination*. Dubuque, IA: Kendall/Hunt.

Acknowledgments

As with any project of this magnitude, I owe a great debt of gratitude to a number of people for their inspiration and support. First, I thank the many students who have engaged in discussions with me around many of the issues in this text. The purpose and structure of this text were framed largely through these discussions and with these students in mind. Second, I thank the many authors who contributed to this text. Thank you for giving voice to the various perspectives that inform the issues addressed. Without your expertise, this book would not have come to fruition. Third, I thank my coeditor, Mark Wagstaff, for taking on this project with me. As always, it has been a pleasure to work with you. Finally, I thank my wife, Sirlei, and my daughters, Isabella and Christiana, for the constant love and support that they offer me. You have filled my life with adventure, making every day a joy to share.

—*Bruce Martin*

For me, the development of this text represents the essence of an adventure experience! I relied on valued group members to achieve success. Thanks to Bruce Martin, a competent writing partner, for leadership and passion for excellence. The impressive group of authors contributing to this text reflects the best of our profession. I must also include my students as critical group members because they constantly stimulate my passion to educate. Finally, I express deep gratitude and love to my spouse, Jenny, who patiently listens and selflessly makes room for my professional life. You gracefully support and value what I do.

—*Mark Wagstaff*

Both editors extend their appreciation to the Human Kinetics staff for supporting this project. Special thanks go to Gayle Kassing for initially embracing the project and to Ray Vallese for seeing the book to fruition. Thanks also to the many other Human Kinetics staff members who worked behind the scenes to make the idea of this book a reality.

Part I

Enduring Issues in Adventure Programming

Controversial Issue 1

Do the benefits of adventure programming outweigh the risks?

Historically, adventure programmers have embraced physical and emotional risk taking as an educational tool because of its potential as a catalyst in facilitating transformational change in the lives of program participants. Risk is considered a central element of adventure and thus is considered a central element of the practice of adventure programming. However, a number of researchers in the field of adventure programming are beginning to question the assumption that risk taking in adventure programming is necessarily a good thing. Wolfe and Samdahl (2005), for example, question whether risk and challenge are always appropriate for every population served by adventure programs. They write, "People have diverse ways of coping with challenge, and some people are more capable than others of internalizing positive lessons from misadventure. The assumption that all people can recover from traumatic events on the challenge course is very dangerous, yet very prevalent in the literature and practice" (p. 34).

This debate helps clarify issues surrounding the use of risk to promote growth and development in program participants. It helps us question some of our underlying and perhaps unspoken assumptions about the use of risk in adventure programming.

Taking a stance in favor of the centrality of risk to adventure programming, Sean Blenkinsop and Chris Beeman embrace the value of risk as a potential catalyst for transformational change and development in program participants. They consider the value of risk along a spectrum of benefits, from the tangible and measurable to the less tangible and immeasurable. The most profound of these benefits is the sense of spiritual invigoration that participants can gain from adventure experience.

Mike Brown, on the other hand, argues that the historical emphasis placed on physical risk taking in adventure programming has diminished the potential for authentic participant experiences in adventure programming and that documented outcomes of adventure programming do not support the continued promotion of physical and emotional risk taking to achieve educational benefits. Further, he argues that the outdoors provides many valuable opportunities to enhance learning without an emphasis on risk taking. This debate addresses underlying assumptions concerning a central construct in adventure programming: the use of risk to facilitate change and development in program participants.

Reference

Wolfe, B., & Samdahl, D. (2005). Challenging assumptions: Examining fundamental beliefs that shape challenge course programming and research. *Journal of Experiential Education, 28*(1), 25-43.

Do the benefits of adventure programming outweigh the risks?

YES The Benefits of Adventure Programming Outweigh the Risks

Sean Blenkinsop, EdD, associate professor of education at Simon Fraser University, Burnaby, British Columbia, Canada

Chris Beeman, PhD, postdoctoral researcher at Simon Fraser University, Burnaby, British Columbia, Canada; adjunct professor, Queen's University, Kingston, Ontario, Canada

"We used to tell them in Outward Bound, when a parent would come and ask us, 'Can you *guarantee* the safety of our son, Johnny?' And we finally decided to meet it head-on. We would say, 'No. We certainly can't, Ma'am. We guarantee you the genuine chance of his death. And if we could guarantee his safety, the program would not be worth running. We do make one guarantee, as one parent to another. If you succeed in protecting your boy, as you are doing now, and as it's your motherly duty to do, you know, we applaud your watchdog tenacity. You should be protecting him. But if you succeed, *we guarantee you the death of his soul!*'"

—William F. (Willi) Unsoeld,
lecture given at Kaiserlautern (emphasis added),
May, 1974. Copyright 1979, J. Unsoeld.

Contemporary Western culture tends to give attention primarily to what is conveniently measurable. As a result, risks and benefits are generally conceptualized as competing columns of figures written on some great accounting ledger. In our litigious, rights-based, and individualized times, risks often have the power to overcome almost all arguments of benefit. This is especially so if benefits and risks are conceptualized as separate from each other and thus discreetly measurable and easily comparable between activities. But, to paraphrase Einstein, "Not all that is measurable is worth measuring and not all that is worth measuring is measurable." Although we acknowledge the context of the discussion and the troublesomeness of our system of accounting, our goal is to offer a perspective that addresses both the measurable and the immeasurable.

We begin with some parameters for our discussion. We understand adventure programming within the context of some form of education. For the purposes of this discussion, we understand risks and benefits to be opposed. However, we think that in some cases this conceptual division may be misleading.

In the first part of this argument, we focus on risk in adventure programming as a continuum of benefits and trace an arc from simpler, more tangible benefits (those of fun or fitness) to more complex benefits that are less easily measurable (those relating to one's soul, humanity, or a life well lived). We divide the continuum into five sections. These sections overlap, but as the benefits accumulate and increase along the continuum, so too does a sense that further risk might be justified. At each layer of benefit we suggest activities that might appear to be less risky for the same return. However, we attempt to show that benefits that are less easily measured may be present in particular contexts in adventure programming, thus tipping the scale to favor higher risk at each layer. In the second part of this argument, our goal is to show that few educational possibilities besides adventure programming offer a benefit such as avoiding the death of one's soul, and that these benefits lie in the realm of the immeasurable.

Along the Benefits Continuum: The Returns of Adventure Programming

On what might be considered the least significant end of the benefits spectrum in adventure programming could be an adrenaline rush, a thrill, or a fun way to spend a few hours. This is not an unusual possibility given the rise of one-off zip trekking or short, guided rafting trips (Holyfield, Jones, and Zajicek, 2005). The goal of these experiences may be as simple as momentary physical enjoyment or what might be called somatic modulation. The question then becomes, as it does for all the possible benefits we refer to at each stop along the continuum, whether this physically risky thing, commonly known as adventure programming, is the only, the best, or the safest way to achieve those particular returns.

At first blush, it would appear that the answer is no. One might argue that viewing three-dimensional IMAX adventure films, riding a roller coaster, or sitting in the front row at a NASCAR race offer qualitatively similar thrills as those attained when engaging in some form of adventure programming but with lessened associated risk. Yet it would appear that differences also exist. At the very least, for example, a raft trip takes place in an environment that is not completely fabricated or controlled by humans. Because of this, the unexpected and uncontrolled may lead to benefits unintended by the human educators. A moment of mist rising out of a canyon, an encounter with a peregrine falcon, or a deep breath of forest air, for example, might catalyze the florescence of a latent biophilia (Wilson, 1984) or love of nature. This benefit, which is less immediately obvious, offers the potential to gain something unexpected that the world outside of adventure programming may not offer. Although not all adventure programming takes place outdoors, much does, and, although potentially risky, the unintended incursion of the more-than-human has deep value that may exceed that of the risks taken.

As we move along the continuum of benefits, we might encounter the role adventure programming can play in physical fitness, in the challenges of obesity, in awareness of self as a body, and in esteem with regard to one's own physical ability and appearance. These are the kinds of returns that longer term wilderness trips can provide. Again, these are all important goals and likely good returns to achieve in any educational setting. Therefore, the question must be posed at this place on our proposed spectrum: Is adventure programming the only, the best, or the safest way to achieve these returns? As before, the answer appears to be fairly easy: no. Almost all sports, whether individual or team, and many body-based activities (e.g., yoga, dance, martial arts, and so on), seem to offer the same return (if one is to believe the advocates of

each activity) and in a way that involves the same, if not less, risk. Yet, as before, might the setting itself offer different returns? Does being outdoors in a less-sculpted environment offer something that these potentially less-risky propositions do not?

Consider what Richard Louv (2005) calls the nature-deficit disorder. If Kellert is right, the average school-age child in the United States spends more than 42 hours per week (Kahn and Kellert, 2002) engaged with electronic media and only 42 minutes outside (Fishman, 1999, as cited by Orr, 2002). What effect does this have on how we understand ourselves as bodies in the world and on what we come to see as important? Work by Cobb (2004), Sobel (2005), and Thomashow (1996) all suggest that students need to spend time outdoors in order to build a relationship with it, which eventually leads them to care about the more-than-human world (Abram, 1996). It is this care that leads them to advocate for and work to protect this place on which all life depends. So, maybe it is not just about making one's body physically fit, but rather allowing that body to find its place within the larger community.

Further considerations exist here with regard to potential benefits in this kind of adventure programming. Following the motif of care are the relationships and shared memories developed among students over the course of a shared activity. In some cases, adventure programming provides a different social environment in which the focus is not on winning or hierarchies established among the participants. Recent work has suggested that many human-constructed environments are sensorially limited. This means that students in schools, even while engaged in physical exercise in gymnasia, are losing their abilities to encounter the world through a full array of possibilities (Livingston, 1994). Quite literally, they are becoming unable to smell the roses, even if they do stop. So, at our second stop on the continuum, we find unexpected benefits of adventure programming that again pertain to the tendency of adventure programming to incorporate the more-than-human.

As we continue on the spectrum, potential benefits become more expansive. Take, for example, an argument that adventure programming might offer people benefits of both technical and personal skills and advance knowledge. Participants learn how to work with others, take care of their own needs, and develop a sense of themselves as capable. They develop resilience and confidence. All of these skills might come in handy practically, in terms of the participants' daily lives, but also in terms of offsetting some of the growing psychological fears manifesting as a result of environmental issues and looming food shortages or other possible crises. Not only might adventure programming offer particular skills, it may also offer an underlying peace of mind, a sense of the self as capable. These qualities, important in achieving an educated citizenry, may begin to justify some of the risks inherent in wilderness travel and longer term adventure programming.

Yet it appears that these skills might be learned in ways that are less risky. Personal skills and knowledge are regularly acquired in all kinds of settings (e.g., classes directly related to a given subject, therapeutic encounters, intentional experiences in group settings, and so on), and the technical skills suggested before might be acquired by growing one's own garden, taking courses at the local technical college, or spending a month car camping at a regional park. It does not appear that adventure programming is required for these benefits to accrue. However, again, these less-risky propositions are limited with regard to some less-measurable benefits. Connection to the natural world (biophilia), the building of relationships, the storehouse of shared memories, immersion in a more diverse sensory world, and the opportunity to become more embodied are all extended possibilities that adventure programming might offer. Also particular to this discussion is the ability to learn to respond in an uncontrolled context. Skills are learned for a reason and are directly applicable. Students encounter the complexities of any given situation by being immersed in a real problem. These situations are not standardized, homogenized, preplanned, or even sanitized but rather are genuine, authentic, and complex. In addition, the qualities at hand in these situations ameliorate risk. As participants become acclimatized, they gain knowledge of how to manage risk and the skills with which to do it.

The fourth stop on our continuum of ever-increasing benefits of adventure programming falls in line with what Kurt Hahn might call the development of character. This might include improved judgment, a sense of self as moral agent, an ability to engage the world with integrity and humility, and the wherewithal to make decisions and take responsibility for the repercussions thereof. Again, all of these are things that can result from an adventure program that is well designed, usually longer, and likely (although not necessarily) wilderness based.

As we make our way along the spectrum, benefits increase, but so do risks. For example, it is hard to imagine major character development as an outcome of half a day on a low ropes course. But again, with regard to character development, the question that remains is whether adventure programming is the only, the best, or the safest way to possibly (we must remember that nothing in education is guaranteed) achieve the benefit. One might suggest that although fewer choices exist, certainly some are arguably equally capable of promoting similar outcomes and carry less risk. One example might be service learning activities. So too, according to moral philosophers, is the ongoing encounter with case studies of moral conundrums. Or how about the role of families and religions in the active formation of the character of people? However, do these options carry with them the holistic properties offered by adventure programming at this level? Although potentially complex in their own right, do service learning, moral case studies, and religious education touch on the same range of benefits as that in our proposed continuum? This brings us back to Willi Unsoeld and the question of soul.

The Benefit That Does Not Exist Without Risk

Willi Unsoeld's point, when it comes to the death of the soul, is that adventure programming has the potential to expand, validate, and expedite the flourishing of the participant. In simpler terms, one of the ostensive benefits of adventure programming is that it offers the possibility of supporting a participant into life—not the biological version, but what might be considered the spiritually mature, humane version. This allows the biologically alive to flourish, to become, to strive, or to attain authenticity rather than remain, as the existentialists might suggest, one of the "living dead," the mob, or non-self-actualized.

We interpret Willi's words to the legitimately concerned mother to mean that risk and benefit cannot be separated in an attempt at self-transformation. What is of value (the benefit) and what is to be avoided (the risk) in self-transformation are two sides of the same coin; one cannot exist without the other. Quantum physics falters at the event horizon of a black hole. In the same way, a standard risk–benefit conversation fails when one approaches the event horizon of self-transformation. If this is an accurate conceptualization, then we are no longer in the realm of what is measurable and what is not, as we suggest above, but of another calculus entirely.

For existential philosophers such as Kierkegaard, Sartre, and even Nietzsche, the human condition is a process of "becoming." As a result of this focus on the process, the human is not a static entity or a noun so much as a journey, a project, or a verb. Nisha is not Nisha so much as "Nisha-ing." However, this process of becoming is not easy. It is littered with fear and trembling (Kierkegaard, 1954), nausea (Sartre, 1964), and absurdity (Camus, 1961). These symptoms, risks, of change are in part a result of coming to know ourselves as being free and active choice-making entities. The challenge of taking responsibility for who we are and what we do—along with who we were and what we did, as well as who we are going to become and what we will do—is steep. For all three philosophers, the project of becoming is very daunting. The payoff, if one survives the journey, is incredible. It is loosely characterized as achieving a more genuine, authentic self. But it tends to come with serious risks that warn us off metaphysically as much as pain or illness does physically. Thus, according to all three of these philosophers, most people avoid taking responsibility for their lives and avoid the ongoing process of self-transcendence (or transformation) and, as a result, live lives that are less robust, less engaged, and less alive than they could be. We are, in Kierkegaard's terms, the living dead. Or, with Willi Unsoeld, we are soulless.

Thus, risk is necessary for self-transformation: risk to an old way of being in the world. This possibility seems to involve, depending upon the student, various levels of risk, both physical and metaphysical. Our job as educators is to mitigate that risk to the lowest possible level while maintaining the possibility of self-transformation. Too much risk and the danger is physical harm and psychological trauma. Too little risk and the danger is inoculation against the possibility of future transformation and the loss of the becoming self. It is also important to remember that the complete avoidance of risk is potentially risky in its own right. If Willi Unsoeld is right, there never is no risk without the death of a soul. And, if the existentialists are correct, by not taking any risks, by not diving into the anguish of freedom, one risks not living one's authentic life. Ultimately, the question becomes, is it worth it to save the physical at the cost of the metaphysical?

Conclusion

What goes missing if risk is not taken? Imagine if any activity perceived as risky was prohibited (e.g., climbing trees, getting dirty, swinging and sliding, and so on). Come to think of it, we don't need to imagine this. Recently, playgrounds in much of North America have been redesigned to minimize the obvious risks to children. But what happens if minor falls at playgrounds could occur? We fall again, and this time we learn again. By the third similar circumstance, we do not fall.

There is a risk associated with *not* developing good judgment in terms of movement, falling, dodging, and so on, judgment that is always needed in unexpected circumstances. For example, imagine an elderly person who still has the physical responses gained in youth that protect them when they slip on ice. Having experienced minor risks earlier in life, they do not break a hip, they do not get an infection in hospital, they do not die. In short, learning to fall well on the playground at age four, although filled with tears and bloody knees, has added 10 years to their happy life. Think of these experiences as a kind of immunization: small doses of the disease (risk) protect us from the more catastrophic possibility. We are not arguing that students should be exposed to megadoses of risk so much as suggesting that certain minor risks, like the ones now being avoided in school yards all over North America, might actually mitigate future ills.

What this suggests further complicates what we have already tried to illustrate as a complex calculus. A more accurate calculus ought not to be based on risk versus benefit, as calculated locally in an activity, but on risk versus the risk of not risking something by doing a "safer" activity. For example, what is the effect of a generation of people who have had few encounters with the more-than-human world? They are kept safe from the potential risks of weather, animals, and disease, and yet something incalculable might be lost over the long run for both the individual and the larger culture. This is very much like the concept of "opportunity cost" in business. According to this view, one ought not simply calculate return from one investment, but rather set this against what would have been the return in a different investment. Opportunity cost is the cost of not doing something. Because one can never tell just which tag that was avoided on the playing field wired which synapses and reactions that 80 years later prevent a broken hip, a wide range of adventurous—and risk-associated—activities may be justified. As we discuss earlier, complex layerings of tangible and intangible benefits may result from any seemingly simple choice between an activity that appears to be safer and an adventure program of supposed comparable return.

So where do we arrive after traveling along the continuum of benefits? It appears that at the lower levels of benefit many contenders offer the same return with arguably less risk. Yet, on closer examination, this conclusion is not so easily justified. Less tangible benefits such as biophilia, sensory diversity, creation of memories, change in community dynamics, and caring relationships all seem to tip the balance in favor of adventure programming. With respect to self-transformation, there appear to be benefits that are almost exclusively the purview of adventure programming. Here, a standard risk–benefit calculus becomes useless.

From here it is a short step back to Willi's story. It might be that, in proposing to the worried parent that he could not guarantee a child's safety, Willi was actually both taking a metaphysically less-risky route and plotting a course for an approach to life that could lead to unimaginable self-transformation. In the same way that certain kinds of "unsafe" playgrounds may lead to the development of healthy reflexes, "unsafe" circumstances may lead to good judgment and even better lives lived. In this view of the world, the discernment that results from gradual introduction to risk appears to be the best protection. Such would not be a risky life, but rather, in both metaphysical and physical senses, ultimately a much safer one that may result in an immeasurable benefit: the flight of a person's soul.

References

Abram, D. (1996). *The spell of the sensuous: Perception and language in a more-than-human world.* New York: Pantheon Books.

Camus, A. (1961). *The rebel.* A. Bower (trans.). New York: Knopf.

Cobb, E. (2004). *The ecology of imagination in childhood.* Putnam, CT: Spring Pub.

Holyfield, L., Jones, L., & Zajicek, A. (2005). Adventure without risk is like Disneyland. In S. Lyng (Ed.), *Edgework: The sociology of risk-taking* (pp. 177-196). New York: Routledge.

Kahn, P., & Kellert, S. (2002). *Children and nature: Psychological, sociocultural, and evolutionary investigations.* Cambridge, MA: MIT Press.

Kierkegaard, S. (1954). *Fear and trembling, and the sickness unto death.* W. Lowrie (trans.). Garden City, NY: Doubleday.

Livingston, J. (1994). *Rogue primate: An exploration of human domestication.* Toronto: Key Porter Books.

Louv, R. (2005). *Last child in the woods: Saving our children from nature-deficit disorder.* Chapel Hill, NC: Algonquin Books.

Orr, D. (2002). Political economy and the ecology of childhood. In P. Kahn & S. Kellert (Eds.), *Children and nature: Psychological, sociocultural, and evolutionary investigations* (pp. 279-304). Cambridge, MA: MIT Press.

Sartre, J.P. (1964). *Nausea.* L. Alexander (trans.). New York: New Directions.

Sobel, D. (2005). *Place-based education: Connecting classrooms and communities.* Great Barrington, MA: The Orion Society.

Thomashow, M. (1996). *Ecological identity: Becoming a reflective environmentalist.* Cambridge, MA: MIT Press.

Wilson, E.O. (1984). *Biophilia.* Cambridge, MA: Harvard University Press.

NO Freeing Ourselves From Narrow Thinking About Risk in Adventure Programming

Mike Brown, PhD, senior lecturer in sport and leisure studies at the University of Waikato, Hamilton, New Zealand

One of the strengths of adventure programming or adventure education is the potential it offers for students to engage in activities that require physical, intellectual, and emotional commitment. To try new ways of acting, to question one's beliefs and attempt to modify behavior, is, in the broadest sense, risky. It involves giving up the known and predictable and embarking on a journey of discovery.

However, the emphasis on physical risk taking in adventure programming has potentially diminished the possibilities for authentic student decision making and the opportunity for students to take responsibility for their actions (Brown and Fraser, 2009; Wurdinger, 1997). In this argument, I contend that the documented outcomes of adventure programming do not support the continued promotion of physical or emotional risk taking (or both) to achieve educational benefits. I argue that the outdoors provides many valuable opportunities to enhance learning that is both relevant in the lives of learners and based on sound teaching and learning principles.

Defining Risk and Its Role in Adventure Programming

Risk, either real or perceived, is positioned as a distinguishing feature of adventure programming (Davis-Berman and Berman, 2002; Miles and Priest, 1990, 1999; Priest and Gass, 1997; Wurdinger, 1997; Zink and Leberman, 2001). Risk has been defined as the potential to lose something of value. The loss may lead to physical or mental harm, social embarrassment, or financial loss (Priest, 1999b). Although the prevention of physical injuries or fatalities receives most attention in the literature, awareness of the potential for emotional harm, through the manipulation of perceived risks, has increasingly received recognition (Davis-Berman and Berman, 2002). The role of risk in adventure programming is well summed up in the following:

To maximize safety, adventure professionals structure risk in a manner that causes participants to perceive it as being enormously high, while in actuality it is much lower than perceived and more acceptable as a medium for producing functional change and growth. By responding to seemingly insurmountable tasks, participants often learn to overcome self-imposed perceptions of their capabilities to succeed. (Priest and Gass, 1997, p. 17)

Thus, the manipulation of risk is seen to be integral to the growth and development of individuals and teams (Haddock, 1993). Brown and Fraser (2009) have suggested that the concept of risk defines much of what happens in adventure programs, from participants taking risks to instructors managing risks.

Questioning Taken-for-Granted Assumptions

The benefits of manipulating and promoting perceived risk to enhance learning are taken for granted in many adventure programming texts. For example, Priest (1999a) suggests, "Adventure programming is the deliberate use of adventurous experiences to create learning. . . . Adventurous experiences are activities with uncertain outcomes (due to the presence of situational risks)" (p. xiii). In a more recent publication, Ewert and Garvey (2007) state, "Inherent in adventure education is the inclusion of activities and experiences that often include elements of danger or risk and uncertain outcomes" (p. 22).

Although many texts promote notions of adventure, risk, and uncertainty, few attempt to provide a sound educational justification for the use of risk as an effective learning strategy (see Beedie, 1994; Beedie and Bourne, 2005; Bunting, 1999;

Wurdinger, 1997). Although the terms adventure, risk, and uncertainty are not necessarily synonymous, in common usage they are frequently used almost interchangeably. Sheard and Golby (2006) highlight the widespread assumption, within Western societies at least, that exposure to challenge can be beneficial. Extended discussions concerning risk tend to focus around strategies relating to the reduction and management of physical harm to participants and the associated legal liabilities (e.g., Brookes, 2007a; Brown, 1999; Dickson, 2005; Martin et al., 2006).

A variety of sources are increasingly questioning the use of activities involving heightened or manipulated risk to enhance learning. Brown and Fraser (2009) suggest that the use of risk in outdoor and adventure education is based on narrow definitions of risk based on historical antecedents that may no longer be relevant and the tendency for adventure programmers to confuse personal preferences and beliefs with sound principles of teaching and learning. Wolfe and Samdahl (2005) question whether risk and challenge necessarily lead to positive outcomes. They assert that there are several underlying assumptions regarding the value of risk in adventure programming. The first is that learners need to learn how to deal with risk and that this will be beneficial for them. The second assumption is that "the potential benefits from an adventure experience outweigh the potential risks. . . . The overt assumption is that participants have the ability to recover from negative situations" (Wolfe and Samdahl, 2005, p. 33).

The use of risk is premised on the belief that people will learn best if they are confronted with a problem or a difficult challenge, if they are placed in a situation involving stress, or if they need to resolve a tension. However, a growing body of literature calls into question the need to create a state of stress or tension as a means to bring about change and growth (Berman and Davis-Berman, 2005; Brown, 2008; Davis-Berman and Berman, 2002; Leberman and Martin, 2003; Zink and Leberman, 2001). Estrellas (1996) argues that the manipulation of risk and the associated stress can be dysfunctional and negatively affect both individuals and groups. Davis-Berman and Berman (2002) argue that if the perceived risk is too high the effect on the student "can be counterproductive, at best, and damaging at worst" (p. 308). Researchers have also indicated that the benefit of manipulating stress to create disequilibrium is questionable and is not a valid rationale for using risk as an aid to learning (Berman and Davis-Berman, 2005; Brown, 2008;

Wolfe and Samdahl, 2005). For example, in a study of Outward Bound students, Leberman and Martin (2003) found that the activities in which students had been pushed outside their comfort zone were not necessarily the activities that resulted in peak learning experiences.

In light of contemporary understandings of the factors that facilitate change, it has been argued that people are more likely to respond positively when they feel safe and secure and a level of predictability exists in the environment (Berman and Davis-Berman, 2005). Using and manipulating risk assumes that the adventure programmer is competent and capable of assessing each individual's level of perceived risk to ensure that optimal learning will occur. It also assumes that this person is able to objectively quantify the real risk and hence avoid harm to participants. This latter assumption is manifestly incorrect as incident records confirm that serious injuries and fatalities have occurred in educational programs. The justification that the benefits of adventure programming outweigh the risks is of little comfort to victims or their families and, as we shall see, is not supported by the research literature.

Benefits of Adventure Programming

It is not necessary to rely on anecdotes or one's gut feelings to justify the potential value of adventure programming. A number of studies have reported on the outcomes of various components of outdoor and adventure education programs. For the purposes of this argument, I briefly draw on the findings of a meta-analysis of outcomes of outdoor education (Hattie et al., 1997). I selected this study because it was conducted by scholars from a range of academic disciplinary areas, it underwent a peer review process and was published in a respected international journal, and it synthesizes the outcomes of almost 100 studies.

Although meta-analytic studies do not provide the fine-grain detail of qualitative studies such as ethnographies (which are very valuable), they do permit a broad view of the educational outcomes. An effect size provides a way to express the magnitude of study outcomes for many types of outcome variables. An effect size of 1.0 indicates an increase of one standard deviation on the outcome (Hattie, 2009). Hattie suggests that, when judging educational outcomes, 0.2 be considered a small change, 0.4 a medium change, and 0.6 a large change.

In this particular meta-analysis, the researchers drew on 96 studies published between 1968 and

1994 that involved more than 12,000 participants. The programs lasted between 1 and 120 days, and the mean length was 24 days. The overall effect size was 0.34, which indicates a 15 percent improvement in the rate of learning. To put this in context, it is worthwhile to compare the magnitude of change of outdoor education with that of other educational programs. In a synthesis of more than 300 meta-analyses of educational interventions, Hattie (1992) determined an effect size of 0.40 for achievement and 0.28 for affective outcomes. "Thus, the overall effect size from the adventure program of 0.34 is most comparable to achievement and affective outcomes from typical educational interventions" (Hattie et al., 1997, p. 55). Interestingly the follow-up effects of adventure programs continued post-program: an effect size of 0.17 was recorded at a mean of 5.5 months after the completion of the course. Of note to outdoor educators working with school students is the finding that the mean effect size was 0.26 (Hattie et al., 1997, p. 70). The findings presented by Hattie and colleagues are similar to those determined by Cason and Gillis' (1994) meta-analysis of outdoor education programs, which returned an effect size of 0.31.

However, one should not interpret a generalized figure derived from a meta-analysis (such as 0.34 or 0.31) as an endorsement that all adventure programs are inherently good. As Hattie and colleagues (1997) point out, only some programs work, and only with some participants and some instructors, and then only on some outcomes. They note a "great deal of variability in outcomes between different studies, different programs, and different individuals" (p. 77). This suggests that an element of caution concerning generalized claims regarding the effectiveness of adventure programming, per se, might be prudent. Space prevents a protracted discussion of individual studies; however, it is worth mentioning that participation in adventure programming may have no significant effect on the participant at all. For example, Sheard and Golby (2006) found no significant difference in several psychological measures between participants in an outdoor adventure education program and a control group. Although the notion that adventure programming leads to the development of desirable psychological characteristics is "intuitively appealing" (p. 189), we should be open to the possibility that no difference or even negative effects may result from participation in adventure programs. This point is also emphasized by Wolfe and Samdahl (2005), who caution that too often research is based on the belief, in challenge courses

at least, that positive change will result from participation.

Given the results of the meta-analysis of Hattie and colleagues, their cautionary rider about the variable effects, the potential for no significant benefits (see Sheard and Golby, 2006), or even the possibility of negative outcomes (Wolfe and Samdahl, 2005), I cautiously suggest that good adventure programmers might reasonably expect to achieve benefits that are similar to those of other educational interventions. Despite passionate advocates and strong beliefs, adventure programmers clearly do not possess a magic educational cure-all.

In a review of fatalities in Australian outdoor education programs, Brookes' (2003a, 2003b, 2004, 2007a, 2007b) response to the question of whether the benefits of adventure programming outweigh the risks is telling. He comments

> These incidents reinforce the observation that, with hindsight, nearly all fatal incidents in outdoor education could be avoided without abandoning the whole enterprise. Usually no educational disadvantage seems attached to action necessary to remove a fatality risk factor. . . . These incidents do not support the view that risks can only be reduced at the expense of educational benefits. (2007b, p. 8)

The author of this detailed and comprehensive review, which covers a 42-year period and 114 fatalities in Australian outdoor education, provides a challenge to adventure programmers to ponder. If no loss of learning appears to occur by removing a risk factor that might lead to a serious incident, why include such risks in your program?

Alternatives to Simplistic Understandings of Risk

In a special issue of the *Journal of Experiential Education*, Sibthorp (2010) noted that young people need "positive, engaging, and challenging experiences to flourish and develop into successful and productive adults" (p. vi). The supports he identifies to assist the developmental outcomes for young people include "multiple supportive relationships with adults and peers, challenging and engaging activities and learning experiences, meaningful opportunities for involvement and membership, and safety" (Sibthorp, 2010, p. vi). It is tempting to infer that this is an accurate description of adventure programming and to equate challenges with activities that involve risk; however, this is but one reading. As Sibthorp notes, relationships lay at the heart of adventure programming. Fostering personal connections and a supportive community may permit and encourage young people to experiment, to try new ways of acting and behaving. This aligns with the findings relating to change conditions identified by advocates of positive psychology (Berman and Davis-Berman, 2005; Passarelli, Hall, and Anderson, 2010; Sammet, 2010). It also finds support in Dewey's (1938) advocacy of continuity in experiences so that they might have educational value.

One of the strengths of adventure programming lies in the provision of experiences that engage students at a variety of levels (physically, emotionally, cognitively, and so on). However, being busy and having fun do not necessarily lead to learning. As Wojcikiewicz and Mural (2010) point out, "The question is not whether learning is or is not experiential: the question is whether the learning experience is of the right sort" (p. 106). In a thoughtful paper drawing together Dewey's framework, positive youth development, and adventure education, Wojcikiewicz and Mural (2010) emphasize a number of key factors in Dewey's educational philosophy. Of note is their call for activities to provide opportunities that allow students to choose and implement means that allow them to reach purposeful ends that have relevance in their lives. They refer to this as "intelligent direction" (p. 110), a notion that incorporates the opportunity to act in a responsible manner and to connect actions with the consequences of those actions. It is here that adventure programmers tread a fine line.

As Wojcikiewicz and Mural (2010) remind us, "Dewey's concept of experience was both specific and demanding, and that it is not necessarily fulfilled just through exciting and unusual activities in exotic settings" (p. 117). The temptation to offer activities that are exciting or unusual, involving technical equipment and high levels of instructor competency, potentially diminishes opportunities for authentic student decision making because the risks may prevent students from experimenting and taking responsibility for their actions (Brown and Fraser, 2009). In Wojcikiewicz and Mural's (2010) terms, we run the risk of eliminating "opportunities for intelligent direction" (p. 117) when we focus on risky activities that require high levels of instructor intervention to ensure safety. Opportunities to learn from cause and effect are negated when consequences of an incorrect choice require intervention and active management. Perhaps the diminishing opportunities that are provided for authentic student decision making and dealing with reasonable consequences are the real risk that we have not paid sufficient attention to in programs that rely on increasingly complex and risky activities.

Conclusion

Priest (1999a) states that "learning is a shift in the way people feel, think, or behave" (p. xiii). He notes that the principal challenge for adventure programmers is how to "create change that is sentient, purposeful, and sustainable" (p. xiii). I concur with Priest's assertions, but, given the issues raised earlier, I suggest that there are more defensible ways to encourage change than by the promotion of risk. An overemphasis on creating situations in which levels of risk are manipulated or in which real risks are present and extensive risk management strategies are required diverts attention from the real issue identified by Priest: How can we best enhance learning?

Adventure programs provide opportunities for social interaction and activities in an outdoor setting that may differ from other institutional forms of education. However passionate we may be about adventure programming, we need to be very careful about the claims we make in regard to the magnitude of the benefits that may result. Over-exaggerated claims are difficult to substantiate and they potentially give tacit approval to engaging in activities that expose students to negative outcomes.

It is clear that adventure programs have the potential to enhance learning. However, these benefits are similar to those of other educational interventions that do not rely on the manipulation of physical or emotional risks as defining features of learning. The consequences of misjudging risk and placing participants' lives in danger for educational gains are not justifiable. This is not a call to place young people in cotton wool; activities do not need to involve physical risk to be challenging and engaging and to provide learning opportunities. Recent research findings from positive psychology may not be a silver bullet or a quick-fix solution, but they do suggest that other ways to enhance learning are worth exploring by adventure programming professionals. As Davis-Berman and Berman (2002) suggest, it may be time "to more clearly advocate for a paradigm shift in the way leaders introduce and conduct outdoor education programs" (p. 308). Other authors have argued that adventure programmers need to broaden their repertoire of teaching and learning strategies and to reconsider the value of engaging in activities that involve high risk (Brown and Fraser, 2009; Bunting, 1999).

Following his comprehensive review of fatalities in outdoor education in Australia, Brookes (2002/2003) came to the conclusion that "as a researcher, outdoor educator, and parent, . . . there is no acceptable rate of accidental deaths in outdoor education" (p. 24). While we acknowledge that taking risks does not necessarily lead to injury or death, we need to remember that misjudgments of risk have led to serious injuries and fatalities. Given that the potential benefits of participation in adventure programs are similar to those of other educational interventions, there is, in my opinion, no justification in the claim that the benefits outweigh the risks.

Adventure programming is one approach to learning in, and from, the outdoors. Perhaps it is an opportune time to engage with other scholars who are interested in how students learn from their experiences in, and about, the outdoor environment. Examples include Beames and Ross' (2010) study of students (aged 8 to 11 years) who planned and undertook journeys in their local environment. The authors found that these journeys encouraged crosscurricular linkages, enhanced levels of student responsibility, and connected the students to their community. The interdisciplinary nature of the journeys, which involved a high degree of student initiative, has the potential to make a valid and valued contribution to student learning. Undoubtedly, programs such as these involve the management of risks. They also require that educators and students be prepared to take risks in negotiating what is important to learn and how it will be learned. This study locates experiential outdoor learning in the discourses of education, curriculum, and pedagogy rather than adventure and risk. This distinction is seemingly small but significant. More recently, in *A Pedagogy of Place: Outdoor Education for a Changing World*, Wattchow and Brown (2011) advocate a form of outdoor education that is responsive to local conditions and cultural traditions. In arguing for the significance of place(s) in learning, they call for a "place-responsive pedagogy" (p. 199) that is able to respond to the contexts and cultures in which students live and learn. Like Beames and Ross (2010), they place learning within the local and emphasize the importance of the relevance of activities to the students' lives as starting points in discussions about what might be learned and how this might best be achieved in a particular locale.

Those who choose to educate in, and about, the outdoors have many ways forward. I suggest that the real risk for adventure programmers is the marginalization of the discipline, and the potential for unwarranted student harm, if it fails to adapt to and adopt changing understandings of how people can best be supported in their endeavors to learn and change.

References

Beames, S., & Ross, H. (2010). Journeys outside the classroom. *Journal of Adventure Education and Outdoor Learning, 10*(2), 95-109.

Beedie, P. (1994). Risk taking: The consensus views. *Journal of Adventure Education and Outdoor Leadership, 11*(2), 13-17.

Beedie, P., & Bourne, G. (2005). Media constructions of risk: A case study of the Stainforth Beck incident. *Journal of Risk Research, 8*(4), 331-339.

Berman, D., & Davis-Berman, J. (2005). Positive psychology and outdoor education. *Journal of Experiential Education, 28*(1), 17-24.

Brookes, A. (2002/2003). Outdoor education fatalities in Australia 1960-2002. Part 1: Summary of incidents and introduction to fatality analysis. *Australian Journal of Outdoor Education, 7*(1), 20-35.

Brookes, A. (2003a). A critique of Neo-Hahnian outdoor education theory. Part one: Challenges to the concept of "character building." *Journal of Adventure Education and Outdoor Learning, 3*(1), 49-62.

Brookes, A. (2003b). A critique of Neo-Hahnian outdoor education theory. Part two: "The fundamental attribution error" in contemporary outdoor education discourse. *Journal of Adventure Education and Outdoor Learning, 3*(2), 119-132.

Brookes, A. (2004). Outdoor education fatalities in Australia 1960-2002. Part 3: Environmental circumstances. *Australian Journal of Outdoor Education, 8*(1), 44-56.

Brookes, A. (2007a). Preventing death and serious injury from falling trees and branches. *Australian Journal of Outdoor Education, 11*(2), 50-59.

Brookes, A. (2007b). Research update: Outdoor education fatalities in Australia. *Australian Journal of Outdoor Education, 11*(1), 3-9.

Brown, M. (2008). Comfort zone: Model or metaphor? *Australian Journal of Outdoor Education, 12*(1), 3-12.

Brown, M., & Fraser, D. (2009). Re-evaluating risk and exploring educational alternatives. *Journal of Adventure Education and Outdoor Learning, 9*(1), 61-77.

Brown, T. (1999). Adventure risk management. In J.C. Miles & S. Priest (Eds.), *Adventure programming* (pp. 273-284). State College, PA: Venture.

Bunting, C. (1999). Have adventure programs eliminated too much risk? In S. Wurdinger & T. Potter (Eds.), *Controversial issues in adventure education* (pp. 129-135). Dubuque, IA: Kendall/Hunt.

Cason, D., & Gillis, L. (1994). A meta-analysis of outdoor adventure programming with adolescents. *Journal of Experiential Education, 17*(1), 40-47.

Davis-Berman, J., & Berman, D. (2002). Risk and anxiety in adventure programming. *Journal of Experiential Education, 25*(2), 305-310.

Dewey, J. (1938). *Experience and education.* New York: Collier.

Dickson, T.J. (2005). Risk management: A 'whole-of organisation' approach. In T.J. Dickson, T. Gray, & B. Hayllar (Eds.), *Outdoor and experiential learning: Views from the top* (pp. 111-122). Dunedin, New Zealand: Otago University Print.

Estrellas, A. (1996). The eustress paradigm: A strategy for decreasing stress in wilderness adventure programming. In K. Warren (Ed.), *Women's voices in experiential education* (pp. 32-44). Dubuque, IA: Kendall/Hunt.

Ewert, A.W., & Garvey, D.E. (2007). Philosophy and theory of adventure education. In D. Prouty, J. Panicucci, & R. Collinson (Eds.), *Adventure education: Theory and applications* (pp. 19-32). Champaign, IL: Human Kinetics.

Haddock, C. (1993). *Managing risks in outdoor activities.* 1st ed. Wellington, New Zealand: New Zealand Mountain Safety Council.

Hattie, J. (1992). Towards a model of schooling: A synthesis of meta-analyses. *Australian Journal of Education, 36*, 5-13.

Hattie, J. (2009). *Visible learning: A synthesis of over 800 meta-analyses relating to achievement.* London: Routledge.

Hattie, J., Marsh, H.W., Neill, J.T., & Richards, G.E. (1997). Adventure education and Outward Bound: Out-of-class experiences that have a lasting effect. *Review of Educational Research, 67*, 43-87.

Leberman, S., & Martin, A. (2003). Does pushing comfort zones produce peak learning experiences? *Australian Journal of Outdoor Education, 7*(1), 10-19.

Martin, B., Cashel, C., Wagstaff, M., & Breunig, M. (2006). *Outdoor leadership: Theory and practice.* Champaign, IL: Human Kinetics.

Miles, J.C., & Priest, S. (Eds.). (1990). *Adventure education.* State College, PA: Venture.

Miles, J.C., & Priest, S. (Eds.). (1999). *Adventure programming.* State College, PA: Venture.

Passarelli, A., Hall, E., & Anderson, M. (2010). A strengths-based approach to outdoor and adventure education: Possibilities for personal growth. *Journal of Experiential Education, 33*(2), 120-135.

Priest, S. (1999a). Introduction. In J.C. Miles & S. Priest (Eds.), *Adventure programming* (pp. xiii-xiv). State College, PA: Venture.

Priest, S. (1999b). The semantics of adventure programming. In J.C. Miles & S. Priest (Eds.), *Adventure programming* (pp. 111-114). State College, PA: Venture.

Priest, S., & Gass, M.A. (1997). *Effective leadership in adventure programming.* Champaign, IL: Human Kinetics.

Sammet, K. (2010). Relationships matter: Adolescent girls and relational development in adventure education. *Journal of Experiential Education, 33*(2), 151-165.

Sheard, M., & Golby, J. (2006). The efficacy of an outdoor adventure education curriculum on selected aspects of positive psychological development. *Journal of Experiential Education, 29*(2), 187-209.

Sibthorp, J. (2010). A letter from the editor: Positioning outdoor and adventure programs within positive youth development. *Journal of Experiential Education, 33*(2), vi-ix.

Wattchow, B., & Brown, M. (2011). *A pedagogy of place: Outdoor education for a changing world.* Melbourne, Australia: Monash University Publishing.

Wojcikiewicz, S., & Mural, Z. (2010). A Deweyian framework for youth development in experiential education: Perspectives from sail training and sailing instruction. *Journal of Experiential Education, 33*(2), 105-119.

Wolfe, B., & Samdahl, D. (2005). Challenging assumptions: Examining fundamental beliefs that shape challenge course programming and research. *Journal of Experiential Education, 28*(1), 25-43.

Wurdinger, S. (1997). *Philosophical issues in adventure education.* 3rd ed. Dubuque, IA: Kendall/Hunt.

Zink, R., & Leberman, S. (2001). Risking a debate—Refining risk and risk management: A New Zealand case study. *Journal of Experiential Education, 24*(1), 50-57.

Controversial Issue 2

Should principles of challenge by choice be integral to all adventure program experiences?

This question relates to Kurt Hahn's assertion that it is morally acceptable (indeed, imperative) to impel students into situations involving real risks in order to facilitate growth and development. This question is pertinent because we currently preach the principles of challenge by choice within the adventure programming industry as a way to avoid miseducative experiences. This juxtaposition of Hahn's assertion concerning the value of risk in adventure programming and the assumptions undergirding the principles of challenge by choice creates a dilemma. We are often in the position of compromising one of these two principles. On one hand, in our adherence to the principle of challenge by choice, we are often reluctant to impel students to participate at a level that would yield significant growth and development. On the other, we often neglect the principles of challenge by choice for the sake of some greater educative or therapeutic ends. A key example of this in the outdoor behavioral health care industry is the "kidnapping" of troubled youth in the middle of the night and sending them to treatment programs. Another example is the use of challenge by choice with developmentally disabled populations who are incapable of making reasoned choices about their degree of participation in a given activity. Adventure programs around the world practice the philosophy of challenge by choice. This practice is so deeply integrated in program philosophy and values that program staff members new and old seldom question its validity.

Jennifer Davis-Berman and Dene Berman argue in support of challenge by choice and assert that participants should have the option to selectively engage in activities that involve perceived or real risks. Adventure activities place participants out of their comfort zones and often create stress and anxiety, which can inhibit meaningful growth and change. Davis-Berman and Berman make a case that challenge by choice must be present to facilitate positive and meaningful change in participants.

Brent Wolfe and Diane Samdahl challenge the basic assumptions of challenge by choice and argue that it ignores the realities of the adventure-based programming. They assert that a lack of research and our profession's blind acceptance prevents a true understanding of the individual's experience during adventure programs. This entire argument merits careful consideration within the profession of adventure programming. Fundamental values at play define who we are and how we serve others. Wrestling with this question offers an opportunity to engage in a more critical analysis of the extent to which program participants should be able to dictate their level of involvement in adventure programs.

Should principles of challenge by choice be integral to all adventure program experiences?

Challenge by Choice: A Positive Model for Change

Jennifer Davis-Berman, PhD, professor of social work at the University of Dayton, Ohio, United States

Dene Berman, PhD, clinical psychologist, Lifespan Counseling Associates, Beavercreek, Ohio, United States

We take the position that adventure program leaders and administrators concerned with participant growth should allow or even encourage participants to selectively engage in activities. This statement is based on the belief that the subjective perception of safety and risk is all-important in creating healthy environments that sustain long-term change. Although it is acknowledged that discomfort, fear, and even life-threatening experiences can facilitate change and growth for some, most people prefer to create change in their lives from positions of relative safety and controllable levels of stress so as to sustain some level of stability. Being placed in situations of perceived or real risk puts some out of their comfort zones and makes them feel unstable, which often creates stress and anxiety, thereby inhibiting change and causing emotional harm.

This argument explores the subjective nature of risk and the experience and meaning of anxiety. We then relate these concepts and experiences to adventure programs. We emphasize reconciling challenge by choice with these ideas about risk and anxiety in adventure programs and support throughout the philosophy of challenge by choice in all settings and situations.

The Subjective Nature of Risk

To begin, consider this quote from an article on peak experiences in a recent issue of the popular magazine *Psychology Today*: "Some people have to climb to the top of a mountain to have a peak moment. For a shy person, reaching out to a stranger is the equivalent of climbing Everest" (Webber, 2010, p. 65). Think about how individualized the notion of risk really can be. We all have different experiences of what brings us out of our comfort zones and how much discomfort we can tolerate. People

have different thresholds at which they begin to feel physically or emotionally threatened. This emphasizes the idea that the experience of risk itself is subjective.

As an example, every semester at a local university one of the authors teaches an experientially based course on death and dying. Although not a traditional adventure course that takes place in the outdoors, this class includes aspects of adventure. For many in the class, this is their first experience with talking about death and sharing their feelings and experiences with a group of fellow students. The course requires many hands-on experiences, including a visit to a local funeral home and touring both the casket selection and embalming rooms. At first, one might think this would be a nonthreatening experience that creates little or no anxiety in students. After all, the funeral director makes sure that the class is not exposed to bodies or anything that would put students at physical risk, and students are not at the funeral home for an actual visitation or service for a loved one.

However, it is a mistake to make these kinds of assumptions about risk. For some students the simple act of visiting a funeral home is way out of their comfort zone and feels extremely risky. Perhaps a student has just lost a loved one to death, or maybe a loved one is currently suffering from a life-threatening illness. It is also possible that a student has had a bad experience at a funeral home in the past. Finally, a student might be so scared of the topic of death that entering a funeral home is overwhelming. Requiring a student to complete the funeral home tour in any of these scenarios could lead to an escalation of stress and anxiety and cause them to shut down emotionally or even be traumatized. After some conversation, some students opt out of this experience and a few ask to be escorted and supported by the professor during the tour.

Another example relates more directly to the process of adventure therapy (Davis-Berman and Berman, 1994, 2008). Even though therapy programs of this sort represent a small number of programs in the larger field of adventure programming, they are nonetheless important; they often have high profiles and the potential to both help and harm participants. This potential to help participants change has been chronicled in such books as *Shouting at the Sky* (Ferguson, 1999) and *Crossing the Water* (Robb, 2002). The potential to harm, including the death of some participants, has been the subject of negative national press and of the book *Help at Any Cost* (Szalavitz, 2006).

From a client's perspective, it is difficult to picture being taken to a therapist's office and forced to participate. Imagine walking into a therapist's office where, instead of being helped to feel safe and comfortable, the setting is harsh or scary or one in which you may even fear for your life. How much would you be willing to share about yourself under these latter circumstances? Wouldn't you want to put up protective psychological walls to keep the threat at a more manageable level? If this were to happen, most mental health professionals would be outraged at the violation of the client's rights. Why, then, would anyone think that it is acceptable to require participation in adventure-based programs?

Traditionally, psychotherapy has been a voluntary activity. Yes, some clients are court ordered or required to participate. However, this situation is far from ideal and therapists often report that those who are forced usually do not work on issues in therapy. Therapists often highlight the importance of readiness to change. People must want to engage in the activity in order to maximally benefit from it.

Moreover, it can be argued that traditional therapists, adventure therapists, or experiential educators have to make a choice about the kind of professionals they want to be. Adventure program leaders and administrators can be professionals who create safe environments and encourage participants who take only those risks that they can be open to, or they can be professionals who push participants into uncomfortable or dangerous places (physically or emotionally). Our position on this issue supports choosing safety. Furthermore, the professional societies affiliated with mental health professionals support this perspective and eschew coercion as a mechanism to therapeutic change. This is an important issue to consider because all psychologists, counselors, and social workers are governed by professional associations and their behavior is governed by codes of ethics.

Because the field of adventure education and therapy is so diverse, it has been difficult to establish a coherent code of ethics that would apply to behavior in a variety of types of programs. It is clear, however, that mental health professionals are bound by their individual code of ethics regardless of the setting of their practice.

Challenge by Choice

The phrase *challenge by choice* is often used in the adventure field as a mantra, yet one might question how often it is actually practiced. This phrase was originally coined by Karl Rohnke (1977, 1984) when he talked about the idea that giving people a choice in adventure programs might lead to greater change than pushing people beyond their limits of coping. He recognized that too much stress could be detrimental.

This philosophy became one of the mainstays of the Project Adventure program, and many still reference this group today as promoting the notion of challenge by choice. According to this group, challenge is a complex experience. In striving for a positive environment, "Out of that wholesomeness, participants will begin to pick and choose for themselves what they need to do to improve" (Schoel, Prouty, and Radcliffe, 1988, p. 130). In the classic text on adventure-based counseling, Schoel, Prouty, and Radcliffe (1988) state that challenge by choice in adventure programs offers a student the following:

- A chance to try a potentially difficult or frightening challenge in an atmosphere of support and caring
- The opportunity to "back off" when performance pressures or self-doubt become too strong, knowing that an opportunity for a future attempt will always be available
- A chance to try difficult tasks, recognizing that the attempt is more significant than performance results
- Respect for individual ideas and choices (p. 131)

This classic statement is still relevant today. This philosophy supports an environment based in care, focuses more on process than outcome, and allows individuals to make choices without reprisal.

Anxiety and Risk

When challenge by choice is not adopted in adventure programs, emphasis is often placed on actual risk or on creating the perception of risk. In a classic reference, Luckner and Nadler (1997) suggest that individuals experience growth and change from a state of dynamic tension. This is best brought out by internal conflict that is created when a person's sense of safety and security is challenged. The following quote illustrates the notion of pushing people out of their comfort zones, a common practice in adventure programs today:

> There are conditions or states that people can be placed in, in order to accentuate disequilibrium, dissonance, disorder, frustration, or anxiety. Enhancing these feelings increases the need to order, restructure, or alter one's cognitive map of the world and oneself in an effort to restore equilibrium. Understanding these conditions and finding ways to create them can increase your ability to promote change. (Luckner and Nadler, 1997, p. 24)

From a psychological perspective, this approach to creating change does not seem reasonable. The danger in creating perceived risk and not allowing challenge by choice is that some participants may be pushed into crisis (Davis-Berman and Berman, 2008). We have talked extensively about the potential dangers in fueling anxiety and creating crisis. Anxiety can cause people to become more closed and withdrawn, clearly affecting them in an adventure program. Others may react with increased agitation, activity, and verbalization (Berman and Davis-Berman, 2002; Davis-Berman and Berman, 2002). These experiences can have lasting effects and cause participants to withdraw from adventure activities altogether. General fears and anxieties can also be increased and generalized to other situations.

Cognitive distortions may also occur when people react with anxiety to being out of their comfort zones. One of the most serious distortions is catastrophizing, where an individual believes that, in essence, "the sky is falling." In other words, the anxiety gets so bad that any sense of personal control or efficacy is lost (Dumont, 1997). This is a potentially serious situation and can contribute to the development of an anxiety disorder or inflame an anxiety disorder that is already present.

Supporting the Challenge by Choice Approach

One of the goals of adventure programs is usually to promote some lasting change or growth in

the participants. We have argued that long-term change may best be achieved by embracing that which people choose. Mitten (1999) has presented a model that stresses flexible, safe leadership within the health-trip community and emphasizes respect and valuing each person. This approach supports the argument that challenge by choice must be present in all adventure-based programs and is very different from pushing individuals out of their comfort zones to facilitate change.

Leberman and Martin (2002) attempt to look at whether activities that pushed participants out of their comfort zones truly led to change or if the more supportive approach previously outlined was more effective. In interviews with Outward Bound students, they found that the activities that students said pushed them out of their comfort zones the most were clearly physical in nature. However, the activities that they identified as most growth enhancing and those that contributed most to permanent and meaningful change in their lives were social, creative, and reflective. Clearly, more research needs to be done in this area to determine what contributes to lasting change. But this study suggests that a safe environment, rather than one fraught with risk, is what facilitates change.

The perspective of challenge by choice is also consistent with a positive psychology approach. This framework is increasingly being used in the field of mainstream psychology. It focuses on strengths rather than deficits and helps people move from a negative or neutral state to a positive one (Seligman and Csikszentmihalyi, 2000). The flow experience is related to positive psychology and has been discussed as it relates to adventure programs. Two of the most important elements of the flow experience are as follows (Csikszentmihalyi and Csikszentmihalyi, 1999, pp. 154-156):

- There is a sense of being in control of one's actions and the environment.
- Being engaged in the activity is so enjoyable and rewarding that the person wants to repeat the experience, which is so different than the mundane aspects of everyday life.

Berman and Davis-Berman (2008) argue that it would be difficult, if not impossible, to achieve this state of flow or this positive movement toward health if put in a position of high perceived risk with no choice about participation.

This is not to say that adventure programs should stop encouraging participants to reach and stretch their physical and psychological limits. To the contrary, for some people this is the best way to promote growth. Leaders could take a personal approach with participants and should attempt to know the strengths and weaknesses of those participating in the program. Leaders should also listen to and respect the personal assessments of the participants. This kind of knowledge could involve in-depth evaluations of program participants. Although this is time consuming, it would help leaders understand the needs of their participants. Perceived risk is a very subjective experience, and leaders should understand and respect the boundaries and limits that participants bring to the program.

Pushing participants to do what feels too risky increases the chance that they will experience an emotional crisis (Berman and Davis-Berman, 2002; Davis-Berman and Berman, 2002). Handling this kind of situation requires a high level of expertise and puts the professional at some risk on two levels. First, the professional must be able to handle participants in crisis and, at the same time, avoid blocking progress for either the individual or those around the person in crisis. This task is not to be taken lightly. Second, there is a risk to the professional's sense of self as an agent of change. Whether it is in the classroom, the therapy office, or in the field, the professional must behave in ways that are seen as growth enhancing yet safe, challenging without being overwhelming, and urging without pushing.

Another concern is the idea of promoting and ensuring lasting change. Ideally, participants should incorporate the changes they have made in adventure programs into their lives in a real way. For that to happen, the experience has to be fully embraced. Experience suggests that people seek to integrate those positive experiences that they actively and positively chose and to reject those that were forced on them by others. Consider the following quote from an article written on positive psychology:

> Instead of trying to create change by increasing risk, outdoor educators can increase autotelic experiences by helping people enjoy the experience and use skills they develop within a context of friendship and support, in which there is emotional release and the ability to measure one's self against their ideals and others. These activities promote . . . feedback and information about one's striving toward the goals. As psychology is moving toward a paradigm of fostering excellence, so too is outdoor education challenged to move away from negative models of change to further help

people find, develop, and use their gifts. (Berman and Davis-Berman, 2008)

Giving participants choice increases their ability to integrate into their lives the power of the experiences. This positive model of change is consistent with mainstream thinking in mental health.

Conclusion

Although many adventure-based programs focus on the value of pushing participants out of their zones of comfort, this argument suggests that doing this is, psychologically, quite risky. Therapists who are bound to a code of ethics must recognize the importance of choice in treatment and participation in activities. As such, a challenge-by-choice approach in all adventure-based programming should be fully endorsed. True and lasting change results from security and safety and giving people the freedom and confidence to stretch themselves and integrate these changes in a permanent way.

Challenge by choice is particularly imperative in adventure-based programs. Pushing people beyond their coping limits or coercing participation can create or add to existing anxiety and crisis. These events can become difficult or even impossible for leaders to manage. The field of adventure programming bears a large responsibility for the health and safety of its program participants. By adopting and following a model of challenge by choice, this safety can be ensured.

References

Berman, D., & Davis-Berman, J. (2002). An integrated approach to crisis management in wilderness settings. *Journal of Adventure Education and Outdoor Learning*, 2(1), 9-18.

Berman, D., & Davis-Berman, J. (2008). Positive psychology and outdoor education. In K. Warren, D. Mitten, & T.A. Loeffler (Eds.), *Theory and practice of experiential education* (pp. 237-243). Boulder, CO: Association for Experiential Education.

Csikszentmihalyi, M., & Csikszentmihalyi, I. (1999). Adventure and the flow experience. In J. Miles & S. Priest (Eds.), *Adventure programming* (pp. 153-158). State College, PA: Venture.

Davis-Berman, J., & Berman, D. (1994). *Wilderness therapy: Foundations, theory and research*. Dubuque, IA: Kendall/Hunt.

Davis-Berman, J., & Berman, D. (2002). Risk and anxiety in adventure programming. *Journal of Experiential Education, 25*, 305-310.

Davis-Berman, J., & Berman, D. (2008). *The promise of wilderness therapy*. Boulder, CO: Association for Experiential Education.

Dumont, R. (1997). *The sky is falling*. New York: Norton.

Ferguson, G. (1999). *Shouting at the sky: Troubled teens and the promise of the wild*. New York: St. Martin's Press.

Leberman, S., & Martin, A. (2002). Does pushing comfort zones produce peak learning experiences? *Australian Journal of Outdoor Education, 7*, 10-19.

Luckner, J., & Nadler, R. (1997). *Processing the experience: Strategies to enhance and generalize learning*. 2nd ed. Dubuque, IA: Kendall/Hunt.

Mitten, D. (1999). Leadership for community building. In J. Miles & S. Priest (Eds.), *Adventure programming* (pp. 253-261). State College, PA: Venture.

Robb, D. (2002). *Crossing the water: Eighteen months on an island working with troubled boys—A teacher's memoir*. New York: Touchstone.

Rohnke, K. (1977). *Cowstails and cobras*. Hamilton, MA: Project Adventure.

Rohnke, K. (1984). *Silver bullets*. Hamilton, MA: Project Adventure.

Schoel, J., Prouty, D., & Radcliffe, P. (1988). *Islands of healing: A guide to adventure based counseling*. Hamilton, MA: Project Adventure.

Seligman, M., & Csikszentmihalyi, M. (2000). Positive psychology: An introduction. *American Psychologist, 54*, 5-14.

Szalavitz, M. (2006). *Help at any cost: How the troubled-teen industry cons parents and hurts teens*. New York: Riverhead Books.

Webber, R. (2010). Big moments. *Psychology Today*, October, 63-69.

Should principles of challenge by choice be integral to all adventure program experiences?

NO | Opposed to Challenge by Choice: An Exploration of Weaknesses and Limitations

Brent Wolfe, PhD, associate professor of recreation therapy at Georgia Southern University, Statesboro, Georgia, United States

Diane M. Samdahl, PhD, professor of recreation and leisure studies at University of Georgia, Athens, Georgia, United States

Challenge by choice (C×C) is one of the first concepts that new adventure program facilitators encounter. In their earliest days of training, facilitators are taught that willing and voluntary participation is central to every aspect of adventure programs. Surprisingly, little research exists to support the legitimacy and effectiveness of C×C. This argument is an attempt to open that discussion.

We contend that C×C should not be promoted, because it conflicts with or ignores the central tenets and experiential realities of adventure programs. We begin by describing the central components of C×C, including the newer variation referred to as "inviting optimal participation." Against that background, we identify what we see as major weaknesses and limitations with C×C. Collectively, these points support our contention that C×C is ineffective and our claim that an unquestioning acceptance of C×C has prevented facilitators from understanding the significant influence that group dynamics has on the individual experiences of participants during adventure activities.

Overview of C×C

One of the earliest references to C×C comes from Rohnke (1989). In that work, Rohnke outlines four main components of C×C:

- the chance to try a potentially difficult or frightening challenge in an atmosphere of support and caring;
- the opportunity to "back off" when performance pressures or self-doubt become too strong;
- the chance to try difficult tasks in an environment where the attempt is more significant than performance; and
- respect for individual ideas and choices. (p. 14)

At first glance, and without doubt by intention, these foundational aspects of C×C are well meaning and noble and are in contrast to then-common leadership practices in adventure programming. Rohnke (1989) stated,

> What a change! What a revelation that the simple affording of that choice could achieve more toward growth of self-awareness and image than what used to require large doses of performance pressure. . . . With the pressure off, the opportunity for growth was palpably different. (pp. 13-14)

Adventure programming itself has a rich history that precedes Rohnke's work. Adventure programming first appeared with the development of Outward Bound, which was initially designed to train and prepare young sailors in the event of abandoning ship (Priest and Gass, 2005). Those early adventure programs simulated emergency situations that might be faced at sea, where there was little room for choice. As this field moved from training for life-and-death situations to the current format as an educational, recreational, developmental, and therapeutic forum, choice and voluntary engagement became more necessary and important (Priest and Gass, 2005). Against this backdrop, the movement to adopt C×C was nothing short of a mammoth paradigm shift.

Since Rohnke first articulated those components of C×C, other authors have attempted to further develop this concept. Carlson and Evans (2001) reframe Rohnke's four concepts into three essential core values. The first core value is that participants should be allowed to establish their own goals and create their own definitions of success. For example, on the pamper pole (in a high ropes course, individuals must ascend a 20- to 30-foot [6 to 9.1

m] pole and jump off it), some participants might feel successful only if they leap from the top of the pole whereas others might be satisfied by climbing halfway up the pole.

The second core value that Carlson and Evans identify is the belief that participants should be allowed to determine how much of an activity or element to complete. This is closely aligned with the notion that participants should be able to establish personal goals, but it emphasizes the need for facilitators to honor participants' decisions to complete only a portion of the intended activity. Whereas some participants might follow an activity from its intended inception to its intended completion, other participants might decide to stop at an earlier point in the activity.

The final core value that Carlson and Evans (2001) discuss is the belief that participants need to be able to make informed choices based on a full understanding of what an activity will entail. To accomplish this, a facilitator must provide the participants with relevant information. It is important to recognize that Carlson and Evans' three core values of C×C are not contrary to Rohnke's original components; rather, they condense and synthesize the original concept.

In response to the idea of C×C, and due to problems with its implementation, Haras, Bunting, and Witt (2005) propose that adventure experiences should be designed to provide a spectrum of challenges that encompass the range of engagements that participants might desire. They refer to this as inviting optimum participation (I-Opt) and suggest it as an alternative to C×C. The principal tenets of I-Opt include the following: creating a multilevel challenge environment that engages all participants, providing inclusive activities that offer simultaneous action opportunities for experiencing adventure, intentionally designing participant choice into the scope of each activity's central task, and presenting comparable interaction that makes it possible for all participants to have an equitable adventure experience (p. 41). Because I-Opt has been identified as an alternative to C×C and has similar foundational beliefs to those of C×C, we at times expand our critique to include both models.

Concerns About C×C

To explore the difficulties with C×C (and to a lesser extent I-Opt), we organize our comments into two categories: general concerns related to the implementation of C×C and more specific concerns about the core assumptions embedded within C×C.

Central to both discussions is the inescapable yet unexamined tension that binds the individual to the group.

Implementing C×C

Our most significant concern with C×C is its widespread acceptance despite the lack of evidence about whether it produces the intended freedom of choice for participants. In fact, Wolfe (2004) found evidence to the contrary. In a study of participants' experiences during a one-day challenge course program, Wolfe uncovered repeated references that participants felt "I've gotta do it." Although the facilitators of this program felt they had effectively implemented C×C, the participants clearly felt pressure to complete the activities as presented to them. This pressure came partly from the facilitators but also from the design of the elements, other members of the group, and even expectations the participants placed on themselves. Because adventure activities are often designed for groups, individual choice may be difficult, if not impossible, to achieve. If that is the case, C×C may be little more than a veneer that makes facilitators feel better about what they do.

This problem stems from the fact that C×C considers only the interaction between the facilitator and a participant. The facilitator must let the participant define success and determine the extent of engagement within an activity, but this model ignores other important factors that limit a participant's ability to make choices. The first example comes from Rohnke himself. When initially describing C×C, Rohnke (1989) states, "Sometimes it may be necessary to say, 'This is the way it's going to be. Do it!' You may seem like a drill-sergeant, but . . . a lot of growth can take place when people have no choice as to whether they are or are not going to do something" (p. 14). Thus, from its inception, the model of C×C has assumed that at times the facilitator has the power and perhaps the responsibility to deny choice.

One troubling example of the ways authority can undermine the intended empowerment of C×C is seen in Wolfe's (2004) study of challenge course participants. Standard safety guidelines require all participants to wear a harness when participating in high elements; this requirement is so basic that every facilitator will enforce it. However, one self-described obese participant in Wolfe's study spoke about her feelings of shame and humiliation because the harness highlighted the size and shape of her body. This participant became painfully aware that participation was not a simple yes–no decision as C×C might imply; rather, the decision to participate entailed a complexity of factors, and negative consequences were associated with either choice.

These problems arise in part because the group is overlooked in the C×C model. This oversight is interesting given that facilitators intentionally use initiatives to build group cohesion before moving into the more central elements of their programs. Because the group becomes so salient, factors like peer pressure, social judgment, pride, and embarrassment are all present in the adventure experience. Participants offer encouragement and enticements to one another to complete a task; likewise, individuals feel they let the group down if their performance becomes problematic to others. Rohnke (1989) acknowledges peer pressure and says it could be positive or negative, but the model of C×C does little to differentiate between those extremes. Does a facilitator's statement about choice truly counterbalance the effect of peer pressure and social comparison? Only the most mature participants can make a dissenting choice without jeopardizing their self-esteem, and only the most skilled facilitators can create an emotionally safe space for choices that go against group norms. We contend that these group influences erode the freedom of C×C for most participants in adventure programs.

Our final concern with C×C is the assumption that it applies equally well to all aspects of adventure programming. In a traditional challenge course with a series of elements, it is feasible that a participant might decide to quit one activity without completing the originally intended goal. However, on a five-day backpacking trip, participants do not have the option of stopping on the third day. Arguing that participants had the option to withdraw before the trip began undermines the basic tenet of C×C that says facilitators should honor a participant's request to stop at any point within the activity and perhaps raises concerns about whether that participant had full information on which to make the initial decision to participate. Even with I-Opt and the intentional provision of a range of activities and challenges, dropping out of a five-day hike is not plausible. C×C may also be weakened in therapeutic programs, not only because of concerns about the amount of risk participants should face (see Berman and Davis-Berman, 2005) but also because those programs might provide less choice for the participants. C×C may not apply equally across different types of adventure activities or during different phases of an adventure program. These nuances are not addressed when C×C is universally applied to all adventure programs.

Assumptions Within C×C

One central assumption within C×C is that participants should be allowed to establish personal goals within each element or activity. On the surface this goal is understandable and noble, but with further examination it becomes problematic.

Many adventure programs are designed for preexisting groups such as a sport team, a business team, or a class of students. The coach, supervisor, or instructor typically has an underlying purpose for engaging this group in the adventure program—that is, there are overriding goals for the group. Encouraging individuals to establish personal goals can quickly undermine that larger group goal. If, for example, the group was brought into the adventure program to build cohesion and unity, an individual who sets increasingly high goals around performance and perfection might create stress and friction within that group. When individual goals conflict with the group goals or group purpose, individuals are typically asked or required to change. If individuals are not asked or required to change their goals, then one must question the whole premise of establishing group goals or establishing a purpose for participating in an adventure program.

Facilitators themselves often impose overarching goals by selecting specific activities or by emphasizing specific points during debriefing. For example, many of the low elements on a challenge course are designed to foster communication and cooperation. The objective is to help members realize that individual goals must be put aside in order for the team to successfully complete the task. In group initiatives such as this, individuals who pursue personal goals are often singled out as the source of a problem. During debriefing, participants are made to see that the group's success began to take shape when participants gave up individual goals and began to work together.

In instances where a facilitator works one-on-one with a participant who is doing an individual activity (e.g., high elements in a challenge course or activities in a therapeutic program), establishing personal goals might truly enhance the experience for the participant. However, most adventure programs require individuals to synchronize their activities and goals with those of a larger group. When that is the case, personal goals can easily become problematic. This premise that individuals should be allowed to establish personal goals is inherently at odds with the group nature of many adventure programs.

A second assumption within C×C is that participants should be allowed to determine how much of an activity they want to complete. Similar to the points made before about personal goals, this appears to honor a participant's right to determine how to engage with an activity, but when examined further, it too is seen as problematic.

Initial problems with selective completion of an activity have been mentioned in the preceding discussions: peer pressure and the social dynamics of a group can undermine a participant's willingness to select anything other than full completion of an activity, and activities designed to build group cohesion often demand the full engagement of all participants. These two aspects of adventure programming suggest that selective completion of an activity is problematic from the start.

Another problem with selective completion is that adventure activities often have an intentional design that includes structured starting and stopping points and clearly articulated rules of engagement. These are not random activities selected simply because they are fun; they entail sequential challenges that reinforce and expand on the lessons from previous activities. Except in therapeutic settings where a facilitator may be working one-on-one with each participant toward predefined goals, a participant's decision to complete less than the intended full activity is often met with negative response from the facilitator and other group members.

We can see this through an example on the catwalk, a high element in a challenge course. During research conducted by Wolfe (2004), facilitators provided the following instructions for this element: climb the tree, walk across a horizontal telephone pole for 20 feet (6 m) to reach a second tree, return to the middle of the pole, and lean backward and be lowered to the ground. As participants performed these activities, an informal norm of success emerged that was associated with reaching the second tree. Whenever a participant reached that stage in the activity, one participant yelled out, "And another success!" while other group members applauded and cheered. Participants who considered stopping before reaching the second tree were often told, "Go just a little farther—you can do it!" These messages came from the facilitator as well as other group members. And when participants elected to stop without crossing the pole, they were met with lowered, less enthusiastic voices that called out statements such as, "That's okay, at least you tried." Though presumably intended as supportive and encouraging, these comments were ultimately demeaning in that they reinforced the fact that this participant did not succeed according to the standards established by the group.

It is clear that selective completion of an activity, which is one of the core principles of C×C, is an exceedingly complex issue. Though facilitators remind participants that they can stop at any point, individuals are directly and indirectly encouraged to "succeed" by completing the entire task in the predetermined fashion. Even if individuals define personal success as completing only a portion of that activity, comments and reactions by other group members (and perhaps by the facilitator) make it clear that these teammates have somehow failed to succeed.

A third assumption in C×C is that participants make informed decisions based on full disclosure about what an activity entails. To allow for informed decisions, adventure program facilitators must provide all information pertinent to each participant's decision to participate. Although this might seem simple at the outset, providing all relevant information is an impossible undertaking. Consider, for example, the woman described earlier who experienced self-consciousness and shame when wearing a safety harness. Should the facilitator have anticipated and described this as a potential risk? If facilitators confine themselves to providing information only about physical risks, truly informed decisions are seriously compromised.

This is not meant as a criticism of program facilitators. One basic tenet of adventure programs (and any other form of experiential education) is that, in order to truly understand, participants need to engage in the experiential learning cycle: experience, reflect, generalize, and apply (Kolb, 1984). Learning occurs not just in the rational brain but through experiential immersion in an activity or, as suggested by Luckner and Nadler (1997), by moving from a comfort zone, through a groan zone, to a growth zone by doing edgework (i.e., participating in experiences that allow for personal growth as individuals move from zone to zone). Thus, the principle of fully informed decision making is profoundly at odds with the core ideology that sets adventure programs apart from other educational, recreational, developmental, and therapeutic venues. In promoting informed decisions, facilitators are attempting to provide information that might not exist in the realm of words and rational thought processes.

Adventure program facilitators have an ethical and moral obligation to minimize the tangible physical risks of an activity. During informed decision making, they describe what an activity will entail and provide information about safety precautions that will prevent injury (e.g., how much weight a rope can hold or how a safety harness works). Even though they take action to minimize real risk, facilitators undoubtedly want the element of perceived risk to remain salient. After all, the entire premise of adventure activities, especially in relation to the potential for personal growth, rests on perceived risk. But how can informed decision making proceed if it requires factual information about real risks that does not reduce or eliminate perceived risk? From an experiential perspective, perceived risk creates the same emotional and biophysical response as real risk—it is, in fact, real. This complex interaction between real and perceived risk has not been fully articulated in C×C, but it has profound implications on informed decision making.

Though facilitators can easily describe safety precautions that prevent or minimize physical risk, they often ignore the overwhelmingly significant realm of social and emotional risks. As mentioned earlier, the social nature of groups affects the freedom of individuals to set personal goals or make decisions about selective participation. Likewise, the social arena produces opportunities and tensions that generate social and emotional risk for participants. Facilitators are not taught, and in fact are often unable to see and unprepared to manage, the complex interactions that produce guilt, shame, or loss of self-esteem when individuals put themselves at risk in a group environment.

It is impossible to anticipate and forewarn participants about the potential social or emotional risks they might encounter. Likewise, it is unrealistic to believe that participants themselves can make rational decisions about an experiential event before engaging in that activity. Like other aspects of C×C, informed decision making is a noble, but impossible, ideal that falls short in the reality of adventure programs.

Conclusion

The intention of C×C is to highlight the right of participants to make their own choices about how they participate in adventure activities (Rohnke, 1989). It is too easy to frame this debate by focusing only on that element of respect for individual decision making. We agree that it is good to allow participants to have a choice, and we see the dangers of forcing participants to take risks they do not embrace. However, we do not agree that programming with C×C will resolve those concerns.

C×C is integrally at odds with central tenets of adventure programming. It rests on a false belief that individuals can make autonomous decisions in social settings that promote group interaction. It is blindly applied to all forms of adventure programs, even those that attempt to promote group cohesion over individual action. It ignores the elements of programming that implicitly define norms of success. And, paradoxically, this belief that individuals can make rational decisions is applied in a professional arena that values experiential immersion over cognition. Despite good intentions, C×C does not occur in adventure programs. The myth of C×C is a veneer that does little more than make facilitators feel good about themselves while preventing them from seeing or addressing more significant factors that influence participants' experiences in adventure activities.

References

Berman, D.S., & Davis-Berman, J. (2005). Positive psychology and outdoor education. *Journal of Experiential Education, 28*, 17-24.

Carlson, J.A., & Evans, K. (2001). Whose choice is it? Contemplating challenge-by-choice and diverse abilities. *Journal of Experiential Education, 24*, 58-63.

Haras, K., Bunting, J.C., & Witt, P.A. (2005). Linking outcomes with ropes course program design and delivery. *Journal of Park and Recreation Administration, 23*, 36-63.

Kolb, D.A. (1984). *Experiential learning: Experience as the source of learning and development.* Englewood Cliffs, NJ: Prentice-Hall.

Luckner, J.L., & Nadler, R.S. (1997). *Processing the experience: Strategies to enhance and generalize learning.* Dubuque, IA: Kendall/Hunt.

Priest, S., & Gass, M.A. (2005). *Effective leadership in adventure programming.* Champaign, IL: Human Kinetics.

Rohnke, K. (1989). *Cowstails and cobras II: A guide to games, initiatives, ropes courses, and adventure curriculum.* Dubuque, IA: Kendall/Hunt.

Wolfe, B.D. (2004). *Participants' perceptions of a one-day challenge course program.* Unpublished doctoral dissertation. Athens, GA: University of Georgia.

Controversial Issue 3

Does the concept of transfer of learning sufficiently explain the way outcomes of adventure programming are generalized to other areas of participants' lives?

An Outward Bound instructor named Rusty Baillie once proclaimed, "Let the mountains speak for themselves!" (Priest and Gass, 2005, p. 184). This statement reflects an approach to facilitation in which program participants independently glean meaning from their program experiences. This approach was commonly used in the early days of Outward Bound and adventure programming. However, researchers and practitioners eventually realized that participants could gain fuller meaning and value from their experiences through more structured reflection. Instructors began to use a range of facilitation techniques to help participants discover from their experiences lessons that might otherwise have gone uncovered. These approaches have evolved in complexity and sophistication over the years, an evolution that Priest and Gass (2005) have characterized in terms of the six generations of facilitation. Yet central in the practice of all forms of facilitation is the notion of transfer of learning (Priest and Gass, 2005), which involves integrating lessons learned from adventure program experiences into the daily lives of program participants.

For more than four decades, adventure programmers have used the concept of transfer of learning to justify the broader value of their work. However, questions have begun to emerge about the ways transfer of learning are understood and implemented in adventure programming experiences. Does the concept of transfer provide a sufficient basis for documenting the effectiveness of our work in the field of adventure programming? These questions are important because, to be taken seriously in the broader domains of education, health care, and other areas of social and environmental concern where we are seeking to make a difference, we must employ concepts that help to demonstrate the efficacy of our work. The questions being raised in this debate speak to the very value and thus viability of adventure programming as a practical discipline. They speak to the very usefulness of the profession in addressing broader societal concerns.

Michael Gass and Jayson Seaman argue that when properly understood and implemented, transfer of learning provides a sufficient basis for documenting the effectiveness of our work. In their argument, Gass and Seaman revisit Gass' (1986) original model of transfer of learning to more fully explain the nature of the concept. They argue that transfer is well established, is supported by research, and accommodates recent advances in theories of learning. They also provide additional explanation and underlying frameworks for future practices based on the idea of transfer as consequential transitions.

Nate Furman and Jim Sibthorp take an opposing stance and argue that evidence to support the primacy of transfer of learning is insufficient in adventure programming. They argue that other theoretical models offer promising alternative ways to conceptualize and document the benefits of adventure programming.

References

Gass, M.A. (1986). Programming the transfer of learning in adventure education. *Journal of Experiential Education, 8*(3), 18-24.

Priest, S., & Gass, M. (2005). *Effective leadership in adventure programming.* 2nd ed. Champaign, IL: Human Kinetics.

Does the concept of transfer of learning sufficiently explain the way outcomes of adventure programming are generalized to other areas of participants' lives?

YES Programming the Transfer of Learning in Adventure Education: An Update

Michael A. Gass, PhD, professor of outdoor education, University of New Hampshire at Durham, United States

Jayson Seaman, PhD, associate professor of outdoor education, University of New Hampshire at Durham, United States

The emerging debate on transfer of learning in outdoor adventure education (OAE) provides a welcome opportunity to revisit this widely used concept. This debate reflects broader criticism of transfer in the learning sciences, which comes from two disciplinary perspectives: cognitivism and situativity theory. Cognitivists, such as Furman and Sibthorp (see page 39), criticize the concept for failing to explain the quality, quantity, and duration of learning following an adventure program. Situativity theorists, such as Brown (2010), criticize the idea that learning is separable from context, as the term "transfer" implies. Cognitivists retain the core assumptions of transfer but propose different mechanisms and outcomes, whereas situativity theorists want entirely different assumptions.

In light of these criticisms, it is fitting for a cognitivist (Gass) and a situativity theorist (Seaman) to jointly advocate for transfer in OAE (see Barab and Duffy, 2000). In the following essay, we elaborate on Gass' (1986) original description of transfer, review empirical research validating transfer in the OAE literature, respond briefly to emerging critiques, and include a revitalized notion of transfer as viewed through the sociocultural lens of consequential transitions (Beach, 1999).

Early Development of the Concept

Gass' (1986) article on transfer presented three forms of transfer: specific, nonspecific, and metaphoric. This article illustrated these processes in a sort of "before and after" process, depicted in a sketch of a human head. This diagram can be misconstrued in the belief that transfer is only a cognitive function, with the additional assumption that individuals function independently of social systems (e.g., group, environment, culture). This was not the intent of Gass' model, and the current debate provides an opportunity to further clarify the concepts of specific, nonspecific, and metaphoric transfer using Bateson's (1972) *levels of learning* paradigm.

Bateson (1972) proposes that human learning occurs at three levels: learning I, learning II, and learning III. He describes learning I as "change in specificity of response by correction of errors of choice within a set of alternatives" (p. 293). In other words, individuals adapt by refining the choices they make within a limited range of options. At this level, specific transfer provides an individual with a new set of specific choices to make in a later situation. For example, climbers learn new knots more easily when they demonstrate associated skills from earlier situations. Specific transfer is achieved when an individual successfully corrects errors of choice with increasing cognitive efficiency.

According to Bateson, learning II is "change in the process of learning I, e.g., a corrective change in the set of alternatives from which choice is made, or it is a change in how the sequence of experience is punctuated" (p. 293). Learning II changes the framework of choices from learning I, which is why Bateson calls it "learning to learn." Nonspecific transfer enhances an individual's capability to imagine unique courses of action and mobilize resources to solve problems. For example, a participant may move from efficiently applying specific skills to developing innovative new solutions, seeking guidance from peers, or even becoming a resource for peers' learning. Nonspecific transfer is evident when individuals interpret situations in novel ways or when groups begin to develop new values and new tools for problem solving.

Bateson defines learning III as "change in the process of learning II, e.g., a corrective change in the system of sets of alternatives from which choice is made" (p. 293). Bateson writes the following:

> Learning II is an economy of the thought processes (or neural pathways) which are used for problem solving or learning I. The premises of what is commonly called "character"—the definitions of the "self" save the individual from having to examine the abstract, philosophical, aesthetic, and ethical aspects of many sequences of life. . . . But learning III will throw these unexamined premises open to question and change. (p. 303)

Learning III is a metalevel awareness of one's habits, character traits, and learning patterns in which routine systems of meaning are reorganized. Metaphoric transfer mirrors this level by applying a metaphor to another system of thought in order to facilitate meta-reflection about such patterns. For example, a metaphor can be applied to a rock-climbing activity such that the activity may cease to be about climbing skills (specific transfer), or even about the achievement of interpersonal trust (nonspecific transfer), but rather about the habitual ways challenges are tackled in everyday life (metaphoric transfer). Metaphoric transfer occurs when a target situation (e.g., challenges at school or family struggles) merges in an analogous manner with the situation at hand (rock climbing) so that the climbing activity takes on the target's figurative meaning.

Although Gass' (1986) conception of transfer can include the classical model of mental representations and situational equivalences (Lobato, 2006, p. 433), it also encompasses cognitive, social, emotional, and kinesthetic dimensions of experiential learning. Its intent was to help leaders think more thoroughly about the range of outcomes they might pursue and the corresponding techniques they could use to achieve them (Gass, 1991; Hirsch and Gillis, 1997, 2004). This is done by centering attention to the very systems where individuals are involved (Gass, 2005), a sentiment also expressed by Bateson (1972):

> The adjectives above which purport to describe individual character are really not strictly applicable to the individual but rather describe transactions between the individual and his material and human environment. No man is

"resourceful" or "dependent" or "fatalistic" in a vacuum. His characteristic, whatever it be, is not his but is rather a characteristic of what goes on between him and something (or somebody) else. (p. 298)

This crucial role of context in transfer might have been a casualty of the "human head" diagram. But even within the diagram, the individual participant is depicted as connected to a variety of systems. Of course, one can place the individual in the foreground of this process (e.g., enhancing someone's skills and knowledge to improve future performances), or one can foreground the systems or contexts in which people participate. In fact, context figures prominently in Gass' work on isomorphs (e.g., Gass and Priest, 1997, 1999), a concept and approach supported by empirical research.

Research on Facilitation

Brown (2010) asks, "Where is the evidence that one generation of facilitation is more effective than others in promoting transfer?" (p. 14). Following is a brief summary of research on facilitation for transfer in the field of OAE.

Early examination of various styles of facilitation failed to find significant differences. Gillis (1985) found no significant differences among couples participating in adventure programs with metaphorically framed experiences compared with participants not receiving metaphorically framed experiences. MacRea and colleagues (1993) examined the effect of a single day of training using a high ropes course on developing positive risk-taking propensity in firefighters. The treatment group showed significantly different positive gains in risk-taking propensity, whereas no significant difference was found between the group receiving metaphoric framing and the group receiving only the adventure training experience.

Learning from this research, Doherty (1995) examined the differences between fifth-generation or metaphoric framing (MF), Outward Bound Plus (OBP) post-experience debriefing, and "mountains speak for themselves" (MST) or no facilitation on a one-day ropes course experience for university students in the northeast United States. Metaphors created for the fifth-generation of facilitation followed the seven-step model developed by Gass (1991) and illustrated in text and video by Hirsch and Gillis (2004). Eighty-four resident assistants participated in the study and were divided into one of three groups. Each group's level of team building was measured immediately before the challenge course experience, immediately after the experience, and 30 days following the training program.

As seen in table 3.1, all three groups showed significant increases in group cohesion from pretest to acquisition. Concerning the facilitation style, the MF model improved group cohesion more than the OBP or MST models. In fact, positive changes in mean scores of the students receiving metaphoric facilitation were more than twice those of students receiving the OBP or MST models (2.50, 1.18, and 1.12, respectively). Scores on 8 of the 10 subscales also revealed greater learning among students receiving metaphoric facilitation, and 7 of the 10 largest improvements in scores were achieved by groups receiving metaphoric facilitation.

In a more rigorous study of European corporate executives, Gass and Priest (2006) measured the type of facilitation offered and when it occurred. Four intact work groups, identical in organizational structure and composition, received a training program with one of four styles of facilitation:

1. No metaphoric framing or debriefing associated with the training
2. Metaphoric debriefing after each training exercise

3. Metaphoric framing before the training experience
4. Metaphoric framing before and debriefing after the training experience

A fifth (control) group received no program. The 72-hour residential program began with goal setting and socialization, continued with group initiatives, and ended with action planning and closure experiences. Levels of teamwork were measured 1 month before, 1 month after, 6 months after, and 12 months after the program.

As shown in figure 3.1, all four groups showed significant increases in teamwork over the two-month period before and after the training program. Teamwork in the control group did not change during the study period, indicating that changes experienced by the other four groups were likely attributable to the particular training program they received rather than extraneous influences.

All groups failed to maintain teamwork levels, likely due to the lack of support at work. Teamwork levels for the group that received no framing or debriefing regressed to near baseline after six months. Teamwork levels for the group that received metaphoric debriefing returned to baseline after 12 months. Teamwork levels for the group that received metaphoric framing remained increased for six months but then decreased significantly at

Table 3.1 Change in Means Between Pretest and Acquisition Test for Each Facilitation Group and Subscale

	MF	OBP	MST
Cohesion	+5.68*	+1.81	+1.81
Leader control[†]	−2.45*	−1.24	+1.28
Anger and aggression[†]	−3.14*	−2.57	−1.10
Order and organization	+0.73	+0.24	+2.38*
Task orientation	+3.46*	+0.62	+1.00
Independence	+1.41*	+1.14	+1.38
Innovation	+1.91*	+1.57	+1.57
Self-discovery	+3.37*	+2.31	+1.43
Expressiveness	+0.46	+0.67	+1.48*
Leader support	+2.41*	−0.38	+0.33
Average change in means	+2.50	+1.18	+1.12

MF = metaphoric framing; OBP = Outward Bound Plus; MST = mountains speak for themselves

* The most beneficial change for each subscale.

† A negative score for leader control and anger and aggression is designated on the GES as a positive change.

Adapted, by permission, from K. Doherty, 1995, "A quantitative analysis of three teaching styles," *Journal of Experiential Education* 18(1): 12-19.

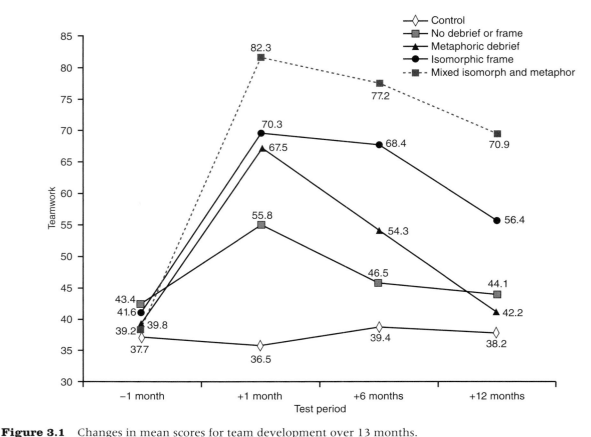

Figure 3.1 Changes in mean scores for team development over 13 months.

Reprinted, by permission, from M.A. Gass and S. Priest, 2006, "The effectiveness of metaphoric facilitation styles in corporate adventure training (CAT) programs," *Journal of Experiential Education* 29(1): 78-94.

12 months; however, they still remained higher than baseline. Teamwork levels for the group that received metaphoric framing and debriefing also remained increased after six months and remained higher than the levels of any of the other groups after 12 months.

This randomized control study showed that type of facilitation made a difference in both initial and maintenance levels, suggesting that the techniques developed on the basis of Gass (1986) produce changes that are consistent with the hypothesized mechanisms of transfer. (For qualitative support, see Gass, Garvey, and Sugerman, 2003.)

Studies of juvenile offenders provide more recent support. Gillis, Gass, and Russell (2008) report statistically significant differences in rearrest rates after one, two, and three years among participants in an adventure-based behavior management program, an outdoor therapeutic camping (no facilitation) comparison group, and a youth development center non-adventure treatment. The differences between the group participating in the adventure-based behavior management program and the other

groups grew even larger with time. Gillis and Gass (2010) found similar statistically significant results when comparing an adventure-based behavior management program for juvenile sex offenders, a traditional treatment-as-usual program (i.e., youth development center), and other specialized programs in the same state to determine program effectiveness (also measured by rearrest rates). In contrast, other approaches (e.g., boot camps and "scared straight" programs) with delinquent youth have, in some cases, produced greater levels of delinquency and cost taxpayers four times more than traditional adjudication approaches.

These findings directly answer Brown's (2010) call for evidence that behaviors observed during a program are sustained after a program in a manner suggestive of transfer. It is also worth making a point here about the policy environment in which adventure-based programs now operate. Brown questions how "transfer became intrinsically linked to notions of learning in the outdoors and critical to the livelihood of outdoor educators" and states, "By inference, if outdoor educators did not foster transfer they would be out of a job" (p. 14). We endorse the idea that adventure programs should expand opportunities for learning. In the United States, however, those working with clients through the outdoors rather than for the outdoors are increasingly held accountable to specific outcomes, not only by policymakers and funders but also according to pressing social needs. In this context, if an individual or institution has contracted with a provider for educational, developmental, or therapeutic reasons, professionals not striving to achieve these outcomes probably should be out of a job.

Critiques of Transfer in OAE

Furman and Sibthorp (page 39) and Brown (2010) both express consternation that transfer has remained prominent despite the larger debate in education and psychology. See *The Journal of the Learning Sciences*, 2006, *15*(4). As the transfer debate escalates, it is important to recognize that the conceptual frameworks presently being proposed move in opposing directions with respect to the transfer problem. In this section, we respond to some of the concerns raised by Furman and Sibthorp and by Brown before discussing transfer as consequential transitions (Beach, 1999).

Cognitivism Versus Situativity Theory

Furman and Sibthorp argue against transfer from the perspective of cognitive constructivism. They state, "Ultimately, what is learned, taken, and applied from an adventure program depends *entirely* on the program participant" (page 42, emphasis added). The implication is that transfer cannot be anticipated with any certainty because learners are always actively constructing knowledge. Their point aligns with one of the central criticisms from the cognitive paradigm, which is that "a novel context is not conceived just as 'given'; using one's prior knowledge and the available resources, one can modify the situation and its perception" (De Corte, 2003, p. 143). This is certainly a problem for the classical notion of transfer. For example, a metaphor might generate insights during a climbing activity, but even the most resolute participant cannot anticipate the new factors he or she might encounter later. Therefore, any imagined parallelism between situations or commitment to carry over what was learned at the climbing site will always be provisional. Furman and Sibthorp therefore doubt that this should qualify as transfer or should preoccupy adventure educators.

They propose transformative learning and turning points as alternative frameworks that would expand the range of outcomes sought by adventure educators. Transformative learning entails perspective transformation, or a change in "sets of beliefs, values, and assumptions held by an individual" (page 42). In this view, learning is not limited to a single skill or concept but rather opens qualitatively new cognitive possibilities. They also offer turning points, in which "adventure programs provide rich experiences that can facilitate changes in a life path or trajectory" (page 43). These frameworks certainly would open up options for programming and research, but, notably, they can also help avoid theorizing the relationship between individual life trajectories and the social ecologies in which people learn and develop—also the major weakness in classical ideas of transfer (Lave, 1988). Furman and Sibthorp's argument therefore represents a compelling move away from transfer but in a highly individualistic direction, which we fear might quickly become detached from social concerns. This seems to us both educationally and epistemologically problematic.

Brown's (2010) argument moves in the opposite direction by maintaining that transfer's "separation of cognition from the social world" (Lave, 1988, p. 43) is fundamentally flawed. Situativity theory instead focuses on the "generative relations between people-in-action and the social world around them" (Lave, 1988, p. 91). Continuity across situations is as much a function of culturally and historically organized ways of being as it is the knowledge, skill, or life trajectories of individuals. Packer (2001) further argues that disputes about transfer are not merely technical (i.e., about the supposed mechanisms of learning) but are also inherently political: "Schools do not simply prepare 'problem solvers' of a particular kind, they help transform children into the workers and citizens who will reproduce our society, or who will help transform it" (p. 502). Rather than transfer, situativity theorists want to focus on changing forms of participation and changing identities in communities of practice that are themselves evolving in relation to broader cultural, historical, and economic trends.

Taking this perspective, Brown (2010) urges adventure educators to consider how "doing something" is always "linked to issues of personal and social identity," and he recommends that they devise practical ways to help participants "recognize the nuanced and dynamic nature of interaction" (p. 18) and "negotiate their way in a variety of communities of practice" (p. 19). These are reasonable priorities. However, the leap Brown makes in his article from analysis to prescription deserves careful attention; in throwing out the bathwater, he also throws out the baby. He writes, "Climbing is not about trusting your belayer and then thinking about how you could use (context free) trust elsewhere, nor is it about creating metaphors that the participant will recall, unprompted, in the future" (p. 18). Brown implies that frank and direct conversations about individuals and their respective social positions are preferable for promoting learning in the moment and enhancing mobility in the future. As educators who have facilitated such conversations, we are dubious of this at face, but we also think that metaphors can be creatively enlisted to serve this goal; indeed, they may already function to "equip students to recognize resources, social configurations, and interactions that might aid or hinder participation in future activities" (p. 18). Although Brown too hastily dismisses the practices historically associated with transfer, he makes a compelling case for reformulating it conceptually.

Transfer as Consequential Transitions

> Why don't you stay in the wilderness? If it does not enable you to cope more effectively with [humankind's] problems—and sometimes it doesn't, sometimes it just sucks you right out into the wilderness and you stay there the rest of your life—then when that happens, by my scale of value it's failed. You go to nature . . . in order to enable you to come back into the world of man and operate more effectively. (Unsoeld, 1976, p. 4)

Unsoeld frames the central problem for adventure educators: how to facilitate people's "continuity and transformation in becoming someone or something new" (Beach, 1999, p. 102) as individuals move across situations. Gass (1986) framed his description of transfer as a means of conceiving and facilitating such continuity and change, and recent theoretical advances make it clear that educators and researchers always deal with mutually changing individuals, social forms, and systems of artifacts that facilitate or complicate learning (Seaman, 2007). The complex relationship among these elements confounds overly cognitive notions of transfer but it does not diminish the importance of "exploring better ways to understand and support learner continuity and transformation across institutions, local practices, problems, and tasks" (Beach, 1999, p. 106)—what the concept of transfer helps accomplish. We introduce Beach's framework of consequential transitions—recognized by Lobato (2006) as one of several promising new approaches to transfer—as a way forward in the debate about transfer in adventure education.

According to Beach, consequential transitions

> involve a developmental change in the relation between an individual and one or more social activities. A change in relation can occur through a change in the individual, the activity, or both. Transitions are consequential when they are consciously reflected on, often struggled with, and the eventual outcome changes one's sense of self and social positioning. (p. 114)

Beach proposed four kinds of consequential transitions: lateral transitions, collateral transitions, encompassing transitions, and mediational transitions.

Lateral transitions "occur when an individual moves between two historically related activities in a single direction" (p. 114). Beach regards lateral transitions as linear, progress-oriented, and irreversible, such as moving from an apprentice to a practitioner, a student to a graduate, or a consumer of outdoor programs to a professional leader.

Collateral transitions "involve individuals' relatively simultaneous participation in two or more historically related activities" (p. 115). Collateral transitions are more complex and nonlinear and have uncertain markers of progress. For example, a teenager enrolled in a wilderness therapy program would be engaged in collateral transitions among treatment, school, and family systems. Analytically, collateral transitions can accommodate the idea of negative transfer, in which dysfunction in one activity can shape individual trajectories in a way that contradicts progress.

Encompassing transitions "occur within the boundaries of a social activity that is itself changing" (p. 117). Encompassing transitions include 1) individual development within relatively stable activities, such as changing one's status from an assistant to a lead instructor in an adventure program, and 2) activities that rapidly change, which necessitates individual adaptations, such as when schools adopt new reform models that teachers must accommodate. These changes provide developmental opportunities and often entail identity changes.

Mediational transitions "occur within educational activities that project or simulate involvement in an activity yet to be fully experienced" (p. 118). Simulation exercises, role playing, and even teambuilding programs are examples of activities that provide mediational transitions between activities.

It is possible to imagine adventure programs facilitating development in each of these forms of transition or to imagine ways individual development can be studied within or across forms of social activity. For example, staff training within a changing organization may be a form of encompassing transition, whereas new programs developed within the same organization for clients may represent mediational transitions. Success in either depends on aligning social resources, individual capacities, and opportunities for growth within and between historically evolving activities. What is important about consequential transitions—and what is downplayed in cognitive theories—is that they situate individual learning, development, and identity in the context of changing social forms of activity. This emphasis enhances the focus on context that is a crucial part of Gass' original work without losing sight of organizationally and individually valued goals—what gets transferred, in other words. In addition, viewing transfer through these lenses does not entail abolishing research-proven methods of facilitation and teaching—such as those articulated in Gass' original work—or resorting to the individual as the unit of analysis. In fact, it opens possibilities for new practices as well as new methods for studying their functioning at individual, group, and social levels.

Conclusion

This issue provides an opportunity to revisit Gass' original work on transfer, validate it by reviewing empirical research, and further support its critical relevance according to new theories of learning. Rather than witnessing the end of transfer in adventure education, we see a rich opportunity for next-generation practices and research foci that accommodate critiques while also building on effective and longstanding practices.

References

Barab, S.A., & Duffy, T.M. (2000). From practice fields to communities of practice. In D.H. Jonassen & S.M. Land (Eds.), *Theoretical foundations of learning environments* (pp. 25-55). Mahwah, NJ: Lawrence Erlbaum Associates.

Bateson, G. (1972). *Steps to an ecology of mind: Collected essays in anthropology, psychiatry, evolution, and epistemology.* Chicago: University of Chicago Press.

Beach, K. (1999). Consequential transitions: A sociocultural expedition beyond transfer in education. *Review of Educational Research, 24*, 101-139.

Brown, M. (2010). Transfer: Outdoor adventure education's Achilles heel? Changing participation as a viable option. *Australian Journal of Adventure Education, 14*(1), 13-22.

De Corte, E. (2003). Transfer as the productive use of acquired knowledge, skills, and motivations. *Current Directions in Psychological Science, 12*(4), 142-146.

Doherty, K. (1995). A quantitative analysis of three teaching styles. *Journal of Experiential Education, 18*(1), 12-19.

Gass, M.A. (1986). Programming the transfer of learning in adventure education. *Journal of Experiential Education, 8*(3), 18-24.

Gass, M.A. (1991). Enhancing metaphor development in adventure therapy programs. *Journal of Experiential Education, 14*(2), 6-13.

Gass, M.A. (2005). Comprehending the value structures influencing the significance and power behind experiential education research. *Journal of Experiential Education, 27*(3), 286-296.

Gass, M.A., Garvey, D.E., & Sugerman, D. (2003). The long-term effects of a first-year student wilderness orientation program. *Journal of Experiential Education, 26*(1), 34-40.

Gass, M., & Priest, S. (1997). Using metaphors and isomorphs to transfer learning in adventure education. *The Journal of Adventure Education and Outdoor Leadership, 10*(4), 18-23.

Gass, M., & Priest, S. (1999). Six generations of facilitation skills. In J.C. Miles & S. Priest (Eds.), *Adventure programming* (pp. 215-218). State College, PA: Venture.

Gass, M.A., & Priest, S. (2006). Effectiveness of metaphoric facilitation styles in corporate adventure training (CAT) programs. *Journal of Experiential Education, 29*(1), 78-94.

Gillis, H.L. (1985). *The strategic use of adventure activities for couples.* Georgia Marriage and Family Therapy Conference, Jekyl Island, GA. ERIC Reproduction Service No. 260 879.

Gillis, H.L., & Gass, M.A. (2010). Treating juveniles in a sex offender program using adventure-based programming: A matched group design. *Journal of Child Sexual Abuse, 19*, 20-34.

Gillis, H.L., Gass, M.A., & Russell, K. (2008). The effectiveness of Project Adventure's Behavior Management Programs for male offenders in residential treatment. *Residential Treatment for Children and Youth, 25*(3), 227-247.

Hirsch, J., & Gillis, H.L. (1997). *Food for thought: A workbook and video for developing metaphorical introductions to group activities.* Dubuque, IA: Kendall/Hunt.

Hirsch, J., & Gillis, H.L. (2004). *Developing metaphors for group activities*. DVD/CD. Boulder, CO: Association for Experiential Education.

Lave, J. (1988). *Cognition in practice: Mind, mathematics and culture in everyday life*. Cambridge, England: Cambridge University Press.

Lobato, J. (2006). Alternative perspectives on the transfer of learning: History, issues, and challenges for future research. *Journal of the Learning Sciences, 15*(4), 431-449.

MacRea, S., Moore, C., Savage, G., Soehner, D., & Priest, S. (1993). Changes in risk taking propensity due to ropes course challenges. *Journal of Adventure Education and Outdoor Leadership, 10*(2), 10-12.

Packer, M. (2001). The problem of transfer and the socio-cultural critique of schooling. *The Journal of the Learning Sciences, 10*(4), 493-514.

Seaman, J. (2007). Taking *things* into account: Learning as kinaesthetically mediated collaboration. *Journal of Adventure Education and Outdoor Learning, 7*(1), 3-20.

Unsoeld, W. (1976). *Spiritual values of the wilderness*. Boulder, CO: Association for Experiential Education.

Does the concept of transfer of learning sufficiently explain the way outcomes of adventure programming are generalized to other areas of participants' lives?

NO Adventure Programs and Learning Transfer: An Uneasy Alliance

Nate Furman, PhD, assistant professor of adventure education, Green Mountain College, Poultney, Vermont, United States

Jim Sibthorp, PhD, associate professor in parks, recreation, and tourism, University of Utah at Salt Lake City, United States

Adventure education programs excel at achieving intrapersonal, interpersonal, and group development outcomes in program participants and groups (Hattie et al., 1997). The application of these outcomes to life postcourse is often referred to as *learning transfer*. Learning transfer is commonly regarded as the foundational purpose of adventure programs and has been touted as the ultimate goal of programs like Outward Bound, the National Outdoor Leadership School (NOLS), and university-based outing programs. In the 2011 NOLS catalog, NOLS executive director John Gans writes about the lasting impacts of a NOLS course:

> Students have continually returned home with the tools needed to succeed in their lives to come . . . you'll become a leader in your own life and connected to the natural world around you. Your strengths will become more noticeable and you'll harness the ability to confront your weaknesses. (National Outdoor Leadership School, 2010, p. 3)

Gans' passage is consistent with the messages sent by many adventure programs and academic publications: program activities such as rock climbing and whitewater rafting are engaged in for the primary purpose of learning life skills that transfer to a postexpedition context. However, focusing on learning transfer as the ultimate indicator of the lasting benefits of participation disregards a number of lasting outcomes that are perhaps equally important. Further, the story of learning transfer is complex and has incited scholars to debate for more than a century; this debate has seen no resolution and has grown only more complex (Barnett and Ceci, 2002). No firm conclusions have been drawn regarding the fundamental purpose of the adventure programming field, and the wealth of research suggesting that students learn skills (McKenzie, 2000; Paisley et al., 2008; Propst and Koessler, 1998) is held in stark contrast to the paucity of research suggesting that said skills transfer to other contexts (e.g., Holman and McAvoy, 2004; Miller, 2001). Given these issues, it may be time to reevaluate the concept of transfer as the ultimate rationale for our work.

Our argument seeks to decentralize the concept of learning transfer as the definitive goal of adventure programming. This argument is based on several contentions:

- Transfer has largely been considered the ultimate goal of adventure programming.
- Learning transfer has not been well explained by empirical evidence in adventure programming.
- Learning transfer is problematic both in theory and in practice in adventure programs.
- Alternative explanations better describe the important and lasting benefits of adventure programming.

The first contention establishes that learning transfer is the primary goal in adventure programming, and the latter three describe why this goal is suspect. These four points do not build sequentially on one another, but rather collectively explain why learning transfer is a problematic concept and that the lasting benefits from adventure programming are constrained by using an explanation that primarily emphasizes transfer.

Transfer in Adventure Education: Why?

By several accounts, the birth of the modern adventure education movement is traced to the founding of the first Outward Bound school in Aberdovey, Wales. Laurence Holt and Kurt Hahn established the school as a response to high death rates among young British mariners during World War II. Holt perceived that young sailors lacked the necessary resilience to survive the ordeals of the North Atlantic in a lifeboat and, partnering with Hahn, began the Outward Bound program to teach young men character and tenacity. This training was conducted primarily through the sea rather than for the sea. Thus the idea of leveraging the rich potential of environmental challenge and developing technical skill to afford transferable life lessons became a central element of adventure programming.

Theoretical underpinnings for transfer in outdoor education were advanced by Walsh and Golins (1975), who suggested that transfer was a result of

a. a learner who is placed into a prescribed environment, then given a
b. set of problem-solving tasks leading to
c. adaptive dissonance and subsequent
d. mastery or competence, and, consequently, a
e. reorganization of meaning and
f. orientation toward change.

This insightful framework has been used as an explanation for lasting outcomes (Ewert and McAvoy, 2000), validated (Sibthorp, 2003a), and adapted (McKenzie, 2003). It stands today as one of the most relevant explanations for how adventure programs foster change in participants.

The contributions of Michael Gass and others cemented the primacy of learning transfer in the collective consciousness of the adventure programming field. Through inclusion in textbooks (Gass, 1985a, 1999) and scholarly publications (Gass, 1985b; Gass and Priest, 1993, 2006), Gass effectively communicated why transfer is critical to the adventure programming field and provided information on how instructors and programs can foster transference in participants. It should be noted that Gass is not the only author to write on the behalf of transfer and that publications by other scholars (e.g., Hammitt et al., 1996; Holman and McAvoy, 2004; Leberman and Martin, 2004; Miller, 2001; Sibthorp, 2003b) have made strong contributions as well. The answer to why transfer is considered the primary goal of adventure programming, then, is a result of historical context, theoretical explanation, and popular academic contributions. Thus, we contend that transfer is largely considered the ultimate goal of adventure programming.

Transfer in Adventure Education: Theoretically Sound But Empirically Elusive

Support for transfer of learning exists in the adventure programming literature. For instance, Mitchell and Mitchell (1988, 1989) found that awareness of others and interpersonal skills were transferred outcomes of participation in Outward Bound courses at two years postcourse. Anderson and colleagues (1997) report that adventure education participants developed friendships and technical skills that transferred as a result of their adventure program. Mazze (2006) found evidence that participants in a NOLS course maintained an increased connection to the outdoors several months after their course. Hammitt and colleagues (1996) report that a sample of NOLS alumni self-reported greater environmentally responsible behavior several months postprogram. Gass and Priest (2006) determined that factors such as trust, communication, collaboration, problem solving, decision making, and task completion could be increased among intact groups up to 12 months after a corporate adventure training program.

Based on these studies, one might reasonably conclude that, indeed, adventure programs are effective at developing and transferring skills to life postprogram. However, the answers to four questions (How many? How frequently? How long? How effectively?) are barely understood. Further, studies need to more frequently offer a standard of comparison in order to communicate a sense of program efficacy. This argument cannot answer these questions, but it can shed light on what it would take to do so.

- **How many?** Studies need to address how many participants use their skills compared with how many do not. One could conclude that communication skills are transferred from an adventure program, but if only 10 percent of program participants report transfer and 90 percent do not, we cannot reliably conclude that the program fosters transfer.

- **How frequently?** Studies need to examine how often transferrable skills are applied by participants postcourse. For instance, if a student reports transferring their communication skills, but they did so only twice in a period of two months, then the program cannot be said to effectively foster the transfer of communication skills.

- **How long?** Studies need to examine the duration of skills transferred from adventure programming. For instance, if a student reports transferring communication skills at one month postprogram but those skills diminish over time, then the effectiveness of the transfer is in question.

- **How effectively?** Studies need to examine the efficacy of transferrable skills applied by participants postcourse. For instance, if a student reports transferring environmental awareness skills but does so ineffectively, then the program cannot be said to effectively foster the transfer of environmental-awareness skills.

- **Comparison standard.** The premise that adventure programs are effective at fostering transfer has less meaning until we have a standard of comparison. For instance, are the communication skills learned during a two-day challenge course transferred better or worse than the communication skills learned during a two-day classroom-based communication seminar?

Although several studies (e.g., Gass and Priest, 2006) have addressed some of these questions, given the multitude of transferrable outcomes and the many types of adventure programs that vary by activity, duration, length, and foci, much more study is needed before we can know in detail how effectively adventure programming fosters transfer. As Brown (2010) states, "Facilitating for transfer and assuming that this learning will continue beyond the course is based more on wishful thinking and observations of behavioural change during the programme than a strong empirical research base" (p. 19). Thus, we contend that learning transfer has not been well explained by empirical evidence in adventure programming.

Problems With Learning Transfer

A number of problems exist with learning transfer, both within the empirical literature and at a pragmatic level in adventure programs. This section explains why parent disciplines, such as educational

psychology and human resource development, have yet to accurately describe transfer and how achieving transfer during adventure programs is challenging.

Theoretical and Empirical Shortcomings

Transfer has been a controversial issue since the beginning of the 20th century. Mestre (2005) notes, "After decades of research and debate, no consensus exists about whether transfer is ubiquitous or rare" (p. 5). Early on, Thorndike (1903) argued that learning in one area did not necessarily improve performance in another area, whereas Judd (1908) counterargued that certain types of learning predisposed the learner to generalization. More current research has led scholars to similar disparate conclusions. Detterman (1993) notes, "Transfer has been one of the most actively studied phenomena in psychology. . . . Reviewers are in almost total agreement that little transfer occurs" (p. 5). Packer (2001) echoes that "transfer has proven hard to define, difficult to investigate, and perplexingly controversial" (p. 493).

These problems with learning transfer have not discouraged scholars from engaging in the discourse; the topic of learning transfer has resulted in thousands of articles from many fields such as human resources, physics, business, mathematics, psychology, and adventure education. Works from Baldwin and Ford (1988), Ford and Weissbein (1997), and Burke and Hutchins (2007) all provide broad reviews of transfer-related research. Readers of these academic works will note that scholars have yet to agree on whether transfer is an outcome or a process (Foxon, 1994), whether transfer can be programmed for (Detterman, 1993), or, indeed, as Mestre (2005) reports, how often transfer occurs. This lack of clarity regarding learning transfer provides a questionable foundation for the central purpose of adventure programming.

Pragmatic Challenges to Programming for Transfer

The many available outcomes from adventure programming—from self-confidence to technical skills to leadership development—make programming for transfer challenging. To clarify why programming for transfer in adventure programming is difficult, we offer the following illustration. In most educational or training contexts, the goal is to learn content, retain the content, and then reapply the content at a later time or setting. This goal, however, is but a small portion of what adventure programs hope to achieve, and this is where the concept of learning transfer gets stretched. Largely, transfer in adventure programming regards "far" transfer, which means that the learned content and context (when and where the content is learned) of acquisition are distal from the content and context of application (see Barnett and Ceci, 2002). For instance, teamwork and communication are commonly learned during adventure programs. Students learn these skills through a variety of means, such as leadership opportunities or small-group interaction (Paisley et al., 2008), and presumably apply them throughout the course. Although application later in the course is certainly desirable, postcourse applications at home or at school are more valued. Applications later in the day or course are less ideal than applications months or years later, and application with the same group of students is typically valued less than application with a different social group and in a different social context (e.g., a group of friends on a recreational trip). These three examples (course–postcourse, recent time–distant time, and same group–different group) highlight that transfer is indeed a "yes-or-no" problem but is also a "how much" problem. Given these issues, it is difficult, if not impossible, to adequately describe how transfer occurs.

Ultimately, what is learned, taken, and applied from an adventure program depends entirely on the program participant. Although some participants certainly learn, transfer, and apply lessons intended by the adventure program, others take away unintentional lessons (see Sibthorp et al., 2011). What people learn, retain, and apply from adventure programs retains elements of individuality and contextual relevance. Thus, the idea of transferring intended outcomes to life postcourse is dicey at best.

Some contend that transfer itself should not be considered an outcome at all. At a fundamental level, transfer is a process in which learning from one context is used in a different context. Foxon (1994) argues that this process consists of several discrete stages, and describing transfer as an ultimate outcome fails to describe the phenomenon. To measure this process, some other outcome (e.g., self-efficacy) is typically assessed at different times, in different social contexts, and in different places. Many behavioral or attitudinal changes that might be evident after a week in the backcountry can likely be lost after a week back in the frontcountry, yet emerge at some later point. This is why transfer, for many of our outcomes, is tricky to document, see, or even define. Attempts to measure transfer may be thwarted when the transferrable outcome has not fully materialized as an observable variable at a discrete point in time—the largely arbitrary time of measurement. Because many issues regarding the characteristics of learning transfer are unresolved, and because it is difficult to program for or assess transfer in the field, we contend that learning transfer is problematic both in theory and in practice.

Alternatives to Transfer

Given the continued theoretical and empirical debates regarding the merits of the concept of learning transfer—and the reality that many adventure program goals function on the periphery of the traditional understanding of learning transfer—it is time to look for alternatives to the traditional understanding of learning transfer. Although the concept of transfer does offer a useful framework in adventure programming, explaining the benefits of participation in adventure programming only through the lens of learning transfer is limiting. We must use other lenses.

It may be that many of the lasting outcomes of adventure programming can be explained by theories of transformative learning (e.g., Dirkx, Friere, Mezirow). Theories of transformative learning suggest that the benefits of education regard perspective transformation (Mezirow, 1991). Perspectives, in this case, are sets of beliefs, values, and assumptions held by an individual. According to Dirkx (1998), the "core of the [transformative] learning process itself is mediated largely through a process of reflecting rationally and critically on one's assumptions and beliefs" (p. 4).

Although transformative learning has been described as an adult learning theory, we suggest that the goals and outcomes of adventure programs are highly consistent with the goals and outcomes of transformative learning. Outcomes from adventure programs, such as a change in life perspective, appreciation for simpler life, appreciation for nature (Sibthorp et al., 2008), challenging assumptions of self and others, profound impacts on life (Gass, Garvey, and Sugerman, 2003), and increased connection with the outdoors (Mazze, 2006), all seem to fit within the context of transformative learning and have been found across a variety of youth- and adult-age groups. Although these outcomes have been studied through the lens of learning transfer, they might be better explained by adopting a transformative learning model.

Transformative learning has not been often used in adventure programming, although D'Amato and Krasny (2011) use transformative learning theory as a lens for studying outcomes from NOLS and Outward Bound programs. The authors determined that the significant elements of the course were

- living in pristine environments,
- living a different lifestyle,
- having a sense of community, and
- having intensity and challenge.

The authors conclude that adventure programming "draws its strength in transformative or emancipatory learning from being situated in a remote setting with a supportive social group" (p. 13).

Another alternative to transfer is to view adventure programs as affording educational experiences that serve as catalysts for growth rather than as direct providers. Such experiences are often termed "turning points" that alter, sometimes subtly, a person's general life trajectory. According to Gotlib and Wheaton (1997):

> A turning point is a disruption in a trajectory, a deflection in the path. Indeed the essential characteristic of a turning point is that it changes the direction of a trajectory. . . . Turning points may be difficult to see as they are occurring, because they are only recognized to be turning points as time passes and as it becomes clear that there has been a change in direction. (p. 1)

According to Yair (2009), educational turning points are characterized by three features: "high level of trust and acceptance, the setting of challenges and high expectations, and extraordinary levels of enthusiasm and seriousness expressed by the teacher" (p. 361). Perhaps such characteristics are more likely in adventure programs given their small-group, expeditionary nature and instructor involvement.

In this view, adventure programs provide rich experiences that can facilitate changes in a life path or trajectory. Many of the targeted outcomes of adventure programs (e.g., self-esteem, character, identity) are constructed from a lifetime of experience and are not easily addressed by a short (e.g., two-week) experience. Rather, these experiences help shape further choices and can change one's life trajectory in a manner that might, over years of living, significantly and meaningfully change some of these targeted outcomes. For example,

some of the recent literature on lifelong learning and self-regulated learning suggests that exposure to an experience with educational opportunities that is both goal-oriented and intrinsically interesting can foster a propensity for lifelong learning (Rathunde, 2009). Like most meaningful outcomes, lifelong learning is distal. However, adventure programs are well situated to afford experiences that are optimally engaging (i.e., goal relevant and intrinsically interesting). Adventure programs may provide a catalyst for growth and change but may not inherently provide immediately meaningful or even recognizable changes.

Finally, it is possible that the most important and lasting lessons from adventure programs are ones of process—that is, changing the ways people approach challenges and problems, rather than fostering skills and applying content. This idea lives in the periphery of the traditional transfer literature, but it has been largely ignored in research specific to adventure programming. This approach to the value of adventure programming defies traditional outcome assessment, because outcomes may not directly change, but the approach toward these outcomes is different. Adventure experiences may lead alumni to approach problems differently, either more efficiently or more effectively. Such process changes are central to how people function, yet challenge traditional ideals of outcomes and benefits of programming.

Given the applicability of transformative learning theory, turning point literature, and process-based explanations of learning, we contend that alternative explanations better describe the important and lasting benefits of adventure programming.

Conclusion

The traditional view of learning transfer is interested primarily in the application of discrete skills and behaviors postprogram. This is certainly a valid and important goal for many adventure programs; however, it is not the only goal. As experiential educators, we tend to place a premium on constructivist approaches to learning and the process of education. This premium makes traditional approaches to transfer incomplete representations of what occurs in adventure programs. To illustrate, if a Navy cadet attends an adventure course through the naval academy and decides to leave the military, or a youth on a church trip decides to leave the church, or a student on an outdoor orientation program decides that their interests are best served at a different school, these behavioral outcomes are not targeted, intended, or valued by the sponsoring organization. They are, however, powerful and individually valuable and are lasting artifacts of adventure experiences. None of these behaviors would generally be described as transfer, but they might be described as transformational turning points in one's life and direct results of an adventure experience.

We believe that learning transfer does not provide a sufficient explanation of the potential and power of adventure programs for human growth and development. The past 25 years of theoretical and empirical work have left our field without a clear understanding of how transfer operates. Simultaneously, other ideas (transformative learning, educational turning points) have emerged that offer strong alternatives to transfer. By broadening our perspective on the lasting outcomes of adventure programming and no longer constraining ourselves to a historical alliance with the concept of learning transfer, we will be more able to understand, explain, and share the power of our programs.

References

Anderson, L., Schleien, S., McAvoy, L., Lais, G., & Seligmann, D. (1997). Creating positive change through an integrated outdoor adventure program. *Therapeutic Recreation Journal, 31*(4), 214-229.

Baldwin, T.T., & Ford, J.K. (1988). Transfer of training: A review and directions for future research. *Personnel Psychology, 41*(1), 63-105.

Barnett, S.M., & Ceci, S.J. (2002). When and where do we apply what we learn? A taxonomy for far transfer. *Psychological Bulletin, 128*(4), 612-637.

Brown, M. (2010). Transfer: Outdoor adventure education's Achilles heel? Changing participation as a viable option. *Australian Journal of Outdoor Education, 14*(1), 13-22.

Burke, L.A., & Hutchins, H.M. (2007). Training transfer: An integrative literature review. *Human Resource Development Review, 6*(3), 263-296.

D'Amato, L.G., & Krasny, M.E. (2011). Outdoor adventure education: Applying transformative learning theory in addressing instrumental and emancipatory EE goals. *Journal of Environmental Education, 42*(4), 237-254.

Detterman, D. (1993). The case for the prosecution: Transfer as an epiphenomenon. In D. Detterman & R. Sternberg (Eds.), *Transfer on trial* (pp. 1-24). Norwood, NJ: Ablex.

Dirkx, J.M. (1998). Transformative learning theory in the practice of adult education: An overview. *PAACE Journal of Lifelong Learning, 7*, 1-14.

Ewert, A., & McAvoy, L. (2000). The effects of wilderness settings on organized groups: A state-of-knowledge paper. In S. McCool, D. Cole, W. Borrie, & J. O'Loughlin (Eds.), *Wilderness science in a time of change conference. Volume 3: Wilderness as a place for scientific inquiry* (pp. 13-26). Washington, DC: USDA Forest Service Proceedings.

Ford, J.K., & Weissbein, D.A. (1997). Transfer of training: An updated review. *Performance Improvement Quarterly, 10*(2), 22-41.

Foxon, M.J. (1994). A process approach to the transfer of training. Part 2: Using action plans to facilitate the transfer of training. *Australian Journal of Educational Technology, 10*(1), 1-18.

Gass, M.A. (1985a). Programming the transfer of learning in adventure education. In R. Kraft & M. Sakofs (Eds.), *The theory of experiential education,* 2nd ed. (pp. 166-172). Boulder, CO: Association for Experiential Education.

Gass, M.A. (1985b). Strengthening adventure education by increasing the transfer of learning. *Journal of Experiential Education, 8*(3), 18-24.

Gass, M.A. (1999). Transfer of learning in adventure education. In J.C. Miles & S. Priest (Eds.), *Adventure education* (pp. 199-208). State College, PA: Venture.

Gass, M.A., Garvey, D.E., & Sugerman, D. (2003). The long-term effects of a first-year student wilderness orientation program. *Journal of Experiential Education, 26*(1), 30-40.

Gass, M.A., & Priest, S. (1993). Using metaphors and isomorphs to transfer learning in adventure education. *Journal of Adventure Education and Outdoor Leadership, 10*(4), 18-24.

Gass, M.A., & Priest, S. (2006). The effectiveness of metaphoric facilitation styles in corporate adventure training (CAT) programs. *Journal of Experiential Education, 29*(1), 78-94.

Gotlib, I., & Wheaton, B. (1997). *Stress and adversity over the life course: Trajectories and turning points.* New York: Cambridge University Press.

Hammitt, J.P., Freimund, W., Watson, A., Brod, R., & Monz, C. (1996). Responsible environmental behavior: Metaphoric transference of minimum-impact ideology: National Outdoor Leadership School (NOLS). Unpublished report. www.nols.edu/resources/research/pdfs/porterhammittpaper.pdf [May 11, 2011].

Hattie, J., Marsh, H.W., Neill, J.T., & Richards, G.E. (1997). Adventure education and Outward Bound: Out-of-class experiences that make a lasting difference. *Review of Educational Research, 67*(1), 43-67.

Holman, T., & McAvoy, L. (2004). Transferring benefits of participation in an integrated wilderness adventure program to daily life. *Journal of Experiential Education, 27*(3), 322-325.

Judd, C.H. (1908). The relation of special training and intelligence. *Educational Review, 36*(1), 42-48.

Leberman, S.I., & Martin, A.J. (2004). Enhancing transfer of learning through post-course reflection. *Journal of Adventure Education and Outdoor Learning, 4*(2), 173-184.

Mazze, S. (2006). *Beyond wilderness: Outdoor education and the transfer of environmental ethics.* Unpublished master's thesis. Eugene, OR: University of Oregon.

McKenzie, M.D. (2000). How are adventure education program outcomes achieved? A review of the literature. *Australian Journal of Outdoor Education, 5*(1), 19-28.

McKenzie, M.D. (2003). Beyond the Outward Bound process: Rethinking student learning. *Journal of Experiential Education, 26*(1), 8-23.

Mestre, J.P. (2005). *Transfer of learning from a modern multidisciplinary perspective.* Greenwich, CT: Information Age.

Mezirow, J.D. (1991). *Transformative dimensions of adult learning.* San Francisco: Jossey-Bass.

Miller, S. (2001). Transferring the benefits from wilderness to the home environment. *Pathways: The Ontario Journal of Outdoor Education, 13*(2), 26-30.

Mitchell, H.A., & Mitchell, M.J. (1988). A study in self-concept, part 1. Unpublished research report for Outward Bound New Zealand. Nelson, New Zealand.

Mitchell, H.A., & Mitchell, M.J. (1989). A study in self-concept, part 2. Unpublished research report for Outward Bound New Zealand. Nelson, New Zealand.

National Outdoor Leadership School. (2010). 2011 NOLS course catalog. www.nols.edu/pdf/2011_NOLS_Course_Catalog.pdf [Accessed May 11, 2011].

Packer, M. (2001). The problem of transfer, and the sociocultural critique of schooling. *The Journal of Learning Sciences, 10*(4), 493-514.

Paisley, K., Furman, N., Sibthorp, J., & Gookin, J. (2008). Student learning in outdoor education: A case study from the National Outdoor Leadership School. *Journal of Experiential Education, 30*(3), 201-222.

Propst, D.B., & Koessler, R.A. (1998). Bandura goes outdoors: Role of self-efficacy in the outdoor leadership development process. *Leisure Sciences, 20*(4), 319-344.

Rathunde, K. (2009). Experiential wisdom and optimal experience: Interviews with three distinguished lifelong learners. *Journal of Adult Development, 17*(2), 81-93.

Sibthorp, J. (2003a). An empirical look at Walsh and Golins' adventure education process model: Relationships between antecedent factors, perceptions of characteristics of an adventure education experience, and changes in self-efficacy. *Journal of Leisure Research, 35*(1), 80-106.

Sibthorp, J. (2003b). Learning transferable skills through adventure education: The role of an authentic process. *Journal of Adventure Education and Outdoor Learning, 3*(2), 145-157.

Sibthorp, J., Furman, N., Paisley, K., Schumann, S., & Gookin, J. (2011). Mechanisms of learning transfer in adventure education: Qualitative results from the NOLS transfer survey. *Journal of Experiential Education, 34*(2), 109-126.

Sibthorp, J., Paisley, K., Furman, N., & Gookin, J. (2008). Long-term impacts attributed to participation in adventure education: Preliminary findings from NOLS. *Research in Outdoor Education, 9*, 86-102.

Thorndike, E.L. (1903). *Educational psychology.* New York: Lemke and Buechner.

Walsh, V., & Golins, G. (1975). *The exploration of the Outward Bound process.* Denver: Colorado Outward Bound School.

Yair, G. (2009). Cinderellas and ugly ducklings: Positive turning points in students' educational career—exploratory evidence and a future agenda. *British Educational Research Journal, 35*(3), 351-370.

Controversial Issue 4

Should there be a professional certification in outdoor leadership?

Simon Priest's 1986 dissertation, *Outdoor Leadership Preparation in Five Nations,* was the first contemporary analysis of issues surrounding outdoor leadership preparation that focused on countries that modeled their systems after the British mountain leadership scheme. Priest surveyed experts from Australia, Canada, Great Britain, New Zealand, and the United States to determine their attitudes and approaches toward outdoor leadership. Priest found experts sharply divided around the issue of certification. He learned that, in general, most were in favor of certifications for specific skills; this is evident by the popularity and abundance of skill certifications today. In the United States, a whole host of certifications exist that reflect various areas of competency and expertise. The American Canoe Association sponsors a variety of instructor certifications in the area of paddle sports. The American Mountain Guides Association (AMGA) and Professional Climbing Instructor Association (PCIA) sponsor widely recognized certification programs in the areas of mountaineering and rock climbing. Land management agencies require group leaders to have either an AMGA or PCIA certification as part of the permitting process. Well-known organizations such as Wilderness Medical Associates, Stonehearth Outdoor Learning Opportunities, and the Wilderness Medicine Institute sponsor certifications in wilderness medicine that many deem essential.

Despite the surge in skill certifications, a central question is worth exploring: "Is there a place for a single, comprehensive certification in outdoor leadership that would serve as a benchmark for entry into the profession?" Many of the questions asked in the 1970s and 1980s still exist today. What does it mean to be certified as an outdoor leader? Does the industry need certification? Has the establishment of program accreditation replaced the need for certification of outdoor leaders? Is a general certification scheme for outdoor leadership feasible? What body should be responsible for overseeing certification? Much in the world of professional outdoor leadership has changed since the 1980s. Revisiting this enduring question with new perspectives may provide answers to these questions. The two arguments in this debate tackle old issues and bring new considerations to the forefront.

Michael McGowan argues in favor of a professional certification as a necessary means to protect the fundamental values of adventure education from commercial influences that are transforming the adventure programming field into an industry. He offers the structure needed to develop a legitimate certification scheme.

Will Hobbs argues the counterpoint by outlining two important points. First, no clear need exists for a national certification. Second, certifying a professional outdoor leader is an impossible task. Hobbs states that our conventional, singular approach to understanding leadership in the outdoor field is insufficient.

Reference

Priest, S. (1986). *Outdoor leadership preparation in five nations.* Unpublished doctoral dissertation. Eugene, OR: University of Oregon.

Should there be a professional certification in outdoor leadership?

YES Certification: Ensuring That Adventure Education Will Be a Force for Human Growth and Development

Michael L. McGowan, PhD, professor, recreation, park, and tourism administration, Western Illinois University, Macomb, Illinois, United States

Professional certification in outdoor leadership must be reexamined in light of developments in the field over the past 20 years. In that time, theory and practice in outdoor leadership have progressed. Outdoor leadership is taught in colleges and universities that include it as an academic major or minor area of study (Martin et al., 2006; Priest and Gass, 2005). Specialized activity certifications now flourish; whitewater, sea kayaking, mountaineering, rock climbing, wilderness medicine, and challenge course facilitation are common examples. Old arguments around professional certification (March, 1985; Priest, 1987) based on outdated perspectives developed 20 and 30 years ago no longer constitute meaningful objection to certification when faced with the transformation of adventure education into a fully commercialized industry.

Two points underlie the affirmative side of this argument. First, the adventure education movement is rapidly becoming an industry that sells service commodities and products. A universal outdoor leadership certification provides a key way to counteract the negative consequences of the commodification and commercialization of adventure programming. It provides a key way to preserve adventure programming's focus on human growth and development as well as its ability to address important educational and societal issues. Second, this argument challenges the assertion that leadership competency is too complex to be evaluated and thus cannot be assessed for the purposes of professional certification. Leadership development is the cornerstone for professional development in our field. Academic texts, curricula, and assessment tools have been developed to promote this important function in the profession. Are we to refute the validity of these efforts? Refusing to acknowledge our ability to develop valid means to facilitate and assess outdoor leadership development seriously impedes further development of the field. It fails to protect the public good. It ensures that the vast majority of outdoor leaders will always be inexperienced youths, working for food service-level wages, who are given only the minimum training they need to deliver the products sold by the business they serve (Ritzer, 2008).

Finally, this argument proposes a logical path forward for our profession in developing a professional certification scheme. Academic programs that focus on outdoor leadership preparation serve as the starting point. Other established professions rely on postsecondary academic preparation coupled with professional certification or licensure as a basis for entry into the profession. So should we! To create such a scheme would require the collective will of our profession and a new way of doing business.

McDonaldization of Adventure Education

The American Outward Bound School, established in 1962, took outdoor recreational pursuits such as backpacking, canoeing, and mountaineering that had always been extracurricular to academics and placed them at the core of leadership and character education (Miner and Boldt, 1981). The approach was novel and exciting and found popularity in documentary films, magazines, and headlines. Thousands of schoolteachers cloned elements of Outward Bound for use in schools. Educational associations hosted workshops and conferences to spread the word. Administrators demanded research to justify budgets, so academicians built theoretical models, tested theories, and evaluated programs. Cottage industries and then corporations sprang up to create and sell cookbooks for building ropes courses, games anthologies, ropes course equipment, professional consultation and facilitation, contractual ropes course construction and inspection, staff training, and even programmed processing cards and rubber chickens. These products made programming easier and a homogenized practice. They enabled anyone to set up and run an "adventure" program, and practically everyone did. Outdoor adventure education exploded during the 1970s and 1980s in schools, camps, colleges, churches, and recreation programs and addressed not just high school kids and youths at risk but every group imaginable (Austin, 2009; Berman and Berman, 1994; Ewert, 1989; Gass, 1993; Schlein et al., 1993; Snyder, Rothschadle, and Marchello, 2006). More than a decade ago, Loynes (1998) sounded a warning concerning the inevitable commercialization of adventure education. Adventure education technology was ripe for entrepreneurial exploitation, and economic exploitation would bring trade associations and professionalization to protect economic interests. Exploitation by corporate training businesses in the 1990s reduced adventure education to a couple of hours in a hotel lobby juggling corporate objectives in matching T-shirts while charging huge fees. The emergence of the Association of Challenge Course Technology and the Professional Ropes Course Association has proved Loynes to be right.

Adventure education began as an educational movement centered on human relationships and skilled adult leadership in consequential human endeavors to promote personal and social growth, maturation, and character development (Ewert, 1989; Gass, 1993; Godfrey, 1980; Graham, 1997; Hogan, 1968; James, 1980; Kalisch, 1979; McGowan, 1997; Meyer, Morash, and Welton, 1987; Miles and Priest, 1999; Miner and Boldt, 1981; Mortlock, 1984). Commodification and commercialization, however, have transformed it into, as Loynes (1998) put it, "adventure in a bun." Adventure guides wearing matching fleeces with corporate logos conduct customers through "the ropes course experience"—a thoroughly contrived apparatus where interactions with the guide, other participants, and nature are rigidly controlled. It is a time-compressed adventure in which the consumer is harnessed and helmeted, read the rules, and queued up to get on course while enjoying a latté and muffin and texting friends. The customer then gets 15 minutes of thrills and chills (but no spills) on the course and celebrates his or her success by posting a picture on Facebook from an iPad. Participants are then debriefed by staff using a carefully scripted interpretation comprising politically correct metaphors that promote archetypal homogenized, predictable, transferable learning outcomes, handed a T-shirt featuring the company logo, and bid farewell. Any chance that customers will be confronted by significant intrapersonal issues or a meaningful, consequential interaction with others or nature has been removed to control litigation by ensuring safety of the product and to make product delivery efficient in the time allotted. Customer-satisfaction surveys replace research in validating claims and justifying programs. Providers are free to offer whatever product they please, call it what they want, and promote it as the solution for whatever problem ails the customer. Consequently, entrepreneurial leadership programs are touted like snake oil as panaceas for virtually every social problem. "Got problems with your high school, neighborhood, dorm floor, or management team? Need enrollment management and retention? Need to address delinquency, post-traumatic stress disorder, juvenile recidivism, drug abuse? What you need is an adventure leadership program."

Others in our industry have recognized the influence of commodification. At the conference of the Association for Outdoor Recreation and Education, Hardy (2001) warned adventure programmers of the McDonaldization of rock climbing. The predictability, control, and objectification brought on by the commercialization of rock climbing leads to rationalization. This commercial transformation we have witnessed within the adventure programming industry meets all of Weber's criteria for rationalization and commodification: efficiency, calculability, predictability, and control (Ritzer, 2008). It has been thoroughly McDonaldized. Human needs that do not lend themselves to product delivery and cannot be commodified are not ignored; rather, they are removed because they interfere with product delivery or customer satisfaction (Ritzer, 2008). Removing human relationships and consequential endeavors thoroughly trivializes the experience. The result is dehumanization of participants to mere consumers, alienation of providers to mere functionaries (Ritzer, 2008), and disenchantment with a potentially introspective experience that becomes a rigidly didactic exercise (Loynes, 1998).

Maslow (1970) points out, "Isolating two interrelated parts of a whole from each other, parts that need each other, parts that are truly parts and not wholes, distorts them both, sickens and contaminates them. Ultimately, it even makes them nonviable" (p. 13). Commodification focuses only on efficiency, predictability, calculability, and control to contrive marketable products for profit, not individuated human needs (Ritzer, 2008). No matter the activity, once the focus shifts from the dynamic needs and creative potential of the individual to efficacy, predictability, controllability, and pricing, it becomes dichotomized, dehumanizing, and alienating (Ritzer, 2008). We lead people, not activities. We teach people, not subjects! Humankind is our business. We must entertain nobler aspirations than mere profit if adventure education is to survive as education and make a real difference in the lives of our participants and communities.

Professional certification provides a key defense against the negative outcomes of the commodification and commercialization within the field of adventure programming. Outdoor leaders trained in the theoretical foundations and methodologies of adventure education possess the tools and knowledge to facilitate a developmental experience. They can readily distinguish between a commercialized leisure experience and the transformational experience made possible through an adventure program experience. This certified professional is not driven by financial motives but by an alternative value system rooted in human services. This entire argument really boils down to a professional discipline dedicated to promoting holistic growth and development through an ethos not governed by economic power. Those that choose to pursue the commercial aspect of adventure should stick with their specialized certifications. The professional outdoor leader represents a discipline that goes far beyond the glamour of adventure sports.

Is Leadership Too Complex to Understand and Assess? No!

It has been asserted that leadership in general, and outdoor leadership in particular, is too complex to understand and thus assess (Hobbs, 2009). The counterargument in this debate by Will Hobbs purports that effective outdoor leadership is so highly complex that it is impossible to distill into a tangible entity that we can understand. Purporting that leadership is too complex to understand suggests that we are unable to define outdoor leadership. It also by extension suggests that standards of practice cannot be established, that practitioners cannot be educated or trained to those standards, and that professional mechanisms such as certification cannot be developed to help regulate the quality of practice. This is misleading and indeed untrue! On the contrary, the scope of the practice in the field of outdoor leadership has been defined, standards of practice have been established, practitioners are trained according to these standards, and it is possible to regulate the quality of practice

through mechanisms such as professional certification. Though they do not offer outdoor leadership certification, organizations such as Outward Bound, the National Outdoor Leadership School (NOLS), and numerous other adventure programs are in the business of outdoor leadership development (National Outdoor Leadership School, 2011; Outward Bound, 2011). The current NOLS catalog reads, "Although there is no universal certification for working within the outdoor industry, having completed a NOLS course is very highly regarded by outdoor professionals worldwide" (National Outdoor Leadership School, 2011, paragraph 30). A refusal to define leadership while simultaneously marketing leadership education as a product would be duplicitous. I am certain that organizations such as Outward Bound and NOLS would stridently object to accusations of such duplicity.

Other professions such as military science, public safety, public administration, recreation education, college life, counselor training, teacher education, and even business and management teach leadership as an essential skill set in undergraduate and graduate professional development programs. They define leadership in their context, teach it, and evaluate it. Governmental agencies license and professional organizations certify these professionals in their fields. Teacher education and certification is the model best suited for examination as a model of professional certification for outdoor leadership. Teacher education and professional certification typically require four years of college; two of those years are spent in focused study of core knowledge and skills requisite to teaching. Embedded in this study are practical observations, supervised practice teaching, laboratory experiences, and mentoring in the core competencies. Concentrated study and training in specialty areas are then completed to enable the student to address specific subjects (e.g., math, earth science, English, speech, drama, or music). Competency testing and student teaching precede certification—the transition from student to teacher. Will every first-year teacher exercise flawless judgment? The answer is no. Still, the state sees fit to certify them because new teachers go through a prescribed process of study, practice, and development and are supervised and mentored by more experienced teachers, principals, and professional associations. Certification in teaching clearly serves the public good and is only one step in professional development—an essential step at that because it marks the transition from student to practitioner. Is outdoor leadership really so much more complex? Does anyone really expect that outdoor leadership certification should not follow the same or a similar model?

In the past 30 years, the core body of knowledge of outdoor leadership has been identified. Technical skills, logistics, instructional methods, leadership theories, and techniques have been formulated, applied, studied, and catalogued (Martin et al., 2006; Priest and Gass, 2005). Competent leadership is the essential human function and relationship that makes a program effective in promoting growth. Times have changed and the need for the development of competent professionals to lead in adventure education has become paramount. Several private colleges and public universities understand this and offer both major and minor concentrations in outdoor leadership, preparing professionals in the core competencies on which all applications of adventure education rely. They identify and address the core knowledge and skills of teaching and leading that are essential and common to working with a variety of people across all outdoor adventure venues and activities. Students in these academic programs undergo supervised practicum experiences and semester-long internships in which they are supervised, mentored, and evaluated by practitioners in the field. They come into the field with a solid foundation in educational theory, human development, group work, leadership programming, and administration and with wilderness first responder certification and instructor-level certifications in a variety of activities. These programs are developing the profession and are establishing the standards that will inevitably lead to the establishment of a core professional certification in outdoor leadership.

So much of the old certification debate was founded on the argument that certification could guarantee professional competency, especially related to safety (Priest and Gass, 2005). A certified outdoor leader would be a safer leader. However, we all know that the quality of a certified leader is reflected by the quality and integrity of the certification system. In the old debates there was little consensus about what the structure of an outdoor leadership certification system should be. Outdoor leadership certification schemes in Canada, the United Kingdom, Australia, the United States, and New Zealand have varied in approach and in degree of success. None of these certification schemes have been built on academic preparation programs (Priest and Gass, 2005). Academic systems are uniquely situated to implement standard curricula in that they adhere to the accreditation model. An accrediting agency focused on adventure education curricula provides the mechanism to standardize a curriculum. The adventure field has the academic support to institute a valid professional certification.

A credible scheme, as seen in other professions, would be built on academic preparation provided through four-year baccalaureate degree programs or master's programs or both. An accumulation of supervised field-experience hours usually serves as a prerequisite before testing. Successful completion of the degree and associated field experiences would be followed by an exam administered through a neutral certification board that might be comprised of industry representatives. These new college graduates and newly certified professionals could then matriculate into the industry. Rather than placing industry players in competition with one another, as is done in the United States and other countries, the certification scheme would use academia and the certification exam to prepare young professionals to go to work for these organizations.

We lack only the collective will to move forward and make it happen. What would it take politically within the adventure programming field to support this type of certification scheme? Obviously, each country that offers university-based leadership preparation programs has its own licensing and certification systems. However, the impetus to create the infrastructure for a legitimate professional certification must come from within our field. Attempts are being made but fall short of a unified national effort. For example, in the United States, the Wilderness Education Association (WEA) has devised an accreditation system that supports outdoor leader certifications. WEA's accreditation model is based on six core competencies in outdoor leadership. Both academic and nonacademic programs can seek accreditation through the WEA Accreditation Council. Once accredited, programs are sanctioned to train and certify outdoor leaders according to the WEA accreditation standards, and students in WEA-accredited programs are eligible to enroll in the International Registry of Outdoor Leaders, an online portfolio-management system overseen by the WEA. Through documentation of field experiences, additional training, and other professional development activities, enrolled members are able to matriculate through various certification levels.

The WEA's current efforts are contributing to the professionalization of outdoor leadership. However, its current approach to outdoor leadership certification falls short of a true professional certification as outlined in this debate because outdoor leadership certifications awarded through WEA-accredited programs are awarded under the banner of those individual programs and not the banner of a national certification board. The certifications bear the brands of the programs through which they were awarded and not the brand of a national certification body. Consequently, the certifications are only as good as the reputations of the programs through which they are earned. One of the implications of this approach is that it pits industry players against one another in vying for market share in the business of outdoor leadership development. Old rivalries within the industry tend to die hard. This approach in many ways perpetuates another aspect of the commodification phenomena in our industry.

Rather than a system that accredits nonacademic programs, the system should be based on the development of professionals through participation in four-year baccalaureate programs. Rather than a system that relies on certification of leaders through accredited programs, certification should be awarded through a national or international certifying body. As noted, many such certification schemes are already in place in other industries. The development of such a system in the field of adventure programming is needed to create a viable national certification in outdoor leadership. In order to create a true national or international outdoor leadership certification, the adventure programming field must unite under one neutral governing body. This governing body should be empowered to dictate standards and a certification process sanctioned by a higher authority typically associated with a governmental infrastructure. As a field, we must be willing to work toward a collective good if a national or international certification scheme is to be viable.

Conclusion

In the world of McVenture, workers belay customer after customer on the climbing wall, day in and day out, supervise grade-school kids in field initiatives and new games five days a week, or run two groups a day through the high ropes course. Many programs rely on in-house staff training and development to properly prepare the outdoor leader. This exacerbates the larger problem because it is limited to training staff to run two or three adventure activities in a limited context. It focuses on the technical skills of activity execution, much like the specialized certifications discussed in this argument, not core knowledge of leadership and understanding of human growth and development. Because virtually no mechanism for professional develop-

ment or advancement exists, staff seasonally move from program to program. They remain indigent, living near or in poverty and serving apprenticeship after apprenticeship as they are retrained in-house. Burned out, frustrated, and fed up with perpetual blocks to professional development and advancement, talented leaders leave the field or strike out on their own to create their own adventure business, which furthers commercial competition and thus commodification within the industry. Professional certification in outdoor leadership can help to remedy this problem.

A foundation already exists to institute a universal outdoor leadership certification. The literature suggests that core competencies serve as the framework for understanding the knowledge, skills, and dispositions that characterize professional outdoor leaders (Martin et al., 2006; Priest and Gass, 2005). Professional competencies provide the framework for defining the scope of the practice of outdoor leadership. Consequently, they also provide a basis for establishing a professional certification in outdoor leadership. A core competencies approach to outdoor leadership development provides a broader, more holistic base compared with the specialized certifications in particular outdoor adventure pursuits such as paddle sports and climbing. Academic preparation programs for outdoor leadership provide the mechanism to begin a serious discussion around a professional certification. Until this happens, outdoor leadership will remain in the wild, wild West where anything goes and vested interests place roadblocks in the way of developing a profession that serves public needs rather than selfish interests. Should there be professional outdoor leadership certification based on academic preparation? It is doubtful that anything less can save adventure education from the barbarians at the gate.

References

Austin, D. (2009). *Therapeutic recreation: Process and techniques.* 6th ed. Champaign, IL: Sagamore.

Berman, J.D., & Berman, D.S. (1994). *Wilderness therapy: Foundations, theory and practice.* Dubuque, IA: Kendall/Hunt.

Ewert, A. (1989). *Outdoor adventure pursuits: Foundations, models, and theories.* Scottsdale, AZ: Publishing Horizons Inc.

Gass, M.A. (1993). *Adventure therapy: Therapeutic applications of adventure therapy.* Dubuque, IA: Kendall/Hunt.

Godfrey, R. (1980). *Outward Bound schools of the possible.* Garden City, NY: Anchor Press.

Graham, J. (1997). *Outdoor leadership: Technique, common sense and self-confidence.* Seattle: The Mountaineers.

Hardy, D. (2001). The McDonaldization of rock climbing: Conflict and counter conflict between climbing culture and dominate value systems in society. In R.A. Poff, A.N. Blacketer, & M.L. Nunnally (Eds.), *Digital archive of the Association of Outdoor Recreation and Education conference proceedings and research symposium abstracts: 1984-2007.* Whitmore Lake, MI: Association of Outdoor Recreation and Education.

Hobbs, W.D. (2009). *An investigation of highly effective leaders in outdoor programs using a multi-method approach.* Doctoral dissertation. Bloomington, IN: Indiana University.

Hogan, J.M. (1968). *Impelled into experiences: The story of the Outward Bound schools.* Wakefield Yorkshire, U.K.: Educational Productions Limited.

James, T. (1980). *Education at the edge: The Colorado Outward Bound school.* Denver: Colorado Outward Bound School.

Kalisch, K.R. (1979). *The role of the instructor in the Outward Bound educational process.* Three Lakes, WI: Honey Rock Camp.

Loynes, C. (1998). Adventure in a bun. *Journal of Experiential Education, 21*(1), 35-39.

March, B. (1985). *Wilderness leadership certification—Catch 22—Assessing the outdoor leader: An insoluble problem?* In J. Miles & R. Walters (Eds.), *Proceedings of the 1984 Conference on Outdoor Recreation* (pp. 37-42). Pocatello, ID: Idaho State University Press.

Martin, B., Cashel, C., Wagstaff, M., & Breunig, M. (2006). *Outdoor leadership: Theory and practice.* Champaign, IL: Human Kinetics.

Maslow, A.H. (1970). *Religions, values and peak experiences.* New York : Penguin Books.

McGowan, M.L. (1997). Thinking outside the box: The role of adventure in spiritual development. *Journal of Experiential Education, 20*(1), 14-21.

Meyer, J., Morash, T., & Welton, G. (1987). *High adventure outdoor pursuits.* Columbus, OH: Publishing Horizons.

Miles, J.C., & Priest, S. (Eds.). (1999). *Adventure programming.* State College, PA: Venture.

Miner, J.L., & Boldt, J. (1981). *Outward Bound U.S.A.: Learning through experience in adventure-based education.* New York: Morrow.

Mortlock, C. (1984). *The adventure alternative.* Milnthorpe, Cumbria, U.K.: Cicerone Press.

National Outdoor Leadership School. (2011). Frequent questions. www.nols.edu/about/faq/#Q30 [December 15, 2011].

Outward Bound. (2011). Home page. www.outwardbound.org [December 15, 2011].

Priest, S. (1987). Outdoor leadership certification: Always an issue, but no longer a trend. *Bradford Papers Annual, 3,* 37-44.

Priest, S., & Gass, M. (2005). *Effective leadership in adventure programming.* 2nd ed. Champaign, IL: Human Kinetics.

Ritzer, G. (2008). *The McDonaldization of society.* Thousand Oaks, CA: Pine Forge Press.

Schlein, S.J., McAvoy, L.H., Lais, G.J., & Rynders, J.E. (1993). *Integrating outdoor education and adventure programs.* Champaign, IL: Sagamore.

Snyder, D.R., Rothschadle, A., & Marchello, M. (2006). *Inclusive outdoor recreation for persons with disabilities: Protocols and activities.* Enumclaw, WA: Idyll Arbor.

Should there be a professional certification in outdoor leadership?

NO Certification: A Solution Looking for a Problem

Will Hobbs, PhD, assistant professor, outdoor education, Georgia College, Milledgeville, Georgia, United States

Two critical elements form the dissenting argument of this question. First, no clear need exists for outdoor leadership certification. During the past 35 years, certification has failed to deliver any lasting value for individual professionals, participants, program providers, or the adventure programming industry as a whole. There is no national call for regulation. Adventure programs are not demanding certification of new employees, and the only existing scheme is experiencing extremely low participation. Ostensibly, the justification for certification is that it will give programs and the public some level of assurance of the competency of the certificate holder. This should equate to a reduced need for training new employees at the program level; however, site-specific training remains a standard condition of employment for most adventure programs.

Second, although appealing in principle, certifying a professional outdoor leader is an impossible task. One cannot officially endorse or guarantee an individual in any capacity (as certification purports to do) without first articulating the expectations in clear, unambiguous, nonsituational terms. However, effective leadership is so highly complex, culturally dependent, and subjective that it is nearly impossible to distill the myriad characteristics, qualities, traits, skills, abilities, dispositions, and knowledge into a comprehensive yet practical (i.e., measurable) understanding (Bolman and Deal, 1991; Hobbs, 2009; Kezar, 2004).

Effective outdoor leadership is more than activity-specific skills (indeed, many organizations already provide excellent activity-specific certifications) or educational skills. It includes higher order cognitive and affective skills such as judgment and decision making, integrity and authenticity, and other-directedness, all of which are highly subjective and mission-defined factors that are incredibly difficult to assess with any intent toward generalization across programs. This is not a new argument; the dissenting positions from the decades-old certification debates still apply. The process of certifying a professional outdoor leader is subjective and confounded by a range of social and environmental variables. Those conducting the assessment are human and thus fallible (i.e., given to stereotyping expected responses and challenged to remain objective in highly subjective situations; Harwell, 1986; Priest, 1987a). Also, the assessment occurs in highly local and isolated contexts and authentic consequences vary across a range of activity-specific skills (Green, 1982; March, 1980, 1984; Priest, 1987b). Consequently, the level of ambiguity that currently exists in our understanding of outdoor leadership severely challenges our ability to assess competency at the level of consistency that a valid professional certification scheme would require—that is, a minimum standard of care cannot be identified. Thus, professional certification is unnecessary and so challenged by ambiguity and subjectivity that it is meaningless. These issues, individually and collectively, challenge the viability of a professional certification program and form the basis for the "no" opinion.

Certification Is Superfluous

Professional certification in outdoor leadership is a vagabond of ideas: intriguing and mysterious, bouncing around between multiple sheltering organizations, yet glinting of potential underneath all the baggage. This has been a common theme since its emergence in the 1970s. The idea took root during a time of explosive and largely unregulated growth in adventure programs. For an emerging profession, articulating a means of self-regulation is crucial (Henderson et al., 2001), and acceptable leadership standards, competencies, and qualifications were common topics in industry circles. Paul Petzoldt (1974) advocated for leadership certification throughout his life, and his definition of outdoor leadership (to deliver safe, sound, and enjoyable expeditions with minimal environmental impact) laid out a very basic framework of accountability for the industry.

Certification certainly seemed to be a viable solution for outdoor leadership at the time. In the early 1980s, a series of scholarly papers and dissertations debated the merits and disadvantages (to start, see Buell, 1981; Cousineau, 1977; Green, 1981; March, 1984; Petzoldt, 1982; Rollins, 1983; Senosk, 1976). Yet, after several contentious discussions at conferences, special issues of scholarly publications (see Robb and Hamilton, 1985; Yerkes, 1985), journal articles, and position pieces (see Cain, 1985, 1988; Cockrell and LaFollette, 1985; Priest, 1987a, 1988), little had been resolved. The energy surrounding certification soon dissipated and programs were left to develop their own trainings, assessments, and other staff development strategies to ensure that safety and quality aligned with their specific mission and population. Since that initial flurry of scholarly activity, only a handful of papers addressing certification have been published (Attarian, 2001; Bassin et al., 1992; Gass, 1999; Teeters, 1994). Thus, rather than look to a homogenized national certification process to define generic best practices, individual programs have drawn on their own creativity and innovation to develop outdoor leaders who are well equipped to design, manage, and evaluate adventure programs.

From a purely pragmatic perspective, the current state of the industry is enough to persuade even the heartiest of certification proponents that the topic is of questionable value, if not completely unwarranted. Consider how few recent job postings list certification as a requirement (or even as a preferred qualification) for a position in outdoor leadership, or reflect on the absence of any data that indicate that participants prefer certified outdoor leaders when choosing an adventure program. Perhaps we should consider how little attention the field has received from government monitors keen on regulating "dangerous" industries.

At the end of the day, program providers need boots on the ground to be able to take customers into the field, provide an enjoyable experience, and bring them back happy and safe so that they return home and tell their friends and neighbors about the program. Program providers are more than willing to spend money on staff training to develop employees who are well prepared to deliver those specific outcomes. But because past certification schemes have failed to provide a consistent product that can be applied across program settings and areas, most practitioners in the United States remain indifferent to certification. Only one organization—the Wilderness Education Association (WEA)—continues to promote a comprehensive leadership certification program in the United States; as of November 2010, fewer than 100 certified leaders were currently active in the field (M. Estock, personal communication, November 17, 2010). In fact, the WEA no longer certifies individual outdoor leaders but rather has placed that responsibility in the hands of accredited institutions (the individual program providers).

Finally, a certification scheme usually stems from the need to justify or verify best practices at the individual level in an industry in which external regulation or oversight is being threatened or implemented. We might experience this in adventure programming if incident or accident rates or negative environmental impacts increase unchecked. But this is purely hypothetical and not reflective of our current reality. The bottom line is this: If program providers are not requiring certification for their employees, if the public is not demonstrating demand by preferring programs that are staffed by certified outdoor leaders, if no incentive exists for current professionals to obtain or maintain the certification, and if no external pressure exists for self-regulation, then certification is unnecessary.

Measuring Effectiveness of Leadership

In the outdoor leadership literature, the concept of effectiveness often takes the form of the successful leader, the need for effective leaders, or becoming an effective outdoor leader (Aguiar, 1986; Bartley and Williams, 1988; Easley, 1985; Martin et al., 2006; Priest, 1999; Priest and Gass, 2005; Raiola and Sugerman, 1999; Riggins, 1986). Perhaps effectiveness describes the extent to which the leader or program is able to assist, facilitate, or otherwise ensure that the participant has a positive experience; however, no clear definition exists. A popular text in the field discusses job requirements in the field (i.e., various skills and techniques for managing participants in outdoor programs, and other constructs), but it stops short of explicitly defining effective leadership (Priest and Gass, 2005). One might assume that an individual can be a successful outdoor leader by obtaining these particular skills, abilities, or knowledge. Few explain what success actually looks like in practice.

However, one simply cannot endorse or guarantee an individual as a professional outdoor leader without articulating the expected qualifications in clear, unambiguous, nonsituational terms. This is the crux of the dissenting position. Effective leadership refuses to be standardized. It is intricately complex, highly situational, and deeply personal and can be understood (i.e., assessed) only in the local and isolated context. It is incredibly challenging to capture all of the characteristics, qualities, traits, behaviors, skills, abilities, attitudes, dispositions, and knowledge in a comprehensive understanding, much less a measurable construct (Hobbs, 2009; Kezar, 2004).

What goes into leadership? It is a Sisyphean topic: questioned repeatedly but never resolved. Every study on the subject concludes something different. Examine a handful of current leadership books and you will be amazed by how different they are. Each claims to reveal the hidden secrets and strategies for effective leadership (see Kaplan, 2011; Kouzes and Posner, 2010; Maxwell, 2007a, 2007b). Each of these books—and the reams of studies striving to identify those key qualities—examines leadership from a theoretical perspective known as essentialism (Popper, 1969). This approach to scientific study argues that the "members of a category [in this case, leaders] have a property or attribute (essence) that determines their identity" (Kezar, 2004, p. 112). According to essentialism, the path to understanding a construct is to simply determine its essence; in our context, we search for those properties or attributes that identify the individual as an outdoor leader (see figure 4.1). Most leadership theories fall under this perspective despite the lack of empirical evidence supporting it—that is, a set of essential qualities has not emerged from the research. In fact, Bolman and Deal's (1991) comprehensive analysis of leadership studies found only one consistent quality: vision.

Conversely, nonessentialism argues that "a complex system of cultural, social, psychological, and historical differences, not a set of pre-existent human essences, position/constitute the subject or human phenomenon" (Fuchs, 2001, as cited in Kezar, 2004, p. 113). Nonessentialism places the role of culture and society at the forefront of any conversation on leadership and argues that essential leadership characteristics are more reflective of current societal opinion than of any empirical truth. Because these local conditions and circumstances can vary tremendously, identifying any essential traits, behaviors, or situations becomes extremely difficult. This may explain the lack of comprehensive research on outdoor leadership and the failure of any one certification scheme to catch on. Leadership is inclusive of local context, culture, and social dynamics and thus resists definition and categorization—critical components for certification. This may explain why individual programs have found

their own perspective on leadership development to be the most appropriate for their setting, culture, and population. Although appealing theoretically, a professional certification scheme that addresses these intricacies is simply not feasible or practical.

A well-designed certification scheme might resolve some of the issues raised in the early debates. For example, the public and program providers may be persuaded by aggressive marketing and promotion followed by tangible evidence of value of a certification program. Generalizability and other assessment problems can be improved with more concrete outcomes and a greater variety and depth of experiences. But no scheme can adequately address the complexity and subjectivity that is inherent in effective outdoor leadership.

Certification ultimately requires a defined set of qualifications or standards against which an individual's performance can be measured (for more information, see the American National Standards Institute [ANSI] at www.ansica.org). Any subjectivity in assessment can be reduced only through a clear reliance on proven assessment models and agreed-upon professional competencies (indeed, some of the critical standards of the ANSI accreditation program). It may be appealing to apply this approach to field leadership and extract the key elements and splay them across an assessment tool, but this is an impossible task because it is just too complex. One can objectively assess only the skills, abilities, and knowledge of basic field management, not true leadership, in the development process.

Field Management Versus Field Leadership

Field management is not leadership. We can measure field management skills, and numerous authors have contributed to this effort (see figure 4.1). These are the simple and clear strategies used to move a group through an adventure experience safely: that is, activity-specific, educational, human, instructional, environmental, organizational, facilitation, technical, and psychomotor skills. These are the skills on which we can base our definitions and assessments of proficiency and thus certify persons. It is interesting to note that the early proponents of certification did not favor awarding certification for any other skills (Priest, 1987b). Conversely, field leadership is more than the sum of its parts. Rather, effective leadership emerges with increasing integration and mastery of the core skills (Nicolazzo, 2007). It is exceedingly more difficult to measure

Experience with accidents, injuries, and death

Survival techniques

Ability to evaluate natural hazards

Recognition of activity problem indicators

Knowledge of group safety

Problem-solving skills

Demonstrates positive environmental ethics

Ability to prepare accident responses

Provision of standard of care

Specialized knowledge of activity

Self-controlled

Recognized level of achievement

Competence in specific outdoor skills

Demonstration of minimum-impact practices

Field experience as a participant and leader

Group management skills

Position or rank (job status)

Experience in supervised leadership positions

Interactions with role models and mentors

Positive attitudes

Experimentation

Creativity

Emotional stability

Outgoing personality

Healthy self-concept and ego

Recognition of own limitations

Integrity

Courage

Brightness

Prevention of injury and illness

Tact

Education

Vision and action

Recognition of indicators of group problems

Acceptance of responsibility

Sense of commitment to the program

Strong belief in the program

Ability to foster teamwork

Identification of individual needs

Aquatic safety procedures

Participation in the skills, personally and professionally

Wilderness emergency procedures and treatment

Ethics and values

Understanding of philosophical foundations

Imagination

Understanding of trends and issues

Outdoor living and travel skills

Preparation for accidents

Organizational skills

Trip planning

Experience-based judgment

Limiting activities to capabilities of participants

Ability to anticipate accidents

Selection and implementation of logistics

Evaluation and assessment

Consideration of legal liability

Honesty

Tolerance for adversity and uncertainty

Caring

Enthusiasm

Flexible leadership style

Awareness of group dynamics

Assessment of group capabilities

Group facilitation and processing skills

Development of safety procedures

Effective communication

Social skills

Emotional intelligence

Assessment of individual capabilities

Awareness and empathy for others

High expectations

Recognition of individual problem indicators

Authenticity

Spending time in the natural environment

Knowledge of local natural and cultural history

Teaching experience

Knowledge of instructional principles

Administration of high-quality learning experiences

Decision-making skills

Ability to clearly identify problems

Recognition of problem indicators

Objective and subjective judgment

Develops environmental awareness, understanding, action

Administration of facilities, equipment, and supplies

Figure 4.1 Outdoor leadership skills, attributes, characteristics, and behaviors.

Sources: Aguiar, 1986; Buell, 1981; Cain, 1988; Cousineau, 1977; Easley, 1985; Green, 1981; Hendy, 1975; Jordan, 1996; Kalisch, 1979; Medina, 2004; Phipps and Swiderski, 1990; Priest, 1984, 1987a, 1987b, 1990; Priest and Gass, 2005; Raiola, 1986; Riggins, 1984; Swiderski, 1981.

Controversial Issues in Adventure Programming

that integration than it is to measure the individual skills of field management (Bassin et al., 1992; Green, 1982; March, 1984; Swiderski, 1985).

Am I proposing that we confine our certification schemes to these distinct, objective skills? Yes. Numerous successful, well-respected certification schemes are already dedicated to these skills. The American Canoe Association (www.americancanoe.org) is the industry standard for paddling skill and safety instruction. The National Ski Patrol (www.nsp.org) manages skill assessments for multiple snow and winter sports as well as emergency response schemes. The American Mountain Guides Association and the Professional Climbing Instructors Association (http://amga.com and http://pcia.us/newpro) address rock and ice climbing as well as mountaineering. Adventure programs have found utility in these credentials based on individual skills because they provide a consistent, reliable product that reduces staff training costs. We have found that it is impossible to design, much less deliver, a single certification system that captures with any degree of success all the activity-specific skill competencies and variations that are required for different physical conditions and client groups. Any certification that ignores those skills is confined to generic backcountry travel skills and the associated safety, instructional, environmental, and organizational skills necessary to manage a group in that setting (Priest, 1988). This is field management, not leadership, and, as we have seen, a certification at this level holds little value for the field.

Conclusion

Field management skills are primarily focused on participant safety and minimizing environmental impact and are well suited for a definitional process. Indeed, these form the baseline sets of skills necessary for any front-line staff member working in an outdoor program. Although a certification scheme could be constructed on this framework, its value and utility would be suspect. Those skills can be assessed and trained by the individual program provider, and an individual without any prior experience can develop adequate competency within a period of time. Professional certification in these skills holds little practical value.

Conversely, field leadership is a comprehensive, integrated approach toward positive outcomes through powerful, human-to-human interaction and influence in an outdoor expeditionary experience—an expression of leadership closely aligned with the philosophical foundations of the field.

Providing opportunities for positive change is a core value regardless of the label (outdoor, adventure, experiential, wilderness leadership, recreation, education, therapy) placed on the field. It can occur indirectly and in minor ways (open recreation programs) and sometimes very overtly and with intense therapeutic design (wilderness therapy). At either extreme and in between, change—be it cognitive, affective, or behavioral—is the central factor that leads to an improved quality of life. It is truly transformational leadership (Bass, 1985; Bass and Riggio, 2006; Burns, 1978). Despite this fundamental core value, outdoor leadership has struggled with its identity as a profession due to the complexity of an incredible variety of human interaction, challenge, uncertainty and risk, physical and social stressors, teaching and learning, and the potential for personal change.

It has long been recognized that a singular approach to understanding leadership in the field is insufficient. Studies have created lists of essentials with regard to what the individual should do and know (those basic competencies according to Buell, 1981) rather than examine the person and character of the leader within the context of adventure programming. In fact, we are beginning to see a growth in research devoted to examining these more latent aspects of outdoor leadership, and some early conclusions on the importance of trust, integrity, character, and authenticity are emerging (Hobbs, 2009; Hobbs and Ewert, 2008; Shooter, Paisley, and Sibthorp, 2010). Any professional certification process must be structured on clear, unambiguous standards; this is a prerequisite that outdoor leadership has not yet fulfilled.

References

Aguiar, J.D. (1986). *Analysis of successful adventure leaders.* Unpublished doctoral dissertation. Boston: Boston University.

Attarian, A. (2001). Trends in outdoor adventure education. *Journal of Experiential Education, 24*(3), 141-149.

Bartley, N.L., & Williams, D.R. (1988). Gender issues in outdoor adventure programming: An outdoor leadership model exploring gender, personality, soft skills training, and leadership style of outdoor leaders. *The Bradford Papers Annual, 3,* 1-9.

Bass, B.M. (1985). *Leadership and performance beyond expectations.* New York: Free Press.

Bass, B., & Riggio, R.E. (2006). *Transformational leadership.* 2nd ed. Mahwah, NJ: Lawrence Erlbaum Associates.

Bassin, Z., Breault, M., Fleming, J., Foell, S., Neufeld, J., & Priest, S. (1992). AEE organizational membership preference for program accreditation. *Journal of Experiential Education, 15*(1), 21-26.

Bolman, L., & Deal, T. (1991). *Reframing organizations.* San Francisco: Jossey-Bass.

Buell, L. (1981). *The identification of outdoor adventure leadership competencies for entry-level and experienced-level personnel.* Unpublished doctoral dissertation. Amherst, MA: University of Massachusetts.

Burns, J.M. (1978). *Leadership.* New York: Harper and Row.

Cain, K. (1985). Wilderness Education Association certification. In J. Miles & R. Watters (Eds.), *Proceedings of the 1984 Conference on Outdoor Recreation* (pp. 53-61). Pocatello, ID: Idaho State University Press.

Cain, K.D. (1988). *A Delphi study of the development, evaluation, and documentation of judgment and decision-making ability in outdoor leaders of adventure education programs.* Unpublished dissertation. Minneapolis: University of Minnesota.

Cockrell, D., & LaFollette, J. (1985). A national standard for outdoor leadership certification. *Parks and Recreation, 20*(6), 40-43.

Cousineau, C. (1977). *A Delphi consensus on a set of principles for the development of a certification system for educators in outdoor adventure programs.* Unpublished doctoral dissertation. Fort Collins, CO: University of Northern Colorado.

Easley, A.T. (1985). *The personality traits of wilderness leadership instructors at NOLS: The relationship to perceived instructor effectiveness and the development of self-concept in students.* Unpublished doctoral dissertation. Blacksburg, VA: Virginia Polytechnic Institute and State University.

Fuchs, S. (2001). *Against essentialism: A theory of culture.* Cambridge, MA: Harvard University Press.

Gass, M. (1999). Accreditation and certification: Questions for an advancing profession. In J.C. Miles & S. Priest (Eds.), *Adventure programming* (pp. 247-249). State College, PA: Venture.

Green, P. (1981). *The content of a college-level outdoor leadership course for land-based outdoor pursuits in the Pacific Northwest: A Delphi consensus.* Unpublished doctoral dissertation. Eugene, OR: University of Oregon.

Green, P. (1982). *The outdoor leadership handbook.* Tacoma, WA: The Emergency Response Institute.

Harwell, R. (1986). Outdoor leadership certification: To be or not to be? In J. Cederquist (Ed.), *Proceedings of the 1986 Conference on Outdoor Recreation.* Salt Lake City: University of Utah.

Henderson, K.A., Bialeschki, M.D., Hemingway, J., Hodges, J.S., Kivel, B., & Sessoms, H.D. (2001). *Introduction to recreation and leisure services.* 8th ed. State College, PA: Venture.

Hendy, C.M. (1975). *Outward Bound and personality: 16PF profiles of instructors and ipsative changes in male and female students 16-19 years of age.* Doctoral dissertation. Eugene, OR: University of Oregon.

Hobbs, W.D. (2009). *An investigation of highly effective leaders in outdoor adventure programs using a multi-method approach.* Unpublished doctoral dissertation. Bloomington, IN: Indiana University.

Hobbs, W., & Ewert, A. (2008). Having the right stuff: Investigating what makes a highly effective outdoor leader. In A.B. Young & J. Sibthorp (Eds.), *Abstracts from the Coalition for Education in the Outdoors ninth biennial research symposium* (pp. 30-32). Martinsville, IN: Coalition for Education in the Outdoors.

Jordan, D.J. (1996). *Leadership in leisure services: Making a difference.* State College, PA: Venture.

Kalisch, K. (1979). *The role of the instructor.* Kearney, ME: Morris.

Kaplan, R.S. (2011). *What to ask the person in the mirror: The seven tests of highly effective leaders.* Cambridge, MA: Harvard Business Press.

Kezar, A. (2004). Philosophy, leadership, and scholarship: Confucian contributions to a leadership debate. *Leadership Review, 4,* 110-131.

Kouzes, J., & Posner, B. (2010). *The truth about leadership: The no-fads, heart-of-the-matter facts you need to know.* San Francisco: Jossey-Bass.

March, B. (1980). Assessing outdoor leaders: The catch-22 of wilderness leadership certification. *Foothills Wilderness Journal, 7*(2), 16-17.

March, B. (1984). Wilderness leadership certification—Catch 22—Assessing the outdoor leader: An insoluble problem? In J. Miles & R. Watters (Eds.), *Proceedings of the 1984 Conference on Outdoor Recreation* (pp. 37-42). Pocatello, ID: Idaho State University Press.

Martin, B., Cashel, C., Wagstaff, M., & Breunig, M. (2006). *Outdoor leadership: Theory and practice.* Champaign, IL: Human Kinetics.

Maxwell, J. (2007a). *The 21 irrefutable laws of leadership: Follow them and people will follow you.* Nashville: Thomas Nelson.

Maxwell, J. (2007b). *The 21 indispensable qualities of a leader: Becoming the person others will want to follow.* Nashville: Thomas Nelson.

Medina, J. (2004). *An exploration of master outdoor leaders' professional development experiences outside of institutional training.* Doctoral dissertation. Fort Collins, CO: University of Northern Colorado.

Nicolazzo, P. (2007). *Effective outdoor program design and management.* Winthrop, WA: Wilderness Medicine Training Center.

Petzoldt, P. (1974). *The wilderness handbook.* New York: Norton.

Petzoldt, P. (1982). The future: Certified wilderness leaders? *Outdoor Communicator, 12*(5), 13-15.

Phipps, M.L., & Swiderski, M.J. (1990). The soft skills of leadership. In J.C. Miles & S. Priest (Eds.), *Adventure education* (pp. 221-232). State College, PA: Venture.

Popper, K. (1969). *Conjectures and refutations: The growth of scientific knowledge*. London: Routledge.

Priest, S. (1984). Effective outdoor leadership: A survey. *Journal of Experiential Education, 7*(3), 34-36.

Priest, S. (1987a). Outdoor leadership certification: Always an issue, but no longer a trend. *Bradford Papers Annual, 2*, 37-44.

Priest, S. (1987b). Agreement reached on the issue of outdoor leadership certification? *Bradford Papers Annual, 3*, 38-43.

Priest, S. (1988). Outdoor leadership training in higher education. *Journal of Experiential Education, 11*, 42-47.

Priest, S. (1990). Outdoor leadership components. In J.C. Miles & S. Priest (Eds.), *Adventure education* (pp. 211-216). State College, PA: Venture.

Priest, S. (1999). Outdoor leadership competencies. In J.C. Miles & S. Priest (Eds.), *Adventure programming* (pp. 237-240). State College, PA: Venture.

Priest, S., & Gass, M. (2005). *Effective leadership in adventure programming*. 2nd ed. Champaign, IL: Human Kinetics.

Raiola, E. (1986). *Outdoor wilderness education: A leadership curriculum*. Doctoral dissertation. Cincinnati: The Union for Experimenting Colleges and Universities.

Raiola, E., & Sugerman, D. (1999). Outdoor leadership curricula. In J.C. Miles & S. Priest (Eds.), *Adventure programming* (pp. 241-246). State College, PA: Venture.

Riggins, R.D. (1984). *An analysis of selected biographical and personality characteristics contributing to the leadership effectiveness of instructors and assistant instructors at the Colorado Outward Bound School: 1982-1983*. Doctoral dissertation. Bloomington, IN: Indiana University.

Riggins, R.D. (1986). Effective leadership in adventure-based education: Setting the directions for future research. *Journal of Environmental Education, 18*(1), 1-6.

Robb, G., & Hamilton, E. (1985). *Issues in challenge education and adventure programming*. Martinsville, IN: Indiana University Press.

Rollins, R. (1983). Leadership certification revisited. *CAPHER Journal, 50*(1), 8-9.

Senosk, E.M. (1976). *An examination of outdoor pursuit leader certification and licensing within the United States in 1976*. Unpublished master's thesis. Eugene, OR: University of Oregon.

Shooter, W., Paisley, K., & Sibthorp, J. (2010). Trust development in outdoor leadership. *Journal of Experiential Education, 33*(3), 189-207.

Swiderski, M.J. (1981). *Outdoor leadership competencies identified by outdoor leaders in five western regions*. Doctoral dissertation. Eugene, OR: University of Oregon.

Swiderski, M. (1985). Stop going around in circles. *Camping Magazine, 57*(6), 20-22.

Teeters, C.E. (1994). *Judgment analysis of outdoor leadership certification decisions: An assessment of WEA certifying instructors*. Unpublished doctoral dissertation. Stillwater, OK: Oklahoma State University.

Yerkes, R. (1985). Certification. *Camping Magazine, 57*(6), 12-13.

Controversial Issue 5

Should programs be accredited to ensure that they adhere to industry standards?

Is national standardization through accreditation the best way to ensure professional competencies and practices? Accreditation has distinct advantages over, and serves a different purpose than, certification. Historically, the adventure programming field has struggled to implement an agreed-upon outdoor leadership certification scheme. As a result, specialized certifications within adventure programming in activities such as kayaking, rock climbing, and mountaineering have flourished. Accreditation negates the need for individual accountability and places responsibility on the agency (program provider) through an established set of standards. The adventure programming field appears to embrace this model as a more realistic way to self-regulate.

Within the adventure programming community, a number of organizations such as, but not limited to, the Association for Experiential Education, the Wilderness Education Association, and the American Camp Association have created their own accreditation standards and program review processes. However, the problem is that no single accreditation adequately embodies the diversity of programming found within the profession. Adventure programmers find themselves confused, financially pressured, and pulled in multiple directions when deciding the best course of action. Yet an accreditation model provides distinct advantages. National standards developed by experts in the profession set the bar for program quality and accountability. Independent reviewers serve as critical eyes to evaluate standards and ensure that they are met. This type of oversight creates a seal of approval for potential participants searching for a quality experience. The following arguments clearly outline the pros and cons associated with adventure program accreditation.

Deborah Bialeschki, Benjamin Hickerson, and Rhonda Mickelson address the value of certification based on their combined experience with the American Camp Association (ACA) accreditation process. ACA accreditation demonstrates the benefits and advantages of a systemwide accreditation scheme. Bialeschki, Hickerson, and Mickelson develop their argument based on four discussion points: 1) they articulate the focus of accreditation, 2) provide reasons agencies seek accreditation, 3) discuss the benefits of accreditation, and 4) outline common arguments against accreditation. The authors expound on the benefits of using performance measures related to industry standards as a healthy mechanism to compare programs. Accreditation also serves as an educational tool and makes sense from a legal perspective. An accreditation system that is well thought out, such as that of the ACA, functions as a legitimate tool to ensure program quality and accountability.

Whitney Ward argues against accreditation based on four confounding factors that negate the purpose and benefits of program accreditation: 1) the notion that accreditation adds value is false; 2) the cost is burdensome; 3) accreditation causes an imbalance in power; and 4) accreditation is contributing to the decline of adventure programming. He supports the argument that accreditation poses an expensive proposition with little benefit. Accreditation does not provide the legal protection that program managers might assume, and smaller adventure programs are discriminated against as a result of the accreditation paradigm. He makes clear that the notion of accreditation as a "value added" entity should be critically questioned. He ends his argument by explaining that accreditation is actually a sign of decline within the outdoor industry.

The adventure programming field as a whole needs to take a critical look at this issue. Are we strengthening or weakening our industry based on the current state of affairs that surround accreditation?

Should programs be accredited to ensure that they adhere to industry standards?

YES Accreditation: A Commitment to Quality Professional Practice

M. Deborah Bialeschki, PhD, director of research, American Camp Association, Bradford Woods, Martinsville, Indiana, United States

Benjamin D. Hickerson, PhD, assistant professor, recreation, park, and tourism management, Pennsylvania State University, University Park, Pennsylvania, United States

Rhonda Mickelson, MEd, director of standards, American Camp Association, Bradford Woods, Martinsville, Indiana, United States

"The camp accreditation process is a necessary catalyst for self-assessment, professional development, and the continuous improvement of organizational best practices."

—Tom Rosenberg, Director,
Blue Star Camps, North Carolina;
personal communication,
January 25, 2011

Accreditation and standards of practice have been around for decades (American Camp Association, 2010; American Camping Association, 1935), yet a discussion of accreditation in outdoor programs often results in strong emotional reactions, both positive and negative, and a level of angst seldom found in other topics. In this debate, we argue that outdoor programs should be accredited as a way to address industry standards. We develop our argument by articulating the focus of accreditation, the reasons why organizations seek accreditation, the benefits that occur as a result of accreditation, and the common arguments against accreditation.

Overview of Accreditation

In many sectors of recreation and leisure services, education, human services, and business, users have shifted from mere consumption to seeking benefits such as developmental outcomes that result from their participation. In this outcomes-oriented environment, organizations are increasingly called upon to demonstrate the impact of their services (Bialeschki, Henderson, and James, 2007). Accredi-

tation has become an effective response to that expectation and is a framework within which an organization can measure a variety of its achievements. The term *accreditation* usually conjures a connection between a process of validation, often done by an outside evaluator, and some established set of standards. Accreditation is usually associated with expected practices implemented within programs (Ball and Ball, 2000) and should not be confused with certification, which is directed toward individuals (Priest and Gass, 1997). A common definition of accreditation is "recognizing or vouching for, as conforming with a standard" (Merriam-Webster, 2005). In simple terms, accreditation has been defined as "a status granted to an institution or a program within an institution that has been evaluated and found to meet or exceed stated criteria of education quality" (Young et al., 1983, p. 443). Accreditation is an iterative process that requires the following:

- The development of standards by a national or regional organization to assess service quality. To secure a valid authorization of accreditation, these standards must be met through assessment by a trained evaluator for an agency or organization.

- The agency or organization must be re-evaluated frequently to monitor their continued adherence to accreditation standards.

The accreditation process usually results in some formal recognition of compliance, such as an accreditation seal and the ability of the organization to set itself apart by showcasing their accredited status (American Camp Association, 2007).

Accreditation has most commonly been applied in the fields of education, human services, and business, so the idea of accrediting outdoor programs seems appropriate. Indeed, it is an option that is currently available through several accrediting bodies (American Camp Association, 2007; Harris and Jago, 2001). Current programs that offer accreditation for outdoor programs include the American Camp Association (2010), the Association for Experiential Education (2010), American Mountain Guides Association (2010), the Council on Accreditation (2010b), and the Wilderness Education Association (2010).

Although the process of accreditation may vary slightly, a general pattern is apparent. Initially, an accrediting body takes on the task of establishing a set of standards that best represents a desired level of practice for that field. This design phase (and later revisions) follows a rigorous process that ultimately reflects the best policies and practices based on research, evidenced-based practice, and the body of knowledge. Once the standards are in place, organizations apply for accreditation. An organization seeking accreditation generally goes through a phase of self-assessment or self-study during which it gathers evidence that demonstrates compliance with the standards. These materials are reviewed by trained visitors or reviewers, and a site visit is usually conducted on an established cycle (e.g., every three years) by a team to verify that the organization has implemented the policies and procedures. Visitor teams generally assign numerical scores for each of the subdomains of performance necessary for accreditation. If the composite score meets the stated levels for acceptable practice, the organization is granted some level of accreditation. If the organization is unsuccessful, it may pursue an appeals process. If accreditation is awarded, the organization is identified as an accredited organization, which carries benefits such as the use of an accreditation seal, special listings or designations, and prestige.

The training of visitors or reviewers is systematic, standardized, and rigorous and requires frequent retraining. Once the content training is finished, a new visitor usually serves an apprentice term for a set number of visits before they are allowed to function as a full member of the visit team. These visit teams are assigned in unbiased, systematic ways that often maximize the expertise of the visitors with the operations of the site. Other considerations (e.g., conflict of interest [real or perceived], cannot visit the same site twice, past connections with the visit site, and so on) are also implemented in order to carry out fair and unbiased visits.

In general, accreditation allows for healthy comparison among organizations around performance measures related to industry standards. The accreditation process can encourage innovation and continuous improvement and help programs move toward higher levels of quality associated with the standards (United States Department of Education, 2006). Ultimately, accreditation is a tangible sign of accountability and an assurance of quality practice. The Council on Accreditation (2010a) views accreditation as a catalyst for change that builds on an organization's strengths and helps it achieve better results in all areas. As with many other accreditation systems, accreditation of outdoor programs should have a rigorous focus on systems of delivery, including employees, facilities and sites, program curriculum, and outcomes associated with the experience (Crouse, 1999; Memon, Demirdogen, and Chowdhry, 2009).

Reasons for Accreditation

From an organizational standpoint, outdoor programs may seek accreditation for a variety of practical considerations. Most of these considerations directly relate to the organization's adherence to professional practice guidelines reflected in specific accreditation standards. For example, one of the American Camp Association (ACA) trip-travel standards requires the program (camp) to have established, written operating procedures for each type of trip and travel program. The operating procedures must include at least the following: safety regulations; provision of appropriate protective or rescue equipment; training for participants to prepare for foreseeable risks such as heat- or cold-related emergencies and other natural hazards; conditioning, warm-up, and activity procedures, where appropriate; and emergency and rescue procedures. Thus, these accredited programs demonstrate adherence to very specific and high levels of professional practice. By doing so, they are prepared for the "if–when" situations in which these practices become imperative. This preparation is evidenced by the following, which was stated after the storms and floods in the Midwest during the summer of 2008:

> Looking back on the last two weeks, I am especially grateful for ACA standards. I'm grateful for SF-3, Contact With Local Officials, because before the chaotic weather started, and before our campers arrived, we took the time to communicate with our local police, fire,

and ambulance services. I am confident that these folks know who we are, where we are, and what kind of help we could need in an emergency. I'm grateful for OM-3, Risk Management Planning, which helped us really sit down and look at our risk exposures and risk control techniques. And, I'm especially grateful for OM-7, Emergency Procedures! Our severe weather plans have been tested and tested again in the early weeks of this summer session. I am so grateful for these standards—helping us make sure we have good plans in place and have considered important possibilities and made good plans *before* we need them. (Ratcliff, 2008)

One of the strongest reasons to support accreditation is that it demonstrates the ongoing professional scrutiny of practice and of the standards themselves. For example, more than 80 percent of management personnel who were involved in seeking accreditation found that the process forced a critical review of all aspects of their operations, heightened their awareness of potential problems, and highlighted strategies that could be used to counter problems (Walker and Johnson, 2009). Internally, the organization has to systematically assess its programs, training, policies, and procedures on an annual basis. At some point within an accreditation cycle, that assessment becomes focused on the accreditation visit, during which those same components are examined by a third party to confirm the organization's efforts.

A second argument for accreditation is that, for most outdoor programs, accreditation indicates the commitment to quality programs and practices to the organization, staff, and, perhaps most importantly, the participants and their families. From the consumer standpoint, accreditation status helps reduce purchase risk by providing evidence that the organization is of certain levels of skill and knowledge (Harris and Jago, 2001).

Once accredited, the organization can display an accreditation logo, which is a visible indication that it has achieved a desired level of quality practice. The seal of approval awarded to an accredited program is often likened to other seals familiar to the public from such groups as Good Housekeeping, Consumer Reports, and the Better Business Bureau. In most circumstances, the seal of accreditation can increase brand recognition and consumer interest (Urgel, 2007). Many people increasingly consider accreditation when choosing a product or service in the current market, where many choices may be available to a consumer (Zammuto, 2008). For many organizations, accreditation becomes a smart business move for marketing purposes, cost-effectiveness, and efficiencies as well as more professionally motivated, philosophical reasons (National Recreation and Park Association, 2010). With the advent of accreditation, competitors must increase the quality of their offerings to compete with one another. Nonaccredited agencies may suffer lesser brand appeal, but many still consult accreditation standards to improve their programs and deliver a message of their commitment to customers (Peer and Rakich, 2000).

For many organizations, a third argument for accreditation is that accreditation makes sense from a legal perspective. For example, in a court of law, plaintiffs claiming negligent behavior of a product or service provider must demonstrate that the organization breached a duty owed to the user. In these cases, accreditation is often viewed as evidence of good practice when subjected to legal procedures (Council on Accreditation, 2010a). Competitors who are not accredited are still affected by accreditation because the standards become the professional standards of practice to which all similar programs or settings are held, especially in a court of law (e.g., Lesser v. Camp Wildwood, 2003). Often, accreditation is used to show that the program meets state laws. In fact, in some states accreditation becomes the doorway to gaining deemed status for state licensure and regulatory purposes or to accessing government grants and other financial awards (e.g., childcare reimbursement in day camps).

Finally, the educational value gained by the organization and its staff when going through the accreditation process is critically important. The following statement is from the *American Camp Association Accreditation Process Guide*:

> The main purpose of the ACA accreditation program is to educate camp owners and directors in the administration of key aspects of camp operation, particularly those related to program quality and the health and safety of campers and staff. (American Camp Association, 2007, p. 11)

In giving attention to policies, procedures, and training needed to meet the established standards, the process guarantees a level of review and revision that organizations may not undertake voluntarily. This education extends beyond the initial accreditation process. Because most accreditation processes mandate some type of annual review of compliance, the educational component is embedded in the accreditation cycle and becomes an ongoing assessment of professional practice. In professions where an accreditation program exists, many educational opportunities and resources support the organization in meeting the accreditation standards. This education is often directed toward how to best meet the standards, but many organizations also address the spirit behind accreditation through professional development opportunities focused on the professionals implementing the accredited program. This approach can boost staff morale and encourage collaboration between departments and staff in the organization (National Recreation and Park Association, 2010) as they work to offer high-quality programs based on the best practices recognized in the field. Tom Riddleberger, owner and director of Campus Kids Summer Camps (New York, New Jersey), shares his perspective on the educational value of the accreditation process:

> Campus Kids Summer Camps has participated in the ACA accreditation program since our founding in 1991. The process of becoming an accredited camp—and maintaining that status—provides the framework that ensures we are doing everything possible for the well-being of our campers and staff. That process engages our staff at every level by challenging us to incorporate the latest information about camp operations into our program. It educates our staff as they prepare for accreditation and helps to create consistency within our organization, and it connects them to the wider world of camp professionalism. Whether parents always realize it or not, we know that our accreditation experience helps give their children a safer, healthier summer. (personal communication, January 26, 2011)

Ultimately, accreditation becomes a hallmark step for defining outdoor programs as a professional practice (Martin et al., 2006).

Countering Common Oppositions

Within many professions, arguments about the value of establishing an accreditation system abound. People who don't see the benefits of accreditation are least likely to pursue accreditation themselves (Kren, Tatum, and Phillips, 1993). For many of these folks who are against accreditation, a common point of contention is that accreditation leads to commoditization of a business that supports a type of status quo (Dillard and Tinker, 1996). They suggest that if an overseeing body (i.e., accreditor) dictates the elements necessary for an experience, all entities providing that service become similar. However, as seen in the description of benefits to accreditation, this consistency in programs is not necessarily a limiting factor. Having a proven model of practice expectations does not necessarily lessen creativity or socially responsible products or services. In fact, contrary to what opponents of accreditation suggest, standards offer the parameters for practice while allowing an administration to fully develop its program in the ways that best reflect its mission and philosophy.

Another criticism is that accreditation standards may incorrectly determine the skills necessary to operate quality programs. However, this problem has a straightforward solution as suggested by Chase and Masberg (2008), who advocate for establishing a greater connection between practitioners and accreditors. Additional research can be conducted to lessen the potential for a disconnect between good practice and standards (Baker, 2002), and existing research can be used when establishing or revising standards. For example, although the accreditation visit seems focused on compliance, the data from the field visits can actually result in new standards or levels adjusted around expectations for professional practice! Standards can *reflect* the expected practice, and, in other cases, the standards *become* the expected practice.

Another issue often raised against accreditation is visitor or reviewer fidelity. This point is a valid concern that is easily addressed with systematic training and unbiased assignment of site visitors or reviewers. All accrediting bodies have stringent guidelines for site visitor training and updates (American Camp Association, 2007). A newly trained accreditation visitor generally serves as an apprentice for a number of site visits before they can assume full visitor responsibilities. Another strategy is to conduct team visits rather than single-person visits. The multiple viewpoints applied during the visit help minimize bias, misunderstandings, visitor fatigue, and scoring errors. Additionally, all accreditation systems have an appeal process in which visitor error can be addressed if the organization feels that it experienced unfairness during the accrediting process.

Another issue commonly raised around accreditation is ongoing compliance after the site visit. For example, once the visitation team leaves the site, staff and administrators could choose to ignore standards. However, data show that external standards and accreditation visits can actually increase a staff's internal motivation to assess and improve the quality of its programs (National Recreation and Park Association, 2010). One can also argue that ongoing compliance is a matter of professional ethics in which the accredited organization is morally (and sometimes legally) bound to uphold the expected standards of practice (American Camp Association, 2010).

Conclusion

Accreditation is necessary to assess standards of practice in outdoor programs. We suggest that the benefits of accreditation offer value around quality and consistency, external (unbiased) scrutiny, legal considerations, and growth through educational opportunities. Rather than being a burden that encourages a status quo approach to practice, accreditation provides opportunities for improving program quality, continually updating and examining relevancy of practice, developing staff, and validating programs to both staff and consumers. Accreditation becomes the proof for the difference between what we think and what we know (National Recreation and Park Association, 2010). The accreditation process is an opportunity to improve the fundamental soundness of the organization and to offer a quality service to discerning consumers who seek seals of approval in order to justify their choice of program or organization. Finally, as suggested by Ann Mulholland, Deputy Mayor of St. Paul, Minnesota, "Accreditation validates our programs. It forces you to think about the future and gives you the structure in which to do this" (National Recreation and Park Association, 2010). We believe that accreditation represents one step toward better defining outdoor programs as a profession and our commitment to a systematic process focused on quality as a result of adhering to professional standards of practice.

References

American Camp Association. (2007). *American Camp Association accreditation process guide.* Monterey, CA: Healthy Learning.

American Camp Association. (2010). Is accreditation right for my program? www.acacamps.org/accreditation/eligible [November 14, 2010].

American Camping Association. (1935). *Suggested tentative standards.* Martinsville, IN: American Camping Association.

American Mountain Guides Association. (2010). Accreditation program. http://amga.com/programs/accreditation.php [November 14, 2010].

Association for Experiential Education. (2010). Accreditation. www.aee.org/accreditation/ [November 14, 2010].

Baker, R.L. (2002). Evaluating quality and effectiveness: Regional accreditation principles and practices. *The Journal of Academic Librarianship, 28*(1), 3-7.

Ball, A., & Ball, B. (2000). *Basic camp management.* Martinsville, IN: American Camping Association.

Bialeschki, M.D., Henderson, K.A., & James, P.A. (2007). Camp experiences and developmental outcomes for youth. *Child and Adolescent Psychiatric Clinics of North America, 16,* 769-788.

Chase, D.M., & Masberg, B.A. (2008). Partnering for skill development: Park and recreation agencies and university programs. *Managing Leisure, 13,* 74-91.

Council on Accreditation. (2010a). About COA. www.coastandards.org/about.php [November 13, 2010].

Council on Accreditation. (2010b). Wilderness and adventure-based therapeutic outdoor services. www.coastandards.org/standards.php?navView=private&section_id=83 2010 [November 14, 2010].

Crouse, J. (1999). Outcomes assessment, quality assurance, and accreditation. *Journal of Family and Consumer Sciences, 91*(4), 114-115.

Dillard, J.F., & Tinker, T. (1996). Commodifying business and accounting education: The implications of accreditation. *Critical Perspectives on Accounting, 7*(1), 215-225.

Harris, R., & Jago, L. (2001). Professional accreditation in the Australian tourism industry: An uncertain future. *Tourism Management, 22*(4), 383-390.

Kren, L., Tatum, K.W., & Phillips, L.C. (1993). Separate accreditation of accounting programs: An empirical investigation. *Issues in Accounting Education, 8*(2), 260-272.

Lesser v. Camp Wildwood. (2003). 282 F. Supp. 2d 139.

Martin, B., Cashel, C., Wagstaff, M., & Breunig, M. (2006). *Outdoor leadership: Theory and practice.* Champaign, IL: Human Kinetics.

Memon, J.A., Demirdogen, R.E., & Chowdhry, B.S. (2009). Achievements, outcomes and proposal for global accreditation of engineering education in developing countries. *Procedia Social and Behavioral Sciences, 1*(1), 2557-2561.

Merriam-Webster. (2005). *Merriam-Webster dictionary.* Springfield, MA: Merriam-Webster.

National Recreation and Park Association. (2010). Video from the Commission of Accreditation for Parks and Recreation Agencies. www.nrpa.org/media/video/capraflv.html [December 12, 2011].

Peer, K.S., & Rakich, J.S. (2000, June). Accreditation and continuous quality improvement in athletic training education. *Journal of Athletic Training, 35*(2), 188.

Priest, S., & Gass, M.A. (1997). *Effective leadership in adventure programming.* Champaign, IL: Human Kinetics.

Ratcliff, R. (2008). "The Current": ACA Great Rivers section newsletter. www.acagreatrivers.org/08_06newsletter_special.pdf [November 14, 2010].

United States Department of Education. (2006). Commission on the Future of Higher Education report. www2.ed.gov/about/bdscomm/list/hiedfuture/reports/final-report.pdf [November 14, 2010].

Urgel, J. (2007). EQUIS accreditation: Value and benefits for international business schools. *Journal of Management Development, 26*(1), 73-83.

Walker, R.H., & Johnson, L.W. (2009). Signaling intrinsic service quality and value via accreditation and certification. *Managing Service Quality, 19*(1), 85-105.

Wilderness Education Association. (2010). Wilderness Education Association accreditation. www.weainfo.org/accreditation [November 14, 2010].

Young, K.E., Chambers, C.M., Kells, H.R., & Associates. (1983). *Understanding accreditation: Contemporary perspectives on issues and practices in evaluating educational quality.* San Francisco: Jossey-Bass.

Zammuto, R.F. (2008). Accreditation and the globalization of business. *Academy of Management Learning and Education, 7*(2), 256-268.

Should programs be accredited to ensure that they adhere to industry standards?

NO **Pay to Play: The Price of Accreditation**

Whitney Ward, PhD, assistant professor, health education and recreation, Southern Illinois University, Carbondale, Illinois

At first glance, it appears that accreditation may be a no-brainer. Literature within the adventure programming industry suggests that the majority of outdoor professionals support the accreditation process (Bassin et al., 1992; Cockrell and Detzel, 1985; Gass, 1999). However, on further investigation, accreditation has serious limitations and some critically question its benefits. Chisholm and Shaw (2004) state, "It is likely that *influential organizations within the outdoor industry will benefit* from the *socially constructed 'need'* for audit and accreditation" (p. 320, emphasis added). Chisholm and Shaw further state that the influential accrediting organizations benefit in terms of both money and power at the expense of the outdoor program provider.

This argument presents a stance against accreditation by outlining four confounding issues that seriously negate the purpose and benefits of accreditation. The first confounding issue is the false notion of added value. Adventure programmers assume that accreditation constitutes a value added by providing a safety guarantee and legal protection. However, the value is questionable given the multiple options for accreditation and the pre-existing government standards. The second confounding issue concerns the associated costs of accreditation. The third issue concerns the unchecked power of accreditation. The final confounding issue concerns the role of accreditation in the overall decline of adventure programming.

Questionable Value

Proponents of accreditation argue that it assures clients, agencies, and the custodians of the lands that a program has clearly defined and appropriate objectives and maintains conditions under which participants can reasonably meet these achievements (Gass, 1999). Additionally, supporters contend that accreditation is an indicator of a commitment to quality and is a seal of approval. Although accreditation does provide objective measures of safety, it can be manipulated to the extent that programs spend more resources pursuing standards than they do delivering the adventure experience itself (Chisholm and Shaw, 2004). This can lead to an environment of suspicion. Furthermore, even with this supposed guarantee and the associated benefits, the track record of accreditation within the adventure programming industry is inconsistent and may be of questionable value.

The American Camp Association (ACA), which has more than 2,400 accredited camps, has been the most successful regarding accreditation (American Camp Association, n.d. a). However, even with their success, only one-quarter of camps in the United States are accredited (Pintas and Mullins Law Firm, 2011). Although the ACA does serve camps that integrate adventure programming into the curricula, their purpose and mission does little to serve the larger adventure programming industry because they focus on organized camping. Even within the organized camping system, large entities such as the Boy Scouts of America (BSA) do not submit to ACA standards. BSA supports a national task force that develops camp standards and trains hundreds of visitation teams to conduct inspections each year.

Other accreditation bodies like the Association for Experiential Education (AEE) and National Recreation and Park Association (NRPA) have not had the same level of success as ACA. AEE provides accreditation in experiential adventure programming, and it has accredited more than 250 programs (Brown, 2007). However, currently only 46 AEE-accredited programs exist in the world (Association for Experiential Education, n.d.). Thus, for whatever reasons, more than 200 programs have decided not to retain AEE accreditation. What may be even more indicative of the value of accreditation is that out of all the adventure organizations, only a few have chosen to pursue accreditation. An AEE board member reflects on AEE's limited growth in the accreditation program: "How long can an organization hang on [to accreditation] with only 40 to 50 organizations? You begin to ask, is this the most effective model?" (A. Bobilya, personal communication, April 11, 2011).

NRPA is the accrediting body for parks and academic programs. Yet, similar to AEE, NRPA has had limited success; only 81 academic programs are NRPA accredited (National Recreation and Park Association, n.d. a). Furthermore, even a smaller percentage of NRPA-accredited park districts exist within the thousands of city and county parks districts in the United States. Several states have only one or two accredited parks, and some states do not have any (National Recreation and Park Association, n.d. b). Does this mean that only a few quality parks exist? The answer obviously is no. Several quality academic programs and parks are not NRPA accredited. Larger universities that primarily focus on research and grant funding as opposed to teaching find little value in an accreditation that is practitioner oriented. In addition, the NRPA accreditation supports the Certified Parks and Recreation Professional (CPRP) certificate. Yet, the vast majority of the recreation and parks agencies do not require the CPRP for employment. Organizations must determine whether the benefits and values received outweigh the costs. Based on the limited success of accreditation, most organizations must not see enough value added to justify accreditation.

The U.S. Department of Education, when addressing accreditation, readily admits that there are "programs that elect not to seek accreditation but nevertheless may provide a quality [experience]" (Office of Postsecondary Education, n.d.). A program dedicated to high standards is going to be a quality program regardless of accreditation. If accreditation is indeed valuable, why do so many organizations choose to forgo the process? The answer can be explained with simple cost–benefit analysis: accreditation does not provide enough perceived benefits for organizations to justify the costs.

The Accreditation Safety Guarantee

Accredited programs are often portrayed as meeting various standards and therefore being safe. Accreditation is by no means a guarantee of prescribed outcomes. Incidents can and do happen to even the best-prepared organization. Having an accreditation will not eliminate incidents. Risk is simply an inherent aspect of adventure programming. Although risk can be managed, safety and risk are mutually exclusive (Gregg, 2007). This point is illustrated by the safety director of a predominant outdoor leader-

ship organization (who asked to remain anonymous for fear of retribution), who stated that accreditation has no effect or would not have prevented past incidents from occurring (safety director, personal communication, April 4, 2011).

In one incident, in 2001 two girls became trapped and drowned in a canoeing accident (Chisholm and Shaw, 2004). After an extensive investigation, authorities determined that the program had followed all the applicable standards, yet an incident still resulted in two fatalities (Chisholm and Shaw, 2004). Another example includes an ACA-accredited camp that was shut down due to allegations of child abuse by staff members. ACA revoked its accreditation because of the allegations. However, the abuse apparently went on for years while the camp was ACA accredited (WBUR, 2011). Accidents and incidents happen regardless of accreditation. Accreditation cannot and does not guarantee safety.

Legal Protection

Legal protection is often touted as a benefit of accreditation. However, the accreditation process that provides legal protection for an organization is also what makes litigation possible. The standards used to determine accreditation are the exact same standards that are used to show negligence. A recent discussion regarding helmet use illustrates this concept of litigation potential:

> As far as standards that affect you folks, there are three organizations that have written standards for helmet use. The ACA, CWA [Climbing Wall Association] and ACCT [Association for Challenge Course Technologies]. All three have standards for helmets around outside programs, some only for minors. Either way it is a perfect opportunity for the plaintiffs [to] find the standard you violated and sue rather than see what you did not screw up. If you are running a program outdoors I would suggest you meet all three standards. The cost of getting the standards is going to bankrupt some of you. (J. Moss, personal communication, April, 6, 2011)

Moss (2011) goes on to say:

> According to evidence presented by the plaintiffs, there was also no rehearsal of any safety plan or communication of the plan to counselors, despite the requirement of training or rehearsal in the ACA

Standards Manual. See Mosley Decl. Exh. N at OM-14 (ACA Accreditation Standards). Simply put the plaintiff's expert used the ACA standards, adopted by the defendant camp, to convince the judge the camp was negligent. Standards are the lowest acceptable level of doing or not doing something. Below that level, if there is an associated injury, someone is negligent. If you do not violate a standard you have not breached the duty of care to someone. No breach, no negligence no matter how bad the injury or how great the damages. Standards are determined by the jury at trial. Normally, the plaintiff and the defendant put witnesses and expert witnesses on the stand to determine what the standard of care is. The jury then decides based on what they've heard. That means the defense has a chance to prove they were not below the standard of care. The defendant loses that chance if your trade association writes standards for you. (paragraphs 22-25)

That is not to say that organizations should not have policies or guidelines that they follow. However, unmet standards that are established by accreditation with the intention of protecting organizations can be used to show negligence.

Accreditation standards can be a double-edged sword: they can protect and they can cut. However, standards become even more legally problematic when they are not mandatory. Each accreditation process has numerous standards. However, accreditation does not require full compliance to the standards, as is seen in the ACA accreditation process: "Accreditation criteria do not require 100 percent compliance with standards. Some nonmandatory requirements, such as shower ratios, can be missed and the camp or conference center can still be accredited" (American Camp Association, n.d. c). Having nonrequired standards begs the question, why have the standard in the first place? Again, an unmet accreditation standard provides an opportunity for litigation against the organization. Rick Curtis, director of Outdoor Action Programs at Princeton University, addresses how standards can cause potential for more liability:

Well, the bad news about protocols is, if you make 'em, you've got to keep 'em. More important in some ways than developing a protocol is seeing to

its implementation. Protocols without the necessary structure behind them to see that they are carried through with are only words on paper. From a Risk Management point of view, poorly implemented protocols can create greater liability for an organization than not having a specific protocol. Having a protocol says, 'we believe that this is the best way to operate.' Ignoring that protocol may leave you more vulnerable for a charge of negligence or even gross negligence. (Curtis, n.d., paragraph 6)

Having nonmandatory standards is equivalent to ignoring protocols and provides the evidence against the organization necessary for it to be found negligent.

Multiple Accreditations

The sheer volume and specialization of accreditation options devalues the intended purpose. The complexity of options has thrown our whole system off balance. An organization could pursue any of multiple accreditations, and additional accreditations are becoming available all the time. Depending on the institution, numerous accreditation schemes related to adventure programming exist in the United States alone. Compound this with other industry accreditations, such as education, human services, and business, and programs have to adhere to a quagmire of accreditations. As the co-chair of the outdoor education department at Montreat College and as a member of the AEE board of directors, Andrew Bobilya feels that as more accreditations become available he starts to question the viability of accreditation in general. An organization can adequately pursue and fund only so many accreditations (A. Bobilya, personal communication, April 11, 2011).

NRPA provides accreditation for institutions that grant undergraduate recreation degrees. Their broad recreation accreditation is granted to institutions that meet specific core requirements. Institutions can also pursue four other NRPA accreditation options in leisure services management, natural resource recreation management, leisure or recreation program delivery, and therapeutic recreation (National Recreation and Park Association, n.d. a). However, if an academic program also wants to be accredited in the area of adventure programming, they would also have to seek an AEE or Wilderness Education Association accreditation. Additionally, departments with therapeutic programs have to meet accreditation standards from the other various therapeutic organizations. This is not just a hypothetical situation; it is a reality for several academic recreation departments. The recreation program at Southern Illinois University is accredited by four accreditation systems (J. Fetro, personal communication, April 7, 2011). Even some smaller departments that offer only specific outdoor-related degrees have to go through at least two accreditations (A. Bobilya, personal communication, April 11, 2011). These numerous accreditations have caused the very situation of "dividing into categories" that Gass (1999) argues accreditation would remedy. Another problem caused by multiple accreditations is that the standards of one accreditation scheme may contradict the standards from another accreditation scheme (M. Malkin, personal communication, September 14, 2011).

False Need

There exists a false notion that accreditation serves a fundamental need that is basic to all adventure-based organizations. For example, as explained by the counterargument to this debate, some argue that accreditation provides an "out-of-the-box" program so that camps do not have to replicate work that has already been done. This may benefit smaller organizations, but it can also provide a cookie-cutter experience. Every program has different needs and objectives. Out-of-the-box programming limits the effectiveness of the provider and may not meet the needs of either the client or provider. For example, a blanket risk-management form may work well for one organization but may be completely inappropriate for another.

Additionally, most seem to overlook the multitude of additional regulatory bodies and laws that dictate adventure-based operations. Each camp, school, or program already must adhere to multiple government-mandated standards; these standards must be met in order to fulfill state licensing requirements (American Camp Association, n.d. c, n.d. d).

Finally, the need for accreditation is lacking; this is especially true for the larger organizations such as BSA, as discussed previously. Also, Outward Bound dropped its AEE accreditation because it felt a lack of need (Brown, 2007). Outward Bound, as one of the original and predominant adventure education organizations, is large enough to influence and develop industry best practices. Their in-house policy and procedure processes may be deemed rigorous enough, especially in a time when financial resources are limited (A. Bobilya, personal communication, April 11, 2011). Organizations such as Outward Bound and BSA develop their own standards, which often drive industry standards, and therefore negate the need for accreditation by an outside accrediting body.

Costs

Accreditation is very costly to both the organization and the members. Even the accreditation organizations realize this: "Accreditation isn't cheap and it isn't easy" (American Camp Association, n.d. b, paragraph 6). Pursuing accreditation is very resource intensive. The amount of time and money varies from accreditation to accreditation, but organizations usually spend a minimum of one year of time, and several accreditations require more time. Admittedly, organizations do not spend the entire time doing accreditation activities, but they are "definitely cumbersome" (A. Bobilya, personal communication, April, 11, 2011). Bobilya comments that he spent 50 hours during a recent semester on projects related to Wilderness Education Association accreditation.

Not only is accreditation time intensive, but it is also very cost intensive. Again, cost varies from accreditation to accreditation, but regardless, accreditation is expensive. According to a camping services director, in regard to ACA accreditation, "There are over three hundred standards to meet, and from what our Executive Director shares with me, it is quite costly to camp. We pay pretty heavy membership dues" (personal communication, April 4, 2011). Furthermore, AEE accreditation can cost an organization more than $2,000 per year and even more in years that require a site visit (Tierney, n.d.). All the various fees of NRPA accreditation are also costly. For example, NRPA charges a $500 fee for filing paperwork late or $1,000 to postpone a site visit (National Recreation and Park Association, n.d. c). When programs and organizations are required to do more and more with less and less, accreditation fees become an unnecessary burden. It causes some to ask, "Can we give the time and resources to [accreditation]? And if so, which accreditation is most important for our organization?" (A. Bobilya, personal communication, April 11, 2011). Some may argue that the cost of accreditation is less than the cost of litigation. However, as discussed previously, accreditation cannot guarantee safety, nor can it prevent litigation. Accredited organizations get sued and lose often. The cost of accreditation by itself would not be a limiting factor if it were justified; however, the costs of accreditation outweigh the benefits received.

Unchecked Power

Accreditation has significant potential to create elitist associations rather than inclusive organizations. This is currently happening with permitting and access. Various agencies allow only groups that have specific accreditations to obtain special-use permits. Joshua Tree National Park issues special-use permits only to groups that have American Mountain Guides Association certifications or AEE accreditation. Essentially, groups must pay to play. Not only does requiring accreditation significantly limit the availability and access to public land, it undermines the trust that experienced practitioners can competently do their job (Chisholm and Shaw, 2004).

Furthermore, one set of standards or accreditation has the ability to set the precedent that all others must adhere to. The American National Standards Institute (ANSI) is a nonprofit organizations that

> oversees the creation, promulgation, and use of thousands of norms and guidelines that directly impact businesses in nearly every sector: from acoustical devices to construction equipment, from dairy and livestock production to energy distribution, and many more. ANSI is also actively engaged in accrediting programs that assess conformance to standards. (American National Standards Institute, n.d. a, paragraph 2)

ANSI tries to establish a national consensus of standards. ANSI does not evaluate the standards that are developed per se; rather, it tries to ensure that the standards are developed in an open, inclusive, transparent way that includes all the various stakeholders:

> [An industry] work[s] cooperatively to develop voluntary national consensus standards. Accreditation by ANSI signifies that the procedures used by the standards body in connection with the development of American National Standards meet the Institute's essential requirements for openness, balance, consensus, and due process. (American National Standards Institute, n.d. b, paragraph 3)

The idea behind the ANSI process is to be commended. However, a significant discrepancy exists in the outdoor industry regarding the ANSI Accredited Standards Developer for the challenge course industry. The Association for Challenge Course Technology (ACCT) was the first organization to submit challenge course standards to ANSI and therefore was granted the Accredited Standards Developer designation for ANSI-recognized challenge course standards. However, the process neglected to include input by the Professional Ropes Course Association (PRCA). Therefore, if PRCA wants to follow the established ANSI standards, it is bound by the standards that ACCT established. The current ANSI accreditation system rewards the individuals or organizations that act first. Furthermore, this system negates collaboration or does not foster necessary collaboration, which is unfortunate considering that adventure programming touts itself as being effective in facilitating team building and collaboration.

Additionally, accreditation is frequently seen as taking control of the industry and developing the standards that govern it, as may be the case in the ACCT example. People often feel that if standards and accreditation are not developed by someone within the industry then they will be developed and imposed on the industry by outsiders less qualified to do so (Chisholm and Shaw, 2004). However, the deep irony within the accreditation process is that none of the accrediting bodies related to adventure programming are recognized by the U.S. Department of Education (DOE) or other governing bodies, as several other industry accreditations are. One could argue that regulation by the DOE is irrelevant to adventure programming, yet accreditation organizations related to adventure programming have little to no oversight from a larger regulatory body (Chisholm and Shaw, 2004).

Finally, the unchecked power of accreditation became evident while writing this issue. Within the outdoor industry, programs "who wish to stay in business will work towards the request of the governing organization without questioning the development of further measures, precisely because they are in the habit of doing so" (Chisholm and Shaw, 2004, p. 322). More importantly, the accreditation process offers few opportunities or options for recourse for those that may not agree with particular standards (Chisholm and Shaw, 2004). The accreditation process very rarely offers opportunities to question the accrediting body, and those that do are seen as rogue or as causing problems. Several individuals interviewed for this issue had plenty to say about the limitations and drawbacks of accreditation. However, when asked whether they were willing for their viewpoint to be included, they immediately declined. They felt that voicing an opinion against accreditation would somehow come back to harm them or that they would be blacklisted by the accrediting body. Names are intentionally left out of the citations to respect wishes and protect the anonymity of individuals when it was requested.

Decline of Adventure Programming

Accreditation changes the nature of professionalism from initiative and discipline to compliance with external standards. Yet accreditation is just one objective measure of quality and safety and neglects to include other measures that may be as equally significant and meaningful (Chisholm and Shaw, 2004). As such, accreditation becomes prescriptive in nature and organizations end up focusing significant resources on pursuing accreditation standards. As resources are used for developing, adhering, and litigating accreditation standards, they are diverted from other areas. According to Neill (2001), "[The outdoor] industry has been seduced into focusing energy and attention on accreditation issues and is now at risk of going too far down this path and killing off growth and development of new and innovative programming methods" (p. 8).

According to Priest (1999), accreditation is indicative of an industry in stagnation or decline. Based on current evidences of the time, Priest (1999) developed a model of the life cycle of adventure programming. Accreditation is an integral part of that model; the voluntary move from certification to accreditation is linked to an outdoor industry in the plateau stage. If this is true, adventure programming in the United States reached the plateau in the later part of the 20th century (see Bassin et al., 1992; Cockrell and Detzel, 1985), and without intervention the adventure programming industry is in the natural cycle of decline. Progressing through the life cycle, mandatory program accreditation and licensing are characteristic of the adventure programming industry in decline (Priest, 1999). Neill (2001) supports Priest:

> There was continued growth [of adventure programming] during the 1990s; however, there are increasing signs of plateauing in the growth curve, with a growing emphasis on accreditation, legalization and consolidation of safety systems, training and program delivery methods. (p. 2)

With the current state of accreditation, the adventure programming industry in the United States appears not too far away from the natural progression of decline.

Conclusion

Accreditation may have some benefits, but they are far outweighed by the disadvantages. The majority of outdoor professionals supported the accreditation process in the 1980s and 1990s (see Bassin et al., 1992; Cockrell and Detzel, 1985). However, much has changed in the past 30 years. When this initial research was conducted in the 1980s and 1990s, ACA accreditation was the only outdoor accreditation available—AEE and Wilderness Education Association accreditations were not established until after this research was conducted.

Since that time very little research has been conducted to determine support for accreditation. Furthermore, several individuals in the industry feel that they cannot speak out against accreditation. This unchecked power (in addition to the multiple accreditation schemes and excessive costs) limits any of the associated benefits of accreditation. By simply looking at the limited number of organizations that have opted to pursue accreditation, one can see the lack of need. Furthermore, the maturation of the accreditation process is a key indicator of the lack of vitality in the outdoor industry. Accreditation is exacting a heavy price: having to pay to play.

References

American Camp Association. (n.d. a). Home page. www. acacamps.org [December 12, 2011].

American Camp Association. (n.d. b). ACA accreditation: Accreditation fees. www.acacamps.org/accreditation/costs [December 12, 2011].

American Camp Association. (n.d. c). Dispelling myths about accreditation. www.acacamps.org/accreditation/myths [December 12, 2011].

American Camp Association. (n.d. d). Is accreditation right for my program? www.acacamps.org/accreditation/eligible [December 12, 2011].

American National Standards Institute. (n.d. a). About ANSI overview. www.ansi.org/about_ansi/overview/overview.aspx?menuid=1 [December 12, 2011].

American National Standards Institute. (n.d. b). Introduction. www.ansi.org/about_ansi/introduction/introduction.aspx?menuid=1 [December 12, 2011].

Association for Experiential Education. (n.d.). AEE accredited programs. www.aee.org/accreditation/programs [December 12, 2011].

Bassin, Z., Breault, M., Flemming, J., Foell, S., Neufeld, J., & Priest, S. (1992). AEE organizational membership preference for program accreditation. *Journal of Experiential Education, 15*(2), 21-27.

Brown, Z. (2007). Managing risk: Adventure schools trying to expand reach of uniform standards. www.dailycamera.com/ci_13082588#ixzz1H0qaHCor [December 12, 2011].

Chisholm, H., & Shaw, S. (2004). Prove it! The 'tyranny' of audit and accreditation in the New Zealand outdoors industry. *Leisure Studies, 23*(4), 317-327.

Cockrell, D., & Detzel, D. (1985). Effects of outdoor leadership certification on safety, impacts, and program. *Trends, 22*(3), 15-21.

Curtis, R. (n.d.). OA guide to building program protocols. www.princton.edu/~oa/safety/protocol.shtml [December 12, 2011].

Gass, M. (1999). Accreditation and certification. In J.C. Miles & S. Priest (Eds.), *Adventure programming* (pp. 247-251). State College, PA: Venture.

Gregg, C.R. (2007). Risk and safety in adventure programming. In D. Proudy, J. Panicucci, & R. Collinson (Eds.), *Adventure education: Theory and applications* (pp. 49-61). Champaign, IL: Human Kinetics.

Moss, J. (2011). Trade association standards sink a summer camp when plaintiff uses them to prove camp was negligent. www.recreation-law.com/2011/02/trade-association-standards-sink-summer.html [December 12, 2011].

National Recreation and Park Association. (n.d. a). Accredited academic programs. www.nrpa.org/Content.aspx?id=1112 [December 12, 2011].

National Recreation and Park Association. (n.d. b). Accredited agencies. www.nrpa.org/media/map/accred-map.htm [December 12, 2011].

National Recreation and Park Association. (n.d. c). COAPRT accreditation fee list. www.nrpa.org/Content.aspx?id=4955 [December 12, 2011].

Neill, J.T. (2001). A profile of outdoor education programs and their implementation in Australia. *Japan Outdoor Education Journal, 5*(2), 1-9.

Office of Postsecondary Education. (n.d.) The U.S. Department of Education database of accredited postsecondary institutions and programs. www.ope.ed.gov/accreditation [December 12, 2011].

Pintas and Mullins Law Firm. (2011). Illinois teen drowns while swimming at Michigan summer camp. www.autoaccidentlawyers-blog.com/2011/07/illinois-teen-drowns-while-swimming-at-michigan-summer-camp.html [December 12, 2011].

Priest, S. (1999). National life cycles in outdoor adventure programming. *The Outdoor Network, 10*(1), 16-17, 34-35.

Tierney, S. (n.d.). The AEE accreditation process. http://iseeninfo.com/annual-institute/.../10/Tierney-AEEAccreditationProcess.ppt [December 12, 2011].

WBUR. (2011). Cape camp to close this summer after sex abuse probe. www.wbur.org/2011/04/08/camp-good-news-accreditation [December 12, 2011].

Controversial Issue 6

Should motorized outdoor adventure pursuits be included in adventure programming?

In an essay titled "The Semantics of Adventure Programming," Priest (1999) defined outdoor pursuits as a subset of outdoor recreation and characterized outdoor pursuits as self-propelled activities such as walking, backpacking, climbing, bicycling, kayaking, and caving. He writes: "They *do not* include other outdoor recreational activities that are motorized (such as snowmobiling, motorcycling, car racing, and power boating) *nor* animal powered (such as horse riding and dogsledding). While the latter are definitely outdoor recreation, they lack the low-impact environmental philosophy that is expected to go hand in hand with outdoor pursuits" (p. 112; italics original).

The phrase "outdoor pursuits" is often used interchangeably with adventure programming. Indeed, many collegiate adventure programs housed within the context of larger campus recreation programs are referred to as outdoor pursuits programs and include an array of activities typical of the definition offered by Priest (1999). This definition creates a conundrum in adventure programming. Should adventure programming include the use of motorized travel in outdoor environments?

The astute adventure programmer can take any activity that contains elements of risk, challenge, and uncertainty in an outdoor setting and facilitate an adventure learning experience. A snowmobile trip or all-terrain vehicle (ATV) experience can provide all the ingredients found in adventure-based activities. Hallmark programs and organizations in the field of adventure programming have embraced the use of pack animals for transportation in their programs, which contradicts Priest's interpretation of outdoor pursuits. Outward Bound Wilderness offers dogsledding programs in the Boundary Waters Canoe Area Wilderness in northern Minnesota. The National Outdoor Leadership School offers programs in which program participants and their supplies are transported on horseback. The Leave No Trace Center for Outdoor Ethics has adapted its seven principles to address impacts associated with the use of livestock in outdoor recreation activities.

Is it now time to consider broadening the scope of outdoor pursuits and adventure programming to include motorized outdoor recreational activities such as snowmobiling, motorboating, and other motorized forms of travel? Robert Dvorak argues that despite historical antipathy to motorized travel, opportunities for motorized pursuits do exist in adventure programming. He argues that recent legislation has provided effective management frameworks for administering motorized travel on public lands and waterways, that technological improvements and education have helped to effectively mitigate environmental impacts, and that adventure programming provides a framework to deliver these activities and experiences in a manner that benefits users.

Philip Cafaro, on the other hand, argues that motorized travel should be strictly limited on public lands because it negatively impacts nature, other users, and the off-highway vehicle (OHV) users themselves. Cafaro's argument is reprinted from an essay published in the book *Thrillcraft: The Environmental Consequences of Motorized Recreation* (2007). The implications of Cafaro's argument are clear for the practice of adventure programming. He suggests that we adhere to our traditional stance on this issue.

Although they technically have different meanings, the arguments that follow use the terms OHV and ORV interchangeably to refer to a broad class of vehicles designed to travel on unimproved roads and trails not suitable for travel by conventional motor vehicles. Examples include all-terrain vehicles, side-by-sides, dirt bikes, 4×4 jeeps and trucks, and snowmobiles. Personal watercraft are another form of motorized travel to which the arguments that follow extend. Personal watercraft are classified by the U.S. Coast Guard as class A inboard boats. They are small vessels propelled by water jet pumps and are designed to carry one to three riders. Considerations for this argument may vary to some degree depending on the different types of vehicles and the intended uses of these vehicles. However, the central question remains: Should motorized outdoor adventure pursuits be included in adventure programming?

References

Cafaro, P. (2007). Teaching disrespect: The ethics of off-road vehicle use on America's public lands. In G. Wuerthner (Ed.), *Thrillcraft: The environmental consequences of motorized recreation* (pp. 31-35). White River Junction, VT: Chelsea Green Publishing Company.

Priest, S. (1999). The semantics of adventure programming. In J.C. Miles & S. Priest (Eds.), *Adventure programming* (pp. 111-114). State College, PA: Venture.

Should motorized outdoor adventure pursuits be included in adventure programming?

YES Opportunities for Motorized Pursuits in Adventure Programming

Robert Dvorak, PhD, assistant professor in recreation, parks, and leisure services administration, Central Michigan University, Mount Pleasant, Michigan, United States

An ongoing debate exists in the fields of outdoor recreation and natural resource management regarding the appropriateness of outdoor motorized pursuits. The conflicts that have historically existed between participants in motorized and nonmotorized recreation continue to fuel this debate. However, this debate has not been fully examined, applied, or understood within an adventure programming context. I suggest that despite historical conflicts, opportunities for motorized pursuits do exist in adventure programming. Through recent legislation and policy, these opportunities have been identified within appropriate contexts. Technological improvements and education also strive to mitigate environmental impacts, and research has found evidence of similar motivations between participants in nonmotorized and motorized recreation. Further, adventure programming provides a framework to deliver these activities and experiences in a manner that benefits users. In this argument, the term "off-highway vehicle" (OHV) refers to all-terrain vehicles, off-highway motorcycles, four-wheel-drive jeeps or sport utility vehicles, jet skis, and snowmobiles.

Historical Growth and Appropriate Contexts

The emergence of motorized recreation pursuits represents a dramatic change in the way individuals experience and engage nature. The traditional modes of experiencing nature via a hike, horseback ride, and canoe are now in the company of the OHV. Yet the emergence of OHV recreation pursuits is not all that surprising. In *Driven Wild*, Sutter (2002) suggests that the economic and infrastructure developments of 20th century America and the proliferation of automobiles provided an opportunity for a larger segment of the population to experience nature. The relationships and meanings individuals associated with nature were achieved by new means and by using the new technologies at hand. Sutter suggests that these developments in part spurred the creation of the Wilderness Act in 1964. However, one can also argue that these changes and technological developments created new forms of access to the outdoors in which OHV became the new way for individuals to interact with and enjoy the outdoors.

These developments have not been just a technological craze. Data from the National Survey on Recreation and the Environment (NSRE) demonstrate that the number of OHV grew from less than 3 million vehicles in 1993 to more than 8 million in 2003 (Cordell et al., 2005). NSRE data also show that "the proportion of people age 16 and older who said they participated in OHV recreation increased from 16.8 percent in 1999–2000 to 23.8 percent in 2003–2004" (Cordell et al., 2005, p. 6). This growth in OHV participants represents a 42 percent increase from 36 million to 51 million participants. As Cordell and colleagues (2005) suggest, this means that 20 percent of the population of the United States or almost one in five people age 16 or older participated in OHV activities in 2003.

Although this growth is significant, we must acknowledge that every motorized pursuit is not necessarily compatible with all contexts. Similarly, because adventure programming is offered across various contexts, limitations exist that constrain which programs are permitted. Sometimes these limitations are based on the landscape or limited public access or are related to resource issues. Other times, use is dictated by legislation. Section 4(c) of the Wilderness Act (1964) states:

> Except as specifically provided for in this Act . . . there shall be no temporary road, no use of motor vehicles, motorized equipment or motorboats, no landing of aircraft, no other form of mechanical transport, and no structure or installation within any such area.

This legislation prohibits motorized recreation in designated wilderness unless other applicable enabling legislation exists. In the case of the Boundary Waters Canoe Area Wilderness, such enabling legislation does exist. Use of motorboats is allowed in certain designated areas that historically allowed recreational motorboat use prior to wilderness designation. In this context, motorized pursuits are considered compatible with the competing goals that natural resources managers balance across the landscape. More recently, the appropriate contexts for motorized recreation pursuits have been outlined in travel management policies. In 2005, the U.S. Forest Service published the Travel Management Rule (36 C.F.R. section 212, subpart B) to govern use of motorized vehicles on national forest lands. The policy requires each national forest to designate which roads, trails, and areas within the forest are open to motor vehicles. Such designations can be based on vehicle classification (ATV, motorcycle, 4×4 vehicle) and, once completed, use of motorized vehicles in nondesignated areas is prohibited.

This policy outlines where motorized pursuits are appropriate across national forests. It provides opportunities for collaboration with local governments and allows for public input and discussion. This framework was further clarified in 2008 when the U.S. Forest Service published Final Travel Management Directives (73 fed. reg. 74,689). These directives clarify terminology in the travel management process and help managers integrate the rule within the agency's other policies on land management planning, environmental analysis, road analysis, and other federal requirements (U.S. Forest Service, 2008).

When considered with growth in OHV use, these recent policies suggest that OHV use is recognized as a compatible recreational pursuit within appropriate contexts on public lands. However, this recognition has raised issues related to environmental degradation, conflict between recreation users, and the benefits of OHV participation. Whether manifested from historical interactions or inappropriate behaviors, users of motorized recreation have received a strong stereotype associated with these issues. In the following sections, I describe how these issues can be reconciled.

Mitigating Impacts With Technology

No matter the recreational pursuit, managers try to communicate to recreationists the importance of minimizing harm to the environment and treating it respectfully. This is necessary because, regardless of the recreational activity, all use causes environmental impacts. The magnitude of these impacts varies by activity, but awareness of these impacts by individual users is still necessary. For example, hikers are directed to avoid trampling fragile soils or vegetation. In backcountry settings, horseback riders are required to use only feed that is certified weed-free. Resource impacts related to OHV use are documented (Stokowski and LaPointe, 2000), but recent technological improvements and education on appropriate behaviors have been important in addressing issues.

Technological advances in OHV design have been partly driven by federal legislation and policy. The Environmental Protection Agency (2007) proposed new emissions standards for many small engines, including those for OHV. This proposed rule targets a reduction in emissions that directly affect air quality. In similar attempts to improve air quality, policies for winter use in Yellowstone National Park require that all snowmobiles entering the park meet emissions standards for best available technology. These policies have caused an industry shift for OHV. Manufacturers have developed four-stroke engine technology with lower emissions than older, two-stroke engines. Studies in Yellowstone National Park have shown that this technology can reduce hydrocarbon emissions per vehicle by a factor of 12 and carbon monoxide by a factor of 2 (Bishop et al., 2006).

OHV manufacturers have also addressed issues related to human-caused wildfire and noise. Spark arrestors, developed to reduce the instance of wildland fires, are now required on most OHV for use on public lands. Related to noise, manufacturers have recently focused on developing eco-friendly, quieter electric OHV. For the past several years, Polaris has offered models such as the EV Electric Side-by-Side and Ranger EV UTV. These fully electric models reduce the carbon footprint from activities and reduce the impact of noise on other recreationists. These developments also represent a commitment, and substantial financial investment, by the OHV industry and its users to minimize their impact on the environment. They are willing to change their use and behaviors as a way to protect the environment and activities they enjoy.

Education and Tread Lightly!

Education is used to change and improve behavior of OHV users. Education has become a core element of park and protected area management and is an effective tool in communicating values, practices, and critical issues. Given the stereotypes and historical conflicts that exist between users of motorized and nonmotorized recreation, educational programs are an important strategy to reduce conflict and increase resource protection. In recent years, many agencies and nonprofit organizations have developed educational programs that target the issues related to motorized use in an effort to increase awareness and influence individual behaviors.

In a review of five such programs, Blahna and colleagues (2005) found four themes: environmental ethics, etiquette, safety, and user images. These themes are communicated through public service announcements, logos, websites, and training presentations. Messages are also tailored for school children and adult riders. Of the various programs, Tread Lightly! has emerged as having the greatest stakeholder involvement by including motorsport manufacturers, federal agencies, and OHV clubs on a national level. Tread Lightly! is a nonprofit organization developed in collaboration with the U.S. Forest Service and Bureau of Land Management. Its educational programs are dedicated to increasing awareness of how to enjoy the outdoors while emphasizing responsible OHV use and low-impact principles (Tread Lightly!, 2005). It emphasizes

- traveling responsibly,
- respecting the rights of others,
- educating yourself,
- avoiding sensitive areas, and
- doing your part to model appropriate behaviors.

Tread Lightly! programs target all OHV pursuits and address such important issues as proper vehicle maintenance, protecting natural soundscapes, and practicing minimal-impact camping.

Tread Lightly! strongly parallels the development of Leave No Trace, the program that teaches environmental responsibility among those who use public lands in nonmotorized ways. The Leave No Trace curriculum teaches planning, proper travel, respecting wildlife, and consideration for other users. Similar to Tread Lightly!, it recognizes that improper use and behaviors create negative impacts. Thus, whether from motorized or nonmotorized recreation, impacts from recreation use are mitigated through good environmental practices. Tread Lightly! and Leave No Trace work to promote these practices and to foster responsible behavior;

however, conflicts do arise among recreation users despite these efforts. These conflicts influence perceptions and perpetuate the existing stereotypes of motorized recreation pursuits.

Overcoming User Conflicts

Conflict between recreational users can be attributed to many factors. Across public lands where competition exists for limited resources, it is easy to understand how users can disagree over what activities are the most appropriate. These disagreements have subsequently led to many of the stereotypes that different users hold of one another. They have also led recreation researchers to examine the source of these conflicts among users.

The classic definition of outdoor recreation conflict proposed by Jacob and Schreyer (1980) is, "For an individual, conflict is defined as goal interference attributed to another's behavior" (p. 369). Assuming that individuals recreate based on motivations and to achieve certain outcomes, conflict is created when the behavior of another individual prevents us from achieving our desired outcomes. For example, I could attribute the fact I did not achieve the escape and sense of solitude I hoped for on my day hike to a large group hiking on a trail, making a lot of noise, and behaving inappropriately. Another factor of conflict may be resource specificity. Resource specificity is the importance individuals attach to the use of a particular resource or place (Jacob and Schreyer, 1980). They may demonstrate a sense of possession for areas (e.g., a certain national forest or park) that play a central role in their lives. They may disagree over what the appropriate uses are for that place and believe that a competing use should not be allowed in the area. Conflict can thus arise over users' different perspectives of what a place is meant for.

Another way to consider conflict is differences in social values of individuals. Conflict in social values is described as conflict that occurs even when no direct contact exists between groups (Carothers, Vaske, and Donnelly, 2001; Vaske, Needham, and Cline, 2007). The phenomenon of "just knowing they are there" causes conflict because different groups have fundamentally different social and cultural values. For example, Vaske, Needham, and Cline (2007) found that skiers expressed conflict with snowmobilers at a Colorado location even when interpersonal contact may not have occurred. This conflict was attributed to skiers feeling that they did not share the same values as snowmobilers. Conversely, snowmobilers exhibited no social value conflicts with skiers and relatively low direct interpersonal conflicts overall. Such an occurrence—where one group has a conflict with another but not vice versa—is often described as asymmetrical conflict. It is essentially a one-way conflict in which only one group is affected. Even groups with similar values (e.g., hikers and mountain bikers) can exhibit asymmetrical interpersonal conflict in which only one of the users demonstrates an issue with the other (Carothers, Vaske, and Donnelly, 2001).

Conceptually, such conflict models make sense. When other individuals prevent us from achieving our desired experience, it is only natural to feel frustration and irritation and to form negative impressions. It is much more difficult, however, to reconcile social value conflicts. When deeply seeded cultural and social values exist, how can managers validate a certain value system? On public lands, managers are asked to balance access and enjoyment with resource protection while accommodating many diverse values. Therefore, how do we move beyond such conflict and stop reinforcing negative stereotypes? I argue that this is achieved through a better understanding and communication of visitor motivations.

Recreational groups in conflict with one another understand only their differences, not their similarities. Many do not realize that they share the same motivations, such as a desire for greater awareness and knowledge of nature. In a study of winter visitors to Yellowstone National Park, Davenport and colleagues (2002) examined differences in experience preferences. Items included viewing wildlife, enjoying natural scenery, having thrills, and being challenged. Regardless of motorized or nonmotorized activities, respondents rated enjoying nature and viewing wildlife as important or very important experiences (Davenport et al., 2002). Values that reflected skill development, challenge, or thrills were less important. To further understand these results, Davenport and Borrie (2005) conducted interviews to investigate whether snowmobiling was an appropriate use of the park. Responses revealed that snowmobilers viewed Yellowstone National Park as a place to experience natural scenery and wildlife. Responses challenged the popular image that snowmobilers in the park are focused merely on thrill seeking. Instead, their motivations and goals were more compatible with, than different from, those who used the park in nonmotorized ways.

Motivations have been examined in other locations with similar results. At Pictured Rocks National Lakeshore in Michigan, Warzecha and colleagues (2001) compared the preferences of snowmobilers, cross-country skiers, and snowshoers. Across all types of use, primary motivations were experiencing and being close to nature and enjoying the scenery. When considered with results from the study at Yellowstone National Park, snowmobiling becomes more a means to achieve desired outcomes. This form of transportation provides the means to have freedom, view wildlife, and gain a certain closeness with nature (Davenport and Borrie, 2005). Although these examples focus on specific contexts and experiences, it is conceivable that OHV use could be considered as "the delivery system" by which recreationists experience nature and achieve their desired outcomes. In this manner, these users are not all that different from the hiker, horseback rider, or paddler. All seek to achieve similar outcomes through a variety of modes of travel and experience.

Despite similar motivations between recreationists, differences in social values have led to conflict between participants in nonmotorized and motorized recreation. Within these conflicts is the argument that OHV use can be detrimental to the participant because it fosters a lack of awareness, or ignorance, regarding environmental impacts and personal behavior. Although this stereotype may seem reinforced by inappropriate individual behaviors, I argue that it does not apply when considered within the framework of adventure programming.

Potential Benefits of OHV Participation

Adventure program participants are not your average recreationists. Although the adventures they take part in emphasize experiencing nature and seeing wildlife, they target additional outcomes. They engage in facilitated experiences that are purposefully structured to empower the individual (Priest and Gass, 2005). Adventure programming is deliberately used for enhancing relationships through active experiences, structure, metaphors, and transference (Priest and Gass, 2005). It uses adventure as a way to achieve valuable educational and developmental goals (Sibthorp, 2003).

To understand the applicability and benefits of adventure programming for OHV participation, it is important to articulate its largely accepted doctrine. This can best be described in light of the Outward Bound process model developed by Walsh and Golins (1976). In their model, Walsh and Golins describe the adventure participant as a motivated learner who is placed in a prescribed social and physical environment to master a specific problem (Sibthorp, 2003). This environment is cocreated by the participants and a leader, who is an essential component of the process. The leader acts as a guide to ensure authenticity, provide feedback, and lead participant development (Sibthorp, 2003). Thus, within a supportive and empowering setting, an optimal learning environment is created that facilitates participant accomplishment (Sibthorp, 2003). It creates an opportunity for individuals to understand their own self, feel empowered, and make significant developmental gains.

Such a model articulates the transformational potential and benefits of adventure programming. It also illustrates a structure in which motorized recreation pursuits can be appropriately delivered. A programmed OHV experience can possess essentially the same elements as nonmotorized pursuits. The OHV becomes a tool to emphasize personal growth and developmental gains within the empowering environment. Thus, the experience becomes the sum of the parts rather than the motorized pursuit itself.

Participants can already realize benefits from OHV participation within the suggested transformational model in various settings and programs. For example, camps have begun offering motorized pursuits (e.g., waterskiing, ATV, off-highway motorcycles) as activities aimed at individual growth and development. These camps are founded on philosophies that encourage children to experience the beauty found in a natural setting and to have personal growth through trust, honest communication, positive leadership, and friendship (Birch Trail Camp for Girls, 2011). They encourage self-confidence, compassion, courage, and perseverance (Camp Sonshine, 2010). Also, as accredited American Camp Association organizations, they are required to meet standards in minimizing the environmental impacts of activities and in providing program activities that help develop appreciation for, awareness of, and responsibility toward the natural environment (American Camp Association, 2007). Based on strong missions and philosophies that guide their adventure programs, these organizations provide benefits from OHV recreation to their participants and empower them to achieve personal growth and development.

Conclusion

Based on legislation and policy, OHV use on public lands is an acceptable and compatible recreational pursuit. This use remains contentious due to concerns over environmental impacts, user conflict, and detrimental personal development. However, many of these concerns can be addressed and mitigated. Emissions standards and policy have called on manufacturers to develop machines that are cleaner, quieter, and eco-friendly. Manufacturers and users have invested to meet these requirements and provide the best available technology. Education programs such as Tread Lightly! promote responsible and ethical behavior of motorized-recreation users. As a dominant education program, Tread Lightly! strives to mitigate environmental impacts and increase the knowledge and awareness of motorized-recreation participants.

Through such education, we can make progress in understanding and alleviating user conflicts. Although some differences in social values may never be overcome, consensus between groups may be possible despite different points of view. Research suggests that users of motorized and nonmotorized recreation might share more motivations than previously thought. Similar to other users, OHV users strive to have freedom, enjoy nature, and enjoy the outdoors. As with all other users, these motivations come with the responsibility to pursue one's preferred activity while protecting the opportunities and enjoyment of future users.

I argue that motorized pursuits can be offered through an adventure programming framework. A model based on a motivated learner in a cocreated social environment with a directing guide has the potential to offer numerous transformational benefits to participants. In such a model, a motorized pursuit becomes more than just riding and thrills; it becomes the mode of travel and experience for individuals to connect with nature. Emphasis is then on personal growth, development, self-efficacy, and usage beyond recreation. Furthermore, such a model provides an opportunity to teach individuals how to participate in these activities in an environmentally responsible way.

Continued efforts are necessary for further implementation of motorized pursuits in adventure programming. Shared knowledge and experience need to be collected by adventure program providers and public land managers if programs are to be developed and implemented effectively. However, with a conscious effort, such programs can provide an important role in providing individual growth, responsible behavior, and environmental stewardship. It is the chance to further build a constituency and advocates for outdoor pursuits. Programs such as Outward Bound and National Outdoor Leadership

School have created many of the current leaders in outdoor recreation and environmental stewardship. Motorized-adventure programs may take the first steps in creating our future leaders.

References

American Camp Association. (2007). Standards at a glance. www. ACAcamps.org/accreditation [January 28, 2011].

Birch Trail Camp for Girls. (2011). Birch Trail Camp for Girls: About our Activities, Camp Philosophy, and Camp Setting. www.birchtrail.com/aboutus.shtml [January 28, 2011].

Bishop, G.A., Burgard, D.A., Dalton, T.R., Stedman, D.H., & Ray, J.D. (2006). Winter motor-vehicle emissions in Yellowstone National Park. *Environmental Science and Technology, 40*(8), 2505-2510.

Blahna, D.J., Reiter, D.K., Absher, J.D., & Cannon, A. (2005). *A review and analysis of five OHV communication programs.* Technical Report RWU-49.2. Riverside, CA: U.S. Department of Agriculture, Forest Service, Pacific Southwest Research Station.

Camp Sonshine. (2010). Camp Sonshine experience. www.campsonshine.org/summer-camp-sonshine-experience.html [January 28, 2011].

Carothers, P., Vaske, J.J., & Donnelly, M.P. (2001). Social values versus interpersonal conflict among hikers and mountain bikers. *Leisure Sciences, 23*, 47-61.

Cordell, H.K., Betz, C.J., Green, G., & Owens, M. (2005). *Off-highway vehicle recreation in the United States, regions and states: A national report from the National Survey on Recreation and the Environment (NSRE).* Athens, GA: U.S. Department of Agriculture Forest Service, Southern Research Station.

Davenport, M.A., & Borrie, W.T. (2005). The appropriateness of snowmobiling in national parks: An investigation of the meanings of snowmobiling experiences in Yellowstone National Park. *Environmental Management, 35*(2), 151-160.

Davenport, M.A., Borrie, W.T., Freimund, W.A., & Manning, R.E. (2002). Assessing the relationship between desired experiences and support for management actions at Yellowstone National Park using multiple methods. *Journal of Park and Recreation Administration, 20*(3), 51-64.

Environmental Protection Agency. (2007). Proposed emission standards rule, 40 C.F.R. Parts 60, 63 et al.: Control of emissions from nonroad spark-ignition engines and equipment. Washington, DC: Environmental Protection Agency.

Jacob, G.R., & Schreyer, R. (1980). Conflict in outdoor recreation: A theoretical perspective. *Journal of Leisure Research, 12*, 368-380.

Priest, S., & Gass, M.A. (2005). *Effective leadership in adventure programming.* 2nd ed. Champaign, IL: Human Kinetics.

Sibthorp, J. (2003). An empirical look at Walsh and Golins' adventure education process model: Relationships between antecedent factors, perceptions of characteristics of an adventure education experience, and changes in self-efficacy. *Journal of Leisure Research, 35*(1), 80-106.

Stokowski, P.A., & LaPointe, C.B. (2000). *Environmental and social effects of ATVs and ORVs: An annotated bibliography and research assessment.* Burlington, VT: University of Vermont, School of Nature Resources.

Sutter, P.S. (2002). *Driven wild: How the fight against automobiles launched the modern wilderness movement.* Seattle: University of Washington Press.

Tread Lightly! (2005). *The Tread Lightly! guide to responsible four-wheeling with minimum impact camping tips.* Ogden, UT: Tread Lightly!

U.S. Forest Service. (2005). Travel management rule, 36 C.F.R. § 212, subpart B: Designation of roads, trails, and areas for motor vehicle use.

U.S. Forest Service. (2008). Final travel management directives 73 fed. reg. 74,689 (proposed Dec. 9, 2008; to be codified at Forest Service manual 2350, 7700, and 7710 and Forest Service handbook 7709.55). Washington, DC: U.S. Forest Service.

Vaske, J.J., Needham, M.D., & Cline, R.C. Jr. (2007). Clarifying interpersonal and social value conflict among recreationists. *Journal of Leisure Research, 39*(1), 182-195.

Walsh, V., & Golins, G. (1976). *The exploration of the Outward Bound process.* Denver: Colorado Outward Bound School.

Warzecha, C.A., Anderson, D.H., James, E.B., & Thompson, J.L. (2001). *Visitor use and Pictured Rocks National Lakeshore: Comparison of snowmobilers and cross-country skiers or snowshoers.* St. Paul, MN: University of Minnesota Cooperative Park Studies Program.

Wilderness Act, 16 U.S.C. § 113 et seq. (1964).

Should motorized outdoor adventure pursuits be included in adventure programming?

NO Teaching Disrespect: The Ethics of Off-Road Vehicle Use on America's Public Lands

Philip Cafaro, PhD, professor of philosophy, Colorado State University, Fort Collins, Colorado, United States

Ethical issues regarding off-road vehicle use center on impacts on nature, impacts on other recreationists, and impacts on off-road vehicle (ORV) users themselves. I argue that all three of these impacts are grounds for strictly limiting ORV use on America's public lands. This conclusion deviates so widely from the status quo that it may indicate a failure in my analysis. Alternatively, it may show an ethical blindness among ORV users and a failure of stewardship by public lands managers. In this argument, the term "ORV" refers to all-terrain vehicles, motorized dirt bikes, and four-wheel-drive vehicles such as jeeps, although many of my conclusions also apply to snowmobiles and jet skis.

Impacts on Nature

Outdoor recreation provides people with a lot, including enjoyment, excitement, physical stimulation, connection to nature, aesthetic and intellectual development, and spiritual awakening. Outdoor recreation also can harm nature. Realizing this, responsible recreationists have developed ethical codes to address these harms.

Consider birdwatchers. One section of the American Birding Association's (2005) "Principles of Birding Ethics" is devoted to "promoting the welfare of birds and their environment." This section, which focuses special attention on the types of harms birding is likely to cause, includes guidelines such as the following: "To avoid stressing birds or exposing them to danger, exercise restraint and caution during observation. . . . Keep well back from nests and nesting colonies, roosts, display areas, and important feeding sites. . . . Stay on roads, trails, and paths where they exist; otherwise keep habitat disturbance to a minimum." Overall, the standard seems to be "do no harm." Many nonconsumptive activities, including wildlife photography, hiking, and rock climbing, can reach or approach this standard.

Now consider hunting. The Izaak Walton League's (2005) "Hunter's Code of Conduct" has sections titled "respect the environment and wildlife" and "support wildlife and habitat conservation." The guidelines, which again pay special, detailed attention to the potential harms of hunting, include the following: "Show respect for the wildlife you hunt by taking only clean, killing shots. . . . Take only what you will use, even if it is under the legal limit. . . . Learn to tread lightly while afield. Use vehicles only on established roads and trails, practice low-impact camping and travel. . . . Provide hands-on and financial support for conservation of game and nongame species and their habitats." Hunters certainly harm individual animals, but they may minimize this harm and treat animals respectfully. Further, ethical hunters limit their "take" of individual animals to protect healthy game populations and threatened species. Hunters, like birders, also provide money for habitat protection. Thus, they can argue that, properly managed, their activities help increase the overall health of species and ecosystems.

Looking at the full range of recreational activities practiced on public lands and the ethical codes that user groups have developed, one finds two types of standards:

- Standard 1: Recreate in such a way that you cause no harm to nature. If an activity cannot be performed in such a manner, do not engage in the activity.
- Standard 2: Recreate in such a way that you cause no significant, permanent harm to nature—or no harm at all from a wider ecological perspective. If an activity cannot be performed in such a manner, do not engage in the activity.

In either case, the motivation seems to be a basic appreciation and respect for the animals hunted or "hunted," the plants gathered, or the rivers floated upon, along with recreationists' self-interested concern of continuing to enjoy themselves. Hence a variety of restraints arise, worked out by recreationists themselves.

Rules and regulations exist because some do not accept such voluntary restraints and because more coordination is needed when recreationists become numerous. State laws limit game takes and require hunting permits, and the U.S. Forest Service implements rules about where to camp or how many horses are allowed per party. If we look at the legal framework behind these management particulars, again we see a concern to limit harms to nature.

The National Environmental Policy Act of 1969 (NEPA) governs all federal environmental activities not specifically excluded from the act, including recreation and transportation decisions on public lands. In its congressional declaration of national environmental policy, NEPA sets as a goal the "creation and maintenance of conditions under which man and nature can exist in productive harmony." It states, "The Congress recognizes that each person should enjoy a healthful environment and that each person has a responsibility to contribute to the preservation and enhancement of the environment" (West Publishing, 1997, p. 641). Here we approach Aldo Leopold's view of land and people as one community, in which we have rights but also responsibilities. The obvious standard for recreation under this sort of view is standard 1: do no harm to nature.

The National Forest Management Act (NFMA) and the Federal Land Policy and Management Act of 1976 (FLPMA) are the main laws governing the decision making of the U.S. Forest Service and Bureau of Land Management, respectively. Both are grounded in the multiple-use, sustained-yield principle, under which all activities, including all forms of recreation, must be part of a balanced use of public lands that preserves their essential natural productivity. The FLPMA defines it as follows:

> The term "multiple use" means the management of the public lands and their various resource values so that they are utilized in the combination that will best meet the present and future needs of the American people . . . a combination of balanced and diverse resource uses that takes into account the long-term needs of future generations for renewable and nonrenewable resources . . . and harmonious and coordinated management of the various resources without

permanent impairment of the productivity of the land. (West Publishing, 1997, p. 1212)

In the present context, "sustained yield" means people can use recreational resources but cannot use them up or use them in a way that degrades them or limits their uses by others, now or in the future. The natural standard for recreation under this utilitarian, managerial view is standard 2: do no significant, permanent harm to nature.

Whether looking at user groups or environmental law, we see divergence about how stringently recreationists should avoid harm. We could debate which of these standards should prevail, but at a minimum, consensus seems to exist that recreation should not cause significant, permanent harm to nature. Recreation user codes and the language of NEPA, NFMA, and FLPMA all support this unequivocally. When recreation does cause significant or permanent harm, it needs to be either reformed or eliminated. That is the minimal standard for ethical recreation on public lands.

How does current ORV use on public lands stack up against this minimal standard? It fails. ORV use causes massive soil erosion. This is partly because the areas that are most challenging and sought by ORV users, such as steep slopes, are also the most vulnerable to erosion (Havlick, 2002, p. 92; Snyder et al., 1976, pp. 78-79). A study of one long-time ORV area documented erosion rates 46 times the tolerance level suggested by the Soil Conservation Service (Wilshire et al., 1979, table 4). For many soil types, no level of ORV use is nondestructive or acceptable (Dregne, 1983, pp. 28-29; Kockelman, 1983, p. 413).

ORV use also fouls rivers, lakes, and wetlands. Many ORV use two-stroke engines, which dump 25 percent of their fuel directly into the environment. Again, user preferences for challenging terrain (desert draws, muddy forest areas, stream fords) compound the problem. The erosion caused by ORV also reduces water quality (Havlick, 2002, pp. 95-96; Kockelman, 1983, pp. 414-416).

ORV use destroys vegetation and degrades wildlife habitat. Losses of shrub biomass of 70 percent or more have been documented in heavily used desert areas, and even lesser vegetation losses destroy plants needed to feed and shelter wildlife. Animals are crushed beneath tires, displaced from burrows and tunnels, harassed by noise, and more easily shot as "varmints." Scientists have found that even moderate ORV use leads to fewer individuals and fewer species for many kinds of animals, from rodents to rabbits to reptiles to birds (Havlick, 2002, pp. 96-100; Sheridan, 1979, pp. 12-22).

ORV use increases the number of roads and motorized trails on public lands, which creates many negative ecological impacts. Roads increase erosion and air and chemical pollution. They fragment wildlife habitat, increase poaching, and help spread noxious weeds. (See Havlick, 2002, chapter 3, for a relatively recent summary of the ecological effects of roads on public lands.) ORV users are a powerful constituency for increased road-building and for keeping roads open that land managers would otherwise close for stewardship reasons. ORV users have also created tens of thousands of illegal roads and trails on public lands; one study estimated more than 60,000 miles of "unplanned or illegal roads" in national forests alone, many created by ORV users (U.S. Forest Service, 2000, pp. 1-5).

In these ways, ORV have degraded millions of acres of our public lands. The damage has not been done by a few bad apples; rather, it is the cumulative effect of the normal use of ORV (Sheridan, 1979, p. 30). Some of the worst damage occurs when ORV are driven cross-country; unfortunately, such abuse is common. According to a recent survey performed for a coalition of ORV advocacy groups, more than two-thirds of Colorado's adult ORV users ride off-trail at least occasionally, and 15 to 20 percent frequently ride off-trail illegally (Frueh, 2001, p. 11).

ORV use causes significant, permanent damage to nature. At a minimum, land managers should not allow ORV users to drive off-road on public lands, nor should users drive ORV off-road even where such use is currently allowed or encouraged. Ethical recreationists realize this, as shown in the excerpts already quoted from the codes of conduct of the American Birding Association and the Izaak Walton League. Given the scientific evidence, a person can drive ORV off-road only if he or she is willing to frankly reject the ethical standard that we should recreate only in ways that do not cause significant, permanent harm to nature.

Impacts on Other Recreationists

Recreational activities can interfere with one another and with nonrecreational uses of forests and rangelands. Hikers scare horses on narrow mountain trails, or horses muddy the trails for hikers. Boaters scare fish and anger anglers, and campers leave gates open and cattle stray. When recreationists negotiate such conflicts, common sense and courtesy can go a long way. Because

these are sometimes in short supply and because, once again, sheer numbers make a difference, land managers must manage recreational conflicts.

Multiple use, sustained yield provides one plausible framework for resolving recreational conflicts. Users are encouraged to recreate in their favored ways, provided they do not significantly harm public lands or other recreationists. When negative impacts to other recreationists occur, attempts are made to eliminate or minimize them. When significant negative impacts to others are unavoidable, segregation of users may be attempted (seasonally, as with hunting, or by zoning, as when fishermen and kayakers are given different stretches of a river). However, because public lands are for public use and people strongly resist being locked out of their favorite places, segregation is at best a last resort.

ORV bring a new dynamic to such conflicts and make management of multiple-use recreation impossible (Kockelman, 1983, pp. 409-410, 423-425; Sheridan, 1979, p. 17). The main reasons are that ORV cause excessive and asymmetrical harms to other outdoor recreationists and that they tend to assert exclusive possession where they are allowed.

The most obvious harm ORV inflict on other recreationists is their noise, which can travel for miles and which interferes with a wide variety of recreational activities. ORV have taught us that quiet is an important recreational resource (as well as a resource for other animals, whose survival and reproduction may depend on it) (Kockelman, 1983, pp. 420-421; Sheridan, 1979, p. 30). A close second in terms of negative impacts is safety, especially for parents recreating with children. ORV tearing along trails are dangerous to other users. Even when ORV are driven responsibly, encounters with them are unpleasant because they force other users off the trail and leave them gagging on exhaust fumes.

ORV transform narrow hiking trails into wide, rutted roads, which are much less enjoyable to hike on. They scare away the wildlife that other users have come to see. The experience and reality of a natural landscape, important to many outdoor recreationists, recedes (Kockelman, 1983, p. 403). One study summarizes these impacts: "Most non-motorized forms of outdoor recreation are disrupted or hurt by the operation of ORV nearby, especially for those whose recreational goals include solitude, tranquility, relaxation, observation of wildlife, and the appreciation of wild environments" (Kockelman, 1983, p. 407).

Research confirms an asymmetry in conflict between ORV users and users of nonmotorized recreation (Havlick, 2002, pp. 100-103). When a 4×4 drives by a hiker on a trail or a snowmobile passes a skier, the meeting typically poses no problem for the ORV user, but it can lessen or ruin the experience of the other. The danger and discomfort is all on one side, as is the desire for quiet, solitude, and communion with nature. Motorized encounters intrude on the essentials of the experience of those who do not use motorized vehicles, but not vice versa. Given the widely different recreational goals of the ORV user, he or she is unlikely to sympathize with or even notice these harms to these recreationists.

This means that ORV users and those who do not use motorized vehicles can't satisfactorily share trails or user areas. Beyond a certain small number of encounters, cross-country skiers will not share trails with snowmobiles and hikers will not hike in areas used by all-terrain vehicles. One researcher speaks of the ISD syndrome—"the progression from Impairment of satisfactions to Suppression of use to eventual Displacement"—as ORV literally drive their recreational competitors from the field (Badaracco, 1976, pp. 73-74). Research has confirmed the ISD syndrome in many areas; readers probably have their own examples of favorite spots that they no longer visit (Sheridan, 1979, pp. 15-17, 29-34). The public is generally hostile to ORV use precisely because these machines, although small in number, powerfully assert their owners' exclusive possession to wide swathes of the public lands. Sheridan (1979, pp. 54-55) cites several studies showing the general public's dislike of ORV. A study in California found a great majority in favor of greater protection for the desert and a majority disapproving of open areas for ORV. A U.S. Forest Service survey in Illinois and Indiana revealed that three times more people opposed motorized use of national forest trails than approved of it.

In thinking about a fair resolution to these recreational conflicts, we should keep two facts in mind. First, ORV users are a small minority of total recreationists on public lands. In Washington State, for example, "hikers outnumber motorized trail users by almost 32 to 1" (Havlick, 2002, p. 114; see also Washington State, 2001). A survey of California desert recreationists "indicated that sightseeing, camping, picnicking, fishing, photography, and hiking were the most popular recreational activities, ranging from one-third to two-thirds of the responses." Motorcycle riding ranked 13th and other ORV uses ranked "close to the bottom of the list" of recreational choices (Field Research Corporation, 1975; summarized in Kockelman, 1983, pp. 404-405).

Second, ORV use demands a disproportionate amount of land compared with other recreational uses. "Loudness and mobility magnify the presence of the individual motorcycle rider in a logarithmic way and diminish the aesthetic satisfactions of other recreationists who may be present over an extensive area" (Badaracco, 1978). A few ORV riders may hog an area where hundreds of birders, hikers, wildflower enthusiasts, wildlife photographers, and cloud watchers could happily coexist.

A small minority of users cause significant harm to the majority on public lands that are ostensibly managed for "the greatest good to the greatest number for the longest time" (Pinchot, 2000). Given these facts, the status quo, under which many national forest lands and most Bureau of Land Management (BLM) lands are open to ORV use, is obviously unfair and directly infringes on the rights of other recreationists to enjoy their public lands. It is a very inefficient use of land if we seek to maximize the recreational enjoyment of the general public.

Common courtesy and multiple use, sustained yield principles suggest two possible standards for limiting harms to others as we recreate on public lands:

- Standard 3: Recreate in such a way that you cause no harm to other people. If an activity cannot be performed in such a manner, do not engage in the activity.

- Standard 4: Recreate in such a way that you cause no significant harm to other people, nor limit the total recreational opportunities available to others. If an activity cannot be performed in such a manner, do not engage in the activity.

Most hikers, fishermen, rock climbers, and other recreationists on public lands have no trouble adhering to something pretty close to standard 3; why should ORV users be held to a lesser standard? Under standard 3, ORV would be prohibited from all trails and all off-road travel on public lands. Given the harmful impacts of ORV on other people, courteous recreationists will hold themselves to this standard right now. Many ways exist to recreate on public lands without annoying others.

Standard 4 represents the minimal standard we would expect any reasonable person to affirm. A generous interpretation of this standard might allow limited ORV use on public lands, provided that sufficient public lands remain available for the majority who do not participate in nonmotorized recreation. ORV would be strictly limited to short trails or small

ORV play areas on our public lands (e.g., five miles of trails or 100 acres of land per national forest). This approach accepts that ORV provide enjoyment to users and accommodates them through creation of sacrifice zones. It also acknowledges that these machines have a large footprint of noise and annoyance, so the amount of land directly sacrificed to ORV would be limited.

Such an application of standard 4 might seem a fair solution to these conflicts among recreational users. Given the status quo, most users of nonmotorized recreation would probably be thrilled to settle for enforcement of this compromise. However, when we consider the impacts that ORV have on nature in addition to their impact on other people, we must ask whether *any* public lands should be set aside as ORV sacrifice zones. Is it fair to the shrubs destroyed, the animals displaced, and the streams and wetlands fouled to do all this damage simply for thrills and fun? (For criticism of such anthropocentrism in ethics and a defense of nature's intrinsic value, see Rolston, 1988, and Agar, 2001.) Is it upholding the letter and spirit of our environmental laws, which speak of minimizing damage to nature and creating harmony between people and the land? Many public land managers argue that providing sacrifice zones protects other areas from ORV use, but I find little support for this practice in the environmental laws guiding public forest and rangeland management. Besides, this tactic doesn't work. ORV users take the sacrifice zones offered, create new ones, and demand more.

For these reasons, we should stick with standard 3. ORV should be prohibited from all trails and all off-road travel on our public lands. They should stay on roads, when they are used at all.

Impacts on ORV Users

We should not ignore the impacts of ORV on ORV users themselves. It is usually assumed, even by critics, that ORV use provides a net benefit to users (see, for example, Sheridan, 1979, p. 5). After all, they spend a lot of money buying and running their machines. The ORV literature and individual riders describe the thrills of breaking new ground, the camaraderie among riders, and the fascination of working on the vehicles. Most simply, ORV provide their users with lots of fun.

But from an ethical perspective, we might tread a little more carefully. There is more to life than fun. Recreational experiences change us, deepening some perspectives and closing off others (Smith, Rexford, and Long, 2001). They help make us certain kinds of people and keep us from becoming others.

Most outdoor recreational activities tend to lead to greater awareness and knowledge of nature. The birdwatcher, hunter, wilderness canoer, and mushroom picker focus on different aspects, but they all delve deeply into nature. You can't be a fly fisherman, certainly not a good one, without learning a lot about fish behavior and ecology. You can't photograph wildflowers without learning a lot about their distributions, habitat preferences, and flowering times. These and many other nonmotorized recreational activities heighten our interest in nature's details and sharpen our abilities to perceive them (Cafaro, 2001).

Motorized recreation is essentially different because experiencing nature is usually secondary (at best) to the thrills and challenges of the ride. Riders typically rush through areas and are often enclosed in a helmet or other cumbersome gear. This cuts them off from the sounds, smells, and textures of nature and renders them oblivious to all but the most obvious sights. Users often claim that ORV are necessary to get into nature, but accounts of their trips on ORV websites and in magazines rarely get past such general comments as "great views" or "saw some elk." The contrast with the detailed, affectionate descriptions of the vehicles is striking. Like other outdoor recreationists, ORV users frequently say they take part in their favored activities in order to "get away from it all," but unlike hunters, anglers, and wilderness backpackers, they don't usually "get back" to nature (Rolston, 1991, p. 393).

First, ORV use promotes ignorance of nature. Compared with those who participate in nonmotorized recreation, ORV users know a lot about carburetors and cam shafts but little about flowers, fish, or forest succession. Indeed, because greater knowledge of nature would often render ORV use morally problematic, this recreational activity comes with a built-in bias in favor of ignorance. Randy Rasmussen (personal communication, June 2005) of the Natural Trails and Water Coalition suggests that this ignorance may be primarily a precursor to ORV use on public lands rather than a consequence of that use. However, he allows that ORV use may compound or prolong such ignorance, and in any case, it does not help alleviate it.

Second, ORV use promotes environmental indifference. Historically, outdoor recreationists have been in the vanguard of the American conservation movement: hunters and birdwatchers during the Progressive Era; hikers and backpackers swelling the ranks of modern environmentalists. Nonmotorized recreation shows people beautiful places that they come to care about. It teaches lessons in appreciation and wonder that often translate into environmental activism. These activities also teach recreationists how to take their pleasure in nature responsibly, a lesson that has wide implications for other areas of life.

ORV use provides none of this. Seeing a dune or ridge as a series of technical challenges or focusing on whether one can get a rig through a muddy trail gives little sense of what animals and plants live there or their requirements for flourishing. Indifference to an area's wildlife may be a prerequisite for using ORV there. As one driver, "classjoe," replied in response to a researcher's question on an ORV listserv:

> I think this environmental stuff is blown out of proportion. Just because we see stuff that we don't like doesn't mean it's necessarily damaging to the environment. Yeah we shouldn't run over trees and stuff but is it really any worse than cutting down trees and tilling up all the weeds and grass and paving a parking lot for a college? (Off-road.com, 2005)

Given this common attitude, it is not surprising that defenders cannot provide a single instance in which ORV users discovered an area and went on to successfully protect it. In a survey of more than 92 national and statewide ORV advocacy groups, the Natural Trails and Water Coalition found only 10 groups whose websites had content that demonstrated any awareness of the environmental impact of ORV use (Randy Rasmussen, personal communication, June 2005). We will likely be waiting a long time for a John Muir or Rachel Carson to emerge from the ranks of ORV users.

Third, ORV use promotes arrogance: a pervasive lack of respect for other people and for nature. Recall how much aggravation ORV use causes other visitors to public lands—then read the ORV literature. At best, you find an occasional tepid admonition not to run people over ("share the trail"). More common are diatribes against the idiots and "eco-wackos" who complain about ORV use. (For a representative sample, visit www.off-road.com and search on "environmentalists" and "environmentalism.") A survey of several dozen ORV magazines and websites for this argument found zero acknowledgments of real harms to other recreationists. When the bar for courteous use is set so low and with so little regard for what others would

consider courteous, these results are not surprising. They merely confirm the antisocial behavior on display on America's public lands every day.

ORV use is also training in disrespect for nature. Crashing through plants, being able to go anywhere without worry about displacing animals, and saying "to hell with rules about where I can and cannot go" is part of the fun—and a big part of how these machines are marketed. When this antienvironmental training occurs on public lands, with the blessing of public officials, this teaches a powerful lesson about the respectability of disrespecting nature. (Why USFS and BLM decision-makers fail to acknowledge this is an interesting question. Perhaps they don't respect nature themselves; perhaps their management of public lands is typically so damaging that ORV use seems benign in comparison.)

In summary, ORV use leads to ignorance, indifference, and arrogance toward people and nature. If we believe we are worse people when we are ignorant, indifferent, or arrogant, then ORV use makes us worse people. Other forms of outdoor recreation are just as fun as ORV, but they teach different lessons about the value of nature and how to get along with our fellow human beings. Properly pursued, they make us better people: physically strong, mentally self-reliant, more knowledgeable about nature, and more likely to treat others with respect (Cafaro, 2001).

Of course, people are free, within legal limits, to recreate any way they want. But once we realize the opportunities and dangers that outdoor recreation poses to our personal development, we may want to set a voluntary standard for ourselves and our loved ones:

- Standard 5: Recreate in ways that make you a better person and avoid recreational activities that make you a worse one.

Following this standard would mean giving up ORV recreation and prohibiting our children from using ORV. It would also mean taking them hiking and camping, teaching them how to hunt and fish, and making more time for the many recreational activities that get us closer to nature. Following this standard would not keep people from enjoying their public lands. On the contrary, it would help many people get more enjoyment, education, and inspiration from them than they do now.

Similarly, federal law affirms ORV as a legitimate recreational activity, "where appropriate," on the public lands (West Publishing, 1997, p. 1251). But managers have broad discretion to encourage or discourage different forms of recreation. Currently,

USFS and BLM land managers encourage ORV use at the expense of nonmotorized recreation. Many national forests spend more money building and maintaining ORV trails than they do hiking trails even though hikers greatly outnumber ORV users. Many forest supervisors reward illegal ORV use by adding user-created roads to their forest transportation systems and by dropping areas from consideration for wilderness designation on the basis of ORV trespassing (Havlick, 2002, p. 116). In contrast, few national forests budget much money or personnel to encourage activities such as birdwatching or wildlife photography that recruit people into the ranks of nature lovers. Land managers who cared about nature would uphold a different standard:

- Standard 6: Encourage recreational activities that lead to love of nature and discourage recreational activities that lead to environmental indifference and harm.

Following this standard would mean setting travel management policies that discourage ORV recreation. A recent rule-making effort by USFS to prohibit most off-road ORV use is a step in the right direction. Much ORV abuse could be prevented simply by enforcing existing laws. Following standard 6 would also mean redirecting recreational dollars to those quiet uses that USFS and BLM have neglected for 100 years but that are favored by the great majority of recreationists. If we can spend tens of millions of dollars annually subsidizing ORV use, we can just as easily spend that money building hiking trails and teaching people how to identify the flowers, birds, fish, and insects living on public lands.

Conclusion

The outlines of a proper ORV ethics for our public lands are clear. Managers should restrict ORV to roads, and ORV users should stay on roads and find better ways to spend their time in nature. Anything less represents a stewardship failure by public land managers and an ethical failure by ORV users. ORV users who reject this conclusion but who still have environmental or social scruples should ask themselves where the foregoing analysis has gone astray and state what standards they would advocate for responsible public lands recreation. In the meantime, they should follow these minimal guidelines on public lands:

- Do not drive ORV off-road.
- Do not cut new roads or trails.

- Use ORV, like other vehicles, to get to nature rather than as a primary recreational activity within nature.

Likewise, federal and state land managers who believe that they are legally required to allow some ORV access but who profess a stewardship ethic should ask whether continued ORV use is compatible with the long-term protection of the lands entrusted to their care. In the meantime, they should follow these guidelines:

- Mandate and enforce the first two user guidelines. ORV users should not be allowed to drive off-road or to cut new roads or trails.
- Do not reward ORV abuse by adding illegally created roads to transportation systems or by removing areas from wilderness consideration based on illegal ORV activity.
- Do not approve permanent ORV sacrifice zones.
- Teach ORV users the real costs of their activities to nature and to other people.

Following even these minimal guidelines would mean drastic changes in how ORV are currently used and managed. But that is what is needed in order to bring ORV use within minimally acceptable standards for ethical conduct.

From P. Cafaro, 2007, Teaching disrespect: The ethics of off-road vehicle use in America's public lands. In *Thrillcraft: The environmental consequences of motorized recreation*, edited by G. Wuerthner (White River Junction, VT: Chelsea Green). Reprinted by permission of the author.

Acknowledgments

Thanks to Nathaniel Bork for the excellent background research used in this essay; to Jerry Freilich, Gary Wockner, Jeremy Bendik-Keymer, and Randy Rasmussen for comments on earlier drafts; and to Kris Cafaro for comments and editorial assistance. None of them agree with everything written here, but they all agree with the parts they think are true. Thanks as well to Bruce Martin and Mark Wagstaff for republishing this essay and to Robert Dvorak for providing an alternative perspective.

References

Agar, N. (2001). *Life's intrinsic value: Science, ethics, and nature.* New York: Columbia University Press.

American Birding Association. (2005). Principles of birding ethics. www.americanbirding.org/abaethics.htm [May 19, 2005].

Badaracco, R. (1976). ORVs: Often rough on visitors. *Parks and Recreation Magazine, 11*(9), 32-35, 68-75.

Badaracco, R. (1978). Conflicts between off-road vehicle enthusiasts and other outdoor recreationists: The ISD syndrome. In K.H. Berry (Ed.), *The physical, biological, and social impacts of off-road vehicles on the California desert.* Los Angeles: Southern California Academy of Sciences.

Cafaro, P. (2001). The naturalist's virtues. *Philosophy in the Contemporary World, 8*(2), 85-99.

Dregne, H. (1983). Soil and soil formation in arid regions. In R. Webb & H. Wilshire (Eds.), *Environmental effects of off-road vehicles: Impacts and management in arid regions* (pp. 15-30). New York: Springer-Verlag.

Field Research Corporation. (1975). Summary of the preliminary desert market analysis of the California desert. Prepared for U.S. Bureau of Land Management, San Francisco.

Frueh, L.M. (2001). Status summary and report: OHV responsible riding campaign. Prepared for the Colorado Coalition for Responsible OHV Riding, Monaghan & Associates, Denver.

Havlick, D. (2002). *No place distant: Roads and motorized recreation on America's public lands.* Washington, DC: Island Press.

Izaak Walton League. (2005). Hunter's code of conduct. www.acs.ucalgary.ca/~powlesla/personal/hunting/text/izaak.txt [May 20, 2005].

Kockelman, W. (1983). Management concepts. In R. Webb & H. Wilshire (Eds.), *Environmental effects of off-road vehicles: Impacts and management in arid regions* (pp. 399-446). New York: Springer-Verlag.

Off-road.com. (2005). Listserv. Accessed May 2005.

Pinchot, G. (2000). Principles of conservation. In P. List (Ed.), *Environmental ethics and forestry: A reader.* Philadelphia: Temple University Press.

Rolston, H., III. (1988). *Environmental ethics: Duties to and values in the natural world.* Philadelphia: Temple University Press.

Rolston, H., III. (1991). Creation and recreation: Environmental benefits and human leisure. In B.L. Driver, P. Brown, & G. Peterson (Eds.), *Benefits of leisure* (pp. 365-368). State College, PA: Venture.

Sheridan, D. (1979). *Off-road vehicles on public land.* Washington, DC: Council on Environmental Quality.

Smith, S., Rexford, K., & Long, R. (2001). Our public lands in twenty years: National parks or amusement parks? In D. Harmon (Ed.), *Crossing boundaries in park management: Proceedings of the 11th Conference on Research and Resource Management in Parks and on Public Lands* (pp. 171-175). Hancock, MI: George Wright Society.

Snyder, C.T., Frickel, D.G., Hadley, R.F., & Miller, R.F. (1976). *Effects of off-road vehicle use on the hydrology and landscape of arid environments in Central and Southern California.* Denver: U.S. Geological Survey.

U.S. Forest Service. (2000). *Forest service roadless area conservation: Final environmental impact statement.* Washington, DC: U.S. Department of Agriculture.

Washington State. (2001). Statewide recreational survey. Olympia, WA: Washington State.

West Publishing. (1997). *Selected environmental law statutes: 1997-98 educational edition.* St. Paul, MN: West Publishing.

Wilshire, H.G., Nakata, J.K., Shipley, S., & Prestegaard, K. (1979). Vehicle impacts on natural terrain at seven sites in the San Francisco Bay area. Cited in D. Sheridan. (1979). *Off-road vehicles on public land.* Washington, DC: Council on Environmental Quality.

Controversial Issue 7

Should individuals with disabilities be fully included in adventure programming?

In 1990, President George H.W. Bush signed the Americans with Disabilities Act (ADA) into law. This law was enacted to prohibit discrimination based on disability, which is defined in the legislation as "a physical or mental impairment that substantially limits a major life activity." This law was extended in 2008 through the ADA Amendments Act, which was signed into law by President George W. Bush. The law prohibits discrimination against individuals with disabilities by all public entities at the municipal, state, and federal levels. The law also stipulates that individuals with disabilities are entitled equal access to any goods, services, facilities, or other accommodations of any place of public accommodation, whether publicly or privately owned. Agencies and organizations that offer adventure programs to the general public are subject to this law, and, in fact, the industry is generally committed to accommodating individuals with disabilities. The American Canoe Association, for example, developed an adaptive paddling curriculum intended to help accommodate individuals with disabilities in paddle sports. A number of efforts have emerged within the adventure programming industry to create access and include veterans wounded in Iraq and Afghanistan. The Special Olympics continues to include adventure sports among the many competitive sports included in the games. Programs such as Wilderness Inquiry, Outward Bound, and others have made concerted efforts to serve the needs of individuals with disabilities in their programs.

Despite the good intentions behind these efforts, is it always desirable to fully include individuals with disabilities in adventure programs? What does it mean to include individuals with disabilities in adventure programming? Is it possible to provide accessibility and fully include individuals with disabilities in adventure programs without compromising the quality and safety of programming for those individuals as well as other participants?

Don Rogers argues that we are morally obligated to fully include individuals with disabilities in adventure programs. Rogers argues moreover that federal law in the United States and other countries provides clear dictates for the inclusion of individuals with disabilities in adventure programming. Finally, he argues that individuals with disabilities are as entitled as any other population to the benefits of adventure programming.

Jennifer Hinton and Danny Twilley, on the other hand, argue that although full inclusion of individuals with disabilities is desirable, valid reasons exist for excluding individuals with and without disabilities from adventure programs. These reasons center on issues of accessibility to natural landscapes, lack of leader competency in addressing the needs of individuals with disabilities, and issues around participants making informed choices in adventure programming.

This issue is important to address not only because accommodation of individuals with disabilities is required by law but also because it strikes to the heart of the humanistic principles on which our discipline is based. It speaks to a leitmotif that largely defined Kurt Hahn's life and educational philosophy: "Your disability is your opportunity" (Miner and Boldt, 2002, p. 30). Hahn was committed to helping others to overcome, as he believed, the sense of defeatism that often accompanies disability by turning the idea of disability on its head. He sought to use the notion of disability as a catalyst for empowerment in the lives of individuals. This same leitmotif is reflected in the underlying values of adventure programming today. It serves to rally our commitment to providing individuals with disabilities opportunities to grow and develop and flourish as humans despite their disabilities. Yet, is our ability to fulfill these values limited in the actual practice of adventure programming? The arguments that follow take up this question.

Reference

Miner, J.L., & Boldt, J. (2002). *Outward Bound USA: Crew not passengers.* 2nd ed. Seattle: The Mountaineers Books.

Should individuals with disabilities be fully included in adventure programming?

YES The Invitation and Obligation of Full Inclusion

Don Rogers, PhD, CTRS, associate professor of recreation therapy, Indiana State University, Terre Haute, Indiana, United States

The question of whether individuals with disabilities should be included in adventure programs could be perceived as naïve or as an intimation of prejudice against people with disabilities. Being a person with a disability (I use a wheelchair) who has worked in the adventure field as a programmer and educator for many years, I admit to mixed feelings at the suggestion that this issue has two sides. More objectively, I understand the need and value for a thoughtful exploration of the basis for inclusion. On the positive side, that this question exists in our literature and our professional dialogue may be interpreted as validation of the issue's significance to the field, and, through the exploration of "why," we strengthen the foundation for implementing inclusive adventure programming.

This argument in favor of fully including people with disabilities in adventure programs is separated into three categories: moral and ethical reasoning, legal requirements, and participant benefits. Each of these categories offers compelling support for inclusion, though in this shortened format each can be explored and developed to only a limited extent. There are numerous program and participant factors that are relevant to a discussion about inclusion in an outdoor adventure program, including the program philosophy and the extent to which this is accurately interpreted by staff, the purpose of the program, the program design and location, participant selection and grouping processes, pre-trip preparations, and staffing requirements. Additional factors include participant functioning levels and requisite skill levels for the activities at hand. These factors provide situational or subjective context for my argument. None of them present insurmountable or unreasonable barriers to inclusion. In fact, the adventure- and recreation-related literature is robust with evidence supporting inclusion, whereas the literature that encourages segregated experiences for participants with disabilities or exclusion is sparse and dated. I do not discount research that reports lack of funding, staffing issues, or inadequate transportation as constraints to inclusion. A constraint, however, does not make inclusion impossible, ill-advised, or even legal; it only presents a challenge that can usually be overcome with creativity and effort if people are committed to doing the right thing.

Inclusion is happening successfully in many recreation and outdoor programs, and full inclusion in these kinds of programs—and, by logical extension, adventure programs—is an achievable goal (Brannan et al., 2003; Devine and King, 2006). Also true is that inclusion is an important concern in the field of adventure programming. Evidence of this is found in the related professional associations, the Association for Experiential Education, the Association for Challenge Course Technology (ACCT), and the American Camp Association. Each of these organizations promotes inclusion to their members and the field through committees, research activities, advocacy, and continuing education. A study of challenge course programs in the United States, supported by ACCT, reported that respondents desired to see the profession continue and expand its support for inclusion and that they wanted to do more in their programs to provide inclusive experiences (Rogers, 2005).

Moral and Ethical Reasoning

The benefits of adventure pursuits broadly affect cognitive, psychosocial, and psychomotor areas of functioning (Ewert, 1989). In other words, participation in adventure experiences is good for people, and people tend to enjoy these programs. The drive to seek adventure is inherent in our species and is for many people quite compelling. Dufrenne (1989) speaks of "the eternal seduction of the hidden" (p. 398) as human motivation for discovery. Quinn (1990) speculates that the essence of adventure is the search for something one senses is missing from one's life. People with disabilities do not define their lives in terms of what is missing; however, they often experience chronic discrimination, exclusion, and dehumanizing stigmatization (Watermeyer, 2009), which compounds disability-specific impairments with concerns for social, emotional, and psychological well-being. Sigurd Olson, the revered North Country writer and philosopher, offers hope through what he describes as the power of outdoor experiences to connect humans with the dynamic, creative natural world. Through that experience, humans can have a similar journey within themselves—through their own internal wilderness—that offers the potential of finding personal meaning and salvation (Backes, 1997).

Exploring a less accommodating view of outdoor adventure pursuits, Ray (2009) exposes a long-standing hidden attachment within environmental thinking and risk-taking culture in the United States: the attachment to a physically fit body that encounters nature purely and unmediated and inspires tales of survival and lives well lived. Ablist thinking has constructed this ideal of outdoor experiences, similar to the way it has constructed this ideal in our architecture and in how people with disabilities are viewed in society. These idealistic conceptualizations and designs have no room for disability. The social model of disability explains this as the outcome of an interaction between actual individual impairments and the environmental and social contexts in which one pursues some activity (Bickenbach, 2001). When an activity is limited or inaccessible, then a disability is imposed upon the person. Therefore, avoiding disability is a responsibility shared by both the person with an impairment and those in position to influence that person's world.

Perhaps the ablist is also concerned about the way a person with a disability violates the purist code of an unmediated relationship with the outdoors. As Ray (2009) points outs, the unmediated encounter is mostly a myth. In fact, outdoor adventures today tend to rely heavily on equipment and technology, as seen in climbing, skiing, rafting, canoeing, and so on. How, then, is a wheelchair that is designed to operate in the outdoors more offensive than an expensive pair of hiking boots, or how is a 4:1 pulley system that helps a person with a physical disability climb too much of a compromise over a 1:1 system that others use? This artificial parameter of purity in the pursuit of outdoor adventure is a self-deluding myth that has no credibility when applied to people with disabilities who venture outdoors.

Making adventure programs available to all members of our communities is a moral and ethical obligation, or, in Kantian terminology, a duty to follow. A duty, according to Kant (as cited in de Colle and Werhane, 2007), is one's reasoning of the right thing to do given that it follows a universal moral principle and is directed to an end that respects others. Including people with disabilities in outdoor adventure programs is the right thing to do, just as including women, African Americans, gays and lesbians, and all others is the right thing to do. Rightness in this context is rooted in social-justice principles of equality and dignity. Although one may offer an emotional or rational (from their perspective) argument against acknowledging the rights of persons with disabilities based on these principles or maxims, the argument does not relinquish them of the duty to abide by the principle (Moore, 2006). Therein lies the challenge and beauty of moral decision making: doing what you know is, or is known as, right (i.e., your duty) even when you do not agree.

The moral philosophy of William James, an American philosopher whose views on education and psychology are influential, has direct bearing on inclusion in adventure programming. He believed that actively engaging others in a natural environment is the way to become fully human and that maturity arises out of difficult experiences in which one directly challenges dehumanizing aspects of the world (Page, 1987). James believed that these actions would contribute to creating a better world.

Brannan and colleagues (2003) state that regardless of the main mission of an outdoor program, it has the potential, when inclusive, to provide a model for "the expression of human rights, the respect of individual differences, and the development of attitudes and values that honor diversity" (p. 8). Through the dynamics of the inclusion efforts of a group, individuals explore and discover their capacity to view others as valued collaborators in ways that are not available in nondiverse groups. The juxtaposition of human differences becomes another dimension of risk in the adventure experience. If a participant experiences discomfort or disequilibrium while interacting with people with disabilities, they will, according to Luckner and Nadler's (1997) adventure learning process, become more open to making accommodations and assimilating new ideas that will facilitate inclusion.

The subject of human rights is at the core of this moral argument. People with disabilities have rights based on laws and their citizenship, but the universal laws of inalienable human rights are not given to them as charity or by the good deeds of others. Their rights to access and participate in activities of their choosing are "entitled to them as equal members of society" (Bickenbach, 2001, p. 566).

Embracing the natural, universal human rights of a person with a disability—rights that all people share equally—over ablism and all other arguments is probably the best hope we have for creating the kind of society that will accept without reservation the full inclusion of people with disabilities.

Legal Requirements

Soon after the Americans with Disabilities Act (ADA) was passed, Richard Thornburg, then the attorney general of the United States, said at an annual gathering of chief executive officers that the law is intended to be "broadening, inclusive, and—if you will—a reawakening" (Thornburg, 1990, p. 36). His comment meant that, upon expanding the civil rights of Americans with disabilities, their contributions "to our economy, our communities, and our individual well-being" (p. 37) would affect all Americans. He even admonishes that it would be un-American to consciously try to circumvent the protections of the ADA.

Passed in 1990, the ADA is perhaps the best-known law that requires accessibility for people with disabilities. It is a positive law that protects people with disabilities from discrimination based on their disability. Previous laws, such as the Architectural Barriers Act of 1968 or the Rehabilitation Act of 1973, applied only to federally funded entities. The ADA extended the protection of equal rights for people with disabilities into the private sector and covers employment, transportation, facilities, programs, and services. An outgrowth of earlier legislation and persistent advocacy, the ADA provided a blueprint for including people with disabilities in the mainstream of American society. Accompanying the ADA is the ADA Accessibility Guidelines, which provide easy-to-follow applications for creating accessibility in the built environment, such as ramps and restrooms.

Since the ADA was passed, substantial work has been done to expand the scope of coverage to include outdoor recreation areas such as boating facilities, fishing areas, and trails. President Barack Obama announced in July of 2010 that new ADA regulations, including many of the recently developed recreation guidelines, will be enforceable as of March 15, 2012. In order to return the ADA to its original intent, the ADA Amendments Act was passed in 2008 and became effective in January of 2009. After years of case law that narrowed the interpretation of disability and blunted the spirit of the ADA, the ADA Amendments Act broadened the scope of who is protected under the law (U.S.

Department of Justice, n.d.). These developments will, in the near future, bring more attention to service provision for and inclusion of people with disabilities in outdoor recreation and adventure areas. Deferring responsibility for including participants with disabilities to those "other programs" that are somehow better equipped is not a defendable or prudent strategy. Outdoor recreation programs are now fully on the ADA radar and should anticipate a greater degree of scrutiny and accountability.

Perhaps some are still skeptical or unsure whether adventure programs are required to comply with the ADA and other accessibility legislation. In short, yes, they are. Even when no guidelines exist for a specific area of programming or activity, such as challenge courses or river rafting programs, it is still a covered entity. Where no ADA guidelines exist, the Department of Justice encourages entities to follow best practices in their field with regard to accessibility. The ADA allows exemption from compliance only if

- making a reasonable accommodation would cause an undue hardship,
- making an accommodation would alter the fundamental nature of the service, or
- barrier removal would not be readily achievable (i.e., removing the barrier would be difficult or expensive) (U.S. Department of Justice, n.d.).

These allowances would likely seldom apply given the ability to adapt multiple factors of an adventure program to the needs of the group or individuals. This is particularly true given the availability of best practices for accommodating participants with disabilities alongside their nondisabled coparticipants in activities such as rock climbing, river rafting, sailing, scuba diving, skydiving, alpine and Nordic skiing, challenge courses (Rohnke et al., 2007), and recreation in general (Miller, Schleien, and Lausier, 2009; Schleien, Germ, and McAvoy, 1996). It is important to note that access to an activity is only part of the inclusion equation. Best practices have also been determined for designing inclusive outdoor program experiences for youths with and without disabilities (Brannan et al., 2003).

Consistent with the idea of reasonable accommodation, the ADA allows providers to offer alternative programs and services when they cannot provide current offerings through readily achievable means (e.g., an inaccessible pharmacy may provide home delivery or a restaurant may provide accessible seating and full service in an area away from an otherwise inaccessible main dining area). These alternative programs and services work in cases such as these, but how would they work for a canoeing, hiking, or climbing program? Perhaps different programs can be offered at different sites and use adapted equipment based on the needs of the group. This would be okay as long as it did not segregate participants with disabilities into disabled-only or disabled-specific programs. The ADA expressly forbids segregation of people with disabilities for the sake of addressing accessibility (U.S. Department of Justice, n.d.). In fact, integrating people with disabilities throughout the community is the expressed purpose of the ADA. As President George H.W. Bush remarked after signing the law, "Let the shameful wall of exclusion finally come tumbling down" (Thornburg, 2010).

For programs in the public sector, like schools, universities, and parks and recreation, the mandate for inclusion is clearer. In addition to the integration requirements of section 504 of the Rehabilitation Act of 1974, Title II of the ADA, which also covers public entities, contains language commonly known as the integration mandate (U.S. Department of Justice, 2011). The language in this mandate is taken from the Rehabilitation Act and specifically requires public entities to "administer services, programs and activities in the most integrated setting appropriate to the needs of qualified individuals with disabilities" (U.S. Department of Justice, n.d.). In this language, the most integrated setting means "a setting that enables individuals with disabilities to interact with non-disabled persons to the fullest extent possible" (U.S. Department of Justice, 2011). This mandate has withstood numerous legal challenges, including the 1999 U.S. Supreme Court decision in Olmstead v. L.C., making it clearly the law of the land. I would also say it expresses a core value of the spirit and intent of the ADA.

It would certainly be out of the question to separate a person with a disability who had signed up for an experience from his or her group or to put that person in a compromised situation because of some unfounded fear for their safety or the safety of others. The currently enforceable and 2010 (addition shown in italics) ADA is clear on this matter:

> In determining whether an individual poses a direct threat to the health or safety of others, a public accommodation (agency or business) must make an individualized assessment, based on reasonable judgment that relies on current medical knowledge or on the best available objective evidence, to

ascertain: the nature, duration, and severity of the risk; the probability that the potential injury will actually occur; and whether reasonable modifications of policies, practices, or procedures *or the provision of auxiliary aids or services* will mitigate the risk. (section 36.208)

Poorly conceived separate experiences would also eliminate a very effective approach to inclusion that was developed by Wilderness Inquiry, a Minnesota-based program that has been running inclusive outdoor adventure programs around the world since 1978. The Wilderness Inquiry approach emphasizes matching participant strengths to create strong duos, teams, or functional units in order for participants to succeed together in an adventure program (Schleien et al., 1993). For example, a person without a disability might help a partner with a physical disability negotiate a very difficult trail, and in turn the latter cooks dinner, fills a Duluth pack, or uses a strong upper body to help power a canoe during a storm. Opting for an alternative experience approach would undermine this very successful model.

An agency has three options: not comply (do nothing), comply according to standards (the minimum), or go beyond the minimum in an effort to include people with disabilities to the greatest degree possible. Not complying is a violation that can result in legal proceedings, particularly if someone (with or without a disability) files a complaint. In fact, an agency is clearly discriminatory if it cannot demonstrate good-faith efforts, not just intentions, to make their facilities, programs, and services accessible (Milani, 1996). Conversely, efforts to exceed the minimum standards are more aligned with the spirit of the ADA and the spirit of full inclusion (Dattilo, 2002; Hughes, 1995; Kockelman, Zhao, and Blanchard-Zimmerman, 2001; Roberts, 2005; Weinum and Mitchell, 1997).

Participant Benefits

Before examining benefits, it is helpful to dispel a couple myths. First is the myth that people with disabilities are not interested in outdoor experiences similar to those pursued by their nondisabled peers. McAvoy (2001) reports that multiple studies indicate that the outdoor and adventure preferences of people with disabilities essentially mirror those of people without disabilities. Second is the myth that people with disabilities do not venture into the outdoors very often. McCormick (2001) analyzed data from the National Survey of Recreation and the Environment, conducted in 1995, on the behavior of more than 17,000 Americans. A total of 1,252 people with disabilities responded to the survey. McCormick found that their participation in outdoor recreation and adventure activities was similar to, and in some cases greater than, that of other respondents. From these findings we can conclude that the assumptions that disability diminishes one's preferences for or are a barrier to participation in outdoor adventure are false.

Research has established that inclusive recreation experiences positively affect all members of the group. Inclusive recreation experiences help participants with disabilities develop friendships (Dattilo, 2002; Schleien et al., 1990) and learn age-appropriate life, leisure, and social skills (Green and DeCoux, 1994; McAvoy, 2001; Miller, Schleien, and Bowens, 2010). When disabled participants experience social acceptance by nondisabled peers, they report more frequent participation in recreation and higher levels of life satisfaction (Devine and Dattilo, 2001; Devine and Lashua, 2002). Dattilo (2002) puts it nicely: "People learn that they are somebody by experiencing positive interactions with others that nurture and support their sense of inherent value as a human being and their sense of self-determination" (p. 194).

For participants without disabilities, inclusive experiences benefit relationships by improving the comfort and confidence that participants without disabilities feel when interacting with their peers with disabilities (Slininger, Sherrill, and Jankowski, 2000; Wilhite, Devine, and Goldenburg, 1999). Interactions between participants with and without disabilities that are cooperative, reciprocal, and of equal status are most likely to produce positive inclusion outcomes (Wilhite, Devine, and Goldenburg, 1999). Participants have reported being more trusting of others who are different and having a better understanding of people with disabilities as a result of their inclusive adventure experience (Holman and McAvoy, 2005). These consequences of interactions align well with the relationships, processes, and outcomes encouraged in adventure programs. Related findings indicate that during inclusive camp programs, youths with and without disabilities worked together to solve problems and developed "appreciation for each others' similarities and differences" (Devine and King, 2006, p. 23). Clearly, ample evidence supports inclusion from a benefits perspective.

Given that approximately 20 percent of people in the United States have a disability (which can be apparent or not apparent), it is hard to imagine that anyone is going to work, school, or recreate without encountering or interacting with people with disabilities. Inclusion in schools is becoming more widespread, and students with disabilities have higher expectations for inclusion in all aspects of their lives. In school they develop social and activity skills in the context of an integrated peer group. In this generation and in upcoming generations, having people with disabilities in the mix will be much more common and acceptable and less anxiety will exist around inclusion. These are the coming generations of adventure program participants.

In diverse groups, labels and stereotypes are broken down and everyone has a new context for knowing and understanding each other (Devine, 2004; Devine and Wilhite, 2000; Sugerman, 1996). During an inclusive activity in which there are preexisting concerns about including or interacting with people with disabilities, there is also new awareness about the actual implications of those concerns, which should make them less threatening and less of an obstacle to inclusion. Learning that a person's interests are similar to yours or that they have strengths that you admire and observing them contributing to the experience in meaningful ways are personal and interpersonal features of an inclusive experience. It would seem likely under these circumstances that such positive effects would diminish the significance of any disability-specific negative aspects. Contact theory supports the potential for activity-based experiences to improve perceptions of others who are different from one's self (Seaman et al., 2009; Wright and Tolan, 2009).

Conclusion

For those still wondering about what is reasonable, consider Mark Wellman, a paraplegic who has climbed El Capitan and Half Dome, or Eric Weihenmayer, a blind mountaineer who has summited Mt. Everest. Where do you think they and others like them draw the line at what is and is not reasonable? Yes, their accomplishments are extraordinary and appear to be an unfair comparison to more typical adventure activities, but they are more alike than different when you gauge the courage and effort it takes for people with severe or multiple disabilities and sedentary lifestyles to take on a whitewater rafting trip or a backcountry expedition. For them, an extraordinary experience is made possible through reasonable means.

A number of programs in addition to Wilderness Inquiry currently offer inclusive wilderness courses. Among these is Outward Bound (OB), a venerable adventure program provider. OB course MD7-1981, Voyager OB, was one of my first programmed adventure experiences designed to be inclusive. It was a tremendous growth experience for me, largely because of the diversity of the group. I saw firsthand how a program can achieve inclusion while remaining true to its philosophy and methods. OB currently provides similar experiences to wounded U.S. veterans. Other programs include the Idaho State University Cooperative Wilderness Handicapped Outdoor Group; SPLORE in Salt Lake City, Utah; and the Bay Area Outreach and Recreation Program in San Francisco, California. These are only a few of the many programs that offer outdoor adventure programming for people with disabilities, and most provide inclusive options. Although these programs emphasize the needs of participants with disabilities, their success with inclusive programming can effectively inform traditional outdoor adventure programs of why and how to implement inclusion.

A succinct summary of these points boils down to the following:

- It is universally the right thing to do.
- It is legally required.
- The benefits are undeniable and significantly compelling and outweigh real or perceived constraints.

Therefore, the answer to the question of whether to provide full inclusivity in adventure programs is an unequivocal yes. This means that any adventure program can provide inclusive experiences based on the essential nature of the program and how it matches up with the needs and abilities of individual participants. This also assumes that no one will be excluded until an individual assessment has been done, the provider of the program has communicated with the individual with a disability, and all reasonable accommodations have been explored.

Richard Thornburg (2010) was invited to speak again about the ADA on the occasion of its 20th anniversary. He shared his observations of the progress toward including citizens with disabilities in our society. Accessibility to public buildings and aspects of community life had greatly improved; however, he expressed disappointments:

> Too many Americans still fail to appreciate the essence of the discrimination that people with disabilities face in their daily lives. Many Americans still don't see barriers to full inclusion, whether based on architecture or attitudes. Many Americans still remain trapped by society's stereotypes about disability. Many Americans still think the barriers faced by people with disabilities stem primarily from their disabilities—not from what we as a society have erected.

I believe that his observations are generally accurate. Despite how morally reprehensible or legally prohibited discrimination is, the disability community still bears an undue discrimination that is one part architectural and two parts attitudinal. At the same time, important advances have improved quality of life for many people with disabilities in a relatively short amount of time.

So where do we go from here? Inclusion still offers a new frontier for our field if we choose to see it that way, but we need to decide soon. The sun is setting on the inclusion question and rising on the actions we need to take in order to make it happen. I say judge a person not by the choices they make when given options; judge them instead by the attitude they take when given only one option.

References

Backes, D. (1997). *A wilderness within: The life of Sigurd F. Olson.* Minneapolis: University of Minnesota Press.

Bickenbach, J. (2001). Disability human rights, law and policy. In G. Albrecht, K. Seelman, & M. Bury (Eds.), *Handbook of disability studies* (pp. 565-584). Thousand Oaks, CA: Sage Publications.

Brannan, S., Fullerton, A., Arick, J., Robb, G., & Bender, M. (2003). *Including youth with disabilities in outdoor programs: Best practices, outcomes and resources.* Champaign, IL: Sagamore.

Dattilo, J. (2002). *Inclusive leisure services: Responding to the rights of people with disabilities.* 2nd ed. State College, PA: Venture.

de Colle, S., & Werhane, P. (2007). Moral motivation across ethical theories: What can we learn for designing corporate ethics programs? *Journal of Business Ethics, 81,* 751-764.

Devine, M.A. (2004). Being a doer instead of a viewer: The role of inclusive leisure contexts in determining social acceptance for people with disabilities. *Journal of Leisure Research, 36*(2), 137-160.

Devine, M.A., & Dattilo, J. (2001). Social acceptance and leisure lifestyles of people with disabilities. *Therapeutic Recreation Journal, 34,* 306-322.

Devine, M.A., & King, B. (2006). Research update: The inclusion landscape. *Parks and Recreation, 41,* 22-25.

Devine, M.A., & Lashua, B. (2002). Constructing social acceptance in inclusive leisure contexts: The role of individuals with disabilities. *Therapeutic Recreation Journal, 36*(1), 65-83.

Devine, M.A., & Wilhite, B. (2000). The meaning of disability: Implications for inclusive services for youth with and without disabilities. *Journal of Park and Recreation Administration, 18*(3), 35-52.

Dufrenne, M. (1989). *The phenomenology of aesthetic experience*. Evanston, IL: Northwestern University Press.

Ewert, A. (1989). *Outdoor adventure pursuits: Foundations, models, and theories*. Scottsdale, AZ: Publishing Horizons.

Green, F., & DeCoux, V. (1994). A procedure for evaluating the effectiveness of a community recreation integration program. *Therapeutic Recreation Journal, 28*, 41-47.

Holman, T., & McAvoy, L. (2005). Transferring benefits of participation in an integrated wilderness adventure program to daily life. *Journal of Experiential Education, 27*(3), 322-325.

Hughes, A. (1995). Interpreting in the spirit of ADA. *Legacy, 6*(3), 6-7.

Kockelman, K., Zhao, Y., & Blanchard-Zimmerman, C. (2001). Meeting the intent of ADA in sidewalk cross-slope design. *Journal of Rehabilitation Research and Development, 38*(1), 101-110.

Luckner, J., & Nadler, R. (1997). *Processing the experience*. Dubuque, IA: Kendall/Hunt.

McAvoy, L. (2001). Outdoors for everyone: Opportunities that include people with disabilities. *Parks and Recreation*, August, 24-29.

McCormick, B. (2001). People with disabilities: National survey of recreation and the environment. Bloomington, IN: National Center on Accessibility, Indiana University. www.indiana.edu/~nca/rec-leisure/nsre.shtml [January 12, 2012].

Milani, A. (1996). Disabled students in higher education: Administrative and judicial enforcement of disability law. *Journal of College and University Law, 22*, 989-1043.

Miller, K., Schleien, S., & Bowens, F. (2010). Support staff as an essential component of inclusive recreation services. *Therapeutic Recreation Journal, 44*(1), 35-49.

Miller, K., Schleien, S., & Lausier, J. (2009). Search for best practices in inclusive recreation: Programmatic findings. *Therapeutic Recreation Journal, 43*(1), 27-41.

Moore, A. (2006). Maxims and thick ethical concepts. *The Author Journal, 19*, 129-147.

Page, H. (1987). William James: An ethical philosopher for experiential education. *Journal of Experiential Education, 10*(1), 34-37.

Quinn, B. (1990). The essence of adventure. In J. Miles & S. Priest (Eds.), *Adventure education* (pp. 145-148). State College, PA: Venture.

Ray, S.J. (2009). Risking bodies in the wild: The "corporeal unconscious" of American adventure culture. *Journal of Sport and Social Issues, 33*(3), 257-284.

Roberts, R. (2005). Boundaries need not apply: Playgrounds are exceeding the Americans with Disabilities Act's guidelines on accessibility. *Parks and Recreation, 40*(8), 49-52.

Rogers, D. (2005). Challenge course operations for including people with disabilities. Bloomington, IN: National Center on Accessibility, Indiana University-Bloomington. www.ncaonline.org/index.php?q=node/735 [January 12, 2012].

Rohnke, K., Rogers, D., Wall, J., & Tait, C. (2007). *Complete ropes course manual*. 4th ed. Dubuque, IA: Kendall/Hunt.

Schleien, S., Fahnestock, M., Green, R., & Rynders, J. (1990). Building positive social networks through environmental interventions in integrated recreation programs. *Therapeutic Recreation Journal, 24*(4), 42-52.

Schleien, S., Germ, P., & McAvoy, L. (1996). Inclusive community leisure services: Recommended professional practices and barriers encountered. *Therapeutic Recreation Journal, 30*(4), 260-273.

Schleien, S., McAvoy, L., Lais, G., & Rynders, J. (1993). *Integrated outdoor education and adventure programs*. Champaign, IL: Sagamore.

Seaman, J., Beightol, J., Shirilla, P., & Crawford, B. (2009). Contact theory as a framework for experiential activities as diversity education: An exploratory study. *Journal of Experiential Education, 32*(3), 207-225.

Slininger, D., Sherrill, C., & Jankowski, C. (2000). Children's attitudes toward peers with severe disabilities: Revisiting contact theory. *Adapted Physical Activity Quarterly, 17*, 176-196.

Sugerman, D. (1996). Diversity: Including people with disabilities in outdoor adventure programs. *Parks and Recreation, 31*(8), 44-47.

Thornburg, R. (1990). The Americans with Disabilities Act: What it means to all Americans. *The Journal of Intergroup Relations, 17*(4), 35-41.

Thornburg, R. (2010). Testimony on the occasion of the 20th anniversary of the signing of the Americans with Disabilities Act. http://judiciary.house.gov/hearings/pdf/Thornburgh100722.pdf [January 12, 2012].

U.S. Department of Justice. (n.d.) ADA homepage: Information and technical assistance on the Americans with Disabilities Act. www.ada.gov [January 12, 2012].

U.S. Department of Justice. (2011). Statement of the Department of Justice on enforcement of the integration mandate of Title II of the Americans with Disabilities Act and Olmstead v. L.C. www.ada.gov/olmstead/q&a_olmstead.htm [January 20, 2012].

Watermeyer, B. (2009). Claiming loss in disability. *Disability and Society, 24*(1), 91-102.

Weinum, T., & Mitchell, M. (1997). Inclusion: Are you ready, willing and able? *Recreation Access in the 90s, 5*(1), 7-8.

Wilhite, B., Devine, M.A., & Goldenburg, L. (1999). Self-perceptions of youth with and without disabilities: Implications for leisure programs and services. *Therapeutic Recreation Journal, 31*, 15-28.

Wright, A., & Tolan, J. (2009). Shared adventure: A qualitative outcome assessment of a multicultural education class. *Journal of Experiential Education, 32*(2), 137-154.

Should individuals with disabilities be fully included in adventure programming?

NO Unquestioned Inclusion: Risks Worth Discussing

Jennifer Hinton, PhD, CTRS, associate professor of recreational therapy, Western Carolina University, Cullowhee, North Carolina, United States

Danny Twilley, MS, lecturer in recreation and sport pedagogy, Ohio University, Athens, Ohio, United States

Choosing to structure a position that focuses on exclusion of any person may seem like a reckless or thoughtless endeavor. Indeed, when we began to construct this argument, a colleague noted that finding reputable resources that cite reasons to not include people with disabilities was like finding articles that state why it is good to be obese. Whereas articles, anecdotes, and textbooks discuss the virtues and details of inclusive programs, virtually none discuss valid reasons for exclusion. We believe that inclusion of persons with and without disabilities is desirable in most instances in adventure programming. However, it is important to push aside the risk of social faux pas and discuss what many believe is the taboo possibility of exclusion.

The benefits of adventure programming for individuals are well known and include improved self-esteem and growth, increased social awareness, improved cooperation skills, increased leisure skills, and greater trust in others (Smith et al., 2005). These benefits come with a certain amount of risk, often through a mix of environmental conditions, leadership competency, and participant readiness (Martin et al., 2006; Paisley, Sibthorp, and Szolosi, 2003; Priest and Gass, 2005). When discussing environmental conditions, we focus on ways that access is created for natural environments and preferences for creating that access. We discuss training for leaders in the adventure field in relation to working with people with disabilities and address specific risks that may occur when information is not clearly conveyed between the adventure provider and participant. Each of these areas may be viewed differently depending on the lens through which it is examined.

Providing Access to Natural Environments

The seminal civil rights laws for people with disabilities—public law (PL) 93-112: The Rehabilitation Act of 1973 and PL 94-142: The Education for All Handicapped Children Act of 1975—were groundbreaking pieces of legislation. For the first time in American history, public schools and facilities that received federal funding could not deny services to persons with disabilities (Bullock, Mahon, and Killingsworth, 2010). These laws referred mostly to programming, but they also addressed the removal of physical barriers and enhancements to improve physical access to facilities. Of course, the Americans with Disabilities Act (PL 101-336), first passed in 1990, has been monumental in changing independent living and inclusion for people with disabilities. It is unprecedented in its scope and level of protections provided to individuals with disabilities. It is also unprecedented in its efforts to truly include people of all abilities in the culture of the United States (Bullock, Mahon, and Killingsworth, 2010). Regardless of these unparalleled and broad-sweeping attempts at inclusion of individuals with disabilities in American society, the laws have limits.

Extensive discussion has taken place regarding how much access can—and should—be created in natural settings for people with disabilities. However, except for specific guidelines for built improvements such as sidewalks, entryways, and the like, nothing in the past disability laws mandates access to outdoor settings for individuals with disabilities. Federal guidelines were proposed in 2007, but, to date, these guidelines have not been adopted. Called "The Draft Final Accessibility Guidelines for Outdoor Developed Areas" (United States Access Board, 2009), the guidelines would apply to all federal agencies managing parks and protected areas in the United States and would regulate camping and picnic facilities, viewing areas, outdoor recreation access routes, trails and trailheads, and beach access routes. In more developed areas, little contention exists concerning these guidelines because the creation of accessible features in these areas would not likely offend one's sensibilities. In more pristine areas, however, greater contention exists.

The reader is encouraged to review "The Draft Final Accessibility Guidelines for Outdoor Developed Areas" (United States Access Board, 2009) and to ponder whether the level of development proposed in these guidelines is prudent for all federally managed parks and protected areas. For example, are the guidelines compatible with the mission of the National Park Service, which is to "preserve *unimpaired* (emphasis added) the natural and cultural resources and values of the national park system for the enjoyment, education, and inspiration of this and future generations" (National Park Service, n.d., paragraph 2)? Although access to the outdoors may be important for everyone, at what cost do we provide access? Waterman and Waterman (1993) attempt to address this issue in *Wilderness Ethics: Preserving the Spirit of Wildness*. The authors ask, should we pave every trail and overlook to provide access for all citizens? How far should we go to provide access but not infringe on the rights of others to enjoy the outdoors in the most natural form possible?

Notably, the proposed accessibility guidelines list four major conditions in which creating access for people with disabilities is not desirable:

1. terrain;
2. prevailing construction practices;
3. fundamental alteration of the function or purpose of the facility or setting; and
4. legislation for wilderness, historic, and environmental protection.

For example, under condition 2, prevailing construction practices, if heavy equipment is prohibited in a wilderness area, then it may not be used to create access even if it would be needed. The access guidelines do not take precedence over the others, and the prevailing construction practice is followed. Similarly, under condition 4, as one of the acts listed in the condition, the National Historic Preservation Act would have primacy. Exceptions are, however, limited to only the segment of the outdoor area that is covered by the condition. All parts of an area that can remain accessible should, even if a substantial barrier exists in another part of the area affected by one of the four conditions. To continue with the National Historic Preservation Act example, another part of the same area may be made completely accessible if a new viewing area is added to a historic site.

User Preferences

Disability is not a collective phenomenon but rather is unique to an individual. Most research shows that people with and without disabilities have similar recreation preferences. Moore, Dattilo, and Devine (1996), for example, assessed the preferences of 1,705 users on trails in 3 states on 27 attributes. Of the 1,608 persons who answered the question regarding disability (which simply asked them to self-report whether they had a disability), approximately 6.7 percent reported having a disability. The authors found that no significant differences in preference existed on 20 of the 27 attributes studied, although users with disabilities tended to prefer historical features and amenities such as food and toilet facilities. This may be connected with the fact that the persons with disabilities in the study were also older; further research is warranted.

Although individual viewpoints vary, evidence exists that some people with disabilities are opposed to "paving the wilderness." For example, in interviews with six individuals with disabilities who attempted through hikes of the Appalachian Trail (AT), Nisbett and Hinton (2005) found that none of these informants believed that the AT should be anything other than the arduous challenge that it currently is. Although these individuals had varying disabilities, some of which were severe enough to prevent them from successfully completing the through hike, none believed that the AT should be changed. One hiker stated, "I mean, there are ways to make trails better for wheelchairs and stuff like that, but I don't think it should be the AT necessarily. I think you can do that other places. The Appalachian Trail is really kind of a special place, and there probably are places where it is really accessible" (Nisbett and Hinton, 2005, p. 232). Another added, "It probably shouldn't be easier. The reason that you are out there is to experience what God is going to throw your way. If you go out with impairments that you already have, then you should know how to cope with those. If you don't know how to do that, then you shouldn't be out there" (Nisbett and Hinton, 2005, p. 233).

The U.S. Forest Service seems to understand this sentiment, as indicated in the following statement (U.S. Forest Service, 2006):

> People using primitive trails, for example, experience the outdoor environment in a nearly natural state, with limited or no development. In these settings, people generally desire challenge

and risk so they can use their outdoor and survival skills. Use of manufactured building materials or engineered construction techniques to comply with accessibility requirements could destroy the natural or undeveloped nature of the setting and change the visitor's experience. (section 2)

In *Inclusive and Special Recreation: Opportunities for Persons With Disabilities,* Smith and colleagues (2005) state that providing access for people with disabilities to outdoor adventure programs is a challenge. However, they reiterate that people with disabilities desire the same natural settings as people without disabilities. "The truth is that people with disabilities do not want these extreme approaches to access any more than many people without disabilities. . . . Improving access while preserving nature is a challenge, but providing people with disabilities with as much information as possible about the level of accessibility of an area can promote inclusion" (Smith et al., 2005, p. 193). They then say that this information can help people with disabilities prepare and make appropriate choices based on available resources.

Leader (In)Competency

Another practical challenge to fully including individuals with disabilities in adventure programs is the lack of adequate education and training of outdoor leaders in addressing the needs of these individuals. When discussing ways that professionals work with people with disabilities, Palley (2009) argues that determining the levels of education services (according to the Individuals with Disabilities Education Act [IDEA] laws in 2004) and medical services (according to the Americans with Disabilities Act [ADA] laws in 1992) in the least restrictive environment or most inclusive setting requires professional assessment. Although both the ADA and IDEA require that people with disabilities be included in essentially all areas of American life, ultimately, Congress and appellate courts "rely on the judgment of professionals to determine what might be appropriate for individuals" (Palley, 2009, p. 48). Educators, medical practitioners, and social workers—all of whom receive education in working with people with a variety of disabling conditions—may be called on to make decisions regarding inclusion needs and adaptations within a medical or education setting. Who, then, is called on to make this determination in a recreational setting? If recreation professionals

are to make these types of decisions, this should be a serious concern to recreation practitioners, educators, and students. Palley (2009) states that "the professional judgment of professionals . . . can have a large impact on the rights available to people with disabilities" (p. 49). The majority of recreation professionals, especially outdoor leaders, continue to have little to no training in working with people with disabilities.

The professional and educational backgrounds of professionals in the field of adventure programming vary widely. A common route into the field is a four-year baccalaureate degree program devoted specifically to preparing professionals for the field; however, little evidence exists of consistency among these programs. These programs are housed within a variety of departments (e.g., kinesiology; recreation, parks, and tourism; environmental education; and so on). The character of a department often tends to shape the character of a program and, consequently, the nature of student experiences in the programs. To complicate matters, many professionals enter the field of adventure programming without formal academic training in outdoor leadership. Untold numbers of professionals working in the field today have baccalaureate and other degrees in history, English, philosophy, art, and a wide range of other disciplines. Indeed, numerous practitioners have only associate degrees from two-year colleges offering professional preparation that leads to employment in the field. These programs are as varied as the four-year programs mentioned previously.

The accreditation standards of two organizations that accredit programs that train outdoor leaders, the Wilderness Education Association and the Association for Experiential Education, do not mention standards or competencies for working with individuals with disabilities. The Council on Accreditation, which operates through the National Recreation and Park Association, is the only accrediting body for academic programs involved in preparing professional outdoor leaders that has a standard that alludes to working with individuals with disabilities:

8.10 Understanding of the importance of leisure service delivery systems for diverse populations.

Content to consider: The impact of leisure service delivery systems on a wide diversity of populations (i.e., mental, physical, aged, youth, multicultural etc.). (Council on Accreditation, 2004, p. 11)

To fulfill this standard, many accredited programs include a course that specifically addresses recreation for people with disabilities. Many programs, however, opt for courses that are broader in scope and cover diverse populations through the lens of race, culture, and subcultural issues. In courses with this broader focus, instructors and students would consider disability as one important issue on which to focus, but the broad scope of such a course would give the issue of disability only cursory attention. Consequently, future practitioners receive too little information about the broad array and complexity of disabilities that they might encounter to make an informed decision regarding inclusion of any individual in a particular activity.

It is clear that the typical outdoor leader, due to a lack of adequate professional preparation, is not qualified to make decisions regarding the needs and rights of people with disabilities. Service providers must be capable of determining who needs accommodations and what accommodations are needed. Palley (2009) argues that service providers "must also assess what is 'reasonable' to alter and what is 'a fundamental alteration'" (p. 47). With the current training available, future recreation professionals may have cursory knowledge of ADA law but not enough knowledge about how the law may be applied to each person with a disability in the vast array of settings in which they will be asked to deliver services. This leaves little doubt that these professionals are not receiving enough education to determine what might be appropriate for individuals in the eyes of Congress and the appellate court.

Participants

We have established that even well-trained outdoor leaders have dubious knowledge and experience regarding working with people with disabilities and making judgments regarding inclusion. We have also discussed the lack of available accessible environments and the dilemma in changing nature to the point that it removes the authentic nature experience. The remaining part of the equation is the person with the disability.

Informed Choice

One of the traditional tenets of the field of adventure programming is that each participant should have the right to exercise challenge-by-choice when determining the level of his or her participation in an adventure program. Smith and colleagues (2005) suggest that providing persons with as much information as possible regarding the nature of the

challenges in a given situation allows persons with disabilities to make decisions about their ability to negotiate the barriers in that situation. Indeed, education about the risks themselves can help all participants negotiate the inherent risk in activities. However, this makes certain assumptions about participants regarding their understanding not only of the nature of the risk but also of themselves and their ability to make sound judgments.

In the case of adventure programming, how do we determine when a person is incapable of exercising the level of judgment required to make informed choices about their involvement in a program? Carlson and Evans (2001) further discuss this point in an article reflecting on the challenge-by-choice philosophy. In itself, challenge-by-choice poses a dilemma for persons with disabilities, whose choices are sometimes limited by personal barriers. Environmental and attitudinal barriers may be removed through universal design or effective facilitation; however, some disability traits may inherently limit choice despite our best efforts. Some of these traits may not allow some consumers, especially those with intellectual impairments, to fully understand all facets of the challenge. Thus, the participant would be unable to make an informed decision. How can a facilitator be sure that a participant is fully aware of all risks, both real and perceived? This poses daunting problems for the outdoor leader, the participant, other group members, and outside personnel providing support to the person with the disability. It also poses a remarkable opportunity for growth, success, and wonder, just as adventure experiences may for anyone. However, it is no wonder that outdoor leaders tend toward overly cautious and paternalistic behaviors when they are undertrained and fearful of litigation.

Obligation to Inform

While it is imperative that instructors ensure that participants are able to make informed choices about the nature and extent of their participation in adventure activities, it is also imperative that program participants provide instructors with honest and accurate assessments of any personal limitations that might inhibit their ability to safely participate in the adventure activities. Such information is typically provided via medical and health history forms prior to the start of adventure programs. However, at times, individuals with disabilities fail to fully disclose information about the nature of their disabilities and thus fail to inform instructors of potential limitations to their ability to safely participate in program activities. A failure to fully disclose information about one's disabilities naturally results in a failure to allow adventure programmers to adequately accommodate for the needs of the individual with disabilities. The reasons that people may not adequately inform service providers about information that may affect their performance in adventure programming activities are complex. There are factors involving fear of exclusion, not understanding what information may be needed, and a number of other considerations that may be involved in the decision not to inform. However, to a certain extent, each person in society has a collective responsibility to ensure not only their own safety but also that of others. When a participant (or guardian) does not inform an adventure program provider fully of his or her needs, whether purposefully or unintentionally, the results can be disastrous. The following is an account of one such instance.

Approximately six years ago, a senior-level college student majoring in an outdoor recreation-related field was participating in a weekend-long wilderness survival trip during a required course. The student had completed almost all of his requisite coursework for the major, had completed other practical and trip-related experiences, and was nearing his internship experience. Before the trip, the student disclosed on the mandated medical form that he had epilepsy but stated that it was under control and that he did not have any other limitations. The student did not disclose to the instructor (though she was to learn later) that he had previously seized on university property and that his driver's license was at that time revoked due to seizures. The student also did not request any accommodations for his disability. During the trip, while participating in a mock solo, the student fell hands- and face-first into a campfire. This caused third-degree burns to his face, hands, and right arm. The student later sued the college, claiming that his fall into the fire was the result of a seizure. The student accused the college of negligence for not providing adequate oversight in light of his disability. Although a seizure was not proven, it was not totally ruled out. The case illustrates the dilemma posed by a failure to fully disclose one's disabilities. How can instructors reasonably be expected to provide adequate accommodation when participants fail to fully disclose the nature of their disabilities and further fail to request adequate accommodations for their disabilities? The case was ultimately settled out of court without an admission of culpability by the college. Additional information about the case is withheld here to protect the student and

all other parties involved. The student continues to heal today.

Of course, countless details would need to be reviewed to have a full discussion of the situation. This tragic story leaves many questions unanswered. However, it gives rise to a number of other questions that are pertinent to this argument. How much information must an adventure program provider request? If a participant gives limited information, should accommodations be required? If accommodations are made, at what point are the modifications taking away from the experience of the individual or group? Is a person, regardless of whether he or she may have any type of disability, in his or her early 20s developmentally capable and knowledgeable enough to make the judgments and decisions required to ensure his or her safety? If not, how are our young adventure program professionals to make these decisions for others? In this case, the student may have soon been leading adventure programs for other participants. Was he competent to ensure the safety of others while guiding a raft? Belaying? Leading a backpacking expedition?

It is no doubt less complex to discuss the ramifications of ADA for environments in which accommodations for people with physical or sensory impairments might be offered. Understanding the nuances of inclusive programming for people with hidden impairments of cognition and judgment that could decidedly affect an adventure experience is much more intricate. As a recreational therapist, one of the authors of this argument has heard parents state that they do not disclose their child's disability to recreation service providers because they do not want them to be treated differently. However, without this disclosure, it is quite possible that their child not only would receive a suboptimal experience but also would face much higher levels of risk due to the lack of preparedness of both the participant and the adventure program leader. Without accurate information, service providers are at a loss as to how they may best include individuals with disabilities. In a group setting, that person's higher risk for failure or injury may also put others in the group in danger. This is unacceptable by any account.

Conclusion

To say that persons of differing ability levels should globally not be included in adventure programming altogether would be a monstrous overstatement. Indeed, the recreational therapy literature states that modifications are meant to be made on an individual level. On an individual level, persons with disabilities or adventure leaders who are knowledgeable can often negotiate questions about the environment, leaders, and participants so that a safe, positive experience can be planned and executed.

Despite the attention given to the issue of access by federal agencies overseeing parks and protected areas, the answers concerning access are not clear and may never be. Waterman and Waterman (1993) offer an insightful overview of the stakes: "Without some degree of management, 'wilderness' cannot survive the number of people who seek to enjoy it. But with too much management, or the wrong kind, we can destroy the spiritual component of wildness in our zeal to preserve its physical side" (p. 47).

A wholesale statement that anyone should be fully included in adventure programming regardless of their (dis)abilities sets everyone up for failure. If you do not allow someone to participate, you may be unfairly denying that person the rightful opportunity to reap the rewards of adventure programming. Indeed, you may also be denying their potential coparticipants the benefit of their presence. On the other hand, if you change the nature of the adventure activity or the nature of nature itself, you may be removing the inherent reasons for participation.

Whose responsibility is it to verify at what level a person with a disability is able to participate in adventure programming? At what point does the person with the disability have enough information about the outdoor area to make an informed decision about participation? At what point does the adventure practitioner have enough—or indeed any—training to ensure access and inclusion? Significant barriers in the environment and leadership remain; therefore, these questions inherently must be answered on an individual basis.

References

Bullock, C.C., Mahon, M.J., & Killingsworth, C.K. (2010). *Introduction to recreation services for persons with disabilities: A person-centered approach.* Champaign, IL: Sagamore.

Carlson, J.A., & Evans, K. (2001). Whose choice is it? Contemplating challenge-by-choice and diverse-abilities. *Journal of Experiential Education, 24*(1), 58-63.

Council on Accreditation. (2004). Standards and evaluative criteria for baccalaureate programs in recreation, park resources, and leisure services. www.nrpa.org/Content.aspx?id=1213 [December 30, 2011].

Martin, B., Cashel, C., Wagstaff, M., & Breunig, M. (2006). *Outdoor leadership: Theory and practice.* Champaign, IL: Human Kinetics.

Moore, R., Dattilo, J., & Devine, M. (1996). A comparison of rail-trail preferences between adults with and without disabilities. *Adapted Physical Activity Quarterly, 13*(1), 27-37.

National Park Service. (n.d.). The National Park Service Organic Act, 16 U.S.C.1. www.nps.gov/legacy/mission.html [December 30, 2011].

Nisbett, N., & Hinton, J. (2005). On and off the trail: Experiences of individuals with specialized needs on the Appalachian Trail. *Tourism Review International, 8,* 221-237.

Paisley, K., Sibthorp, J., & Szolosi, A. (2003). *How different programs manage field risks.* Paper presented at the Wilderness Risk Management Conference, State College, PA.

Palley, E. (2009). Civil rights for people with disabilities: Obstacles related to the least restrictive environment mandate. *Journal of Social Work in Disability and Rehabilitation, 8,* 37-55.

Priest, S., & Gass, M.A. (2005). *Effective leadership in adventure programming.* Champaign, IL: Human Kinetics.

Smith, R.W., Austin, D.R., Kennedy, D.W., Lee, Y., & Hutchison, P. (2005). *Inclusive and special recreation: Opportunities for persons with disabilities.* 5th ed. New York: McGraw Hill Higher Education.

United States Access Board. (2009). Draft final accessibility guidelines for outdoor developed areas. http://access-board.gov/outdoor/draft-final.htm [December 30, 2011].

U.S. Forest Service. (2006). Accessibility guidebook for outdoor recreation and trails. Department of Agriculture. www.fs.fed.us/recreation/programs/accessibility/htmlpubs/htm06232801/page22.htm [December 30, 2011].

Waterman, L., & Waterman, G. (1993). *Wilderness ethics: Preserving the spirit of wildness.* Woodstock, VT: Countryman Press.

Controversial Issue 8

Should people of color be encouraged to participate in current outdoor adventure programs?

Outdoor adventure professionals readily acknowledge the lack of participation by people of color. This important issue receives attention among our professional networks; however, little progress has been made to include people of color. A few adventure programmers have devoted themselves to activities such as developing social-justice texts, promoting diversity through national conferences, or producing research around the topic. Unfortunately, these activities have not created enough momentum to affect a systemwide change. As a profession, we agree all must have access to programs and to the corresponding benefits. We embrace a moral imperative to create and operate a field that is inclusive. Yet we seem to be lost on how to effectively act on this ethical obligation. Occasionally, an adventure-based organization that purposefully targets a population of color achieves success. Unfortunately, these isolated successes do not reflect a desperately needed approach on which we can all agree.

Jo Ann Coco-Ripp and Karen Warren offer two distinct options to tackle the issue. Coco-Ripp offers what would seem to be a realistic approach that focuses on individual encouragement. She introduces contact theory and shows that implementing it within the adventure-based programming industry is feasible and complements what we do best. She offers a systematic approach that is realistic to implement within our industry's existing infrastructure. Coco-Ripp argues that if our adventure programmers would follow the well-researched tenets of contact theory, we could encourage and achieve meaningful participation by people of color.

Warren argues that without dramatic, systemwide change, inviting people of color is a solution that will not work. She pushes for systemwide change by advocating for Kuhn's ideas about paradigm change and implementing concepts found in the social-justice literature. Although some would consider this a more radical approach, Warren makes a case that individual or personal invitations to people of color to participate are not effective unless the institutional culture of outdoor adventure programs changes by shifting from currently entrenched paradigms.

Careful attention to this debate is a must if we are to affect change in outdoor adventure programming. Serious discussion and unified action must occur in order to confront this chronic issue. Warren and Coco-Ripp provide two distinct options that would require unified agreement if adventure programs want to affect real change. Many would argue that the future of our field hangs tenuously as demographic trends in society shift. By not including people of color in a predominately white, privileged participant base, we will never actualize the true potential of our field.

Should people of color be encouraged to participate in current outdoor adventure programs?

YES Outdoor Adventure Experiences and People of Color

Jo Ann Coco-Ripp, PhD, assistant professor of therapeutic recreation, Winston-Salem State University, Winston-Salem, North Carolina, United States

Participation by people of color in outdoor adventure experiences needs to be encouraged at the individual and personal levels within the existing structure of the adventure programming industry. Despite acknowledgment of the need to change, evidence shows a surprising lack of diversity among staff and participants and in many other areas within the outdoor adventure field (Floyd, Bocarro, and Thompson, 2008; Frazer, 2009; Kerr, 2009). Involvement by members of diverse ethnic and racial groups will increase when information and messages persuade individuals, through their affiliation as members of various familial, ethnic, and friend groups, to participate in outdoor adventure experiences. Benefits to the individual, groups, and society will follow. Concurrent systemic changes can contribute to increased involvement, yet the primary emphasis needs to be placed at the individual and personal levels.

The premise of intergroup contact theory, developed by Gordon Allport (1954), is that under appropriate conditions interpersonal contact is one of the most effective ways to reduce prejudice between group members. Nonparticipants and participants in outdoor adventure experiences may be viewed as two distinct groups. Based on the depth of research (Pettigrew and Tropp, 2006) and current applications of contact theory (Devine and O'Brien, 2007; Seaman et al., 2010) in the outdoor adventure industry, contact theory holds the greatest promise to effectively change participation patterns. The adventure programming industry must embrace and apply contact theory in order to be inclusive and ensure participation. The theory does not require larger systemic changes that many social-justice advocates propose for our industry. It uses strengths innately found in adventure experiences. One difficulty is the variety and differences in the field—not all adventure programs are equal. However, careful industrywide attention through accreditations, certifications, and other quality-enhancement measures in conjunction with focused application of contact theory can resolve some of the issues that lack of diversity brings to the adventure industry.

This argument looks at connecting contact theory across five key areas targeted for improvement at the individual level: role models, leadership, the message being communicated, multiple methods of communication, and producing evidence in various ways. In addition, application of contact theory can effectively increase involvement of people of color in outdoor adventure experiences when combined with the positive results from four conditions (covered later in this argument) that maximize intergroup contacts and minimize circumstances that diminish the contact (Devine and O'Brien, 2007; Pettigrew and Tropp, 2006; Seaman et al., 2010).

Current Status of Diversity

Despite acknowledgment of the need to change, evidence points to a lingering lack of diversity across many areas within the outdoor field. Larson (2010) conducted an adventure education study using online surveys and follow-up interviews with participants from the listservs of the Association for Challenge Course Technology, the Association for Outdoor Recreation and Education, and the Association for Experiential Education. Among the 96 respondents, the demographic majority was white (93 percent), male (64 percent), and college educated (all had some level). Two highlights from the most recent Outdoor Recreation Participation Report (Outdoor Industry Association, 2010a, p. 5), which identifies many demographic trends in outdoor recreation, include the following:

- In 2009, in nearly all age groups, participation in outdoor activities was significantly higher among Caucasians than among any other ethnicity and lowest among African Americans.

- Whereas 67 percent of Caucasian kids ages 6 to 12 participated in some form of outdoor recreation in 2009, only 50 percent of Hispanic kids and 39 percent of African American kids in the same age range participated.

A recent *New York Times* article (Navarro, 2010) discussed visitation of national parks by ethnic population groups and specifically focused on African American visitors to more wilderness-oriented parks. Various surveys reveal low general attendance (e.g., 13 percent of all respondents over a two-year span for African Americans) in some areas. At Yosemite National Park, a 2009 survey found that 77 percent of visitors were white, 11 percent were Latino, 11 percent were Asian, and 1 percent was black. In another survey, blacks were three times as likely as whites to report that they felt that parks were not comfortable places to be. Social scientists do not report any changes in the past 10 to 15 years in this underrepresentation of ethnic groups. In seeking to understand or explain this pattern, barriers such as cost, travel distance, and lack of information are often cited.

Application of Contact Theory

Application of contact theory can effectively increase involvement of people of color in outdoor adventure experiences. Contact theory asserts that interaction between people from different groups has the potential to change people's attitudes, and perhaps behavior, toward one another (Devine and Wilhite, 1999). These groups could be male and female, black and white, English-speaking and non-English-speaking, or any number of self- or society-defined groups. Outdoor Nation (Outdoor Industry Association, 2010b) advocates turning insiders to outsiders; thus, two groups could be labeled: outsiders and insiders. According to contact theory, some conditions encourage positive interactions and some conditions discourage positive interactions or lead to negative outcomes (Pettigrew and Tropp, 2006). For the most favorable outcomes, this intergroup contact needs to occur under certain conditions. Intergroup contact will likely lead to reduced prejudice if the contact meets these four conditions:

1. Participants from different groups must perceive that they have *equal status* within the situation.

2. They must work interdependently toward *common goals*.

3. They should have the opportunity to associate and possibly become *friends without competition*.

4. They must experience the normative support of *authorities*.

Contact under less-desirable conditions can lead to negative effects or no impact (Coco-Ripp, 2003). Unfavorable conditions include the following: contact between the group is competitive (e.g., competing for limited resources); the environment is unpleasant, involuntary, or tense; a state of frustration exists among group members; and standards held by groups are objectionable to each other. A large body of empirical research supports intergroup contact theory. Pettigrew and Tropp's (2006) meta-analysis demonstrates that programs that maximized most or all of the contact conditions yielded significantly higher reductions of prejudice. When any unfavorable condition presents itself, even when the four main conditions are met, the results are less than satisfactory (Devine and O'Brien, 2007).

In a study using adventure-based activities with adolescents, Seaman and colleagues (2010) found that contact theory as the designing framework provided a viable approach to diversity education in nonformal settings. The authors found that the cross-group interactions under the four optimal conditions led to favorable results. Additionally, their study indicated that application of contact theory to experiential activities can successfully decrease bias. Therefore, it could be effective to view outdoor adventure experiences using a contact-style approach that primarily alters the structure of interpersonal relationships. Assuming that the study analysis is correct, careful attention to the four optimal conditions of contact theory is important in achieving desired results from most experiential activities (Seaman et al., 2010, p. 218). In a qualitative approach, through one-on-one interviews, Devine and O'Brien (2007) collected data related to contact occurring naturally in a camp setting. The authors used contact theory to ground the research, minimize the voice of the researcher, and represent the participant's perception. Findings from this study suggest that optimizing contact in a camping setting has huge potential to foster positive intergroup experiences.

Both studies emphasize structuring contact using the four conditions for successful results. Support by authorities and opportunities for developing friendships are critical in encouraging people of color to participate in outdoor adventure experiences. The equal status condition can be applied to the participants and the facilitators or leaders. Many experiences in outdoor adventure programming already fulfill the cooperation or interdependence condition. Further attention to the four conditions in all aspects of outdoor adventure experiences is important. Additionally, eliminating unfavorable conditions will lead to positive results. Less-than-desirable conditions might include lack of information on gear or terrain, insufficient knowledge about the cultural background of a group, or poor planning for the environment.

In an experiential program for urban youths, Kerr (2009) found several guidelines to encourage future participation. Program aspects that participants associated with positive relationships were the length and consistency of the program, overcoming group challenges, and discussing their lives together during free time in cabins. Participants claimed that they would not have been able to form such strong peer relationships without the long-term, consistent nature of this program. This type of association fostered positive relationships.

Space for groups seems to be an important consideration. Floyd and Shinew (1999) suggest that spatial separation (in neighborhoods and other group spaces) leads to social isolation and to fewer opportunities for interracial contacts for African Americans. Findings suggest that when interracial contact is taken into account, most differences in outdoor recreation preferences between blacks and whites disappear.

Contact theory has persisted for more than 50 years and has generated a huge body of cross-disciplinary research. It is a promising theory for reducing prejudice and encouraging positive intergroup communication practices. Harwood (2010) asks how we might shift around the space to achieve maximum positive effects of intergroup contact. Outdoor adventure experiences might be the ideal setting for achieving positive results based on use of contact theory. Taking advantage of the outdoors as a space for positive intergroup contact seems like a great way to encourage increased participation by people from various racial and ethnic backgrounds.

Five Areas for Improvement

Connecting contact theory in five areas targeted for improvement (role models, leadership, the message, methods of communication, and producing evidence) can provide direction and focus.

I provide a brief discussion of each area and give suggestions for effective contact and other ideas to improve attitudes that may foster increased positive intergroup relations.

Role Models

Positive role models are important in application of contact theory. President Obama's Great Outdoors Initiative (America's Great Outdoors Initiative, 2010), Oprah Winfrey's recent visit to Yosemite National Park, and Shelton Jackson (Navarro, 2010) are three examples of role models that can influence participation by diverse groups in outdoor adventure experiences. I discuss the Great Outdoors Initiative later. Oprah's visit was initiated by a letter from Shelton Jackson, an African American who has been a Yosemite park ranger for more than 20 years. His appeal as an individual has had a ripple effect. His action and interests in outdoor experiences led to two episodes of Oprah's television show and her visit.

Exposure to outdoor spaces and activities can lead to curiosity about them. Authentic positive experiences structured by conditions of contact theory can result in increased participation. Role models can serve as supportive norms or authority sanction (one of the four conditions). Role models sometimes can function as leaders. Shelton Jackson's job as a park ranger influenced his coworkers to gain new perspectives and act on them. For example, Jackson helped facilitate incorporating stories into tours and other interpretive venues about diverse groups who have had an impact on the national parks, such as the Buffalo Soldiers (Navarro, 2010). Targeting role models does not have to be on the celebrity level. Many assume it would be most effective to solicit the assistance of a popular public figure or a famous person to have an impact. A common person of color is able to role model just as effectively. Nevertheless, role models from nonparticipant or diverse groups should be more evident in outdoor adventure experiences.

Outdoor Leadership

A shift in leadership styles is needed, and it is best done within the framework of the conditions of contact theory. Outdoor leadership typically focuses on the skills level and competencies or performance of the individual leader (Martin et al., 2006; Priest and Gass, 2005). Shooter, Sibthorp, and Paisley's (2009) view of leadership focuses on skills of a program rather than of an individual leader. Most outdoor programs can use leadership teams and match skill sets in ways that maximize success for the specific goals of the program. This programmatic approach to leadership would be ideal for enhancing tenets of contact theory. Several leaders collaborating for the success of an activity or program have the potential to work toward one goal and bring a more diverse leadership to the venture.

For the leader, becoming a group participant is a skill to develop. According to Ina (2009), in outdoor education the traditional role of the facilitator is outside the group of participants. The leader often either is in a position of power over the participants or is detached and passive. A very different role emerged in results of an ethnographic study Ina (2009) conducted. In-depth analysis of the facilitation process showed that the facilitator is always part of the group. The way a facilitator approaches their role within the group determines the influence that they have on the outdoor learning process. The facilitation process provides a tremendous opportunity to embed conditions of contact theory into outdoor programs. The facilitator or leader can buffer larger institutional messages projected by an agency, especially if it does not fully embrace diversity at the experience level. Facilitators need to develop skills that go beyond their traditional roles in order to encourage friendship development and cooperation in activities that might become competitive.

Messages in Outdoor Adventure

The messages being communicated need to change in order to increase participation in outdoor adventure experiences. Messages about outdoor adventure experiences are complex and often difficult to discern. This area should be explored in much more detail and greater depth than this venue allows. Nevertheless, I offer brief comments on self-determination and self-identity and discussion from Outdoor Nation (2010) regarding messages about inside–outside participation.

Self-Determination and Self-Identity

Self-determination theory can be intertwined with contact theory to increase participation levels. Legault (2009) examined self-determination theory in relation to intergroup attitudes and found that internal regulation provided by self-determination served in a powerful manner to regulate an individual's negative regard for groups. Emphasizing this aspect of self-determination may provide an effective path to decreasing prejudice, stereotypes, and other negative influences for youths as well as adults (Sklar, Anderson, and Autry, 2007). Spending time and effort to help members of diverse groups become self-determined can affect change more efficiently than can laws or regulatory methods.

Identity formation is an area of difference across groups. Getting to know others is important in identity development. Many outdoor adventure experiences can foster identity development in a variety of ways (Bell, 2006). Outdoor experiences led by a facilitator who is similar to the participants can lead to positive results and encourage further participation. In designing outdoor experiences, activity implementation can lead to positive or negative outcomes in relationships within groups. Phillipp (1998) found that black and white teen groups operated in quite different ways to encourage or discourage participation choices. Intentionally exploring identity development using cooperative activities with two groups can potentially decrease bias and increase positive attitudes across the groups.

Insiders and Outsiders

One major challenge, uncovered in youth listening sessions held June of 2010, is for the outdoor community to engage new audiences—especially minorities and insiders—in outdoor activities. The Outdoor Nation Special Report generated from this session recommends the following for increasing participation (Outdoor Industry Association, 2010b):

- Increase the number of safe and accessible green spaces, particularly in low-income communities with significant health disparities.
- Support close-to-home outdoor recreation that allows unstructured outdoor play.
- Strengthen outreach to new audiences by integrating 21st-century communication tools that will increase the visibility of parks and natural spaces.
- Use free incentives—in multiple languages— to engage minority groups. The recommendations also state that providing mentorship and gear subsidies or cooperation would be the most effective ways to reach underserved populations.

Even though these suggestions were generated by federal agencies, individual involvement in communicating messages can be effective in changing attitudes about participation in the outside environment. Communications from outsiders to insiders need to highlight the message that activity can be done in an outdoor environment to increase health outcomes and the idea that outdoor experiences can be shared with friends and family. Applying the cooperative condition and the authority sanction of contact theory will strengthen the positive effect of contact between insiders and outsiders.

Methods of Communication

Multiple methods of communication must be used to connect individuals to outdoor adventure experiences. Expanding ways to communicate can be a form of encouragement and can be viewed as a collaborative effort or cooperation. Using varied tools can be beneficial. Social media sites can help people make connections across groups. Outdoor Afro (Mapp, n.d.) is a website that supports diverse participation in the great outdoors. On November 9, 2010, a commenter stated that she was proud to see black people doing things they enjoy instead of being called white for exploring the outdoors.

Audio (e.g., podcasts or radio broadcasts) is another means of communicating to diverse groups the benefits of participating in outdoor adventure experiences. In a recent interview (Burke and Cavanaugh, 2010) with Audrey Peterman on KPBS radio, the host asked about the fact that national parks are not proportionately visited by blacks, Latinos, and other minorities. Peterman responded that one of the reasons is lack of information; unless you know about the parks or the benefits of being in the outdoors, it is hard to know what you are missing. Peterman and her husband, both Americans who are black, wrote *Legacy on the Land* about their experiences traveling across the United States to many of the national parks. They provide a unique perspective that includes stories of people and ethnic groups who contributed to the development of the United States. They say that this rich history of diversity is not reflected in traditional history texts.

In April of 2010 the Obama administration established America's Great Outdoors Initiative, the purpose of which is to develop a 21st-century conservation and recreation agenda and reconnect Americans with our great outdoors (America's Great Outdoors Initiative, 2010). Listening sessions have been held in about 20 urban and rural sites across the nation to gather information from individuals. Even though it is a national project, people are affected at the individual level through their involvement in sessions. Using multiple, diverse methods of communication relates directly to the application of contact theory. Exposing two groups to each other through varied methods of communication can improve attitudes of one group toward the other and can increase familiarity with members of the group.

Producing Evidence

Evidence can highlight or limit perceptions. Expanding perceptions from studies conducted using less-traditional methods such as ethnography or case studies (Cavert, 2009; Dieser, 2002; Hatch, 2005; Sylvester, 1996) provides information about experiences that studies with quantitative results cannot. For example, in an extensive study focused on practices of college faculty in outdoor education studies, Frazer (2009) uncovered many influential beliefs and practices. In particular, he found that those who train future staff in the outdoor field can be a positive influence for increased involvement by diverse groups. Outdoor education may serve "as a vehicle for leaving the world a better place, particularly for the students and clients of outdoor education who for whatever reason are marginalized, underserved, oppressed, or left out altogether" (p. 345). Delving into ways that training and research affect practices, both Larson (2010) and Wu (2007) discovered that preparation for outdoor leaders did not often include methods or practical help for change at the individual level.

In a review by Floyd, Bocarro, and Thompson (2008), less than 5 percent of articles in five journals relevant to outdoor researchers were related to race and ethnicity. Very few articles focused on explanation of behaviors; instead, most used descriptive survey approaches. In terms of the methodologies used, no empirical studies were reported and ethnological approaches were nonexistent. In another study related to adolescents and ethnicity, Phillipp (1998) brought up the major concern that using categories of ethnicity or socioeconomic class instead of race in considering issues related to group interactions can obscure the power of race in the dynamics; race may be hidden and discrimination overlooked. Traditional statistics and quantitative data-collection methods may not yield information that can lead to practices needed for including individuals who currently do not participate in outdoor adventure experiences. Encouraging researchers to use contact theory and intentionally make the effort to change to more nontraditional or qualitative methods can uncover critical evidence.

Conclusion

Despite continued acknowledgment of the need for change, evidence continues to show a lack of diversity among staff and participants and in many other areas within the outdoor field. One of the most effective paths to support increased involvement of diverse groups in outdoor adventure experiences is the application of contact theory. Taking advantage of the positive results of structured use of the four conditions that maximize intergroup contacts, minimizing less favorable conditions, and connecting contact theory to five key areas will enhance participation.

Positive role models are important in application of contact theory. Encouragement from role models can represent supportive norms or positive authority sanction. Connecting role models to leadership changes can also be advantageous. A shift in leadership styles is needed and it is best done within the framework of the conditions of contact theory so that the equal status condition is supported. To increase participation by members of diverse groups, messages being communicated about outdoor experiences need to change. Messages should be communicated using multiple methods to connect individuals and groups to outdoor adventure experiences. Expanding ways to communicate can be a form of encouragement and viewed as a collaborative effort or cooperative action. Outcomes from evaluation and research studies will help us to understand obstacles as well as means to increase participation by individuals and diverse groups in outdoor adventure. Moving beyond traditional methods of data collection can broaden information and extend perceptions of how outdoor adventure experiences benefit diverse populations.

Shifting focus in these five key areas and incorporating contact theory will expand long-established expectations. Shifts can begin immediately and simultaneously with systemic changes. Integrating the four optimal conditions—supportive norms, cooperation, equal status, and friendship opportunities—is important in achieving the desired results of increased participation by people of color in outdoor adventure experiences.

References

Allport, G. (1954). *The nature of prejudice.* Reading, MA: Addison-Wesley.

America's Great Outdoors Initiative. (2010). www.greatoutdoorsamerica.org [December 20, 2010].

Bell, S.A. (2006). *Effect of challenge initiative and facilitator ethnic similarity to explore ethnic identity among adolescents who are ethnic minorities.* Doctoral dissertation. Salt Lake City: The University of Utah.

Burke, M., & Cavanaugh, M. (2010). Legacy on the land [radio transcript from interview on KPBS]. www.

kpbs.org/news/2010/feb/09/legacy-land [December 27, 2010].

Cavert, C. (2009). *Entry-level challenge course facilitator training programs: A multiple site case study.* Doctoral dissertation. Flagstaff, AZ: Northern Arizona University.

Coco-Ripp, J. (2003). *The effect of awareness training and planned contact on the provision of an inclusive environment for persons who are deaf.* Doctoral dissertation. Salt Lake City: The University of Utah.

Devine, M., & O'Brien, M. (2007). The mixed bag of inclusion: An examination of an inclusive camp using contact theory. *Therapeutic Recreation Journal, 41*(3), 201-222.

Devine, M., & Wilhite, B. (1999). Theory application in therapeutic recreation practice and research. *Therapeutic Recreation Journal, 33*(1), 29-46.

Dieser, R.B. (2002). *Understanding how the dominant discourse of individualism within therapeutic recreation affects leisure education intervention, the utilization of therapeutic recreation practice models, and the therapeutic recreation certification process.* Doctoral dissertation. Edmonton, AB: University of Alberta.

Floyd, M.F., Bocarro, J.N., & Thompson, T.D. (2008). Research on race and ethnicity in leisure studies: A review of five major journals. *Journal of Leisure Research, 40*(1), 1-22.

Floyd, M.F., & Shinew, K.J. (1999). Convergence and divergence in leisure style among Whites and African Americans: Toward an interracial contact hypothesis. *Journal of Leisure Research, 31*(4), 359-384.

Frazer, R. (2009). *Toward a theory of critical teaching for social justice in outdoor education studies: A grounded theory study of philosophical perspectives and teaching practices.* Doctoral dissertation. Madison, WI: The University of Wisconsin.

Harwood, J. (2010). The contact space: A novel framework for intergroup contact research. *Journal of Language and Social Psychology, 29*(2), 147-177.

Hatch, K.D. (2005). *An evaluation of a supplemental procedure geared toward prolonging challenge course benefits.* Doctoral dissertation. Austin, TX: The University of Texas.

Ina, S. (2009). Recontextualizing the role of the facilitator in group interaction in the outdoor classroom. *Journal of Adventure Education and Outdoor Learning, 9*(1), 23-43.

Kerr, R. (2009). *The view from here: The perspectives of inner city youth in experiential education programs.* Doctoral dissertation. Kingston, ON: Queen's University.

Larson, S.W. (2010). *Adventure education and social justice: An investigation into the status and integration of social justice in the field of adventure education.* Doctoral dissertation. Prescott, AZ: Prescott College.

Legault, L. (2009). *Internalizing and automatizing motivation to be nonprejudiced: The role of self-determination in stereotyping, prejudice, and intergroup threat.* Doctoral dissertation. Ottawa, ON: University of Ottawa.

Mapp, R. (n.d.). So what is outdoor afro? www.outdoor-afro.com/about/ [December 15, 2010].

Martin, B., Cashel, C., Wagstaff, M., & Breunig, M. (2006). *Outdoor leadership: Theory and practice.* Champaign, IL: Human Kinetics.

Navarro, M. (2010). National Parks reach out to Blacks who aren't visiting. *New York Times.* www.nytimes.com/2010/11/03/science/earth/03parks.html?_r=1&partner=rss&emc=rss&pagewanted=print [December 12, 2011].

Outdoor Industry Association. (2010a). 2010 outdoor recreation participation report. www.outdoorindustry.org/images/researchfiles/TOF_ResearchParticipation2010.pdf?121 [December 15, 2010].

Outdoor Industry Association. (2010b). Outdoor nation special report: Turning insiders out. www.outdoorindustry.org/images/researchfiles/TOF_research_insideout2010.pdf?120 [December 15, 2010].

Outdoor Nation. (2010). National youth summit summary. www.outdoornation.org/images/mainPage/ONYSSummary.pdf [December 15, 2010].

Pettigrew, T.F., & Tropp, S. (2006). A meta-analytic test of intergroup contact theory. *Journal of Personality and Social Psychology, 90*(5), 751-783.

Phillipp, S.F. (1998). Race and gender differences in adolescent peer group approval of leisure activities. *Journal of Leisure Research, 30*(2), 214-232.

Priest, S., & Gass, M. (2005). *Effective leadership in adventure programming.* Champaign, IL: Human Kinetics.

Seaman, J., Beightol, J., Shirilla, P., & Crawford, B. (2010). Contact theory as a framework for experiential activities as diversity education: An exploratory study. *Journal of Experiential Education, 32*(3), 207-225.

Shooter, W., Sibthorp, J., & Paisley, K. (2009). Outdoor leadership skills: A program perspective. *Journal of Experiential Education, 32*(1), 1-13.

Sklar, S., Anderson, S., & Autry, C. (2007). Positive youth development: A Wilderness intervention. *Therapeutic Recreation Journal, 41*(3), 223-243.

Sylvester, C. (1996). Instrumental rationality and therapeutic recreation: Revisiting the issue of means and ends. In C. Sylvester, J. Hemmingway, R. Howe-Murphy, K. Mobily, & P. Shank (Eds.), *Philosophy of therapeutic recreation: Ideas and issues,* Volume II (pp. 92-105). Arlington, VA: National Recreation and Park Association.

Wu, G. (2007). *Exploring outdoor leaders' cross-cultural experiences in the wilderness education setting.* Doctoral dissertation. Bloomington, IN: Indiana University.

Should people of color be encouraged to participate in current outdoor adventure programs?

NO Paradigms of Outdoor Adventure and Social Justice

Karen Warren, PhD, outdoor program and recreational athletics instructor, Hampshire College, Amherst, Massachusetts, United States

At first glance, this seems like an easy question to answer with a resounding yes, but a deeper critical analysis of the issue brings me to this "no" position. It is imperative that outdoor adventure programs include all people who wish to partake in them, but we will not achieve social justice by encouraging people of color to participate in outdoor adventure experiences as they are presently conceived and constructed in the United States. Due to entrenched notions of the nature of outdoor adventure, which I call paradigms, current programs may not appeal to certain racial and ethnic groups. I argue that these traditional paradigms about outdoor adventure are both overtly and subtly exclusionary and need to be critically examined and changed to be truly welcoming of all people (Warren, 1998b). Therefore, institutional change systemwide is the most productive way to actualize multicultural outdoor adventure experiences.

A paradigm is an overarching worldview that a culture holds, a baseline assumption we act on without being conscious of its implications. According to the work of Thomas Kuhn (1962), a paradigm is abruptly transformed by new information and thinking; therefore, although not everyone supports the values that sustain the paradigm, it persists until enough people consciously commit to change it. A closer look at five paradigms underlying the delivery of outdoor adventure in programs in the United States forms the basis of this "no" position.

Paradigm of Diversity

The paradigm of diversity is a foundation for the paradigms that follow. It is an orientation in the field that influences the way people of difference are included in outdoor adventure. In comparing diversity with social justice, Yeskel (1995) calls diversity the great Crayola crayon box. Each color is different and unique, but in the 64-crayon box, no crayon is less or more important than any other—burnt sienna has no more power than cerulean, magenta

no more than lime green. In a social-justice orientation, unlike in a crayon box, certain categories are weighted more than others. Institutional power and privilege is held by dominant groups—white, male, able-bodied, heterosexual, Christian, middle or owning class, and young. The outdoor adventure field continues to distance itself from the real issues of creating socially just programs by being trapped in the diversity paradigm, which posits that we will have diversity if we incorporate a multitude of difference and thus fails to take power differentials into account.

Chavez (2008) offers the "I" triad as a way to ensure that nondominant groups are represented in programs. According to Chavez, programs need to invite, include, and involve members of different racial and ethnic groups. The programs must *invite* members of oppressed groups to participate, *include* them in programs by asking what they have to say about services, and *involve* these groups in decision making at the highest level.

The outdoor adventure field is caught in the invite leg of the triad. It uses brochures, advertising, and scholarships to invite people of color to participate in one-size-fits-all programs (Warren, 1998a). The outdoor adventure field is sustained by the persistent false notion that getting more people of color as participants and staff will solve the diversity dilemma. Instead of examining existing courses for suitability to the cultural conditions important to oppressed people, we invite oppressed people to traditional programs without critically analyzing the program components or embedded assumptions. We neglect to include the opinions of people of color in program development and delivery and we do not ask them what outdoor adventure means to them. As O'Connell and colleagues (2005) point out, "A 'universal' definition of leisure and recreation seems to exist in many outdoor recreation programs, with little or no attention paid to the different ways in which non-Caucasian cultures perceive 'recreation' and 'leisure'" (p. 83).

We are not involving people of color in decision making, as demonstrated by their stark absence at the administration and board levels within our field. Encouraging people of color to join currently constructed adventure programs without giving them actual power to determine their orientation and direction is discriminatory assimilation. We must all work together to ensure the true inclusivity of adventure programming by cocreating new programs with people of color. Moreover, to move the outdoor adventure field from an ethnocentric melting pot to a more multicultural practice, people of privilege need to work to prioritize the "include" and "involve" legs of Chavez's model.

Paradigm of Wilderness Adventure

The allure of high mountaintops, deep woods, and rushing rivers has been the holy grail of outdoor adventure programs. Outdoor adventure has evolved from a history of wealthy white people finding leisure in the sublime wilderness (Nash, 2001). This schism in values positions the sublime view of nature against the utilitarian view that advocates the usefulness of nature. A prevalent view of wilderness, rooted in the dominant group culture, favors a more sublime immersion into wilderness as opposed to a utilitarian approach that is often the orientation of ethnic and racial minorities. Many communities of color have traditionally used the wilderness for hunting, fishing, gathering, and surviving (Johnson et al., 2005).

The idea of wilderness as a majestic, empty place is echoed in the definition from the Wilderness Act of 1964—"a land untrammeled by man, where man himself is a visitor who does not remain." Some scholars suggest that this view of wilderness is an artificial construct used to create a rationale for the genocide of indigenous people who populated the entire American continent upon the arrival of Europeans (Jaimes, 1992; Weatherford, 2010). If we create an idea that wilderness landscape, the frontier, is a lonely, empty place, it allows us to be excused for not seeing the people who did live there. "What better way to deny genocide than to ignore the existence of the human residents of the 'wilderness'?" (Fink, 1999, p. 167).

Wilderness values that deny that people are an integral part of the landscape privileges the sublime view of wilderness over the utilitarian, which results in wilderness values that may not be shared by oppressed groups. The popular Leave No Trace philosophy used in many outdoor programs is an example of a construct of the sublime valued over the utilitarian. I am not questioning the value of Leave No Trace; rather, I am suggesting that we need to look critically at all theory and practice in outdoor adventure to see how it perpetuates paradigms that inhibit the participation of people of color.

The location of outdoor adventure course areas is called into question by the fact that white people favor more remote outdoor experiences whereas African Americans seek out more developed recreation settings (Virden and Walker, 1999). However, the outdoor profession is drawn to using remote wilderness areas for programming. In addition, wilderness access historically has depended on resources to get there, money to buy specialized gear, and access to leisure time. The last time I checked, there was no subway to Yellowstone. As a mother in Erickson, Johnson, and Kivel's (2009) study points out,

> First of all, you have to have the type of car . . . you know . . . and then there's gas. . . . I don't have the right gear to go up to the mountains. I have to wear another jacket other than the one I am wearing to school every day. . . . Oh, then gloves. Earmuffs . . . who can afford it? I've got a decision here, you have choices. Do we eat, or do we go to the mountain? (p. 542)

Although the concept of urban adventures has been well established, the major outdoor adventure programs have been slow to embrace this arena. The insistent draw of the sublime locks outdoor adventure programming into "untamed" areas worthy of a Sierra Club calendar. The total-immersion attitude pervasive in long-term wilderness trips could be changed to short-term courses with progressive challenges.

Encouraging people of color to participate in outdoor adventure programs with restrictive access based on logistical, philosophical, and cultural factors is quietly, yet profoundly, unwelcoming and not conducive to people of color enjoying future outdoor adventure experiences or feeling a sense of self-identity in the outdoors.

Paradigm of Individualism

Rugged individualism is a defining hallmark of North American culture and the pioneering spirit of westward expansion. Outdoor adventure programs have embraced the ethos of rugged individualism and it has been strongly ensconced in the outdoor adventure worldview.

The hero of the wilds captures our imagination, whether he is a canyon hiker who cuts off his arm to survive, the solitary climber who stands atop Mt. Everest, or a college dropout who ventures into the wild to live off the land in backcountry Alaska. A preoccupation with the individualism embedded in the heroic-quest literature rests at the very core of U.S. culture (Bellah et al., 1985) and has served as a guiding metaphor for many outdoor programs (Bacon, 1983; Warren, 1996).

Self-reliance, one of the pillars of Outward Bound founder Kurt Hahn's philosophy, is a key goal of many adventure programs (Miner and Boldt, 1981). Program components such as solos, individual elements on the high ropes course, and first ascents and descents emphasize individualism. Yet the values of many racial and ethnic groups focus on community and family. A long history of oppression has encouraged people of color to form strong communities as a way to have power within white culture. For example, Hispanics have strong family bonds (Carr and Williams, 1993) that may not be encouraged on outdoor courses. Communities often serve as a guard against discrimination and marginalization; therefore, a program that emphasizes self-reliance and individualism may be antithetical to the lived experience of people of color.

For people of color, individualism in a privileged culture can be lonely. An outdoor instructor told me the story of a Hispanic man on an outdoor course who had just returned from the solo with an experience that was very different from that of the rest of the participants:

> We're back sitting around base camp checking in, and he's talking about his experience, saying it's the most painful, difficult night he's ever spent in his life, while there are other people saying it was wonderful, and they got to commune with nature and wrote this great stuff in their journals. But for him it was, "This was exactly how I grew up. I grew up in a dirt shed with a tarp over my head, and that's how I spent the first 18 years of my life, and I never, ever want to do that again." So that was basically a night of misery because he was reliving what he'd spent his whole lifetime escaping. It's this whole notion that being in the woods, the outdoors, is the reverential spiritual commune, when for a whole number of people presently in

the population, it's not that. (Warren, 1999, p. 117)

Targeted groups rely on a community structure to survive and prosper in light of an oppressive society with a long history of colonialism. Although outdoor adventure courses can and do offer aspects of community building, there remains an emphasis on individualism that is foreign to the experience of communities of color. Outdoor experiences that are family oriented or neighborhood-community focused need to be brought into the standard outdoor adventure curriculum in order to counter the emphasis on individualism. However, until we are ready to unpack this paradigm, examine how often unseen structures of white privilege inundate outdoor adventure, and make foundational changes, we have no business encouraging people of color to partake in a system that further disadvantages them.

Paradigm of Physical Risk

I introduce this paradigm with a story I call "Willi's Promise." Willi Unsoeld, renowned mountaineer and educator, was a member of the first American expedition to summit Mt. Everest. Later, as a speaker for Outward Bound and professor at Evergreen State College, Unsoeld's exchange with a parent of a student contemplating an outdoor course is the foundation of ideas about risk in outdoor adventure today.

> Parent: Can you guarantee the safety of our son Johnny?
>
> Willi: No, we certainly can't, ma'am. We guarantee you the genuine chance of his death. And if we could guarantee his safety, the program would not be worth running.
>
> Parent: Well! If that's all you have to say. . . .
>
> Willi: No, I have one more thing to say. We do make one guarantee as one parent to another. If you succeed in protecting your boy as you're doing now . . . we guarantee you the death of his soul.

Willi's promise underlies strongly held beliefs about risk and challenge in the outdoor adventure field. The outdoor adventure field dedicated itself to the idea of challenge and risk by advocating its educational value and potential to contribute to individual improvement. Perceived risk is a revered concept that is held onto even while outdoor adventure practitioners and directors attempt to manage risk in a litigious society.

Although outdoor adventure is traditionally viewed as a site of growth-producing risk and challenge, many people of color report feelings of discomfort and fear in the great outdoors. Some research suggests that the African American experience may be the cultural memory of slavery, lynching, and violence that occurred in the outdoors (Erickson, Johnson, and Kivel, 2009; Holland, 2002; Johnson and Bowker, 2004). As Evelyn C. White (1995) explains,

> My genetic memory of ancestors hunted down and preyed upon in rural settings counters my fervent hope of finding peace in the wilderness. Instead of the solace and comfort I seek, I imagine myself in the country as my forebears were—exposed, vulnerable, and unprotected—a target of cruelty and hate. (p. 378)

Hispanics (Carr and Williams, 1993) and Asians (Johnson et al., 2005) also experience an exclusionary fear about venturing into the wild outdoors. The Native American experience has been one of forced removal from outdoor areas (DeLuca and Demo, 2001) and ongoing battles to retain access to public lands that are important to their heritage (Roberts, 2003). Outdoor adventure programs that emphasize physical risk and challenge may not seem welcoming to groups whose historical orientation to the outdoors has been tainted by racism and violence. For people of color, risk, as codified in contemporary outdoor adventure, may not have the great soul- and character-building features of Willi's promise.

Therefore, I suggest we question the concept of risk as an organizing principle of outdoor adventure in favor of self-selected challenge, valuing simple natural experiences, and reframing physical risk to include emotional risk while at the same time appreciating the huge risks of oppression people of color face in considering participating in outdoor adventure. We need to find ways to make programs adventurous without putting undue emphasis on physical risk as the foundation that defines adventure. For example, challenges in deriving health benefits from the outdoors or in creating positive social interactions within the group may be alternatives to risk in adventure programs (Kellert, 1998); these alternatives might alleviate current problems with the risk orientation for people of color in outdoor adventure.

Paradigm of Outdoor Identity

This paradigm concerns the image held about people who lead and participate in outdoor adventure. To imagine being part of outdoor adventure, we need to believe that people like us are involved.

In an exercise I use in my outdoor class, I ask students to draw life-size representations, including all social identity characteristics, of a typical image of an outdoor leader (Warren, 2009). Without fail they draw a young, heterosexual, athletic, white male with snazzy outdoor gear and a pickup truck. Although we know that many different outdoor leaders exist, the activity shows the persistence of the image. In the popular notion of outdoor adventure, a common belief is that outdoor leaders just run around the woods and have a good time. Maverick, informal, unconventional, transient, nonmainstream, and anti-intellectual are words that have been used by some outdoor professionals to describe the image of an outdoor leader in the United States. This conception of who leads in the outdoors is highly exclusionary for anyone who does not match the normative stereotype.

For people of color to join adventure experiences in which other participants and leaders have a stylized identity is alienating. Cosgrove (1995) points out this disconnect:

> The highly elaborated codes of conduct and dress for these areas can be as rigid and exclusive in their moral message as in their expense. They articulate an individualistic, muscular, and active vision of bodily health largely derived from Anglo socio-psychological culture. (p. 37)

Ironically, it is problematic to summon a politics of resistance when a field self-identifies as apolitical, maverick, and outside the mainstream. Societal marginality of a profession gives it little power in responding to social marginality within its ranks. If people of privilege in the field position themselves on the margins, it is difficult to use the dominant privilege they have to address discrimination within the outdoor field or society in general.

Messages about identity in the outdoors come from a variety of sources. Martin (2004) did a content analysis of three popular magazines (*Time*, *Outside*, and *Ebony*) and examined how African Americans were depicted in ads about the outdoors. He found a racialized outdoor identity—a kind of apartheid in the great outdoors in which the outdoors was viewed as white space that included very little representation of African Americans. To further Martin's analysis, I contend that outdoor adventure has its own racialized identity and a long history and practice of whiteness. Given the Native American experience with the cultural commodification and misappropriation of sacred native traditions in outdoor adventure (Oles, 2008), would Native Americans want to be encouraged to attend a traditional outdoor adventure course that incorporates a sweat lodge or a rites-of-passage ceremony?

The history of outdoor adventure is also problematic in that it covers the works of a few prominent men. Early pioneers such as L.B. Sharp of the American camping movement, Kurt Hahn and the establishment of Outward Bound, Paul Petzoldt's influence on the National Outdoor Leadership School and the Wilderness Education Association, and the founders of Project Adventure show that the Euro-American male model defines outdoor adventure (Miles and Priest, 1999; Warren, Mitten, and Loeffler, 2008). That the experience of people of color is invisible and stripped from history is reprehensible. Harris (1997) points out that African Americans have always been aligned with the outdoors but are not perceived as connected to the current white view of enjoying the outdoors:

> We have always been, in fact, a rural, outdoor people—from when we were African to the time when we were uprooted and shipped to this new land to work as sharecroppers. But like the natives of North America who likewise lived for countless generations on the land, or Hispanics, or Middle Easterners, or Laotians, or Polynesians, or just about anyone of color, blacks are not thought of in the context of this new love affair with the recreational outdoors. (p. 110)

To break through this paradigm of normative outdoor identity, it is necessary to critically question the image of who leads and participates in outdoor adventure and whose history is privileged. We must take steps to revise program values by including people of color in the history of outdoor adventure or by providing nonstereotypical images of many different participants and leaders. It is a slow process and constant attention is required for change to occur, but being aware of how white privilege paints the picture of who is included is an essential first step.

Conclusion

In the outdoor adventure field, recognizing who has been included and excluded from the dialogue affects the production of knowledge and, consequently, practice. If the paradigms of outdoor adventure as argued here keep people of color from feeling a sense of belonging, encouraging people of color to join outdoor adventure programs as they are currently constructed will be more damaging to the future of outdoor adventure and contrary to a beneficial experience for all.

Concerns about race and ethnic oppression in outdoor programs should not operate in isolation; they often interact with other identities of privilege and oppression such as class, gender, ability, age, and so on. For outdoor adventure programs to be completely multicultural, the intersections of all social identities need to be considered for inclusive programming. Furthermore, I certainly do not suggest that people of color should not participate in current programs; personal agency and power to make one's own choices are paramount to social justice. Yet, if practitioners in outdoor adventure continue to be vested in inviting and encouraging people of color to participate instead of working for foundational change and paradigm busting, the field of outdoor adventure will never solve this participation gap.

Paradigm shifts are monumental, but if the outdoor adventure field is to include and involve people of color rather than just invite people of color to participate, the worldviews that direct theory and practice must be radically revised and replaced by alternative paradigms. Some of these alternative paradigms include family involvement in outdoor adventure courses, community-based activities rather than individual-based activities, revisiting notions of risk and adventure, urban outdoor adventure, same culture space in groups, culturally sensitive and contextualized models of knowing and teaching, and attention to how white privilege defines outdoor adventure (Warren, 1999).

Fortunately, hope lies in the commitment of many outdoor adventure leaders who seek to educate themselves and act on their understandings. The outdoor adventure field promises to be stronger and more robust when barriers to participation at all levels are consciously removed.

References

Bacon, S. (1983). *The conscious use of metaphor in Outward Bound.* Denver: Colorado Outward Bound School.

Bellah, R.N., Madsen, R., Sullivan, W., Swidler, A., & Tipton, S.M. (1985). *Habits of the heart.* New York: Harper and Row.

Carr, D.S., & Williams, D.R. (1993). Understanding the role of ethnicity in outdoor recreation experiences. *Journal of Leisure Research, 25*(1), 22-38.

Chavez, D.J. (2008). Invite, include, and involve! Racial groups, ethnic groups, and leisure. In M.T. Allison & I.E. Schneider (Eds.), *Diversity and the recreation profession: Organizational perspectives* (pp. 179-191). State College, PA: Venture.

Cosgrove, D. (1995). Habitable earth: Wilderness, empire, and race in America. In D. Rothenberg (Ed.), *Wild ideas* (pp. 27-41). Minneapolis: University of Minnesota Press.

DeLuca, K., & Demo, A. (2001). Imaging nature and erasing class and race: Carleton Watkins, John Muir, and the construction of wilderness. *Environmental History, 6*(4), 541-560.

Erickson, B., Johnson, C.W., & Kivel, B.D. (2009). Rocky Mountain National Park: History and culture as factors in African-American park visitation. *Journal of Leisure Research, 41*(4), 529-545.

Fink, C. (1999). Denials of the genocide of Native Americans. In I.W. Charney (Ed.), *Encyclopedia of genocide* (pp. 166-167). Santa Barbara, CA: ABC-CLIO.

Harris, E.L. (1997). Solo faces. *Outside,* December, 105-110, 177-178.

Holland, J. (2002). *Black recreation: A historical perspective.* Chicago: Burnham.

Jaimes, M.A. (Ed.). (1992). *The state of native America: Genocide, colonization, and resistance.* Cambridge, MA: South End Press.

Johnson, C.Y., & Bowker, J.M. (2004). African-American wildland memories. *Environmental Ethics, 26,* 57-75.

Johnson, C.Y., Bowker, J.M., Cordell, H.K., & Bergstrom, J.C. (2005). Wilderness value differences by immigration, race/ethnicity, gender, and socioeconomic status. In H.K. Cordell, J.C. Bergstrom, & J.M. Bowker (Eds.), *The multiple values of wilderness* (pp. 143-159). State College, PA: Venture.

Kellert, S. (1998). *A national study of outdoor wilderness experience.* New Haven, CT: Yale University.

Kuhn, T. (1962). *The structure of scientific revolutions.* Chicago: University of Chicago Press.

Martin, D.C. (2004). Apartheid in the great outdoors: American advertising and the reproduction of a racialized outdoor leisure identity. *Journal of Leisure Research, 36*(4), 513-535.

Miles, J.C., & Priest, S. (Eds.). (1999). *Adventure programming.* State College, PA: Venture.

Miner, J.L., & Boldt, J. (1981). *Outward Bound USA.* New York: William Morrow.

Nash, R. (2001). *Wilderness and the American mind.* New Haven, CT: Yale University Press.

O'Connell, T.S., Potter, T.G., Curthoys, L.P., Dyment, J.E., & Cuthbertson, B. (2005). A call for sustainability education in post-secondary outdoor recreation program. *International Journal of Sustainability in Higher Education, 6*(1), 81-94.

Oles, G.W.A. (2008). "Borrowing" activities from another culture: A Native American's perspective. In K. Warren, D. Mitten, & T.A. Loeffler (Eds.), *Theory and practice of experiential education* (pp. 423-428). Boulder, CO: Association for Experiential Education.

Roberts, N.S. (2003). Teaching about diversity issues in natural resources and outdoor recreation course. In W.M. Timpson, S.S. Canetto, E. Borrayo, & R. Yang (Eds.), *Teaching diversity, challenges and complexities, identities and integrity* (pp. 227-246). Madison, WI: Atwood.

Virden, R.J., & Walker, G.J. (1999). Ethnic/racial and gender variations among meanings given to, and preferences for, the natural environment. *Leisure Sciences, 21,* 219-239.

Warren, K. (1996). Women's outdoor adventure experience: Myth and reality. In K. Warren (Ed.), *Women's voices in experiential education* (pp. 10-17). Dubuque, IA: Kendall/Hunt.

Warren, K. (1998a). A call for race, gender, and class sensitive facilitation in outdoor experiential education. *Journal of Experiential Education, 21*(1), 21-25.

Warren, K. (1998b). Old paradigms, new visions: Social justice in outdoor adventure. *Ziplines, 37*(1), 54-55.

Warren, K. (1999). *Unpacking the knapsack of outdoor experiential education: Race, gender, and class sensitive outdoor leadership.* Unpublished doctoral dissertation. Cincinnati: Union Institute & University.

Warren, K. (2009). Introduction to social justice in outdoor adventure education. In B. Stremba & C.A. Bisson (Eds.), *Teaching adventure education theory: Best practices* (pp. 221-231). Champaign, IL: Human Kinetics.

Warren, K., Mitten, D.S., & Loeffler, T.A. (Eds.). (2008). *Theory and practice of experiential education.* Boulder, CO: Association for Experiential Education.

Weatherford, J.M. (2010). *Indian givers: How Native Americans transformed the world.* New York: Random House.

White, E.C. (1995). Black women and the wilderness. In T. Jordan & J.R. Hepworth (Eds.), *Stories that shape us: Contemporary women write about the west* (pp. 376-383). New York: Norton.

Yeskel, F. (1995). Breaking the taboo: Discussing power in the classroom. *Holistic Education Review, 8*(3), 38-46.

Controversial Issue 9

Can adventure programming make a meaningful difference in promoting health and wellness in society?

Concerns regarding health and wellness have occupied the field of adventure programming since its beginnings. Organizations such as the Boy Scouts and Outward Bound emerged in large part as a response to the debilitating influences of modern society. Lord Robert Baden-Powell's *Scouting for Boys* (1908), for instance, lists physical health as one of the four aims of the Boy Scouts. The book includes a chapter detailing daily exercise routines and a number of games and outdoor activities that promote physical strength and endurance. The book includes information on maintaining a healthy diet and warns against the perils of overeating as well as eating the wrong kinds of foods. To this point, Baden-Powell (1908) writes: "If you have lots of fresh air you do not want much food; if, on the other hand, you are sitting indoors all day, much food makes you fat and sleepy" (p. 201). The emphasis on health and wellness in scouting became even more pronounced following World War I when, in 1918, the "healthy man" badge was introduced (Zweiniger-Bargielowska, 2005). To earn the badge, scouts had to demonstrate an understanding of how to remain healthy as well as "evidence of at least twelve months following the prescribed health rules" (Zweiniger-Bargielowska, 2005, p. 267).

Kurt Hahn held similar concerns about health and wellness among modern youth. Hahn identified a number of "social declines" or social diseases that he believed were a result of modern lifestyles that emerged during the Industrial Revolution. Among these was a "decline of fitness due to modern methods of locomotion" (Richards, 1999, p. 66). Hahn addressed this concern by emphasizing physical fitness in his various educational endeavors, including the County Badge scheme, the Duke of Edinburgh Award, and Outward Bound. Indeed, physical fitness is one of the four pillars of Outward Bound (McKenzie, 2003). Baden-Powell's and Hahn's concern with health and wellness in Great Britain during the early 20th century reflected broader public health concerns at the time. Zweiniger-Bargielowska (2005) notes, "From the 1880s onward, the medical profession and policy makers became concerned about perceived physical degeneration due to the corrupting influence of modern urban lifestyles in general and an unhealthy diet in particular" (p. 242). Scouting and Outward Bound were just two of a number of approaches that emerged in response to this issue.

Health and wellness remain prevalent social concerns today. On February 9, 2010, the Obama administration announced a new initiative to address the problem of childhood obesity in the United States. Called Let's Move, the initiative was slated to receive nearly $1 billion a year for the first 10 years and to involve the U.S. Department of Education, the U.S. Department of Health and Human Services, the U.S. Department of Agriculture, and the U.S. Department of the Interior. The initiative is based on four core pillars: nutrition education, increased physical activity, easier access to healthy foods, and personal responsibility. First Lady Michelle Obama is currently leading the initiative, and the stated goal is to eliminate childhood obesity in a generation. The problem of childhood obesity has reached epidemic proportions. According to the Centers for Disease Control and Prevention (2011), approximately 17 percent of children and adolescents in America aged 2 to 19 years are currently obese, three times the rate of obesity among children and adolescents a generation ago. The percentages are higher among children and adolescents within minority communities. Being overweight or obese can lead to future health problems, including diabetes, heart disease, and a host of other illnesses. The aim of the initiative is to get people to think differently about eating and fitness.

The question for adventure programmers is whether the adventure programming industry can effectively contribute to addressing this and other health concerns in society. Many are trying. Project Adventure, for example, has worked to promote physical fitness through the use of adventure activities in physical education in schools. It has developed several programs and published numerous texts to this end, including *Adventure Curriculum for Physical Education* (Panicucci et al., 2003) and *Creating Healthy Habits: An Adventure Guide to Teaching Health and Wellness* (Kilty, 2006). Summer weight-loss camps, many of which are adventure based, have emerged in recent years as a popular approach to addressing the issue of child and adult obesity. Scouting and Outward Bound both remain committed to promoting health and wellness in youths. Despite these efforts, can the industry really make a difference in addressing issues related to health and wellness in society?

Alan Ewert argues unequivocally that adventure programming is positively associated with issues related to human health and wellness and that this connection is greatly strengthened when these programs occur in natural and outdoor environments. He attributes this positive relationship between human health and wellness and adventure programming to the restorative value of natural environments, physiological benefits that can result from the physically active nature of adventure programs, and a range of psychosocial benefits that can result from group interactions in adventure program contexts.

Andy Szolosi, on the other hand, argues that although the contention that adventure programming can make a meaningful difference in promoting health and wellness in society may seem compelling, the very premise fails to recognize the full scope and complexity that surrounds many of the issues related to health and wellness in our society. Szolosi argues that adventure programming professionals are ill equipped to address the daunting health challenges that our public health system has struggled to overcome and that such challenges exceed the scope of the adventure programming industry.

References

Baden-Powell, R. (1908). *Scouting for boys.* London: C.A. Pearson Ltd.

Centers for Disease Control and Prevention. (2011). Childhood overweight and obesity. www.cdc.gov/obesity/childhood/data.html [December 21, 2011].

Kilty, K. (2006). *Creating healthy habits: An adventure guide to teaching health and wellness.* Beverly, MA: Project Adventure Inc.

McKenzie, M. (2003). Beyond "The Outward Bound Process": Rethinking student learning. *Journal of Experiential Education, 26*(1), 8-23.

Panicucci, J., Constable, N., Hunt, L., Kohut, A., & Rheingold, A. (2003). *Adventure curriculum for physical education.* Beverly, MA: Project Adventure Inc.

Richards, A. (1999). Kurt Hahn. In J.C. Miles & S. Priest (Eds.), *Adventure programming* (pp. 65-70). State College, PA: Venture.

Zweiniger-Bargielowska, I. (2005). The culture of the abdomen: Obesity and reducing in Britain, circa 1900-1939. *Journal of British Studies, 44*(2), 239-273.

Can adventure programming make a meaningful difference in promoting health and wellness in society?

YES Take a Park, Not a Pill: Promoting Health and Wellness Through Adventure Programming

Alan Ewert, PhD, professor of recreation, park, and tourism studies, Indiana University, Bloomington, Indiana, United States

"Climb the mountains and get their good tidings. Nature's peace will flow into you as sunshine flows into trees. The winds blow their own freshness into you and the storms their energy, while cares drop off like autumn leaves."

—John Muir

John Muir's often-quoted statement not only elegantly describes his belief in the power of natural landscapes but also characterizes one of the questions facing our society: what is the value of experiencing undeveloped natural environments through personal visitation, structured programs, or simply knowing that they are there? More specifically, does a connection exist between human health and adventure-based programs that occur in natural environments? We argue that the answer to this question is unequivocally yes. The extant literature and personal experience suggest that adventure programming is positively associated with issues related to human health, and this connection is greatly strengthened when these programs occur in natural and outdoor environments. Moreover, three factors make adventure programming effective in promoting health and wellness:

1. the environment in which most adventure activities take place;
2. the activities themselves, which typically require physical activity and movement; and
3. participation in adventure activities, which often helps develop social networks and support that is conducive to personal health.

To build this case, we start with a brief synopsis of natural environments and the values that society places on them. We expand on this thinking by summarizing some of the major theories underlying the belief that nature can be exceptionally potent in promoting characteristics associated with positive human health. These include biophilia, psychoevolutionary theory, and attention restoration theory. Following this, we discuss the specific benefits of adventure programming as related to health and wellness. Finally, we explore the concept of intentionally designed experiences. It is through these intentionally designed experiences that adventure programming can serve as a particularly effective catalyst in promoting behaviors that lead to positive human health.

Natural Environments and Societal Values

Society places value on different components associated with nature and natural environments. Historically, this worth was measured in the form of goods such as board feet of timber, cubic feet of free-flowing water, or tons of a particular mineral; this worth has now extended to other, less-tangible benefits. In addition, natural settings provide a substantial number of functions related to ecosystem processes such as the absorption of pollutants and nutrient recycling. However, beyond the obvious material outputs that natural environments provide, there also exist a number of values that are either ethereal or difficult to measure (Harmon and Putney, 2003).

For example, individuals value their visit to the local park or forest. Likewise, society places value on many of the functions that naturally functioning ecosystems inherently perform, such as the fresh air or fresh water that we all need and enjoy. Some values, however, present a more complicated picture in that they have both intrinsic and extrinsic worth. For example, natural environments are valued by some individuals because of the therapeutic impacts they may have (Bandoroff and Newes, 2004). Others would place an economic value on adventure programming in natural environments (Hanley, Shaw, and Wright, 2003). And herein rests the two assumptions of interest in this argument. First, a substantial amount of past and ongoing research posits and supports that natural environments have the capacity to promote health and wellness in societies across the globe (Frumkin, 2001). Second, although nature can be good for you, structured programs such as those offered through adventure education can make it even more effective. These two points constitute the bulk of our argument.

Benefits Associated With Nature

"The enjoyment of scenery employs the mind without fatigue and yet exercises it; tranquilizes it and yet enlivens it; and thus, through the influence of the mind over the body, gives the effect of refreshing rest and reinvigoration to the whole system."

—Frederick Law Olmstead

As this quote illustrates, Frederick Law Olmstead (1822-1903) certainly thought that viewing scenes depicting nature was extremely beneficial to individuals and, more collectively, to communities and groups (aesthetic value). Yet, beyond the aesthetic quality and tranquility associated with a beautiful natural scene, do natural environments have any redeeming qualities and contributions relative to human health and wellness? One can pose this question in three ways:

1. Is nature beneficial?
2. How is nature beneficial?
3. Why is nature beneficial?

The literature follows what most of us have already suspected: that nature provides individuals with positive and beneficial experiences. Moreover, natural environments mediate these experiences in essentially five ways:

1. Recovery from stress and attention fatigue
2. Encouraging physical activity
3. Facilitating social contact
4. Encouraging optimal development
5. Providing opportunities for personal development and sense of purpose

Of these five mediating factors, recovery from stress and attention fatigue has received the most research attention (Bowler et al., 2010), followed by increased physical activity (Kaczynski and Henderson, 2007). Within the contexts of stress and attention fatigue, three theoretical pathways—biophilia hypothesis, psychoevolutionary theory, and attention restoration theory—serve to provide the explanatory foundation.

Biophilia Hypothesis

The biophilia hypothesis, first described by E.O. Wilson (1984, 1993), states that humans have innate tendency to affiliate with natural things and that this mind–body connection reacts fully to nature. Thus, when humans are exposed to natural objects or views, a response is elicited within the physiological, psychological, and emotional domains. When placed in natural environments, individuals experience a wide range of emotions including attraction, aversion, peacefulness, and fear-driven anxiety (Wilson, 1993). In turn, these emotions are linked to adaptive learning rules that govern how we learn about and from nature. Wilson captures this belief in the adaptation of humans through learning in and about the natural environment when he suggests that this "learning" about the natural environment took thousands of years to develop and is with us, as a species, yet today.

Kellert (1993) furthered this thinking by surmising that people have a biological need to feel connected to the natural world. As a result of this linkage, the response to a nonthreatening natural environment stimulus has a positive effect on an individual's emotional state, which, in turn, affects their physiological activity levels and autonomic responses (Berto, 2007).

Psychoevolutionary Theory

Folding into the biophilia hypothesis is the psychoevolutionary theory. Based on the proposition that affect precedes cognition (Ulrich, 1983), psychoevolutionary theory emphasizes emotions and the immediacy of affect or feeling. In turn, this connection between natural environments and affect or feelings serves to reduce stress reactions. That is, because of our ancestral direct connection to natural landscapes, humans can experience immediate reactions to natural environments well before they have had a chance to analyze these environments through cognitive processes. Stress connotes a physiological response to situations that threaten well-being and often manifests in physiological

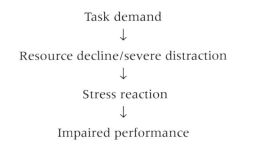

Task demand
↓
Resource decline/severe distraction
↓
Stress reaction
↓
Impaired performance

Figure 9.1 Generalized model of stress and individual performance.

indictors such as increased autonomic arousal (e.g., increased heart rate or elevated blood pressure). Figure 9.1 illustrates a generalized model of stress.

Conversely, stress recovery occurs in settings that evoke interest, pleasantness, and calm. This is where biophilia and psychoevolutionary theory integrate; that is, humans are attracted to natural environments, and this attraction helps reduce negative factors such as stress. Indeed, natural landscapes contain a number of dimensions that are associated with restoring scenes, including

- moderate complexity;
- a focal point; and
- natural contents, most notably vegetation and water.

Thus, natural environments serve as stress recovery settings and point to a number of important outcomes for humans under stress. These dimensions involve replacing negative affect with positive feelings, inhibiting negative thoughts, and decreasing autonomic and cortical responses such as fight, flight, or freeze. Psychoevolutionary theory can be conceptualized as shown in figure 9.2.

One of the most salient studies that supports the concept of the psychoevolutionary theory investigated the effect of viewing nature on recovery rates of surgery patients. After randomly assigning surgery patients to either a hospital room with a view of nature or a hospital room without such a view, Ulrich (1984) found evidence that the patients with the view of nature had shorter recovery times, required less pain medication, and had fewer incidents of medical issues associated with their surgery compared with the patients without the view of nature. Ulrich (1981) suggests the results from this study point to a proposition that people benefit most from visual contact with nature as opposed to urban environments lacking nature. Moreover,

for individuals experiencing stress or excessive arousal, nature views appear to reduce arousal more effectively than urban scenes and hence are more beneficial in a psychophysiological sense.

Attention Restoration Theory

Based on the work of William James (1842-1910), attention restoration theory presupposes that attention is either voluntary or directed (involuntary). Directed attention requires effort, plays a central role in achieving and maintaining focus, is usually under a cognitive-control process, controls distraction through the use of inhibition, plays a central role in problem-solving, and is susceptible to fatigue. This susceptibility to fatigue forms the underlying role of natural environments in attention restoration theory. Essentially, the attention restoration theory model assumes the components shown in figure 9.3.

According to Kaplan and Kaplan (1989), restorative settings, as provided through natural environments, can effectively aid in the recovery from directed-attention fatigue through the following properties:

- Fascination: engages attention effortlessly and thus allows directed attention to rest
- Being away: physically or conceptually different from one's usual environment
- Extent: setting is rich and coherent enough to engage the mind and promote exploration
- Compatibility: implies a good fit between one's inclinations and purposes and the activities supported by the setting

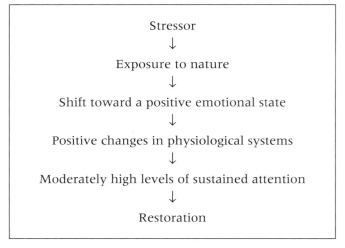

Stressor
↓
Exposure to nature
↓
Shift toward a positive emotional state
↓
Positive changes in physiological systems
↓
Moderately high levels of sustained attention
↓
Restoration

Figure 9.2 A model describing the psychoevolutionary theory process.

Directed attention requires effort to maintain focus and avoid distractions.

↓

Directed attention fatigues and results in difficulty in focusing, irritability, and distraction.

↓

Involuntary attention results in a replenishment of directed attention mechanisms.

Figure 9.3 A generalized model of the attention restoration theory.

Moreover, fascination can take two forms: hard fascination and soft fascination. Hard fascination refers to experiences or activities that are intense and riveting and allow limited space or time for reflection or cognitive activity. Soft fascination involves activities or experiences that are moderate in intensity and can focus an individual's attention while allowing for reflection and cognition. Peaceful, natural settings are often thought to be good locations for experiencing soft fascination.

A substantial amount of research has demonstrated the efficacy of the attention restoration construct. For example, people exposed to natural settings generally report better performance on tasks that demand attention (Taylor, Kuo, and Sullivan, 2001, 2002). Natural views from home are positively related to effective functioning and feeling at peace and are negatively related to distraction (Kaplan, 2001). People who live near nature report improved interpersonal relations and the ability to effectively handle major life issues (Kuo, 2001). Exposure to natural environments may be related to improved self-control, reduced attention-deficit disorder symptoms, and improved care in treating dementia (Bossen, 2010).

The Health Benefits of Adventure Programming

The literature and our own personal experiences generally point to a connection between human health and natural environments. Does the same connection carry over to experiences and activities associated with adventure programming? For example, aspects of quality of life that are often influenced by natural environments include perceived safety, physical health and exercise, emotional well-being, a sense of community, social interaction, enjoyment, appropriate levels of stimulation, and a sense of autonomy and control. Beyond the fact that most adventure activities occur in natural or outdoor environments, do some underlying commonalities link adventure programming, natural landscapes, and human health? Louv's (2005) *Last Child in the Woods* effectively promotes the idea that nature is desirable and even necessary for the proper development of children but is relatively silent on the issue of adventure education and health-related issues. However, as mentioned in Louv (2005, p. 225), Taylor and Kuo point out that some of the most exciting findings of a link between contact with green space and developmental outcomes come from studies examining the effects of outdoor challenge programs on children's self-esteem and sense of self.

Drawing back to Berlyne's (1960) arousal theory, to be restorative, levels of arousal must be sufficiently but not overly complex or intense and have understandable consequences that are somewhat under the control of the participant. Likewise, participation in adventure programs has often been associated with developmental outcomes such as personal growth, enhanced interpersonal skills, and group development (Ewert and Garvey, 2007; Passarelli, Hall, and Anderson, 2010). McKenzie (2000) attributes these outcomes to four characteristics that are common to many adventure program experiences:

1. the unfamiliar nature of the physical environment;
2. the incremental and progressive sequencing of the challenges presented through the adventure program experience;
3. the processing of the experience in order to identify and organize meaning to the participant; and
4. the use of small groups to facilitate issues such as reciprocity, group cohesiveness, interpersonal relationships, and balance between group belonging and individual autonomy.

Thus, many of the attributes associated with adventure program activities and experiences are similar to those attributed to healthy lifestyles or behaviors.

The field of adventure programming has an historical literature base that supports the efficacy of these areas in promoting human health. For example, Eastman (1921) extols the importance of out-of-door activities in maintaining good health, especially of the physical and nervous systems. Fast forward to the present and one can find a plethora of studies and papers that examine the impacts of adventure-based activities on a number of variables often associated with either actual health conditions (e.g., level of fitness) or health promotion (e.g., variable associated with making decisions about health behavior, such as smoking cessation). For example, Ewert and Yoshino (2011) found increases in levels of resilience of college students after they participated in an adventure education program. In addition, Grocott and Hunter (2009) found that participation in an adventure-based sailing program enhanced both global and domain-specific attributes of self-esteem. Both self-esteem and resilience are often linked to health behaviors and healthy lifestyles.

Moreover, not just the adventure activities serve as the vehicles to influence human health attitudes and behaviors. The location in which these adventures take place can also play a critical role. Cole and Hall (2010) investigated the connection between Wilderness landscapes and restoration. Their findings pointed to substantial reductions in stress levels and increases in mental rejuvenation following visits to wilderness areas. Miles (1987) provided the foundation of this work by examining the way that wilderness or wilderness-like areas contribute to physical, emotional, or spiritual health.

Not surprising, research demonstrates a consistent link between physical exercise and human health (Pretty et al., 2007). In addition, a number of physiological health-related benefits are linked to participation in adventure programming. For example, Russell and Phillips-Miller (2002) found that hiking and physical exercise were critical components of a wilderness therapy program. Jelalian and colleagues (2006) found that an adventure therapy program patterned after Outward Bound served as an effective adjunct therapy for reducing weight in adolescents. In a similar fashion, Caulkins, White, and Russell (2006) report that physical exercise plays an important role in wilderness therapy for adolescent women.

It seems clear that the physical activity inherent in most adventure programming activities contributes to human health in a variety of ways, such as enhancing fitness, aerobic training, and balance. However, the often short-term and episodic nature of these activities suggests that the true power of adventure programming in affecting health and wellness lies not just in the physicality of the activities but also in the promotion of health-enhancing behaviors. For example, Bowler and colleagues (2010) found less consistency in the evidence supporting the idea that natural environments affect variables such as blood pressure, hormone levels, or immune functioning and much more consistency in positive changes in self-reported variables such as revitalization, reductions in anger and anxiety, levels of attention, and lower depression. Marcus and Forsyth (2009) suggest that the most important variables related to health behaviors such as physical activity include self-efficacy, a sense of achievement, and social support systems. Thus, the true value of adventure programming may lie in the affective outcomes it often produces in addition to the movement and activity inherent in the experiences.

A Model Linking Human Health and Adventure Programming

With few exceptions, the research and subsequent literature strongly suggest that adventure programming is linked to human health in a variety of ways, such as physicality, emotional health, spiritual development, resilience, and attitude. One key component in this linkage between health and adventure is the use of intentionally designed experiences. Although psychoevolutionary theory, biophilia, and attention restoration theory provide a foundation of understanding relative to the relationship between human health and natural environments, they remain somewhat passive. That is, they provide a backdrop for understanding the impact of people simply being in a natural environment. Intentionally designed experiences, on the other hand, provide an active component; that is, people are engaged in programmed and structured activities in natural environments. Thus, the intentionally designed experience builds on the power of the natural environment to enhance its benefits to human health. Figure 9.4 illustrates this model.

As figure 9.4 shows, psychoevolutionary theory, biophilia, and attention restoration theory serve as the foundational theories for understanding the connection between natural environments and human health—the very places where most adventure programming takes place. These inputs are passive, however, in that they provide a pos-

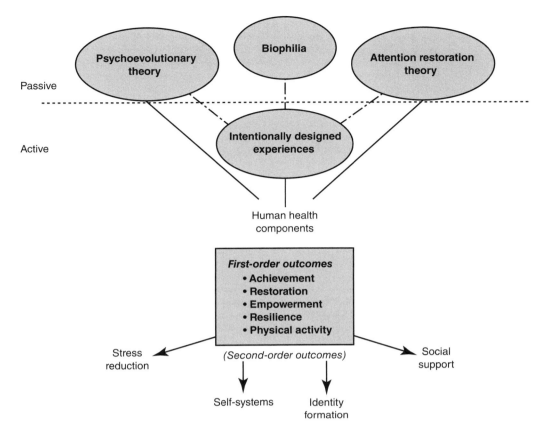

Figure 9.4 Model of the relationship between intentionally designed experiences and natural environment theories.

Reprinted from A. Ewert, J. Overholt, A. Voight, and C.C. Wang, 2011, Understanding the transformative aspects of the Wilderness and Protected Lands experience upon human health. In *Science and stewardship to protect and sustain wilderness values: Ninth World Wilderness Congress symposium, November 6-13, 2009, Merida, Yucatan, Mexico* (Proceedings RMRS-P-64), compiled by A. Watson, J. Murrieta-Saldivar, and B. McBride (Fort Collins, CO: U.S. Department of Agriculture, Forest Service, Rocky Mountain Research Station), 142.

sible explanation of what happens when individuals are exposed to natural environments. Natural environments can powerfully induce positive benefits to a person; however, intentionally designed experiences are often critical to combining the affect of the natural setting with the effectiveness of structured and purposely designed experiences. In turn, these designed experiences result in a set of first-order outcomes that provide a foundation for subsequent outcomes. These primary outcomes include achievement, restoration, empowerment, resilience, and physical activity. For example, return to the Cole and Hall (2010) study that found that wilderness environments can provide restoration and mental rejuvenation. Second-order outcomes that emerge from the primary outcomes and that connect to human health and well-being include self-systems, identity formation, social support, and stress reduction. For example, Holman and McAvoy (2005) report that beneficial outcomes from participation in an integrated adventure program included achievement and self-awareness.

Conclusion

It seems clear and more than self-evident that the plethora of information constructed from personal experience, anecdotal records, and systematic research points to an important and beneficial effect of adventure-based programs on the factors that are considered important in maintaining or promoting human health and wellness (e.g., self-concept, sense of control, personal responsibility, and so on). Moreover, these effects often occur in tandem with the use of a natural environment to provide a setting or backdrop for these types of programs.

The answer to the root question posed in this chapter—can adventure programming make a meaningful difference in promoting health and wellness in society?—is multidimensional but also very clear: yes. The multidimensional aspects of the answer present themselves in a number of follow-up questions. Although the answer to the question remains yes, the extent of this impact can be appended by "it depends." For example, the magnitude of the difference that adventure programming in natural environments can make depends on a number of factors and variables, including the following:

- Novelty: Are these effects primarily due to the presence of novelty or a systematic effect from program, nature, or both?

- Dosage: What role does length of the adventure experience and the intensity of that experience play in the outcomes related to human health?

- Fidelity: What effect will changes in variables such as program, externalities such as weather and instructor type, and student mix have on the reported or experienced outcomes from the program?

In conclusion, adventure-based programming and natural environments can provide a spectrum of powerful synergistic outcomes related to human health and wellness. These outcomes can often far exceed those alluded to in the concept of nature-deficit disorder and have served societies across the world with health-enhancing experiences and activities.

References

Bandoroff, S., & Newes, S. (2004). *Coming of age: The evolving field of adventure therapy.* Boulder, CO: Association for Experiential Education.

Berlyne, D. (1960). *Conflict, arousal, and curiosity.* New York: McGraw-Hill.

Berto, R. (2007). Assessing the restorative value of the environment: A study on the elderly in comparison with young adults and adolescents. *International Journal of Psychology, 42,* 331-341.

Bossen, A. (2010). The importance of getting back to nature for people with dementia. *Journal of Gerontological Nursing, 36*(2), 17-22.

Bowler, D.E., Buyung-Ali, L.M., Knight, T.M., & Pullin, A.S. (2010). A systematic review of evidence for the added benefits to health of exposure to natural environments. *BMC Public Health, 10,* 456.

Caulkins, M.C., White, D.D., & Russell, K.C. (2006). The role of physical exercise in wilderness therapy for troubled adolescent women. *Journal of Experiential Education, 29*(1), 18-37.

Cole, D.N., & Hall, T.E. (2010). Experiencing the restorative components of Wilderness environments: Does congestion interfere and does length of exposure matter? *Environment and Behavior, 42*(6), 806-823.

Eastman, C.A. (1921). What can the out-of-doors do for our children? *Education, 41*(9), 599-605.

Ewert, A., & Garvey, D. (2007). Philosophy and theory of adventure education. In D. Prouty, J. Panicucci, & R. Collinson (Eds.), *Adventure education: Theory and applications* (pp. 19-32). Champaign, IL: Human Kinetics.

Ewert, A., Overholt, J., Voight, A., & Wang, C. (2011). Understanding the transformative aspects of the Wilderness and Protected Lands experience upon human health. In A. Watson, J. Murrieta-Saldivar, & B. McBride (compilers), *Science and stewardship to protect and sustain wilderness values: Ninth World Wilderness Congress symposium, November 6-13, 2009, Merida, Yucatan, Mexico* (Proceedings RMRS-P-64). Fort Collins, CO: U.S. Department of Agriculture, Forest Service, Rocky Mountain Research Station.

Ewert, A., & Yoshino, A. (2011). The influence of short-term adventure-based experiences on levels of resilience. *Journal of Adventure Education and Outdoor Learning, 11*(1), 35-50.

Frumkin, H. (2001). Beyond toxicity: Human health and the natural environment. *American Journal of Preventative Health, 20,* 234-240.

Grocott, A.C., & Hunter, J.A. (2009). Increases in global and domain specific self-esteem following a 10 day developmental voyage. *Social Psychology of Education, 12,* 443-459.

Hanley, N., Shaw, W.D., & Wright, R.E. (2003). *The new economics of outdoor recreation.* Cheltenham, U.K.: Edward Elgar.

Harmon, D., & Putney, A.D. (Eds.). (2003). *The full value of parks: From economics to the intangible.* Boulder, CO: Rowman and Littlefield.

Holman, T., & McAvoy, L.H. (2005). Transferring benefits of participation in an integrated wilderness adventure program to daily life (SEER 2004 Abstract). *Journal of Experiential Education, 27*(3), 322-325.

Jelalian, E., Mehlenbeck, R., Lloyd-Richardson, E.E., Birmaher, V., & Wing, R.R. (2006). 'Adventure therapy' combined with cognitive-behavioral treatment for overweight adolescents. *International Journal of Obesity, 30,* 31-39.

Kaczynski, A.T., & Henderson, K.A. (2007). Environmental correlates of physical activity: A review of evidence about parks and recreation. *Leisure Sciences, 29,* 315-354.

Kaplan, R. (2001). The nature of the view from home: Psychological benefits. *Environment and Behavior, 33*(4), 507.

Kaplan, R., & Kaplan, S. (1989). *The experience of nature: A psychological perspective.* Cambridge, U.K.: Cambridge University Press.

Kellert, S. (1993). The biological basis for human values of nature. In S. Kellert & E.O. Wilson (Eds.), *The biophilia hypothesis* (pp. 42-69). Washington, DC: Shearwater Books/Island Press.

Kuo, F.E. (2001). Coping with poverty: Impacts of environment and attention in the Inner City. *Environment and Behavior, 33,* 5-34.

Louv, R. (2005). *Last child in the woods: Saving our children from nature-deficit disorder.* Chapel Hill, NC: Algonquin Books of Chapel Hill.

Marcus, B.H., & Forsyth, L.H. (2009). *Motivating people to be physically active.* Champaign, IL: Human Kinetics.

McKenzie, M.D. (2000). How are adventure education program outcomes achieved? A review of the literature. *Australian Journal of Outdoor Education, 5*(1), 19-28.

Miles, J. (1987). Wilderness as healing place. *Journal of Experiential Education, 10*(3), 4-10.

Passarelli, A., Hall, E., & Anderson, M. (2010). A strength-based approach to outdoor and adventure education: Possibilities for personal growth. *Journal of Experiential Education, 33*(2), 120-135.

Pretty, J., Peacock, J., Hine, R., Sellens, M., South, N., & Griffin, M. (2007). Green exercise in the UK countryside: Effects on health and psychological well-being, and implications for policy and planning. *Journal of Environmental Planning and Management, 50*, 211-231.

Russell, K.C., & Phillips-Miller, D. (2002). Perspectives on the wilderness therapy process and its relation to outcome. *Child and Youth Care Forum, 31*(6), 415-437.

Taylor, A., Kuo, F., & Sullivan, W. (2001). Coping with ADD: The surprising connection to green play settings. *Environment and Behavior, 33*(1), 54.

Taylor, A., Kuo, F., & Sullivan, W. (2002). Views of nature and self-discipline: Evidence from inner city children. *Journal of Environmental Psychology, 22*(1-2), 49-63.

Ulrich, R. (1981). Natural versus urban scenes: Some psychophysiological effects. *Environment and Behavior, 13*(5), 523-556.

Ulrich, R.S. (1983). Aesthetic and affective response to natural environments. In I. Altman & J.F. Wohlwill (Eds.), *Behavior and the natural environment* (pp. 85-125). New York: Plenum Press.

Ulrich, R.S. (1984). View through a window may influence recovery from surgery. *Science, 224*, 420-421.

Wilson, E.O. (1984). *Biophilia: The human bond with other species.* Cambridge, MA: Harvard University Press.

Wilson, E.O. (1993). Biophilia and the conservation ethic. In S. Kellert & E.O. Wilson (Eds.), *The biophilia hypothesis* (pp. 31-40). Washington, DC: Island Press.

Can adventure programming make a meaningful difference in promoting health and wellness in society?

NO Adventure Programming and Public Health: Dreaming Big or Just Dreaming?

Andrew Szolosi, PhD, assistant professor of recreation and sport pedagogy, Ohio University, Athens, Ohio, United States

Richard Louv, a renowned author best known for his work *Last Child in the Woods* (2005), has helped to popularize the notion that interaction with nature can promote a variety of benefits related to health and wellness. The major premise underlying Louv's argument stems from studies that have indicated that contact with the natural world can provide a person with a multitude of emotional, cognitive, and physical benefits (Kaplan and Kaplan, 1989; Mackay and Neill, 2010; Ulrich, 1983). People often attribute these same types of benefits to adventure-based programs. Adventure-based programs tend to be socially oriented and physically demanding and take place in natural surroundings. Those characteristics presumably create a set of conditions that can serve as a catalyst for change (Walsh and Golins, 1976). Much of the evidence garnered from studies that have examined adventure experience outcomes supports that notion (Hattie et al., 1997). Connecting these dots, some have generalized that adventure-based programs can make a meaningful difference in areas related to health and wellness (Hattie et al., 1997; Jelalian et al., 2006). Although that contention may seem compelling, its very premise fails to recognize the complexity that surrounds many issues related to health and wellness in our society.

Promoting health and wellness is by no means an easy task. Public health agencies charged with promoting healthy behavior are often rightly the target of a great deal of criticism that stems from the failure of different agencies to effectively and efficiently deliver the outcome desired for the public's health (Sultz and Young, 2011). Given this, how can we reasonably expect adventure programming to make a meaningful contribution to promoting health and wellness when government-funded organizations established expressly to accomplish those purposes have struggled to meet such objectives? Although adventure programming may at times offer participants an array of benefits, it is not currently and likely never will be positioned to effectively address problems related to health and wellness in society. Understanding the limitations of adventure programming within the context of public health may perhaps best illustrate that point.

This argument addresses current challenges facing our public health system and examines why adventure programming is ill equipped to address those challenges. This analysis begins with what is possibly the most fundamental aspect of the issue: how do we define health? After we establish a foundational understanding of that concept, the discourse then focuses on three prominent health challenges that society currently faces. The examination of each health challenge includes a corresponding argument that outlines the obstacles adventure programming is likely to face in addressing that health issue. Those arguments are based on one of two positions:

1. Challenges associated with adventure programming interventions
2. The limited reach of adventure programming

In carefully examining each of these themes within the context of the health challenges identified, one can begin to understand the reality of the situation. Adventure programming, as an industry, is overmatched and unqualified to address the prominent issues currently confronting the health and wellness needs of the public. Although advocates of the adventure programming profession have never shied away from dreaming big, any notions they have about the industry having a meaningful effect on public health may in fact be just a dream.

Models of Public Health

From a distance, the definition of *health* may seem obvious: the simple absence of illness or disease. However, as one attempts to more precisely define that concept, the complexities surrounding the term become apparent. For example, a person can be ill without having a disease or can have a disease without being ill. Such intricacy tends to highlight the challenges that are often associated with defining health. For some people, health may refer to having strength or a high quality of life. For others, the term may more accurately correspond to the absence of a physical disability, a mental disability, or even pain. These and other divergent views of health have led to the conceptualization of health into more formal models: the medical model, the World Health Organization (WHO) model, the wellness model, and the environmental model.

The medical model, which views health as the absence of disease or disability, has historically been the predominant view of health (Larson, 1999). Under this paradigm, there is an acute focus on objective measures that lead to the diagnosis and treatment of an ailment. Given this narrow view of the concept, other models of health have adopted a more holistic position.

The constitution of the WHO defines health as "a state of complete physical, mental, and social well-being" (World Health Organization, 1947, p. 100). Although this conception is widely considered the most popular today, the WHO model has received criticism for its lack of practicality (Saracci, 1997). Critics suggest that rather than providing a specific course of action, the WHO model more closely embodies a utopian view of health that is near impossible for anyone to truly realize, attain, or even measure (Larson, 1999).

Later interpretations of health have taken a slightly different approach to the concept. For instance, the wellness model tends to emphasize the link between the mind and the body. From this perspective, health is a feeling or experience that is internal to an individual (Marvin and Crown, 1976). Such experiences or feelings, when they do occur, can presumably affect even the simplest of physical processes. Consequently, this stance on health tends to focus on subjective perceptions such as happiness and other personal feelings.

The environmental model asserts that health exists to the extent an organism can grow, thrive, and function within its environment (Abanobi, 1986). Although each of the described models provides a means by which to organize and understand the parameters of human health, the conflicting value systems that exist within each model tend to underscore the incessant challenges related to the health domain.

Current Challenges to Public Health

During the past century, numerous advancements have been made in direct response to the challenges that have confronted the broader public health community, such as childhood immunization, fortified foods, and clean water (Koplan and Fleming, 2000). Although there is certainly good reason to be proud of the progress made, the issues confronting the public health sector are unrelenting. The Centers for Disease Control and Prevention has identified a number of public health challenges that will need continued attention in the decades to come (Koplan and Fleming, 2000). Though the list of health challenges is extensive, a few profound public health issues are regularly at the forefront of discussion. The health challenges selected as part of this review represent issues that tend to elicit or dominate discussion in the health sector (Marmot, 2007; McCray, 2005; Wadden, Brownell, and Foster, 2002). As well, each of the presented health challenges focuses on aspects of the public health crisis that relate to the origin of the problem, factors contributing to the problem, or the resultant consequences.

Public Health Literacy

According to the American Medical Association, health literacy is a strong predictor of a person's health (American Medical Association, 1999). The term "health literacy" refers to a person's ability to obtain, comprehend, and make use of basic health information (U.S. Department of Health and Human Services, 2000). A person must have health literacy in order to be able to make informed health decisions. Regrettably, a large majority of people in our society possess low or inadequate health literacy. For some, this is a result of having limited access to health information. For many others, the information presented does little to motivate them toward a healthier lifestyle either because they do not understand the information or they do not know how to use the information. In essence, health information by itself is often insufficient and futile in developing a sense of health literacy. Approaches that allow for longer periods of time and that are more comprehensive in nature tend to be the most effective in promoting health literacy (Nutbeam, 2000). Such an approach provides a person with opportunities to build skills that are critical to sustaining a healthy lifestyle. Although effective, these sorts of methods have a number of inherent challenges, especially within the context of adventure programming.

Challenges Associated With Adventure Programming Interventions

The existing research in the area of adventure programming has largely supported adventure as a vehicle for change (Cason and Gillis, 1994; Goldenberg, McAvoy, and Klenosky, 2005; Hattie et al., 1997). Despite that espousal, the literature often identifies clear limitations and weaknesses that are worthy of some consideration. One of the more prominent issues discussed within the literature deals with durability—that is, the extent to which the changes accrued from an adventure experience are lasting. Very few studies have actually examined the long-term effects that an adventure-based program can have on a person (Hattie et al., 1997). As a result, the utility of a program may come into question if the health education outcomes achieved are hardly sustainable or integrated into a person's everyday life. Engineering adventure experiences that can have a lasting impact requires an approach that focuses just as much on the process as it does on the outcome (Ewert, 1987; Tucker and Rheingold, 2010). Until recently, researchers had largely ignored this area of study (Sibthorp, Paisley, and Gookin, 2007). Understanding the mechanisms of change is certainly necessary if adventure programming is to stand even with other health-related interventions. One such mechanism that may hinder adventure programming's ability to promote health literacy is the length and duration of an adventure experience.

Length and Intensity of Interventions

Adventure programming experiences are heterogeneous in nature; they often involve a variety of activities, take place in dissimilar locations, and occur over a period varying in length or intensity. Each of those program characteristics can play a vital role in the process by which participants achieve certain adventure experience outcomes (Sibthorp, Paisley, and Gookin, 2007). The length and intensity of an adventure experience are important components that deserve attention. In previous studies, longer and more substantial adventure experiences tended to produce the greatest effects on targeted outcome measures (Cason and Gillis, 1994; Hattie et al., 1997; Sibthorp, Paisley, and Gookin, 2007). Certain adventure programming experiences are likely to rival other types of health and wellness interventions in their length and intensity; however, experiences such as these are very much the anomaly. By and large, most adventure programming experiences are of a very short length and of low intensity and consist of aims in which health

and wellness may not even be explicit (Hattie et al., 1997). Such realities become even more striking when compared with traditional health and wellness interventions.

Within a more conventional context, an abundance of research has addressed the efficacy that specific types of interventions can have on factors related to health and wellness. One of the more prominent studies in this field of inquiry is the HERITAGE Family Study. As part of the study, a consortium of researchers examined the effect that regular physical activity could have on a number of variables. One facet of the study aimed to address the effectiveness of a 20-week training session on a series of factors related to body composition (Wilmore et al., 1999). The data indicated that a 20-week, short-term exercise intervention could lead to changes in body composition; however, the magnitude of those changes was of limited significance. As a result, the researchers concluded that physical activity was likely to have a major effect on body composition and other aspects related to human health, but only if that activity was of greater intensity and sustained over a longer period of time. Studies such as this provide a point of reference from which one can truly surmise the efficacy of adventure programming in promoting human health and developing a sense of health literacy. Of course, that assessment is contingent on a person's interpretation of the meaning of health.

Adventure Programming: How Do We Define Health?

Adventure-based programs are inherently physical by design; however, physical fitness and other health-related outcomes are not often the primary aim of those types of programs. In fact, many adventure-based programs tend to focus solely on measures related to self-concept or closely related constructs (Cason and Gillis, 1994; Hattie et al., 1997). Although it is a valuable component within most models of health, that approach does not fully take into account the complexities of the concept. Attempts to compensate for that shortcoming have led some researchers to focus solely on certain physical fitness indicators as part of their assessment (Hattie et al., 1997). Although noble, those efforts have often lacked validity. For instance, changes in a person's blood pressure, although important, can occur from interventions of even the shortest length or intensity (Roberts, Vaziri, and Barnard, 2002). As a result, relying on those types of physiological indicators, which are likely not reflective of a lifestyle change, could be an erroneous approach from which to construct an argument in favor of the impact of adventure programming on health and wellness. If adventure programming is to have the type of impact that so many people readily want to assign it, a more comprehensive approach and understanding of health is required.

Traditional health and wellness interventions have largely been successful due to their comprehensive nature. Such programs tend to combine dietetic counseling, behavior therapy, and other relapse-prevention strategies with exercise to help promote more long-term change (Rieb et al., 2003). In this way, programs are able to retain certain objective measures of assessment and adapt to the emotional and psychosocial aspects of health. In the end, these strategies aim to create a greater sense of empowerment and allow participants to become more independent and to self-manage their health—a primary aim of health literacy (Nutbeam, 2000). When integrated with family, school, and community efforts, interventions of this type are apt to be even more effective. Unfortunately, approaches such as these are in no way commonplace in adventure programming. In fact, this area of adventure programming is in need of significant progress (Sibthorp, 2010). With so much room for advancement, it is premature to advertise adventure programming as making a difference in the health and wellness movement. In order to become truly effective, the adventure industry will also have to account for other factors that contribute to the public health crisis, including health inequities.

Health Inequities Among Marginalized Populations

The uneven distribution of health between and within populations has become a major issue in our society (Reidpath and Allotey, 2007). Although attaining equal health status for all members of a population is an unrealistic aim, systemic factors related to fairness can affect a person's health. The most obvious of those factors is poverty. Existing research tends to show that a population's health hinges on that population's economic capacity (Gwatkin, 2000). In fact, evidence has strongly indicated that the lower a person's socioeconomic status, the worse that individual will likely be in terms of physical and mental health (Marmot, 2007). As is often the case with such groups, a variety of factors contribute to that result, some of which include barriers or constraints that tend to prevent a person from obtaining access to quality health care and prevention. Those barriers or constraints often revolve around issues of supply (i.e.,

location) and demand (i.e., cultural background). Efforts to alleviate these types of health inequities will require improving those groups' access to health services and increasing the availability of resources and opportunities to promote a healthy lifestyle.

For many people, parks and recreation agencies provide both the resources and the opportunities they need to sustain a healthy lifestyle. The vast majority of programs and facilities offered by such agencies are located in close proximity of most community members and exist at no or very little cost (Payne et al., 2005). Despite these factors, residents from areas of lower socioeconomic status tend to report less access and use of a recreational agency's resources than residents from areas of higher socioeconomic status (Abercrombie et al., 2008). Additional constraints such as transportation and limited financial resources often prevent this segment of the population from seeking out alternatives that are better in terms of quality or security. Consequently, low-income individuals often have the lowest levels of recreational physical activity. Given these considerations, what reasonable health expectations should we have for adventure programming, an industry that caters to the more affluent or elite?

One of the major criticisms against forms of recreation that possess an element of adventure is that most are elitist by design. That is, participation in such activities typically requires a person to have a specialized skill set, specific and sometimes expensive technical equipment, and the discretionary money required to travel to and participate in the adventure activity. The commodification of adventure has made it possible for people to participate in activities that they would otherwise not be able to do; however, that luxury is usually not without a hefty price tag. As a result, large segments of the population likely have limited, if any, access to adventure programming experiences. In fact, people from lower socioeconomic classes are most often the recipients of this inadvertent discrimination. Without the resources necessary to participate, marginalized groups are unlikely to ever view adventure programming as a viable option for addressing their health and wellness needs.

As the adventure industry continues to move toward a business model that focuses on revenue production, the market segments (i.e., the affluent) that that industry serves will only continue to shrink (Cloutier, 2003). In the end, the population segments that likely could benefit the most from adventure programming experiences are only further alienated from participating. These types of inherent inequities that exist within adventure programming do little to address the health and wellness needs of the public at large. If adventure programming is to have a meaningful effect on people's health and wellness, a venue that serves a much broader segment of the population and bridges the gap between such inequities is necessary. Only then will interventions of this sort be able to tackle the more global health problems such as physical inactivity and obesity.

Physical Inactivity and the Obesity Epidemic

The obesity epidemic is perhaps one of the more publicized health issues in recent years. In the past decade, the number of adults and children who are obese has doubled (Byers and Sedjo, 2007). Identifying the source of this problem is often complex and tends to involve a number of social, cultural, and economic factors. From a very fundamental perspective, however, the cause would seem somewhat straightforward: people today have increased their consumption of food and decreased their levels of physical activity. Other than in the rarest of circumstances, the outcomes associated with this type of behavior are all detrimental to a person's health and wellness. For example, an obese person is at greater risk for a number of health conditions, including type II diabetes, heart disease, stroke, certain cancers, and many other ailments (Koplan and Fleming, 2000). In addition, a person may experience psychological effects as a result of being obese, including feelings of depression and anxiety (Puhl and Heuer, 2009). Reversing the global obesity epidemic requires individuals to implement a plan of action that integrates lifelong nutrition and regular physical activity. Implementing obesity-prevention programs that promote these types of healthy habits will require the collective efforts of many individuals and organizations if meaningful change is to occur. Schools conceivably represent an ideal option for that purpose; however, those types of establishments are not without their challenges.

Educational Policy: A Disconnect

According to Larson and Verma (1999), children and adolescents spend one-quarter of their waking hours at school. As a result, schools play a prominent role in developing in their students healthy lifetime habits and addressing health issues such as obesity. Teaching students health and wellness concepts early on through a physical education (PE) program can increase the prospect that those students will lead physically active lifestyles in adulthood (Lee et al., 2007). Unfortunately, too many schools across the world deny children the opportunity for PE (Hardman, 2004). Many schools have for various reasons substantially reduced the time allocated to PE in favor of academic subjects that are seemingly superior (Hardman, 2008). In a report published by the Center of Education Policy (McMurrer, 2008), 46 percent of school districts in the United States indicated an increase in the amount of time allotted to subjects such as math and language arts. In order to accommodate those changes, schools had to simultaneously decrease the amount of time devoted to PE, in some cases by 50 minutes per week. With much of society lamenting the increasingly sedentary lifestyle of youths, the sacrifice of PE in the name of traditional academic learning sends an incredibly mixed message.

This current disconnect in educational policy is a hurdle that likely precludes adventure programming from having an impact on the child obesity epidemic that plagues many school students—a very large, accessible, and captive population. Without the resources, the time, and the institutional commitment, physical educators will be slow to adopt or even embrace an approach to PE that engages students in adventure-based tasks such as initiatives or climbing. Some people are quick to tout the emotional and physical benefits of these types of experiences (Warner, 2010); however, the effectiveness of using adventure has also come into question (Brown, 2006). Certain studies have found that the use of adventure in PE produced no noticeable differences in students' actual or perceived levels of physical fitness when compared with a control group (Gehris, Kress, and Swalm, 2010). Results such as these give cause for hesitation and suggest that integrating adventure programming into PE may not provide the greatest return on a school's investment of time and resources. Taking that into consideration, are adventure programmers guilty of putting the cart before the horse? The answer to that question is in fact an emphatic *yes* when one begins to consider the many limitations that are often inherent in adventure programming experiences.

Conclusion

Significant anecdotal and empirical evidence demonstrates that adventure programming experiences can offer a person a wide range of benefits. Despite this, the evidence that points to the efficacy of adventure programming in promoting health and wellness to the population as a whole is woefully lacking. Research on adventure-based programs has rarely accounted for the complexities that surround issues related to public health. The most glaring of those issues deals with the differences between population segments that have historically participated in adventure programming and those that have not. Because adventure programs, almost by design, cater to only a select group of people, adventure programming cannot realistically make a meaningful difference in promoting health and wellness to the population as a whole.

That limitation alone defeats any claim that adventure programming can meaningfully impact the health and wellness of the general population. Other factors more specific to the adventure interventions themselves further hinder the ability of adventure programming to have any meaningful impact. The duration and length of those programs are insufficient in relation to prescribed interventions because the bulk of adventure programming experiences are of a short duration or length. Even those we might consider to be long are relatively short by conventional standards. As a result, affecting meaningful change in a person's health and wellness is likely more a dream than a reality. If we are to adequately answer Louv's call and absorb all of the benefits that nature has to offer, adventure programmers will have to take a hard look at how the industry is currently packaged. Through that process of reflection, adventure programmers can begin to address the validity of making changes and determine what actions, if any, can lead to this ultimate public health outcome.

References

Abanobi, O. (1986). Content validity in the assessment of health states. *Health Values, 10*, 37-40.

Abercrombie, L.C., Sallis, J.F., Conway, T.L., Frank, L.D., Saelens, B.E., & Chapman, J.E. (2008). Income and racial disparities in access to public parks and private recreation facilities. *American Journal of Preventative Medicine, 34*(1), 9-15.

American Medical Association. (1999). Report on the Council of Scientific Affairs, Ad Hoc Committee on Health Literacy for the Council on Scientific Affairs. *Journal of the American Medical Association, 281*(6), 552-557.

Brown, M. (2006). Adventure education and physical education. In D. Kirk, D. McDonald, & M. O'Sullivan (Eds.), *The handbook of physical education* (pp. 685-702). London: Sage.

Byers, T., & Sedjo, R.L. (2007). Public health response to obesity epidemic: Too soon or too late? *Journal of Nutrition, 137*, 488-492.

Cason, D., & Gillis, H.L. (1994). A meta-analysis of outdoor adventure programming with adolescents. *Journal of Experiential Education, 17*(1), 40-47.

Cloutier, R. (2003). The business of adventure tourism. In S. Hudson (Ed.), *Sport and adventure tourism* (pp. 241-272). New York: Haworth Hospitality Press.

Ewert, A. (1987). Research in experiential education: An overview. *Journal of Experiential Education, 10*, 4-7.

Gehris, J., Kress, J., & Swalm, R. (2010). Students' views on physical development and physical self-concept in adventure-physical education. *Journal of Teaching in Physical Education, 29*(2), 146-166.

Goldenberg, M., McAvoy, L., & Klenosky, D.B. (2005). Outcomes from the components of an Outward Bound experience. *Journal of Experiential Education, 28*(2), 123-146.

Gwatkin, D.R. (2000). Health inequalities and the health of the poor: What do we know? What can we do? *Bulletin of the World Health Organization, 8*(1), 3-18.

Hardman, K. (2004). *An update on the status of physical education in schools worldwide: Technical report for the World Health Organization.* Copenhagen: WHO, International Council for Sport Science and Physical Education.

Hardman, K. (2008). Physical education in schools: A global perspective. *Kinesiology, 40*(1), 5-28.

Hattie, J., Marsh, H.W., Neill, J.T., & Richards, G.E. (1997). Adventure education and Outward Bound: Out-of-class experiences that make a lasting difference. *Review of Educational Research, 67*(1), 43-87.

Jelalian, E., Mehlenbeck, R., Lloyd-Richardson, E.E., Birmaher, V., & Wing, R.R. (2006). 'Adventure therapy' combined with cognitive-behavioral treatment for overweight adolescents. *International Journal of Obesity, 30*, 31-39.

Kaplan, R., & Kaplan, S. (1989). *The experience of nature: A psychological perspective.* New York: Cambridge University Press.

Koplan, J.P., & Fleming, D.W. (2000). Current and future public health challenges. *Journal of American Medical Association, 284*(13), 1696-1698.

Larson, J.S. (1999). The conceptualization of health. *Medical Care Research and Review, 56*(2), 123-136.

Larson, R., & Verma, S. (1999). How children and adolescents spend time across the world: Work, play and developmental opportunities. *Psychological Bulletin, 125*, 701-736.

Lee, S., Burgeson, C., Fulton, J., & Spain, C. (2007). Physical education and physical activity: Results from the school health policies and programs study 2006. *Journal of School Health, 77*(8), 435-463.

Louv, R. (2005). *Last child in the woods: Saving our children from nature-deficit disorder.* Chapel Hill, NC: Algonquin Books of Chapel Hill.

Mackay, G.J., & Neill, J.T. (2010). The effect of green exercise on state anxiety and the role of exercise duration, intensity, and greenness: A quasi-experimental study. *Psychology of Sport and Exercise, 11*, 238-245.

Marmot, M. (2007). Achieving health equity: From root causes to fair outcomes. *Lancet, 370*, 1153-1163.

Marvin, R., & Crown, R. (1976). *Concepts and surveys for health care planners*. Ames, IA: Center for Agriculture and Rural Development.

McCray, A.T. (2005). Promoting health literacy. *Journal of American Medical Infomatics Association, 12*(2), 152-163.

McMurrer, J. (2008). *Instructional time in elementary schools: A closer look at the changes for specific subjects*. Washington, DC: Center on Education Policy.

Nutbeam, D. (2000). Health literacy as a public health goal: A challenge for contemporary health education and communication strategies in the 21st century. *Health Promotion International, 15*(3), 259-267.

Payne, L.L., Orsega-Smith, E., Roy, M., & Godbey, G.C. (2005). Local park use and perceived health among older adults: An exploratory study. *Journal of Park and Recreation Administration, 23*(2), 1-20.

Puhl, R.M., & Heuer, C. (2009). The stigma of obesity: A review and update. *Obesity, 17*, 941-964.

Reidpath, D., & Allotey, P. (2007). Measuring global health inequity. *International Journal for Equity in Health, 6*(1), 16-22.

Rieb, D., Greene, G.W., Ruggiero, L., Stillwell, K.M., Blissmer, B., Nigg, C.R., & Caldwell, M. (2003). Evaluation of healthy-lifestyle approach to weight management. *Preventive Medicine, 36*, 45-54.

Roberts, C.K., Vaziri, N.D., & Barnard, J. (2002). Effect of diet and exercise intervention on blood pressure, insulin, oxidative stress, and nitric oxide availability. *Circulation, 106*, 2530-2532.

Saracci, R. (1997). The World Health Organization needs to reconsider its definition of health. www.bmj.bmj-journals.com [December 28, 2011].

Sibthorp, J. (2010). Letter from the editor: Positioning outdoor and adventure programs within positive youth development. *Journal of Experiential Education, 33*, vi-ix.

Sibthorp, J., Paisley, K., & Gookin, J. (2007). Exploring participant development through adventure-based programming: A model from National Outdoor Leadership School. *Leisure Sciences, 29*, 1-18.

Sultz, H.A., & Young, K.M. (2011). *Health care USA: Understanding its organization and delivery*. Sunbury, MA: Jones and Bartlett Learning.

Tucker, A.R., & Rheingold, A. (2010). Enhancing fidelity in adventure education and adventure therapy. *Journal of Experiential Education, 33*(3), 258-273.

Ulrich, R.S. (1983). Aesthetic and affective response to natural environment. In I. Altman & J.F. Wohlwill (Eds.), *Behavior and the natural environment* (pp. 85-125). New York: Plenum.

U.S. Department of Health and Human Services. (2000). *Healthy People 2010: With understanding and improving health and objectives for improving health*. 2nd ed. Vol. 2. Washington, DC: Government Printing Office.

Wadden, T.A., Brownell, K.D., & Foster, G.D. (2002). Obesity: Responding to the global epidemic. *Journal of Consulting and Clinical Psychology, 70*(3), 510-525.

Walsh, V., & Golins, G. (1976). *The exploration of the Outward Bound process*. Denver: Colorado Outward Bound School.

Warner, L. (2010). A place for healthy risk-taking. *Educational Leadership, 67*(4), 70-74.

Wilmore, J.H., Despres, J., Stanforth, P.R., Mandel, S., Rice, T., Gagnon, J., & Bouchard, C. (1999). Alterations in bodyweight and composition consequent to 20 wk of endurance training: The HERITAGE Family Study. *American Journal of Clinical Nutrition, 70*, 346-352.

World Health Organization. (1947). *The constitution of the World Health Organization*. Geneva: WHO Basic Documents.

Controversial Issue 10

Does technology compromise the wilderness experience?

The average adventurer entering wilderness areas today is armed with technological advances that would boggle the minds of the most successful earlier explorers. Versatile synthetic clothing, communication devices, route-finding systems, high-tech food preparation systems, lightweight shelters, and specialized gear have transformed the wilderness experience. The advantages of these amazing technological advances are innumerable. They promote access. Many more people are able to experience the wilderness through the gift of technological support. Technology has vastly improved safety. Adventure programmers are able to manage risks on a whole new level. Communication systems, satellite support, and other electronic wonders ensure a more controlled experience. Technology has been the great equalizer. The average person can access remote places that were once off limits, and more are able to experience and appreciate the wild places we hold sacred. Access breeds awareness and appreciation of our wild places. Although some may believe that technology has compromised the experience, the truth is that technology may be the very thing that saves these special places.

However, this story has another side. What is a true wilderness experience? Our wild places are vanishing at a staggering rate. A true wilderness experience requires vast expanses of contiguous, untouched natural systems. Such experiences challenge our survival on a primitive level. They also connect us to life beyond ourselves. Unfortunately, few, if any, places left on the surface of the Earth remain untouched by human activity. Consequently, as modern-day adventurers, we have lost the ability to experience wilderness at a fundamental level and to experience the rhythms of life or interact with the environment in a natural way. Technology protects but separates us from what is real. We operate in a technological bubble of perceptions that prevents a fundamental connection with nature.

Howard Welser argues that technology is becoming so pervasive in human society that it will eventually result in the extinction of wilderness spaces and the loss of our collective capacity to enjoy the aesthetic and practical dimensions of wilderness experience. His argument highlights four inherent conflicts between the progressive development of technology and the individual and collective capacity for wilderness experience.

Todd Miner argues that romanticized notions of wilderness have caused technology to be broadly vilified in the adventure programming industry. Miner argues that technological improvements have, for the most part, led to safer and more enjoyable wilderness experiences as well as a better understanding of backcountry resources.

This issue raises interesting questions and dilemmas for the adventure programming industry. To what extent should we rely on various forms of technology in facilitating adventure programs? What are the implications for risk management and legal liability associated with choices around the use of technology in adventure programming? What are the implications concerning the way we market and frame wilderness experience for program participants? Grappling with this issue is crucial to sorting through these and other questions that have profound implications for the practice of adventure programming.

Does technology compromise the wilderness experience?

YES The Growth of Technology and the End of Wilderness Experience

Howard T. Welser, PhD, assistant professor of sociology, Ohio University, Athens, Ohio, United States

Between 1993 and 1998, my climbing friends and I would spend the month of January bouldering and camping at Hueco Tanks State Park near El Paso, Texas. The warm sun, brilliant problems, supportive climbing culture, and stark desert beauty brought us back. Every year, more climbers made the pilgrimage, inspired by advances in bouldering pad technology, the rapid expansion of indoor climbing gyms, and promotion of the bouldering scene in the popular climbing press. These technological developments helped spur the growth of a worldwide bouldering community, which increased demand for more bouldering, which spurred even more development of technology. Eventually, campsites were always full, the water supply started to dry up, portable toilets overflowed, litter proliferated, and vegetation was trampled. The overuse led the state park to sharply restrict the access of all users, and the locust swarm of winter bouldering shifted elsewhere.

Of course, Hueco Tanks State Park was not a wilderness area, nor were the climbers interested in wilderness experience per se. Climbers came to boulder and camped for comfort in the improved sites with electric space heaters, espresso machines, and automatic bread makers. The wilderness sensibilities of the climbers ranged from urban punk rockers to professional outdoor leaders, and most were appreciative of the natural world. Despite a general desire among climbers to minimize the negative effects of climbing in the park, the collective effect of the uncoordinated actions of all led to crowding, degradation of the resource from overuse, and an inescapable awareness of the presence and impact of people in the natural environment. Beyond the park, suburban El Paso encroached, lowering the aquifer and increasing the desertification of the surrounding plains. In the popular media, photo essays and stories continued to trumpet the virtues of Hueco bouldering even as access was sharply curtailed. The popularity experiment at Hueco Tanks does not simply represent problems of overuse in recreation areas. It highlights how our actions can be unintentionally detrimental to recreation and wilderness and how technology used inside and outside of wilderness spaces can accelerate those losses.

The Hueco Tanks bouldering example is a small part of a much larger trend. In large and small ways, technological development is leading to the unintended yet inevitable degradation of wilderness spaces and the demise of the potential for wilderness experience on Earth. To the extent that technological development continues unabated, this progress will eventually result in the extinction of wilderness spaces and the loss of our collective capacity to enjoy the aesthetic and practical dimensions of wilderness experience. The degradation of our collective capacity for wilderness is a particular example of a large class of situations characterized as "tragedies of the commons" (Hardin, 1968). Such tragedies involve people pursuing individually reasonable courses of action that inadvertently and inexorably lead to negative collective outcomes. The tragic dimension of the phenomenon is that although we might be aware of the negative collective implication, we are unable to prevent it (Kollock, 1998). Use of common pool resources does not always entail tragic ends (Manning, 2005; Ostrom et al., 1999). However, the challenges of preserving wilderness spaces are especially daunting.

This argument highlights four inherent conflicts between the progressive development of technology and the individual and collective capacity for wilderness experience:

1. Nonrecreational technological development is increasing the potential for high-impact instrumental use of wilderness spaces.
2. Technology used in recreation has the potential to expand the range, intensity, and scope of recreational uses.
3. In the larger society, the development of social media and increased communication technology is driving increased interest in and use of unusual wilderness destinations.

4. The increasingly unavoidable use of and access to mobile communication technology in wilderness recreation undermines core dimensions of the wilderness experience.

Defining Wilderness

Wilderness has both practical and aesthetic dimensions. On a practical level, wilderness spaces can be defined as geographic contexts where the processes, conditions, and organisms of the natural world predominate and where the infrastructure, alterations, and organizations of human society are absent or severely minimized. Recreation in wilderness implies reliance on the self for basic needs—food, shelter, and safety—because the external systems we rely on in civilization are largely absent in wilderness. The Antarctic Treaty System (since 1959; Secretariat of the Antarctic Treaty, 2011) and the Wilderness Act of 1964 contribute notions that wilderness should be untrammeled, that instrumental uses should be curtailed, and that permanent human constructions should be minimized. Although treaties and acts such as these helped establish guidelines for the defense and maintenance of wilderness in a practical sense, they also reinforce the notion that the aesthetic dimensions of wilderness should be valued. Contemporary organizations such as the Wild Foundation advocate for practical and aesthetic values of wilderness as well as the notion that wilderness spaces should be biologically intact (Wild Foundation, 2011). This notion reflects that the survival of the ecological living systems is a value that takes priority.

Somewhat in contrast to that notion, advocates of wilderness recreation are more focused on the impact of human actions on human users of wild spaces. This focus results largely from considering how aesthetic arguments relate to recreation in the wilderness experience (Nash, 1967). Notably, Aldo Leopold (1949) offers several justifications for wilderness, two of which are especially relevant to the aesthetic dimensions of wilderness recreation: recreation in wilderness opens our historical imaginations by giving us a sense of what things used to be like, and, contextually, the physical reality of the wilderness gives us a sense of perspective that transcends the limitations of our current social world. By contrasting with business as usual, wilderness space offers an external perspective on the social reality of civilization, our cultural heritage, our place in the universe, and the potential for a higher purpose. The sense of distance from our historical moment and our social world is a key source of the aesthetic dimension or art (Marcuse, 1978) and potentially of wilderness recreation. One key virtue of that aesthetic dimension is the capacity to view our everyday lives from the outside and develop an independent set of values.

One of the best contemporary examples of extensive wilderness space is Antarctica. The majority of the continent remains unimproved by infrastructure, alterations, or social organizations. In wilderness such as the Antarctic, the conditions and influences of the natural world predominate. The Antarctic Treaty attempts to maintain this condition through prohibiting military, extractive, and proprietary ownership claims and valorizing peaceful and scientific uses while extending environmental protections. The reliance on a treaty to enforce the wilderness state of Antarctica and to restrain parties from unilateral exploitation demonstrates some of the difficulty inherent in maintaining wilderness in general. Without the imposition of formal agreements, social actors tend to use spaces for purposes that undermine the wilderness attributes. Many extant wilderness spaces are also formally designated wilderness areas that prohibit substantial human alteration, restrict the use of particular tools, and limit access.

What are the defining attributes of wilderness experience in outdoor recreation? If a geographic space lacks infrastructure, alterations, and organizations of society, wilderness users will not have access to the advantages those resources normally provide. As wilderness users, we must either forgo or be prepared to provide our own medical care, food, shelter, and security. The act of entering a wilderness space for recreation then entails, to varying extents, both a practical reality of self-reliance and a subjective awareness of the need for such self-reliance. It also entails an aesthetic dimension where we recognize and reflect on the relative absence of human infrastructure, alterations, and organizations. For instance, a telephone booth in the wilderness damages the wilderness experience of hikers on three of these dimensions: it robs us of the necessity for self-reliance, it prevents us from experiencing our connection to "how it used to be," and it intrudes on the aesthetic of wilderness, which is defined partly by the absence of such alterations (figure 10.1).

Lasting Evidence of Instrumental Uses

Technological development increases incentives for instrumental use of remaining wilderness spaces. Numerous social and corporate actors have strong

Figure 10.1 Hikers enjoy an ironic wilderness experience in the Pacific Northwest.

material interests that motivate them to use wilderness spaces in ways that can seriously compromise the practical and symbolic attributes of existing wilderness spaces. Advances in technologies of resource extraction, communication, energy generation, travel, agriculture, and development will increase the pressure to open more of the landscape to high-impact, instrumental uses.

The aesthetic dimensions of wilderness experience are susceptible to spoilage due to prominent signs of human impact and alteration. For example, not only do oil-covered beaches degrade the environment, they can signify the conflict between the instrumental use of technology for private gain and risk of public loss. Unlike crowding, which can abate, spoilage in the forms of visible infrastructure, waste, and destruction of natural terrain can have long-lasting effects.

The potential for spoilage derives from the meaning of wilderness experience. To the extent that we value aesthetic dimensions that connect us to the historical absence of human impact and that connect us to the capacity to feel nature without the intervention of the impacts of civilization, wilderness experience will remain an extremely fragile type of public good.

The tragic oil spill in Prince William Sound presents a lasting reminder that the largest and most serious technological threats to the preservation of wilderness spaces and to our capacity for wilderness experience come from social actors who do not share wilderness values (figure 10.2). The expansion of human infrastructure and the effects of resource extraction, agriculture, manufacturing, and transportation indelibly touch an increasing portion of the globe every year. Increases in technology expand the reach and impact of these endeavors. For instance, on the U.S. coast of the Gulf of Mexico, more than 3,800 oil-drilling platforms are currently active, and many operate in conditions that were technologically prohibitive in earlier decades (see Boland, 2006). Each platform brings immediate localized impacts as well as potential for much broader degradations to the environment. Green power, derived from the wind, rivers, or tides, is not impact-free: technological advance and profit motives bring extensive infrastructure that invades view-sheds and natural systems.

The geographic area that lacks substantial infrastructure, usage, or impacts is constantly decreasing. Technology exaggerates the loss of wilderness space in both a direct sense and an indirect sense

Figure 10.2 An oil-covered inlet in Prince William Sound.

in that technology enables population growth and encourages further uses. Organizations apply pressure to open access to wilderness spaces in order to further their interests. The geographic area that combines all formal wilderness areas and informal wilderness spaces represents the maximum size of future wilderness space; this area is likely to continuously shrink as organizations compete for increasingly rare opportunities in our finite world. Even formally designated wilderness areas, such as the Arctic National Wildlife Refuge, remain under constant threat of being opened to uses that would bring significant practical and symbolic degradations. Other areas, such as the Everglades, are subject to the inadvertent effects of agriculture and water uses in adjacent territory, which degrade the wilderness attributes of the protected area.

Public Goods at Risk From Technologically Enabled Use

Technological development results in direct and indirect applications that alter how people recreate, often in ways that undermine the wilderness experience. In the field, advances in equipment can expand, alter, or extend usage; degrade resources; and spoil our capacity to see our recreation as wilderness experience due to presence of other people or the remnants of their actions. Technology used outside of wilderness areas—for instance, the technological advances applied in indoor climbing gyms—can reverberate into wilderness spaces even if the technology is not applied there. Capacities, norms, practices, and expectations fostered in urban environments alter behavior in wilderness spaces and tend to turn recreation into an extension of the domesticated version.

Officially designated wilderness areas and other spaces that offer wilderness experiences are a type of public good or common pool resource (Ostrom et al., 1999). These goods are, to varying degrees, available to a broad public and are subject to uses that alter the nature and potential value of that good to others. Wilderness enthusiasts are consumers of these goods and, through their consumption of the good, have the potential to create negative externalities or impacts that detract from the utility derived by other wilderness users. Three distinct types of problems confront these resources: crowding, degradation, and spoilage. Spoilage, discussed previously, refers to how human alterations to wilderness spaces undermine the potential for recreationists to derive wilderness aesthetic values from their experience. Crowding and degradation are two related results of resource usage that can lead to both spoilage and reduction in users' capacity to participate in the recreation.

Crowding occurs when concurrent use of a resource either prevents or diminishes the quality of usage by others. Wilderness campsites can become filled, climbing routes can develop queues, and waves can become crowded. Crowding can diminish the recreation value of wilderness spaces, and it can have an even stronger effect on the potential for wilderness experience in the aesthetic sense. How crowded can a resource become before it is no longer a wilderness? When does the experience become just another social experience that keeps us embedded in the normal life of civilization? For example, a busy weekend surf session at Mavericks (see figure 10.3) has become a strongly social experience that is unlikely to lead to the aesthetic dimensions of wilderness. Similarly, for surfers on the north shore of Oahu, the advent of tow surfing means that surfers are constantly drawn back to society by the sound and smell of motorized tow vehicles.

In a direct sense, technological advances lead to greater crowding by making it easier to access wilderness recreation, democratizing the population of users, and expanding the scope of activity. Sea kayaking is a great avenue to wilderness experience, but not when one is surrounded by crowds. Motorized vehicles may be restricted from some areas, but a host of technical advances in equipment expand the reach of mountaineers, divers, cavers, skiers, and hikers and increase the chances that in any recreation users will conflict with other users for access, if not for solitude.

Degradation of wilderness spaces occurs when use of the resource alters the resource in a way that diminishes the future recreation value or the potential for wilderness experience. Surfing leaves no lasting marks on the waves. However, many other uses of wilderness lead to visible physical degradation of the resource. Users of hiking,

Figure 10.3 Surfers crowd the break at Mavericks, an isolated, big-wave surfing resource off the coast of California. After years of being used by a single intrepid surfer, Mavericks has become an international surf destination where rampant crowding occurs during prime conditions (Warshaw, 2000).

biking, climbing, horse, and jeep trails each leave a residue of use. Users of a resource can degrade it simply through use (e.g., the partial destruction of popular crack climbs in Yosemite before the clean-climbing movement, or the polishing of footholds on popular routes). Degradation can also have a symbolic dimension. Hiking trails are constructed to reduce the effects of degradation due to overuse. However, these trails and other marks of use can create for subsequent users of wilderness spaces salient features that detract from the wilderness experience. The Bridger Wilderness Area in Wyoming includes more than 600 miles of established trails, but most users are unlikely to object to their presence because they allow access to so much terrain and they help disperse users. A trail system also rises along the flanks of Mount Rainier; the first stretch of the summit trail is paved to reduce erosion and increase access. In Europe and increasingly in the United States, "via ferrata" trail systems that incorporate bolts, cables, and metal rungs fastened to cliff sides are seen as acceptable improvements that allow access. How much infrastructure is enough to undermine the wilderness experience of users?

Technology Is Expanding the Market for Exotic Goods

Communication technology is changing the social structure, behavior, and size of populations that consume wilderness recreation. By drastically reducing the costs of storing, transmitting, and finding cultural goods the digital information revolution has eroded the cost advantage of mainstream cultural goods and spurred a flood of interest in the long tail of diverse niche activities (Anderson, 2007). Like other cultural goods, remote and unusual recreational locations are subject to increasing attention and use. At market level, promotion of attractive natural features encourages popularity and overuse of many of the most impressive wilderness spaces. Promotion of some resources may be necessary to maintain public support for designated wilderness spaces (see Manning, 2005). However, user-generated content and expanding communication technology can lead to increased awareness of particular wilderness areas, increased demand for travel to those locales, increased usage rates, and, therefore, degraded wilderness experience. This means, for instance, that the high-altitude trash heaps made famous on Mt. Everest are spreading to peaks that are less well known, such as Gasherbrum II (Horrell, 2011).

The growth of long-tail consumption patterns has profound implications for all kinds of cultural activities (Anderson, 2007). Consider that in 1983, the final episode of *MASH* captured 61 percent of the viewing public's attention. In 2010, the final episode of *Lost* captured only about 7.5 percent of the viewing public's attention (Nielsen, 2011). Both were the most popular finales of their eras, but current blockbusters must stand out in a much more complex and competitive market for attention. As the costs of search and distribution of information have decreased essentially to zero, the potential market for all things exotic or unusual has increased. Correspondingly, some of the people who once went to Disneyland for vacation are now hiking through the Bridger Wilderness Area, others are diving with whale sharks in Belize, and others are free-heel skiing in British Columbia. Not only are information search and distribution essentially free, but feedback and reviews are also readily available through and propagated by online communities.

Evidence of this shift is as close as your computer. Open Flickr and search for the name of any wilderness destination. Photos from Baffin Island? Wrangel Island? Attu Island? Check, check, check. On Flickr, the search term "wilderness" results in more than half a million hits. The "many to many" technology of the Internet has fostered the growth of large-scale systems of collaboration and creation in which ordinary people can contribute and, crucially, share insights from their own experiences (Shirky, 2010). This freedom of collaborative creation leads to promotion of attractive natural features and wilderness destinations. This promotion encourages popularity and, potentially, overuse of many of the most impressive wilderness spaces and experiences.

If you search online for the phrase "dive with whale sharks," you will get dozens of commercial hits, including vacation packages to destinations worldwide like Honduras, Belize, the Galapagos, Thailand, Mexico, and Mozambique. Amateur photos of dives with whale sharks are tagged as favorites by hundreds of Flickr users. In this and thousands of other examples, exotic activities and distant destinations gain prominence and attract more participants. The promotion, whether organized or grassroots, may well be necessary to maintain public support for designated wilderness spaces, but user-generated content combined with expanding communication technology can lead to increased demand for travel to those locales, increased usage rates, and, through increased usage, increased potential for crowding, degradation, and spoilage of key dimensions of wilderness experience.

Ubiquitous Communication: Visible and Invisible Bridges to Civilization

Some of the most profound erosions of the practical and aesthetic dimensions of wilderness experience come from the progressive expansion of mobile communication technology. Global positioning system (GPS) devices and mobile phones bring into wilderness spaces access to infrastructure, organizations, and social networks. In their comfort and convenience, these tools reduce our opportunity to experience the self-reliance, isolation, adventure, exposure to the wild, and natural consequences that define the wilderness experience for recreationists. In a pragmatic sense, the presence of these tools in the wilderness is inevitable. If you do not bring your phone, someone else will. Indeed, outdoor professionals are often obligated to bring location and communication technology with them. The presence and potential presence of these technologies alter participation by eroding the need for self-reliance and blocking our capacity to experience wilderness as an escape from the mindset of contemporary modern life.

I frequently hike near my home in Athens, Ohio. The combination of Appalachian geography (tight, twisty hills) and regional poverty makes it easy to slip out of reach of the nearby cell towers. Apparently, reception is better on Mt. Everest (Bly, 2010), in the Grand Tetons (Alltrips, 2011), or in Kruger National Park (Kruger Park, 2011). Access to mobile communication infrastructure is rapidly extending to many wilderness destinations. Profit motives and safety justifications ensure that this access will only increase. Around the world, cellular network towers encroach on the edges of wilderness areas; this infrastructure potentially disturbs the view-shed and spreads communication access into wilderness areas.

Recent efforts of land managers to restrict access to communication systems in wilderness areas in Yosemite National Park are based on the concern that communication access itself, and not simply aesthetic impacts, undermine wilderness experience in the park. However, such restrictions may be moot as early as 2016. In fall of 2010, a Virginia-based firm launched a communications satellite, promising to drench North America with 4G broadband access regardless of location: urban, rural, or wilderness area (Clark, 2010). Across the globe, areas designated as wilderness and areas where people seek wilderness experiences will eventually be blanketed with the same wireless connections available in the hearts of civilization.

At a practical level, ubiquitous communication technology will erode wilderness experience much more powerfully than the most unsightly cell tower. Wireless technology creates an invisible bridge to civilization that includes the support, resources, and potential intervention of organizations. Wherever people have access to these resources, they tend to act as if they are not self-reliant, not remote, and not fully exposed to natural consequences. And, in fact, they are not. Numerous anecdotes show that access to communication technology alters behavior in ways that are consistent with reliance or assumed reliance on the invisible bridge. Already, GPS devices and rescue beacons are eroding our collective capacity for self-reliance and encouraging irresponsibility and exploitive use of rescue support in wilderness spaces. An especially abusive example is noted by Cone (2009), who describes inexperienced hikers who attempted to hike the Royal Arch Loop in the Grand Canyon. In just three days they summoned rescue personnel for trivial matters on three occasions, which eventually resulted in their forced evacuation.

Another technological intrusion on the capacity for wilderness experience comes in the form of the growing use of wearable digital cameras. Anderson (2010) describes how digital video is driving the evolution of culture. Some of the most striking examples of this evolution are found in areas of outdoor recreation. This digital documentation and global sharing may accelerate cultural innovation, but it does so at the cost of the nature of the recreation. By focusing on producing videos for online distribution, recreationists (and new recruits) are likely to conceive of their recreation simply as a social and competitive process and ignore the potential for reflecting on wilderness experience. YouTube is flooded with amazing videos of surfing, skiing, mountain biking, and various forms of skydiving that illustrate this performative recreation. Because of the social reinforcement available from the large crowds of online viewers, these recreational performances are likely to increasingly define participation in recreation. In wilderness spaces, away from crowds or cameras, surfers and skiers have the potential to transcend the everyday social world in wilderness experiences. Without their phones and emergency beacons, hikers and climbers can experience the self-reliance and obligation for personal responsibility that wilderness recreationists have long assumed. Yet who among us will continue to go without those handy gadgets?

To avoid these degradations of wilderness experience, advocates for wilderness could leave their phones at home. However, this situation takes the form of a prisoner's dilemma, where the collective optimum would be the absence of cell phones in wilderness but the individual optimum is to cheat and bring your own phone, just in case. Extended to the population, most people will not leave their phones behind, and those who do will still know that other people will likely have phones, and thus the invisible bridges are still potentially accessible. Furthermore, experience shows us that most people will carry and use their phones wherever and whenever they are able to. Consequently, the potential social negatives of cell access in wilderness spaces will occur regardless of whether some individuals unilaterally abstain.

Contemporary smart phones are portable computers. Through web-based applications they augment wilderness recreation with tools, social worlds, and knowledge of civilization. Such resources can help recreationists identify plants, navigate terrain, and avoid dangerous weather situations in natural spaces. However, as our capacity to understand, document, and communicate about natural spaces expands, these smart phones will impede our ability to gain an external sense of perspective on ourselves and our position in the world. These wonderful tools tie us to society in a way that is antithetical to the aesthetic dimensions of wilderness. Wilderness, as Leopold and Nash experienced it, retreats in direct proportion to advances of the visible and invisible infrastructure of the modern world.

Conclusion

The four types of technological development that undermine wilderness experience are not just likely to continue, they will most likely accelerate. It would seem that all hope is lost for a future with wilderness and wilderness experience. In a sense, that hope is already lost. The self-reliance and the sense of distance from the modern world that accompanied recreation in remote parts of North America in the days of Nash and Leopold are nearly extinct. Domesticated and trammeled wilderness spaces are becoming the default, and even these will largely recede in the face of development and instrumental use. Ultimately, we will have to accept the fact that wilderness is an aesthetic ideal that we are increasingly unable to achieve and learn to appreciate the values that we can still draw (Pollan, 2003) from recreation in the world we are creating.

References

Alltrips. (2011). Cell phone coverage. www.jackson-holewy.net/essentials/cell_phone_coverage.php [December 29, 2011].

Anderson, C. (2007). *The long tail. Why the future of business is selling less of more.* New York: Hyperion.

Anderson, C. (2010). How web video powers global innovation. *Ted: Ideas worth sharing.* www.ted.com/talks/chris_anderson_how_web_video_powers_global_innovation.html [December 29, 2011].

Bly, L. (2010). 3G service on Mount Everest takes cellphone debate to a new level. *USA Today.* http://travel.usatoday.com/destinations/dispatches/post/2010/11/3g-service-on-mount-everest-takes-cellphone-debate-to-a-new-level/129481/1#uslPageReturn [December 29, 2011].

Boland, G. (2006). Oil and gas exploration. *NOAA.* http://oceanexplorer.noaa.gov/explorations/06mexico/background/oil/oil.html [December 29, 2011].

Clark, S. (2010). Multi-billion dollar broadband dream rockets into reality with launch. www.space.com/9528-multi-billion-dollar-broadband-dream-rockets-reality-launch.html [December 29, 2011].

Cone, T. (2009). Tired from a tough hike? Rescuers fear yuppie 911. *Arizona Daily Sun.* http://azdailysun.com/sports/article_ee562fc5-1910-5b5a-85d0-3be-d2914eb22.html [December 29, 2011].

Hardin, G. (1968). The tragedy of the commons. *Science, 162*(3859), 1243-1248.

Horrell, M. (2011). Turning mountains into trash heaps. *Footsteps on the mountain.* www.markhorrell.com/blog/2011/turning-mountains-into-trash-heaps [December 29, 2011].

Kollock, P. (1998). Social dilemmas: The anatomy of cooperation. *Annual Review of Sociology, 24,* 183-214.

Kruger Park. (2011). Kruger park cell phone coverage map. www.krugerpark.co.za/Maps_of_Kruger_Park-travel/cellphone-map-knp.html [December 29, 2011].

Leopold, A. (1949). *A sand county almanac.* Oxford, U.K.: Oxford University Press.

Manning, R. (2005). The limits of tourism in parks and protected areas: Managing carrying capacity in the U.S. National Parks. In C. Ryan, S.J. Page, & M. Aicken (Eds.), *Taking tourism to the limits: Issues, concepts and management perspectives* (pp. 129-139). New York: Pergamon Press.

Marcuse, H. (1978). *The aesthetic dimension: Toward a critique of Marxist aesthetics.* Boston: Beacon Press.

Nash, R. (1967). *Wilderness and the American mind.* New Haven, CT: Yale University Press.

Nielsen. (2011). Television measurement. www.nielsen.com/us/en.html [December 29, 2011].

Ostrom, E., Burger, J., Field, C., Norgaard, R., & Policansky, D. (1999). Revisiting the commons: Local lessons, global challenges. *Science, 284*(5412), 278-282.

Pollan, M. (2003). *Second nature: A gardener's education*. New York: Grove Press.

Secretariat of the Antarctic Treaty. (2011). ATS—The Antarctic Treaty. www.ats.aq/e/ats.htm [December 29, 2011].

Shirky, C. (2010). *The cognitive surplus*. New York: Penguin.

Warshaw, M. (2000). *Maverick's: The story of big-wave surfing*. San Francisco: Chronicle Books.

Wild Foundation. (2011). What is a wilderness area? www.wild.org/main/how-wild-works/policy-research/what-is-a-wilderness-area/ [December 29, 2011].

Does technology compromise the wilderness experience?

NO Electronic Boogeyman: Technology and the Wilderness

Todd Miner, EdD, executive director of Cornell Outdoor Education, Cornell University, Ithaca, New York, United States

Over the past few years, an explosion has occurred in the number of media stories sounding a warning cry about the use of technology in the wilderness (Cone, 2009; Greenwald, 2000; Kaufman, 2010; Repanshek, 2008). Likewise a number of academic journal articles, texts, and research papers (Borrie, 1998; Holden, 2004; Pope, 2010; Shultis, 2000; Strong, 1995) have warned about technology's negative effect on the wilderness experience. Others, not taking a stance on whether technology is a detriment or asset, have emphasized how critical the role of technology is to the future of wilderness (Eldred, 2010; Freimund and Borrie, 1997; Stankey, 1999).

Clearly, the role of technology in the wilderness is an important and growing issue that demands attention and discussion. Unfortunately, much of the discussion to date has focused on the negatives of technology and has been at best irrational and subjective, and at worst elitist. To some, technology has become a kind of boogeyman that threatens the very existence of wilderness. A neo-luddite (Shultis, 2001), romanticized notion of wilderness has caused technology to be vilified and rejected in a skewed, illogical, and broad-brush manner.

Although misuse of technology can be problematic, technological improvements have for the most part led to safer and more enjoyable wilderness experiences and a better understanding of backcountry resources and have helped to create more wilderness advocates. Rather than compromising wilderness experiences, technology has largely enhanced them.

Our society will continue to spawn technological advances, likely at an increasing rate. Fighting technology in the wilderness is a futile and ultimately misplaced, curmudgeonly struggle. Trying to divorce technology from the wilderness is counterproductive to users' experiences and it is unfeasible due to human nature, definitions, practical applications, and societal trends. Rather than fight technology, wilderness advocates should embrace appropriate technology, which benefits both users and the land.

Man the Tool Maker

Humans cannot escape technology because it is basic to our nature. Tool making and technology are a major part of what defines our very being. As noted anthropologist Jane Goodall (2010) puts it, "Our species was defined as 'Man the Tool Maker'" (p. 1). The term, first popularized by British anthropologist Kenneth Page Oakley (1976), highlights how we evolved on the subtropical plains of Africa, where we could not survive without tools and technology. Not equipped with fur, claws, teeth, speed, or flight, humans have survived and found a niche through tool making and technology. If dropped naked into a wilderness, the only way a human could survive would be to make tools (shelter, digging sticks, hunting tools, and so on), and thus technology creeps in. Given the basic premise that our very survival depends on tools, how could we make a case for divorcing technology from a wilderness experience? Unless humans are totally kept out of the wilderness, technology will inevitably be part of the wilderness experience. Divorcing technology from the wilderness would mean banning humans.

While critics of technology believe that the wilderness should remain "pure" and that only some technology (perhaps what they use?) should be allowed, the reality is that the wilderness experience is rife with technology. "Far from the match-less, animal skin-clad primitives that wilderness critiques might have us imagining, most wilderness visitors appear to be well aware that they are carrying a considerable assortment of 21st-century contraptions with them into the wild" (Havlick, 2006, p. 56). Wilderness users have broadly and apparently enthusiastically accepted technology as part of their wilderness experience. As Havlick (2006) notes, "the widespread acceptance of [technology] suggests that wilderness users are not as devoted to the idea of a retreat to a pre-industrial setting as Cronon and similar critics indicate" (p. 55).

Drawing the Line

Some argue that technology interferes with our wilderness experience (Cone, 2009; Kaufman, 2010; Strong, 1995). But if we are to ban technology, where do we draw the line? Do we allow a global positioning system (GPS)? If not, how about a compass? Maps? Are these not all examples of technology? Can we only enter the wilderness naked and use what we can craft with our bare hands? Only natural fibers and materials? Nothing with a battery? No motors? No firearms? How about a knife? Technology is a continuum; as noted before, we absolutely require it, so where do we draw the line? More importantly, on what do we base the decision to forbid technology in the wilderness experience? What is the principle or philosophical basis for the decision? Basic outdoor clothing, general backpacking gear, and a simple canoe are all technologies, and who among us is going to forsake these tools? More importantly, why would we want to? What is the rationale of banning some technologies (assuming they do not leave a mark on the land) while allowing others? Who defines what is acceptable and what is not? Technology itself is neither good nor bad; it is neutral. Certainly, technology can be misused, but the human action, not the technology, causes the problem. As Freimund and Borrie (1997) note, "the discussion about technology is more one of values than of technological devices" (p. 23).

Other challenges exist in drawing a line regarding technology in the wilderness. Some technology (such as lifejackets with canoes and kayaks) is legally required. Other technology is viewed differently depending on the terrain or activity. For example, radio is considered normal gear by prudent sea kayakers but overkill by most climbers.

In addition, where do we draw the line that defines wilderness? Is that wilderness with a capital W, those lands officially given "wilderness" status, or simply those wild lands and backcountry areas that are commonly considered wilderness? If "wilderness" refers to officially designated wilderness areas where technology is not appropriate, then wilderness makes up only 2.5 percent of the contiguous United States, or an area about the size of South Dakota (National Park Service, 2010). Does that mean that technology is acceptable in all other wild lands?

Welser (page 148) defines wilderness as "geographic contexts where the processes, conditions, and organisms of the natural world predominate and where the infrastructure, alterations, and organizations of human society are absent or severely minimized." Is technology, at least as used in the wilds, an "organization of human society"? If so, this definition demands that technology be either absent or severely minimized. The real issue is not forbidding technology in the wilderness or even severely minimizing it—that would effectively ban humans—but rather is where we draw the lines in terms of appropriate or inappropriate technology. And at best, whether discussing technology or wilderness, such lines involve artificial or arbitrary definitions based on often competing values of different users of these areas.

Cultural Biases and Wilderness Myths

A number of cultural perspectives or myths create subtle but powerful societal opposition to technology in the wilderness. These underlying storylines are powerful precisely because they are deeply ingrained in our worldviews and thus are largely undetected. We are unaware of their effect on our perspectives.

Perhaps the most significant of these hidden perspectives is that of the "no pain, no gain" mentality. Many writers, in both the general media (Cone, 2009; Kaufman, 2010) and academic press (Dustin and McAvoy, 2000; Knapp, 2000; Strong, 1995), warn about the encroachment of technology in the wilderness, particularly that technology makes the experience easier. This is not a new argument; Aldo Leopold was making it in the early part of the 20th century (Marafiote, 2008). However, it appears even stronger today, particularly in regard to communication technology. The premise, at times explicit and other times implicit, is that a wilderness experience is better if it involves more struggle or more danger (Dustin and McAvoy, 2000; Knapp, 2000). For instance, Strong (1995) criticized upscale llama packing, stating, "It insulates one from the conditions of the place, smoothing out even the forbidding ruggedness of the Crazies, narrowing one's contact with them, and making wilderness an easily consumable package" (p. 93). Whether this mentality comes from a kind of puritanical perspective or a kind of patriarchal machismo (Marafiote, 2008), it has helped to create an unwarranted bias against technology in the wilderness. Why is portaging an 80-pound (36 kg) canoe a better experience than portaging a 40-pound (18 kg) canoe? How does someone in my party carrying a cell phone lessen my experience?

Perhaps the concept of the noble savage living in an idyllic primitive existence—Nash's (1982) romantic wilderness—sets up technology to be the enemy. Think of how Tarzan is glorified in contrast to the decadent and comfort-loving jungle explorers who have baggage, porters, and especially guns. Is technology viewed as the forbidden fruit in the Garden of Eden? Does the glow surrounding "the good ol' days" make people yearn for some mystical golden time when life was somehow better? None of these are solid, rational reasons to assume that technology is inappropriate for the wilderness, but they all may well color society's view of technology and wilderness.

Wilderness for the Elite

More than three-quarters of a century ago, Aldo Leopold worried about elitism in the wilderness as technology was excluded (Havlick, 2006). That concern should be even stronger today as purists attempt to portray technology as inappropriate in the wilderness. It is elitist, or at best subjective, to state that a hike without a cell phone is better than one with a phone. Is using dead reckoning better than using a compass? Is using a compass better than using a GPS? Who is to say which leads to a better experience?

If technology is divorced from wilderness, then wilderness will increasingly become the haunt of the elite outdoors people. Such a result would be a social injustice because only a few, mainly privileged, individuals would take advantage of a common good supported by taxes paid by all. In addition to the social injustice, if only a few experience the wilderness, the wilderness will lose the benefit of the many who, if they were exposed to its beauties and wonders, would become its advocates. Technology is the great equalizer. Without technology the wilderness becomes the exclusive domain of experts, of the very fit and hardcore. Technology allows a more diverse group of citizens to use our national treasures. Whether it is beginners, senior citizens, or the disabled, technology provides a gentler start to encourage use of the wilderness.

Technology can also provide solutions that allow busy working people to experience the wilderness. Think of how a cell phone allows a working mother to get outside for a quick one-hour hike after work because she feels connected to the rest of her family. "Bringing a cell phone into the wilderness may change the intensity of your experience but enable you to go on a trip that you otherwise wouldn't be able to experience at all" (Freimund and Borrie, 1997, p. 22). A lightweight 40-pound (18 kg) high-tech Kevlar canoe that can easily be thrown on top of a car by one person, compared with a traditional 80-pound (36 kg) beast that one must wrestle up top, might make the difference between spending a few hours paddling on Sunday afternoon or giving up and watching football on television.

Technology and the internet open up a whole world of information about where to go, local conditions, the weather, and what to bring. This can be particularly helpful for beginners of all kinds. Lack of information is a major barrier to minority populations' participation in the outdoors and wilderness (Roberts, 2010). According to the Outdoor Foundation (2010b), "A major challenge for the outdoor community is to engage new audiences in outdoor activities—especially minorities and 'insiders'" (p. 1). One of the main strategies of their study "Inside Out" is "forming key partnerships and using a diversity of media to communicate how *indoor activities can be enjoyed outdoors*" (p. 1). In other words, technology can serve as an effective bridge between young people's infatuation with screen time and getting outdoors.

In particular, technology can assist those with physical limitations. The ultralight revolution that has hit backpacking has cut the weight of packs in half and the weight of tents by even more. Lighter, higher tech gear can help the growing population of senior citizens continue to do as much as they could when their bodies were younger. They started with wool, leather, wood, and steel; now they have fleece, Gore-tex, titanium, and Kevlar.

Using biking and paddling as examples, Ewert and colleagues (2006) described how

> The mountain bike revolutionized cycling. Likewise, high travel shocks have revolutionized mountain bikes and allow bikers to get into remote locations faster and more comfortably. In a similar case, new generation kayaks allow novice or intermediate kayakers to paddle extremely difficult whitewater and perform stunts previously unattainable even by expert boaters. (p. 130)

And it is not just for experts or the hardcore. In a similar fashion, new ski designs, bindings, and boots have made learning to ski much easier for beginners. These new technologies do not compromise the wilderness experience; they enhance it!

Technology as Benefit to Wilderness

Technology has benefited wilderness participation by making the backcountry more accessible, easier to experience, and safer. As Ewert and colleagues (2006) state, "Advances in technology in the last two decades have given individuals opportunities to enhance their participation in different recreational experiences through improvements in communication and information, access, transportation, comfort, and safety" (p. 127).

Technology has also helped develop a constituency of support for wilderness because it encourages more outdoor participation. Outdoor participants are in turn more likely to believe that preserving outdoor space is important (Outdoor Foundation, 2010a). Building political support for wilderness rests in part on "building a clientele for it" (Nash, 1982, p. 316). And that clientele grows not just from abstract ideas and philosophies about nature and wilderness but from involvement in outdoor recreation. Technology, rather than being a detriment to wilderness, has helped spawn a new generation of wilderness consumers and, thus, advocates. "A *revolution in equipment* has facilitated the implementation of love for wilderness" (Nash, 1982, p. 317 [italics in original]). What Nash means is that by creating lighter weight tents, more efficient stoves, and higher performance clothing, technology has made it easier to get out to the wilderness and has thus spawned more participation. Even as far back as the early 20th century, the founders of the Wilderness Society recognized that technology can increase support for wilderness (Marafiote, 2008). By encouraging more participation in the wilderness, technology has created more advocates to save the newly discovered and revered resource.

Some have worried that technology, by making the wilderness easier to experience, will somehow create too many users and stress the very values that makes wilderness so attractive (Ewert and Shultis, 1999; Shultis, 2001). However, the reality is that in the past few years, participation in traditional backcountry activities such as hiking, canoeing, skiing, mountaineering, and rafting has actually decreased (Ewert et al., 2006), as has youth interest in outdoor recreation in general (Outdoor Foundation, 2010a). The problem is not so much overuse of wilderness as it is nature-deficit disorder (Louv, 2005) or disconnect from the natural world and wilderness.

Technology can attract users, particularly young people, back to the wilderness. Young people are particularly and increasingly disengaged from outdoor recreation (Outdoor Foundation, 2010a). How can we reverse that downward slide so that we continue to have strong wilderness advocates? One of the most common reasons cited by youths ages 6 to 17 as to why they do not participate in outdoor activities is because they "would rather spend time watching TV, on a computer, or playing video games" (Outdoor Foundation, 2010a, pp. 55-56). If that is the case, either those young people can be written off or land managers and wilderness proponents can try to use technology to encourage them to experience the outdoors. Chavez (2009) demonstrated that youths prefer technology-dependent activities over more traditional outdoor activities and suggests using technology to get youths outdoors. Activities such as geocaching and digital photography or equipment-intensive sports such as ice climbing can and should be used to encourage our future citizens and voters to go out into the wilderness and thus become its future advocates.

Technological advances have also helped reduce the brunt of wilderness use. Using examples of backpacking cook stoves versus campfires and of modern tents versus cutting tent poles, Freimund and Borrie (1997) found that "through the use of some technologies, many wild places are impacted less now than they were in 1964" (p. 23). Lightweight approach shoes versus big waffle-stomper boots, or chocks and cams versus pitons, are other examples of how technology is reducing the footprint of wilderness users.

Technology is also an important asset to research in the wilderness. This includes research and education in biology, geology, hydrology, oceanography, and astronomy (Chang, 2009). More recently, remote sensing of wildfires—the modern equivalent of the old fire warden and firetower—is being used as a tool in understanding and managing brush and forest fires. Technology is ever more important to scientists trying to understand wilderness areas and their resources. The use of technology for research can also involve citizenry, thus strengthening their connection to wilderness and their support for the resource (Harmon and Gleason, 2006). We should not handcuff the researchers and public officials who are responsible for managing our wilderness treasures by banning technology. For research in the wilderness, technology is an asset rather than a detriment.

Safety

Forget the philosophical or ethical rationales for the benefits of technology in the wilderness and consider the black-and-white issue of safety. How many lives have been saved by technology in the wilderness? Radios, cell phones, personal locator beacons (PLBs) or emergency position-indicating radio beacons (EPIRBs), avalanche beacons, helicopters, and even tools as simple as lifejackets or helmets have all provided for safer wilderness experiences. According to Ewert and colleagues (2006), "the use of this technology (cell and satellite phones) allows backcountry visitors to expand their 'bubble of safety' by allowing emergency calls to be placed from virtually anywhere in the world" (p. 128).

In U.S. National Parks alone, between 1992 and 2007 more than one-fourth of the 65,000 search and rescue missions were initiated by a cell phone, satellite phone, or marine radio. Of the 78,000 individuals who were involved in search and rescue over that time period, the fatality rate was just 3.3 percent and, more importantly, 16.8 percent or more than 13,000 were classified as saves (from death or serious injury) (Heggie and Amundson, 2009).

Extrapolating from those figures, between 1992 and 2007 more than 3,000 people were saved by the use of high-technology communications in national parks alone. Given that today a much higher proportion of people carry and use cell phones than did in the 1990s, that national park acreage makes up only about 14 percent of total federally protected wild lands (Jensen, 1995), and that many more wild-land acres are in local, state, and private hands, the total number of people saved by high-technology communications is very significant. Technology does not compromise the wilderness experience; it enhances the experience. Moreover, it does so by enhancing the physical and psychological safety of the users of wilderness areas, particularly beginners or those with minimal wilderness experience. Holden (2004) movingly described an example of a young woman from urban Los Angeles who in an Outward Bound program went from being miserable to well acclimated when she learned the instructors carried a cell phone. Purists can decry the use of technology in the wilderness, but if an accident occurs and a cell phone would save a life, who among us would not wish for or use one?

Conclusion

In his seminal work, *Wilderness and the American Mind*, Nash (1982) states, "Dams, mines, and roads are not the basic threat to wilderness quality of the environment. Civilized people are" (p. 317). Surely,

cell phones, snow machines, and GPS units do not impact the wilderness as much as dams, mines, and roads; thus, they also are not the basic threat to the wilderness.

The threat is not from the boogeyman of technology. People can misuse technology, but blanket statements such as "technology compromises the wilderness experience" do more harm than good. Technology has produced a net benefit to the wilderness experience by encouraging more participants and thus advocates, by making the experience safer and more enjoyable, by lessening individuals' impact on the resource, and by giving land managers and policy makers powerful tools to manage wilderness. The impact of technology on the wilderness is only going to grow. Wilderness advocates who push a broad-brush, luddite opposition to technology are fighting a losing battle. Rather than blindly fighting technology, those who cherish wilderness should, while resisting the few misuses, accept and embrace the many benefits.

References

Borrie, W.T. (1998). The impacts of technology on the meaning of wilderness. In A.W. Watson, G.H. Aplet, & J.C. Hendee (Eds.), *Proceedings of Sixth World Wilderness Congress Symposium on Research, Management, and Allocation*, Volume II (pp. 87-88). Fort Collins, CO: USDA Forest Service.

Chang, I. (2009). Wiring the wilderness. www.livescience.com/technology/091120-bts-wireless-internet-remote-location.html [November 23, 2010].

Chavez, D. (2009). Youth Day in Los Angeles: Evaluating the role of technology in children's nature activities. *Children, Youth and Environments, 19*(1), 102-124.

Cone, T. (2009). Wilderness rescuers fear 'yuppie 911' makes calling for help too easy. *The Seattle Times.* http://seattletimes.nwsource.com/html/travel/2010171491_trhikingemergency01.html [November 22, 2011].

Dustin, D.L., & McAvoy, L.H. (2000). Of what avail are forty freedoms? The significance of wilderness in the 21st century. *International Journal of Wilderness, 6*(2), 25-26.

Eldred, S. (2010). Wireless in the wilderness brings risks, rewards. *USA Today.* www.usatoday.com/travel/destinations/2010-04-14-wireless-state-national-parks_N.htm [November 23, 2010].

Ewert, A., Attarian, A., Hollenhorst, S., Russell, K., & Voight, A. (2006). Evolving adventure pursuits on public lands: Emerging challenges for management and public policy. *Journal of Park and Recreation Administration, 24*(2), 125-140.

Ewert, A., & Shultis, J. (1999). Technology and backcountry recreation: Boon to recreation or bust for management? *Journal of Physical Education, Recreation, and Dance, 70*(8), 23-28, 31.

Freimund, W., & Borrie, B. (1997). Wilderness @ Internet: Wilderness in the 21st century—Are there technical solutions to our technical problems? *International Journal of Wilderness, 3*(4), 21-23.

Goodall, J. (2010). Toolmaking. www.janegoodall.org/chimp-central-toolmakers [November 24, 2010].

Greenwald, J. (2000). The future of adventure. *Sierra, 85*(1), 30-39.

Harmon, L., & Gleason, M. (2006). Using technology to interact with the natural environment: Part II. In R. Burns & K. Robinson (Eds.), *Proceedings of the 2006 Northeastern Recreation Symposium* (pp. 540-544). Bolton Landing, NY, Gen. Tech. Rep. NRS-P-14. Newton Square, PA: U.S. Department of Agriculture, Forest Service, Northern Research Station.

Havlick, D. (2006). Reconsidering wilderness: Prospective ethics for nature, technology, and society. *Ethics, Place and Environment, 9*(1), 47-62.

Heggie, T.W., & Amundson, M.E. (2009). Dead men walking: Search and rescue in U.S. national parks. *Wilderness and Environmental Medicine, 20*(3), 244-249.

Holden, G.T. (2004). *The impacts of satellite phone technology on a North Carolina Outward Bound School experience.* Unpublished doctoral dissertation. Raleigh, NC: North Carolina State University.

Jensen, C.R. (1995). *Outdoor recreation in America.* Champaign, IL: Human Kinetics.

Kaufman, L. (2010). Technology leads more park visitors into trouble. *New York Times,* August 21, A1.

Knapp, D. (2000). Technology and wilderness in the 21st century. *International Journal of Wilderness, 6*(2), 20.

Louv, R. (2005). *Last child in the woods: Saving our children from nature-deficit disorder.* Chapel Hill, NC: Algonquin Books.

Marafiote, T. (2008). The American dream: Technology, tourism, and the transformation of wilderness. *Environmental Communication: A Journal of Nature and Culture, 2*(2), 154-172.

Nash, R. (1982). *Wilderness and the American mind.* New Haven, CT: Yale University Press.

National Park Service. (2010). Wilderness: Gateway to National Park Service Wilderness—Where is wilderness? http://wilderness.nps.gov/where.cfm [November 24, 2010].

Oakley, K.P. (1976). *Man the tool-maker.* 6th ed. Chicago: University of Chicago Press.

Outdoor Foundation. (2010a). *Outdoor recreation participation report.* Boulder, CO: The Outdoor Foundation.

Outdoor Foundation. (2010b). *Inside out: Outdoor nation special report—Turning insiders out.* Boulder, CO: The Outdoor Foundation.

Pope, K.E. (2010). *Visitor perceptions of technology and rescue in the wilderness.* Unpublished master's thesis. Arcata, CA: Humboldt State University.

Repanshek, K. (2008). Is technology compatible with the National Park wilderness experience? *National Parks Travel.* www.nationalparkstraveler.com/2008/08/technology-compatible-national-park-wilderness [November 23, 2010].

Roberts, N. (2010). Third annual Trends and Issues in Outdoor Education Programs panel discussion. Workshop conducted at the 2010 Association for Experiential Education International Conference, Las Vegas, NV.

Shultis, J. (2000). Gearheads and golems: Technology and wilderness recreation in the 21st century. *International Journal of Wilderness, 6*(2), 17-18.

Shultis, J. (2001). Consuming nature: The uneasy relationship between technology, outdoor recreation and protected areas. *The George Wright Forum, 18*(1), 56-66.

Stankey, G.H. (1999). Future trends in society and technology: Implications for wilderness research and management. In D.N. Cole, S.F. McCool, W.A. Freimund, & J. O'Loughlin (compilers), *Wilderness science in a time of change conference: Changing perspectives and future directions* (pp. 10-23). Volume 1. RMRS-P15-VOL-1. Ft. Collins, CO: U.S. Department of Agriculture, Forest Service, Rocky Mountain Research Station.

Strong, D. (1995). *Crazy mountains: Learning from wilderness to weigh technology.* Albany, NY: State University of New York Press.

Part II

Contemporary and Emerging Issues in Adventure Programming

Controversial Issue 11

Should extreme sports, such as BASE jumping and other high-risk sports, be included in adventure programming?

This argument represents a continuation of the debate concerning the appropriate role of risk in adventure programming. However, in this debate, the question is not simply whether the risks outweigh the benefits in adventure programming. Here, the question is whether adventure programming should include adventure pursuits that involve *extreme* levels of risk that entail the very likely consequence of severe injury or death as a result of an accident.

In "The Essence of Adventure," William Quinn (1999) notes that adventure is inspired by an inherent human desire to discover the unknown. One of the key outcomes of adventure experience, according to Quinn, is peace. He quotes D.H. Lawrence to illustrate this point: "Peace is the state of fulfilling the deepest desires of the soul. It is the condition of flying within the greatest impulse that enters us from the unknown" (Lawrence, 1936, pp. 117-118; as cited in Quinn, 1999, p. 150). Quinn (1999) states, "To fly, wrapped in an impulse from the unknown towards the unknown, lies close to the heart of the experience of adventure. Peace comes from the confidence gained and the fulfillment of success" (p. 150). Yet Quinn (1999) introduces a measure of controversy to his definition of adventure by drawing a distinction between what he considers to be thrill seeking and adventure. He writes, "The reward of peace is the difference between adventure and thrill seeking. The thrill seekers find no peace" (p. 150).

Although Quinn does not explicitly define thrill seeking in relation to adventure, he implies that individuals who engage in pursuits involving extreme risks to fulfill thrill-seeking desires are not true adventurers. This statement is controversial because it excludes the reward of peace from those participating in adventure sports to fulfill thrill-seeking desires. It implies that participation in extreme sports cannot yield the kinds of positive, transformational benefits that adventure experiences can yield. Consequently, one can conclude that no place exists for pursuits that give rise to such sensations in the field of adventure programming.

Quinn clouds the issue when later in his essay he writes, "Grand adventurousness is recognized in those who confront death while seeking excitement. The price of a mistake is so great" (p. 150). He refers to climbing Mt. Everest and dogsledding to the North Pole as examples of this type of adventurousness. However, Quinn's assertion concerning the distinction between thrill-seeking and adventure gives rise to a number of questions. Does participation in extreme sports qualify as thrill seeking? What motivates people to engage in extreme sports? What are the rewards of participation in extreme sports? More importantly, should extreme sports be included in adventure programming?

Eric Brymer argues that participation in extreme sports does yield positive benefits and that these benefits might not be attainable in other mediums. As such, these benefits far outweigh the risks or detrimental consequences associated with extreme sports. Brymer further argues that the formalization of training and education offered through adventure programs can reduce any negative effects.

Tara Allman and Marni Goldenberg, on the other hand, argue that including extreme sports in adventure programming is unethical on a number of grounds. They contend that participation in extreme sports should be accessible only to elite athletes and not to the public at large. Inclusion of such activities in adventure programming is likely to result in serious injuries or deaths and thus should not be permitted.

Reference

Quinn, W. (1999). The essence of adventure. In J.C. Miles & S. Priest (Eds.), *Adventure programming* (pp. 149-151). State College, PA: Venture.

Should extreme sports, such as BASE jumping and other high-risk sports, be included in adventure programming?

Transforming Adventures: Why Extreme Sports Should Be Included in Adventure Programming

Eric Brymer, PhD, lecturer in human movement and sports science, Queensland University of Technology, Brisbane, Australia

Extreme sports are fast becoming sporting activities of choice (American Sports Data, 2002; Pain and Pain, 2005). It seems that participants, both male and female, come from a broad cross-section of society and from various age ranges and income and educational levels (Creyer, Ross, and Evers, 2003). According to Puchan (2004), participation rates in extreme sports are increasing, and involvement seems "not to be just a 'flash in the pan' but a sign of the times" (p. 177).

However, what constitutes an extreme sport is still unclear (Brymer, Downey, and Gray, 2009; Olivier, 2006). Self-directed activities that necessitate a high level of training, personal skills, preparation, and commitment (e.g., extreme skiing and rope-free climbing) are assumed to be in the same class as activities that are led and require no participant skill, dedication, or prior knowledge (e.g., commercial rafting and bungee jumping) (Brymer, 2009b; Palmer, 2004; Wheaton, 2004). Equally, some activities require dedicated technological aids (e.g., the BASE jumping parachute), other activities require less equipment than might be common to their less-extreme cousins (e.g., rope-free climbing), and still other activities do not require any special paraphernalia (e.g., parkour). Also, a lack of clarity about what exactly is meant by *extreme* exists within the same sport. For example, although maneuvering a kayak down a grade 3 rapid as defined by the international river grading system (Berry, 2002) might be exhilarating, the results of an accident or mistake are relatively harmless. The result of an accident or mistake at grade 6, on the other hand, is most likely death (Hunt, 1995; Slanger and Rudestam, 1997).

I argue that extreme sports should be included in adventure programming. I demonstrate that the current presupposition that extreme sports are about undesirable risk taking is misplaced. This is important because participation in these activities is growing and policies and practices for an activity that is considered deviant, socially unacceptable, and focused on risk will differ from those for an activity that is considered socially beneficial and developmentally focused. Based on current understandings, extreme sports have been banned in many areas around the world (Ewert et al., 2006; Soreide, Ellingsen, and Knutson, 2007). For example, in the United States, the National Park Service has instigated a policy that prohibits BASE jumping (U.S. Department of the Interior, 2006), though in practice the National Park Service does allow some BASE jumping events. In another instance, in February of 2010 the Italian government presented an amendment to the civil protection law that effectively renders off-piste (skiing in virgin snow away from the regular runs) skiers subject to criminal conviction (Day, 2010).

I also show that participation in extreme sports promotes environmental, social, and individual benefits that might not be attainable in any other medium. These benefits far outweigh any suggested detrimental consequences. Further, I show that the relationship between extreme sports and risk may not be as solid as is traditionally assumed. Finally, I argue that formalization of training and education may reduce any potential negative effects, which suggests that it is essential to include extreme sports in adventure programs.

To make these arguments I focus on research that includes the most extreme of extreme sports, in which the most likely outcome of a mismanaged mistake or accident is death (Brymer, 2009a; Brymer and Oades, 2009). Typical activities that fall into this category are self-directed and include BASE jumping, extreme skiing, waterfall kayaking, big-wave surfing, high-level mountaineering, and climbing without ropes (also known as free solo climbing). This definition might also include activities such as free running or parkour (Miller and Demoiny, 2008).

The Presumption of Risk

The traditional standpoint on participation in extreme sports supports a widely held, theory-driven presupposition that extreme sports are deviant manifestations of a drive to take risks or search for an adrenaline surge (Allman et al., 2009; Brymer, 2010; Delle Fave, Bassi, and Massimini, 2003; Lambton, 2000; Olivier, 2006; Pizam, Reichel, and Uriely, 2002; Rinehart, 2000; Self et al., 2007; Simon, 2002). From the traditional perspective, participation in extreme sports is most often judged as pathological, socially unacceptable, negative, and deviant (Elmes and Barry, 1999; Monasterio, 2007; Pain and Pain, 2005; Self et al., 2007). Participants are frequently described as selfish teenage boys who are "fascinated with the individuality, risk, and danger of the sports" (Bennett, Henson, and Zhang, 2003, p. 98). Media, advertising representations, and management practices have mirrored these presuppositions (Bennett, Henson, and Zhang, 2003; Davidson, 2008; Pollay, 2001; Puchan, 2004; Rinehart, 2005; Soreide, Ellingsen, and Knutson, 2007; Tomlinson et al., 2005).

The dominant theories focus on psychological and sociological explanations. These perspectives propose that personality traits (e.g., Breivik, 1996; Hunt, 1996; Self et al., 2007), socialization processes (e.g., Allman et al., 2009; Fletcher, 2008; Laurendeau, 2008), and previous experiences work to compel a participant to put his or her life at risk through extreme sports (Brymer, 2010). Psychological theories include type T (Self et al., 2007), psychoanalysis (Hunt, 1996), and sensation seeking (Breivik, 1996; Goma, 1991; Robinson, 1985; Rossi and Cereatti, 1993; Schrader and Wann, 1999; Shoham, Rose, and Kahle, 2000; Slanger and Rudestam, 1997; Straub, 1982; Zarevski et al., 1998; Zuckerman, 2007).

Those espousing type T theory explain participation in extreme sports as the realization of a deviant personality trait (Self et al., 2007) and a need for uncertainty, novelty, ambiguity, variety, and unpredictability (Farley, 1991). The psychoanalytic perspective (Elmes and Barry, 1999; Hunt, 1996) views participation in extreme sports as a pathological and unhealthy narcissistic tendency in which participants are "denying limitations and vulnerabilities, rationalizing unacceptable behavior and feelings, overestimating abilities and accomplishments, and offering consistently self-serving explanations for successes and failures" (Elmes and Barry, 1999, p. 165). Those holding the sensation-seeking standpoint argue that participation in extreme sports is driven by an inbuilt need for novel experiences and intense sensations (Rossi and Cereatti, 1993; Schroth, 1995). Participants search for new outlets to obtain thrills and excitement and alleviate boredom.

The main sociological theory is termed "edgework" (Laurendeau, 2008). From this perspective, risk taking is the principal goal (Lyng, 2008). According to Laurendeau (2008), edgework includes the theoretical explanation of voluntary risk taking where "it is not simply that danger is associated with the activity, but that practitioners have a particular interest in courting danger while still maintaining control over themselves, their equipment, their surroundings, and/or their sanity" (p. 294). That is, the edge in edgework describes the point at which participants are in danger of losing control. From this perspective, participation in extreme sports is about walking a fine line between control and chaos.

Some suggest that a genetic reason exists for participation in extreme sports. From this perspective, a gene (usually understood as the alleles of the D4DR gene and its variants) somehow directs individuals to undertake extreme sports. Most applications of this perspective are based on research on drug taking, gambling, and sex (Zuckerman, 2000); theorists have often made a huge leap in assuming that extreme-sport participants are somehow the same as these other populations. Those who have studied extreme-sport populations indicate that no conclusive evidence supports this notion (Thompson, 2008). Despite the plethora of seemingly negative connotations that link extreme sports to personality types or social processes, the risk perspective also presents a tantalizing glimpse into a potential positive side of extreme sports. For example, Self and colleagues (2007) write that extreme sports are a positive outlet for those who were born with a personality type that needs to take physical risks. That is, extreme sports might be an ideal outlet for those who would otherwise take physical risks in a negative manner (e.g., crime or delinquent behaviors) (Brymer, 2002). Allman and colleagues (2009) argue that traversing the edge allows participants to experience profound transformation. Participants perceive themselves as free from societal norms while "releasing potentials that they did not even know they possessed" (Lyng, 2008, p. 101).

From these theoretical, risk-taking perspectives, participation in extreme sports is traditionally perceived as follows:

- a need or search for novelty, uncertainty, and uncontrollability;

- a pathological and unhealthy activity that is rationalized by self-deception; and
- a selfish focus on undertaking for thrills and excitement an activity in which death is probable.

However, these same risk perspectives also offer a glimpse of extreme sports as a positive outlet for those who might be driven to spurn traditional recreational pursuits or undertake delinquent activities. Equally, the risk perspectives present participation in extreme sports as a unique way of realizing human potential that would otherwise remain dormant. However, according to Breivik (2007), this risk point of view presents two important arguments against participation in extreme sports. The first, paternalism, argues that participants need to be saved from themselves by wiser and more rational guides. The second, moralism, argues that extreme-sport participants are bad social examples, are selfish, and have little concern for family, friends, and potential rescuers. However, perhaps the real question is what these arguments say about our society, that we fear and wish to sanction those things that we feel uncomfortable undertaking (Brymer, 2005). After all, for many people on the planet everyday life is more extreme that any extreme sport (Zuckerman, 2000).

Although for some the initial motive to participate might be the risk, thrills, glamour, and excitement of these activities, some evidence contradicts the risk-taking focus (Celsi, Rose, and Leigh, 1993; Delle Fave, Bassi, and Massimini, 2003). For example, Slanger and Rudestam (1997) found no relationship between sensation seeking and experienced extreme-sport participants. They suggest that this supports Breivik's assertion that "maximising risk is not the goal of their activities" (Breivik cited in Slanger and Rudestam, 1997, p. 369). Pain and Pain (2005) write:

> Despite the public's perception, extreme sports demand perpetual care, high degrees of training and preparation, and, above all, discipline and control. Most of those involved are well aware of their strengths and limitations in the face of clear dangers. Findings of extensive research in climbers suggest that the individuals do not want to put their lives in danger by going beyond personal capabilities. (p. S34)

From this perspective, participants are described as self-aware, careful, disciplined, and in control,

not risk-takers on the edge. Danger is not central to the experience of extreme sports but rather is peripheral in the same way that danger is not central to the driving experience. Many extreme-sport participants consider socially acceptable activities such as driving to be more dangerous than extreme sports. For example, JM, a mountaineer in his early 40s, explains:

> You know, some of the biggest risks I face are on the roads because . . . the most dangerous thing I encounter [is] people. . . .

For JM, the "normal" social environment is perceived to be less safe than the extreme-sport environment:

> I don't feel like I'm putting my life in any greater danger going on an adventure, whether it's climbing Mt. Everest or walking across the desert. But I do when I get out on the road. So we face risks in our lives every day, and I don't really draw a big distinction. I do feel safer when I'm in the natural world. I do feel safer when I'm on the Arctic Ocean or in the Himalayas than I do out in the home environment when I'm driving around.

For Lynn Hill, danger and risk are not central to the experience, as is true for most who participate in extreme sports:

> Extreme to me means doing something that is dangerous and risky. And that was never my motivation as a climber. The reason I climb is more about learning about myself as well as the sense of partnership with my climbing partners within the natural environment. It has nothing to do with how dangerous it is. (cited in Olsen, 2001, p. 59)

Brymer (2010) confirmed this perspective and found that extreme-sport participants clearly determine that they function well within their individual capabilities and do not believe that they live on the edge.

Statistics on fatal and near-fatal injuries support this notion. It seems that socially accepted activities that are not negatively labeled as risk-taking activities, such as scholastic football or riding a motorcycle, present more chance of paralysis or death than do climbing or BASE jumping (Horton, 2004; Ramsey, 2003; Soreide, Ellingsen, and Knutson,

2007; Storry, 2003). Brymer (2010) argues that extreme-sport participation is not about the need to take risks, and the search for explanations that focus on risk and risk taking is more likely a reflection of modern society's desperate need for control and morbid aversion to uncertainty. Thus, the presumption that extreme sports are about a search for risk might be completely misguided (Storry, 2003). Nevertheless, the assumption that extreme sports must be about risk has proven incredibly seductive and difficult to reframe. For example, although Brymer and Oades (2009) are careful not to present extreme-sport participation as a search for risks, Allman and colleagues (2009) interpret the findings of Brymer and Oades as "participants purposefully take risks" (p. 230).

The focus of the risk-taking perspective is that participants undertake extreme sports because they need or desire to search for danger. This perspective, often theory driven and the presupposition of naïve nonparticipants, is inconclusive and often based on assumptions that do not reflect reality (Brymer, 2005, 2010; Delle Fave, Bassi, and Massimini, 2003; Lyng, 2008; Willig, 2008). According to Brymer (2010), numerous problems exist with the risk-taking presupposition, including the following:

- Some of the literature reveals characteristics and statistics that do not fit with the traditional assumption about risk (Celsi, Rose, and Leigh, 1993; Soreide, Ellingsen, and Knutson, 2007; Storry, 2003).

- A focus on risk means that the experience has been largely ignored (Brymer, Downey, and Gray, 2009; Brymer and Oades, 2009; Willig, 2008).

- Definitions used to explain extreme sports are imprecise. For example, whitewater kayaking can be mild at grade 2 of the international whitewater grading system (Berry, 2002) but potentially deadly at grade 6.

- Tools such as the sensation-seeking scale have been designed for the general public and not for those participating in extreme sports.

- Extreme sports may not be just further along a risk continuum, and the evidence suggests that many activities considered socially acceptable and not associated with risk are far more dangerous (Brymer, 2010).

- The commitment, training, and skill required for successful participation receive little recognition (Brymer, 2009a).

- The current focus on risk might actually be attracting the adrenaline junkie who has a taste for risk and danger but little skill or understanding of the commitment necessary for successful participation (Brymer, 2009a).

- Theory-driven methodologies reflect judgments that do not necessarily relate to the lived experience of participants (Brymer, 2005, 2010; Celsi, Rose, and Leigh, 1993; Ogilvie, 1974; Weber, 2001).

In essence, the presumption that taking part in an extreme sport is about risk entirely misses the point. Although the consequences of extreme-sport participation might be devastating, the evidence suggests that these consequences are less likely to occur than they are in traditional, socially accepted activities that are not associated with risk.

Individual, Social, and Ecological Benefits of Extreme Sports

The idea that extreme sports might correlate with individual, social, and ecological benefits is not new. Ogilvie (1974) found that male and female extreme-sport participants shared positive personality constructs, including above-average intelligence, above-average independence, self-assertiveness, and forthrightness. Brannigan and McDougall (1983) highlighted special emotions, solitude, harmony with nature, and self-reliance and made no mention of a desire to take risks. Celsi, Rose, and Leigh (1993) made comparisons to plastic surgery and concluded that self-change in this instance was an external, superficial process that an individual hoped would change something inside, whereas the changes resulting from participation in extreme sports involved a deep, internal process. However, research has only recently conceded that extreme-sport participation might be a unique way to generate desirable qualities. From this perspective, extreme-sport participation is not about risk or the desire to walk the edge of control (Brymer, 2010).

As with the risk viewpoint, this perspective argues that extreme sports present unique challenges that facilitate positive individual changes. However, this perspective also argues that extreme sports transform a participant's relationship with others and the environment. Willig (2008) concludes that taking part in extreme sports has the potential to enhance a participant's life in ways that cannot be achieved elsewhere. She suggests that extreme sports could be considered transformational and therapeutic activities that might be a way of "re-establishing psychological balance" (p. 700). Other researchers have observed this positive transformation (Allman et al., 2009; Breivik, 2007; Brymer, 2009a; Brymer and Oades, 2009). Brymer and Oades (2009) draw on the literature from positive and transpersonal psychology to propose that some events enable one to appreciate the reality of one's own impermanence, which might activate positive personal changes. They argue that extreme sports are such an event and show how participation triggers deep personal transformations and the development of humility and courage.

Delle Fave, Bassi, and Massimini (2003) found that extreme climbers use the challenges inherent in their chosen activity to cultivate personal growth. Brymer (2009c) shows how extreme-sport participation can lead to a profound sense of wellness and life enhancement. For some, participation "stripped away the socio-cultural noise" (Brymer, 2009c, p. 294) and allowed a connection to a deep sense of self beyond social and cultural expectations. This experience reflects Heidegger's (1996) authentic self. According to Heidegger, the realization of an authentic sense of self also opens a door to authentic relationships with others and perhaps even encourages others to live more authentic lives.

Indeed, participants describe how extreme sports have enhanced their interactions with others. For example, Cotter (cited in Spence, 2001), an extreme mountaineer, reports that instead of making quick judgments about right and wrong, he now welcomes different perspectives—a change he attributes to participation in extreme sports. This is echoed by the words of GS, a BASE jumper and medical doctor in his mid 40s, who narrates how extreme-sport participation changed how he relates to patients:

> Pretty well every aspect I handle differently now. For example, when I practice medicine now, I'm a lot more aware of a patient . . . not just bed four's got a stroke. I'm much more aware that Mrs. so and so is a lady who's got a lot of other things and just happens to have a stroke right now.

Still, for Breivik (2007) the question is not whether participation benefits society but "whether concerned and worried families can cripple a person's right to flourish and live a life that is rich for him/her" (p. 175).

Research also shows that participation in extreme sports can elicit harmonious relationships with the natural world and promote sustainable practices (Brymer, Downey, and Gray, 2009; Brymer and Gray, 2010). For example Brymer, Downey, and Gray (2009) demonstrate that participation in extreme sports can foster a desire to look after the natural world. They argue that the extreme-sport experience is an essential catalyst that facilitates an experience of vulnerability and therefore feelings of psychological connection with the natural world. Extreme sports are a means to reconnect with an aspect of ourselves that was once deeply connected to the natural world but has been forgotten as society has become fearful of uncertainty and desperate for control. In turn, a participant is more likely to partake in sustainable practices.

Extreme Sports in Adventure Programming

Participation and interest in extreme sports are increasing (Delle Fave, Bassi, and Massimini, 2003; Pain and Pain, 2005), yet many activities have been banned around the world. Even when participation is tolerated, the current focus of adventure programming is risk protection; therefore, extreme sports are not considered viable (Delle Fave, Bassi, and Massimini, 2003). Extreme sports are relegated to a category of alternative recreational pursuits despite the exponential increase in participation numbers.

This approach has numerous problems. First, participants are often forced to undertake their chosen activity illegally (Allman et al., 2009). Second, those searching for thrills attempt to undertake extreme activities without possessing the required skills, and many die as a result (Brymer, 2009a; Delle Fave, Bassi, and Massimini, 2003). This irony has not been lost on participants. For example, TB, a BASE jumper in his late 30s who is also responsible for safety matters for the Australian BASE jumping association, says:

> The trouble with BASE as it gets more well-known is it starts to attract extremists—people who want that edge thing, that sort of high-risk adrenaline, are coming across and they're dying.

Third, serious novices interested in participating in an extreme sport already develop skills through informal channels (Nimmo et al., 2007). According to TB, a fortunate novice will find an experienced and skilled mentor; however, this is not guaranteed.

Delle Fave, Bassi, and Massimini (2003) argue that this paradox cannot be sustained. Instead, they recommend that a more useful way to manage the potential negative outcomes is for programs to get involved and facilitate a process "to match participants' skills with appropriate activity settings" (p. 95). Nimmo and colleagues (2007) conclude that participation

> provides physical activity benefits to a wider section of the community, who may not be interested in conventional organised sports. These benefits make it an important area for organisations and government, particularly the Department of Sport and Recreation to recognise and support. (p. 41)

In this way the individual, social, and ecological benefits can be maintained and the individual learns how to participate effectively. Equally, the participant is introduced in an organized and effective manner to an activity that has the potential to transform an individual and benefit society and the natural world.

Conclusion

Extreme sports are here to stay, and participation rates will inevitably continue to grow. In the current climate, extreme sports are considered socially unacceptable at best and the potential benefits of these activities are ignored. However, novices are still being introduced to activities in an informal way. A formalization of this process will help novices match skill levels with activity levels and ground their future development based on an understanding of the knowledge, commitment, and skills required for successful participation. A formal process of training might also present extreme sports as more socially acceptable and less threatening. This positive representation might even serve to reframe the current image of extreme-sport participants as thrill seekers and risk takers into an image that is more productive. This in turn might reduce the number of nonskilled participants trying extreme sports because of the risk-taking and thrill-seeking image. These points suggest that extreme sports should be included in adventure programming.

References

Allman, T.L., Mittlestaedt, R.D., Martin, B., & Goldenberg, B. (2009). Exploring the motivations of BASE jumpers: Extreme sport enthusiasts. *Journal of Sport and Tourism, 14*(4), 229-247.

American Sports Data. (2002). "Generation Y" drives increasingly popular "extreme" sports. www.americansportsdata.com/pr-extremeactionsports.asp [November 14, 2002].

Bennett, G., Henson, R.K., & Zhang, J. (2003). Generation Y's perceptions of the action sports industry segment. *Journal of Sport Management, 17*(2), 95-115.

Berry, M. (2002). Reading white water. In F. Ferrero (Ed.), *Canoe and kayak handbook* (pp. 280-292). Bangor, North Wales, U.K.: Pesda Press.

Brannigan, A., & McDougall, A.A. (1983). Peril and pleasure in the maintenance of a high risk sport: A study of hang-gliding. *Journal of Sport Behavior, 6*, 37-51.

Breivik, G. (1996). Personality, sensation seeking and risk taking among Everest climbers. *International Journal of Sport Psychology, 27*, 308-320.

Breivik, G. (2007). Can BASE jumping be morally defended? In M.J. McNamee (Ed.), *Philosophy, risk and adventure sports* (pp. 168-185). London: Routledge.

Brymer, E. (2002). *Extreme sports: Theorising participation—A challenge for phenomenology*. Paper presented at the ORIC research symposium, University of Technology, Sydney.

Brymer, E. (2005). *Extreme dude: A phenomenological exploration into the extreme sport experience*. Unpublished doctoral dissertation. Wollongong, Australia: University of Wollongong. http://ro.uow.edu.au/theses/379 [December 20, 2005].

Brymer, E. (2009a). Extreme sports as a facilitator of ecocentricity and positive life changes. *World Leisure Journal, 51*(1), 47-53.

Brymer, E. (2009b). The extreme sports experience: A research report. *IFPRA World*, March, 6-7.

Brymer, E. (2009c). The role of extreme sports in lifestyle enhancement and wellness. Paper presented at Creating Active Futures. *Edited proceedings of the 26th ACHPER International Conference*, Brisbane, Australia.

Brymer, E. (2010). Risk and extreme sports: A phenomenological perspective. *Annals of Leisure Research, 13*(1&2), 218-239.

Brymer, E., Downey, G., & Gray, T. (2009). Extreme sports as a precursor to environmental sustainability. *Journal of Sport and Tourism, 14*(2-3), 1-12.

Brymer, E., & Gray, T. (2010). Dancing with nature: Rhythm and harmony in extreme sport participation. *Journal of Adventure Education and Outdoor Learning, 9*(2), 135-149.

Brymer, E., & Oades, L. (2009). Extreme sports: A positive transformation in courage and humility. *Journal of Humanistic Psychology, 49*(1), 114-126.

Celsi, R.L., Rose, R.L., & Leigh, T.W. (1993). An exploration of high-risk leisure consumption through skydiving. *Journal of Consumer Research, 20*(1), 1-23.

Creyer, E., Ross, W., & Evers, D. (2003). Risky recreation: An exploration of factors influencing the likelihood of participation and the effects of experience. *Leisure Studies, 22*(3), 239-253.

Davidson, L. (2008). Tragedy in the adventure playground: Media representations of mountaineering accidents in New Zealand. *Leisure Studies, 27*(1), 3-19.

Day, M. (2010). Jail threat to skiers who go too far off-piste. *The Independent.* www.independent.co.uk/news/world/europe/jail-threat-to-skiers-who-go-too-far-offpiste-1893331.html [February 15, 2010].

Delle Fave, A., Bassi, M., & Massimini, F. (2003). Quality of experience and risk perception in high-altitude climbing. *Journal of Applied Sport Psychology, 15*(1), 82-98.

Elmes, M., & Barry, D. (1999). Deliverance, denial, and the Death Zone: A study of narcissism and regression in the May 1996 Everest climbing disaster. *The Journal of Applied Behavioral Science, 35*(2), 163-187.

Ewert, A., Attarian, A., Hollenhorst, S., Russell, K., & Voight, A. (2006). Evolving adventure pursuits on public lands: Emerging challenges for management and public policy. *Journal of Park and Recreation Administration, 24*(2), 124-140.

Farley, F. (1991). The type-T personality. In L. Lipsitt & L. Mitnick (Eds.), *Self-regulatory behavior and risk taking: Causes and consequences* (pp. 371-382). Norwood, NJ: Ablex Publishers.

Fletcher, R. (2008). Living on the edge: The appeal of risk sports for the professional middle class. *Sociology of Sport Journal, 25*(3), 310-330.

Goma, M. (1991). Personality profiles of subjects engaged in high physical risk sports. *Personality and Individual Differences, 12*(10), 1087-1093.

Heidegger, M. (1996). *Being and time: A translation of Sein and Zeit* (J. Stambaugh, trans.). Albany, NY: State University of New York.

Horton, D. (2004). Extreme sports and assumption of risk: A blueprint. *University of San Francisco Law Report, 38*, 599-664.

Hunt, J.C. (1995). *The neutralisation of risk among deep scuba divers.* Unpublished manuscript.

Hunt, J.C. (1996). Diving the wreck: Risk and injury in sport scuba diving. *Psychoanalytic Quarterly, LXV*, 591-622.

Lambton, D. (2000). Extreme sports flex their muscles. *Allsport*, September(SB49), 19-22.

Laurendeau, J. (2008). "Gendered risk regimes": A theoretical consideration of edgework and gender. *Sociology of Sport Journal, 25*(3), 293-309.

Lyng, S. (2008). Risk-taking in sport: Edgework and the reflexive community. In M. Atkinson & K. Young (Eds.), *Tribal play: Subcultural journeys through sport* (pp. 83-109). Bingley, U.K.: Emerald.

Miller, J.R., & Demoiny, S.G. (2008). Parkour: A new extreme sport and a case study. *The Journal of Foot and Ankle Surgery, 47*(1), 63-65.

Monasterio, E. (2007). The risks of adventure sports/people. *The Alpinist.* www.alpinist.com/doc/web07f/rb-erik-monasterio-mountaineering-medicine [June 11, 2008].

Nimmo, L., Stewart, J., McNamara, J., & Leaversuch, P. (2007). *Research into status of challenge/extreme sport and activities in Western Australia.* Perth, Western Australia: Royal Life Saving Society (WA Branch).

Ogilvie, B.C. (1974). The sweet psychic jolt of danger. *Psychology Today, 8*(5), 88-94.

Olivier, S. (2006). Moral dilemmas of participation in dangerous leisure activities. *Leisure Studies, 25*(1), 95-109.

Olsen, M. (2001). *Women who risk: Profiles of women in extreme sports.* New York: Hatherleigh Press.

Pain, M.T.G., & Pain, M.A. (2005). Essay: Risk taking in sport. *The Lancet, 366*(1), S33-S34.

Palmer, C. (2004). Death, danger and the selling of risk in adventure sports. In B. Wheaton (Ed.), *Understanding lifestyle sports: Consumption, identity and difference* (pp. 55-69). New York: Routledge.

Pizam, A., Reichel, A., & Uriely, N. (2002). Sensation seeking and tourist behavior. *Journal of Hospitality and Leisure Marketing, 9*(3-4), 17-33.

Pollay, R.W. (2001). Export "A" ads are extremely expert, eh? *Tobacco Control, 10*, 71-74.

Puchan, H. (2004). Living "extreme": Adventure sports, media and commercialisation. *Journal of Communication Management, 9*(2), 171-178.

Ramsey, C.B. (2003). Homicide on holiday: Prosecutorial discretion, popular culture, and the boundaries of the criminal law. *Hastings Law Journal, 54*, 1641-1703.

Rinehart, R. (2000). Emerging arriving sports: Alternatives to formal sports. In J. Coakley & E. Dunning (Eds.), *Handbook of sports studies* (pp. 501-520). London: Sage.

Rinehart, R. (2005). "BABES" & BOARDS: Opportunities in new millennium sport? *Journal of Sport and Social Issues, 29*(3), 232-255.

Robinson, D.W. (1985). Stress seeking: Selected behavioural characteristics of elite rock climbers. *Journal of Sport Psychology, 7*(4), 400-404.

Rossi, B., & Cereatti, L. (1993). The sensation seeking in mountain athletes as assessed by Zuckerman's sensation seeking scale. *International Journal of Sport Psychology, 24*(4), 417-431.

Schrader, M.P., & Wann, D.L. (1999). High-risk recreation: The relationship between participant characteristics and degree of involvement. *Journal of Sport Behaviour, 22*(3), 426-431.

Schroth, M.L. (1995). A comparison of sensation seeking among different groups of athletes and nonathletes. *Personality and Individual Differences, 18*(2), 219-222.

Self, D.R., Henry, E.D., Findley, C.S., & Reilly, E. (2007). Thrill seeking: The type T personality and extreme sports. *International Journal of Sport Management and Marketing, 2*(1-2), 175-190.

Shoham, A., Rose, G.M., & Kahle, L.R. (2000). Practitioners of risky sports: A quantitative examination. *Journal of Business Research, 47*(3), 237-251.

Simon, J. (2002). Taking risks: Extreme sports and the embrace of risk in advanced liberal societies. In T. Baker & J. Simon (Eds.), *Embracing risk: The changing culture of insurance and responsibility* (pp. 177-208). Chicago: University of Chicago Press.

Slanger, E., & Rudestam, K.E. (1997). Motivation and disinhibition in high risk sports: Sensation seeking and self-efficacy. *Journal of Research in Personality, 31*(3), 355-374.

Soreide, K., Ellingsen, C., & Knutson, V. (2007). How dangerous is BASE jumping? An analysis of adverse events in 20,850 jumps from the Kjerag Massif, Norway. *Journal of Trauma-Injury Infection and Critical Care, 62*(5), 1113-1117.

Spence, A. (2001). Into the mountains. *North and South,* April, 52-62.

Storry, T. (2003). The games outdoor adventurers play. In B. Humberstone, H. Brown, & K. Richards (Eds.), *Whose journeys? The outdoors and adventure as social and cultural phenomena* (pp. 201-228). Penrith, U.K.: The Institute for Outdoor Learning.

Straub, W.F. (1982). Sensation seeking among high and low-risk male athletes. *Journal of Sport Psychology, 4*(3), 246-253.

Thompson, C.J. (2008). *The genetics of sport behavior: The role of the DRD4 gene in sensation seeking in skiers.* Unpublished thesis. Vancouver, BC: The University of British Columbia.

Tomlinson, A., Ravenscroft, N., Wheaton, B., & Gilchrest, P. (2005). *Lifestyle sports and national sport policy: An agenda for research.* Eastbourne, U.K.: University of Brighton.

U.S. Department of the Interior. (2006). Management policies 2006: The guide to managing the national park system. In National Park Service (Ed.), *Use of parks.* www.nps.gov/policy/mp/chapter8.htm [May 30, 2008].

Weber, K. (2001). Outdoor adventure tourism: A review of research approaches. *Annals of Tourism Research, 28*(2), 360-377.

Wheaton, B. (2004). Introduction. In B. Wheaton (Ed.), *Understanding lifestyle sports: Consumption, identity and difference* (pp. 1-28). New York: Routledge.

Willig, C. (2008). A phenomenological investigation of the experience of taking part in "extreme sports." *Journal of Health Psychology, 13*(5), 690-702.

Zarevski, P., Marusic, I., Zolotic, S., Bunjevac, T., & Vukosav, Z. (1998). Contribution of Arnett's inventory of sensation seeking and Zuckerman's sensation seeking scale to the differentiation of athletes engaged in high and low risk sports. *Personality and Individual Differences, 25*(4), 763-768.

Zuckerman, M. (2000). Are you a risk taker? *Psychology Today, 33*(6), 52.

Zuckerman, M. (2007). *Sensation seeking and risky behavior.* Washington, DC: American Psychological Association.

Should extreme sports, such as BASE jumping and other high-risk sports, be included in adventure programming?

NO A Case for Why Extreme Sports Should Not Be Permitted in Adventure Programming

Tara L. Allman, MS, adventure programmer for the department of family, morale, welfare, and recreation (DFMWR) at Fort Carson Adventure Programs and Education (APE), Colorado Springs, Colorado, United States

Marni Goldenberg, PhD, associate professor in recreation, parks, and tourism administration, California Polytechnic State University, San Luis Obispo, California, United States

Adventure programming should not include extreme sports because it would be difficult for adventure professionals to mitigate the amount of risk associated with these activities. Elite athletes are the only group who should participate in extreme sports; the public at large should not. Increased participation in these risky activities presents the opportunity for serious injuries or death. If they include extreme sports in their programming, adventure programmers will experience adverse consequences that may also negatively affect the public and other user groups, such as climbers, that lobby for access.

Extreme sports are synonymous with action, lifestyle, or adventure sports. Bennett, Henson, and Zhang (2003) interpret action sports as "mostly individual sports that have danger or unconventional rules or techniques which differ from dominant team sports" (as cited in Park, 2004, pp. 6-7). Practitioners of extreme sports perform stunts or use specific equipment and rely heavily on technological advances. Sagert (2009) defines an extreme sport as an individualistic activity with an element of danger in which participants often rely on creativity to master an activity. Groups that most frequently participate in extreme sports are young subcultures interested in breaking records or exceeding previous limitations of human endeavor. Brymer (2005) defines an extreme sport as an activity in which an accident would almost certainly result in severe injury or death. Common examples of extreme sports include BASE jumping, big-wave surfing, extreme skiing, high-level mountaineering, rope-free solo climbing, and waterfall kayaking. Bungee jumping, controlled freefalling, cave diving, desert racing, hang gliding, heli- and speed skiing, street luging, and wingsuit flying are also examples of extreme sports.

Edgeworkers Versus Adventure Programming Participants

Extreme-sport athletes are edgeworkers who have extremely high levels of risk acceptance and who voluntarily take risks. Lupton and Tulloch (2002) define a voluntary risk-taker as an individual who intentionally chooses to participate in activities they view to be somewhat dangerous. Edgeworkers are voluntary risk-takers because they push the limits by maintaining control while exploring the capabilities of technology and their skill (Laurendeau, 2006). They overcome their fears by controlling feelings of discomfort and chaos as they move closer to the edge (Laurendeau, 2006). Every edgeworker explores this boundary, but in different ways and to different degrees (Laurendeau, 2006). This notion coincides with Varley's (2006) adventure commodification continuum, in which crowding the edge constitutes an original adventure at the deep end of the spectrum.

Some edgeworkers crowd the edge more than others and increase the potential for catastrophic outcomes (Laurendeau, 2006). The edgeworkers who operate where mishaps occur more commonly are extreme-sport athletes. Some examples include a big-wave surfer taking increasingly greater risks, such as surfing 20-foot (6 m) waves at high tide, or a mountaineer who begins climbing to high altitudes without oxygen after previously climbing with oxygen. Each edgeworker establishes their individual perception of risk. Edgeworkers combine extremely risky circumstances with the rewards of self-discovery and elite skill (Ferrell, 1995, 1996, 1997; Ferrell, Milovanovic, and Lyng, 2001; Lyng,

1990, 1998). Lyng (1990) explains that edgeworkers, like extreme-sport athletes, often perform at such a high level of risk that they have an "illusory sense of control" (p. 872) in which they believe they have a survival instinct. Laurendeau (2006) explains that participants attribute deaths to fate as a means to make sense of situations that are beyond their control. As such, it would be difficult to mitigate the risk of extreme sports enough to safely offer programs to the public.

Adventure programmers, because they are responsible for the lives of others, are not in the business of creating risky situations. But edgeworkers *do* create risky situations for themselves and others; they are willing to walk the fine line between life and death. Extreme-sport participants often become interested in the sensations of the sport, which can lead to residual risk taking. Those with no prior experience need to have a safe training ground or a dedicated mentor in order to develop the judgment needed to participate in extreme sports. A novice does not have the judgment of an extreme, or elite, sport practitioner. This experience is difficult to get, and most errors in judgment are seen among novices and are the result of a lack of experience or a failure to analyze the entire situation in a methodical way (McCammon, 2002). Therefore, including extreme sports in an adventure programming context would be a recipe for disaster.

The Ethics of Promoting Addiction

Some researchers describe edgeworkers as sensation seekers. Zuckerman (1994) defines sensation seeking as "the seeking of varied, novel, complex, and intense sensations and experiences and the willingness to take physical, social, legal, and financial risks for the sake of such experience" (p. 27). People who are sensation seekers appear to have a novelty-seeking trait, which means they "poorly tolerate a monotonous mode of life and seek the new and unusual" (Golimbet et al., 2007, p. 601). According to Golimbet and colleagues (2007), these individuals tend to enjoy dangerous sports. Michel, Carton, and Jouvent (1997) and Hymbaugh and Garrett (1974) observed that people engaged in bungee jumping and skydiving, respectively, have high sensation-seeking behaviors. Zuckerman's (1990) sensation-seeking scale is complex and has many dimensions that seek to measure a person's eagerness to pursue sensations. According to Jack and Ronan (1998), "in a study comparing 166

athletes participating in high- and low-risk sports, athletes participating in high-risk sports scored significantly higher in total sensation seeking than those participating in low-risk sports" (p. 1079). One can presume that extreme-sport enthusiasts such as BASE jumpers are among the sensation, or novelty, seekers.

By looking at the brain, many researchers have found evidence of a genetic link to novelty-seeking behavior (Baron, 1998; Berns, 2005; Ebstein and Belmaker, 1997; Ebstein, Benjamin, and Belmaker, 2000; Golimbet et al., 2007; Malhotra and Goldman, 2000; Paterson, Sunohara, and Kennedy, 1999; Zuckerman, 1994). These researchers believe that D4DR, a dopamine receptor, generates strong feelings associated with pleasure and emotion (Alvear, 1999; Brisley, O'Hearn, and Vagg, 2008; Roberts, 1994; Toufexis, 1996; Zuckerman, 2000). Brisley, O'Hearn, and Vagg (2008) reveal that a release of dopamine neurotransmitters happens in anticipation of the BASE jump—as a motivator, for instance. Over time, the repeated exposure to an anticipated pleasure causes physical changes in the brain, often creating satisfying feelings of transcendence and euphoria (Berns, 2005). This provides evidence that sensation seekers become addicted to the chemical response the body provides (Golimbet et al., 2007) during their quest for novel experiences.

Many extreme-sport participants acknowledge that the adrenaline rush can be quite addictive. Stranger (1999) recognized the addictive quality of the adrenaline rush among the surfing community. Celsi, Rose, and Leigh (1993) report that both the baseline adrenaline rush and a person's perception of the risk decrease with more experience. As participants take greater risks, they become desensitized to those risks because the dopamine response decreases as exposure to risk increases (Brisley, O'Hearn, and Vagg, 2008). According to Wilde (1982), "sensation seekers, especially extreme sport participants, may have higher levels of target risk (acceptable perceived risk)" (cited in Napier, Findley, and Self, 2007, p. 1). Furthermore, Griffith and Hart (2005) found that skydivers had lower levels of death anxiety than non-skydivers.

To further illustrate this point using reversal theory, Pain and Kerr (2004) affirm that a "paratelic protective frame" often develops among arousal seekers. This falsely gives the person feelings of safety when real dangers exist and produces a paradox that a danger is not a danger. In their study, one such case involved a skydiver who had suffered numerous injuries but still found it vitally important to continue participating despite his doctor's recommendation to cease. Reversal theory has an additional construct, in which "continued participation may lead to dependence on the high levels of arousal associated with such activities" (Pain and Kerr, 2004, p. 339). This is congruent with comparisons of how dopamine and other stimulant drugs affect the body. Brisley, O'Hearn, and Vagg (2008) reveal that dopamine is the same chemical that releases when individuals use cocaine and the other stimulant drugs that produce an overwhelming experience of ecstasy and energy. Because novelty seekers can become chemically addicted to the adrenaline rush, adventure programmers should not promote sports that produce extremely high adrenaline. As a service to the public, the adventure industry should provide an appropriate level of adventure activities that do not subject participants to such a high level of risk that they seek the sensations associated with dopamine release in the body.

Measurable scientific evidence shows that extreme-sport participants can become addicted to their chosen sports. The need to fulfill the adrenaline rush causes many participants to take greater risks to derive the same dopamine release in the brain. So, where should programmers draw the line for which adventure activities they offer?

The Ethics of Exposing Participants to Experiences Involving Extreme Risk

Determining what is morally right for adventure programming is difficult when it comes to issues involving safety and risk management because adventure programming involves an inherent paradox in relation to the role of risk in the adventure experience (Hunt, 1990). We embrace risk to a degree to enliven participants' souls, yet we avoid excessive risk to safeguard participants' bodies. This paradox gives rise to an interesting moral dilemma in adventure programming. As Hunt (1990) states, "The ethical issue that raises its head, therefore, is whether it is morally acceptable to expose students to educational activities that might very well harm or kill them in order to achieve good educational ends" (p. 34).

Historically, professionals in the adventure programming industry have adopted ethical principles and guidelines that are congruent with those of other disciplines, such as psychology. Due to the considerable risk inherent to extreme sports, it would be difficult for adventure program professionals to follow these principles and guidelines

and offer a safe experience for participants. Some of the guidelines for professional outdoor leaders that have gained attention in the field of adventure programming include the following (Martin et al., 2006; Priest and Gass, 2005; Williamson and Gass, 1993):

- competence (maintaining and working only within the bounds of their knowledge base and practice),
- integrity (being honest and respectful to clients about their services),
- professional responsibility (for the client and the environment),
- respect (for people's rights and dignity, including nondiscriminatory practices against people with disabilities or a lower socioeconomic status, and obeying the law),
- concern for welfare (of clients' physiological and psychological needs), and
- social responsibility (to the community, regarding the interest of participants and the public).

Many participants of extreme sports breach the ethical principles and guidelines set forth by outdoor professionals. The first issue is that extreme sports, by their very nature, involve putting participants' lives or well-being at risk. This violates the guideline of having concern for the welfare of the client. Above all else, it is important that "no matter what the course of action you select, the *summum bonum* (i.e., do no harm) ethic you as a professional follow to resolve dilemmas should be guided by empathy for the client" (Priest and Gass, 2005, p. 290). Hunt (1990) states, "We put our students in situations that could harm or kill them, but we do everything reasonable in our power to prevent harm" (p. 39). The inability to mitigate the risks associated with extreme sports (for instance, the numerous tragedies associated with BASE jumping) is one of many ethical reasons why it is difficult to include extreme sports in the context of adventure programming.

At the Go Fast Games in 2003, a famous BASE jumper, Jeb Corliss, witnessed the death of his best friend and fellow jumper, Dwain Weston, as they attempted a stunt that no one had before performed. Weston attempted to fly over the Royal Gorge Bridge in a wingsuit but died instantly when he struck the bridge railing while traveling 120 miles (193 km) per hour. Corliss does not deny the severe risks associated with extreme parachuting stunts, and he continues to accept those risks.

Karnia Hollekim, another BASE jumper, suffered a near-fatal crash in 2006 and has since regained mobility of her legs after being told she would never walk again. In a recent documentary about her road to recovery, *20 Seconds of Joy*, Corliss recalls telling her the three rules of BASE jumping:

1. If you jump long enough, you will break bones.
2. If you're in the sport long enough, you're going to watch people die.
3. It's kind of pointless to talk about, but you're gonna die, too. Do this long enough, it's gonna kill you. If you can't handle that, then don't get into BASE jumping.

These three rules are clearly inconsistent with the ethical principles and guidelines for adventure programming listed previously.

A number of tragedies have been attributed to the commercialization of extreme sports, including many of the tragedies that have occurred on Mt. Everest. One of the most infamous commercial-climbing tragedies in history happened on Mt. Everest during the Mountain Madness Expedition in May of 1996. As detailed in Boukreev and DeWalt (1999), eight climbers died at extreme elevations during a blizzard. The lead expedition guide, Anatoli Boukreev, received much criticism for his actions that perilous day, most notably from Jon Krakauer (1998) in his book *Into Thin Air*. Krakauer's two main criticisms are that 1) Boukreev climbed without supplemental oxygen when guiding his clients, which Krakauer argues compromised his ability to guide effectively, and 2) Boukreev descended the mountain alone before the storm, abandoning his clients.

Boukreev rebuts these criticisms in his book, *The Climb*. He explains that he did not use supplemental oxygen because he did not want to risk the sudden loss of acclimatization should supplemental oxygen supplies run out. He argues, moreover, that after he descended and resupplied, he was able to save three climbers during five solo rescue attempts in which he suffered frostbite and risked his own life (Boukreev and DeWalt, 1999). Even though this tragedy stirred a heated ethical debate within the climbing community, Boukreev remained firm that he would have died in the storm had he not descended early.

Another such incident on Mt. Everest in 2006 involved experienced climber David Sharp, who died while attempting a solo climb of the mountain. More than 40 climbers saw Sharp alive and walked by him without attempting to rescue him. Sharp ultimately died on the mountain. The other climbers claimed that they thought he was beyond help or that he was already dead. This tragedy raised questions about "how ethical climbers should act and respond in emergency situations" (Sagert, 2009, p. 55). The commercialization of Mt. Everest has gained criticism from top mountaineers, who say that they would never leave a person unless the person was confirmed dead and that, given the amount of money people pay guides, too much pressure exists to complete a climb, no matter the human cost (Sagert, 2009).

Cost to the Public, Family, and Friends

As participation in extreme sports increases and accidents like the examples above increase, it will ultimately affect the public as well as family and friends. As extreme-sport accidents that require rescues increase, the forefront issue will become the burden to the taxpayer instead of the welfare of the participant. This will limit the access of using land to other user groups (such as climbers) and will cause increased litigation against rescuers. The effects on family and friends could become overwhelming. A loved one's injury or death would undoubtedly result in a high emotional toll. Relatives can suffer significant financial consequences and social exclusion due to a poor decision made by a friend or family member while performing an extreme sport. Outdoor professionals should not include extreme sports as a part of their programs because the cost to others is so great.

Costs to Rescuers

Excessive risk is put on the people who perform rescues. Although many rescuers accept that level of risk, it may increase the public's perception of a rescuer's level of responsibility. For 20 years, Mike Gauthier was a supervisor of search and rescue for Mount Rainier National Park. At the 2010 Wilderness Risk Management Conference, he revealed that the U.S. National Park Service spent only $4 million on search and rescue per year, but he emphasized the importance of not introducing the cost of a rescue into the decision-making matrix. He emphasized doing what is best for his staff and saving the person (Gauthier, 2010). His fear was that the public would question every expenditure. Litigation against rescuers, for instance, could increase, and the quality of rescues could be based on economic factors alone, leaving some injured at higher risk than others (e.g., helicopter versus ground-crew rescues).

Toll on Family and Friends

Participation in extreme sports also includes an emotional risk to the families involved. Breivik (2003) explains that the extreme-sport athlete can be selfish because each time they choose to participate they could die and leave their families and friends alone. This has happened to famous extreme athletes such as free solo climber Dan Osman, who died in his attempt to reset the world record for controlled freefalling. It also happened to Shane McConkey, a professional ski BASE jumper for Red Bull in Canada who died while filming an extreme video in the Italian Dolomites. These stories are incredibly tragic because both of these athletes had started families. Extreme athletes have to weigh the benefits of participating in their sport against the costs to their families and friends should they have an accident. Creyer, Ross, and Evers (2003) state, "Clearly when an injury or death occurs . . . the economic and psychological costs to the individual and that individual's family can be high" (p. 240).

Much like a soldier's family and friends, family and friends of extreme-sport participants have the stress of wondering whether their loved one will come home. The reality always exists that a soldier might not come home from a deployment. But because more of a stigma is attached to participation in extreme sports, many families fear that they will lose social support if their loved one dies. They might be blamed or blame themselves for not stopping the actions of the participant. The family might also lose economic support; most life insurance policies will not cover extreme-sport participants. Insurance companies in Belgium have already introduced an unintentionally discriminatory genetic-testing policy to detect those who are susceptible to high-risk behaviors. Andy de Klerk (2007) frames his previous experiences as a BASE jumper best when he states, "When I look at my small children and their perfect little bodies, BASE jumping no longer makes sense" (p. 21). This extreme athlete realized that his family is more important than seeking out the adrenaline rush that might kill him.

Conclusion

Including extreme sports in an adventure programming context would be detrimental. Professionals should abide by the ethical standards set forth by other professionals to maintain the best practices in order to offer the best quality program for their clients. The risks of extreme sports are just that: extreme. The job of professionals is to mitigate as much risk as possible. Priest and Gass (2005) state, "Adventure professionals structure risk in a manner that causes participants to perceive it as being enormously high, while in actuality it is much lower than perceived and more acceptable for producing functional change and growth" (p. 17). In this sense, extreme sports are the antithesis of adventure programming.

Our position addresses the many good reasons for excluding extreme sports from adventure programming. Extreme-sport programs violate numerous ethical guidelines set forth by previous outdoor professionals. As participation in extreme sports increases, so will the number of injuries to participants. If a participant involved in an extreme sport makes even a small mistake in judgment, it can cost a life. Practitioners would have to be completely honest about the probable chance of the client becoming addicted to the risk or about the likelihood of incurring significant losses due to a serious injury or death. Offering a program such as this does not practice *summum bonum* (i.e., do no harm) and lacks concern for the welfare of participants. Increased participation in extreme sports will put the livelihood of rescuers and other user groups at risk. It can have upsetting consequences and create emotional and economic risk for friends and families of participants. None of this is practicing good social responsibility.

Extreme sports should continue only within the elite subcultures that practice them. It is the duty of adventure programming professionals to minimize the risks of all the adventures on which they take their clients. Extreme sports have no place in adventure programming because they ignore many of the ethical guidelines developed by professionals within the industry. Adventure programmers should strive for a professional standard. The reality is that if a sport becomes safe enough to be a part of an adventure program, then it is no longer an extreme sport.

References

Alvear, M. (1999). Risky business. www.salon.com/health/feature/1999/07/22/risk [August 20, 2010].

Baron, M. (1998). Mapping genes for personality: Is the saga sagging? *Molecular Psychiatry, 3,* 106-108.

Bennett, G., Henson, R.K., & Zhang, J. (2003). Generation Y's perceptions of the action sports industry segment. *Journal of Sport Management, 17*(2), 95-115.

Berns, G. (2005). *Satisfaction: The science of finding true fulfillment.* New York: Henry Holt and Co.

Boukreev, A., & DeWalt, G.W. (1999). *The climb: Tragic ambitions on Everest.* New York: St. Martin's Griffin.

Breivik, G. (2003). Can BASE jumping be morally defended? The International Association for Philosophy in Sport Conference, University of Gloucestershire, Cheltenham.

Brisley, T., O'Hearn, D., & Vagg, R. (2008). *The brain.* [Documentary]. A&E Television Networks. Documentary AAAE146470. Toronto: Paradox Entertainment Group.

Brymer, E. (2005). *Extreme dude! A phenomenological perspective on the extreme sport experience.* Doctoral dissertation. Wollongong, Australia: University of Wollongong. www.library.uow.edu.au/adt-NWU/uploads/approved/adt-NWU20060508.145406/public/02Whole.pdf [October 24, 2007].

Celsi, R.L., Rose, R.L., & Leigh, T.W. (1993). An exploration of high-risk leisure consumption through skydiving. *Journal of Consumer Research, 20*(1), 1-24.

Creyer, E.H., Ross, W.T., & Evers, D. (2003). Risky recreation: An exploration of factors influencing the likelihood of participation and the effects of experience. *Leisure Studies, 22,* 239-253.

de Klerk, A. (2007). *Sharper edges.* Cape Town, South Africa: Sunbird Publishers.

Ebstein, R.P., & Belmaker, R.H. (1997). Saga of an adventure gene: Novelty seeking, substance abuse and the dopamine D4 receptor (D4DR) exon III repeat polymorphism. *Molecular Psychiatry, 2,* 381-384.

Ebstein, R.P., Benjamin, J., & Belmaker, R.H. (2000). Personality and polymorphisms of genes involved in aminergic neurotransmission. *European Journal of Pharmacology, 410,* 205-214.

Ferrell, J. (1995). Urban graffiti: Crime, control, and resistance. *Youth and Society, 27*(1), 73-92.

Ferrell, J. (1996). *Crimes of style: Urban graffiti and the politics of criminality.* Boston: Northeastern University Press.

Ferrell, J. (1997). Criminological Verstehen: Inside the immediacy of crime. *Justice Quarterly, 14*(1), 3-23.

Ferrell, J., Milovanovic, D., & Lyng, S. (2001). Edgework, media practices, and the elongation of meaning: A theoretical ethnography of the Bridge Day event. *Theoretical Criminology, 5*(2), 177-202.

Gauthier, M. (2010). *Conference opening.* Keynote speaker of the 2010 Wilderness Risk Management Conference, October 14-16, Colorado Springs, CO.

Golimbet, V.E., Alfimiva, M.V., Gritsenka, I.K., & Ebstein, R.P. (2007). Relationship between dopamine system genes and extraversion and novelty seeking. *Neuroscience and Behavioral Psychology, 37*(6), 601-606.

Griffith, J.D., & Hart, C.L. (2005). Collegiate skydivers: Do they fear death? *Journal of Worry and Affective Experience, 1*(2), 71-76.

Hunt, J.S. (1990). *Ethical issues in experiential education.* Dubuque, IA: Kendall/Hunt.

Hymbaugh, K., & Garrett, J. (1974). Sensation seeking among skydivers. *Perceptual and Motor Skills, 38,* 118.

Jack, S.J., & Ronan, K.R. (1998). Sensation seeking among high- and low-risk sports participants. *Personality and Individual Differences, 25,* 1063-1083.

Krakauer, J. (1998). *Into thin air: A personal account of the Mt. Everest disaster.* New York: Anchor Books.

Laurendeau, J. (2006). "He didn't go in doing a skydive": Sustaining the illusion of control in an edgework activity. *Sociological Perspectives, 49*(4), 583-605.

Lupton, D., & Tulloch, J. (2002). "Life would be pretty dull without risk": Voluntary risk-taking and its pleasure. *Health, Risk, and Society, 4*(2), 113-124.

Lyng, S. (1990). Edgework: A sociological analysis of voluntary risk taking. *American Journal of Sociology, 95*(4), 851-886.

Lyng, S. (1998). Dangerous methods: Risk taking and the research process. In J. Ferrell & M.S. Hamm (Eds.), *Ethnography at the edge* (pp. 221-251). Boston: Northeastern University Press.

Malhotra, A.K., & Goldman, D. (2000). The dopamine D(4) receptor gene and novelty seeking. *American Journal of Psychiatry, 157,* 1885-1886.

Martin, B., Cashel, C., Wagstaff, M., & Breunig, M. (2006). *Outdoor leadership: Theory and practice.* Champaign, IL: Human Kinetics.

McCammon, I. (2002). Evidence of heuristic traps in recreational avalanche accidents. *Proceedings of the International Snow Science Workshop, Penticton, British Columbia.* http://monosar.org/avalanche_safety/article_avalanche_study_mccammon_human_factors_traps.pdf [January 6, 2012].

Michel, G., Carton, S., & Jouvent, R. (1997). Sensation seeking and anhedonia in risk taking. Study of a population of bungy jumpers. *Encephale, 23,* 403-411.

Napier, V., Findley, C.S., & Self, D.R. (2007). Risk homeostasis: A case study of the adoption of a safety innovation on the level of perceived risk. *Proceedings of the American Society of Business and Behavioral Sciences.* February 22-25, Las Vegas, NV. www.vicnapier.com/Risk/4%20Risk%20Homeostasis.doc [January 6, 2012].

Pain, M., & Kerr, J.H. (2004). Extreme risk taker who wants to continue taking part in high risk sports after serious injury. *British Journal of Sports Medicine, 38,* 337-339.

Park, H. (2004). *Analyzing motivational factors of action sports participants.* Unpublished masters thesis. Pullman, WA: Washington State University. www.dissertations.wsu.edu/Thesis/Fall2004/h_park_122104.pdf [October 13, 2007].

Paterson, A.D., Sunohara, G.A., & Kennedy, J.L. (1999). Dopamine D4 receptor gene: Novelty or nonsense? *Neuropsychopharmacology, 21,* 3-16.

Priest, S., & Gass, M.A. (2005). *Effective leadership in adventure programming.* Champaign, IL: Human Kinetics.

Roberts, P. (1994). Risk (the leisure pursuit of danger is a growth industry). *Psychology Today, 24*(6), 50.

Sagert, K.B. (2009). Ethics and extreme sports. In K.B. Sagert (Ed.), *The encyclopedia of extreme sports* (pp. 53-55). Westport, CT: Greenwood Publishing.

Stranger, M. (1999). The aesthetics of risk. A study of surfing. *International Review for the Sociology of Sport, 34*(3), 265-276.

Toufexis, A. (1996). Risk compensation: Implications for safety interventions. *Organizational Behavior and Human Decision Process, 66*(1), 73-88.

Varley, P. (2006). Confecting adventure and playing with meaning: The adventure commodification continuum. *Journal of Sport Tourism, 11*(2), 173-194.

Wilde, G.J.S. (1982). The theory of risk homeostasis: Implications for safety and health. *Risk Analysis, 2,* 209-225.

Williamson, J., & Gass, M.A. (1993). *Manual of program accreditation standards for adventure programs.* Boulder, CO: Association for Experiential Education.

Zuckerman, M. (1990). The psychophysiology of sensation seeking. *Journal of Personality, 58,* 313-345.

Zuckerman, M. (1994). *Behavioral expression and biosocial bases of sensation seeking.* New York: Cambridge University Press.

Zuckerman, M. (2000). Are you a risk taker? *Psychology Today, 33*(6), 52.

Should nonprofit and educational programs be required to obtain permits to use public land?

Public land managers struggle under the weight of budget cuts, lack of resources, and chronic overuse. Regulation is one of the most effective ways to manage recreational use of public lands. One aspect of regulation includes limiting and controlling use through permitting systems. Access to many of the most heavily used outdoor recreation areas is restricted completely unless those wishing to use the land obtain the proper permit. In some cases, private individuals and groups must wait years before they are able to obtain a coveted permit. Although this may seem unfair, many land managers argue that a permitting system is the best option for providing equitable access to outdoor recreation resources while at the same time protecting environmental integrity. Permits also provide a revenue stream to supplement government funding, allow land managers to ensure that users are prepared and properly trained, and provide a layer of legal protection that otherwise would be difficult to obtain. The permitting process offers tremendous advantages and serves as an important management tool for natural resources.

Although one can make a logical argument for implementing a permitting process, a select group of users is quickly losing access to public resources. Land managers do not typically distinguish between commercial enterprises, nonprofit organizations, and educational institutions. Camps, school groups, university programs, youth organizations, and others must adhere to the same permit requirements as private businesses. The issue becomes one of exclusion because nonprofit and educational institutions already operate on shoestring budgets. The added burden of permit fees makes it impossible to program on public lands. Many of these organizations serve populations that would otherwise not have access to public lands. Introducing an increasingly diverse society to the wilderness is of critical importance if we hope to preserve our nation's unique natural heritage.

There also exists a select group of educational institutions that specifically train professional outdoor leaders. The very students who engage in these courses enter the outdoor profession as environmental stewards. Public land managers must realize that this army of trained, qualified professional outdoor leaders could be one of their most important assets. However, the existing permitting process excludes universities and other professional preparation programs. In some cases, permits are not available. In other situations, land-management insurance requirements inhibit the ability of nonprofit and educational programs to obtain permits. Agencies that manage public land must take a harder look at who is required to operate under a permit.

Michael Gassner argues in favor of requiring permits for nonprofits and educational groups. He outlines the ethical and environmental rationale that defends the necessity of permits. Gassner emphasizes the ethical imperative that adventure programmers have as environmental stewards. He forces us to take a critical look at our responsibility to protect our finite and unique resources.

John Peden outlines four arguments against permit requirements for nonprofit and educational groups. Peden focuses on lack of evidence to support use limits, the underlying rationale for permit systems, inconsistent definitions of commercial use, and unreasonable indemnification requirements. He makes clear that recent changes in the outfitting and guiding policies on public lands need critical review.

The serious ramifications of this argument directly affect the adventure programming industry. We need careful consideration and a unified course of action to protect what we as a profession deem valuable.

Should nonprofit and educational programs be required to obtain permits to use public land?

YES Permits Required for All: The Right Thing to Do

Michael Gassner, PhD, instructor of tourism and outdoor leadership, Oregon State University–Cascades, Bend, Oregon, United States

Lani teaches undergraduates in a recreation degree program at a university in the United States. She recently posed the following question to students in one of her classes: "Do you think we as a class should be required to obtain and pay for a permit to run our outdoor classes in a publically designated Wilderness area?" Lani's students could actually see from their classroom part of the Wilderness area in question. The response from students taking both sides of the issue sparked a passionate, unexpected debate.

- One student said that if we can't get a permit, we should just go anyway because we are taxpayers and should have the liberty and freedom to use the Wilderness. We are a university class and are not in the business of making a profit and should be exempt.

- Another said that if we can't experience our own unique Wilderness that is right out there, how can we teach others to be advocates for Wilderness?

- Another student said that permits are necessary; otherwise, how can land managers know who and how many people use the Wilderness?

- Another student shouted that permits should be required of any group because there is only so much Wilderness and not everyone can be out there at the same time.

- Nearly coming unglued in her chair, another student screamed that groups should have to get a permit because hordes of groups will trash the place!

To Lani's surprise, no clear consensus existed among the students. Toward the end of class, after emotions settled, Lani thanked the students for sharing their views. She, however, did not share her own mixed feelings. She could not cognitively commit to a resounding *yes* or *no* to the question.

Lani, like many other professional outdoor leaders, understands the perspectives of both the user and land manager.

I argue that nonprofit and educational adventure programs should be required to obtain special-use permits to access public lands regardless of whether fees are charged. The issue of whether fees should be assessed for recreational use is still being discussed (Moore and Driver, 2005). This important topic goes hand in hand with special-use permits but is outside the scope of this discussion. The major premise of this argument is based on the concept that our public lands are *finite* and *unique* resources that are best protected and sustained by limiting use. Natural resource managers use permit systems to ensure the integrity of these two critical variables that define the state of our public lands. In addition, I argue that obtaining a special-use permit is an ethical imperative for any professional outdoor leader. I conclude by arguing that adventure programs need to go beyond the current structural processes and embrace a more collaborative and service-oriented vision for the future use of public lands.

Overview of the Public Permitting Process

In general terms, a special-use permit is "a formal agreement between an agency and a partner that authorizes the partner to undertake a relatively unique operation within the agency's jurisdiction" (Moore and Driver, 2005, p. 331). The Bureau of Land Management (BLM), the United States Forest Service (USFS), the United States Fish and Wildlife Service, the National Park Service, the United States Corps of Engineers, and the Bureau of Reclamation are the primary agencies that manage public lands in the United States. Together, these agencies manage approximately 651 million acres of land (Moore and Driver, 2005). The special-use permits granted by the BLM and the USFS are central to this argument. These two agencies are the largest owners of public lands that are managed for recreational use in the United States.

The BLM requires special-recreation permits for "commercial use, competitive use, vending, special area use, and organized group activity and event use" (Bureau of Land Management, 2007, p. 9). Under BLM requirements, adventure programs are considered to be partaking in an organized group activity. The USFS is required to issue special-use permits for nonprofit and educational adventure programs because these programs are classified as outfitters or guides. The USFS considers that outfitting and guiding include but are not limited to "packing, hunts, education, float trips, canoe or horse liveries, shuttle services, ski touring, helicopter skiing, jeep tours, boat tours, and fishing trips and may be conducted by, among others, educational, rehabilitation, and interpretive ventures and outdoor institutional organizations, including both for-profit and non-profit entities" (U.S. Forest Service, 2008, p. 27).

Finite and Unique Resources

The amount of public land available for recreation use is finite. The percentage of private land owners who allow the public to recreate on their lands is also decreasing. Approximately 40 percent of open land in the United States is publicly owned and 60 percent is privately owned. However, only about 28 percent of public land owned by the federal government is available for recreational use (Moore and Driver, 2005). At the same time, the demand for recreational lands is high and increasing, the lands are not distributed equally across the United States, and use is uneven (Betz, English, and Cordell, 1999; Teasley et al., 1999). Nonprofit and educational adventure programs often seek to use public lands designated as Wilderness areas, which have particularly scarce overall land area. For example, "Alaska contains just over half of America's Wilderness; only about 2.7 percent of the contiguous United States—an area about the size of Minnesota—is protected as Wilderness" (wilderness.net, 2010). The finite nature of our public lands necessitates that resource managers must somehow control and monitor use of our limited resources. Permitting is the most powerful way to accomplish this grave and nearly impossible task. An increasing and active population also threatens these finite resources.

The population of the United States has increased by 13.4 percent since 1982 (NSRE, 1994-95, p. ii) and reached 272,690,813 by July of 1999 (U.S. Census, 1999). On November 11, 2010, the population of the United States was 310,684,108 and counting (U.S. Census, 2010). Current birth rates in the United States are also well above death rates (infoplease.com, 2010). Our population will continue to grow, yet public lands are not increasing at an appreciable rate. Recreational use of public lands has also increased and is projected to continue (Moore and Driver, 2005). When one considers these disturbing trends, it is not unreasonable to expect protection for these resources. Special-use permits offer some protection to public lands and are part of land managers' responsibility to manage public lands for recreational purposes.

One tool for natural resource management that is analogous to special permits is the permit system for hunting. Obtaining a special-use permit to use public lands is no different from having to obtain a hunting permit. Permits are required in the United States to hunt animals such as deer, elk, and water fowl. These permits are a way to limit the type and number of animals killed and provide a record of kills. In some areas in the United States, strict quotas exist for the number of hunting permits issued and the number of animals that can be taken. Imagine the scenario that would play out if one did not need a permit to hunt wolves. Many years ago, Aldo Leopold witnessed firsthand the deer population explosion that occurred with devastating results when too many wolves were killed in the Gila National Forest of New Mexico. The hunting permit system ensures a level of protection that enhances the natural resource and meets user needs. We would all like to believe that everyone will behave in an altruistic manner and do nothing to harm a resource. History has shown, however, that species and resources become devastated if no limits are in place. Special-use permits for nonprofits and educational programs exist to ensure protection and meet user needs.

In addition to the critical issue of finiteness, our public lands are unique. Public lands that are open for recreational use exist as unique entities based on specific characteristics that are distinctive to each entity. The distribution of special-use permits is associated primarily with scarcity of resources. However, USFS administrators deem the permitting system necessary based on the finite and unique variables of these resources and differing use pressures (S. Moore, personal communication, October 20, 2010). Each piece of public land differs in aspects such as land area, proximity to heavily populated areas, ecological conditions, and type of recreational use. For example, the urban area of Los Angeles has a population of more than 9 million (U.S. Census, 2009a) and is nearly adjacent to the San Bernardino National Forest (800,000 acres). The Boundary Waters Canoe Area Wilderness (BWCAW), within the Superior National Forest (1.09 million acres) in northeastern Minnesota, belongs to a state that has a population of approximately only 5 million (U.S. Census, 2009b). The unique mountain and desert environment of the San Bernardino National Forest attracts multitudes of hikers, whereas others are more likely to canoe in the BWCAW because of the abundance of lakes. These two examples show that the uniqueness of individual public lands and their corresponding characteristics dictate types of use. Each potential permit and resource must be carefully analyzed to ensure a good fit between user behavior and protection of the area's unique resource.

As they wrestle with the validity of special-use permits, adventure programs should consider the idea of carefully matching a potential user group to a resource. Often, those charged with acquiring special-use permits for adventure programs become frustrated at the vast array of responses given by different special-use administrators concerning public lands and wish for a more standardized and transparent application process for all public lands. This notion of standardizing the permitting process is impossible. All public lands are different and require specific decision-making criteria to protect and sustain the unique features associated with each resource. In addition, decision making must take into account the diverse demographics of people and groups that use each resource.

Land managers need time to analyze each potential user group. A special-use administrator with more than 15 years of experience acknowledged that the special-use permit process is a management tool that allows land managers time to formulate an informed decision (R. Wesseler, personal communication, October 19, 2010). Congressional laws and codes of federal regulations are frameworks for the initial screening of applicants. Subsequent decisions are based on specific forest plans or land-use plans. Finally, land managers consider other variables such as desired conditions in the area, possible duplication of existing permits, user days not utilized, existing and potential type of pressure on resources, and the competency, safety, and knowledge of potential applicants. The limits of acceptable change system (Stankey et al., 1985) used by the USFS is an example of a tool that is available to assist land managers in analyzing the desired conditions of a resource. The limits of acceptable change system focuses on human-induced impacts to a resource and is "a framework for establishing acceptable and appropriate resource and social conditions in recreation settings" (Stankey et al., 1985, p. iii). This nine-step process requires citizen involvement throughout the entire process, which facilitates collaboration, transparency, and understanding of the process. This is one of the many management tools available to land managers, but it takes time to implement properly.

All these variables assist the land manager in the decision-making process, but the onus falls on land managers to make the final call. The subjective nature of a permit decision is a strength of the system because it allows human judgment to apply the global issues of finiteness and uniqueness. Special-use permits ensure that finite and unique resources match the ever-increasing and diverse user pool. As the Bureau of Land Management (2007) states, special-use permits are "a tool for managing recreation use; reducing user conflicts; protecting natural and cultural resources; informing users; gathering use information; and obtaining a fair return for commercial and certain other uses of public land" (p. 7). A fair return for commercial and other uses may need to be construed not only in economic terms but also in terms of what users can return to the resource.

A Professional Ethic

Permits in general and special-use permits in particular are intended to limit use in an effort to protect and sustain a finite and unique resource. Use levels are addressed in a number of ways. Some of these methods, such as mandatory Wilderness permits, have been viewed as extreme and have caused individuals to describe certain public lands as police states (Behan, 1974). Less-extreme alternatives to mandatory permitting of public lands noted by Hammitt and Cole (1998) include request, reservation, lottery, first come first serve, and merit (pp. 256-264). Other means to limit use are geographic quotas, limiting frequency of visits, and time rationing (Dustin, 1977). Many of these limiting techniques were introduced either directly or as concepts in a seminal essay by Hardin (1968) titled "The Tragedy of the Commons," which discusses the likely degradation of resources if unlimited access to public resources were to occur. Hendee and Dawson (2002), Hammitt and Cole (1998), and Manning (2007) have extensively discussed methods to limit visitor use. The literature has also extensively discussed and critiqued which specific tools are appropriate to measure, and subsequently manage and limit, impact on public lands (Buckley, 1999; Lindberg, McCool, and Stankey, 1997; Manning, 1997, 2005). To date no clear consensus exists regarding the best way to measure, manage, and limit use on public lands.

Inconclusive research could form the basis of an argument to exempt nonprofits and educational groups from permits; however, it is secondary in importance to an ethos of environmental stewardship that adventure programmers profess to embrace. Unclear and contradictory research is no excuse to exempt nonprofit and educational adventure programs from obtaining a special-use permit. A technical solution based on empirical research demands "little or nothing in the way of change in human values or ideas of morality" (Hardin, 1968, p. 1243). The fundamental question that permeates my argument boils down to, What is the right thing to do? At its core, the question of permit exemption is not just a pragmatic or technical matter; it is an ethical one. Hunt (1994) states, "Questions of ethics or values are not settled exclusively by means of empirical inquiry. To attempt to answer the question of what ought to be requires a philosophical response rather than an empirical response" (p. 6).

Generally, public lands are supposed to be managed for "the greatest good to the greatest number for the longest time" (Pinchot, 2000, p. 34). The National Forest Service Management Act is the main law governing U.S. Forest Service decision making regarding the public lands under its jurisdiction. The Federal Land Policy and Management Act of 1976 is the BLM's equivalent law. Both laws aim to manage public lands from a utilitarian perspective. Utilitarianism is a consequentialist theory of ethics that argues that "actions are good if, and only if, they bring about the greatest good for the greatest number" (Hunt, 1994, p. 15). Ethical consequentialists are concerned with the results of an act, not the act itself. In other words, do the ends justify the means? One then needs to ask, in the case of special-use permits, what is the greatest good for the greatest number and do the ends justify the means?

Users should obtain special-use permits because the greatest good for the greatest number is the protection of the resource for society now and in the future. This greatest good (the end) is brought about through a special-use permit process (the means) administered by government land manag-ers. Manning (2007) states, "Government ownership allows for a broad and long-term management perspective that is focused on the ultimate welfare of society as a whole (as opposed to the individual), thus offering protection for resources that are ultimately important to society" (p. 9). Public lands are important not only to adventure programs but also to society. Unfortunately, individuals or individual adventure programs often want the maximum good for themselves, not necessarily for the resource. The maximum good for an individual or individual program may not be the maximum good for society.

Conclusion

We cannot wait to ponder inconclusive research while our public lands become degraded. The finite and unique nature of our resources requires that land managers apply all tools at their disposal. It may be time to change the language of special permits to something that suggests benefit to public lands and society rather than restrictions. The word "permit" implies permission to partake in something and a power differential between those issuing the permit and those being permitted. The word "special" suggests that some person or group is special, or possibly apart from the general public. What if public land managers were to use the phrase "stewardship pass"? Stewardship implies collective care of something that we all hold in common and carries with it a connotation of responsibility, collective ownership, and collaboration. Nonprofit and educational adventure programs would then have the opportunity to become stewards of public lands in partnership with land managers instead of being special users who use the land only in special instances. This approach has been voiced by others who have encouraged individuals to become "actively involved in the care, maintenance, and study of wilderness landscapes" (Simon and Alagona, 2009, p. 32). The word "pass" implies that someone or something is temporary and travels through an area. This would emphasize the transitory nature of adventure program use.

The word "special" warrants an additional mention. It may imply too much individuality, but admittedly, individuality is revered in American society. Someone may perceive not being considered special as an affront to their very notion of freedom and liberty. The idea of individual freedom and liberty is deeply ingrained in the psyche of the American people. Recall Lani's student who said that she should have the liberty and freedom to use a Wilderness area. Nash (1987) states,

"Liberty is the single most potent concept in the history of American thought" (p. 10); however, it comes at a price. As Hardin (1968) notes, "We are locked into a system of 'fouling our own nest,' so long as we behave only as independent, rational, free-enterprisers" (p. 1245). It is possibly time for adventure programs and public land managers to think more collectively. As a nation, only recently have we become acutely aware that the conundrum of finite and unique public lands and an ever-increasing population are impinging on our conceptions of liberty and freedom. Personal liberty may be infringed on each time someone is asked to obtain such a stewardship pass. In an alternative paradigm, however, a stewardship pass may also give an adventure program the liberty to serve the public land that it wishes to use.

The challenge that I now put forward to land managers and adventure programs is to develop a service ethic that goes beyond Leopold's (1949) land ethic to incorporate the value of service. In this way, the land is not just taken care of, but served. In this service paradigm, some sort of service that benefits the resource would be required in order to obtain the stewardship pass. Is it really right for adventure programs to reap the benefits of using public lands without doing their fair share for the resource itself? We as a society need to do what is right for public lands and think about how we can give a fair return to the land.

A service ethic is needed whereby adventure programs understand the need for serving the resource for which a pass is sought and develop the desire to do so. As in the spirit of Aldo Leopold, who first developed the idea of a land ethic, users could come to understand that although they may have the liberty and right to use public lands, with this liberty comes a responsibility to serve and help sustain the lands on which they travel. Adventure programs must become active players for the collective betterment of the resource, not merely passive special users who give nothing in return for the benefits they accrue. For example, adventure programs could work in collaboration with land mangers on restoration or maintenance projects, data-collection efforts, trail adoptions, search and rescue operations, or other services that benefit the land. In the end, special-use permits are the right thing to do.

References

Behan, R. (1974). Police state Wilderness: A comment on mandatory Wilderness permits. *Journal of Forestry, 72*, 98-99.

Betz, C., English, D., & Cordell, H. (1999). Outdoor recreation resources. In H.K. Cordell, C. Betz, J.M. Bowker, D.B.K. English, S.H. Mou, J.C. Bergstrom, J.R. Teasley, M.A. Tarrant, & J. Loomis (Eds.), *Outdoor recreation in American life: A national assessment of demand and supply trends* (pp. 39-182). Champaign, IL: Sagamore.

Buckley, R. (1999). An ecological perspective on carrying capacity. *Annals of Tourism Research, 26*, 705-708.

Bureau of Land Management. (2007). Recreation permits and fees manual (2930). www.blm.gov/pgdata/etc/medialib/blm/wo/Planning_and_Renewable_Resources/recreation_images/trip_planning.Par.69375.File.dat/2930%20Manual.pdf [October 22, 2010].

Dustin, D. (1977). *Gaming-simulation in the college classroom: An assessment of Quagmire, a recreation resource management game.* Unpublished doctoral dissertation. Minneapolis: University of Minnesota.

Hammitt, W., & Cole, D. (1998). *Wildland recreation: Ecology and management.* 2nd ed. New York: Wiley.

Hardin, G. (1968). The tragedy of the commons. *Science 162*, 1243-1248.

Hendee, J., & Dawson, C. (2002). *Wilderness management: Stewardship and protection of resources and values.* 3rd ed. Golden, CO: Fulcrum Publishing.

Hunt, J. (1994). *Ethical issues in experiential education.* Boulder, CO: The Association for Experiential Education.

infoplease.com. (2010). Crude birth and death rates from selected countries. www.infoplease.com/ipa/A0004395.html [November 1, 2010].

Leopold, A. (1949). *A sand county almanac: And sketches here and there.* New York: Oxford University Press.

Lindberg, K., McCool, S., & Stankey, G. (1997). Rethinking carrying capacity. *Annals of Tourism Research, 24*, 401-465.

Manning, R. (1997). Social carrying capacity of parks and outdoor recreation areas. *Parks and Recreation, 32*, 32-38.

Manning, R. (2005). The limits of tourism in parks and protected areas: Managing carrying capacity in the U.S. national parks. In *Taking tourism to the limits: Concepts, management, practice* (pp. 129-139). New York: Pergamon Press.

Manning, R. (2007). *Parks and carrying capacity. Commons without tragedy.* Washington, DC: Island Press.

Moore, R., & Driver, B. (2005). *Introduction to outdoor recreation: Providing and managing natural resource based opportunities.* State College, PA: Venture.

Nash, R. (1987). *The rights of nature. A history of environmental ethics.* Madison, WI: University of Wisconsin Press.

NSRE. (1994-95). Executive summary. www.srs.fs.usda.gov/trends/fsexecsum.pdf [November 11, 2010].

Pinchot, G. (2000). Principles of conservation. In P. List (Ed.), *Environmental ethics and forestry: A reader* (pp. 32-35). Philadelphia: Temple University Press.

Simon, G., & Alagona, P. (2009). Beyond leave no trace. *Ethics, Place, and Environment, 12*(1), 17-34.

Stankey, G., Cole, D., Lucas, R., Petersen, M., & Frissell, S. (1985). *The limits of acceptable change (LAC) system for wilderness planning.* General technical report INT-176. Ogden, UT: Intermountain Forest and Range Experiment Station.

Teasley, R.J., Bergstrom, J.C., Cordell, H.K., Zarnoch, S.J., & Gentle, P. (1999). Private lands and outdoor recreation in the United States. In H.K. Cordell, C. Betz, J.M. Bowker, D.B.K. English, S.H. Mou, J.C. Bergstrom, J.R. Teasley, M.A. Tarrant, & J. Loomis (Eds.), *Outdoor recreation in American life: A national assessment of demand and supply trends* (pp. 183-218). Champaign, IL: Sagamore.

U.S. Census. (1999). Population clocks. www.census.gov/popest/archives/1990s/popclockest.txt [November 11, 2010].

U.S. Census. (2009a). Los Angeles County, California. http://quickfacts.census.gov/qfd/states/06/06037.html [November 11, 2010].

U.S. Census. (2009b). Minnesota population. www.google.com/publicdata?ds=uspopulation&met=population&idim=state:27000&dl=en&hl=en&q=minnesota+population [November 11, 2010].

U.S. Census. (2010). Home page. www.census.gov [November 11, 2010].

U.S. Forest Service. (2008). *Forest Service handbook* (2709.11, 41.53). WO amendment 2709.11-2008-2 FSH 2709.11—Special use handbook chapter 40—Special use administration. Washington, DC: U.S. Forest Service.

wilderness.net. (2010). Creation and growth of the national wilderness preservation system. www.wilderness.net/index.cfm?fuse=NWPS&sec=fastfacts [November 1, 2010].

Should nonprofit and educational programs be required to obtain permits to use public land?

NO · Special Use Permit Requirements: The Prisoner's Dilemma

John Peden, PhD, associate professor of recreation and tourism management, Georgia Southern University, Statesboro, Georgia, United States

In October of 2007, the U.S. Forest Service issued proposed directives for revisions to outfitting and guiding policies on public land (Proposed Directives for Forest Service Outfitting and Guiding, 2007). The proposed changes set off a firestorm of controversy within the outdoor education community and outfitter–guides in general. The U.S. Forest Service claimed that changes were necessary to protect public health and safety and the environmental resources necessary for high-quality visitor services. Much of the contention surrounded the definition of commercial use, the establishment of temporary and priority use allocations, and related indemnification requirements. Professional associations that represented outfitters, guides, educational institutions, and nonprofit organizations moved quickly to provide public input within the 90-day comment period. The vigorous public debate that surrounded the proposed revisions was symptomatic of a larger problem that has pervaded outdoor recreation planning and management for decades: How can federal land-management agencies meet increasing demands for recreational access while protecting the natural and cultural resources under their jurisdictions?

This position addresses current approaches to commercial-use allocation on federal lands and presents four arguments against special-use permit requirements for nonprofit and educational adventure programs. First, evidence to support use limits and related allocation decisions is lacking; second, special-use permit requirements are being used to generate revenue; third, the definition of commercial use as applied by the Bureau of Land Management (BLM) and the U.S. Forest Service is inappropriate; and finally, indemnification requirements preclude many nonprofit and educational programs from acquiring special-use permits.

Tragedy of the Commons

Garrett Hardin (1968) argues that the definitive question in environmental management is how best to promote the conservation of common pool resources. In his classic thesis, Hardin uses the analogy of a cattle pasture to illustrate the difficulty of limiting human population growth. He notes that a herdsman would attempt to maximize individual self-interest by adding as many cattle to the pasture as possible. The herdsman would retain the economic benefits derived from selling these animals, but the commons would collectively bear much of the cost in the form of a degraded pasture. Other herdsmen were bound to conclude that the only rational course of action was to follow the example set by the original herdsman, thereby further degrading the commons. Hardin believes that technology alone could not solve the problem and concludes that the only solution is government regulation, or "mutual coercion, mutually agreed upon." As is the case in the current dispute over special-use permits, the government would ultimately define acceptable levels of impact, allocate use, and enforce decisions accordingly.

Robert Manning is a noted scholar and professor of natural resource management at the Rubenstein School of Environment and Natural Resources at the University of Vermont. In a recent work, Manning (2007) challenged Hardin's assumption that individuals are motivated primarily by economic self-interest. Manning argues that people are capable of altruistic behaviors and other actions that transcend short-term gain. He uses the prisoner's dilemma (Kuhn, as cited in Manning, 2007) to illustrate how cooperation can overcome the limitations of self-interested behavior. Two prisoners who are accused of the same crime have the options of remaining silent, confessing, or implicating each other. Although each option has advantages and disadvantages, the solution to the problem is to work together to achieve mutual gain: the release of both prisoners. Manning concludes "that the model of human behavior proposed by Hardin may be too rigid and limiting, at least in certain contexts" (p. 11). Perhaps solutions to disputes over recreation access lie not in government regulation but in educating outdoor enthusiasts about the necessity of working together to ensure equitable access to public lands. This will prove exceedingly difficult if land-management agencies continue to alienate nonprofit and educational adventure programs through existing commercial-use policies.

A Question of Capacity

Manning (2007) emphasizes that the tragedy of the commons is based on the assumption that unchecked growth is unsustainable. Few would argue with this point of view. However, the need to establish or maintain an economically viable business has led many organizations to seek larger and larger use allocations. The U.S. Forest Service and other federal agencies are now faced with the challenge of preventing the tragedy on public lands. The predominant strategy has been to focus on the management of recreational carrying capacities. Early approaches to capacity focused on use levels that areas could sustain without adverse effects on the environment (Manning, 2007; Moore and Driver, 2005). Such approaches were formula based (i.e., mathematical) and have largely been discredited (Moore and Driver, 2005).

Wagar (1964) may have been the first to note that questions of capacity also involve social and managerial components. In other words, capacity is influenced by conditions such as conflict and crowding as well as the management strategies to mitigate these impacts. Federal agencies now rely on standards-based approaches such as the Limits of Acceptable Change and the Visitor Experience and Resource Protection frameworks. These approaches 1) define desirable biophysical, social, and managerial conditions; 2) establish indicators and standards of quality; and 3) employ monitoring and management actions to ensure that standards are not exceeded (Hendee and Dawson, 2002; Manning, 2007; Moore and Driver, 2005). Unfortunately, the scope of existing capacity studies appears to be insufficient to justify limitations on use in many of the areas under the jurisdictions of federal land-management agencies. Manning (2007) reported that 57 percent of National Park Service areas were unable to estimate carrying capacity as of 1993. Of the remaining 43 percent, less than half based their capacity decisions on scientific evidence. More recently, more than 76 percent of National Park Service managers stated that they were unable to estimate carrying capacity; only 5 percent reported capacity assessments that were based on scientific

data (Abbe and Manning, 2007). Nonprofit and educational providers have also raised concerns about capacity studies. In comments on the Proposed Directives for Forest Service Outfitting and Guiding, the American Mountain Guides Association (2008) states, "Across the national forest system, the status of needs assessments, capacity analyses, and commercial allocations vary widely. The Directives are vague and leave a great deal of discretion to the field" (p. 7). The Association of Outdoor Recreation and Education (2008) echoes similar sentiments:

> The inability of the agency to actually perform such studies is often used as a rationale for not considering new priority or temporary use permits. The language in the directive should acknowledge the resources required to develop credible data to ensure that such studies will be conducted as a means of fairly allocating use and facilitating the growth of new guiding business on Forest Service Lands. (p. 3)

The lack of existing capacity studies and insufficient resources to conduct future assessments is the first argument against special-use permit requirements for nonprofit and educational adventure programs. I use a recent decision for appeal regarding access to the Chattooga National Wild and Scenic River as an example.

For more than 30 years, whitewater boating has been banned on the Headwaters section of the Chattooga National Wild and Scenic River. In 2004, the American Whitewater Association appealed the Sumter National Forest Revised Land and Resource Management Plan on the grounds that it violated the Wilderness Act, the National Wild and Scenic Rivers Act, and related legislation. The American Whitewater Association sought access to the Headwaters section for private parties of kayakers and canoeists. Although the appeal did not pertain to commercial access, it is relevant to the current debate over allocations of special-use permits. Gloria Manning, reviewing officer for Chief Forester Dale Bosworth, concludes:

> The Regional Forester does not provide an adequate basis for continuing the ban on boating above Highway 28. Because the record provided to me does not contain the evidence to continue the boating ban, his decision is not consistent with the direction in Section 10(a) of the

WSRA or Sections 2(a) and 4(b) of the Wilderness Act or agency regulations implementing these Acts. (Manning, 2005, p. 5)

This decision is of critical importance. The administrative rules of the U.S. Forest Service state that the agency must use indirect management strategies (e.g., education, interpretation, and site design) to control impacts before relying on direct management strategies such as use-allocation systems. Furthermore, the decision to limit use must be based on periodic capacity assessments. Thus, the chief forester mandated that a visitor-use capacity analysis be conducted to determine whether acceptable levels of impact had been exceeded. Although a temporary ban on boating on the Headwaters remains in place, this case clearly illustrates that decisions to limit use cannot be arbitrary and must be supported by capacity assessments. At the present time, it is questionable whether such studies exist to support special-use permit requirements for nonprofit and education adventure programs.

Environmental Protection or Revenue Generation?

Thomas More's (2002) controversial article, "The Parks Are Being Loved to Death, and Other Frauds and Deceits in Recreation Management," raises an interesting question: "Are the parks being loved to death, or is overuse mostly a manifestation of the interests of agencies and researchers?" (p. 60). More argues that the federal agencies are primarily concerned with justifying budget requests and maintaining political influence. More states, "As a problem, overuse helps justify budgets. Positions are needed, regulations must be passed and enforced, and facilities and environments must be repaired or restored, all serving to enhance agency power (control) and prestige" (p. 59). Although More's argument may sound contradictory to the missions of our federal land-management agencies, it is worth considering.

The BLM, the National Park Service, and the U.S. Forest Service derive their authority to charge fees for public access primarily from the Federal Lands Recreation Enhancement Act of 2004 (REA). This act authorizes four types of fees: entrance fees, standard-amenity recreation fees, expanded-amenity recreation fees, and special-recreation permit fees. The act prohibits entrance fees and standard-amenity recreation fees for "outings conducted for noncommercial educational purposes by schools or bona fide academic institutions" (section 803d3B). However, section 803(h) states, "the Secretary may issue a special recreation permit, and charge a special recreation permit fee in connection with the issuance of the permit, for specialized recreation uses. . . ." This directive allows federal agencies to charge nonprofit and educational adventure programs for access to federal lands and waters.

An important question is whether fees are used to offset the costs of allocation systems or to generate revenue from outdoor recreation. The BLM's *Recreation Permits and Fees Administration Handbook* (H-2930-1) states that one of the objectives of BLM permit policy is to ensure a fair return on commercial uses of public lands. More specifically, the "BLM uses special recreation permits to implement REA's Special Recreation Permit Fees" (Bureau of Land Management, 2007, section .06A2b). This seems to suggest that use-allocation systems, at least on BLM land, have more to do with generating revenue than protecting the environment and the quality of visitor experiences.

Similar concerns were expressed by nonprofit and educational institutions during the open-comment period on proposed revisions to U.S. Forest Service outfitter–guide policy. Respondents commented that use of the REA as the primary authority for issuing special-use permits would provide incentives for the agency to increase commercial access for organizations with higher gross revenue (priority-use permit holders are charged a 3 percent fee on gross receipts). Educational and nonprofit organizations argued that the emphasis on fees would result in a competitive disadvantage because they typically do not generate as much revenue as for-profit outfitters of similar size. The U.S. Forest Service responded by stating, "To address the concern regarding the competitive disadvantage of institutional outfitters and guides, the agency has revised section 41.53g, paragraph 3a, to clarify that the return to the government is not a selection criterion for outfitting and guiding permits at this time" (Final Directives for Forest Service Outfitting and Guiding, 2008, p. 53830). This statement does little to reassure smaller outfitters—educational, nonprofit, or otherwise—that the agency will make equitable allocation decisions. The phrase "at this time" also suggests that revenue generation could become an allocation criterion in the future. Thus, a second argument against special-use permit requirements for nonprofit and educational adventure programs is that the policy is designed primarily to generate revenue, which has placed and continues to place these organizations at a competitive disadvantage when applying for access to public land.

Problems With the Current System

The U.S. Forest Service estimated that more than 5,000 outfitting and guiding permits had been issued for access to lands under its jurisdiction as of October of 2007 (Proposed Directives for Forest Service Outfitting and Guiding, 2007). This number did not account for unauthorized commercial use. In response to the proposed directives, the Association of Outdoor Recreation and Education (2008) acknowledged that its membership accounted for approximately 1.1 million service days in 2006 alone. They noted that much of this use would be unauthorized under the proposed directives and expressed concerns about members' ability to obtain access due to moratoriums on new special-use permits:

> It is believed that these moratoriums have driven educational and institutional groups into the margins as much as any other factor. . . . If the agency wants educational and institutional users to come into compliance with this directive, the agency must also facilitate the process by actively re-allocating use or creating additional use for such groups. (p. 5)

The U.S. Forest Service responded by adding an objective to section 41.53b: "Facilitate greater participation in the outfitting and guiding program by organizations and businesses that work with youth and educational groups" (Final Directives for Forest Service Outfitting and Guiding, 2008, p. 53824). The primary mechanisms for accomplishing this objective appear to be the establishment of a temporary use permit pool, the exclusion of tuition in the fee-calculating process for priority-use permits (U.S. Forest Service, 2008, FSH 2709.11, section 37.21k), an increase in the proposed number of temporary service days, and assurances that revenue generation will not be considered in allocation decisions. The U.S. Forest Service is to be commended for addressing the concerns of nonprofit and educational outfitters; however, important issues remain unaddressed. Specifically, the definition of commercial use is inappropriate, and many organizations are unable to comply with existing indemnification requirements.

Definition of Commercial Use

Both the U.S. Forest Service and the BLM define nonprofit and educational adventure programs as commercial users. These agencies do not consider the nonprofit status and unique mission of these organizations when determining whether to require a special-use permit (U.S. Forest Service, 2008, FSH 2709.11; Bureau of Land Management, 2007, H-2930-1). Many respondents supported this decision in comments on the proposed directives and argued that such a distinction would provide an unfair competitive advantage to 501(c)(3) organizations. However, many nonprofit and educational programs remain fundamentally opposed to definitions of commercial use that fail to distinguish between the nonprofit and for-profit sectors of provision. Under the approved directives, any organization that derives revenue in exchange for services is required to obtain a special-use permit, even in cases where tuition is excluded from fee calculations. Federal agencies argued that permits are necessary to protect the environment and the quality of visitor experiences. Yet, in many cases, no capacity analyses justify direct management approaches such as use allocation. The U.S. Forest Service clearly states in the final directives that it does not generally allocate noncommercial use (Final Directives for Forest Service Outfitting and Guiding, 2008, p. 53826, 53827). What then, is the justification for allocating commercial use, other than revenue generation? Interestingly, the National Park Service does distinguish between the different sectors of provision: "Nonprofit institutions are not required to obtain commercial use authorizations unless taxable income is derived by the institution from the authorized use" (National Parks Omnibus Management Act of 1998). Why the difference in policy? It may have something to do with the fact that the BLM and the U.S. Forest Service are prohibited from charging entrance fees under the REA. In short, they are more dependent on special-use permit fees to ensure a "fair return" on access to public land. Thus, a third argument against special-use permit requirements for nonprofit and educational adventure programs is that these providers do not derive taxable income in exchange for services. They are not commercial users and should not be treated as such for purposes of generating revenue.

Indemnification Requirements

The federal agencies use a tiered scale to determine the minimum amount of insurance coverage necessary for acquiring special-use permits. Different activities are assigned to different risk categories;

each category specifies the minimum amount of coverage necessary per individual and per occurrence. In most cases, this does not present a problem for nonprofit and educational adventure programs. However, public providers at the state and local levels, educational institutions in particular, may be precluded from complying with indemnification requirements due to sovereign (state) or governmental (local) immunity. If state tort claims legislation limits damages at a level below the minimum indemnification requirements specified by agency policy, the program will be unable to enter into a special-use agreement. Furthermore, the BLM, the National Park Service, and the U.S. Forest Service all require that applicants for special-use permits name the United States as an additional insured. Many states have refused to do so, which presents another barrier to complying with agency directives. The option to secure supplemental insurance (Final Directives for Forest Service Outfitting and Guiding, 2008, p. 53841) is simply not feasible for many programs.

A final observation on indemnification requirements is warranted. The Federal Tort Claims Act of 1946 considers the federal government comparable to a private individual when considering liability exposure. Agencies such as the BLM, the National Park Service, and the U.S. Forest Service are afforded immunity protection under state recreational-user statutes (Kozlowski, 1998). Although all 50 states have such statutes, the relationship between the visitor and the land manager changes when a fee is charged (Cotten, 2003; Kozlowski, 1998). Carroll, Connaughton, and Spengler state, "Most states hold that a person classified as a recreational user by statute is not given invitee or licensee status and is owed a duty comparable to a trespasser" (as cited in Grady, 2010, p. 123). However, such immunity does not apply when a fee is charged for access to the site (Kozlowski, 1998). This may be an underlying consideration for the revised indemnification requirements. Thus, a fourth argument against special-use permit requirements for nonprofit and educational adventure programs is that many organizations are unable to comply with indemnification requirements due to existing state laws. Furthermore, the cost of increased liability exposure resulting from the fee policy is passed on to nonprofit and educational providers, further constraining their ability to access public land.

Conclusion

Our federal land managers have a difficult job. They have been charged with resolving an enduring problem that has no clear solution: the tragedy of the commons. To date we have been content to rely on mutual coercion, mutually agreed upon. But coercion has limits. We are now faced with the prisoner's dilemma. We can confess to the impacts that our programs have on the land and give up access to the commons. We can implicate others and continue fighting for increased access that promotes our own self-interest. We can remain silent and accept what we have been afforded. Or we can find a way to work together, to increase access for all, while protecting the commons on which we depend. More (2002) argues that we need additional access, not less. Through connections with the outdoors, an interested public will muster the political will to fight for the protection of our federal lands. In this sense, nonprofit and educational adventure programs are the greatest allies of land managers. If Manning (2007) is correct and we are truly capable of altruistic acts and enlightened self-behavior, we can solve the prisoner's dilemma. Otherwise, we can expect more of the same: more regulation, more disputes over access, and more complaints about the fairness of it all. In the words of Thomas More (2002), "Indifference, rather than excessive recreation use, is the real long-term enemy of natural environments" (p. 61).

References

Abbe, J.D., & Manning, R.E. (2007). Wilderness day use: Patterns, impacts, and management. *International Journal of Wilderness, 13*, 21-38.

American Mountain Guides Association. (2008). *Public comments. USDA Forest Service. RIN 0596-AC50. Proposed Directive for Forest Service Outfitting and Guiding.* Boulder, CO: American Mountain Guides Association.

Association of Outdoor Recreation and Education. (2008). *AORE draft comments for the USFS directives published October 19, 2007.* Whitmore Lake, MI: Association of Outdoor Recreation and Education.

Bureau of Land Management. (2007). *Recreation permits and fees* (H-2930-1). Washington, DC: Bureau of Land Management.

Cotten, D.J. (2003). Immunity. In D.J. Cotten & J.T. Wolohan (Eds.), *Law for recreation and sport managers* (pp. 91-104). 3rd ed. Dubuque, IA: Kendall/Hunt.

Federal Lands Recreation Enhancement Act of 2004. Pub. L. No. 108-447, § 804.

Federal Tort Claims Act of 1946. 28 U.S.C. § 2671-2680(b).

Final Directives for Forest Service Outfitting and Guiding. (2008). Special Use Permits and Insurance Requirements for Forest Service Special Use Permits, 73, Fed. Reg. 53823-53845 (Sept. 17, 2008).

Grady, J. (2010). Premises liability. In D.J. Cotten & J.T. Wolohan (Eds.), *Law for recreation and sport managers* (pp. 121-133). 5th ed. Dubuque, IA: Kendall/Hunt.

Hardin, G. (1968). The tragedy of the commons. *Science, 162*, 1243-1248.

Hendee, J.C., & Dawson, C. (2002). *Wilderness management: Stewardship and protection of resources and values.* 3rd ed. Golden, CO: Fulcrum.

Kozlowski, J.C. (1998). State recreational use laws on federal sites. *Parks and Recreation, 33*, 46-50.

Manning, G. (2005). Decision for appeal of the Sumter National Forest Land and Resource Management Plan revision. www.fs.fed.us/r8/fms/sumter/resources/documents/appealdecision_001.pdf [January 30, 2011].

Manning, R.E. (2007). *Parks and carrying capacity: Commons without tragedy.* Washington, DC: Island Press.

Moore, R.L., & Driver, B.L. (2005). *Introduction to outdoor recreation: Providing and managing natural resource based opportunities.* State College, PA: Venture.

More, T.A. (2002). "The parks are being loved to death" and other frauds and deceits in recreation management. *Journal of Leisure Research, 34*, 52-78.

National Parks Omnibus Management Act of 1998. Pub. L. No. 105-391, § 1693.

Proposed Directives for Forest Service Outfitting and Guiding. (2007). Special Use Permits and Insurance Requirements for Forest Service Special Use Permits, 72, Fed. Reg. 59246-59251 (Oct. 17, 2007).

U.S. Forest Service. (2008). *Forest Service handbook* (FSH 2709.11, §37.21k). Washington, DC: U.S. Forest Service.

Wagar, J. (1964). *The carrying capacity of wildlands for recreation. Forest Science Monograph 7.* Washington, DC: Society of American Foresters.

Should Wilderness First Responder be the standard of care for wilderness leadership?

This contemporary debate has gained significant national attention in the United States over the past few years. Although many in the adventure programming industry adamantly defend Wilderness First Responder (WFR) as the definitive standard of care for outdoor leaders, others challenge this assertion and question its validity and practicality. Adventure programming job descriptions commonly require applicants to possess a WFR certification as a minimum requirement. Many professionals acknowledge that field staff are more confident and prepared when armed with the knowledge and skills found in WFR curricula. Wilderness medicine providers specifically designed the curriculum to administer care in remote settings or until more advanced care can be arranged. Supporters argue that those trained in WFR have the clear evacuation guidelines and tools needed to make sound decisions about patient care.

The literature does not clearly document the history and origin of the WFR certification. Buck Tilton (personal communication, March 30, 2011), a well-known figure and pioneer in the wilderness medicine field, believes that the first public course was offered by Peter Goth and Frank Hubbell in 1984. Goth and Hubbell observed a need and a market for WFR training in addition to the Wilderness EMT and Wilderness First Aid courses already in place. After that initial course, Goth and Hubbell moved on to form their own organizations: Wilderness Medical Associates and the Stonehearth Open Learning Opportunities (SOLO), respectively. Tilton, a student in the 1984 course, was hired by SOLO to teach, and he subsequently helped develop SOLO's WFR curriculum in conjunction with the first responder curriculum of the New Hampshire Department of Transportation. Since those early days, numerous WFR providers have established national and international businesses. These companies compete for market share and are not bound by national standards or regulatory agencies. Some consumers perceive inconsistency among the providers in terms of curriculum, training methods, and instructor qualifications. Regardless of its vague inception and current consumer perceptions, WFR has become the de facto standard of the profession.

Tod Schimelpfenig and Thomas Welch provide excellent viewpoints for both sides of the debate. Schimelpfenig argues that WFR should be the standard of care for those who lead wilderness trips. He bases his argument on decades of outdoor leadership and field medical experience and on persuasive accident and injury data collected by the National Outdoor Leadership School.

Welch argues the opposite and critiques five assumptions that serve as the basis of the acceptance of WFR as the standard of care in the industry. Welch approaches the argument from the perspective of a medical doctor and the experience of a seasoned outdoor leader.

As you read these two compelling points of view, weigh the pros and cons of whether WFR should serve as the national standard for those leading wilderness experiences. The adventure programming industry is significantly influenced by this issue, and movement toward a solution would bring needed consistency to the profession and clarify an important minimum competency for outdoor leaders in the United States.

Should Wilderness First Responder be the standard of care for wilderness leadership?

YES Wilderness First Responder: A Valid Standard

Tod Schimelpfenig, WEMT, curriculum director at Wilderness Medical Institute of the National Outdoor Leadership School, Lander, Wyoming, United States

The fundamental duty of an outdoor leader is to ensure the safety of his or her expedition members. In order to be able to meet this seemingly straight-forward responsibility, a leader must possess a wide variety of competencies: outdoor living and travel skills; technical skills; risk- and group-management skills; and, most important, leadership and judgment. An outdoor leader must also be prepared to manage the medical situations and the health care needs that inevitably arise in the outdoors. I argue that an outdoor leader should be trained as a Wilderness First Responder (WFR) from the point of view that the WFR scope of practice is practical and relevant to the needs of the wilderness trip leader. Before I start, I clarify the names of and the context for the primary training courses that are currently available for laypeople, comment on the present state of national standards for medical training for outdoor leaders, define a wilderness context, and focus this argument on the needs of a trip leader in remote wilderness. I also speak to the history of the WFR course and its value to the profession and the concept of first aid, and I discuss some areas of concern.

Definitions

To put my argument into context, I must provide an overview of the training options associated with wilderness medicine. Although this argument focuses on WFR, the catalog of courses commonly used to train laypeople in wilderness medicine also includes Wilderness First Aid (WFA) and Wilderness Advanced First Aid (WAFA). The relevant training depends on how deep into the wilderness one plans to venture and the reliability of rescue and medical support. Some outdoor leaders are never far from the umbrella of the local emergency medical system (EMS) response and may need only the basic 16-hour WFA certification. Some outdoor leaders work on trips with sound rescue response and communication options and may need a 40-hour WAFA certification. For others who lead in a remote

wilderness context, the 70- to 80-hour WFR is the suitable credential.

I am not aware of an agreed-upon, industry-wide national standard for wilderness medicine training for outdoor leaders. In *The New Wilderness Handbook*, Petzoldt (1974) recommends that "one or two persons on every expedition should be knowledgeable about accepted first aid procedures concerning splints, treating shock, closing cuts, and detailed symptoms indicating appendicitis, pulmonary edema, and hypothermia" (p. 220). He also advocates for leaders being certified in "second aid and evacuation" (Petzoldt, 1974, p. 230). Currently, programs make individual choices. These choices are occasionally driven by accreditation, insurance, or land-management permit requirements, although these stipulations tend to be vague and allow almost any credential to meet first aid training requirements. Outdoor programs, land managers, and national organizations may choose to require any of a variety of credentials (Welch, Berman, and Clement, 2009).

- The Association for Experiential Education has program accreditation standards. One standard requires a wilderness program to have at least one leader with WFR certification if the program is at least 4 to 6 hours from definitive care.

- The American Camp Association requires a minimum of a 16-hour wilderness medicine course when access to EMS takes more than one hour.

- The National Outdoor Leadership School (NOLS) requires WFR for its field staff.

- Outward Bound requires WFR of the field staff if a program is more than one hour from definitive medical care (M. Lindsey, personal communication, September 24, 2010).

In this argument, I define a wilderness context as multiday or multiweek domestic or international backcountry trips during which communication is unreliable or medical or rescue support is delayed or both. Evacuations are primarily walkouts or carry-outs performed by the group or with the assistance of local resources. In these settings the leader may be called on to make independent decisions about the need for and urgency of evacuation and calls for outside assistance. As well, medical equipment is limited, communication is unreliable, transportation is delayed and difficult and often by human power. As a result, patient care takes place in austere or harsh environments (Johnson et al., 2010).

A Practical and Relevant Curriculum

After decades of small-scale educational programs on mountain medicine, often hosted by large outdoor organizations such as the Seattle Mountaineers or the Adirondack Mountain Club, modern wilderness medicine programs began in earnest in the 1970s. This development occurred in tandem with the growth of the outdoor education industry to meet the needs of trip leaders who shook their heads in frustration when attending an irrelevant, urban-oriented first aid course.

In the early years of modern wilderness medicine programs, the instructors were often experienced outdoor education practitioners—passionate about wilderness, medicine, and education—who took what they had learned in urban-oriented advanced first aid or emergency medical technician courses and adapted this curriculum, based on experience and opinion, to fit their needs. Published research was sparse and courses evolved based on experience, opinion, and the available literature. Many of the credible textbooks of the time contain techniques—such as incision and suction for snakebite, suturing wounds, and administering a plethora of medications—that are now considered ineffective or beyond the scope of practice of a lay medical provider. At the time it was the best advice available (Forgey, 1979; Lentz, MacDonald, and Carline, 1972; Wilkerson, 1967).

In 1984, NOLS began carefully collecting data on the illnesses and injuries reported by course instructors. It was clear that small wounds, sprains and strains, diarrhea, and flu-like illness were the day-to-day experience of the outdoor leader and that serious injury and illness were rare. This observation was confirmed in the first publication of the data (Gentile et al., 1992) and has subsequently been seen in other publications (Islas, 2008; Schimelpfenig, 2006). NOLS began to develop an informed perspective of what is common. In the

WFR courses taught internally by NOLS for staff training, dramatic, unrealistic scenarios were set aside and the focus moved toward developing the patient-assessment skills needed to gather the information to make sound decisions and addressing prevention of wound infections, sprains and strains, diarrhea, and flu-like illness.

The NOLS field incident database remains the largest and longest running data set on injury and illness on organized wilderness educational expeditions. It is currently in its 26th year and includes more than 3 million person-days of experience and 13,000 incidents. The first paper—the database has now generated three—has been called a seminal publication on wilderness injury and illness. In the past decade, the pace of research and textbook publication has increased, and now a substantial body of work can inform our practice and help us focus our training and decision-making tools (McIntosh, 2009). We can also study incident data collected by youth groups, outdoor programs, park visitors, search and rescue teams, climbing programs, trekking organizations, or boating groups. We still lack credible incidence data from large segments of the outdoor recreation community, including college-based programs, Scouts, and many camps.

The literature on specific issues in wilderness medicine, and first aid in general (Circulation, 2005), is growing. We are peeling the onion and asking critically whether traditional techniques work and whether hallowed information is accurate. We study the arguments on the need for and efficacy of traction splints, on which dislocation techniques are relevant and realistic for an outdoor leader, and whether prehospital providers can make accurate decisions on the need for spine immobilization. We're seeing rational discussion on wilderness water quality, hygiene, and water disinfection (Derlet and Carlson, 2004; Welch, 2004).

In addition to the science, these courses continue to reflect the direct experience of outdoor leaders whose expertise is in the outdoors, not medicine. They can often do little for a patient besides provide comfort while evacuating, and the crux they face is the decision whether to evacuate, and if so, how quickly. This decision affects the expedition, the rescuers, and the patient. Guidance on evacuation is not found in urban first aid courses, which assume ready access to a physician. This difference is crucial. Wilderness medicine weaves judgment and decision making into first aid training. To ignore judgment and decision making in a leader's training is to ignore a reality of the field. Our data and experience tell us that decisions on patients with abdominal pain and minor head injury, for example, remain vexing for outdoor leaders, unless they want to simply evacuate every patient. Decision tools such as protocols have been tightened over the years based on experience, and communication from the wilderness to the physician is more likely, although not guaranteed. In the future, accurate case reports may allow us to validate or abandon these decision tools.

The data also show that mental health and behavioral concerns—topics that are often given short shrift in first aid courses and outdoor instructor training—are part of the field experience, and leaders tell us of the challenge of managing these problems. This topic is beginning to find its way into wilderness medicine curriculum and has been integrated into the WFR scope-of-practice document (Johnson et al., 2010). Wilderness Medical School of NOLS began intentionally addressing this topic in 2008 in its WFR curriculum and devoted a chapter of the WFR textbook to mental health concerns (Tilton, 2010).

Wilderness medicine courses remain evidence informed, perhaps a more honest phrase than evidence based, and reflect the limits and biases of the science and the ever-present influence of human experience and opinion. I review many field incidents through NOLS and the risk management community and as an active search and rescue practitioner. Many of the directors of the prominent wilderness medicine schools do the same. We see what these outdoor leaders are capable of doing. We listen to them explain how they made their decisions about the need for and the urgency of evacuation. These observations inform our decisions on what to include in our programs. The curriculum is dynamic and continues to thoughtfully evolve to meet the current needs of the outdoor leader. The WFR instructor of today does not teach a 1976 curriculum.

WFA Versus WFR

NOLS decided in the early 1980s to make its staff-training standard WFR and not Emergency Medical Technician, which at that time was the gold standard in prehospital medicine. WFR focuses on information and skills and on scenario-based training relevant to the typical setting in which a wilderness leader practices. Wilderness First Aid, the 16-hour introductory course, is used by some programs for leader training. This may be appropriate for people assisting a more highly trained leader or in a front-country context, but it is insufficient for wilderness

trip leaders. No evidence demonstrates that one credential is better than another. However, the WFA course lacks ample time to practice skills, which is a cornerstone of the WFR experience. It also does not address the breadth of medical situations that a wilderness trip leader may experience. Although flu-like illness, gastrointestinal complaints, sprains, strains, and small wounds are common, the available evidence shows that illness with history will present while on an expedition and illness without history will reveal itself for the first time.

Some argue that the WFA concisely presents all that the trip leader really needs to know. As a veteran of 35 years in the outdoor field, I have seen more than my share of diarrhea, flu-like illness, blisters, and minor cuts and burns and I have made evacuation decisions on people who suffered a blow to the head, had acute abdominal pain, and had a mechanism for a spine injury. I have reduced dislocations and splinted fractures and have seen urinary tract infections and testicular pain, frostbite and immersion foot, acute mountain sickness and high altitude pulmonary edema, spontaneous pneumothorax and broken ribs, asthma, hyperventilation, and stomach aches from too many nonsteroidal anti-inflammatory drugs. The list goes on and on. I have always appreciated my wilderness medical training. Last summer I participated in a search and rescue event in which WFA-trained leaders, in the middle of the Wind Rivers, overreacted to a participant's injury and insisted, in multiple satellite phone calls, on a helicopter evacuation. The weather precluded flying for several hours. When we were finally able to land near the group after a hair-raising flight, we found a young woman without injury who did not need to be evacuated. These young leaders were not prepared to manage the situation. An outdoor leader or program manager may see first aid training as a necessary evil and choose the shorter program, but they change their tune when they experience their first challenging medical event in a true wilderness context.

First aid, defined as "assessments or interventions that can be performed by the bystander (or by the victim) with minimal or no equipment," is at one end of a loosely defined continuum of care that ends with the physician (Circulation, 2005). One of the criticisms of WFR is that people are trained in skills beyond first aid. This is not the case. As I have argued before (Schimelpfenig, 2007), almost everything in the WFR scope of practice is accepted first aid practice for laypeople. The American Red Cross are recognized experts in the science and teaching of first aid and are often cited as the source of what is and what is not first aid. Their wilderness first aid course (directly based on the WFA curriculum of the major wilderness medicine programs), taught to people as young as 14 years of age, includes skills and knowledge widely taught in WFA and WFR as well as the more controversial topics of medication administration, dislocation reduction, and selective spine immobilization. Obviously, the American Red Cross considers this body of practice to be first aid (American Red Cross, 2010).

Serving the Outdoor Community

Risk managers for outdoor programs do not argue the necessity of wilderness medicine training. Rather, their conversations center around which course is relevant for the program staff, which trainings are required or could be considered standards, and which topics should be covered.

As an active field instructor in the early years of this profession (the 1970s), poor decisions and poor patient care were part of my learning curve. Students became ill because we did not appreciate the importance of washing hands or cleaning wounds. Students who should have been able to complete their programs left the field because we could not handle their medical problems. Our medical training was not taught well, was not focused on what we needed to know, and did not prepare us for the realities of the field. My NOLS instructor course in 1973 included two days of poorly taught advanced first aid curriculum. Paul Petzoldt, then director of NOLS, would have appreciated a more relevant and practical course. Indeed, I obtained an emergency medical technician certificate and began to volunteer in EMS, something I do to this day, to gain experience and remedy this training deficit.

The theme of prevention in wilderness medicine courses separates these programs from urban-based courses. Drew Leemon, risk management director of NOLS, says this is a clear benefit of these programs, a sentiment recently echoed by members of the Association for Outdoor Recreation and Education (D. Leemon, personal communication, September 21, 2010).

The literature lacks longitudinal studies that evaluate the effect of training on medical care on wilderness trips, but we can look at the impact on prevention. The NOLS database shows clear trends of a reduced evacuation rate and reduced incidence of the commonly reported incidents: athletic injury, wound infection, and hygiene-related illness (Gentile et al., 1992; Leemon and Schimelpfenig, 2003;

McIntosh et al., 2007). We learned that these incidents were common and we have educated staff on how to prevent and manage them. The data demonstrate that our students are in better hands now because of wilderness medicine training that is relevant and practical.

Areas of Concern

What remains a challenge in wilderness medicine, and in all forms of medical education, is the consistency and skill of instruction. No matter what is written in curriculum documents, control of the instructor's teaching style, instructional methods, and general behavior in front of the students is elusive. As Steve Donelan (2010) wrote in a recent edition of *Journal of Wilderness and Environmental Medicine,* "even an evidence based, standardized curriculum cannot guarantee that students will learn (as the many studies of CPR performance and training testify). Whether our classes are effective in preparing students for real emergencies still depends more on how we teach than on what we teach" (p. 66).

Instructor qualifications differ vastly among organizations offering training. I recently obtained a credential to teach for a major national wilderness first aid provider through a 90-minute online course that did not assess my medical experience or skills competence, my outdoor experience or skills competence, or my efficacy as an educator. Compare this with providers who require extensive outdoor and medical experience and train their instructors for seven days to teach a basic 16-hour WFA course.

Also, those involved in prehospital medicine know that problems exist at all levels with uniform outcomes and that detailed curriculums and lesson plans are not a panacea. Content is remarkably consistent among the major wilderness medicine schools. This may be due in part to ongoing informal sharing of curriculum among providers and the material's sharp focus on wilderness medicine.

The major wilderness medicine programs, on their own initiative, recently embarked on a scope-of-practice project intended to clarify what skills and knowledge a person with a WFA and WFR credential should have. This seemed to be a logical point of departure for the next phase in development of wilderness medicine courses. The programs engaged a wide number of providers and consumers in multiple drafts of a consensus document. The intent is for this document to standardize these credentials and to serve as a base for future development of the content of these courses. This will evolve into a consensus position statement by the Wilderness Medical Society and make clear to outside audiences the content of these programs. The Wilderness Medical Society will also host regular meetings to continue the conversations about the relevant and practical skills for a lay wilderness medical provider and to continue the evolution of the course content.

It is clear that medical decisions remain challenging to people whose expertise and experience is in the outdoors, not medicine. It is also clear that what we think our WFR students are capable of doing in a classroom and what they can realistically do in the field can be two very different things. Only a few studies of learning retention in medical education inform us of the limits of instruction. Several projects on retention of wilderness medicine skills are in progress. When complete, these projects may help us further refine our courses.

Conclusion

Petzoldt notes that diarrhea is often due to hygiene, minor accidents due to fatigue and haste, and hypothermia due to "inappropriate time, energy and climate control plans" (Petzoldt, 1974, p. 219). Wilderness medical events are often problems of leadership, judgment, and competence in fundamental outdoor skills long before they become an injury or illness. Wilderness medicine training is but a subset of these far more important competencies.

WFR should be the standard of care for outdoor leaders in the remote wilderness context. WFR curricula have evolved to reflect program experience, expert opinion, and data-driven evidence, and the result is training that is practical and relevant to the needs of outdoor leaders. The widespread endorsement of WFR training for outdoor leaders has been a sound risk-management tool.

WFR and its companion courses, WFA and WAFA, will continue to evolve as more evidence becomes available on the incidence of various problems, the efficacy of treatments, and the efficacy of our instruction. As well, they will remain practical and relevant through the ongoing dialogue between those who teach wilderness medicine and those who practice it.

References

American Red Cross. (2010). *Wilderness and remote first aid.* Yardley, PA: StayWell Publications.

Circulation. (2005). *Guidelines for first aid.* 112:IV-196-IV-203. doi: 10.1161/CIRCULATIONAHA.105.166575. Hagerstown, MD: Lippincott Williams and Wilkins.

Derlet, R.W., & Carlson, J.R. (2004). An analysis of wilderness water in Kings Canyon, Sequoia, and Yosemite National Parks for coliform and pathologic bacteria. *Wilderness and Environmental Medicine, 15,* 238-244.

Donelan, S. (2010). Classroom and reality: What should we teach in wilderness first aid courses? *Wilderness and Environmental Medicine, 21,* 64-66.

Forgey, W. (1979). *Wilderness medicine.* Pittsboro, IN: Indiana Camp Supply Books.

Gentile, D., Morris, J., Schimelpfenig, T., & Auerbach, P. (1992). Wilderness injuries and illness. *Annals of Emergency Medicine, 21,* 853-861.

Islas, T. (2008). What kills us in the woods. In *Syllabus, 25th annual meeting of the Wilderness Medical Society.* Snowmass, CO: Wilderness Medical Society.

Johnson, D., Schimelpfenig, T., Nicolazzo, P., McEvoy, D., Hubbell, F., Fizzell, L., Weil, C., Malone, P., Padgett, J.P., Cull, A.D., Kimmel, N., Ditolla, M., Webster, M., & Yacubian, D. (2010). Wilderness First Responder scope of practice draft. www.outdoored.com/Community/blogs/wildmed/archive/2010/05/21/wfr-scope-of-practice-draft.aspx [December 12, 2011].

Leemon, D., & Schimelpfenig, T. (2003). Wilderness injury, illness and evacuation: NOLS incident profiles 1999-2002. *Wilderness and Environmental Medicine, 14,* 174-182.

Lentz, M., MacDonald, S., & Carline, J. (1972). *Mountaineering first aid.* Seattle: The Mountaineers.

McIntosh, S. (2009). The top 10 articles in wilderness medicine. In *Syllabus, 25th annual meeting of the Wilderness Medical Society.* Snowmass, CO: Wilderness Medical Society.

McIntosh, S., Leemon, D., Schimelpfenig, T., Visitacion, J., & Fosnocht, D. (2007). Medical incidents and evacuations on wilderness expeditions. *Wilderness and Environmental Medicine, 18,* 298-304.

Petzoldt, P. (1974). *The new wilderness handbook.* New York: Norton.

Schimelpfenig, T. (2006). Evidence informed wilderness medicine: What really happens out there? https://rendezvous.nols.edu/content/view/1748/713 [December 12, 2011].

Schimelpfenig, T. (2007). Wilderness medicine practices and protocols. https://rendezvous.nols.edu/content/view/1748/713 [December 12, 2011].

Tilton, B. (2010). *Wilderness first responder.* Guilford, CT: Falcon Guides.

Welch, T. (2004). Evidence-based medicine in the wilderness: The safety of backcountry water. *Wilderness and Environmental Medicine, 15*(4), 235-237.

Welch, T., Berman, D., & Clement, K. (2009). Wilderness first aid: Is there an "industry standard"? *Wilderness and Environmental Medicine, 20*(2), 113-117.

Wilkerson, J. (1967). *Medicine for mountaineering.* Seattle: The Mountaineers.

Should Wilderness First Responder be the standard of care for wilderness leadership?

NO: Woof(er), Woof(er): The Wilderness First Responder Dog and Pony Show

Thomas Welch, MD, professor and chair of Department of Pediatrics SUNY Upstate Medical University, Syracuse, New York, United States; Wilderness Education Association instructor at Denali Education Center, Denali, Alaska, United States

Paul Petzoldt professionalized outdoor leadership in the United States. More than 35 years ago, he authored one of the first comprehensive textbooks in the field, *The New Wilderness Handbook* (Petzoldt, 1974). The topic of mountain medicine and first aid consumes about 10 pages, the bulk of which deals with preventing accidents. He opines that he has "little faith in pills and medications in the wild outdoors" and recommends that first aid kits contain only "tape, a small roll of gauze, moleskin, Band-Aids, pain pills, and sleeping pills." For those interested, he recommends that they study a book (Forgey, 1999), but he stresses that "quality judgments" are more important.

In many outdoor programs today, Paul Petzoldt would not be eligible to lead an expedition. Despite his legendary accomplishments as a mountaineer, educator, and environmentalist, Petzoldt lacked a *sine qua non* for a contemporary wilderness leader in some programs: graduation from a 70-hour wilderness first responder (WFR) course. The man who held the record for safely guiding folks up the Grand, whose reconnaissance laid the foundation for the ultimate ascent of K2, and whose system of climbing communication is used daily throughout the world would today be considered unqualified to lead a group of young adults into his beloved Wind River Range.

This odd state of affairs has a long and complicated history but ultimately is predicated on five assumptions that I believe are fundamentally flawed. In this argument, I outline the five assumptions as an argument against WFR as the industry standard.

Assumption One

Wilderness recreation carries a substantial risk of serious injury and illness.

Wilderness recreation encompasses a broad range of activities. Clearly, one cannot lump BASE jump-ing or hunting, which is responsible for an average of about 30 deaths annually in the United States (International Hunter Education Association, 2008), with backpacking or mountaineering. For purposes of this discussion, wilderness recreation includes extended treks into remote areas; during these treks, the activity mostly consists of traveling over terrain of variable difficulty and setting up and taking down campsites and occasionally consists of skill-specific tasks such as rock climbing or flat-water canoeing. This definition includes most of the wilderness education programs offered by colleges and universities, courses offered to the public by various providers of outdoor adventure travel, and activities sponsored by organizations such as the Boy Scouts of America.

Unfortunately, obtaining complete national data on serious medical problems in such venues is impossible. The administrative data sets that are used by epidemiologists for such studies are mined by ICD-9 codes (Gindee et al., 2008). Because no codes or modifiers specifically identify wilderness recreation, comprehensive analysis of hospital or death-certificate data can never be performed.

On the other hand, investigators have used a number of techniques, such as regional or organizational registries, to obtain data on wilderness medical incidents. Published data addressing the risk of injury and illness in such pursuits is strikingly consistent: wilderness recreation is one of the safest recreational activities on which data are maintained.

One attempt at using an administrative database to collect incidence data on outdoor recreational injuries used the National Electronic Injury Surveillance System All Injury Program (NEISS-AIP), a 63-hospital stratified probability sample of all U.S. hospitals that is maintained by the U.S. Consumer Product Safety Commission (Flores, Haileyesus, and

Greenspan, 2008). This database is used by investigators to project the incidence of various injuries throughout the United States. Unfortunately, the outdoor recreation activities in this database include sports such as skiing, snowboarding, snowmobiling, and surfing. Additionally, there is no way to identify where in the wilderness these injuries occurred. Despite these limitations, the total burden of outdoor recreational injuries in the United States was small (roughly 100,000 per year for the entire country, or about 25/100,000 of the population) and the severity of the vast majority of the injuries was modest (only 5 percent were hospitalized).

Although the NEISS-AIP data are the most robust global estimate of the burden of outdoor injuries, data from organizational databases provide much better information on the incidence of specific injuries, albeit without the context of population frequency. A recent example of this is a 2003 study that prospectively examined medical incidents occurring during more than 20,000 participant days in a Minnesota canoe and backpacking camp (Elliott, Elliott, and Bixby, 2003). Most of the incidents studied were minor: only 12 in the entire series required evacuation for definitive care and, apparently, none of these 12 was serious enough to require hospital admission.

A larger database examines the injury and illness experience of the National Outdoor Leadership School (NOLS) (McIntosh et al., 2007). This report, derived from a database, covers a three-year period from 2002 through 2005. The report cites injury and illness rates of 1.18 and 1.08, respectively, per 1,000 participant days; this is similar to the findings of Elliott, Elliott, and Bixby's (2003) report on the Minnesota camp. No deaths occurred. About half of the incidents resulted in leaving the field, and less than 5 percent required hospital admission. As is the case in most such reports, the majority of injuries were soft-tissue injuries, mostly in the lower extremity. The catalog of injuries and illnesses (authors' tables 2 and 3) list few if any conditions that would call for much in the way of knowledge or skill competency beyond basic first aid.

The most recent attempt to establish incidence rates from a well-defined cohort came from a college program, Cornell Outdoor Education. During a five-year period encompassing more than 74,000 participant days, this program experienced an illness and injury rate of 1.5 per 1,000 participant days; this is strikingly consistent with other data (Gaudio, Greenwald, and Holton, 2010).

The most serious wilderness injury, of course, is death. Although examination of death rates may not be an appropriate way to inform discussion of specific backcountry injuries, it is ideal for putting the health risks of the activity into perspective. Deaths are dramatic events that are uniformly reported and, consequently, quite reliable.

At least two studies have examined death rates from wilderness recreation in defined populations. Paton (2007) recently updated his report of deaths among participants in Outward Bound courses. In the most recent period examined (1999 through 2005), no fatal accidents occurred in 1,347,587 participant days. In this report, Paton also revisited an analysis of deaths in this program in an unfortunate era in which such events were more common. Of 12 deaths in Outward Bound programs between 1971 and 1980, at least 7 deaths were the result of situations that even the most exemplary wilderness first aid training could not have prevented (multicasualty drowning, motor vehicle accidents, sudden cardiac death, and a suicide).

Complementing this organization-based study is a population-based report from Victoria, Australia (Gabbe et al., 2005). Using data from the Victoria State Trauma Registry and the National Coroner's Information Service, this study examined deaths and serious injuries from sport and recreation over a two-year period. Merging these data with information about the populations engaging in various activities, the investigators calculated rates of serious injury and death per 100,000 participants per year. The activities associated with the greatest risk of injury or death were those associated with powercraft and horses. The most common mechanism of death was drowning. Backpacking, camping, hiking, and mountaineering were not included in the activities associated with serious injury or death. Two percent of the cases were associated with rock climbing, but it is impossible to tell from the study whether these cases were associated with a wilderness location.

Assumption Two

A defined set of competencies exists between standard first aid and definitive medical care, and these competencies can be used in situations in which such definitive care is substantially delayed.

This assumption undergirds the entire WFR education industry, which seems at first glance to be eminently reasonable. Knowledge and procedures typically considered within the purview of first aid assume that the patient will either have a benign, self-limited condition that requires no further medical care or be able to connect with definitive care in a brief period of time (often one hour or less). The nature of wilderness activity is such that extended periods of time may pass before definitive care can be accessed. Thus, it makes sense that a body of knowledge and skills short of the practice of medicine but beyond first aid might have application in the backcountry.

Although eminently reasonable, minimal evidence shows that such a set of competencies exists. Consider shock. Most first aid texts have an approach to shock that boils down to a few points: keep warm, keep hydrated, keep dry, treat other problems, watch for deterioration, and get to definitive care. Once the patient reaches definitive care, our options are legion: volume expansion and pressors titrated to cardiac output and perfusion, antibiotics and blood products based on the underlying cause of the shock, ventilatory support to maintain peripheral oxygenation, extracorporeal support to other target organs (e.g., hemofiltration), and correction of underlying processes, to name just a few. It is difficult to identify any evidence-based intervention between the basic first aid for shock and its definitive care.

Sure, the patient with shock who is a day from a trailhead will require a longer period of first aid (if he or she survives, which is highly unlikely in bona fide shock). In reality, however, the actual care we can offer the patient continues to be nothing beyond the aforementioned basics (warm, dry, hydrated, and so on). Ensuring these basic comforts in a remote location and orchestrating evacuation requires much more in the way of general outdoor skills, judgment, and leadership than specific medical competencies.

The example of shock can be extended to the panoply of catastrophic (albeit extraordinarily rare) events that are included in the curriculum of WFR courses. Closed head injury, surgical abdominal emergencies, multiple traumas, respiratory failure—beyond basic first aid, provision of comfort, and orchestration of evacuation, no evidence-based intervention exists that a layperson could use in the backcountry for an individual with one of these conditions.

Assumption Three

Competencies in medical procedures can be taught to and meaningfully retained by laypersons who do not regularly use them.

Much of the curriculum of contemporary WFR courses deals with the pathophysiology and recognition of rare (in the backcountry) conditions and a variety of specific interventions. One published curriculum (keep in mind that there is absolutely no standard WFR curriculum to which U.S. providers or regulatory bodies have agreed) listed goals for a WFR course; these goals included such complex issues as the management of diabetes, chest trauma, and alterations in consciousness (Wilderness Medical Society Curriculum Committee, 1999). The idea that laypersons could meaningfully retain the bulk of this material is implausible and certainly has never been systematically tested.

In this context, we must remember that these concepts and competencies are not only taught to individuals with no medical background, they are taught to individuals who will not have regular opportunities to use them in the course of their daily work. Courses of similar length are used for entry-level providers in the Department of Transportation emergency medical system (EMS). Individuals completing these programs, however, will generally be working in the EMS industry on either an employed or a volunteer basis. Thus, they will have ongoing, regular exposure to the medical problems included in their initial course, and their practice will include direct oversight and regular opportunities for feedback and continuing education. An outdoor educator will never encounter the vast bulk of the content of a typical WFR course in his or her lifetime. The belief that such an individual could meaningfully apply skills from a remote course—skills that had not been used since course completion—when suddenly confronted with a crisis defies everything we know about pedagogy.

Although the modern wilderness medicine education industry emphasizes its expertise in education, the reality is that it is completely disconnected from contemporary scholarship in medical education. The American Heart Association and the American Red Cross are the recognized experts in the science and teaching of cardiopulmonary resuscitation skills to professional medical personnel and to the general public. The research of these organizations has led to discontinuation of teaching to laypersons the pulse check (Cummins and Hazinski, 2000) and airway management skills (Svensson et al., 2010) during basic cardiopulmonary resuscitation (CPR) courses because these organizations recognized that meaningful skill retention does not occur.

The issue of skill retention has become a major subject for research and practice among personnel working full time in clinical medicine. Nurses working regularly in intensive care have demonstrated deterioration in airway-management skills (Hamilton, 2005), and initiatives now promote regular workplace assessment of CPR skills for critical-care unit personnel who regularly use these skills in the course of their jobs (Niles et al., 2009). These issues are being addressed with high-fidelity simulators and dedicated clinical educators in advanced clinical education laboratories. In light of developments such as this, the notion that laypersons with no continuing oversight or practice can master and retain vastly more complex clinical skills is preposterous.

Assumption Four

The costs (direct, indirect, and opportunity) are in alignment with their benefits.

The costs of taking a WFR certification or recertification course today are not inconsequential. Tuition, room, board, travel, and materials may easily push the cost of a course to more than $1,000 per participant. These costs are borne either by the educators themselves or by their programs. If the latter, the costs will of course pass to program clients. Given the precarious financial situations of many outdoor education programs today, it would be irresponsible to make such investment without compelling evidence of its appropriateness.

In particular, if a program is going to make an investment in safety and risk management for its clients, one might ask whether a blanket requirement for WFR certification is the most responsible use of this investment. For example, automotive accidents are the largest cause of accidental death and severe injury among young adults in the United States today (Heron et al., 2010). However, a recent survey of college wilderness education programs showed that the students who drive participants to wilderness activities receive little if any formal driver education (Welch, Clement, and Berman, 2009). It seems curious that a program would insist that its instructors complete a 70-hour course dealing with esoteric aspects of human physiology while permitting them to, with no or minimal structured instruction, drive clients in multiperson vans on interstate highways.

Although fatalities in wilderness recreation are extraordinarily rare, when they do occur, drowning is one of the most commonly reported incidents (Gabbe et al., 2005; Paton, 2007). Beyond treks involving water travel, many backcountry expeditions provide opportunities for swimming. The evidence-based practitioner might reasonably question why training and certification in water safety and rescue have not infiltrated the outdoor education industry to the degree that wilderness medicine has.

Recent reports of evacuations from wilderness education programs have highlighted the role of emotional and psychological crises in such incidents. Indeed, much-publicized (and litigated) fatalities have occurred consequent to trek leaders (including some with WFR credentials) failing to appreciate clients' emotional distress (Szalavitz, 2006). It would seem that a place exists for structured training for backcountry educators in areas such as conflict resolution and the approach to psychic trauma. Textbooks used in some WFR training programs (Carline, 2004; Schimelpfenig, 2006) do not even reference such situations.

In the very rare event that a severe injury occurs in a remote location, the skill set required for dealing with the situation is broad and first aid training is only a part of it—a small part. We have already demonstrated that few medical competencies beyond standard first aid have an evidence basis in the backcountry. Advanced navigational skills, complex decision making, organizational skills and communication, and the basic campcraft competencies requisite to ensuring warmth, nutrition, hydration, dryness, and comfort are vital to the resolution of a wilderness disaster. Yet few instructors come into programs with a uniform skill set in these areas, and we are unaware of any broad initiative to require regular recertification or skill updating in these areas.

The toolbox required by the outdoor educator today is large and varied. I find it curious and unsupported by the evidence that such an emphasis is placed on one very small part of this toolbox.

Assumption Five

WFR certification is a standard in the adventure programming industry.

Despite these rather incontrovertible points, debates about this topic ultimately move to the conclusion that, rightly or not, WFR certification has become an industry standard. This, too, is clearly incorrect. A recent study (Welch, Clement, and Berman, 2009) shows that no governmental jurisdiction in the United States recognizes the WFR certification as a requirement for guides or outfitters. The national organizations that provide the vast majority of guided wilderness expeditions in the country (e.g., Boy Scouts of America, Sierra Club) have no such requirement. A minority of college outing programs prescribes WFR certification for trek leaders. Indeed, the largest organization that does require this certification for its outdoor instructors (NOLS) also happens to be a major provider of WFR courses.

Although course providers market these programs as providing a credential, the certification is not recognized by any government entity in North America (unless the specific course also provides Department of Transportation certification, which is rarely the situation today). States vary somewhat in the ways in which they regulate the practice of medicine, but all enforce such regulation through medical practice acts and pharmacy acts. In no jurisdiction is the holder of a WFR or similar certification granted authority to independently undertake any procedure beyond standard first aid—indeed, anything that could be done by any layperson.

Conclusion

Wilderness pursuits are among the safest forms of recreation. Serious injuries and death are exceedingly rare, and most often the latter are relatively instantaneous and not amenable to intervention. Absolutely no evidence shows that competencies beyond those of standard first aid could be useful in backcountry incidents. Current scholarship suggests that the likelihood is nil that laypersons can meaningfully retain medical information and skills that they do not use regularly. Devotion of time and resources to lengthy courses and refreshers in first aid may detract from acquiring and maintaining skills in more important areas. The WFR credential is not a recognized certification by any legal jurisdiction, does not endow on its holder any additional legal authority, and is not required by any state agency.

Paul Auerbach (2010), author of the leading textbook of wilderness medicine and a past president of the Wilderness Medicine Society, provides a final word to this debate: "What should be taught to guides, instructors, and trip leaders who are responsible for the care of their participants in the outdoors? The best we can advise right now is that basic first aid with augmentation about wilderness-specific concerns seems reasonable. . ." (paragraph 5).

References

Auerbach, P. (2010). Wilderness first aid. www.healthline.com/blogs/outdoor_health/2010/03/wilderness-first-aid.html [November 18, 2010].

Carline, J.L. (2004). *Mountaineering first aid.* Seattle: Mountaineers Books.

Cummins, R.O., & Hazinski, M.F. (2000). Guidelines based on fear of type II (false negative) errors: Why we

dropped the pulse check for lay rescuers. *Circulation, 102,* 1377-1379.

Elliott, T.B., Elliott, B.A., & Bixby, M.R. (2003). Risk factors associated with camp accidents. *Wilderness and Environmental Medicine, 14,* 2-8.

Flores, A.H., Haileyesus, T., & Greenspan, A.I. (2008). National estimates of outdoor recreational injuries treated in emergency departments, United States, 2004-2005. *Wilderness and Environmental Medicine, 19,* 91-98.

Forgey, W. (1999). *Wilderness medicine.* Guilford, CT: Globe Pequot Press.

Gabbe, B.J., Finch, C.F., Cameron, P.A., & Williamson, O.D. (2005). Incidence of serious injury and death during sport and recreation activities in Victoria, Australia. *British Journal of Sports Medicine, 39,* 573-577.

Gaudio, F., Greenwald, P., & Holton, M. (2010). Injury and illness in college outdoor education. *Wilderness and Environmental Medicine, 21,* 363-370.

Gindee, A.A., Blanc, P.G., Lieberman, R.M., & Camargo, C.A. (2008). Validation of ICD-9-CM coding algorithm for improved identification of hypoglycemia visits. *BMC Endocrine Disorders, 8,* 4.

Hamilton, R. (2005). Nurses' knowledge and skill retention following cardiopulmonary resuscitation training: A review of the literature. *Journal of Advanced Nursing, 51,* 288-297.

Heron, M., Sutton, P.D., Xu, J., Ventura, S.J., Strobino, D.M., & Guyer, B. (2010). Annual summary of vital statistics: 2007. *Pediatrics, 125,* 4-15.

International Hunter Education Association. (2008). Incident reports. www.ihea.com/news-and-events/incident-reports/index.php [November 18, 2010].

McIntosh, S.L., Leemon, D., Visitacion, J., Schimelpfenig, T., & Fosnocht, D. (2007). Medical incidents and evacuations on wilderness expeditions. *Wilderness and Environmental Medicine, 18,* 298-304.

Niles, D.S., Sutton, R.M., Donoghue, A., Kalsi, M.S., Roberts, K., Boyle, L., Nishisaki, A., Arbogast, K.B., Helfaer, M., & Nadkarni, V. (2009). "Rolling refreshers": A novel approach to maintain CPR psychomotor skill competence. *Resuscitation, 80,* 909-912.

Paton, B.C. (2007). Health and safety in Outward Bound. *Wilderness and Environmental Medicine, 18,* 146.

Petzoldt, P. (1974). *The new wilderness handbook.* New York: Norton.

Schimelpfenig, T. (2006). *NOLS wilderness medicine.* Mechanicsburgh, PA: Stackpole Books.

Svensson, L., Bohm, K., Castren, M., Pettersson, H., Engerstrom, L., Herlitz, J., & Rosenqvist, M. (2010). Compression-only CPR or standard CPR in out-of-hospital cardiac arrest. *New England Journal of Medicine, 363,* 481-483.

Szalavitz, M. (2006). *Help at any cost.* New York: Riverhead Books.

Welch, T.R., Clement, K., & Berman, D. (2009). Wilderness first aid: Is there an "industry standard"? *Wilderness and Environmental Medicine, 20*, 113-117.

Wilderness Medical Society Curriculum Committee. (1999). Wilderness first responder: Recommended minimum course topics. *Wilderness and Environmental Medicine, 10*, 13-19.

Controversial Issue 14

Should wilderness program staff always accompany their participants?

Adventure-based programs such as Outward Bound and the National Outdoor Leadership School engage in a well-known practice steeped in tradition. Instructors purposefully leave their participants without direct supervision for multiple days in a wilderness setting. These experiences are commonly known as individual solos, group solos, independent student group travel, or final expeditions. These unaccompanied expedition components provide participants with a unique situation that could result in rich learning or unsupervised disaster. Currently, programs are re-evaluating these practices and in some cases eliminating unaccompanied components. Accidents and injuries have influenced policy changes within organizations, resulting in curriculum revisions. Some organizations hold steadfast and believe that these course components provide significant educational benefits for participants. Are these unsupervised experiences too dangerous? As a curricular component, do the benefits of unaccompanied experiences outweigh the risks? Does our profession have an accurate understanding of risk versus benefit in this area of programming?

Ken Kalisch argues that the absence of direct staff supervision is an unnecessary risk and should no longer be practiced in adventure-based programs. He explains that the benefits of unaccompanied experiences do not outweigh the emotional and physical risks to participants. In addition, the organization opens itself to legal risks that far exceed program benefits. Kalisch rounds off his argument by explaining that society is becoming more risk averse and intolerant of incidents resulting from unaccompanied educational activities.

Brad Daniel and Andrew Bobilya take the opposing view. They argue that adventure-based staff should not be required to accompany participants at all times, provided that proper precautions are taken. They document the educational value of unaccompanied components by sharing recent research. They claim that much of this debate is driven by fear of litigation and lack of understanding regarding the educational value of this type of programming and the actual risks involved.

This debate is especially significant to adventure-based programs that integrate unaccompanied experiences into their curricula. We as a profession must decide what stance to take: to support or eliminate unaccompanied experiences.

Should wilderness program staff always accompany their participants?

YES One Question You Don't Want to Hear: Where Were the Instructors?

Ken Kalisch, associate professor of outdoor education and outdoor ministry, Montreat College, Montreat, North Carolina, United States

Where were the instructors? The question is appropriate because wilderness program instructors have traditionally varied their roles with a student expedition group. It is typical for instructors to be more engaged with members at the beginning and become less engaged over time. During some programmed components, students might rarely see their instructors.

For the past 40 years, prominent international organizations such as Outward Bound (OB), the National Outdoor Leadership School (NOLS), and countless adaptations of them have used these unaccompanied activities. The two traditional unaccompanied events are the solo and final expedition. The OB solo is a one- to three-day separation from instructors during which students camp alone at a specified site with minimal food and equipment. The OB final expedition or NOLS student-led expedition is group travel without direct instructor supervision from one to five days. These two practices have been justified on the basis that they enhance student learning (Bobilya, Kalisch, and Daniel, 2010; Bobilya, McAvoy, and Kalisch, 2005a; Daniel, 2003; Kalisch, Bobilya, and Daniel, in press; Sibthorp et al., 2008). I argue that the absence of direct staff supervision during these expedition components is unnecessarily risky and should no longer be practiced in wilderness education programs.

Time for a Change

Although many wilderness programmers value and utilize these unaccompanied events, it is time to change the manner in which these events are conducted. A history of tragic injuries and deaths surrounds them, even at NOLS and OB. Though few in number, these accidents involved young people who were severely hurt or lost their lives when unaccompanied by their instructors.

- A young woman was raped on her North Carolina OB solo in 1971 (Hunt, 2000).

- In the same year, two young women died from exposure on their Northwest OB final expedition in the Cascade Mountains (Hunt, 2000).

- Three young adults on a Southwest OB final expedition drowned in 1978 while kayaking in the Gulf of California (Morganthau, 1979).

- A young man on his Voyageur OB solo was viciously attacked by a predatory black bear in 1987 (Rogers and Garshelis, 1988).

- A young female on a NOLS student-led expedition drowned while crossing a Wyoming river in 1996 (McCarthy, 2009).

- A New Hampshire teenager on a NOLS student-led expedition fell to his death down a deep glacial hole in 1999 (Komarnitsky, 1999).

- A young female on a 2006 OB final expedition died of heatstroke in Utah's canyon country. She leaves behind an anguished brother who asks, "Where were the instructors when (my sister) was dying in Lockhart Canyon?" (Ketcham, 2007, p. 55).

- Four young men were attacked and mauled by an Alaskan grizzly bear on a student-led expedition at NOLS in 2011 (Grove, 2011).

It is difficult to determine whether similar incidents involving students intentionally separated from their instructors have occurred in smaller and less-recognized programs across the country. Further, little documentation exists of near misses in wilderness programs, especially in these activities. However, Haddock (1999a) suggests that the epic tales and close calls recited by instructors and students after trips provide evidence. Although often unverified, these tales indicate that incidents with a high potential for harm do occur and may be indicators of serious accidents to come. There are stories of solo students who became sick after foraging for food and those who injured themselves due to emotional distress. There are epic tales of student-led expeditions that became lost and ventured over treacherous terrain and those who divided into subgroups due to unresolved conflict. The latter circumstances led to the 2006 death in the Utah wilderness (Ketcham, 2007). Direct supervision by instructors largely prevents such tragic incidents. Davidson (2004), after studying trip accidents in New Zealand and Australia, argues:

> While there are many methods employed to assist in managing the risk in outdoor education activities such as providing good equipment, sequencing programs, gaining the most recent weather forecasts, etc., the most powerful tool to reducing the risk in an outdoor education activity is by providing supervision for those taking part in the activity with someone with an assessed level of skill and experience. . . . The duty of the skilled supervisor is to be in a position to intervene if a dangerous situation arises and prevent harm from occurring. (p. 2)

One might argue that a few serious injuries and deaths are acceptable losses when compared with the positive experiences that thousands of students have had as a result of these two program components. This position advocates the high educative value inherent in legitimate risk taking. It is represented by Willi Unsoeld's classic response to the mother of a prospective OB student who requested a guarantee of safety for her son: "No. We certainly can't, Ma'am. We guarantee you the genuine chance of his death. And if we could guarantee his safety, the program would not be worth running" (cited in Hunt, 1999, p. 119). A difference exists between guaranteeing safety and trying to provide the safest program possible. Removing the direct supervision of instructors for an extended period of time does not contribute to guarding safety. A more ethical position would argue that the traditional educational strategy used for these trip components is an act of negligence and is unjustified for pedagogical, legal, and moral reasons (Davidson, 2004).

Three Pillars of Support

Three predominant principles support this argument. When aptly considered, they facilitate an understanding of this more ethical position.

Risk Versus Student Competency

First, real risk exists in wilderness programs, and it increases when program instructors do not directly supervise novice students for a lengthy time. A staff trainer for Outward Bound USA describes the risk involved in wilderness programs:

> Risk is at the very center of the Outward Bound experience. We lead our students through natural and social environments in which we encounter inherently risky situations. There are the risks that derive from rocky terrain and inclement weather, the risks stemming from the kinds of activities and testing situations we devise to stretch our students physically and mentally, and those that come from the interpersonal dynamic of placing a small and diverse group together in stressful circumstances. . . . Instructors must make frequent decisions as they encounter the myriad risks their course provides, and all without benefit of the resources—the help—of the personnel back at the base; they are quite literally on their own; they are the on-the-scene risk managers. Will they know what to do? Will they have the knowledge, the skills, and the judgment to make good decisions when faced with the challenge of choosing the best course of action in the face of a potentially dangerous situation? (Garrett, 2008, p. 1)

. This concern for the exercise of good judgment by staff is commendable. It has caused OB and NOLS to conduct judgment-training workshops for their instructors in recent years. But what about students left alone on a solo or final expedition? Will *they* have the knowledge, skills, and judgment to make good decisions? What judgment training do novice students receive before they are sent out alone? Is their preparation by staff sufficient to ensure wise decisions?

Two distinct factors combine to make indirectly supervised students a high-risk event. First, the wilderness is a dynamic environment that includes endless physical challenges and potential threats to the traveler. The wilderness is a world of constant, often unexpected, change. Second, novices in this dynamic environment are challenged to exercise adequate judgment in decision making. It is likely that a novice will not perceive some perils as being high risk. Some rapid rivers look easy to cross, and some rocky slopes look easy to climb down. The reality is that students will potentially make many errors in judgment. According to Udall (1995), it takes much experience to accurately observe the dynamics of wild places, to understand the frailty of humans in it, and to respond wisely in each moment. If students misread the situation, it can result in "a series of seemingly inconsequential decisions . . . that stack up one-on-another until the entire pattern totters and collapses under the weight of the wind or of human fatigue or of an unexpected stumble" (p. 67).

Research studies have suggested some predictors of serious accidents in wilderness programs. Liddle and Storck (1995) report that "one of the most frequent contributing factors to accidents is lack of knowledge of an environmental hazard, or a lack of appreciation of its danger" (p. 5). Haddock (1999b) determined that "unsafe acts by students" is the second-highest contributing factor (after weather) in high-potential incidents. Davidson's (2004) analysis of 1,908 incidents indicates "a higher chance of a serious incident occurring if the level of supervision is removed or reduced" (p. 1). Brookes (2003) concluded that indirectly supervised teenagers on wilderness expeditions presented "a clear fatality risk if . . . the group encountered moving water or steep ground" (p. 38).

It takes much experience to develop sound judgment that adequately responds to a variety of wilderness hazards. This is the necessary role of competent instructors. For students, there is no substitute for having immediate access to a skilled and knowledgeable leader in high-risk circumstances. Opportunities for independent student decision making might be educational, but they may come with a high cost, even death. And then people will certainly ask, "Where were the instructors?"

Risk Versus Educational Benefits

Second, the benefits of unaccompanied experiences do not outweigh the emotional and physical risks to students or the legal risks to the educational organization.

When instructors distance themselves from students, it tends to violate the expectations associated with an acceptable standard of care. There exists a legal and moral obligation to provide consistent supervision while students are participating in an educational program (Davidson, 2004). Hunt (1990) states, "The ethical issue that raises its head, therefore, is whether it is morally acceptable to expose students to educational activities that might very well harm or kill them in order to achieve good educational ends" (p. 51). More directly, irrespective of the program's educational aims and accompanying hopes for student learning, is it worth the risk? Hunt (1998) further writes:

> There is a threefold concern here. First, and most important, is the impact of an accident upon the person affected and its impact on his or her family, relatives, and others close to him or her. Second, is the impact of the accident upon the students, staff, and administrators of the program involved. Third, is the impact of the accident upon the profession of wilderness education in general. (p. 8)

These questions deserve consideration: How can instructors know whether the benefits of an unaccompanied experience outweigh the risks? Is it conceivable that the solo and final expedition are being programmed for uncertain and unquantifiable educational benefits? According to Hunt (1990), "the quantification of benefits is even more elusive than the quantification of risks. . . . In order to quantify a benefit, there must exist some objective source of benefit. But, the concept of a benefit is quite subjective" (p. 36). So, how does one pedagogically justify offering unaccompanied experiences when subjective, elusive benefits are weak compared with clearly defined, objective risks? This risk–benefit question is truly problematic when a student dies or is seriously injured.

Furthermore, one can likely achieve the educational objectives of unaccompanied events by modifying them to include direct staff supervision or by participating in other activities. The best educational scenario is when an outdoor experience is perceived as risky but has a low real risk. Hunt (1990) concurs, "Ethically, it can be argued that if the educational goals can be accomplished by using situations that are not in fact risky, then that is the way to go, rather than using methods that are really risky in order to accomplish the exact same goals" (p. 38).

Student autonomy is often identified as a key goal of unaccompanied activities. A growing body of research indicates that opportunity for autonomy is a catalyst for participant learning and growth (American Camp Association, 2006; Gambone, Klem, and Connell, 2002; Witt and Caldwell, 2005). It promotes pedagogic outcomes related to perceived competence and self-esteem (Reeve, 2002; Sibthorp et al., 2008). But simply removing instructors does not necessarily support or enhance autonomy. Other studies indicate that students can experience autonomy and increased responsibility when the instructors are present but have limited involvement (Bobilya, Kalisch, and Daniel, 2010; Bobilya, Kalisch, and Sperry, 2009). Davidson (2004) suggests that instructor presence may have little or no diminishing influence on the quality of the student experience and that the same sense of accomplishment persists on completion. Traditionally, programs have offered autonomy to students at the expense of direct supervision; this practice surely increases the risk associated with the activity. What if this practice is unnecessary?

The debate over the pedagogical value of unaccompanied activities loses meaning when one major accident can bankrupt a program. This can occur in both direct and indirect ways. The direct financial impact of a lawsuit can drive a smaller program out of business, or the perceived lack of safety and supervision that one well-publicized accident can create can greatly reduce customer support and cause the organization to fail. Either way, the loss is great. The organization must carefully manage risk so that it can serve others in the future.

Risk Versus Cultural Intolerance

Third, current culture is risk averse and intolerant of the incidents resulting from unaccompanied educational activities.

Ongoing staff supervision is a reasonable expectation of novice students (and their parents) when paying for a wilderness or adventure program. In the past, the public was more understanding of occasional incidents that resulted from inadequate supervision. However, the current parental, legal, and media expectations are much more conservative. According to Schimelpfenig (2007), former NOLS risk management director, "We operate in a climate, in both our profession and society, of growing intolerance to the adverse consequences of risk. . . . [T]his present generation of parents is especially protective of and adverse to negative consequences, or even some discomfort, for their children" (p. 2).

Wilderness programs attempt to close this gap by warning participants of the real risks involved, including the potential for death. Admissions personnel require students and parents or guardians to sign documents that enumerate the risks associated with various activities, including solos and student-led expeditions. This is the common legal practice of gaining informed consent and a release of liability. But this practice is not without its inherent weakness: most participants and their parents do not (and cannot) comprehend the actual risks involved. Despite signing documents, most students and parents are *not* willing to accept the

possibility of crippling injury or death. No public support exists for a program that is perceived as compromising safety for the sake of education. As Hunt (2000) explains:

> There is a cultural gap between the people who do wilderness programming for a living and those who come on courses. . . . It is very easy for those who do risky activities for a living to grant a level of ethical acceptability or tolerability to accidents that might not be even remotely shared by the broader public. (p. 167)

More conservative legal decisions and increasing public expectations clearly call for a high duty of care for students. For this reason, program administrators hire the most experienced and competent instructors they can find. They also provide a high instructor-to-student ratio in each group. Then, they proceed to do the unthinkable by removing the presence of these instructors during some of the most challenging and potentially hazardous events of the program. Regardless of its educational justification, this is illogical and contrary to the cultural norm of moving expert resources closer to students in the midst of increased risk taking and providing more protective care.

This rightly raises the question of legal negligence, which NOLS legal counsel Reb Gregg (1999) defines as follows:

> Negligence has to do with the failure to behave reasonably toward another person to whom a duty is owed. To be charged with negligence, 1) you or the school must have a duty of reasonable care, 2) that duty must have been violated, and 3) damages, reasonably arising out of that breach of duty, and reasonably foreseeable, must have been incurred. (p. 83)

In other words, one is accused of negligence when a perceived breach of duty has allowed another to experience unreasonable harm, especially if the person was dependent on the care of another. Because most wilderness program students are young and inexperienced, they are quite dependent. Some would argue that these minors are deserving of the "highest degree of care." This legal standard reflects what an extremely cautious person would do in caring for another (Gregg, 2008, p. 2). The question becomes, Would a reasonable person define the highest degree of care to include the direct supervision of students?

Where were the instructors? Again, this will be the first and most damning question asked following a serious injury or death. Offended clients and lawyers will likely pursue liability claims based on negligent supervision. Regarding the 2006 OB death cited previously, Ketcham (2007) states, "When I contacted (the mother), a few days after her daughter was found, she was outraged. 'They told me my daughter was going to be well supervised . . . and she obviously wasn't,' she said. 'They killed my baby'" (p. 49). Ketcham (2007) quotes the family lawyer as saying, "My goal is to get the family money. . . . Having a kid hike in 110-degree heat, in a canyon, with a backpack that's nearly half her weight, without appropriate supervision checking in on her is gross negligence—and by that I mean negligence that was disgusting" (p. 54). Ken Stettler, director of Utah's Department of Human Services, agrees: "There's no question that this was a case of negligence" (Voss, 2007, p. 6).

The inability to acknowledge the responsibility of supervisors angers the public, especially the victim's parents and friends. Lawsuits tend to follow. Despite OB and NOLS program traditions, one must acknowledge that much has changed in the public's perceptions of unaccompanied activities. The helicopter parent of modern times, characterized by extremely close attention to his or her child's experiences and concerns, strongly expects a helicopter instructor in the wilderness.

Alternative Supervision Strategies

What does this helicopter instructor act like during solos and student-led expeditions? Staff can provide direct supervision of students by being within sight and sound of them at all times. Acting as shadow instructors, they can intervene on occasion to debrief students or provide expert counsel. Research suggests that this higher interaction with students does not diminish the educational quality of these experiences (Bobilya, Kalisch, and Daniel, 2010; Bobilya, McAvoy, and Kalisch, 2005b). Many students report positive outcomes when instructors visit them on solo or travel with them on the final expedition. For Davidson (2004), the "high quality feedback from skilled practitioners" (p. 9) during these events enhances the students' learning.

The physical presence of instructors can provide extra care to unmotivated or incapable students. The staff can act as ghost instructors by sitting quietly in proximity to all solo students or traveling in silence with final expedition students, offering no assistance in order to foster independence. Or the staff can choose a more personal style of interaction as friend instructors by systematically visiting with nearby solo students or amicably engaging them on final expedition without providing assistance. Each supervision strategy minimizes incident potential while preserving essential student autonomy. The instructor is also in an excellent position to facilitate learning by encouraging students to pursue the activity objectives. The role of the instructor in wilderness programs is influential and greatly shapes the student experience through intentional intervention (Kalisch, 1999; Outward Bound USA, 2007). Why not offer educational facilitation during the solo and student-led expedition?

Conclusion

This argument supports the educational value of autonomous educational experiences in wilderness programs such as the solo and student-led expedition, but it challenges instructors to minimize risk to the greatest extent while providing for autonomy. As discussed, instructors can meet this objective when they modify their role of direct supervision. The risk to students who are alone in the wilderness and under distant or indirect supervision will always be higher than the risk to students when staff are present. Therefore, any decision to allow students to be unaccompanied for any extended time represents less-than-good judgment and perhaps negligence. In the current culture, indirect supervision by staff violates a prudent standard of care that the public will not tolerate. Although some argue that direct supervision diminishes student learning, the potential for growth is eliminated entirely if the program is terminated. Isn't it better for a program to modify its practices than to be eliminated due to an accident and subsequent lawsuit? Davidson (2004) concurs:

> If someone places themselves in your care, do not you have the moral duty to be there to ensure they do not do anything that would cause them serious harm? Will you sleep well at night knowing that if you had been present you could have prevented that injury from occurring? . . . Further, I believe that management personnel who condone (unaccompanied) practices are placing themselves at risk of criminal prosecution by doing so. (p. 4)

The time has come to embrace a new kind of solo and final expedition that is accompanied by expert risk managers and educational facilitators. The wilderness education profession and its programs will become more ethical by making this necessary change.

References

American Camp Association. (2006). *Innovations: Improving youth experiences in summer programs*. [Brochure]. Martinsville, IN: American Camp Association.

Bobilya, A.J., Kalisch, K.R., & Daniel, B. (2010). *An investigation of the Outward Bound final expedition*. Paper presented at the Association for Experiential Education International Conference: Symposium on Experiential Education Research (SEER), Las Vegas, NV.

Bobilya, A.J., Kalisch, K.R., & Sperry, D. (2009). *Where are the instructors? Benefits of unaccompanied program components*. Paper presented at the Wilderness Risk Management Conference, Durham, NC. www.nols.edu/wrmc/resources.shtml [December 12, 2011].

Bobilya, A.J., McAvoy, L., & Kalisch, K.R. (2005a). Lessons from the field: Participants' perceptions of a multi-day wilderness solo. In C. Knapp & T. Smith (Eds.), *Exploring the power of solo, silence, and solitude* (pp. 103-120). Boulder, CO: Association for Experiential Education.

Bobilya, A.J., McAvoy, L., & Kalisch, K.R. (2005b). The power of the instructor in the solo experience: An empirical study and some non-empirical questions. *Journal of Adventure Education and Outdoor Learning, 5*(1), 35-50.

Brookes, A. (2003). Outdoor education fatalities in Australia 1960-2002. Part 2: Contributing circumstances: Supervision, first aid and rescue. *Australian Journal of Outdoor Education, 7*(2), 34-42.

Daniel, B. (2003). The life significance of a wilderness solo. In C. Knapp & T. Smith (Eds.), *Exploring the power of solo, silence, and solitude* (pp. 85-102). Boulder, CO: Association for Experiential Education.

Davidson, G. (2004). Unaccompanied activities in outdoor education: When can they be justified? *New Zealand Journal of Outdoor Education, 4*, 5-25.

Gambone, M.A., Klem, A.M., & Connell, J.P. (2002). *Finding out what matters for youth: Testing key links in a community action framework for youth development*. Philadelphia: Youth Development Strategies, Inc. and Institute for Research and Reform in Education.

Garrett, J. (2008). *The case study discussion method as used by Outward Bound for instructor judgment training*. Paper presented at the Wilderness Risk Management Conference, Jackson, WY. www.nols.edu/wrmc/resources.shtml [December 12, 2011].

Gregg, C.R. (1999). Liability issues for NOLS instructors. In *1999 Wilderness Risk Management Conference proceedings* (pp. 83-84). Lander, WY: Wilderness Risk Managers Committee.

Gregg, C.R. (2008). *Understanding your legal duty of care*. Paper presented at the Wilderness Risk Management Conference, Jackson, WY. www.nols.edu/wrmc/resources.shtml [December 12, 2011].

Grove, C. (2011). Grizzly attacks teens in wilderness school. *Anchorage Daily News*. www.adn.com/2011/07/24/1983379/grizzly-sow-attacks-group-of-seven.html [December 12, 2011].

Haddock, C. (1999a). Epics, lies, and hero stories: The folklore of near misses in the outdoors. In *1999 Wilderness Risk Management Conference proceedings* (pp. 22-32). Lander, WY: Wilderness Risk Managers Committee.

Haddock, C. (1999b). High potential incidents—Determining their significance. In *1999 Wilderness Risk Management Conference proceedings* (pp. 33-46). Lander, WY: Wilderness Risk Managers Committee.

Hunt, J. (1990). *Ethical issues in experiential education*. Boulder, CO: Association for Experiential Education.

Hunt, J. (1998). Ethically tolerable accidents. In *1998 Wilderness Risk Management Conference proceedings* (pp. 7-12). Lander, WY: Wilderness Risk Managers Committee.

Hunt, J. (1999). Philosophy of adventure education. In J. Miles & S. Priest (Eds.), *Adventure education* (pp. 115-122). State College, PA: Venture.

Hunt, J. (2000). Ethical foundations of wilderness risk management. In D. Ajango (Ed.), *Lessons learned: A guide to accident prevention and crisis response* (pp. 157-175). Anchorage, AK: University of Alaska Anchorage.

Kalisch, K.R. (1999). *The role of the instructor in the Outward Bound educational process*. Kearney, NE: Morris.

Kalisch, K.R., Bobilya, A.J., & Daniel, D. (in press). The Outward Bound solo: A study of participants' perceptions. *Journal of Experiential Education*.

Ketcham, C. (2007). A death at Outward Bound. *National Geographic Adventure* (special report). www.national-geographic.com/adventure/news/outward-bound.html [December 12, 2011].

Komarnitsky, S.J. (1999). Visiting teen disappears, likely fell in glacier hole. www.alaska.net/~jlanders/Fatal/Nazzaro.htm [December 12, 2011].

Liddle, J., & Storck, S. (1995). *Adventure program risk management report: 1995 edition*. Boulder, CO: Association for Experiential Education.

McCarthy, A. (2009). Going back in. *National Geographic Adventure,* August/September, 66-70.

Morganthau, T. (1979). Risky or reckless? *Newsweek,* December 3, 72.

Outward Bound USA. (2007). *Leadership the Outward Bound way*. Seattle: Mountaineers.

Reeve, J. (2002). Self-determination theory applied to educational settings. In E.L. Deci & R.M. Ryan (Eds.), *Handbook of self-determination research* (pp. 183-203). Rochester, NY: University of Rochester Press.

Rogers, L., & Garshelis, D. (1988). The BWCAW bear attacks of 1987. *Boundary Waters Journal, 2*(1), 48-56.

Schimelpfenig, T. (2007). *Fostering student leadership, competence and independence: NOLS student supervision practices.* Paper presented at the Wilderness Risk Managers Conference, Alberta, Canada. www.nols.edu/wrmc/resources.shtml [December 12, 2011].

Sibthorp, J., Paisley, K., Gookin, J., & Furman, N. (2008). The pedagogic value of student autonomy in adventure education. *Journal of Experiential Education, 31*(2), 136-151.

Udall, J. (1995). Thinking about safety. In *1995 Wilderness Risk Management Conference proceedings* (pp. 66-69). Lander, WY: Wilderness Risk Managers Committee.

Voss, G. (2007). Dangers that can cause or lead to. . . . *The Boston Magazine.* www.bostonmagazine.com/articles/dangers_that_can_cause_or_lead_to [December 12, 2011].

Witt, P., & Caldwell, L. (2005). *Recreation and youth development.* State College, PA: Venture.

NO Guarding Safety Without Compromising Learning: The Value of Unaccompanied Components

Brad Daniel, PhD, professor of environmental studies and outdoor education (cochair), Montreat College, Montreat, North Carolina, United States

Andrew Bobilya, PhD, associate professor and cochair of outdoor education, Montreat College, Montreat, North Carolina, United States

"I most enjoyed testing myself and discovering that I am made of thicker skin than I might have assumed. It gives me confidence for whatever future endeavors I undertake."

—North Carolina Outward Bound final expedition participant, 2008 (cited in Bobilya, Kalisch, and Daniel, 2010)

Should wilderness program instructors always accompany their groups? In the coming pages we argue that wilderness staff should not be required to accompany their participants at all times, provided that proper safety precautions are taken. The literature supports the fact that wilderness experience programs should continue to incorporate unaccompanied expedition components because such components have educational value (Bobilya, 2004; Daniel et al., 2010; Sibthorp et al., 2008). Further, we argue that unaccompanied wilderness program components should continue as traditionally practiced by Outward Bound and the National Outdoor Leadership School (NOLS) and modified only as a last resort to avoid removing the component from program design or when other circumstances warrant it. Anticipating and minimizing risk can help maximize learning during unaccompanied expedition components. This argument puts forth two main propositions:

- Research indicates that unaccompanied components (e.g., solo, final expedition) where the instructors are not present provide valuable educational experiences that are not easily replicated with instructor supervision.
- The trend toward eliminating or minimizing unaccompanied components is driven

by fear of litigation, not by an understanding of the components' educational value or the actual risk involved. Risk related to unaccompanied wilderness expedition components generally can be managed in a way that is relatively safe.

Educational or Pedagogic Value

The literature suggests that the times when the instructors are not present provide powerful learning opportunities for wilderness program participants. The solo experience is regarded as one of the most influential components in wilderness programs (Bobilya, 2004; Daniel, 2003; Fredrickson and Anderson, 1999; Griffin, 2000; McAvoy, 2000; McFee, 1993; Stringer and McAvoy, 1992). In addition, recent research has shown the final expedition, or any independent group travel, to be one of the most memorable and significant course components according to postcourse surveys at Outward Bound Singapore (Gassner, Kahlid, and Russell, 2006), NOLS (Sibthorp et al., 2008), and Montreat College's Discovery Wilderness Expedition (Daniel, 2003). These two course components have one thing in common: the instructors either are not present or significantly alter their role within the group to allow for increased student autonomy.

A recent study on the final expedition component of North Carolina Outward Bound courses found that minimizing instructor involvement enhanced personal growth by increasing self-reliance and self-awareness and enhanced group development by encouraging greater group reliance, responsibility, and cohesion (Bobilya, Kalisch, and Daniel, 2010). Personal growth was expressed in terms of increased self-reliance and self-awareness.

In the words of one student, "The final expedition helped me to trust myself, made me realize that my thought and my voice is worthwhile and that I am perfectly capable of working interdependently" (North Carolina Outward Bound School participant, 2008, cited in Bobilya, Kalisch, and Daniel, 2010). Another student commented on the impact of the final expedition on his group's development: "The [freedom from instructors] was good. It made me/us feel like independent, mature adults, like we don't need people telling us what to do" (North Carolina Outward Bound School participant, 2008, cited in Bobilya, Kalisch, and Daniel, 2010).

Qualities that enhance learning from unaccompanied components include autonomy, empowerment, choice, and a measure of control over the outcomes. One of the most valuable aspects of these components is that they increase student autonomy (the participant's perception of having some control). Students on solo, final expedition, or other unaccompanied expedition components have more autonomy to make their own decisions and experience the consequences. The value of autonomy has been noted and supported in a variety of fields, including the youth-development literature (American Camp Association, 2006; Gambone, Klem, and Connell, 2002; Sibthorp, Paisley, and Gookin, 2007; Witt and Caldwell, 2005), which indicates that these types of outcomes (e.g., responsibility, leadership development, self-reliance) are what young people need in contemporary culture. Bobilya, Kalisch, and Daniel (2010) found that for youth attending North Carolina Outward Bound School, the top three most enjoyable characteristics of the final expedition were autonomy, accomplishment, and teamwork—all characteristics that are critical to positive youth development (Gambone, Klem, and Connell, 2002).

A growing body of research has documented the benefits of student autonomy in outdoor programming (Allan, 2005; American Camp Association, 2006; Paisley et al., 2008; Ramsing and Sibthorp, 2008; Sibthorp et al., 2008). Unaccompanied program components afford students the opportunity to have a measure of control and choice that they do not often experience over the outcomes in their daily lives. Choice and control have been identified as factors that influence the effectiveness of autonomous student experiences (Sheldon, Williams, and Joiner, 2003). By providing a measure of choice and control, unaccompanied components empower students. A goal of the NOLS curriculum—and of many outdoor and adventure programs worldwide—is to "develop students as leaders who make

decisions and lead without the direct guidance of their instructors" (Schimelpfenig, 2007, p. 4). Many young people today say they want more of this type of empowerment (American Camp Association, 2006), and many cultures need this type of empowerment in order to develop future citizens who are engaged leaders.

Experiences that are perceived as meaningful empower students to engage (Leffert, Benson, and Roehlkepartain, 1997). This would include such things as the ability to determine what to do, when to do it, and for what purpose. Students on a final expedition could determine such things as their route and time-control plan, their decision-making process, and their goals for traveling together. Some of the more commonly used course components, such as a student serving as the leader of the day, help to empower students (Gookin and White, 2006) and often culminate in students traveling without their instructors. NOLS expedition students have opportunities to "display competencies necessary for wilderness travel, to better understand their abilities and limitations and to gain valuable experience upon which to further develop their self-awareness and judgment, and accomplish a realistic and achievable goal" (Schimelpfenig, 2007, p. 1). Participants on NOLS courses who had more days of autonomous student expedition reported higher levels of empowerment (Sibthorp et al., 2008). The autonomy resulting from unaccompanied components is pedagogically valuable and necessary in our culture (American Camp Association, 2006; Sibthorp et al., 2008).

Some have suggested that instructor presence may have little or no influence on the quality of student learning in unaccompanied components and may result in the same sense of accomplishment at completion (Davidson, 2004). In reality, very little research indicates that participants learn just as much from experiences when accompanied by an instructor. Others have noted that freedom from instructors has a positive influence on personal growth and group development (Bobilya, Kalisch, and Daniel, 2010), life significance (Daniel, 2003), group development (McFee, 1993), and spiritual growth (Griffin, 2000). More often today, however, people argue that despite the educational value, the benefits can never outweigh the potential risk. It is to that concern that we now turn our attention.

Risk and Fear of Litigation

The word *risk* inherently has a negative connotation, yet any risk of loss also implies a potential for gain (Cline, 2007). Many programs in operation today have either minimized or eliminated unaccompanied expedition components, primarily due to concerns over risk and liability. The trend is driven by fear of litigation, not by a full understanding of the educational value of unaccompanied expedition components or perhaps even their true risk. Schimelpfenig (2007) states, "We operate in a climate, in both our profession and society, of growing intolerance to the adverse consequences of risk. Sociologists tell us that this present generation of parents is especially protective of and adverse to negative consequences, or even some discomfort, for their children" (p. 2). It would appear that what has come to be called helicopter parenting has influenced wilderness programming.

One might assume that the rate of serious accidents or deaths would be significantly higher when the instructors are absent. Brookes (2003) and others have suggested that lack of supervision is a predictor of serious accidents. Despite the concern about risks involved in wilderness experience programming, "national [Outward Bound] statistics show that the risk of serious accidents is very low" (Paton, 1992, p. 141). Paton's (1992) study also looked at injury rate by activity type at Outward Bound in the United States. The unaccompanied expedition components did not rank highly when activity at the time of accident was taken into account. In fact, the final expedition did not rank at all, and the solo was 10th in the list and reported at only one of the five Outward Bound USA schools. A recent study at NOLS from a sample of 17,887 program days in 2005 and 2006 indicated that "the incident rates do not appear to be greater during unaccompanied portions of the course" (Sibthorp et al., 2008). This could be due to differences in how thoroughly these programs prepare the participants beforehand and how carefully they evaluate the potential hazards. Some have argued that potential hazards and skill requirements are intentionally reduced during autonomous student expeditions in order to enhance safety (Sibthorp et al., 2008). However, these modifications appear to vary by program (Davidson, 2004).

As discussed later, programs use a variety of methods to reduce the risks involved in such expedition components. However, one of the central tenets of adventure education is the idea that taking on some risk has inherent value and that in doing so the learner can better distinguish between real risk and perceived risk.

Unaccompanied expedition components have come under increased scrutiny in recent years due to several well-publicized accidents. Davidson (2004) asserts that the lack of supervision in unaccompanied components can pose significant risks and that these risks cannot be justified pedagogically. Lack of supervision does, indeed, pose risks, but to varying degrees depending on how well the group or individuals have been prepared to take on the task and whether the instructors properly evaluated the potential risks beforehand. Allowing students to do solo without sufficient access to water or allowing groups to conduct autonomous expeditions in steep or otherwise treacherous terrain would pose exceptional risk.

In many expedition designs, the skill level of the participants increases through sequenced programming until the point at which, if deemed ready by the instructors, they are afforded the opportunity to experience unaccompanied components. The critical component, and one that we would argue is important in all wilderness experience programming, is the instructor. Much responsibility rests on the field instructors, who make the decisions regarding a student group's readiness for the final expedition or an individual's readiness for solo (Bobilya, McAvoy, and Kalisch, 2005). We argue that one should not uniformly remove the educational benefit of such experiences because of the risks involved. On the contrary, instructor training and supervision should be increased to ensure that program safety expectations are being administered in the field. For example, NOLS allows its instructors to modify the experience in the field instead of eliminating the program component from their courses. Whether autonomous student travel occurs is up to the judgment of the instructors. If the terrain is too unforgiving, the required skills are too technical, or the group has not demonstrated the knowledge, skills, and judgment to make good decisions, the instructors may choose to shorten, modify, or eliminate the experience (Schimelpfenig, 2007).

One cannot eliminate all potential hazards and, therefore, the risk associated with them, for to do so would mean eliminating the activity altogether. Still, those arguing this position insist that one cannot remove the instructor or supervisor without significantly increasing the risk. We argue that with proper training, the risks involved are not significantly increased and that the educational benefit exponentially increases. Research has confirmed higher student outcomes as a result of NOLS autonomous student expeditions while trying to "balance the likelihood and cost of a beginner's error against the benefit of the activity" (Schimelpfenig, 2007,

p. 2). The most important factor affecting those outcomes was personal empowerment gained from independent decision making (Schimelpfenig, 2007); this factor was confirmed more recently by Bobilya and colleagues' (2010) study of the North Carolina Outward Bound final expedition.

The presence of one or more instructors does not guarantee safety because one cannot completely eliminate risk from wilderness expedition design. One can, however, take steps to minimize it. Studies have identified a number of tangible ways to reduce risk on various unaccompanied components (Brookes, 2003; Daniel, Kalisch, and Bobilya, 2009; Schimelpfenig, 2007). These include the following:

- Equip participants with the requisite equipment, skills, knowledge, and practice time beforehand and assess them on these factors.

- Sequence skill acquisition and development so that participants build toward a final challenge for which they have been well prepared.

- Know the terrain where the unaccompanied components will take place.

- Direct the group from potential hazards (e.g., valleys prone to flash flooding, steep terrain with many cliffs, avalanche areas) while remaining close enough to intervene if needed.

- Monitor predicted weather before and during these components and adapt the group's route, avoiding areas that might flood or be prone to lightning strikes.

- Review safety protocols with the group and obtain a copy of their route and time-control plan for final expedition. Ensure that solo participants know not to wander away from their campsites and to follow emergency communication protocols if needed.

- Shadow a group fairly closely on final expedition.

- Use a star or circular arrangement so that basecamp is at the center of the solo spots when choosing solo locations. This shortens the distance between instructors and all participants.

- Prevent students from attempting highly technical skills or any skills that they have not been able to demonstrate under instructor supervision.

- Provide the means for students to get help quickly if needed via satellite phones, cell phones, radios, satellite tracking devices, and other technology. Train students in first aid, emergency, and lost-person procedures before they travel unaccompanied.

- In program promotional literature and precourse communication, inform students, and their parents if required, of the potential risk of harm, injury, and death.

- Consider the age, skill level, and ability to function as a team based on direct observations.

- Do not allow participants to attempt unaccompanied components if they have not demonstrated an ability to make good decisions.

Instructors must try to provide students with maximum autonomy while minimizing risk as much as possible. Schimelpfenig (2007) writes, "Instructors need to be able to articulate, with supporting examples, why we think they have earned independence" (p. 3). NOLS instructors look for key strategies for preparing students for autonomous student experiences, including "clarity of expectations and curriculum progression, observation of performance and the decision on student readiness for independence" (p. 2).

Some evidence suggests that the actual risk of such activities might be exaggerated for a variety of reasons. Bad news, such as the death of a wilderness participant, is often reported through a variety of media outlets. Reporting the death of any one participant, although undoubtedly tragic, fails to recognize the thousands who have safely and successfully completed various unaccompanied wilderness program components. In reality, the number of deaths is very small when compared with the number of participants who successfully complete unaccompanied components. This statement is certainly not meant to minimize a tragic loss of life but simply to suggest that the media has incredible power to shape perception and opinion using worst-case scenarios. This tendency likely increases the perceived risk of those components during which the instructors are not with the group (e.g., Voss, 2007).

In the United States, the inherent risks involved in the final expedition and solo wilderness experience program components have not been shown to lead to more injuries or deaths when compared with other program components. Furthermore, with proper training, students can, should, and must be allowed to be independent. The key is instructor judgment. For NOLS, "observations and demonstrated competence are foundations of a decision that students are ready to be independent" (Schimelpfenig, 2007, p. 3).

Current Trends

Unaccompanied components within outdoor and adventure programs have decreased in frequency through the years. It is becoming more common today to use a variety of modified instructional techniques to promote student independence and autonomy. The North Carolina Outward Bound School, for example, facilitates student-led expeditions in one of four ways:

- unaccompanied by instructors (adult groups only),
- instructors travel within sight or sound of the crew,
- instructors travel within sight *and* sound of the crew, and
- instructors travel with the group (Bobilya, Kalisch, and Daniel, 2010).

In the last three cases, the word "unaccompanied" is not completely accurate; NOLS adjusts the level of instructor supervision based on student performance. These supervision methods include ghost instructors, shadowing, meeting at hazards, and daily debriefing (Schimelpfenig, 2007). It would be more precise to describe these components as having limited instructor involvement. Even when the instructors travel with the group, they often minimize their involvement by remaining silent (Bobilya, Kalisch, and Daniel, 2010). All of these methods attempt to provide a final, culminating experience for students that fosters leadership, competence, and independence—qualities that the program hopes students will transfer to their daily lives at home (Schimelpfenig, 2007). However, are they equal in pedagogic value? Some evidence suggests they are not. Attention and focus are enhanced when no perceived safety net exists in the form of the instructors standing nearby. Therefore, any adjustments to instructor positioning should be considered as a last resort and used only when truly unaccompanied experiences cannot be maintained in the program design. Further, to deny participants who have the required skills the right to experience true autonomy and real choice does not adequately prepare them for the inevitability of dealing with risk in everyday life.

In an address to the Inaugural Outdoor Education Australia Risk Management Conference, Preston Cline, a risk management consultant and past risk management director at Project U.S.E., argued:

> For too long we have been viewing risk as something to be feared and without intending it we have passed that fear onto our students and their parents. In doing so, we have moved steadily away from trying to teach our students, toward a belief that we should protect them at all costs. Yet the truth is that we cannot protect them, and all we are doing is denying them access to the very skills they will need to move from relative security into adventure. To learn how to manage the exceptions, paradoxes and mysteries that makes the authentic life so rich and rewarding. (Cline, 2007, p. 7)

We agree and argue that we must move beyond concerns about risk and consider the value of unaccompanied wilderness experience components.

Conclusion

Should students ever be allowed to experience unaccompanied components, such as solo and the final expedition? This is an important question in today's world, where one lawsuit can drive a program out of business. In a business-oriented model, taking what are perceived as unnecessary risks will seem illogical; however, from a program-oriented model, the pedagogical value of the risk exceeds the potential ramifications if the risk is managed properly. Accidents still will happen, and no amount of preparation or precaution will eliminate them entirely, regardless of whether the instructors are present. One cannot and should not remove the challenge from what is essentially challenge education, and some of the most challenging aspects of a wilderness expedition occur when the instructors are not present or are present in a very limited form. Challenge is a key ingredient in personal growth. When challenge is eliminated or, more commonly, minimized in expedition design, the educational value is somewhat compromised. One of the proponents of experiential education, the legendary mountaineer Willi Unsoeld, once responded to a mother asking whether he could guarantee her son's safety. He replied that he could not guarantee the safety of her son and went on to say, "If you succeed in protecting your boy, as you are doing right now. . . . If you succeed, we guarantee the death of his soul" (cited in Hunt, 1990, p. 123).

Unaccompanied expedition components, such as solo and the final expedition, provide important educational opportunities for students to learn more about their own strengths and limitations and how they interact with others in group settings. By holding firm to the value of these components, wilderness expeditions offer powerful, countercultural experiences in a world driven more and more by fear of litigation. Program managers should consider the value of components that allow student autonomy despite the inherent risks. Decisions regarding whether to employ unaccompanied components should be based on evidence and grounded in research into the educational value and actual (not perceived) risk of such components.

Instructors should carefully assess student readiness in order to determine the appropriate level of autonomy to be granted instead of providing a standardized experience to all students. Paton (1992) states, "The safety record of Outward Bound is as good as, or better than, the safety record of many other recreational activities in which young people indulge, which justifies the continued use of the wilderness as a classroom and potentially dangerous activities for achieving the aims of the programs" (p. 143). Students should be given the opportunity to experience true autonomy instead of a facsimile of it, provided they have proven themselves capable. Our position is clear: Unaccompanied student experiences should not be uniformly eliminated from program design. They should be used whenever it is prudent to do so. This position is similar to that of NOLS's perspective on autonomous student expeditions:

> Throughout our history, the education, training, and experience provided through a NOLS course has developed competent graduates capable of leading and conducting their own outdoor trips and expeditions. . . . It is no less true today than when NOLS was founded in 1965 that people, especially young people, need, want, and respond well to this educational approach. NOLS's use of independent student group travel has a profound effect in the development of desired leadership attributes in our students. Our alumni tell us this. Our observations tell us this. Research into the educational outcomes from a NOLS course consistently correlate both daily and multi-day independent travel by student groups with higher

student outcomes. Personal empowerment that comes from independent decision making is the most significant course-level factor affecting all student outcomes. (Schimelpfenig, 2007, p. 1)

Risk will always be involved in wilderness expeditions regardless of whether the instructors are present. We must take steps to minimize risk as much as possible; however, we should not negate the significant, positive outcomes associated with components that increase student autonomy. The potential benefits of unaccompanied components far outweigh the risks.

References

Allan, S. (2005). Unaccompanied activities: Notes from the footpath. *New Zealand Journal of Outdoor Education, 5,* 5-9.

American Camp Association. (2006). *Innovations: Improving youth experiences in summer programs.* [Brochure]. Martinsville, IN: American Camp Association.

Bobilya, A.J. (2004). *An investigation of the solo in a wilderness experience program.* Unpublished doctoral dissertation. Minneapolis: University of Minnesota.

Bobilya, A.J., Kalisch, K., & Daniel, B. (2010). *An investigation of the Outward Bound final expedition.* Paper presented at the Association for Experiential Education International Conference: Symposium on Experiential Education Research (SEER), Las Vegas, NV.

Bobilya, A.J., McAvoy, L.H., & Kalisch, K.R. (2005). The power of the instructor in the solo experience: An empirical study and some non-empirical questions. *Journal of Adventure Education and Outdoor Learning, 5*(1), 35-50.

Brookes, A. (2003). Outdoor education fatalities in Australia 1960-2002. Part 2: Contributing circumstances: Supervision, first aid and rescue. *Australian Journal of Outdoor Education, 7*(2), 34-42.

Cline, P. (2007). *Learning to interact with uncertainty.* Keynote address at the Inaugural Outdoor Education Australia Risk Management Conference, Ballarat, Victoria, Australia.

Daniel, R.B. (2003). *The life significance of a spiritually oriented outward bound-type wilderness expedition.* Unpublished doctoral dissertation. Keen, NH: Antioch New England Graduate School.

Daniel, B., Bobilya, A.J., Kalisch, K., & Lindley, B. (2010). Lessons from the Outward Bound solo: Intended transfer of learning. *Journal of Outdoor Recreation, Education and Learning, 2*(1), 37-58.

Daniel, B., Kalisch, K., & Bobilya, A.J. (2009). *The final expedition: What happens when we leave students alone?* Session presented at the Association for Experiential

Education International Conference, Montreal, Quebec, Canada.

Davidson, G. (2004). Unaccompanied activities in outdoor education: When can they be justified? *New Zealand Journal of Outdoor Education, 4*, 5-25.

Fredrickson, L.M., & Anderson, D.H. (1999). A qualitative exploration of the wilderness experience as a source of spiritual inspiration. *Journal of Environmental Psychology, 19*, 21-39.

Gambone, M.A., Klem, A.M., & Connell, J.P. (2002). *Finding out what matters for youth: Testing key links in a community action framework for youth development.* Philadelphia: Youth Development Strategies, Inc. and Institute for Research and Reform in Education.

Gassner, M., Kahlid, A., & Russell, K. (2006). Investigating the long-term impact of adventure education: A retrospective study of Outward Bound Singapore's Classic 21-Day Challenge Course. In K. Paisley, L. McAvoy, A. Young, W. Shooter, & J. Bochniak (Eds.), *Research in outdoor education: Vol. 8* (pp. 75-93). Cortland, NY: Coalition for Education in the Outdoors.

Gookin, J., & White, T. (2006). Empowering and engaging NOLS students. In J. Gookin (Ed.), *Wilderness educator notebook* (pp. 35-38). Lander, WY: NOLS.

Griffin, W.J. (2000). *Effects of an adventure based program with an explicit spiritual component on the spiritual growth of adolescents.* Unpublished doctoral dissertation. Albuquerque, NM: University of New Mexico.

Hunt, J. (1990). Philosophy of adventure education. In J. Miles & S. Priest (Eds.), *Adventure education* (pp. 115-122). State College, PA: Venture.

Leffert, N., Benson, P., & Roehlkepartain, J. (1997). *Starting out right: Developmental assets for children.* Minneapolis: Search Institute.

McAvoy, L. (2000). Components of the outdoor trip: A response to the papers. In L.A. Stringer, L.H. McAvoy, & A.B. Young (Eds.), *Coalition for Education in the Outdoors Fifth Biennial Research Symposium proceedings* (pp. 12-14). Cortland, NY: Coalition for Education in the Outdoors.

McFee, M. (1993). *The effect of group dynamics on the perception of positive learning experience in the outward bound process.* Unpublished doctoral dissertation. Wheeling, IL: Forest Institute of Professional Psychology.

Paisley, K., Furman, N., Sibthorp, J., & Gookin, J. (2008). Student learning in outdoor education: A case study from the National Outdoor Leadership School. *Journal of Experiential Education, 30*(3), 201-222.

Paton, B.C. (1992). Health, safety and risk in Outward Bound. *Journal of Wilderness Medicine, 3*, 128-144.

Ramsing, R., & Sibthorp, J. (2008). The role of autonomy support in summer camp programs: Preparing youth for productive behaviors. *Journal of Parks and Recreation Administration, 26*(2), 61-77.

Schimelpfenig, T. (2007). *Fostering student leadership, competence and independence: NOLS student supervision practices.* Paper presented at the Wilderness Risk Management Conference, Banff, Alberta, Canada.

Sheldon, K.M., Williams, G.C., & Joiner, T. (2003). *Self-determination theory in the clinic: Motivating physical and mental health.* New Haven, CT: Yale University.

Sibthorp, J., Paisley, K., & Gookin, J. (2007). Exploring participant development through adventure-based recreation programming: A model from the National Outdoor Leadership School. *Leisure Sciences, 29*(1), 1-18.

Sibthorp, J., Paisley, K., Gookin, J., & Furman, N. (2008). The pedagogic value of student autonomy in adventure education. *Journal of Experiential Education, 31*(2), 136-151.

Stringer, L.A., & McAvoy, L. (1992). The need for something different: Spirituality and wilderness adventure. *Journal of Experiential Education, 15*(1), 13-20.

Voss, G. (2007). Dangers that can cause or lead to. . . . *The Boston Magazine.* www.bostonmagazine.com/articles/dangers_that_can_cause_or_lead_to [December 12, 2011].

Witt, P., & Caldwell, L. (2005). *Recreation and youth development.* State College, PA: Venture.

Controversial Issue 15

Should transgender youths be encouraged to favor specialized camps over mainstream camps?

Serving transgender and transgender nonconforming youths has received little discussion in the larger context of the adventure programming industry. This emerging issue is worthy of discussion to help better serve this diverse and growing population of participants. Attention has been directed to the Lesbian, Gay, Bisexual, Transgender, Queer, and Allies community; however, the transgender population deserves special attention. The term "transgender" refers to individuals who identify or express a gender identity that differs from the larger social view that equates sex with gender. This group tends to experience higher levels of exclusion as members of society. Harassment of transgender youths is pervasive in mainstream schools. In general, society does not understand the transgender population and related issues.

Adventure-based programs, which include summer camps, face some distinct challenges when serving transgender youths. Most commonly, program administrators and staff wrestle with issues of appropriate sleeping arrangements and bathroom facilities. However, larger issues are at stake beyond basic programming logistics. How do adventure-based programs holistically include rather than exclude transgender youth participants? Is integration into mainstream programs the best route to take from a developmental perspective? Is it best to provide a specialized environment specifically designed for the well-being and growth of the transgender camper? The two arguments featured in this debate provide an excellent overview of the issues and a deeper understanding of transgender and gender-variant populations.

Jackson Wilson and Stephen Lewis argue in favor of promoting specialized camps for transgender youths. They acknowledge that although traditional summer camps promote positive youth development, escaping from climates of oppression is very difficult. Transgender youths should not have to fight against exclusion from basic needs such as sleeping and going to the bathroom when attending adventure-based experiences. Wilson and Lewis acknowledge that little research focuses specifically on transgender participants in adventure-based programming. However, the related literature regarding specialized camps, such as single-gender programming, documents beneficial outcomes. Transgender youths face extraordinary challenges in our society and would benefit from the safe, accepting, and developmentally rich atmosphere of specialized camps. Wilson and Lewis structure their argument around the well-being of the individual within the complex issues that surround transgender youths and society.

Denise Mitten argues the opposing view by promoting participation in mainstream summer camps. She makes it clear that her argument includes only programs accredited by American Camp Association or Association for Experiential Education. Mitten claims that the benefits far outweigh the risks and takes a social justice viewpoint in her argument. Accredited camps offer an inclusive atmosphere and allow transgender youths to explore issues of identity in the context of an integrated society. Mitten structures her debate on the benefits to the individual, the camp community, and society at large. All campers and staff that experience the rich diversity of a mainstream program are more likely to return home and into society to make positive change.

As adventure programmers, we need to be realistic and do what is best in the way of service to all of our participants. You decide whether we as a profession should take a stance.

Should transgender youths be encouraged to favor specialized camps over mainstream camps?

YES Transgender-Specific Programming: An Oasis in the Storm

Jackson Wilson, PhD, assistant professor of recreation, parks, and tourism, San Francisco State University, San Francisco, California, United States

Stephen Lewis, PhD, assistant professor of recreation management and therapeutic recreation, University of Wisconsin–La Crosse, La Crosse, Wisconsin, United States

Faggot! Tranny! Freak! Robin's parents shuddered when they looked at the cell-phone photo of her epithet-covered middle-school locker. Robin seemed rather apathetic toward this recent act of bullying but was still somewhat relieved that the school year was drawing to a close. However, this new harassment further complicated her parents' decision about what to do about summer camp. Robin loved some things about the two week-long summer camps she previously attended, but, unfortunately, she had to balance her enjoyment with harassment by some for being considered too much of a "sissy." Now that she had grown a little older and was outwardly expressing herself as female, the terminology and types of harassment had grown worse, at least at school.

Although her parents want Robin to have an opportunity to express herself and develop self-confidence, they are concerned that camp might not offer those opportunities to Robin as it does to other campers. Their concerns are further heightened by their knowledge that bullying extends beyond schools and into camp settings (Carney and Nottis, 2008). Her parents are also afraid that the more intimate living arrangements in an overnight camp will create stressful situations for Robin. They are concerned about her physical and emotional safety during routine tasks such as going to the bathroom, changing clothing, and sleeping and during extended periods of unstructured time. Given all of the energy Robin will have to exert in navigating these potential challenges, they wonder when she would possibly find time to enjoy herself. Her parents wonder which would be better for Robin to attend: a mainstream camp or a camp that specifically serves transgender and gender-variant children.

Even in the current age of "inclusivity," we assert that the benefits of camps specifically for transgen-

der and gender-variant youths greatly outweigh the risks of participating in mainstream camps. We begin our argument by explaining relevant terminology and describing the social climate that transgender youths currently experience in their daily lives. We then explore research regarding separate recreational programming for groups based on gender and sexual identity. Finally, we end with a discussion that synthesizes all of this information into our stance that separate adventure-based programming is the best option for youths like Robin.

Exploring Gender Diversity

When Robin was born, her sex and assumed gender were declared based on the doctor's observation of her external genitalia ("it's a boy!") (Girschick, 2008). Although this simple litmus test is widely accepted within American culture, it may not perfectly correlate with other biological markers of sex such as chromosomal makeup, gonadal differentiation (ovaries or testes), and hormonal levels and cannot predict the way a child will eventually feel about and express their gender (Cho et al., 2004; Girschick, 2008). In contrast to biological sex, gender is more difficult to evaluate because it implies socially constructed roles created within a given culture (American Psychological Association, 2010; Cho et al., 2004; Grossman, O'Connell, and D'Augelli, 2005).

Children begin developing a gender identity early in life (Girschick, 2008; Grossman, O'Connell, and D'Augelli, 2005). This is true for children who fit with the dominant male or masculine and female or feminine paradigms as well as children who identify as transgender or gender variant (Girschick, 2008; Grossman and D'Augelli, 2007). For most people, gender is correlated strongly with sex, whereas others find it difficult to conform to prescribed gender roles and may internally feel that they were born the "wrong" sex (Cho et al., 2004). Gender identity refers to the internal feelings and image one holds for one's self in relation to cultural representations of sex and gender (Cho et al., 2004). Gender expression involves the external presentation of one's internal gender identity. Although many Native American cultures celebrated gender variance (Gilley, 2006), today's dominant American culture positions gender identity and expression dichotomously as "masculine" or "feminine." Some people identify and express themselves in less-conventional ways that may be considered as cross-gender, androgynous or ambiguous, or gender-blending or genderqueer type behaviors. For example, a young boy who prefers to dress up as a princess and collect dolls rather than focus on sports and toy cars may be perceived as gender variant if this behavior is prolonged, regardless of the child's actual gender identity (Cho et al., 2004). However, recent media coverage has increased awareness of children who identify differently than their assigned sex (Siebler, 2010).

The transgender (or "trans") experience is extremely diverse and ranges from the expression of some level of queer gender identity and infrequent cross-dressing to hormonal or surgical intervention and lifelong quest to match the external appearance with internal gendered feelings (Whittle, 2006). "Transgender" is an umbrella term for those individuals whose gender identity does not fit within the larger social view that equates sex with gender. Transgender individuals may or may not have sex reassignment surgery or identify within the traditional male–female binary. Genderqueer, gender nonconforming, bigender, and androgynes are some of the other terms that individuals have claimed to identify themselves (Dean et al., 2000). Just as an array of diverse expressions and ideologies of masculine and feminine exists within the more heteronormative population, a spectrum of trans embodiments exists that is further constituted by intersections of race, ethnicity, socioeconomics, sexual orientation, and other demographic factors. Further, one cannot assume the sexual orientation or identity of a person who identifies as transgender (Israel and Tarver, 1997).

Even though transgender is lumped together with sexual orientation in the well-known acronym LGBTQA (representing a lesbian, gay, bisexual, transgender, queer, and allies collective), gender is different than sexual orientation. Sexual orientation refers to one's romantic and sexual drives in relation to sex and gender. The heteronormative norm within our culture is for a (male-bodied) man to romantically partner with a (female-bodied) woman. However, people may be exclusively attracted to the same sex, be equally attracted to men and women, or even identify as pansexual and base sexual attraction on factors other than sex and gender (Israel and Tarver, 1997). Notions of sexual orientation are further complicated by trans identities. If two women date each other, they would be considered to be in a lesbian relationship. But if one of them transitioned to a male identity, this situation could be considered to be a heterosexual attraction. The taboo surrounding such diversity may be decreasing because examples of trans identities are much more widely available than they once were (Whittle, 2006).

Although the reality for transgender and gender-variant individuals in American society may be improving, transgender individuals are still stigmatized by mainstream America. Cohen and Semerjian (2008) state, "Those individuals who do not claim matching biology and gender identity are often written as outlaws living within pathologized bodies" (p. 133). The level of ostracism most transgender individuals face is associated with many negative medical, economic, and social issues that are even more extreme than those faced by others within the LGBTQ community (Dean et al., 2000, p. 5).

The situation is especially difficult for youths in schools. A recent study found that harassment of transgender students was pervasive across all of the schools studied; this level of harassment diminished transgender and gender-variant students' sense of safety (McGuire et al., 2010). Moreover, students who violate traditional gender boundaries often face consequences from adults in addition to those incurred by peers (Bochenek and Brown, 2001). Due to a lack of support, victimized transgender students often have a difficult time dealing with the effects of this pervasive discrimination (Greytak, Kosciw, and Diaz, 2009). According to O'Shaughnessy and colleagues (2004), 53 percent of California students reported that school is not safe for "effeminate" guys and 34 percent of California students reported that school is not a safe place for women who were considered to be more "masculine." Transgender students report even higher levels of victimization at school than do lesbians or gay males (Kosciw, Greytak, and Diaz, 2009).

Although transgender youths experience high levels of abuse in and out of school, the nation's courts have upheld the rights of transgender youths to not be harassed (Flores v. Morgan Hill Unified School District, 2003; Nabozny v. Podlesny, 1996) and to be treated equally with other students (Doe v. Yunits, 2000). The majority of transgender youths currently face an extremely harsh climate at school. Given this reality, is it better for them to be social activists and constantly fight for their rights and attempt to educate others at a mainstream camp, or for them to go to a camp specifically for transgender and gender-variant youths?

Benefits Extend to Transgender Participants

Research suggests that participation in camp has many benefits (e.g., Henderson et al., 2007; Readdick and Schaller, 2005; Thurber et al., 2007). On the American Camp Association (2010) website, camp participants state that benefits include feeling wanted, respected, proud of one's self, connected to others, and in tune with one's self. One particular response states, "I don't have to be fake to anyone. Everyone here accepts me as I am, and I'm not judged or criticized" (American Camp Association, 2010). Would Robin get these same benefits at summer camp? Would she develop the same social connections, have similar opportunities for self-expression, and blossom in an environment of unconditional peer support? Or would Robin be ostracized, ridiculed, and bullied by the other camp participants and camp staff because she identifies as a gender that is different than is normally associated with her male anatomy?

A selection of summer camps have been identified as being friendly to the LGBTQA community (LGBT Families, 2009). Moreover, authors such as Meyer (2010) have written about the possible value that wilderness programs offer LGBTQA participants. However, testimonials from transgender individuals point out that camps may be more accepting of lesbians, gay men, and bisexual individuals than of transgender individuals. Nick Teich, founder of a camp for transgender youths, has recited his own story of being shunned from the camp that he had worked at for years after he transitioned from a female to a male gender identity (Teich, 2010b).

Very little research focuses specifically on transgender participants in outdoor education (Meyer, 2010). One of the few outdoor education studies that specifically includes transgender individuals is a longitudinal study of a series of Outward Bound courses for LGBTQA participants. These courses were shown to consistently lead to statistically significant increases in participants' self-confidence and time-management skills (Neill, 2002).

In 2010, the first summer camp specifically for transgender and gender-variant youths opened. Camp Aranu'tiq is a week-long summer camp for transgender and gender-variant children age 8 to 15. Aranu'tiq is a Chugach (Alaska Native) term for a person who has been blessed with both the male and female spirit. This program is structured much like any other summer camp; however, therapists are on staff given the unique social and psychological pressures this group of campers faces. The founder of the camp explained that he was inspired to create the camp based on his own background as a camper and counselor and his first exposure to transgender children. Excerpts from the Camp Aranu'tiq website suggest that the programming, specific to transgender and gender-variant youths, creates a positive environment for self-expression and confidence:

> I saw incredible things happening as I looked around. I saw trans and gender-variant kids, some of whom had never met someone else like them, beginning to open up and be themselves. I saw campers using new pronouns and names that they never before felt like they were able to use. I saw thousands of smiles throughout the week. I saw kids getting more comfortable dressing in what made them comfortable, not in what society tells them to. (Teich, 2010a)

Both mainstream summer camps and Camp Aranu'tiq appear to positively develop self-concepts in their youth participants. Given the social stigmatization that many transgender youths face, opportunities to positively develop self-concept may be especially crucial for transgender youths. The next section offers a closer look at summer camps and the challenges that they may face in promoting positive developmental opportunities for transgender youths.

Gender-Identified Space

Outdoor education programs that serve youths often have sex-segregation rules that are based on hegemonic notions that girls and women need to be protected from boys and men. These rules are often to protect women from males who may get them pregnant or who may dominate them in sports and other activities. Previous court cases and demonstrated limitations within sport were to protect women from female impersonators, working under a system of belief that female athletes are, by nature, weaker and more prone to being taken advantage of than their male (read: more well equipped) counterparts (Cohen and Semerjian, 2008, p. 134).

This fear of men and boys preying on women and girls is based on a reality of victimization that transgender and gender-variant individuals share. "Victimization is widely recognized in the literature, and the implication exists that virtually every transgender person is likely to experience some form of victimization as a direct result of his or her transgender identity or presentation" (Dean et al., 2000, p. 40). The dichotomous separation during the mundane experiences of sleeping and going to the bathroom to protect women and girls may have the secondary effect of excluding transgender and gender-variant participants.

Sleeping Arrangements

Bedtime should be a restful time. However, the traditional separation of campers based on sex (girl cabins and boy cabins) excludes transgender and gender-variant individuals. Moreover, the potential lack of supervision during that period of time may create a void of leadership that creates opportunities for harassment, especially because bullying typically takes place during times of lower supervision (Carney and Nottis, 2008).

As do many other programs serving youths, Outward Bound, the largest adventure education organization in the United States, provides separate sleeping areas for boys and girls (Outward Bound, 2010). This classic sleeping arrangement that splits participants into a binary based on sex is troubling because it assumes a heterosexual norm. This binary also leaves transgender participants out in the cold. In contrast, Camp Aranu'tiq places campers in cabins based on their gender expression and focuses on providing campers with personal privacy. Half of the cabins are dedicated to campers identifying in the "transmasculine spectrum" and half to campers identifying in the "transfeminine spectrum." It may be more difficult for camps that don't specialize in transgender and gender-variant populations to fully understand this issue and make appropriate arrangements.

Where Do I Go to the Bathroom?

The first author was recently having lunch with a friend, J.P. (who self-identifies as "gender ambiguous"), and they got on the topic of bathrooms. J.P. recounted a familiar transgender tale of being very conscious about whether to use the bathroom (Cho et al., 2004; Lewis and Johnson, 2011). J.P. stated, "I usually try to not go to the bathroom until I get back home or I can go to a unisex bathroom." This is partly about personal comfort and security, but it is also about the comfort and security of the other bathroom users. "I've had women come into the bathroom, look at me, and then walk out and check the sign on the door." Transgender and gender-variant individuals who don't fall within the male–female binary may face the negative health ramifications of not having a place to use the bathroom or the possibility of harassment for using a bathroom.

This issue is moot for outdoor education programs that are expedition based. Out in the wilderness, no signs state that a certain bush is for women. However, built camps often have sex-specific group restrooms. Camps can resolve this issue by providing more gender-neutral single-occupancy restrooms or providing many fully enclosed bathroom stalls in gender-neutral bathrooms (Transgender Law Center, 2005). Unfortunately, not all camps may offer convenient restroom facilities that Robin could use without being harassed. This would not be an issue at a transgender-specific camp because the camp's restrooms are designed with this issue in mind.

Single-Gender Programming

Even within traditional binary notions of gender, similar debates surround mixed- versus single-gender programming. In the world of outdoor education, single-gender programming normally refers to programs for women and girls. Programs such as Girlventures in San Francisco or Northwest Passages in Seattle provide outdoor education programming for women and girls. The literature on this topic provides many good reasons that support single-gender programming.

Authors have claimed that single-gender programming is essential because the outdoors has traditionally been a "masculine space" (McDermott, 2004) dominated by males (Allin and Humberstone, 2006). If it is true that women and girls have felt like an "other" who is not welcome in the dominant male culture of outdoor education, it is easy to extrapolate that research would likely find very similar results for transgender and gender-variant individuals.

Research on outdoor programming for women and girls also shows that single-gender programming eliminates the potential for boys and men to disempower girls and women through chauvinistic actions and that it decreases the disempowering reactions of girls and women to the presence of boys and men. One participant states, "I would tend to hang back more if guys were there" (McDermott, 2004, p. 290). This level of internalized chauvinism that some females may feel may be even more intense for transgender women. Cohen and Semerjian (2008) report the story of a transgender woman who works to express extremely stereotypical feminine behavior in order to be seen by others as a woman and not a "male in disguise." This includes not competing in hockey as fiercely as she is capable of for fear of being accused of being a female impersonator. A single-gender program allows transgender and gender-variant individuals to express themselves without constantly needing to react to the presence of the dominant gender binary.

Allin and Humberstone (2006) describe the historical dearth of female role models in the outdoor industry. Even fewer transgender outdoor leaders exist for transgender youths to model themselves after. Therefore, it may be advantageous for youths to have outdoor education experiences with other transgender and gender-variant youths and leaders who can support them based on a firm foundation of knowledge about the transgender experience. In programming that is specific to transgender and gender-variant individuals, transgender leaders and participants can serve as role models for transgender and gender-variant youths to learn healthy recreational and lifestyle choices.

Conclusion

Where should Robin go to summer camp? The introduction relates an incident of abuse that is pervasive in the educational experience of transgender youths (Greytak, Kosciw, and Diaz, 2009; Kosciw, Greytak, and Diaz, 2009). Research shows that summer camps have the potential to develop a positive self-concept in participants (e.g., Henderson et al., 2007; Readdick and Schaller, 2005; Thurber et al., 2007). However, outdoor education and recreation experiences may be an extension of the climate of oppression that Robin commonly experiences rather than an opportunity for emancipation and self-development. Robin may need to continually fight against her exclusion from basic needs such as sleeping and going to the bathroom.

Transgender and gender-variant youths have the right to participate in mainstream adventure programming, but that right doesn't necessarily translate into the most rewarding option for the child. If the purpose of a youth going to camp is to participate in social activism to educate others about the transgender experience, then perhaps the best option is to go to a mainstream camp. But if the purpose is for the youth to have an enjoyable experience, make some friends, and learn to express and appreciate him or herself, a transgender youth may have a more difficult experience at mainstream camps and other outdoor education experiences.

Robin's parents felt a little panicked as they walked across the camp to find Robin. They picked up their pace as they witnessed more children and adults crying uncontrollably. Suddenly, Robin ran and crashed into her father, burying her face into the side of his shirt. "What's wrong? What happened?" her mother blurted out. In between sobs, Robin explained how sad she was for camp to be over because it exceeded her expectations in every way. She was going to miss the friends that she had made. During closing circle, the campers put on a short skit, sang the camp song, and showed off some of the arts and crafts they made during the week. Robin's parents realized that the camp wasn't about being transgender; it was about providing the space for their child to be just another camper. Emotions ran high as both children and parents exchanged contact information and animatedly discussed how awesome next year's camp session would be.

References

Allin, L., & Humberstone, B. (2006). Exploring careership in outdoor education and the lives of women outdoor educators. *Sport, Education and Society, 11*(2), 135-153.

American Camp Association. (2010). Kids speak: What is camp all about? www.campparents.org/expert/kids-speak [November 10, 2010].

American Psychological Association. (2010). *Publication manual of the American Psychological Association.* 6th ed. Washington, DC: American Psychological Association.

Bochenek, M., & Brown, A. (2001). *Hatred in the hallways: Violence and discrimination against lesbian, gay, bisexual, and transgender students in US schools.* New York: Human Rights Watch.

Carney, A., & Nottis, K. (2008). No vacation from bullying: A summer camp intervention pilot study. *Education, 129*(1), 22.

Cho, S., Laub, C., Wall, S.S.M., Daley, C., & Joslin, C. (2004). *Beyond the binary: A tool kit for gender identity activism in schools.* San Francisco: Gay-Straight Alliance Network, Transgender Law Center, and National Center for Lesbian Rights.

Cohen, J.H., & Semerjian, T.Z. (2008). The collision of trans-experience and the politics of women's ice hockey. *International Journal of Transgenderism, 10,* 133-145.

Dean, L., Meyer, I., Robinson, K., Sell, R., Sember, R., Silenzio, V.M.B., Bowen, D.J., Bradford, J., Rothblum, E., & White, J. (2000). *Lesbian, gay, bisexual, and transgender health: Findings and concerns.* Conference edition. San Francisco: Gay and Lesbian Medical Association; New York: Center for Lesbian, Gay, Bisexual, and Transgender Health, Columbia University's Joseph L. Mailman School of Public Health.

Doe v. Yunits. (2000). 2000 33162199.

Flores v. Morgan Hill Unified School District. (2003). 324 1130, Court of Appeals, 9th Circuit, 2003.

Gilley, B.J. (2006). *Becoming two-spirit: Gay identity and social acceptance in Indian country.* Lincoln, NE: University of Nebraska Press.

Girschick, L. (2008). *Transgender voices: Beyond women and men.* Lebanon, NH: University Press of New England.

Greytak, E., Kosciw, J., & Diaz, E. (2009). *Harsh realities: The experiences of transgender youth in our nation.* New York: Gay, Lesbian and Straight Education Network.

Grossman, A., & D'Augelli, A. (2007). Transgender youth and life-threatening behaviors. *Suicide and Life-Threatening Behavior, 37*(5), 527-537.

Grossman, A.H., O'Connell, T.S., & D'Augelli, A.R. (2005). Leisure and recreational "girl-boy" activities—Studying the unique challenges provided by transgendered young people. *Leisure/Loisir, 29*(1), 5-26.

Henderson, K., Whitaker, L., Bialeschki, M., Scanlin, M., & Thurber, C. (2007). Summer camp experiences: Parental perceptions of youth development outcomes. *Journal of Family Issues, 28*(8), 21.

Israel, G.E., & Tarver, D.E. (1997). *Transgender care: Recommended guidelines, practical information, and personal accounts.* Philadelphia: Temple University Press.

Kosciw, J., Greytak, E., & Diaz, E. (2009). Who, what, where, when, and why: Demographic and ecological factors contributing to hostile school climate for lesbian, gay, bisexual, and transgender youth. *Journal of Youth and Adolescence, 38*(7), 976-988.

Lewis, S.T., & Johnson, C.W. (2011). "But it's not *that* easy": (Trans)gender negotiations of leisure spaces. [Special issue on Leisure Space and Social Change.] *Leisure/Loisir, 35*(2), 115-132.

LGBT Families. (2009). Gay-friendly day and overnight camps. http://web.me.com/ecortez1/lgbtfamilies/Community/Entries/2009/2/28_Annual_gay-friendly_private_schools_listing_-_NY_2.html [November 10, 2010].

McDermott, L. (2004). Exploring intersections of physicality and female-only canoeing experiences. *Leisure Studies, 23*(3), 283-301.

McGuire, J., Anderson, C., Toomey, R., & Russell, S. (2010). School climate for transgender youth: A mixed method investigation of student experiences and school responses. *Journal of Youth and Adolescence, 39*(10), 1-14.

Meyer, A.M. (2010). *For refuge, connection, and ecological belonging.* Unpublished thesis. Missoula, MT: University of Montana.

Nabozny v. Podlesny. (1996). 92 446, Court of Appeals, 7th Circuit, 1996.

Neill, J.T. (2002). *A brief report on the short-term changes in the personal effectiveness of young adult gay, lesbian, bisexual and transgendered participants in a 2002 Colorado Outward Bound school program.* Durham, NH: University of New Hampshire, Department of Kinesiology, James Neill.

O'Shaughnessy, M., Russell, S.T., Heck, K., Calhoun, C., & Laub, C. (2004). *Safe place to learn: Consequences of harassment based on actual or perceived sexual orientation and gender non-conformity and steps for making schools safer.* San Francisco: California Safe Schools Coalition.

Outward Bound. (2010). What to expect. www.outwardbound.org/index.cfm/do/exp.attend_expect [November 10, 2010].

Readdick, C.A., & Schaller, G.R. (2005). Summer camp and self-esteem of school-age inner-city children. *Perceptual and Motor Skills, 101*(1), 121-130.

Siebler, K. (2010). Transqueer representations and how we educate. *Journal of LGBT Youth, 7*(4), 320-345.

Teich, N. (2010a). Camp 2010: Letter from Nick. http://camparanutiq.blogspot.com [November 10, 2010].

Teich, N. (2010b). Camp Aranu'tiq. www.socialworker.com/home/Feature_Articles/General/Camp_Aranu%27tiq [November 10, 2010].

Thurber, C., Scanlin, M., Scheuler, L., & Henderson, K. (2007). Youth development outcomes of the camp experience: Evidence for multidimensional growth. *Journal of Youth and Adolescence, 36*(3), 241-254.

Transgender Law Center. (2005). *Peeing in peace: A resource guide for transgender activists and allies.* San Francisco: Transgender Law Center.

Whittle, S. (2006). Foreword. In S. Stryker & S. Whittle (Eds.), *The transgender studies reader* (pp. xi-xvi). New York: Routledge.

Should transgender youths be encouraged to favor specialized camps over mainstream camps?

NO Transgender and Gender-Nonconforming Participation in Outdoor Adventure Programming: Let's Go Mainstream!

Denise Mitten, PhD, chair of MAP Adventure Education, Prescott College, Prescott, Arizona, United States

Robin loves many things about the two-week-long summer camp she has previously attended. Even though she is expressing herself as female more now than she has in the past, Robin has chosen to attend that same camp this summer. Over the years, Robin, biologically a male, has felt more comfortable with a female gender identity. Coming to terms with this aspect of her development has caused her to re-evaluate decisions that she used to take for granted, including where to attend summer camp. Robin is looking forward to seeing her old friends and participating in a week-long backpacking trip now that she is old enough to do so. Robin has a history of positive experiences at camp. People there know and like her. For two weeks each summer, many of the same children return and renew their friendships. Over the years, they have seen each other change and grow and have listened to each other talk about divorced parents, deceased grandparents, and parents who have come out. One of her friends has two dads. In a sense these children have grown up together; some keep in touch over the winter on Facebook. Many claim they are "camp sick" all winter until they can return to their summer retreat. Robin knows that some people at the camp may treat her with disrespect—she has certainly experienced that at school—but the true friends she has there and the call of the tradition have overpowered that negative aspect.

Robin's reasons for choosing her tried-and-true camp are based on emotions and hope; in addition, her parents weighed in with thoughtful considerations. This argument highlights the reasons why her decision to attend a mainstream summer camp should be supported. Robin has decided to attend a mainstream camp for her personal goals; however, important developmental, ethical, and cultural reasons reinforce her decision. I argue against the notion that it is better for transgender campers to go to camps that serve only transgender and gender-nonconforming children, and I support the notion that transgender youths should be encouraged to participate in mainstream adventure-based programming experiences. I describe the individual, camp culture, and societal benefits that derive from Robin attending a mainstream camp, argue that mainstream camps are inclusive, and explore the drawbacks of camps that serve only transgender children. For the purpose of this debate, this argument pertains to camps accredited through either the American Camp Association or the Association for Experiential Education.

Types of Camps

Mainstream camps are organized camps that are available to the general public. Camps vary by residency, length, and programming. Organized camps generally focus on the natural environment, revolve around a group-living experience in an organized community, and rely on trained and well-qualified staff. When I taught camp administration as a university professor, I defined a traditional camp as a community of people living together in an outdoor setting with leaders who are well trained in facilitating community experiences in order to enhance wellness in group members' emotional, social, intellectual, spiritual, and physical dimensions in line with the values of the camp owner or sponsoring body. The program consists of the total of all the experiences or events in the camp, whether structured or not; therefore, staff supervision during nonstructured time is expected. The American Camp Association database lists 2,365 such camps.

In addition to traditional camps, one can choose from many special-interest camps and special-purpose camps (the American Camp Association database lists 499 such camps). Special-interest camps are defined by either the environment (e.g., ranch camps, farm camps, coastal camps, or submarine camps) or the activity (e.g., field hockey, rock climbing, language study, or dance). Special-purpose camps serve select clientele, such as certain populations of children with common family backgrounds or religious beliefs, children who are examining issues of identity, or children working with grief or another specific emotion. Other special-purpose camps may be organized around children who have asthma, limb differences, or cancer. A camp specifically for transgender youths would be a special-purpose camp. For the purposes of this argument, a mainstream camp includes traditional camps and special-interest camps. When a child with special needs or from certain populations goes to one of these camps, it may be referred to as mainstreaming the child.

Parents and children often decide between a mainstream camp and a specialized camp. For many it is a matter of whether the special interest or the special population is more attractive than a general program or a wider diversity of campers. For example, a basketball enthusiast might choose a basketball camp because focusing on improving that skill to the exclusion of other activities is appealing. On the other hand, a basketball enthusiast might attend a mainstream camp and think that playing basketball several times during the camp session would be plenty. In another example, a Jewish child might choose a mainstream camp because the Jewish aspect of a camp is not that important to the child, or because of location, cost, or some other reason. Another Jewish child might choose a special-purpose camp for Jewish youths because of the draw of associating with other Jewish children. Either choice can result in a positive experience. In any case, a youth with a special interest or need should not categorically avoid mainstream or traditional camps.

Whether a child should be encouraged to attend a camp only for transgender youths depends on the goals of the person attending camp. Some children may prefer special-purpose camps for transgender youths, whereas other children have their hearts set on the camp they have always known or a special-purpose camp specializing in kayaking or backpacking, or they simply do not want to put a great deal of emphasis on that aspect of their identities. Although many camps specialize in specific populations such as veterans, cancer survivors, or lesbian, gay, bisexual, transgender, queer, and allies (LGBTQA), limiting options to only specialized camps is not constructive. When possible, the child and the parents should work together to make

a decision. As Peg Smith (2010), chief executive officer of American Camp Association (ACA), says, "The best camp experience for your child is one born out of an informed family decision."

Mainstream Camps Are Inclusive

Inclusion in the United States has been a long process, and the same is true for inclusion in camps. Mainstream camps have moved from serving solely white, male, primarily Christian youths to being coed and more inclusive of campers from many racial, ethnic, and religious or spiritual backgrounds, campers who choose nontraditional sexual and gender identifications, and campers of varying abilities and exceptionalities. The camping movement in the United States began in the late 1800s. Miranda and Yerkes (1996) note that girls' and women's camp programs were originally framed as providing a time for networking, relaxation, skills acquisition, and civic engagement. The Girl Scouts of America have a large camping program that from the beginning sought to help girls be caring and active citizens. This more feminine take on being outdoors and in a camp environment has greatly influenced mainstream camps today. An ethic of care and social responsibility, captured in the phrase "in an accepting and nurturing environment, girls build character and skills for success in the real world" (Girl Scouts of America, 2009), is now a sought reality for many camps. Today camps strive toward inclusivity, care, and social responsibility in addition to healthy outdoor activity.

Complementing the development of camps, recreation in the United States has a strong ethic of care and social justice dating at least from when Nobel Peace Prize recipient Jane Addams and Ellen Gates Starr opened Hull House in Chicago in 1889. People working in recreation and specifically the adventure education field have demonstrated an ethical consciousness that is higher than the United States norm and even higher than that of graduates in theology, which sets the stage for inclusivity and appropriate leadership and guidance for the campers (Mitten, 2002). Jacobs and McAvoy (2005) found that working at camps helps counselors develop emotional intelligence. Therefore, counselors who return multiple years help influence a positive camp culture. When well-intended leaders receive proper education and training, camps can and do help campers understand, accept, and embrace diversity (DeZeeuw, 2002; Mitten, 2002).

Organized camps benefit both the campers and staff (Henderson et al., 2007; Jacobs and McAvoy, 2005; Readdick and Schaller, 2005). A remaining question is whether transgender campers can receive these documented benefits if they attend a mainstream camp. Although more research needs to be completed in order to confidently respond to this question, for at least the past 20 years the literature has engaged in specific dialogue about LGBTQ participants on outdoor trips and in camps (Alexander and Kriesel, 2003; Mitten, 1997; Ohle, 1990). These authors focus on inclusivity of campers who do not fit the stereotypical heteronormality and offer guidelines for positively and productively framing discussions.

Mainstream camps currently serve transgender youths. Susan Yoder (personal communication, 2010), chief public policy and outreach officer at ACA, says that parents and camp staff ask about accommodations and other considerations for transgender children. *Camp Line,* the quarterly newsletter for ACA, offered a case study titled "Transgendered Camper Enrolling in an All-Girls Resident Camp" (American Camp Association, 2010). The demand for accommodating transgender youths is growing, and transgender youths could be well served by taking advantage of the opportunity to participate in mainstream camps.

Benefits to the Individual

In the past Robin has probably witnessed other campers grow and transform. Now, when staff and other youths witness Robin's process of thinking about her gender, it enriches their personal processes. Through this camp experience, the other campers and staff can expand their views about transgender people. If Robin is required or encouraged to attend a camp specifically for transgender campers, messages potentially sent to her and the other campers and staff include "people who are different get shipped away" or "it is not okay to be different."

Gender exploration is a healthy part of human development. Currently, mainstream culture in the United States sees gender as either male or female; this binary of thinking that a person is either female or male needs to be questioned and problematized. Gender exploration at mainstream camps can help people have a healthy view of gender as fluid and help disengage the predominant belief that gender is static and binary. Attending the mainstream camp can help Robin and others have a lived experience and understand that at different times an individual

may be comfortable expressing gender at different places on a gender continuum or in some other way altogether.

Robin has experienced camp as a place to experiment with who she is in a supportive environment. This positive experience in both trying out changes and witnessing the changes of others sets a positive example for healthy exploration, and individuals can make other healthy changes with confidence and security. They know they can ask for support. People unconsciously engage in parallel process, and how the campers are treated at camp will likely influence how they treat others later in life. This supportive community experience helps develop compassionate people who can live harmoniously in community, thus laying the foundation for sustainable community building.

The staff has opportunities to grow professionally. Staff training around various aspects of diversity is abstract until people with various backgrounds, sexual and gender identities, and other differences actually attend the camp. Because Robin would be at the camp, it is imperative that staff is trained in the sorts of inclusivity and practical issues that need to be addressed when serving a transgender population. As much as we like to believe that we would train about these inclusivity issues, unless faced with an actual transgender camper coming to camp, the specific training rarely happens and theory does not evolve into practice.

In summary, although not a conscious goal for Robin, she would be a peer role model. She would grow and learn from this role and the other campers would see that it is okay to explore gender and other questions about identity and see transgender as part of "normal." Robin's presence and sharing about her exploration would help campers learn through experience that people change, thus normalizing growth and change. Campers would get to dialogue about gender in a supportive environment and may decide to explore areas of their identity or question the rigid gender binary in U.S. culture. Robin also may find that other individuals at camp are exploring gender identity.

Benefits to the Camp Culture

The camp community benefits from the diversity Robin's presence brings. Having more diversity at the table, so to speak, allows more voices to be heard and more overall growth to take place for the transgender youth as well as the other campers and staff. It does not mean that the transgender youth is either a spokesperson for gender-fluid youths or a poster child for transgender youths (nor should Robin ever be made to feel that way). Rather, it means that the richness of diversity adds to the pluralistic atmosphere.

Camps are making strides to be even more inclusive to many different people. Requiring or implying that transgender youths should go to specialized transgender camps permits mainstream camps to not move forward on inclusive practices and, in fact, contributes to marginalizing these special populations. Edler and Irons (1998) say that we move forward on discriminatory issues when people with differences are present. Like racism, discrimination based on gender identity cannot be undone at a distance. All people need to sit through their emotions and listen to others. This includes the transgender person as well, who in all likelihood will have internalized discrimination based on gender identity. The richer the diversity in people present at camp, the more opportunities there will be to understand and practice truly living in community with pluralistic values.

As shown through organizations such as Play for Peace (2010), in which youth leaders from many countries organize play days that include children from other cultures, and the Zeitouna story of six Arab and six Jewish women becoming friends as portrayed in the movie *Refusing to be Enemies* (White, 2010), friendship is a sound way to get past oppression. Through living and playing with others, Robin will continue her friendships and make new friends and thus help lighten the load of oppression for herself and the other campers while at camp and after returning home.

The benefits Robin and the other individuals at camp experience are in essence magnified because they can now help transform society. Any gains in understanding and overcoming oppressive behaviors, understanding gender issues, and embracing diversity in general extend to the greater society.

Drawbacks of a Transgender Camp

Some are concerned that camps only for transgender children promote the idea that the child is one-dimensional, put too much emphasis on one aspect of development, inappropriately try to protect the child from the messiness of life, and send a message to the child that greater society will not support gender exploration.

Attending a camp for transgender youths may give Robin the idea that she is seen as one-dimen-

sional, which may lead to the loss of understanding herself as a whole person. It is possible that she may have less in common with other transgender youths than she does with the youths at the summer camp she has been attending.

At Robin's age she will explore many aspects of her life, and gender is one area. If her parents encourage her to attend a special camp for people who are transgender, they may be putting too much emphasis on this aspect of Robin's development. I am not minimizing the importance of gender exploration, but this situation may be similar to a child saying that she wants to have 25 children and her parents either getting overly worried and sending her to therapy or getting overly indulgent and getting her 25 dolls. At this point in her life, one doesn't want to make everything about her gender exploration.

Being transgender is one way of being different and perhaps of being discriminated against. At the same time, all space is gendered, classed, raced, and sexualized (Green and Singleton, 2006) and we need to cope with this. Some parents and youths choose a special-interest or special-purpose camp because they feel it is a safer decision. One might think that camps for transgender youths are an oasis of utopia, only to find that the same age-related behavior and the same problems from the greater society are brought to camp. Mitten (1992) said the same thing about women's outdoor trips. Although women's trips encourage an accepting environment, women still bring with them the challenges of society. Life will be messy at times at a camp for transgender youths, just as it is messy at times in a mainstream camp. Although it is natural for parents to want to protect children from this messiness, it is also not fair to give potential campers a utopian forecast that cannot be met.

Additional Considerations

It is Robin's legal right to choose to go to a mainstream camp. As Wilson and Lewis write in the "yes" argument for this issue, the nation's courts have upheld the rights of transgender youths to not be harassed. Robin should not to have to fight for her rights; rather, she should have the choice to be present and part of the community. When the Supreme Court ruled that separate is not equal in terms of race, some African American children chose to integrate white schools. Before bussing, the African American children wanted to break the mold for themselves. The children were not trying to educate others, but they did.

Dewey's theory of valuation comes into play here. He says that we have to judge an activity in context to determine whether the intended outcome outweighs the costs or negative risk. Any alternative will likely satisfy some interests and frustrate others for both the decision maker and other people. Dewey wanted educators to teach the skill of using valuation as part of experiential education (Dewey, 1978). In the case of African American youths choosing to integrate white schools, they decided that the potential gains were worth the pain. Robin's parents can work with Robin and openly discuss the potential benefits and the potential costs or risk. Using the theory of valuation, Robin can make a decision about camp that she feels is best for her.

Bullying is problematic in U.S. culture. Although Carney and Nottis (2008) found that bullying occurs at day camps, they found that with minimal training bullying decreased by 60 percent at these camps. Overnight camps may or may not have the same rate of bullying as day camps. Regardless, although bullying behaviors may come up at all camps, camps with best practices have involved leaders who do not tolerate bullying. ACA standards for accreditation address inclusivity and bullying prevention through HR-11 Pre-Camp Staff Training. Currently, HR-11 says, among other things (Susan Yoder, personal communication, December 17, 2010):

> A camp should have written evidence of pre-camp training for all camp staff directly involved in camp programming and camper supervision that includes at least the following topics:
>
> - ... Developmental needs of campers to be served and the resulting differences for program, structure, and behavior management. ...
> - Behavior management and camper supervision techniques to create a physically and emotionally safe environment
> - Clear expectations for staff performance and conduct, including sexual harassment policies
> - Recognition, prevention, and reporting of child abuse, child-to-child, as well as adult-to-child, both outside of and during the camp setting

Currently, choices are limited for youths looking for a camp that serves transgender youths.

A child would have to want to be with other transgender youths more than any other aspects of camp, including location, activity emphasis, or other friends. For example, if a youth wants to go to a horsepacking camp, the youth likely will not find one especially for transgender youths. Choosing a camp for transgender youths may be preferable for some children; however, a wider range of camp choices is available if mainstream camps are included.

One must be concerned about a gendered mentality at camps for transgender children and mainstream camps. All camps need to be conscious of not gendering space and language. Gendered spaces at camps usually include sleeping quarters, showers, program areas such as dance, language such as gender-based jokes, and more. As an example, sleeping arrangements are thought to be a problem for mainstreaming a transgender child. However, the same worry about power differences and unsupervised sleeping is appropriate at a transgender camp. Some camps are beginning to offer personal sleeping areas and higher supervision at night. Some camps require one or two counselors to sleep in the same cabin as the campers. In these instances cabins do not have to be separated by sex. Higher staff supervision at night can decrease nighttime bullying at any camp.

Finally, the word "transgender" is inherently based on a gender binary. It means transitioning from one to another. Postmodern feminist work notes that gender is neither biologically based nor based on a binary. The word "trans" perpetuates a gender binary. Calling a camp a transgender camp perpetuates the notion that two genders exist. All camps need to go beyond the trans concept even before mainstream society does in order to truly provide ethical and safe space for campers to learn, grow, and transform.

Conclusion

Transgender youths are going to mainstream camps, and current programming and infrastructure at many camps support integration. Diversity at mainstream camps benefits the individual, the camp community, and society. Many camps are mini incubators for a positive society, and the youth and staff have more experience with diverse people when camps are more pluralistic. This diversity promotes better staff training, dialogue, awareness, and appreciation of others. Through interaction with people who are different and intentional facilitation, campers and staff can grow on a personal level, become more compassionate, gain community-living skills, and better understand social justice issues. As the campers and staff return to the greater society, they bring their experiences and skills to their home communities and are better able to help make positive changes. As Warren and Loeffler (2000) assert, outdoor experiential and adventure education practitioners (of which camps are a part) must be concerned with social justice issues.

Mainstream camps that use best practices offer opportunities for transgender youths to experience a supportive environment as they explore issues of identity in the context of an integrated society and often with friends from previous summers. Youths learn through experience that gender exploration is normal and that it is normal to view gender as fluid.

Whether a child who identifies as transgender attends a camp specifically for transgender youths depends on the child's goals for attending camp. For some youths, a camp serving only transgender youths may provide the environment they seek. For others, downsides of choosing such a camp include the limited choices, expectations to focus on sexual or gender identity, limited understanding of plurality, and the false hope of a utopia-like camp. Parents and campers need to investigate camps, specialized or mainstream, to make sure that the camp meets emotional, social, spiritual, intellectual, and physical safety aspects to a high degree. If the youth can gain similar benefits at a mainstream camp and the youth prefers a mainstream camp, then the mainstream camp is the better choice. If Robin wants to go to the mainstream camp, it is important to support her decision.

References

Alexander, R., & Kriesel, C. (2003). Don't assume I'm straight: Providing a safe environment for GBLQ youth at camp. *Camping Magazine, 76*(6), 1-6.

American Camp Association. (2010). Campline case study. Camps in crisis: ACA's annual review of the Camp Crisis Hotline. www.acacamps.org/campline/fall-2010/camps-in-crisis-annual-hotline-review-2010 [December 14, 2011].

Carney, A., & Nottis, K. (2008). No vacation from bullying: A summer camp intervention pilot study. *Education, 129*(1), 22.

Dewey, J. (1978). *The middle works: Vol. 5. Ethics.* (J.A. Boydston, Series Ed.). Carbondale, IL: Southern Illinois University Press. (Original work published 1908.)

DeZeeuw, J. (2002). *An examination of the impact of experiential education methodologies used in cross-cultural programs on the moral reasoning of high school students.* Unpublished graduate thesis. Durham, NH: University of New Hampshire.

Edler, J., & Irons, B. (1998). Distancing behaviors often used by white people. In E. Lee, D. Menkart, & M. Okazawa-Rey (Eds.), *Beyond heroes and holidays: A practical guide to K-12 anti-racist, multicultural education and staff development* (p. 114). Washington, DC: Network of Educators on the Americas.

Girl Scouts of America. (2009). About Girl Scouts of the USA. www.girlscouts.org/WHO_WE_ARE [December 14, 2011].

Green, E.E., & Singleton, C. (2006). Risky bodies at leisure: Young women negotiating space and place. *Sociology, 40*(5), 853-871.

Henderson, K., Whitaker, L., Bialeschki, M., Scanlin, M., & Thurber, C. (2007). Summer camp experiences: Parental perceptions of youth development outcomes. *Journal of Family Issues, 28*(8), 21.

Jacobs, J., & McAvoy, L. (2005). The relationship between summer camp employment and emotional intelligence. *The Journal of Experiential Education, 27*(3), 330-332.

Miranda, W., & Yerkes, R. (1996). The history of camping women in the professionalization of experiential education. In K. Warren (Ed.), *Women's voices in experiential education* (pp. 63-77). Dubuque, IA: Kendall/Hunt.

Mitten, D. (1992). Empowering girls and women in the outdoors. *The Journal of Physical Education, Recreation, and Dance, 63*(2), 56-60.

Mitten, D. (1997). In the light: Sexual diversity on women's outdoor trips. *Journal of Leisurability, 24*(4), 22-30.

Mitten, D. (2002). An analysis of outdoor leaders' ethics guiding decisions. In M. Bialeschki, K. Henderson, A. Young, & R. Andrejewski (Eds.), *Research in outdoor education, Volume 6* (pp. 55-73). Bradford Woods, IN: Coalition for Education in the Outdoors.

Ohle, L. (1990). Putting everyone in the picture: Countering homophobia in the camp setting. *Camping Magazine, 63*(2), 30-31.

Play for Peace. (2010). About us. www.playforpeace.org/who-we-are-1 [December 14, 2011].

Readdick, C.A., & Schaller, G.R. (2005). Summer camp and self-esteem of school-age inner-city children. *Perceptual and Motor Skills, 101*(1), 121-130.

Smith, P. (2010). Do your homework: Find the right camp for next year now. www.campparents.org/content/do-your-homework-find-right-camp-next-year-now [December 14, 2011].

Warren, K., & Loeffler, T.A. (2000). Setting a place at the table: Social justice research in outdoor experiential education. *Journal of Experiential Education, 23*(2), 85-90.

White, L. (2010). Refusing to be enemies. http://refusingtobeenemies.org/film.html [December 14, 2011].

Controversial Issue 16

Does Leave No Trace make a difference beyond the scope of backcountry environmental practices?

The Leave No Trace (LNT) Center for Outdoor Ethics has had a profound effect on the adventure programming industry. Until LNT, outdoor educators had limited access to environmental curricula and standardized practices to guide environmental stewardship. The success of LNT has infiltrated the vast majority of adventure programs in North America, and it is spreading internationally. Based on partnerships between federal agencies, state organizations, educational institutions, private businesses, and myriad other agencies, LNT has become the accepted standard for outdoor ethics in the United States and elsewhere around the world. LNT has transformed the way that outdoor recreationists interact with the natural environment.

Despite LNT's history of success in promoting an ethic of stewardship among outdoor recreationists, questions have arisen about the scope of LNT's influence and effectiveness in contributing to the resolution of broad environmental concerns. LNT was originally designed to influence attitudes and practices of visitors to backcountry recreation areas. However, as the success and influence of LNT have grown, so too have the scope of its message and its range of curricular options. For example, LNT has designed curricula that now address recreation behaviors in "frontcountry" day-use recreation areas as well as suburban and urban open spaces. In fact, in 2011, LNT introduced a new social activism and environmental stewardship program called Backyard Sessions. The program is designed to help communities determine how to incorporate the principles of LNT into the ways that they generally live and play. This program has given legs to the old LNT expression "From Our Backcountry to Your Back Yard."

Professional adventure programmers strive to influence environmental values, attitudes, and behaviors of their program participants beyond the field and in society more generally. And the LNT message is typically integral to these efforts. However, many argue that the LNT curriculum as it stands is not positioned to address more universal environmental concerns, such as global climate change. As such, we are falling short in addressing these broader concerns as a result of our reliance on LNT in promoting change. The assertion is that the success of LNT has led to stagnation in the adventure programming community by not allowing it to keep up with current, pressing environmental issues beyond the relatively localized concerns of recreational use of natural areas.

Garrett Hutson and Elizabeth Andre take up this issue by addressing the question: Does Leave No Trace make a difference beyond the scope of backcountry environmental practices? Hutson argues that LNT is a viable and effective foundation to move learners beyond the backcountry context. He bases his rationale on three important points: 1) LNT is explicitly and implicitly centered on protecting nature as a whole; 2) LNT has a broad focus, which includes settings beyond the backcountry; and 3) LNT backcountry principles are an effective form of place-based outdoor education. Hutson places responsibility on outdoor educators to solidify lessons beyond the backcountry to address larger global environmental challenges. LNT serves as a powerful tool to help others make the connection.

Andre discusses the ineffectiveness of LNT as a means to instill a global environmental ethic in our participants. She argues that LNT is unable to promote substantive environmental ethics because of its historical design, philosophical underpinnings, misrepresentation of ecological principles and supply chains, and pedagogical shortcomings. Andre argues that LNT is ineffective at promoting more far reaching environmental ethics. She argues further that its rhetoric lulls leaders into believing that, by incorporating LNT into their programming, they are fulfilling their responsibility to teach environmental ethics. This belief undermines the profession's ability to critically assess whether it is meeting its goals for environmental stewardship and teaching, thereby standing in the way of the evolution of a more appropriate ethic.

Because LNT is so prevalent in the adventure programming industry, this topic deserves careful attention. After reading these two arguments, you can decide the best course of action.

Does Leave No Trace make a difference beyond the scope of backcountry environmental practices?

YES **The Seeds of Leave No Trace Grow Well Beyond Backcountry Boundaries**

Garrett Hutson, PhD, assistant professor of recreation and leisure studies, Brock University, Ontario, Canada

Whether Leave No Trace (LNT) practices make a difference beyond backcountry experiences is a topic that has received increased attention in recent years (Simon and Algona, 2009). I argue that LNT does make a difference beyond backcountry experiences for three important reasons. First, the LNT curriculum explicitly and implicitly centers on protecting nature as a whole. The LNT focus on minimizing the impacts on particular places is also framed within a whole-world context throughout the LNT curriculum. Second, the broad focus of LNT includes frontcountry settings, urban settings, and outreach initiatives. This form of LNT outreach connects with a wide range of people and places well beyond backcountry settings. Third, LNT backcountry principles are an effective form of place-based outdoor education that provides a necessary platform for long-term environmental ethics and place connections to take hold. Thus, LNT practices are prime examples of effective place-based outdoor learning in action.

I expand on each of these three points to make a case for why LNT is a useful and constitutive part of outdoor education pedagogy. In what follows, LNT refers to the Leave No Trace program, curriculum, and principles. For a brief history of LNT, see Marion and Reid (2001).

A Holistic Curriculum

The LNT curriculum explicitly and implicitly centers on protecting nature as a whole. The seven LNT backcountry principles are as follows:

1. Plan ahead and prepare.
2. Camp and travel on durable surfaces.
3. Dispose of waste properly.
4. Leave what you find.
5. Minimize campfire impacts.
6. Respect wildlife.
7. Be considerate of other visitors.

Although these principles are meant to be applied to a variety of backcountry environments, the framing of the curriculum explicitly centers on protecting the natural world (Leave No Trace Inc., 2008). LNT practices give people the tools to experience natural areas responsibly and sustainably and are framed to deepen relationships with nature (Leave No Trace Inc., 2008). For example, LNT's teaching literature suggests that educators introduce the seven LNT principles after an experiential "web of life" activity to highlight human–nature connections and the fragile and indispensable nature of those connections (Leave No Trace Inc., 2008). Another popular LNT learning activity that introduces the seven principles is titled "Things in Nature, Things We Have in Common, How It Helps Me" (e.g., respectively: a tree, we both have an outer layer to protect us, and a tree gives me oxygen) (Leave No Trace Inc., 2008, p. 24). This activity gives learners an opportunity to articulate their commonalities with and dependence on the natural world. These are just a few examples of how the seven principles are simple and effective to protect natural areas but also flow from a whole-world context and aim to explicitly promote lifelong outdoor ethics (Hampton and Cole, 2003).

Implicitly, although the mission of minimizing backcountry impacts drives LNT, much of the spirit or ethos of LNT is about protecting and heightening connections to the natural world as a whole (Hampton and Cole, 2003; Leave No Trace Inc., 2008). The LNT curriculum promotes through its educational literature a broad, nature-based ethic. For instance, the first paragraph of *Teaching Leave No Trace* (Leave No Trace Inc., 2008), a book that is often distributed to and used by LNT trainers and educators, stresses this wider view toward the natural world:

> As cities grow and populations encroach on wildlands and recreation areas, we must do more than just pick up litter

and extinguish campfires. We must learn how to maintain the integrity of all living things. Leave No Trace is not simply a program for visiting the backcountry, it is an attitude and a way of life.

Similarly, in the beginning of *NOLS Soft Paths: How to Enjoy Wilderness Without Harming It*, the executive director of LNT suggests that readers should "settle down with this book, get a sense of the ethic, learn the finer points, and then ask yourself, what would my last outing say about me? You will never 'get outside' the same way again" (Hampton and Cole, 2003, p. viii).

These passages suggest that LNT is not just a set of mechanical practices; rather, LNT is positioned to be tied to one's identity and way of being in nature. These suggestions are not limited to the backcountry alone but instead rely on implicit notions that LNT should become part of one's larger relationship to nature both in and out of the backcountry.

This notion of deepening one's relationship to nature as a whole—even after the backcountry experience has ended—continually permeates LNT philosophy and is further accentuated in LNT literature with assertions such as "a wildland ethic may be the most important item we carry into the backcountry, as well as the most important lesson we take back home to our everyday lives" (Hampton and Cole, 2003, p. 206). Further, the LNT literature emphasizes transforming people's broader awareness of environmental ethics by highlighting convictions of well-known environmental philosophers such as John Muir, Aldo Leopold, and Barry Lopez. Asides include quotes such as, "And what will be the disposition of the landscape? Will it be used, as always, in whatever way we will, or will it one day be accorded some dignity of its own?" (Lopez, 1986, cited in Hampton and Cole, 2003). Lopez's perspective in particular strengthens the notion that the LNT ethos is not only about minimum-impact backcountry practices but is also centered on transforming thinking about how to relate to nature beyond the backcountry.

Furthermore, germane examples in the research literature show how LNT can transform thinking about human–nature relations beyond backcountry experiences. A study conducted by Boland and Heintzmen (2009) explored how LNT practices transfer to everyday life from the perspectives of outdoor education program participants. One student who took part in the program remarked afterward, "My behaviors changed in general, as I mentioned, no littering and pollution. You can't leave anything behind" (Boland and Heintzmen, 2009, p. 32). Another student remarked, "Maybe things like picking up after yourself, like if you go to a park . . . I know that eventually if one person does it, then everyone is going to do it. . . ." (Boland and Heintzmen, 2009, p. 32). The words of these students indicate a wider perspective toward environmental care that began when LNT practices were introduced during an outdoor education program and ended with proenvironmental actions. Clearly, the LNT curriculum in the previous context explicitly and implicitly centers on protecting nature beyond backcountry boundaries.

A Broad Focus

LNT has evolved a broad focus to include frontcountry settings, urban recreation settings, and outreach initiatives that reach a wide range of people and green spaces (Marion and Reid, 2001). Frontcountry and urban LNT programs are designed for city and state parks that are not considered backcountry environments. This emphasis broadens the scope of LNT by helping a larger number of recreationists minimize impacts on natural areas that are closer to where they live (Marion and Reid, 2001). This broader focus helps people bring LNT into the context of their everyday lives. It is estimated that day hikers in the United States will increase from 47 million to 74 million over the next 40 years; this number far surpasses the number of backpackers who travel into backcountry environments (Leave No Trace Center for Outdoor Ethics, 2008b). LNT frontcountry and urban programs help the LNT message reach far more people—all outside of backcountry settings—than ever before.

Additionally, it seems reasonable to suggest that frontcountry and urban LNT programs provide backcountry travelers other contexts closer to home in which to practice the LNT outdoor ethics they were introduced to in the backcountry. Pragmatically speaking, this may be some of the strongest evidence for how LNT makes a difference beyond backcountry settings. The phrase "leave no trace" has become part of many smaller, local park settings. Through these settings, LNT provides a backcountry-to-frontcountry connection and a common language that people recognize. Seeing LNT principles expressed in frontcountry settings gives backcountry travelers a common point of reference and an impetus to further their minimum-impact practice.

Further, LNT outreach initiatives include hotspot programs, which give communities, government agencies, and other environmental agencies the tools they need to protect natural areas that suffer from recreational overuse (Leave No Trace Center for Outdoor Ethics, 2008a). These types of outreach initiatives, which evolved from LNT backcountry principles, transfer the principles to local natural areas. For example, the Red River Gorge in Kentucky is a designated LNT hotspot because of its proximity to urban centers and its popularity for recreational activities such as rock climbing. The purpose of the program in Kentucky is to bring all stakeholders together to protect a local recreational resource through LNT practices and philosophy (Leave No Trace Center for Outdoor Ethics, 2008a). This community-driven change is facilitated by individuals and agencies outside of backcountry environments that want to protect local natural areas. Moreover, LNT hotspot programs have the potential to drive further LNT evidence-based research projects that demonstrate how LNT education translates directly to limiting ecosystem degradation (for a recent discussion, see Marion and Reid, 2007). LNT hotspot programs also strongly encourage recreationists to become involved in local park clean-up programs, land management issues, and other environmental initiatives in order to express their feelings about the treatment and management of specific natural environments. The purpose of hotspot programs is to promote and encourage long-term proactive thinking and actions in community members who will sustain and protect their local outdoor environments.

Finally, LNT has recently added a sustainability ethos to its website. This site gives followers of LNT other outlets for exploring environmental and outreach initiatives and ways to positively affect local and global environmental change (Leave No Trace Center for Outdoor Ethics, 2008b). Marion and colleagues (2010) argue that LNT has been so successful in part due to its mission and focus of promoting responsible behaviors in specific outdoor environments. Through the focused introduction of these behaviors combined with its sustainability ethos, LNT enables others to broadly apply its principles to other sustainability issues and contexts (Leave No Trace Center for Outdoor Ethics, 2008b). Thus, LNT is an ethical platform that can, through a broad focus, drive participatory environmental change, action, and engagement to venues outside of backcountry environments while still remaining mission driven (Marion et al., 2010).

Place-Based Outdoor Education

LNT backcountry principles are an effective form of place-based outdoor education. Place-based educational approaches connect learners to local environments and communities through teaching and learning strategies that emphasize and evolve from the particular needs of specific places (Sobel, 2004). As previously mentioned, LNT is mission driven and focuses primarily on responsible use of the outdoors (Marion et al., 2010). Critics of LNT have suggested that it is time for LNT to broaden its focus to more explicitly confront global social and environmental injustices and to reposition LNT as a "radical form of political action" (Simon and Algona, 2009, p. 17). Others suggest that LNT contributes to a human–nature divide and assert that LNT practices create a barrier between people and nature—a place they are not necessarily a part of (Moskowitz and Ottey, 2006). I argue against these claims by presenting a case for why LNT backcountry practices are an effective form of place-based outdoor education that provides a necessary platform for long-term environmental ethics and place-connections to take hold beyond backcountry environments.

Practicing LNT puts people into a unique relationship with the natural world around them and thrusts them into a particular set of ethics. For the unfamiliar, LNT may seem foreign, unreasonable, and at times uncomfortable—perhaps like it would feel to move to a new city in a different country and not know your way around or how to speak the language. Take pooping in the woods, for example (part of LNT principle 3). I bet that outdoor educators who have taught others how to properly dispose of their waste remember many looks of disbelief after explaining this LNT principle to the uninitiated. However, that look of disbelief holds power and has the potential to shift one's gaze toward a different view of nature. Properly disposing of our waste transforms into intentional environmental ethics involving practices that protect water (e.g., depositing solid human waste in a cathole at least 200 feet (61 m) away from water sources and trails), practices that protect people and wildlife (e.g., packing out toilet paper and hygiene products), and practices that minimize introducing foreign substances to natural areas (e.g., using a small amount of biodegradable soap to wash hands). King (2003, p. 163) offers a useful perspective on Western society's ability to grapple with environmental ethics:

It's not that we don't care about ethics or ethical behavior. It's not that we don't care about the environment, about society, about morality. It's just that we care more about our comfort and the things that make us comfortable. (p. 163)

LNT practices interrupt our state of comfort. LNT practices put us back in our place in nature, both literally and figuratively. LNT reminds us that we have an impact on the world and that we will have to make sacrifices that will likely make us uncomfortable if we are to create a more sustainable existence for all living things. However, LNT's mission is not to get us to think this way—LNT's mission is to get us to behave in the moment, *in response to the needs of a specific place*, with sustainable, caring, and thoughtful actions that have the potential to shift from discomfort to compassion. The culmination of these place-based actions and responses (inspired by LNT) may act as a platform from which a long-term environmental ethic can take hold (Cameron, 2003; King, 2003).

One of the pillars of place-based education is the process of helping people to learn or relearn "how to reinhabit our communities and regions in ways that allow for sustainable relationships now and in the long run" (Gruenwald and Smith, 2008, p. ix). I introduce place-based education here in the context of a backcountry environment as a region with which to become acquainted through LNT ideals. Vast literature exists about place-based education and its implications for global perspectives; however, place-based practices are first anchored in the needs of particular settings (Gruenewald and Smith, 2008). Relating to backcountry environments through LNT can serve as a model for action in one's own community. LNT principles present an advantageous framework for helping people to understand what it feels like to have a sustainable and honest relationship with a particular place.

An honest relationship with a place means confronting one's impacts. Although critics enjoy pointing out that it's nearly impossible to "leave no trace" (see Moskowitz and Ottey, 2006), it is common to find within the LNT curriculum and literature place-specific details that highlight the very traces we leave (Hampton and Cole, 2003). For example, camping and traveling on durable surfaces (LNT principle 2) helps people to confront their impacts and to see and have a direct relationship with the ways they impact certain environments. Furthermore, the LNT literature highlights that different environments call for different behaviors (Hampton and Cole, 2003) or place responsiveness that is congruent with the particular needs of a particular place (Cameron, 2003). One example of how LNT facilitates this type of responsiveness is the different ways backcountry travelers are advised to operate in black bear country versus in grizzly bear country. Travelers should respond appropriately depending on the species of wildlife found within the region.

Backcountry travelers who make these ethical choices about what is right and good for land and wildlife, which depend on the particular needs of a place, are engaged in a type of place responsiveness that is rarely experienced elsewhere (Cameron, 2003). This relationship to the details of a place makes practicing LNT in the backcountry such a unique and powerful form of place-based education. Furthermore, Stewart (2004) strongly argues that understanding the details and needs of a place makes a person aware of the vulnerabilities that exist within particular environments. Not only does LNT promote an understanding of the details and particulars of natural environments, but it also illuminates differences between environments, which provides people with a more accurate frame of reference about where they recreate, find meaning, and find joy in the outdoors compared with other places and contexts. Therefore, I argue that LNT inspires a special type of place-based learning that encourages a connection to nature as a whole through knowing and acting on the specific needs of particular places. Thus, by practicing thoughtful behaviors that respond to the specific needs of places, backcountry travelers are in a position to re-envision their views toward environments beyond the backcountry that demand attention to the details and particulars that sustain them. I suggest that LNT makes this possible, and I believe this gives LNT the license to ignore its critics. Overall, LNT should remain true to its mission and vision.

Conclusion

LNT makes a difference beyond backcountry experiences for three important reasons: 1) its curriculum explicitly and implicitly centers on protecting nature as a whole; 2) LNT has a broad focus that includes frontcountry settings, urban settings, and outreach initiatives; and 3) LNT backcountry principles are an effective form of place-based outdoor education that provides a necessary platform for long-term environmental ethics and place-connections to take hold. Some argue that LNT perpetuates a human–nature divide (Moskowitz and Ottey, 2006); however, I have presented an alternative LNT place-based perspective (much of which is inherent in LNT philosophy, literature, and principles) that shows how LNT brings humans and nature closer together; this is extended both explicitly and implicitly beyond the backcountry.

It is up to outdoor educators to help learners find ways to solidify these "beyond backcountry" connections. Outdoor educators should teach learners about global environmental issues and responsibilities and should use LNT (in part) as a tool to do so. In its current form and structure, LNT is well poised to address larger global environmental challenges. This does not require dismantling or re-envisioning LNT as a whole; rather, it means that outdoor educators should more rigorously and metaphorically apply the LNT curriculum instead of merely brushing over the principles in a haphazard way. The metaphorical value of LNT can extend the meaning of the principles to other contexts. For example, learners can be shown that the importance of camping on durable surfaces can transfer to the importance of using sustainable construction materials from renewable resources (e.g., bamboo). The importance of traveling on durable surfaces in the backcountry can also be applied to using sustainable transportation in the frontcountry (e.g., walking and biking instead of driving). Respecting wildlife can transfer to supporting global initiatives that protect at-risk species. Disposing of waste properly can transfer to global issues relating to landfill and waste concerns. Finally, being considerate of other visitors can transfer to being a compassionate and sensitive human being. These are only a few examples. Ask learners to metaphorically apply the LNT principles to everyday life and they will come up with imaginative ideas of their own.

Helping people to make lasting proenvironmental decisions and engage in proenvironmental behaviors is a major undertaking that involves larger issues such as a need for additional process and outcomes research within outdoor experiential programs, further understanding of the nature of person–place relationships, the topics of environmental and social justice, and further societal place-based education. LNT is part of the solution, but outdoor and environmental educators are ultimately the ones responsible for developing, structuring, and delivering a global environmental pedagogy. Re-envisioning or developing a new form of LNT is limiting and would dismantle a curriculum that in its current form represents a best practice for outdoor education.

In conclusion, the LNT program and curriculum is strong where it currently stands, and outdoor educators should continue to use it to help others make lasting connections to nature that extend both to and beyond backcountry environments.

References

Boland, H., & Heintzmen, P. (2009). The perceived impact of a university outdoor education program on students' environmental behaviors. In *Proceedings of the 2009 Northeastern Recreation Research Symposium* (pp. 31-35, Gen. Tech. Report NRS-P-66). Newtown Square, PA: U.S. Department of Agriculture, Forest Service, Northern Research Station.

Cameron, J. (2003). Responding to place in a post-colonial era: An Australian perspective. In W. Adams & M. Mulligan (Eds.), *Decolonizing nature: Strategies for conservation in a post colonial era* (pp. 172-196). London: Earthscan.

Gruenewald, D., & Smith, G. (2008). *Place-based education in the global age.* New York: Lawrence Erlbaum.

Hampton, B., & Cole, D. (2003). *NOLS soft paths: How to enjoy Wilderness without harming it.* Mechanicsburg, PA: Stackpole Books.

King, T. (2003). *The truth about stories.* Toronto: House of Anansi Press.

Leave No Trace Center for Outdoor Ethics. (2008a). Hot spots. www.lnt.org/01_community/hotspots.php [December 14, 2011].

Leave No Trace Center for Outdoor Ethics. (2008b). Sustainability. www.lnt.org/aboutUs/sustainability.php [December 14, 2011].

Leave No Trace Inc. (2008). *Teaching Leave No Trace.* Boulder, CO: Leave No Trace Inc.

Marion, J., Lawhon, B., Vagias, W., & Newman, P. (2010). Revisiting "Beyond LNT." *Ethics, Place, and Environment, 13*(2), 1-6.

Marion, J.L., & Reid, S. (2001). Development of the United States Leave No Trace programme: A historical perspective. In M.B. Usher (Ed.), *Enjoyment and understanding of the natural heritage* (pp. 81-92). Edinburgh, Scotland: The Stationery Office Ltd., Scottish Natural Heritage.

Marion, J., & Reid, S. (2007). Minimising visitor impacts to protected areas: The efficacy of low impact education programmes. *Journal of Sustainable Tourism, 15*(1), 5-27.

Moskowitz, D., & Ottey, D. (2006). Leaving LNT behind: Towards a holistic land use ethic. *Green Teacher, 78*(Spring), 16-19.

Simon, G.L., & Algona, P.S. (2009). Beyond Leave No Trace. *Ethics, Place, and Environment, 12*(1), 17-34.

Sobel, D. (2004). *Place-based education: Connecting classrooms and communities.* Great Barrington, MA: Orion Society.

Stewart, A. (2004). Decolonising encounters with the Murray River: Building place responsive outdoor education. *Australian Journal of Outdoor Education, 8*(2), 46-55.

Does Leave No Trace make a difference beyond the scope of backcountry environmental practices?

NO It Is Time for a Global Ethic, Not Just Local Etiquette

Elizabeth Andre, PhD, assistant professor of outdoor and environmental education, Northland College, Ashland, Wisconsin, United States

The Environmental Stewardship Committee of the Association of Outdoor Recreation and Education recently polled the membership of the association about efforts their programs were making to be more sustainable, to reduce their environmental footprint, and to educate their participants about environmental ethics. Many of the respondents cited adoption of the Leave No Trace (LNT) principles as evidence of their program's care for the environment.

Although the LNT program has successfully contributed to a reduction in visible impacts of recreation on backcountry areas, the LNT program does not contribute to overall environmental sustainability or to far-reaching environmental ethics. Practitioners believe that it does and thereby neglect to implement more substantive efforts at sustainability and education. Therefore, the ubiquity of LNT may undermine the ability of the profession to contribute to real environmental progress.

The LNT program was never intended to contribute to environmental sustainability or to protect the larger environment outside of recreation areas. To appreciate the inadequacy of LNT as an environmental ethic or program of sustainability, one must understand its historical foundations and philosophical underpinnings, its misrepresentation of ecological principles and supply chains, its pedagogical practices, and the difference between ethics (which LNT claims to be) and etiquette (which more adequately describes the LNT principles). To further demonstrate the weakness of LNT as a far-reaching environmental ethic, we can also compare and contrast the LNT program with other models that strive to develop more comprehensive environmental ethics.

Historical Foundations

During the early 20th century, woodcraft was a popular wilderness recreation movement. The woodcraft movement valued an intimate knowledge of nature and a frontiersman's work ethic. A true woodsman rejected the many gadgets available in camping stores and relied instead on his craftsmanship with primitive tools and his knowledge of local flora and fauna. Woodsmen used axes to cut tree branches for lean-tos, tripods, utensils, and bedding. Woodsmen hunted, tanned hides, gathered edible plants, and cooked over open fires (Turner, 2002).

The number of people participating in backcountry recreation increased dramatically during the middle of the 20th century. In the decade following the 1964 passage of the Wilderness Act, recreational use of national forest wilderness and primitive areas tripled (Simon and Alagona, 2009). Increasing numbers of visitors, many still using the heavy-handed camping methods from the legacy of the woodcraft movement, degraded popular backcountry areas. Americans were "loving their wilderness to death" (Nash, 1982, p. 316).

The Wilderness Act encompassed two competing notions of wilderness: a recreational resource and a scientific preserve. Land managers were challenged to solve the riddle of how to make Wilderness areas available for public use while still preserving them. The U.S. Forest Service's first attempt at a solution was a restrictive quota system that limited recreational use (Turner, 2002). Environmental groups such as The Sierra Club and the Wilderness Society worried, however, that limiting the number of people who could experience Wilderness firsthand would limit the popular support for wilderness. Starting in the 1970s, they advocated instead for increasing the carrying capacity of Wilderness areas by training users in new, minimum-impact camping techniques (Turner, 2002).

Minimum-impact camping techniques continued to gain popularity and acceptance. In 1993, the U.S. Forest Service, the National Outdoor Leadership School, the Outdoor Recreation Coalition of

America, and the Sporting Goods Manufacturing Association came together to create Leave No Trace Incorporated (Simon and Alagona, 2009). LNT has since been adopted by the Bureau of Land Management, the National Park Service, the U.S. Fish and Wildlife Service, and the state parks system. The focus of LNT has expanded from solely Wilderness areas to include frontcountry and urban recreation settings. The LNT program has been successful in reducing the direct impact of visitors on recreation areas and in allowing a greater carrying capacity in these areas (Marion and Reid, 2007).

The LNT program never intended to constitute an environmental ethic that reached beyond recreation areas. The LNT organization has made clear that it believes the program's success is "tied to its narrower mission and focus" and that it has no desire to expand its ethical considerations (Marion et al., 2010, p. 5).

Philosophical Underpinnings

The words "leave no trace" are catchy, have a pleasant acronym, and even lend themselves to being used as a verb, as in, "Did you LNT the campsite?" Those of us who have grown up in the era of LNT likely accept these three words uncritically. Words, however, shape our ideas and our understanding of the world. Our ideas and understandings, in turn, determine the options available to us. We must, therefore, ask which values and assumptions are inherent in these words.

Asking people to leave no trace sends the message that humans are merely visitors who do not belong in natural areas. LNT principles, for example, encourage visitors to travel and camp on durable surfaces and to avoid damaging live trees. Other animals, in contrast, leave visible traces on these areas—beavers build dams and lodges, woodpeckers drill for insects, and deer bed down in tall grasses. The unintended message to campers is "we humans are bad, don't touch that, don't pick that up, and we need to tiptoe around the woods because we don't really belong here" (Weiss cited in Moskowitz and Ottey, 2006, p. 17). This view of humans as separate from nature is embedded in our Western culture. One definition of nature is "the world apart from the features or products of civilization and human will" (Snyder, 1990, p. 7).

These arguments are of more than just theoretical significance. Although this question needs to be studied in more depth, one researcher found that the LNT program taught in Outward Bound courses actually led students to feel disconnected from the environment (Lemburg cited in Moskowitz and Ottey, 2006). Environmental historian William Cronon (1995) argues that "any way of looking at nature that encourages us to believe we are separate from nature . . . is likely to reinforce environmentally irresponsible behavior" (p. 87). If people believe that nature is "out there" and they can protect it by adopting simple LNT principles while camping, they may abandon their care for the environment once they leave the recreation area and return to the city. They may not make the connections between their lifestyle choices and larger environmental issues that threaten not only individual recreation areas but also the ecological integrity of the entire planet.

The advent of minimum-impact camping techniques in the 1970s replaced the ideal of the woodsman, who must know and appropriately use local flora and fauna. The minimum-impact backpacker, who can "spring a temporary camp from a backpack of modern gear," does not need the same intimate knowledge of his or her surroundings (Turner, 2002, p. 474).

Few would advocate, however, that we return en masse to the techniques of the woodcraft movement; our recreation areas would quickly be damaged by the large numbers of people they currently accommodate. Minimum-impact camping techniques have a place within a modern environmental ethic. We must, however, re-examine the underlying philosophy and language of the LNT program if we are to connect people emotively with the environment, help them understand that they are part of nature, and assist them in developing a broad environmental ethic. We must make people believe, as poet Gary Snyder (1990) asserts, that "nature is not a place to visit, it is *home*" (p. 7, emphasis in the original).

Misrepresentation of Ecological Principles and Supply Chains

One of the tenets of ecology is that organisms are connected to each other and to their surroundings. From an ecological perspective, the idea that an organism can leave no trace on its environment makes no sense. Human beings consume resources, dispose of waste, and modify natural processes. We impact the entire ecosystem. For example, when campers who practice LNT use a stove that burns fuel refined from petroleum instead of cooking over a fire, they are not "leaving no trace." They are, instead, transferring their impact from the backcountry to the oil fields, the refineries, the factories that make the stoves, the highways that transport the items, the stores that exist to sell camping supplies, and, ultimately, to our atmosphere.

LNT principles and practices do not protect the larger environment. In an ironic twist, they may even contribute to increased resource use and environmental degradation. The LNT program was developed and is promoted in concert with the outdoor-products industry. Many of the LNT practices depend on modern gear—stoves, nylon tents, synthetic clothing, plastic utensils—that contributes to globalized production and distribution chains. Yet as environmental historian Jay Turner (2002) argues, "to the extent that backpackers actually embrace the notion that they 'Leave No Trace,' they risk divorcing themselves from their actions as consumers outside wilderness . . . in turn dismissing larger questions of the modern economy, consumerism, and the environment" (p. 479).

One can argue that LNT practices do not protect the environment in the actual recreation areas. In reality, the purpose of the principles is to protect the experience of other people recreating in that area. Eroded trails, compacted soil in campsites, numerous campfire scars, broken tree limbs, and toilet paper left by the trail do not significantly affect the overall function of the ecosystem. Compare the scale of these human impacts with the scale of erosion from landslides and rivers, scarring from forest fires, and broken limbs and downed trees from windstorms. The human impacts do, however, significantly affect the aesthetic experience of people recreating there in a way that nonhuman impacts do not (Wuerthner, 1986).

Minimum-impact camping techniques are desirable in that they allow larger numbers of people to enjoy recreation areas without degrading the experience of those areas for others. The way LNT frames these techniques, however, obscures larger ecological concepts, divorces participants from their roles as consumers in global supply chains, and misrepresents the actual intent of the minimum-impact camping practices. This shortcoming is exacerbated if outdoor educators assume that by teaching LNT principles they are fulfilling their duty to environmental education and, as a result, neglect to teach about larger principles.

A more far-reaching educational program, in contrast, would promote ecological literacy. Educational philosopher David Orr (1992) argues that ecological literacy "is not [only] comprehension of how the world works, but in light of that knowledge a life lived accordingly" (p. 87). By connecting the environmental and social considerations, ecological literacy can help bridge the psychological divide between humans and nature (Cachelin, Paisley, and Dustin, 2009).

Pedagogical Practices

Although we sometimes use the words "education" and "training" interchangeably, their meanings are different. Training helps people master how to *do* something. Education helps people learn how to *understand* underlying principles, connections, and implications and to think critically. The LNT program is one of training, not of education. LNT focuses on behaviors—disposing of waste properly, respecting wildlife, minimizing campfire impacts. This focus on behavioral outcomes denies students the opportunity to gain a deeper understanding of why certain choices and actions are more appropriate than others. Sherman (2008), professor of environmental policy and decision making, calls this an "intellectual shortcut" around the "more complex, pedagogically rich relationship between natural limits and value systems that underlies the human impact on the environment" (cited in Cachelin, Paisley, and Dustin, 2009, p. 144).

We can compare LNT to Nancy Reagan's "Just Say No" antidrug campaign from the 1980s. Reagan's campaign avoided discussing the complex reasons children might experiment with drugs and instead advocated for a particular behavior—just saying no. This campaign failed to achieve any long-term reduction in rates of drug use among participants (Cachelin, Paisley, and Dustin, 2009).

A constructivist approach, in contrast, would assume that students seek to learn rather than simply react. It would assume that students are not blank slates but rather are learners who carry a host of understandings and opinions that influence how they make sense of new information. A constructivist approach would explore participants' prior knowledge, identify any misconceptions, and help students form more accurate models of the world. It would not present disconnected facts and ask students to commit, through repetition and drilling, these facts to rote memory, just as flat pieces of paper are added to a file folder. It would, instead, develop three-dimensional understandings that are connected to prior knowledge and to affect. These understandings would be durable and adaptable and form the foundation for continued learning. These understandings would be far more likely to contribute to a substantive environmental ethic than the flat information promoted by behavior-based approaches such as LNT (Cachelin, Paisley, and Dustin, 2009, pp. 145-146).

Delivering a constructivist approach to education takes far more time than delivering a behavioralist approach to training. The constructivist approach is, however, a better investment if our desired outcome is a populace that is educated rather than well trained. Outdoor educators and recreation professionals are in a position to deliver this kind of education. We have our participants' unfettered time and attention while they are with us, we have their respect and trust, and we have the assistance of nature—perhaps the greatest educator of all.

Ethics and Etiquette

Ethics are sets of moral principles that evolve within communities of interdependent individuals and groups. Aldo Leopold (1949), father of the modern land ethic, regards ethics as "a mode of guidance for meeting ecological situations so new or intricate, or involving such deferred reactions, that the path of social expediency is not discernable to the average individual" (p. 202). If we examine our current environmental situation in light of Leopold's words, the need for an environmental ethic becomes evident. This planet is home to a quintessential community of interdependent individuals and groups. Our ecological situation is intricate and involves deferred reactions, meaning that the effects of our actions are often hidden from us through time, space, and scale. In this situation it is difficult for individuals to discern which actions are best. It is for these reasons that we need an environmental ethic.

Leopold (1949) presents his land ethic as a "product of social evolution" rather than as a "law" that is unchanging. He asserts that this is "because nothing so important as an ethic is ever 'written' . . . evolution never stops" (p. 225). Ethics evolve as our understandings evolve. Our society's understanding of complex human–environment interactions continually increases. Our ethics must keep pace with these increased understandings. For example, environmentalism in the 1960s and 1970s focused on visible, isolated, and comparatively simple issues—acid rain, water pollution, pesticides, deforestation (Kline, 2007). The 1973 Endangered Species Act is representative of the level of understanding of that era in that the act focuses on individual species rather than on functioning ecosystems. The LNT program grew out of the understandings developed during this same era.

The current level of environmental understanding recognizes the interconnectedness and complexity of human–environment interactions. For example, we know we can't designate nature preserves and expect them to indefinitely protect the species within. We must consider drivers of extinction, such as invasive species, pollution, and climate change, that do not obey the artificial boundaries we create (Quammen, 1998).

We need an environmental ethic that has evolved to match our current level of understanding. LNT is well intentioned. However, "conservation is paved with good intentions which prove to be futile, or even dangerous, because they are devoid of critical understanding" (Leopold, 1949, p. 225).

One could also argue that although LNT claims to be outdoor ethics, the more appropriate label would be etiquette. Etiquette is a customary code of polite behavior. LNT principles merely extend to recreation areas the etiquette that people follow in town. Just as we do not loudly blast our music toward our neighbors' house on a weeknight or dump our garbage in their yard, we do not shout loudly while in camp and strew our waste along the trail. This hardly constitutes an ethical code; it is merely the minimum expected among polite company. Again, Leopold (1949), whose words are as true today as when he penned them, provides insight:

> We have been too timid, and too anxious for quick success, to tell [ourselves] the true magnitude of [our] obligations. Obligations have no meaning without conscience, and the problem we face is the extension of the social conscience. . . . No important change in ethics was ever accomplished without an internal change in our intellectual emphasis, loyalties, affections, and convictions. . . . In our attempt to make conservation easy, we have made it trivial. (p. 209)

An ethic, in contrast to a mere etiquette, would demand more from the backcountry enthusiast both in level of understanding and in depth of effort.

Alternative Models

As ethics evolve, individuals and groups propose new models. Three current examples are As Sustainable As Possible (ASAP), Beyond Leave No Trace (BLNT), and Conscious Living Impact. Contrasting these models with the LNT program can help us envision progress toward an educational approach that will more successfully develop substantive environmental ethics that make a difference beyond the confines of recreation areas.

Students at Northland College in Ashland, Wisconsin, developed the ASAP model (Bulger, Sveum, and Van Horn, 2008). The model considers the impacts of recreation choices on the immediate areas in which we recreate and on the world at large. The model asks participants to consider the ecological footprint of recreation choices in three areas: food, gear, and transportation. ASAP, for example, encourages participants to buy bulk, local, and organic food, to eat low on the food chain, and, when feasible, to grow their own food. It also encourages participants to purchase secondhand items, to maintain and repair their gear, and, when new purchases are necessary, to make responsible choices (made easier now that the Outdoor Industry Association is developing an eco index to measure the footprint of individual items).

Gregory Simon and Peter Alagona at Stanford University and the University of California Santa Barbara, respectively, developed the BLNT model. It includes the areas addressed by the ASAP model and extends the ethic to include active participation in collaborative processes of land management, information gathering and scientific study, and design and production of outdoor products. The authors envision "a more democratic, more participatory, and more radical vision of outdoor recreation as a form of political action" (Simon and Alagona, 2009, p. 29).

Kroka Expeditions in Vermont developed Conscious Living Impact as a vision for how participants could "address the immediate land management goals of the Leave No Trace program and at the same time place [their] experience within a larger, more holistic context" (Moskowitz and Ottey, 2006, p. 18). Conscious Living Impact echoes what Snyder (1990) calls the lessons of the wild: "that we must try to live without causing unnecessary harm, not just to fellow humans, but to all beings" (p. 4). The seven principles of Conscious Living Impact are as follows (Moskowitz and Ottey, 2006):

1. Live simply.
2. Think globally and plan ahead.
3. Follow the precautionary principle.
4. Reduce, reuse, recycle, relearn.
5. Follow nature's lead and blend into your surroundings.
6. Use appropriate technology and use technology appropriately.
7. Show respect and compassion for all forms of life.

These three models demonstrate forward and expansive thinking. Unlike LNT, they develop an environmental ethic that reaches beyond individual recreation areas.

Conclusion

LNT has been successful in reducing the visible impacts of visitors on recreation areas and has allowed these areas to increase carrying capacity. However, LNT was never intended to make a difference beyond individual recreation areas. LNT cannot promote substantive environmental ethics because of its historical design, philosophical underpinnings, misrepresentation of ecological principles and supply chains, and pedagogical shortcomings. LNT is not a code of ethics but rather of etiquette. However, many practitioners believe that by training participants in LNT they are fulfilling their duty to teach environmental ethics. If they neglect to teach more substantive and holistic principles, the ubiquity of the LNT model may, paradoxically, undermine the ability of the profession to contribute to meaningful environmental progress. Alternative models suggest more effective ways forward.

References

Bulger, H., Sveum, P., & Van Horn, P. (2008). *As sustainable as possible: A working model to assess and improve the sustainability of outdoor education and recreation.* Presented at the National Conference of the Wilderness Education Association, San Diego.

Cachelin, A., Paisley, K., & Dustin, D. (2009). Opportunity and obligation: A role for outdoor educators in the sustainability revolution. *Journal of Outdoor Recreation, Education, and Leadership, 1*(2), 141-150.

Cronon, W. (1995). The trouble with wilderness; Or, getting back to the wrong nature. In W. Cronon (Ed.), *Uncommon ground: Toward reinventing nature* (pp. 69-90). New York: Norton.

Kline, B. (2007). *First along the river: A brief history of the U.S. environmental movement.* 3rd ed. Lanham, MD: Roman and Littlefield.

Leopold, A. (1949). *A Sand County almanac, and sketches here and there.* London: Oxford University Press.

Marion, J.L., Lawhon, B., Vagais, W.M., & Newman, P. (2010). Revisiting "Beyond Leave No Trace." *Ethics, Place and Environment, 13*(2), 1-6.

Marion, J.L., & Reid, S. (2007). Development of the United States Leave No Trace programme: A historical perspective. In M.B. Usher (Ed.), *Enjoyment and understanding of the natural heritage* (pp. 81-92). Edinburgh, Scotland: The Stationery Office.

Moskowitz, D., & Ottey, D. (2006). Leaving "Leave No Trace" behind: Towards a holistic land use ethic. *Green Teacher, 78*, 16-19.

Nash, R. (1982). *Wilderness and the American mind*. 3rd ed. New Haven, CT: Yale University Press.

Orr, D.W. (1992). *Ecological literacy: Education and the transition to a postmodern world*. Albany, NY: State University of New York Press.

Quammen, D. (1998). Planet of weeds. *Harper's, 297*(1781), 57-70.

Simon, G.L., & Alagona, P.S. (2009). Beyond Leave No Trace. *Ethics, Place, and Environment, 12*(1), 17-34.

Snyder, G. (1990). *Practice of the wild*. San Francisco: Northpoint Press.

Turner, J.M. (2002). From woodcraft to "Leave No Trace": Wilderness, consumerism, and environmentalism in twentieth-century America. *Environmental History, 7*(3), 462-484.

Wuerthner, G. (1986). The natural role of humans in wilderness. *Western Wildlands,* Summer, 26-30.

Controversial Issue 17

Are educational reform policies that stress standards and accountability compatible with pedagogical aims and practices in outdoor education?

On January 8, 2002, President George W. Bush signed into law the No Child Left Behind Act (NCLB). For the past 10 years, this law has dictated the nature of the federal government's role in public education in the United States. Originally proposed by President Bush, NCLB received strong bipartisan support from the U.S. Congress. In the final Senate debate over the bill, Massachusetts Senator Edward M. Kennedy stated, "The legislation before us today is about America's future. It is about enabling all children to fulfill their dreams and to build a future for themselves, their families, their communities, and our country" (Dewar, 2001). In short, the purpose of the legislation was to close the achievement gap between minority and nonminority schools in America.

NCLB promotes a standards-based approach to education, which is based on the assumption that the best way to ensure high levels of achievement in schooling is to develop measurable outcomes by which to gauge student success in schooling. Under NCLB, each state must develop standards that delineate the knowledge and skills that students in public schools are expected to learn in such core academic subjects as science, mathematics, English, and history. Each state must also develop standardized assessments to determine the extent to which students fulfill these standards of learning. Many advocates of standards-based approaches to learning believe that such approaches provide a basis for accountability and, subsequently, quality control in public schools. It is an effort, stemming from various political and economic influences, to ensure that the nation receives the most for its money in public education and that schools help students to fulfill their potential. When schools fail to help students achieve basic levels of proficiency, school interventions are initiated to help improve student performance. In cases where school failure is persistent and pervasive, students are awarded vouchers and transportation that allow them to attend a school of their choice, including public charter schools and private schools, within their school district. Currently, approximately 30,000 schools throughout the United States are considered failing schools.

While maintaining a commitment to standards-based learning in public schools in the United States, the Obama administration has proposed broad changes to the NCLB law. These proposed changes are intended primarily to alter the way in which school success or failure is judged and to eliminate the requirement that every child in the United States be brought up to a basic level of proficiency in reading and math by 2014. When announcing the proposed changes, U.S. Secretary of Education Arne Duncan stated, "We want accountability reforms that factor in student growth, progress in closing achievement gaps, proficiency towards college and career-ready standards, high school graduation, and college enrollment rates. We know that's a lot to track, but if we want to be smarter about accountability, more fair to students and teachers and more effective in the classroom, we need to look at all these factors" (Dillon, 2010). The Obama administration is proposing to waive the 2014 timeline for states "that have adopted their own testing and accountability programs and are making other strides toward better schools" (Dillon, 2011). If the 2014 timeline remains enforced, thousands of additional schools will likely be labeled failing schools once this deadline has passed.

In light of monumental efforts at school reform in the United States, Britain, and elsewhere around the world, the question for adventure programmers is whether and how we as an industry can contribute. Can Expeditionary Learning and other curricular models based on the principles of outdoor education meaningfully contribute to educational reform in a climate predominated by standards and accountability?

Jayson Seaman and Alison Rheingold argue that if outdoor educators continue to emphasize "adventure, romance, and life in community" without a "corresponding emphasis on academic rigor," they will be complicit in maintaining the educational and social disparities that standards-based reforms are meant to redress. Likewise, unless standards-based reforms engage students through thoughtful pedagogy, they will fail to reach their own aims. Consequently, Seaman and Rheingold argue for greater integration of standards-based reforms and outdoor education aims and practices.

Tony Rea and Sue Waite, on the other hand, argue that complicity with an educational reform movement that is generally antithetical to the principles and practices of outdoor education appears to have resulted in a landscape of educational colonization, which has devalued and diminished key pedagogical principles that underpin many outdoor education programs. Their analysis focuses on what they view as the deceptive rationality of "effective" education policy and the potential dangers of accountability and performativity.

References

Dewar, H. (2001, December 19). Landmark education legislation gets final approval in Congress. *The Washington Post,* A8.

Dillon, S. (2010, February 2). Administration outlines proposed changes to 'No Child' law. *The New York Times,* A16. www.nytimes.com/2010/02/02/education/02child.html [February 2, 2010].

Dillon, S. (2011, August 8). Overriding a key education law. *The New York Times,* A12. www.nytimes.com/2011/08/08/education/08educ.html?pagewanted=all [August 8, 2011].

Are educational reform policies that stress standards and accountability compatible with pedagogical aims and practices in outdoor education?

Selling Out or Buying In? Imperatives for Outdoor Education in the Age of Accountability

Jayson Seaman, PhD, assistant professor of outdoor education, University of New Hampshire, Durham, New Hampshire, United States

Alison Rheingold, MEd, doctoral candidate in education, University of New Hampshire, Durham, New Hampshire, United States

Our debate question has a modern ring to it, but its core concerns are not new. It is the latest foray into "the long conversation" about Progressive reforms that Adams and Reynolds outlined in 1981. They concluded:

> It is evident that [current experiential reforms] have retained what Ed Yeomans, an historian of the progressive movement, fondly refers to as the 'adventure, romance, and life in community' reminiscent of the early Romantics. But the corresponding emphasis on academic rigor and an integrated approach to the arts in many instances has been minimized or eliminated. Not only is there no longer an implicit belief in the validity of education for social reform, but in fact, many experiential programs function completely independently of schools. (p. 27)

As experiential education developed a "strong commitment to developing the powers of the individual" (Adams and Reynolds, 1981, p. 27), it became less common to imagine it as a systemic reform. This was a break from earlier Progressive ideals. An editorial written a quarter-century later by Sean Blenkinsop (2006) suggests that the break endures:

> I think part of the reason we are not more involved in producing change is that it is sometimes easier to be in the opposition benches but, more substantively, it is because we do not have a comprehensive and consistent enough philosophy of education to do the job that is currently being asked of the mainstream. (p. vi)

We see this as the root issue in our question: Should outdoor education (OE) primarily be conceived as a means of personal and affective development among individuals or as a means of educational and social reform at a broader level? If Adams and Reynolds are correct, the former has come to dominate thinking; if Blenkinsop is correct, this prevents OE from contributing much to the latter.

Despite their flaws, reforms that emphasize standards and accountability represent systemic efforts to accomplish an unprecedented societal goal: expanding opportunities for educational attainment for all children (Darling-Hammond, 2007). By establishing guidelines for subject-matter content and proposing metrics for achievement, standards and accountability reforms are intended to help overcome the unjust distribution of educational access and opportunity. How will OE contribute to this goal? Our concern is that, if outdoor educators continue to prioritize adventure, romance, and life in community without a corresponding emphasis on academic rigor, they will be complicit in maintaining the educational and social disparities that standards-based reforms are meant to redress. Conversely, unless standards-based reforms engage students through thoughtful pedagogy, they will fail to reach their own aims. For these reasons, we argue for more incorporation of standards-based reforms and OE aims and practices, not less.

Our argument consists of two parts. First, we discuss the break from Progressive ideals that Adams and Reynolds describe, namely that OE has become preoccupied with developing the powers of the individual without sufficiently considering how this addresses broader educational priorities. We provocatively cast this as a mismatch between the conception of education that commonly appears in OE texts and John Dewey's philosophy on which the field is supposedly founded. Second, we present a case example drawn from our ongoing research in an urban middle school that demonstrates how OE aims and practices can merge with reforms emphasizing standards and accountability, indicating that no inherent incompatibility exists between the two. We conclude by returning to Dewey in order to express the need to consider reforms at a systemic level.

Outdoor Education, Individualism, and John Dewey's Philosophy of Education

We trust it is not necessary to detail OE's claims to Deweyan foundations (see, for example, Breunig, 2008; Priest and Gass, 2005; Smith and Knapp, 2008; Wojcikiewicz and Mural, 2010). In light of this purported lineage, we are struck by a contrast between Dewey's conception of education and the way it is often construed in major OE texts. Dewey conceived of education as a social institution responsible for the expansion of democratic culture. Outdoor educators seem to conceive of education as a democratic process of individual learning. These represent different philosophical priorities and entail different curricular logics.

In "The Four Uses of Outdoor Adventure Programming," Stremba (2008) states that adventure or outdoor education differs from recreation, development, and therapy in its emphasis on "activities aimed at understanding concepts" (p. 101). Concepts are defined as "learning the importance of working together as a team and of support (interpersonal relationships) or the value of healthy risk taking (intrapersonal relationships)" (p. 101). Furthermore, adventure education "changes the way people think—new attitudes that can transfer to daily life" (p. 101). Research by Brookes (2004) suggests that this characterization is prototypical. Surveying common OE texts, Brookes found a catalog of socially altruistic aims that were expressed in "purely personal" terms, such as "the tremendous value of utilizing the outdoors for . . . trust, ownership, personal achievement, teamwork, leadership, determination, strategic planning and motivation" (Gair cited in Brookes, 2004, p. 28). Likewise, Lynch and Moore (2004) found a similar "orientation towards the individual" across OE texts (for further examples, see Bailey, 1999; Raiola, 2003; Sheard and Golby, 2006). Thus, although the OE literature emphasizes many socially altruistic

aims, it is often guided by an underlying methodological individualism, or "the belief that all social phenomena should be understood as resulting from the psychological processes of individuals" (Hong et al., 2007, p. 336). It also demonstrates little regard for knowledge of subject matter as central to education.

In contrast, Dewey did not discuss education primarily in terms of individual growth and he did not define "concepts" as interpersonal or intrapersonal skills; he conceived both as a matter of culture. The third paragraph of *My Pedagogic Creed* (1897) begins, "I believe that knowledge of social conditions, of the *present state of civilization*, is necessary in order properly to interpret the child's powers" [italics added]. The first paragraph of the section titled *What the School Is* reads:

> Education being a social process, the school is simply that form of community life in which all those agencies are concentrated that will be most effective in *bringing the child to share in the inherited resources of the race*, and to use his own powers for social ends. [italics added]

Dewey wrote this in 1897. One could argue that his emphasis later shifted from knowledge of the present state of civilization to knowledge of how individuals relate to themselves and others, or that he equated knowledge with civic attitudes, as in the final clause above. But these arguments would also need to explain the cultural–historical themes that permeate his writing as well as his ongoing preoccupation with how disciplinary knowledge should be organized (see Dewey, 1896; Dewey, 1938, p. 74). For example, in *Underlying Philosophy of Education* (1933), he writes, "Economic forces are at the present time *superior to others in causal power*. They condition what people can do and how they can develop more than other forces" (p. 85, italics added). He further writes:

> The liberation of individual creative activity and elevation of esthetic taste which would follow the reconstruction of the economic system is moreover an illustration of the position we have taken as to the relation of the individual to the social. (p. 86)

The continuity of such themes gives reason to believe that his primary educational focus was never on individuals as such but rather on altering their historical relation to the social and economic spheres.

He defined "concepts" according to this relation. The following passage follows a discussion about westward American pioneers (Dewey, 1929/1999):

> But it is no longer a physical wilderness that has to be wrestled with. Our problems grow out of social conditions: they concern human relations rather than man's direct relationship to physical nature. The adventure of the individual, if there is to be any venturing of individuality and not a relapse into the deadness of complacency or of despairing discontent, is an unsubdued social frontier. (pp. 45-46)

So far the ideas seem congenial to OE. But then he elaborates:

> The issues cannot be met with ideas improvised for the occasion. The problems to be solved are general and not local. They concern complex forces that are at work throughout the whole country, and not those limited to an immediate and almost face to face environment. . . . A new individualism can be achieved only through the controlled use of all the resources of the science and technology that have mastered the physical forces of nature. (p. 46)

Dewey's insistence that social and economic changes are needed before the liberation of individual creative activity suggests that the cultural function of knowledge, not individual psychology, was primary in his educational thinking.

Once one recognizes Dewey's priorities, his curricular logic appears backward to that of OE. Equipped with anthropological insights, he saw education as the vehicle for "controlling use" of science and technology so they could serve more humane, noneconomic ends (Fallace, 2008; Seaman and Nelsen, 2011). An educator's job was to design "active centers of scientific insight into natural materials and processes, points of departure whence children shall be led out into a realization of the historic development of man" (Dewey, 1899, p. 462). Experiences were to be "permeated throughout with the spirit of art, history and science" (Dewey, 1899, p. 467). To teach in this manner, educators would need to anticipate the scientific and historical concepts that children would learn as they worked through problems at hand. In OE, the logic is reversed; the persons and problems at hand are all that is required for interpersonal or intrapersonal concepts to emerge, and it is the participant's responsibility to work out any scientific or cultural significance (see Voyer, 2009, for a similar analysis). Whereas outdoor educators want to educate the whole child but eschew imposing preordained concepts for fear of squelching growth, Dewey wanted to help the historical child bring the "inherited resources of the race" into being as concepts and practices and, in so doing, realize him or herself as growing. For Dewey, no personal development occurs apart from cultural knowledge and practices (Schecter, 2011). This poses a dilemma for outdoor educators: they can either shed the pretenses of alignment with Dewey or feature culture and subject matter more prominently in their conception of education.

Our purpose here is not to scold outdoor educators for being inconsistent with their foundations; rather, it is to point toward several contradictions that arise when socially altruistic aims are promoted within an individualistic framework that does not emphasize the cultural importance of knowledge. First, Brookes (2002) argues that the geographical expansion of modern OE follows that of other Western institutions and that its cultural impact has been similarly detrimental (see also Zink and Burrows, 2008). He argues that universalist OE supplanted indigenous forms of outdoor learning in Australia and converted the land into a blank canvas for self-discovery rather than a physical and cultural geography with its own stories that link development to specific locations and customs. Traditional forms of outdoor learning receded in favor of practices modeled on universalist ideals—that "what is learned in the bush" can be applied anywhere, thus freeing the individual from the contingencies of local experience. The idea became that where learning occurs is less important than what you, personally, learn about yourself. In direct contrast to Rea and Waite's argument in this issue, Brookes casts modern OE as the colonizing agent.

Second, no inherent connection exists between socially altruistic attitudes and progress toward a just democracy. As Apple (1996) writes:

> Practical and "progressive" teaching and curricula are not always socially critical. In a highly stratified society such as the one in which we live, "experiential, affective, and emotional learning can shape dispositions and loyalties" just as easily in directions favoring the powerful as the least advantaged. . . . Thus we

need to ask of each and every proposed "reform" in schools whether its analysis and proposals are indeed linked to the development of such critical dispositions. (p. 103)

Other critical educators have made similar points. On Western adaptations to Paolo Freire's literacy programs, Macedo (cited in Freire, 1998) writes, "The sharing of experiences should not be understood in psychological terms only . . . it must always involve a political project with the object of dismantling oppressive social structures and mechanisms" (p. xiv). Kincheloe (2004) cites Freire as saying, "No teacher is worth her salt who is not able to confront students with a rigorous body of knowledge" (p. 21). Although it would be flatly wrong to imply that accountability-based reforms match with the priorities of critical theorists, any socially altruistic reform that does not take knowledge seriously—including instrumental knowledge aimed solely at completing school—might appear liberating on its face but is unlikely to change the status quo.

Finally, despite the serious flaws of programs such as No Child Left Behind in the United States and the English National Curriculum (Coulby, 2000; Ravitch, 2010), they at least represent attempts to deal with educational problems such as minority underachievement, what Luke, Green, and Kelly (2010) call "the most durable and robust problem facing education research" (p. vii)—and, we add, educational practice—since the mid-20th century. It is highly unlikely that even nonacademic outcomes can be adequately understood or addressed without attention to the way the lives of youths are shaped by the social distribution of educational opportunities (Ladwig, 2010). Thus, although we understand the desire for outdoor education to resist contamination, we are concerned that successful resistance will ensure its irrelevance.

What Successful Incorporation Can Look Like: King Middle School

We have become convinced that OE aims and practices can be incorporated with reforms that emphasize standards and accountability through our ongoing research at King Middle School, the most diverse public middle school in the predominantly white, rural state of Maine (see Expeditionary Learning, n.d., and http://king.portlandschools.org for details about King Middle School). King is ordinary in the sense that it faces challenges similar to those of other highly diverse urban schools. But it is extraordinary because it surpasses state and district averages on standardized metrics and achieves national prominence for the quality of work its students produce, its role in the community, and its highly supportive internal culture. These strengths did not develop overnight or by accident; they have been cultivated through years of implementing the aims and practices commonly associated with outdoor education and by taking the intent of standards and accountability reforms seriously.

King was one of 10 schools initially to adopt the Expeditionary Learning (EL) reform model. EL grew from Outward Bound's urban education initiatives and in 1992 was established with funding from the New American Schools Foundation. King is now considered one of EL's flagship schools. Mike McCarthy, King's principal of 22 years, still draws inspiration from his early participation in an Outward Bound course to create a school in which "all students reach the top of the mountain" (McCarthy, 2010). Owing to this history, much of what happens at King would look familiar to outdoor educators: students are crew, not passengers; they embark on learning expeditions; they build close relationships with each other; they learn in the field; they help one another step out of their comfort zones; they take craftsmanship seriously; they capably perform challenging culminating events; and they reflect on and celebrate their accomplishments. King is also recognizable to educationists and policy makers: it was recently heralded by U.S. Secretary of Education Arne Duncan on his 2010 Courage in the Classroom tour (Billings, 2010).

Case Example: Small Acts of Courage

Throughout the spring of 2010, we observed a diverse seventh-grade class as they embarked on the Small Acts of Courage learning expedition. Instead of studying the larger-than-life heroes of the civil rights movement, Small Acts focused on local individuals involved in the movement from 1954 to 1964. Students began by learning the dynamics of political movements, examining specific events in Portland and nationally, and conducting primary research at a university library's African American collection. This prepared them for face-to-face interviews with community members active in civil rights. These interviews generated narratives that students wrote up, edited, and had professionally bound; these books were given to both the interviewees and the library for future research. The expedition culminated in a stage performance in which all 80 students read excerpts from the narratives before an audience of civic leaders, parents, and the interviewees themselves. It also employed OE practices in a more conventional sense. When students needed reminders about care and community, the teacher, Caitlin, routinely invoked their culture-building work at a nearby camp. For instance, as one group containing recently mainstreamed English Language Learners prepared for the stage presentation, she said:

> Now, remember, for those of us in this group, where we're leaving our comfort zone by a huge stretch here—it's like when we were at [camp], and we did something that was a little scary for us, but we all had the support of each other—we're here to support each other. And if you are nervous about coming up and speaking, that's why we're doing this practicing. We're here to support one another, right? (class observation, April 4, 2010)

Through our research we met Michael, an African-American boy whose family immigrated to the United States from the Congo in 1998 to escape the atrocities of civil war. Their immigration was part of a larger movement of Africans to cities in the northeast throughout the 1990s. As he explained it, "There was a war and genocide going on and [my family] left for the United States . . . because they thought it would be a better place to live" (personal interview, October 22, 2010). Many King personnel consider Michael to be "at risk": he is sometimes disruptive in the hallway, his attention in class is intermittent, and he brings neighborhood conflicts into the school. In these ways, he fits Wortham's (2005) model of an "unpromising boy" and Ferguson's "bad boys": black males caught in spirals of conflict and discipline with consequences that reproduce historical patterns of inequality (in Thorne, 2005, p. 72). Ordinarily, Michael's chances of succeeding in school would be low.

Michael played a pivotal role in the expedition, however, as if "a spotlight was turned on behind him" (teacher interview, May 18, 2010). He regularly shared insights beyond most of his peers in whole-class conversations, appropriately advanced small-group work, and expended considerable effort to skillfully write his interviewee's narrative. At the culminating performance, Michael assumed two crucial but challenging roles: he was one of three student announcers and also sang solo

during a freedom song. He articulately described the value of creating new historical information and connecting with local community leaders: "[the interviewees] helped us get to where we are today . . . everyone has equal rights and anyone can sit where they want . . . and it's just fair because of what they all did." He also said after their presentation, "an interviewee came up to me and shook my hand and said, 'Great job. Keep doing what you're doing.' And that was a very, like, inspiring moment for me" (personal interview, October 22, 2010). When asked why it was inspiring, he said, "Just to know that they appreciated what we did. And knowing that they helped us, like they helped change the way things were . . . to make it better now. And, knowing that they appreciated what we're doing and they know that we appreciate what they did for us is very inspiring."

Through this expedition Michael became part of a much larger "crew": local community members with a personal and collective stake in civil rights work. From Caitlin's perspective, the expedition "brought that piece of history alive. There's nothing like sitting down with a person who has a story to tell, that has lived through or witnessed a piece of this time period . . . to not only feel the history and connect with the person but also to be a part of the process and the understanding of the importance of capturing that" (personal interview, May 18, 2010).

We suspect that Michael's exceptional performance throughout this expedition was motivated by the kind of communal recognition he described (Miettinen, 2005). This social experience is unavailable to many students in schools that follow heavily prescribed curricula. But Michael's feelings of personal accomplishment and connectedness can hardly be considered nonacademic; they were enabled by the legitimate skill he demonstrated in interpreting his interviewee's life through a historical lens. His care for historical knowledge was invaluable in forging a connection with his interviewee. Michael's social experience would therefore also be unavailable in a program that did not take knowledge seriously. High standards were central not only to Michael's growth but to the sense of accomplishment felt across the entire seventh-grade class.

Conclusion

We close by returning to Dewey (1899):

> Whenever we have in mind the discussion of a new movement in education, it is especially necessary to take the

broader, or social view. Otherwise, changes in the school institution and tradition will be looked at as the arbitrary inventions of particular teachers, at the worst transitory fads, and at the best merely improvements in certain details. . . . (p. 455)

When Dewey urges reformers to take the social view, he is not calling for a broader disbursement of socially altruistic attitudes. Rather, he is asking them to consider the implications of their aims and practices if brought to scale. It is easy for us to imagine Michael's experience functioning at a systemic level to help address persistent educational problems, especially among urban minority students. Success at this level will come from understanding that social altruism and academic rigor must be considered jointly. This is not a matter of programmatic freedom but of educational necessity, particularly for children like Michael.

References

Adams, A., & Reynolds, S. (1981). The long conversation: Tracing the roots of the past. *Journal of Experiential Education, 4*(1), 21-28.

Apple, M. (1996). *Cultural politics and education.* New York: Teacher's College Press.

Bailey, J. (1999). A world of adventure education. In J.C. Miles & S. Priest (Eds.), *Adventure programming* (pp. 39-42). State College, PA: Venture.

Billings, R. (2010). Education secretary impressed by expeditionary learning in Portland. www.theforecaster.net/content/p-duncan-090110 [September 15, 2011].

Blenkinsop, S. (2006). Experiential education: A short story about transforming the mainstream. *Journal of Experiential Education, 29*(2), vi-ix.

Breunig, M. (2008). The historical roots of experiential education. In K. Warren, D. Mitten, & T. Loeffler (Eds.), *Theory and practice of experiential education* (pp. 77-92). Boulder, CO: Association for Experiential Education.

Brookes, A. (2002). Lost in the Australian bush: Outdoor education as curriculum. *Journal of Curriculum Studies, 34*(4), 405-425.

Brookes, A. (2004). Astride a long-dead horse: Mainstream outdoor education and the central curriculum problem. *Australian Journal of Outdoor Education, 8*(2), 22-33.

Coulby, D. (2000). *Beyond the National Curriculum: Curricular centralism and cultural diversity in Europe and the USA.* Abingdon, U.K.: RoutledgeFalmer.

Darling-Hammond, L. (2007). Race, inequality and educational accountability: The irony of "No Child Left Behind." *Race, Ethnicity and Education, 10*(3), 245-260.

Dewey, J. (1896). Interpretation of culture-epoch theory. In J.A. Boydston (Ed.), *John Dewey, the early works. Volume 5: 1895-1898* (pp. 247-253). Carbondale, IL: Southern Illinois University Press.

Dewey, J. (1897). My pedagogic creed. *The School Journal, LIV*(3), 77-80.

Dewey, J. (1899). The school and social progress. In J.J. McDermott (Ed.), *The philosophy of John Dewey* (pp. 454-467). Chicago: University of Chicago Press.

Dewey, J. (1929/1999). *Individualism old and new.* Carbondale, IL: Prometheus Books.

Dewey, J. (1933). Underlying philosophy of education. In J.A. Boydston (Ed.), *John Dewey, the later works. Volume 8: 1933* (pp. 77-103). Carbondale, IL: Southern Illinois University Press.

Dewey, J. (1938). *Experience and education.* New York: Macmillan.

Expeditionary Learning. (n.d.). King Middle School profile. http://elschools.org/evidence/school-profile-king-middle-school [September 20, 2011].

Fallace, T.D. (2008). John Dewey and the savage mind: Uniting anthropological, psychological, and pedagogical thought, 1894-1902. *Journal of the History of the Behavioral Sciences, 44*(4), 335-349.

Freire, P. (1998). *Teachers as cultural workers: Letters to those who dare to teach.* Boulder, CO: Westview Press.

Hong, Y.-Y., Wan, C., No, S., & Chiu, C.-Y. (2007). Multicultural identities. In S. Kitayama & D. Cohen (Eds.), *Handbook of cultural psychology* (pp. 323-345). New York: The Guilford Press.

Kincheloe, J. (2004). *Critical pedagogy primer.* New York: Peter Lang.

Ladwig, J.G. (2010). Beyond academic outcomes. *Review of Research in Education, 34*, 113-141.

Luke, A., Green, J., & Kelly, G.J. (2010). Introduction: What counts as evidence and equity? *Review of Research in Education, 34*, vii-xvi.

Lynch, P., & Moore, K. (2004). Adventures in paradox. *Australian Journal of Outdoor Education, 8*(2), 3-12.

McCarthy, M. (2010). Principal Mike McCarthy sustains a culture of collaboration. Schools that work: Project-based learning in Maine. www.edutopia.org/maine-project-learning-leadership-collaboration-innovation-video [February 15, 2011].

Miettinen, R. (2005). Object of activity and individual motivation. *Mind, Culture, and Activity, 12*(1), 52-69.

Priest, S., & Gass, M. (2005). *Effective leadership in adventure programming.* Champaign, IL: Human Kinetics.

Raiola, E. (2003). Communication and problem solving in extended field-based outdoor adventure education courses. *Journal of Experiential Education, 26*(1), 50-54.

Ravitch, D. (2010). *The death and life of the great American school system: How testing and choice are undermining education.* New York: Basic Books.

Schecter, B. (2011). "Development as an aim of education": A reconsideration of Dewey's vision. *Curriculum Inquiry, 41*(2), 250-266.

Seaman, J., & Nelsen, P.J. (2011). An overburdened term: Dewey's concept of *experience* as curriculum theory. *Education and Culture, 27*(1), 2-25.

Sheard, M., & Golby, J. (2006). The efficacy of an adventure education curriculum on selected aspects of positive psychological development. *Journal of Experiential Education, 29*(2), 187-209.

Smith, T., & Knapp, C. (Eds.). (2008). *Beyond Dewey and Hahn: Foundations for experiential education. Vols. 1 & 2.* Lake Geneva, WI: Raccoon Institute Publications.

Stremba, B. (2008). The four uses of outdoor adventure programming. In B. Stremba & C. Bission (Eds.), *Teaching adventure education theory* (pp. 99-102). Champaign IL: Human Kinetics.

Thorne, B. (2005). Unpacking school lunch time: Contexts, interaction, and the negotiation of difference. In C. Cooper (Ed.), *Developmental pathways through middle childhood: Rethinking contexts and diversity as resources* (pp. 63-87). Mahwah, NJ: Lawrence Erlbaum Associates.

Voyer, A. (2009). *Doing difference: Diversity training, diversity talk, and Somali immigrant incorporation in Lewiston, Maine.* Unpublished dissertation. Madison, WI: University of Wisconsin.

Wojcikiewicz, S.K., & Mural, Z.B. (2010). A Deweyan framework for youth development in experiential education: Perspectives from sailing instruction. *Journal of Experiential Education, 33*(2), 105-109.

Wortham, S. (2005). *Learning identity: The joint emergence of social identification and academic learning.* Cambridge, U.K.: Cambridge University Press.

Zink, R., & Burrows, L. (2008). "Is what you see what you get?" The production of knowledge in-between the indoors and the outdoors in outdoor education. *Physical Education and Sport Pedagogy, 13*(3), 251-265.

Are educational reform policies that stress standards and accountability compatible with pedagogical aims and practices in outdoor education?

NO Taken Over? Schooling and Outdoor Education

Tony Rea, PhD, freelance academic, Ivybridge, United Kingdom
Sue Waite, BA, research fellow at School of Education, Plymouth University, United Kingdom

In this issue, we argue that a policy of educational reform that places too great an emphasis on standards and accountability is generally incompatible with the pedagogical aims and practices of outdoor education. Outdoor adventure programs and outdoor centers, especially those in the public sector, cannot expect to be immune from wider societal and governmental influences and would not wish to be insulated from improvements. However, the impact of reform imposed from outside appears to have been so wide reaching that a landscape of colonization seems to have been created, thus devaluing and diminishing key pedagogical principles that underpin many outdoor and adventurous education programs.

We preface our argument with some definitions. We then argue our position, weaving within it explanation and examples of the fundamental concepts and values that underpin it. In doing so, we point out why we consider accountability and standards regimes problematic in outdoor education. Our argument then turns away from a somewhat pessimistic critique to outline how, if openness, fluidity, and distinctiveness of outdoor learning can be maintained and developed, adventure programming and outdoor learning can make a positive and unique contribution to the education of young people. We believe that this distinctive, constructive contribution derives from providing grounded experiential learning, opportunities for affective education and the development of autonomy, and the introduction of children to discourses and practices rarely encountered in schools. In conclusion, we reflect on what we see as the deceptive rationality of "effective" education policy and the potential dangers of accountability and performativity.

Performativity

Performativity (Lyotard, 1984; Usher, 2006) represents a critical perspective on modern measures of standards, accountability, and performance management. Currently, schools in the Western world are subject to increasing levels of audit, curricular control, pedagogic control through state-sponsored strategies, initiatives and best practice orthodoxies, surveillance through testing, self-review and inspection, the production of comparison tables, and the publication of inspectorial reports. These measures, intended to optimize efficient performance in education and prominent within the "schools effectiveness" culture, are what Foucault (1977, 1981) terms "technologies of control." The term "performativity" has been used in other senses in the literature; however, Ball's (2003, 2004) deployment of Lyotard's term is most pertinent to our argument. For Lyotard and Ball, performativity defines a culture where second-order practices (e.g., audit, surveillance, accountability, and so on) assume a greater importance than the first-order practices (in this case, learning) that they purport to enhance and thus become "a technology, a culture and a mode of regulation," (Ball, 2004, p. 143). Thus, what is currently measured is conformity to an imposed orthodoxy.

Policy makers are beginning to recognize problems with the current accountability system. In June of 2011, the new coalition government in England ordered an inquiry into whether primary schools in England drill their pupils rather than teach them. Au (2009) claims that high-stakes testing has had a similar effect in the United States. On the other hand, Finland, which is widely considered to have high-quality educational provision (e.g., OECD PISA results in Sahlberg, 2008, p. 53), samples only some schools with standardized tests each year as a tool to inform improvement confidentially, thus encouraging teachers to use their own values and professionalism in creating excellent learning opportunities for students rather than maintaining apparent performance of their school in league tables (Sahlberg, 2008). This is an excellent illustration of how sampled measurement can yield indicators to support schools' improvement without the negative narrowing effects on curricular and extracurricular enrichment of universal testing.

Performativity has become dominant in many areas of education in developed countries. Yet Gorard (2010) argues that school effectiveness models fail to calibrate with anything other than themselves, thus calling into question their usefulness for affecting change. Indeed, the complexity of such large-scale analyses is so fraught with potential errors that it begs the question as to whether they might in fact misdirect efforts for greater improvement and accountability. One might better achieve improvement and accountability through more situated interrogation of values and purpose and the subsequent qualitative evaluation of whether the practice is fit for those articulated purposes (Niikko and Havu-Nuutinen, 2009). We contend that even this might pose a challenge for outdoor learning, which has more fluid, experiential emergent outcomes. Loynes (2000) suggests that experiential learning should offer a source of *emerging* ideas rather than a place to prove others' ideas.

What Is Happening to Outdoor Learning?

Performativity acts negatively on outdoor learning in two principal ways: the colonization of the outdoors and the adoption of schooling orthodoxy, including learning goals, audit of children's performance, and the yoking of outdoor centers' practice to the national curriculum.

Colonization of the Outdoors

The British government's manifesto for education outside the classroom (Department for Education and Skills, 2006) presents an argument that all are entitled to outdoor learning and states, "learning outside the classroom is about *raising achievement* through an *organised*, powerful approach to learning in which direct experience is of prime importance" [our italics].

This quote, welcome as it was at a time when risk aversion was reducing the opportunities for outdoor education in the United Kingdom, demonstrates how the process of colonization works. The dominant discourse of mainstream schooling thus provides legitimate cognitive aims for outdoor education practices, but these practices originate from a recognition of the role of affect in human development. This is not to say that cognitive aims may not also be achieved by outdoor education.

However, we argue that outdoor learning can resist being overtaken by others' goals only by maintaining an ambiguity that refuses to be limited by measurement and accountability. Postcolonial theorist Spivak (1988, p. 205) suggests that the possibility of alternative purposes and practices in education can be created only through "strategic essentialism" of dominant and marginalized groups. However, this process of colonization may be largely subconscious and unnoticed. Said (1978) argues that postcolonial attitudes might work to reimpose colonial domination by unwittingly working with stereotypes and assumptions. A similar process may be at work in the relationships between national and local governments and those professionals working in and making use of outdoor centers.

Whatever the cause, strategic or unwitting, outdoor learning is prescribed as an entitlement for all but is also now defined in terms of school effectiveness and provides an example of how government policy and agenda are quick to colonize the language and territory of others. This move presents the risk that schooling orthodoxies may become embedded in the practices of outdoor centers. It completely fails to specify "achievement" of what or what role the "organization" of learning might have in supporting that achievement. The ways in which outdoor learning can make a difference to the future life chances of students, described earlier by Seaman and Rheingold, appear to support our analysis. Their examples of integrating standards and outdoor education center on social dimensions that, we wholeheartedly concur, do indirectly support academic goals. However, in a climate where standards testing focuses on aggregated but essentially individual scores, such social and emotional aspects of learning are often squeezed out of classrooms in favor of a direct focus on cognitive and academic outcomes. If academic outcomes also become the primary focus for outdoor centers, then a similar constriction of opportunities for social development may result.

Outdoor centers in the public sector are subject to inspections by the state apparatus for performance management, audit, and account that places massive importance on quantifiable outcomes, principally test results and improvement in national examinations. Yet, as Waite and Davis (2007) argue, the narrowness of current testing of parcels of defined knowledge fails to encompass broader benefits and affective outcomes of education (see, for example, Duckworth et al., 2009). In considering European responses to measurement of educational standards, Waite and Davis (2007) note:

It seems as though educational systems in our various nations may be circling on a merry-go-round of pedagogical approaches from whole-class instruction to child-centred and personalized learning with corresponding emphases on cognition and affect. As perceived academic standards rise and fall like the painted horses in the different countries, greater emphasis is placed on whole-class or whole-child approaches, often representing a move away from the prevailing system which is seen as failing to reach educational targets. (p. 259)

Furthermore, measurement in itself is problematic because it assumes a finished measurable state rather than a potential, which may be situated, complex, and fluid. Watson and Emery (2010) suggest that if outcomes are social and emotional, it makes no sense to impose normalized standards to quantify them. These kinds of outcomes can be evaluated only through assessment that acknowledges the shifting and socially constructed nature of outcomes. Thus, intuitive formative assessment, widely practiced by outdoor learning professionals in adaptive and personalized pedagogy that is responsive to the contingencies of different people and situations, might better reflect accountability than a spurious objective measurement. Despite research that has sought to define attributes of meaningful learning experiences in outdoor education programs (e.g., Taniguchi, Freeman, and LeGrand Richards, 2005), one could argue that the variation in the offerings and outcomes of different programs and centers makes a universal accountability system an impossible and, moreover, undesirable dream.

Even the voluntary sector has not escaped colonization. For example, the U.K. Scouts website states that taking part in a residential or day program will broadly meet the overall aims of the National Curriculum as well as some specific subject areas. This claim is followed by a list of 28 activities linked to key stages 2 and 3 (Scouts, 2010), and the scouts "teacher zone" includes links to the National Curriculum and Every Child Matters (Department for Education and Skills, 2003). Similarly, the website of the Duke of Edinburgh's Award Scheme includes reference to impact research and meeting U.K. government education agenda (Duke of Edinburgh, 2010). We might anticipate that the power and influence of governmental accountability regimes would be attenuated when funding and training are

separate and independent. However, colonization works not only directly through top-down guidance but also indirectly through expectations and values of the consumer within the system, expressing cultural values that permeate public life (Said, 1978).

Schooling Orthodoxy

A recent study of an English residential outdoor education center (Rea, 2011b) revealed a disturbing phenomenon. This research was undertaken at a residential outdoor education center in Southwest England that is maintained by an English local authority. This center accommodates approximately 30 children ages 9 to 11. Center activities include those undertaken on site (e.g., climbing, orienteering, outdoor games, problem solving) and others based in the local surroundings (e.g., beach adventure, canoeing, coasteering, farm visits, gorge walking, local history trails, moorland walks, mountain biking, river walks, surfing). The work and life of the center are more fully described and discussed elsewhere (e.g., Rea, 2008, 2011a, 2011b; Waite and Rea, 2007).

The center seemed to be adopting a number of schooling orthodoxies:

- Adopting the current schooling practice of overtly telling children what they are expected to learn.
- Auditing children's attainment against these intended outcomes.
- Tailoring activities to the school curriculum.

These moves tend to increase instrumental attitudes of staff and children toward demonstrating their achievement. This tension is implicit even in qualitative evaluative techniques. For example, Taniguchi, Freeman, and LeGrand Richards (2005) ask participants in a wilderness experience to write an essay about it. This free writing is then used to analyze key attributes or outcomes of the experience. Although the task is apparently open ended, by virtue of participation, the "correct" or expected responses to the event would be very clear to those taking part, thus perhaps leading the participants to conform to orthodoxy rather than give to authentic answers.

The Schooling Orthodoxy of Learning Goals

Hayes (2007) expresses concern about current best practice in schools of teachers who share their intended learning outcomes with children. Note the pronoun Hayes uses to draw attention to the practice of teachers defining learning. He argues that this learning is articulated in the adult-oriented language of the National Curriculum. As such it may make little connection with children's own understanding and agenda for learning. Although few objections can exist to teachers discussing with pupils what might be or has been learned, the rigidity of these practices may commit children to a passive role. The imposition of preordained learning objectives fails to recognize that meaning and therefore learning is filtered and constructed through multiple discourses to which children contribute as much as adults (Waite and Pratt, 2011). Furthermore, Watson and Emery (2010) contend in relation to social and emotional learning that "programmes and policies aimed at young people generate far more outcomes and benefits than are currently recorded and these are highly contested and often poorly recorded" (p. 768). Therefore, accountability that is based on flawed and misdirected measurement fails to recognize the extent and true value of programs.

Instructors at the center follow the current schooling orthodoxy of telling children what they are to learn by explaining learning goals to the children. The center staff ask teachers in schools to introduce these learning goals to the children the week before the visit. However, the narratives of both children and adults in the research (Rea, 2011b) indicate that other learning took place—learning that stands apart from the intended learning outcomes articulated to the children. Because respondents in these interviews chose not to mention the intended learning goals, we might conclude that other learning was more important to them.

Outdoor educators have long advocated an approach to learning that recognizes the cyclical nature of the learning process (e.g., Kolb, 1984) rather than linear approaches with discrete end points of knowledge. Sahlberg and Boce (2010) argue that "'knowledge tests' and assessments . . . rather than looking for growth in skills aptitudes or personal characteristics of students, almost solely address academic mastery or recalling knowledge" (p. 34). Unfortunately, although the authors advocate enhancing qualitative knowledge about teaching and learning in schools, they fail to acknowledge that this aim is often in dynamic tension with increasing quantitative data about student achievement. Furthermore, from young people's perspective, Quinn (2010) observed that those in jobs without training in the southwest of England frequently and spontaneously referred to nature as a place of value to them. However, this sustaining relationship with the outdoors is seldom acknowledged in the rush to "push them back from the outside into classrooms and training centers" (p. 76). This tends to support the argument that what is important and significant in young people's lives may not coincide with the educational goals championed by educational reform policies of standards and accountability. This also indicates a need for a broader understanding of accountability that addresses what learners deem important.

Auditing Children's Performance

Some centers also set out to track, or audit, children's performance against imposed learning goals. In a letter to schools, the head of one center explains that they are undertaking a long-term investigation to assess what impact a residential experience can have on its participants (Rea, 2011b). Schools are asked to select three children; the criteria for selection are left open to them. At the end of each day's activity, the center asks accompanying teaching staff to comment on the form on how the pupil has made progress against three of the learning goals that will be introduced to the group at the start of the course. "These are the times we live in!" is the rationale that the head of the center gives to the teachers.

Tracking progress and trying to demonstrate impact on a day-to-day basis are the discursive practices of performativity. However, if impact assessment was tailored to broader goals negotiated between the staff and students, this process could serve to reinforce shared values and motivation and have an educational purpose beyond generating questionable evidence for accountability. In a study of quality in Finnish preschools, Niikko and Havu-Nuutinen (2009) argue that multiple perspectives from stakeholders, including children, parents, and educators, are more helpful in determining quality than apparently objective measures because they incorporate communication, interaction, and participation. This process yielded information that showed that the social environment of Finnish preschools was the most important aspect for children, parents, and teachers.

Tailoring Outdoor Activities to the School Curriculum

The prominence of affective aspects of education in the Finnish study raises questions about why many outdoor centers try to link to the schools' curricular needs, perhaps appealing to those teachers who require taking pupils to a center to enhance their achievement on tests and exams. At one level, this is not problematic and may be of benefit, for evidence exists that participation in an outdoor adventure program may improve general academic performance in curriculum areas (e.g., Christie, 2004; Dismore and Bailey, 2005). Evidence also exists that studying geography and environmental sciences in the field promotes acquisition of procedural knowledge and subject-specific skills and enhances understanding of the subjects (e.g., Ewert, 2004; Knapp and Barrie, 2001; Nundy, 1999).

Yet, in a recent U.K. case study of assessment in an outdoor context, Edwards-Jones, Kelly, and Waite (2010) found that when primary school teachers began working with an outdoor center, they specified in fine detail the many ways the outdoor activities could be linked to the National Curriculum and tried to micromanage the outdoor program. However, following that initial visit, the teachers perceived that that level of school intervention actually reduced positive impacts on children. It interfered with the very qualities of the outdoor center that they valued: for the children, the freedom to explore nature and to develop inquiry and personal and interpersonal skills; and, for the teacher, the opportunity to observe the whole child. Their motivation for making these links seems to stem from school performativity culture leaking into outdoor education. Outdoor centers often now claim links to the curricula of schools to make their offerings more "salesworthy," but, in doing so, may lose sight of the affective values on which their work is founded.

Why Are Paradigms of Performativity Problematic?

We are concerned that efforts to align with paradigms of performativity may damage outdoor education. The primary school staff who participated in the assessment project (Edwards-Jones, Kelly, and Waite, 2010) now eschew using schoolroom assessment practices in the outdoor center. They relish instead the opportunity to see the child in the round and to discover both cognitive and affective capabilities that are invisible within the constrained performances inside the classroom (Waite and Davis, 2007). A head teacher (Rea, 2011b) who had been taking his school to the same outdoor center for 18 years witnessed an increasing willingness of the center to play the same game as schools, namely manufacturing explicit targets to satisfy a demand for evidence. Clearly, some schoolteachers are critical and skeptical about this shift to absorb centers within their own customs and practices. Furthermore, Collins, Reiss, and Stobart

(2010) report that high-stakes testing narrowed the teaching of science and that practical investigatory science was revived when testing was abolished in Wales in 2004.

Insufficient space exists within this argument to enumerate the myriad aims and practices that populate the rich field of outdoor education (see, for example, James and Henderson, 2007; Ward Thompson, Travlou, and Roe, 2006), but practical experiential learning is clearly a major feature. We contend that outdoor education centers contribute to learning principally through their distinctive aims and practices. Central to this argument is that previously unencountered practices and experiences are very important in enabling learning in outdoor education centers. So, despite a wide variety of aims, outdoor contexts tend to disrupt the expectations of roles and ways of working in schools, thereby creating new spaces to coconstruct pedagogy (Waite, 2010). In outdoor centers, the role of the adult is generally to facilitate learning rather than transmit knowledge (Thomas, 2010). Participants have more responsibility for learning because fostering independent learning is often a primary goal. The research of Ciani and colleagues (2010) has established that supporting student autonomy is more influential in motivating students to learn beyond the classroom than a focus on mastery goals, which are implicit in performativity approaches. It follows from this that the degree to which centers engage in facilitative pedagogies, in contrast to the majority of schooling in performance-driven cultures, is vital to their effectiveness in motivating lifelong learners.

Therefore, we suggest that staff at outdoor centers should be alert to colonization where it occurs and reflect on its potential effects. They might reconsider the use of long, sedentary plenary sessions in their delivery of health and safety advice and learning goals to children. Furthermore, learning goals should not be imported from schools but rather should be negotiated between those participating in the particular context of the place.

We suggest that adoption of schooling practices and orthodoxies by outdoor centers is inappropriate and that measurement against standards should be deferred until further research findings become available. We need to establish first whether outdoor centers and programs are indeed working well by virtue of their distinctive offer to schools and, second, precisely what they are working at or toward well. Furthermore, situated approaches to this research are vital to define the benefits of different programs so that any accountability applied is congruent with substantive aims and particular places (Lugg and Slattery, 2003). Based on existing research (e.g., Waite, 2010), one could consider shifting focus away from classroom discourse and cognitive outcomes and toward affective changes through enjoyment, challenge, and independent learning.

Policy makers in private and third-sector organizations should resist the temptation to imitate schooling discourses when developing their programs and pedagogy. Rather, they should explore the effectiveness of their programs and pedagogy in terms of their difference to schools. Evidence shows that, beneath the brittle surface of standards compliance, mainstream schooling itself harbors pockets of resistance and unaccounted-for intuitive practice (e.g., Wrigley, 2003, 2007). Teachers' personal values have always presented a counterbalance to received policy (Kirk and Macdonald, 2001), and, in situations where children are allowed greater freedom in their learning, a flowering of alternative or additional outcomes and larger promises for education may be fulfilled (Duckworth et al., 2009; Waite, 2010).

A Plea for the Place of Affect in Effective

We accept that notions such as accountability and effectiveness are apparently virtuous and therefore highly seductive. Who would argue against effectiveness in a broad and general sense? Who could suggest that public education should not be accountable? We too want "no child left behind" (U.S. Department of Education, 2006). We believe fervently that "every child matters" (Department for Education and Skills, 2003). Yet we think that this calls for a deeper, critical discussion of performativity. First, we need to develop a more complex but clearly articulated understanding of what it is that education should be held accountable for, and this implies a shared definition of the intended purposes of education, which are highly contested. Second, the current doctrine of "schools effectiveness" should be questioned in the light of this properly examined, values-based, morally sound conceptualization and application of accountability. The purposes of educational endeavor need to be very clear. Indeed, we contend that measurement of educational effectiveness that excludes socially just aims, such as developing all young people's potential for social and personal fulfillment, cannot be compatible with the fields of adventure programming and outdoor learning because these fields

are ultimately founded on precisely such affective principles.

Conclusion

In conclusion, we suggest that Jayson Seaman and Alison Rheingold's argument supports our own case regarding the powerful role of affect through experiential learning on mainstream education, but we advise considerable circumspection and caution in that school effectiveness strategies can deflect and distort outdoor and experiential learning pedagogies and purposes. A tendency to homogenize and increase uniformity across experiential learning provision would strike at the heart of its potential for creative flexibility to respond to local and situated needs.

References

Au, W. (2009). *Unequal by design: High stakes testing and the standardization of inequality*. Abingdon, U.K.: Routledge.

Ball, S. (2003). The teacher's soul and the terrors of performativity. *Journal of Educational Policy, 18*, 215-228.

Ball, S. (2004). Performativity and fabrications in the education economy: Towards the performative society. In S. Ball (Ed.), *The RoutledgeFalmer reader in sociology of education*. London: RoutledgeFalmer.

Christie, E. (2004). *Raising achievement through outdoor experiential learning? A case study of Scottish secondary school students*. Edinburgh, U.K.: Edinburgh University.

Ciani, K., Ferguson, Y., Bergin, D., & Hilpert, J. (2010). Motivational influences on school-prompted interest. *Educational Psychology, 30*(4), 377-393.

Collins, S., Reiss, M., & Stobart, G. (2010). What happens when high stakes testing stops? Teachers' perceptions of the impact of compulsory national testing in science of 11 year olds in England and its abolition in Wales. *Assessment in Education: Principles, Policy and Practice, 17*(3), 273-286.

Department for Education and Skills. (2003). *Green paper: Every child matters: Change for children*. Nottingham, U.K.: Department for Education and Skills Publications.

Department for Education and Skills. (2006). *Learning outside the classroom manifesto*. Nottingham, U.K.: Department for Education and Skills Publications.

Dismore, H., & Bailey, R. (2005). "If only": Outdoor and adventurous activities and generalised academic development. *Journal of Adventure Education and Outdoor Learning, 5*, 9-20.

Duckworth, K., Akerman, R., MacGregor, A., Salter, E., & Vorhaus, J. (2009). *Self-regulated learning: A literature review*. London: Institute of Education, Centre for Research on the Wider Benefits of Learning.

Duke of Edinburgh. (2010). Duke of Edinburgh's award scheme website. www.dofe.org [January 3, 2011].

Edwards-Jones, A., Kelly, O., & Waite, S. (2010). *Assessment of learning outdoors.* Unpublished analysis report. Plymouth, U.K.: University of Plymouth.

Ewert, A. (2004). The effect of outdoor experiential programs upon environment beliefs: Do they make a difference? *Research in Outdoor Education, 7,* 32-39.

Foucault, M. (1977). *Discipline and punish.* Harmondsworth, U.K.: Penguin.

Foucault, M. (1981). *The history of sexuality.* Harmondsworth, U.K.: Penguin.

Gorard, S. (2010). Serious doubts about school effectiveness. *British Educational Research Journal, 36,* 745-766.

Hayes, D. (2007). What Einstein can teach us about education. *Education 3-13, 35,* 143-154.

James, P.A., & Henderson, K.A. (2007). *Camps and nature report.* North Martinsville, IN: American Camp Association.

Kirk, D., & Macdonald, D. (2001). Teacher voice and ownership of curriculum change. *Journal of Curriculum Studies, 33*(5), 551-567.

Knapp, D., & Barrie, E.U. (2001). Content evaluation of an environmental science field trip. *Journal of Science Education and Technology, 7,* 55-65.

Kolb, D.A. (1984). *Experiential learning: Experience as a source of learning and development.* Englewood Cliffs, NJ: Prentice-Hall.

Loynes, C. (2000). The values of life and living: After all, life is right in any case. In P. Barnes (Ed.), *Values and outdoor learning.* Penrith, Cumbria, U.K.: Association for Outdoor Learning.

Lugg, A., & Slattery, D. (2003). The use of national parks for outdoor environmental education: An Australian case study. *Journal of Adventure Education and Outdoor Learning, 3*(1), 77-92.

Lyotard, J.-F. (1984). *The postmodern condition: A report on knowledge.* Manchester, U.K.: Manchester University Press.

Niikko, A., & Havu-Nuutinen, S. (2009). In search of quality in Finnish pre-school education. *Scandinavian Journal of Educational Research, 53*(5), 431-445.

Nundy, S. (1999). The fieldwork effect: The role and impact of fieldwork in the upper primary school. *International Research in Geographical and Environmental Education, 8,* 190-198.

Quinn, J. (2010). *Learning communities and imagined social capital: Learning to belong.* London: Continuum.

Rea, T. (2008). Alternative visions of learning: Children's learning experiences in the outdoors. *Educational Futures: e-journal of the British Education Studies Association, 2.*

Rea, T. (2011a). Outdoor centres. In S. Waite (Ed.), *Children learning outside the classroom: From birth to eleven* (pp. 149-151). London: Sage.

Rea, T. (2011b). *Wild Country Hall: Children's learning at a residential outdoor education centre.* Unpublished PhD thesis. Plymouth, U.K.: University of Plymouth.

Sahlberg, P. (2008). Rethinking accountability in a knowledge society. *Journal of Educational Change, 11*(1), 45-61.

Sahlberg, P., & Boce, E. (2010). Are teachers teaching for a knowledge society? *Teachers and Teaching. Theory and Practice, 16*(1), 31-48.

Said, E. (1978). *Orientalism.* Harmondsworth, U.K.: Penguin.

Scouts. (2010). Curriculum links. www.scouts.org.uk/cms.php?pageid=2436 [January 3, 2012].

Spivak, G.C. (1988). Subaltern studies: Deconstructing historiography. In G.C. Spivak (Ed.), *In other worlds: Essays in cultural politics* (pp. 197-221). London: Routledge.

Taniguchi, S.T., Freeman, P.A., & LeGrand Richards, A. (2005). Attributes of meaningful learning experiences in an outdoor education program. *Journal of Adventure Education and Outdoor Learning, 5*(2), 131-144.

Thomas, G. (2010). Facilitator, teacher, or leader? Managing conflicting roles in outdoor education. *Journal of Experiential Education, 32*(3), 239-254.

U.S. Department of Education. (2006). No Child Left Behind. www.ed.gov/nclb/landing.jhtml?src=pb [November 11, 2010].

Usher, R. (2006). Lyotard's performance. *Studies in Philosophy and Education, 25*(4), 279-288.

Waite, S. (2010). Teaching and learning outside the classroom: Personal values, alternative pedagogies and standards. *Education 3-13, 39*(1), 65-82.

Waite, S., & Davis, B. (2007). The contribution of free play and structured activities in forest school to learning beyond cognition: An English case. In B. Ravn & N. Kryger (Eds.), *Learning beyond cognition* (pp. 257-274). Aarhus, Denmark: Danish School of Education Press.

Waite, S., & Pratt, N. (2011). Theoretical perspectives on learning outside the classroom—Relationships between learning and place. In S. Waite (Ed.), *Children learning outside the classroom: From birth to eleven* (pp. 1-18). London: Sage.

Waite, S., & Rea, T. (2007). Enjoying teaching outside the classroom. In D. Hayes (Ed.), *Joyful teaching and learning in the primary school.* Exeter, U.K.: Learning Matters.

Ward Thompson, C., Travlou, P., & Roe, J. (2006). *Free-range teenagers: The role of wild adventure space in young people's lives.* Edinburgh, U.K.: Openspace: The Research Centre for Inclusive Access to Outdoor Environments.

Watson, D.L., & Emery, C. (2010). From rhetoric to reality: The problematic nature and assessment of children and young people's social and emotional learning. *British Educational Research Journal, 36*(5), 767-786.

Wrigley, T. (2003). *Schools of hope: A new agenda for school improvement.* Stoke on Trent, U.K.: Trentham.

Wrigley, T. (2007). *Another school is possible.* Stoke on Trent, U.K.: Trentham.

Controversial Issue 18

Are rational decision-making models the most effective method to train novice outdoor leaders?

Training and developing outdoor leaders are integral parts of the adventure programming industry. Professional preparation programs such as university academic programs, specialized outdoor schools, association certifications, and governmental certification schemes represent the various entities dedicated to preparing professional outdoor leaders. Curricula and training methods vary widely among organizations. However, one outdoor leadership competency—judgment and decision-making—is consistently recognized and accepted by the outdoor leadership community as an attribute that all outdoor leaders must possess. Making quality decisions as a professional outdoor leader requires extensive practice and experience. An early pioneer in the industry, Paul K. Petzoldt, placed judgment and decision-making at the center of his philosophy of the development of outdoor leaders. The current outdoor leadership literature firmly supports decision making as a foundational skill. Competency-based models routinely include judgment and decision making as critical skills. The overall emphasis and importance placed on this attribute drive the contemporary paradigm for outdoor leadership development.

Due to the enormous emphasis placed on this leadership competency, those who prepare professional outdoor leaders have a serious obligation to critically assess their training methods. Developing a novice leader's decision-making skills is a complex task. Are organizations that are in the business of training outdoor leaders taking this task seriously? Are training methods conducive to developing quality decision-makers? Are organizations following best practices when developing this critical leadership competency? These questions drive the current debate. Jack Drury, Bruce Bonney, and Shayne Galloway argue two fundamental viewpoints at the root of this discussion.

Drury and Bonney argue that rational decision making (RDM) is the most effective way to select and evaluate a course of action. They argue that RDM provides a superior methodology for training novice outdoor leaders. RDM constitutes a straightforward, simple process for those who lack fundamental skills. Many entry-level texts within the outdoor leadership profession use RDM models as logical starting points for developing judgment and decision-making competency in novice outdoor leaders. Others, such as the military and policy makers, find RDM models to provide a better-quality approach to structuring the decision-making process. Drury and Bonney are quick to point out weaknesses of the RDM approach but clearly make a case that, in the context of developing novice leaders, RDM is the most practical route.

Galloway takes the opposing stance and argues that rational decision-making methods do not fit the real-world context. He makes the case that RDM models are too artificial and mechanistic in nature. Galloway argues in favor of developing a trainee's cognitive abilities through naturalistic decision making (NDM). NDM and other macrocognitive functions take into account the actual context of a high-stress, high-stake leadership decision. Conversely, RDM serves only as a reflection tool once decisions are made.

This debate directly affects those in the business of training professional outdoor leaders. Professional certifications and organizational accreditations do not tend to mandate particular training methodologies or even provide direction concerning development of decision-making skills for novice leaders. The adventure programming industry would advance further if it could make progress on this issue.

Are rational decision-making models the most effective method to train novice outdoor leaders?

YES It's Natural to Be Rational

Jack Drury, cofounder of Leading E.D.G.E. LLC, Saranac Lake, New York, United States

Bruce Bonney, cofounder of Leading E.D.G.E. LLC, Norwich, New York, United States

We view the rational decision-making (RDM) model as a straightforward, logical, step-by-step framework for both guiding the selection of a course of action and assessing the quality of that action after the fact. In contrast, we see the naturalistic decision-making (NDM) model as a complex and sophisticated description of the actual mental and emotional processes of veteran decision-makers as they make their choices in the fast-moving, high-stakes environment of real life. The RDM model is more appropriate to use when working with novice decision-makers. We define RDM as a structured, step-by-step cognitive process that ensures that one gives due consideration to the relative merit of available options when making a decision. One can use a similar protocol to assess or reflect on the quality of past decisions.

Three fundamental ideas support our view. First, RDM is the most effective model to use when teaching novices because it constitutes a comprehensive intellectual framework for considering all the crucial elements necessary for making a quality decision and for systematically assessing the quality of the decision. Professions other than outdoor leadership rely heavily on the RDM model to produce quality decisions. The most effective public policies are generated by policy makers through a rational process (Davies, Nutley, and Smith, 2000; Everett, 2003; Sanderson, 2004). Policy makers work in a group context and assimilate massive amounts of evidence and options within a specified framework to make the best choice. As Kosseff (2003) explains, RDM in an outdoor context is most effective in a group situation in which a framework is needed to support the decision-maker. Whether one is developing effective public policy or making an outdoor leadership decision, a structured process provides systematic guidance to achieve a desired outcome. As an example, let's look at this very important argument point in a slightly different context. A beginning carpenter benefits when he or she has simple directions and a clear blueprint to follow when building their first toy chest for a kid's room. A novice decision-maker can benefit similarly when they use an intellectual blueprint such as the RDM model to guide their thinking.

Second, RDM is the most effective model to use when teaching novices because its straightforward simplicity is developmentally appropriate for the new learner. No experienced coach would start the training of a novice ice skater with an airborne triple salchow. The coach would instead start the student with a rudimentary exercise that is fundamental to ice skating (such as a figure 8) because it is developmentally appropriate for the skill level of the skater. When instructors use the RDM model to guide their students' thinking through the processes of brainstorming, filtering through feasible options, choosing options using relevant criteria, and evaluating results, they too are introducing fundamentals that are developmentally appropriate for a novice decision-maker.

Third, RDM is the most effective model for teaching novices because it provides a mechanistic process for drilling patterns of thought and action that must be developed in novices who lack the experience and internalized repertoire of the expert. Basketball, for instance, comprises the fundamentals of shooting, ball handling, passing, stance, positioning, and footwork in addition to the cognitive skills associated with game strategy and situational awareness. Like the ice-skating instructor, a basketball coach breaks down each fundamental into its simplest components so that players can perfect each part through constant repetition and drilling under increasingly challenging circumstances. We contend that the RDM model lends itself to a similar type of drill and practice that develops the capacity of novice decision-makers.

Keeping It Simple: Drill the Skill

We must make a few things clear regarding our professional point of view. All that follows in this discussion proceeds from our fundamental assumption that quality decision-making is a skill. By "skill" we mean that it is a capacity to bring about a desired outcome through the smooth execution of coordinated physical and intellectual processes that one learns and that one can develop over time with practice. To be sure, one's genetic inheritance and cultural context (intelligence, physical size, family background, and so on) play a role in the ultimate expression of our skills. Individuals clearly have different personal gifts, and no matter how hard one might train and persevere, only a few are destined to be world-class athletes, kayakers, or cooks. However, many of us can be *very good* athletes, kayakers, and cooks if we have a useful mental model of what "good" looks like in the skill area, understand the fundamentals that make up the skill, and get well-informed guidance and quality feedback as we gain experience practicing the skill. We do not see a significant difference between successful strategies for developing psychomotor skills and those for developing metacognitive skills. Whether it is navigation or decision making, the novice learner must understand the basics, drill the fundamentals, and practice putting them together as a whole.

Popular texts in the outdoor leadership field routinely use forms of RDM as a fundamental starting point to address decision-making skills. Drury and colleagues (2005) outline a classic RDM model in a lesson-plan format to train novice leaders. Graham (1997) outlines a risk–benefit model that describes a clear, user-friendly process for a novice learner. Kosseff (2003) articulates the weaknesses of RDM but also singles out significant strengths. Kosseff states that an analytic process "can be a valuable experience for the less-experienced group members as the various aspects of the decision are vocalized and discussed" (p. 121). Our proposition is supported by commonly used outdoor leadership texts written to educate the novice leader and our combined 75 years of experience as educators in the classroom, on the athletic field, and in the wilderness. Many of our points are based primarily on our practical experiences as teachers and coaches in the field. We believe that most professionals in the business of training novice outdoor leaders will relate to our practical perspective.

With those caveats in mind, this discussion centers on two related questions:

- To what extent is RDM or NDM more or less useful as a characterization of quality decision making?

- What are the implications of using one or the other of these models for teaching novices in the field?

Based on our understanding of NDM, we concede that NDM is no doubt a much more accurate description than is RDM of the actual thought process that experts use in complex, high-pressure, time-constrained situations. From our own professional experience, we know that seasoned decision-makers in any situation seem to intuitively grasp familiar patterns that might suggest successful strategies or solutions that have worked before. Clearly, the effective decisions that experts make under stress are much too fast and efficient to be the product of a process that is as linear and all-inclusive of possible options as that described in *The Backcountry Classroom* (Drury et al., 2005, p. 156). We readily concede this point.

It is important, however, to note the obvious. The brain of an expert in almost any field—outdoor leader, college basketball coach, airline pilot, and so on—possesses a tremendous advantage over that of a novice. Having "been there, done that" many times before, the expert's brain has well-established habits of mind and neural pathways that help him or her very quickly recognize familiar patterns in events and narrow the range of choices to a selection of options that they have used with success before. Dealing with circumstances that seem familiar, the expert brain copes with the pressure by using an internalized process that is highly efficient and effective. In other words, experts have both an internal framework for analyzing a situation (they have an organized way of thinking about situations and way of knowing what variables are important or not important, what information is credible or not credible, and so on) and a history of experiences from which to draw patterns of recognition and choices that let them function much better than other folks in stressful situations.

In short, experts have a repertoire. For them, the process of decision making is not a struggle because it is part of their professional being—intuitive, natural, and organic. Novices have no such repertoire (Fernandez, 2008; Westerman, 1991). The military recognizes the value of both rational decision-making processes and naturalistic decision-making processes and feels that each has its own strengths. They also recognize that the naturalistic approach requires two things: information and experience (Marr, 2001). Novice outdoor leaders have very little of either. Klein (1989), a military analyst, does not support the RDM model as an effective process for experienced decision-makers. However, he points out that the RDM model "is more helpful for novices who lack an experience base and for seasoned decision-makers confronting novel situations" (p. 61).

Novice decision making is often a struggle: painful, laborious, energy consuming, confused, and inconclusive. Lacking an overarching framework of understanding, when facing a decision novices typically do not know what to think about, how to distinguish between important and unimportant variables, what to look or listen for as evidence, or how to separate truth from fiction, especially when confronted with information that is incomplete or contradictory. Because their personal experience is usually very limited, they discern few patterns in the cavalcade of events streaming before them. Like a 13-year-old falling in love for the first time, everything seems brand new, unfamiliar, and a touch overwhelming. Even if they have experienced something similar before, they do not have a menu of options from which to snatch a solution. Lacking internal resources, the novice often looks for external support or group consensus to help them make a judgment. For instance, how many times on an expedition have we seen a leader of the day (LOD) inappropriately put up for a vote a decision that she should make herself (Martin, Schmid, and Parker, 2009)?

The conundrum for leadership development and the heart of this debate is how to best guide our future outdoor leader along the winding trail from novice to expert. This is where we see the RDM model as useful. Note that we say useful rather than technically accurate. NDM is clearly more technically accurate than RDM as a sophisticated description of expert decision making. However, in our view, RDM is a more useful model of quality decision making for novices to study because it provides two things they desperately need: a conceptual framework or mental model that is simple enough to grasp, and procedures that are mechanistic enough to replicate and perfect through practice (Graham, 1997).

In our view, it is clear that to learn how to do something complex (play basketball, write a novel, lead a mountaineering expedition) one needs a mental model. A mental model is the big mental picture that helps a person grasp an understanding of the unique characteristics of the activity (what makes basketball different from writing or leading an expedition) and how to do the activity (how to dribble, pass, shoot, play defense). To be truly helpful, a model for beginners must be simple and developmentally appropriate for the learner to access yet be faithful to the essential truths or principles of the more sophisticated big picture we hope the learner will eventually acquire. For example, when outdoor educators teach novices how to use a map

and compass, most start by asking students to make broad interpretations of the topography rather than complex ones and by challenging students to find their way about in safe and nonthreatening environments. This introductory activity is obviously rudimentary and in no way approaches the complex work of map and compass use in the deep woods far from the trailhead. Nonetheless, the essentials of knowledge and skill are there.

Its very simplicity makes the RDM model attractive as a teaching tool for novices. Although NDM is more accurate, we think most would agree that, compared with the RDM model, the internalized and organic processes of experts described in the NDM model are more complex to understand, difficult to explain to the uninitiated, and, most importantly, hard for a novice to replicate through drill and practice. In contrast, the RDM model is relatively straightforward, structured, and linear in its procedure. It is just what a novice needs to get started—a mechanistic approach to a complex skill (i.e., one that is prescriptive and relies on external protocols, standard operating procedures, defined tasks, checklists of things to think about, and so on). In short, RDM is a mental model that the novice learner can embrace and mimic until his or her maturity, sophistication, and breadth of experience create a personal repertoire worthy of the challenge.

Teaching Strategies With RDM

Whether in the classroom or in the field, we approach teaching as constructivists. We seek to meet students where they are intellectually and emotionally; tap into their prior experience; provide them with clear and comprehensible models, examples, and criteria by which to process their experience; engage them in the process of thought with challenging questions and experiences; and provide them with constant and relevant feedback (Brooks and Brooks, 1993). We have found the RDM model useful for achieving all of these ends.

Almost all of our students come to us with some familiarity with the RDM approach to decision making, even though they may not be aware of this familiarity until we point it out to them. Examine the science curriculum of any reputable public or private school system in the country and we are quite confident that the scientific method of inquiry will be prominently featured as a key area for study. We are not arguing that school systems do a great job of helping students internalize this habit of thought, so fundamental to Western civilization, beyond its recitation in the next exam. Nonetheless, the scientific method is extremely close to the RDM model in both substance and process, and many students find it easy to make the connection.

Similarly, whenever we debrief a decision-making process, we invariably revisit every one of the considerations outlined in the RDM model: "Did you clearly understand the decision you faced? Did you consider all the factors bearing on the decision (time, space, resources, and so on)? What information did you have and was it reliable? Did you consider the available options and their plausible consequences?" Students who have connections to the military, emergency health care systems, or law-enforcement agencies recognize that the types of questions we ask are similar to those inquiries posed in the "after action" reports or case reviews in other fields and organizations. In essence, whenever we debrief an experience or event using the questions or protocols of the RDM model, we are reinforcing it as a model by which to assess the quality of a decision. The bottom line is, if you debrief or reflect on your decision making, you are using RDM.

Reflective journaling, which has always been a major component in our teaching toolbox, is a means of revealing the thought processes of students as they review their own decision making or that of their peers. The structured and linear list of considerations and the need to process several options as featured in RDM have provided students with clear guidelines for thinking and writing about their insights. Many students who have difficulty organizing their thoughts have found the clearly organized structure and its relatively simple graphic representation in *The Backcountry Classroom* (Drury et al., 2005) to be helpful.

The RDM model is also tailor made for novices who require checklists to help them think their way through a problem or plan for future action. We are confident that almost any instructor can easily make the link between RDM and the airline industry, which believes that a systematic review of what to think about before takeoff increases the odds of a successful flight. Similarly, NASA uses exhaustive checklists to inform the decision-making process throughout every segment of a mission (Cass, 2005). One only needs to watch the movie *Apollo 13* to see how NASA, under the most extreme constraints of time and resources, used institutionalized checklists and protocols to force a review of every conceivable option to work toward a life-saving solution that would bring the astronauts home

alive. We contend that using the RDM model as a template to help a novice practice and develop his or her own internalized checklist of what to think about before launching into an important decision serves a similarly practical purpose.

We can see how all these considerations come into play when examining how we, the authors, have used the RDM model on the 33-day Wilderness Education Association expeditions we have instructed. Usually, we start asking students right away to identify some of the decisions they are making. In some of the early daily debriefings, we ask them to place these decisions along a continuum from very simple to very complex and their reasons for placing them so. We also ask them to reflect on their decisions in their journals and to analyze the factors that led them to their final choices.

At some point in the first 10 days of the expedition, we introduce RDM as a concept and illustrate the components of RDM in a graphic format. As the expedition proceeds, we constantly encourage the LOD to reference the RDM model almost as a checklist as he or she thinks through the decisions throughout the day. We also, of course, use the RDM model as a reference while debriefing the decisions of an LOD. Admittedly, at times this feels cumbersome and almost like a fill-in-the-box approach. Yet this structure seems to give comfort to those students who are not used to thinking for themselves. And, most importantly, it works!

On one expedition, a group wrestled its way, off trail, through a typically dense Northeastern spruce fir forest that covered the slopes of the 4,500-foot (1,372 m) peak it hoped to summit. The LOD had assigned a scout and was working closely with her to make sure the group was heading in the correct direction. The group was struggling through incredibly thick terrain and walking in the brook because it was the path of least resistance. The brook abruptly split into two branches. The scout and LOD were unable to determine their exact location from the map or see any hint in the mass of green before them to suggest which path to take. The LOD decided to send a lone scout up each branch of the brook. The LOD neglected to tell each scout how far to go (in either time or distance) or what to look for. One scout completed his assignment in 10 minutes and returned breathlessly to the group with little to share. The other scout took almost an hour to finish his task. The group became concerned as the minutes ticked away. The scout eventually returned just as the LOD was considering whether to send out a search party. The scout had clearly taken his assignment seriously and reported back with a wealth of valuable and detailed information. It came as no small shock to him when, rather than expressions of appreciation for the thoroughness of his report and sincere effort, he was greeted with frustration and comments that were almost hostile in tone from some group members who asked, "Where the hell have you been?"

As instructors, we anticipated that the debriefing of this event the following morning could include some extremely valuable, though potentially emotional, teachable moments. In preparation, we asked the students to reflect on the decision making of the day in their journals and use the RDM model to guide their thinking. Further, we asked them to come to the debriefing prepared to share their thoughts and defend their conclusions. The conversation that ensued was lengthy, spirited, and emotionally draining. It was also extremely valuable, in large measure because we had the formality of the RDM model to prompt an examination of many assumptions, misunderstandings, and issues that may well have gone unexplored otherwise. No doubt many of the students on that trip—as do we—still carry with them valuable lessons learned about decision making because we used the RDM model to process that day.

Conclusion

As the reader has no doubt discerned, our perspective tilts toward "nuts and bolts" practical. "What will work for the student and instructor in the field?" is the question that guides our choice of strategy. Although the RDM model has its shortcomings as an elegant and sophisticated expression of the latest understanding of expert decision making, it nonetheless is true to the essential elements of quality decision making. Like the trusted stick-shift vehicle sitting in the garage, it is not fast, sophisticated, or stylish, but you can get behind its wheel, learn how to drive in it, and, with some focused practice, take yourself almost anywhere you want to go.

References

Brooks, J.G., & Brooks, M.G. (1993). *In search of understanding: The case for constructivist classrooms.* Alexandria, VA: Association for Supervision and Curriculum Development.

Cass, S. (2005). Apollo 13, we have a solution: Rather than hurried improvisation, saving the crew of Apollo 13 took years of preparation. http://spectrum.ieee.org/aerospace/space-flight/apollo-13-we-have-a-solution/0 [September 22, 2011].

Davies, H.T.O., Nutley, S.M., & Smith, P.C. (Eds.). (2000). *What works?: Evidence-based policy and practice in public services.* Portland, OR: The Policy Press.

Drury, J.K., Bonney, B.F., Berman, D., & Wagstaff, M.C. (2005). *The backcountry classroom: Lessons, tools and activities for teaching outdoor leaders.* 2nd ed. Helena, MT: Globe Pequot.

Everett, S. (2003). The policy cycle: Democratic process or rational paradigm revisited? *Australian Journal of Public Administration, 62*(2), 65-70.

Fernandez, A. (2008). Your trading brain: Expert or novice. www.sharpbrains.com/blog/2008/06/05/your-brain-on-trading-101 [September 22, 2011].

Graham, J. (1997). *Outdoor leadership: Technique, common sense and self-confidence.* Seattle: The Mountaineers.

Klein, G.A. (1989). Strategies of decision making. *Military Review,* May, 56-64.

Kosseff, A. (2003). *AMC guide to outdoor leadership.* Boston: Globe Pequot Press.

Marr, J.J. (2001). The military decision making process: Making better decisions versus making decisions better [monograph]. Fort Leavenworth, KS: United States Army Command and General Staff College School of Advanced Military Studies.

Martin, B., Schmid, D., & Parker, M. (2009). An exploration of judgment and decision making among novice outdoor leaders: A dual-processes approach. *Journal of Outdoor Recreation, Education and Leadership, 1*(1), 38-54.

Sanderson, I. (2004). Getting evidence into practice: Perspectives on rationality. *Evaluation, 10*(3), 366-379.

Westerman, D.A. (1991). Expert and novice teacher decision making. *Journal of Teacher Education, 42*(4), 292-305.

Are rational decision-making models the most effective method to train novice outdoor leaders?

NO Macrocognition: A Naturalistic Approach to Outdoor Leader Development

Shayne Galloway, PhD, lecturer, school of physical education, University of Otago, Dunedin, New Zealand

Contemporary outdoor leader degree programs and outdoor leadership schools need to critically question their curricula and methods for developing a leader's decision-making process. Embedded within these curricula and programs are untested assumptions regarding decision making that rely on outdated and wrongly applied theoretical perspectives that run contrary to the findings of empirical research focused on how professionals actually make decisions and use their judgment.

To me, this argument is straightforward. The classical and rational decision-making (CRDM) models focus on how optimal decisions are made statistically and in laboratories rather than on how they are made in real-world contexts. These models assume that the decision-maker is completely rational (none of us are) and uses an orderly search pattern to analyze all available options in an unbiased fashion (few of us can actually do this) and that all the necessary information and time is available (which it never is). It prescribes a sequence of problem identification, development of criteria for comparing all available options, identification and evaluation of all the options, the selection of the best option—a process that is developed for laboratory studies and economic decisions and that is antithetical to wilderness leadership experience. Rather than impose an artificial and mechanical system on trainee outdoor leaders, I propose that we, as educators, help them develop their own innate cognitive abilities within a richly nuanced professional training context. To support my argument I draw extensively on theory related to macrocognition, which Cacciabue and Hollnagel (1995) define as "the role of cognition in realistic tasks, that is, in interacting with the environment" (p. 57).

Why Take a Macrocognitive Approach?

The study of naturalistic decision making (NDM) originated as an effort to understand how profes-

sionals "make decisions under conditions of uncertainty and time pressure that preclude any orderly effort to generate and evaluate sets of options" (Kahneman and Klein, 2009, p. 516). Instead of exhaustively generating multiple options—the expected finding of the early research—the experienced professionals "usually generated only a single option, and that was all they needed" (p. 516). These operators relied on a depth of pattern recognition provided by their real and virtual experience to identify a plausible option. The operators evaluated the option by mentally simulating it to determine whether it would work in the current situation. If the option seemed appropriate, they would try it; if it had flaws, they would adapt it; and if it could not be adapted easily, they would shift to the next most plausible option. This process, known as progressive deepening (de Groot, 1946/1978) or satisficing (Simon, 1957), has been identified in outdoor leaders in terms of the serial processing of options (Boyes and O'Hare, 2003) and the influence of only a few elements of the situation (Galloway, 2007).

We must acknowledge that CRDM and NDM arise from separate theoretical and applied perspectives and that this has important implications for the field of outdoor leadership. CRDM was developed to help understand decision error and nonoptimal decision making, often in economic or clinical settings without time stress, high stakes, or other complexities; this renders it unusable by experts in the field. Martin, Schmid, and Parker (2009) acknowledge this limitation in research conducted during a Wilderness Education Association National Standards course, in which participants stated that they would have made decisions differently had they been leading an actual trip (p. 52). This implies that the members of the class brought with them sufficient experience to be able to recognize the static and artificial limitations of the CRDM model. Furthermore, Martin, Schmid, and Parker (2009) suggest that the use of dual-process cognition is voluntary, whereas the literature suggests that these processes are innate and involuntary (Kahneman and Klein, 2009).

I argue that we should free ourselves from considering CRDM as a decision-making method in the field of outdoor leadership. Instead of aiding the development of judgment, CRDM hinders it by raising unrealistic, counterintuitive expectations that if actually practiced—by anyone—would result in far more accidents and deaths, far less achievement of program goals, and ultimately a diminished, marginalized outdoor leadership profession. Zakay and Wooler (1984) estimate that methods such as CRDM cannot be faithfully and effectively used in less than 30 minutes, a consideration that eliminates most decisions made by outdoor leaders. Klein (2009) points to a distinct lack of evidence that "these analytical methods help people make better decisions, or that training in formal decision making results in better decision performance" (p. 86). Instead of making decisions by generating several options and comparing them to choose the best one, Klein (2009) observes that "good decision-makers use their experience to recognize an effective option and evaluate it through mental simulation" (p. 91).

When we talk about developing judgment and decision making in outdoor leaders, we often fail to acknowledge that judgment and decision making are embedded in a professional context with a repertoire of practice (Seaman and Coppens, 2006), ethical frameworks (Mitten, 2002), and adaptive expertise (Tozer, Fazey, and Fazey, 2007). This context defines what we accept as an expert. Shanteau (1992) provides an operational definition of experts as "those who have been recognized within their profession as having the necessary skills and abilities to perform at the highest level" (p. 255). His review of the literature indicates that many studies that are meant to explore differences between experts and novices in fact investigate the difference between novice and naïve individuals. The CRDM literature emphasizes expertise in terms of optimal decisions based on maximum utility (de Groot, 1970) or those that adhere to a statistical efficiency standard that is not available to outdoor leaders—of any level of expertise—in the field.

Based on Shanteau's (1992) research, Kahneman and Klein (2009) coined the term "fractionated expertise" to describe professional domains where professionals display genuine expertise in some areas of their practice but not in others. Experience in outdoor leadership crosses many domains of expertise. Generally, outdoor leaders operate in complex, inherently risky environments that involve participants, nature (usually), and programming or curricular goals. They must navigate challenging physical environments, maintain a high degree of psychological and physical safety for those involved, and achieve the ends for which the program is designed. The field of outdoor leadership spans the complete range of outdoor and adventure recreation activities and natural environments as well as the recreational, educational, and therapeutic domains of expertise. Very few, if any, individuals achieve mastery in all these domains of knowledge, skill, and ability.

Although a profession with such a scope of operation may seem unique, many other occupations operate in naturalistic environments: those with ill-structured problems, uncertain and dynamic environment, shifting or competing goals, action–feedback loops, time stress, high stakes, multiple players, and organizational goals and norms (Klein, 1998). Research in NDM and outdoor leadership supports the applicability of NDM to the field in terms of training and development (Beare and Lynch, 2005; Galloway, 2002) and the complexity of judgment in the field (Boyes and O'Hare, 2003; Galloway, 2007). I am aware of no evidence that the use of CRDM models improves the decision making of outdoor leaders at any level of expertise.

An important premise for this argument is that the novice outdoor leader does not operate alone or without at least adequate supervision and support. The literature on NDM and macrocognition focuses on professional environments, and one can only conclude that placing inexperienced outdoor leaders alone in inherently risky field settings will result in tragedy sooner rather than later. Although I argue against a prescribed, ritualistic reduction of a contextual situation into a spectrum of options and their component values, I do not propose depending people into situations with which they are not reasonably prepared to cope. Sink-or-swim pedagogy falls outside the bounds of credible outdoor leadership education.

However, our goal should be to develop the ability of novice outdoor leaders to think and act as professionals and to rely on their innate human abilities to learn, use available recourses, and adapt with a high degree of confidence. I propose a macrocognitive approach such as that proposed by Klein and colleagues (2003). Macrocognition operates via the following functions: NDM, sense making and situation assessment, planning, adaptation and replanning, problem detection, and coordination. The processes of mental simulation and storyboarding, maintaining common ground, developing mental models, managing uncertainty, managing attention, and turning leverage points into courses of action support and develop these functions to a professional level. Development of the processes of macrocognition enables the appropriate use and development of the functions of macrocognition. Fortunately, our classroom makes available vast opportunities for the development of both, and, in fact, we already take advantage of these in the field.

Novice outdoor leaders do not struggle to make decisions in the field because they lack a process or model for making decisions. They struggle because they do not have the mental models, rules of association, sense of typicality, and so on associated with the environments in which they operate. By suggesting that CRDM offers a better way to make decisions, trainers influence outdoor leaders at the beginning of a career to ignore or devalue their naturally evolved cognitive and affective processes rather than to develop these innate abilities into a competence in which the outdoor leader can be reasonably confident. Martin, Schmid, and Parker (2009) state that rational decision-making models "provide basic frameworks for initially learning and practicing judgment and decision making," but they may overreach in claiming that the use of NDM and—arguably—macrocognition is a choice that one can make; evidence indicates that it is an innate process. Furthermore, the basic framework they suggest does not align with the cognitive processes observed to be naturally used by a wide array of professionals in contexts very similar to those of outdoor leaders.

NDM and Macrocognition Versus CRDM

The macrocognitive approach relies on recognition-primed decision making (RPD) as its functional theory. Klein and colleagues (2003) developed RPD around four main constructs: prototypicality, situation assessment, singular evaluation, and mental simulation.

- Prototypicality refers to the normalcy of the situation and operates on the schemata and rules of association that an individual invests in an object or event based on his or her experience. Recognition of a prototypical event primes the cognitive space with the relevant expectancies related to that prototype.

- Situation assessment is the recognition of elements in the perceptual environment (e.g., students, rope, 10-meter cliff, and so on), the value and relationships of these objects or events in the current context, and the mental projection of what will likely occur next (Endsley, 1995).

- Professionals tend to rely on singular evaluation of the most likely viable option and will attempt to make that option work before discarding it rather than attempt to fairly weigh all possible options.

- Mental simulation refers to the projection of events into the future in a predictive sense.

RPD, in turn, operates within what psychologists refer to as the dual-system approach. Evans (2008) provides a lengthy analysis of research into this approach. Generically, two major cognitive systems (or sets of systems) have emerged: type 1 (intuitive) processes (which include fast, effortless, and unconscious cognition related to the automaticity of recognition or learned behaviors such as driving a car) and type 2 (reflective) processes (which include slow, effortful, and conscious cognition that involves working memory and its limitations). Linkages exist between these processes such that type 2 (reflective) processes can move to type 1 (intuitive processes); consider the effort involved with learning to drive a car compared with the effort of driving a car after having learned. Conversely, type 1 (intuitive) processes shift to type 2 (reflective) processes in cases in which the situation is not recognized or is novel enough to emerge into conscious deliberation. These processes occur across the range of human experience, may not rise to the level of conscious thought, and form the basis of the macrocognitive argument that individuals innately move from a form of analysis to intuition as they become familiar with the context. These processes reduce the cognitive load, thereby freeing resources for other, perhaps less familiar, tasks.

Singular Evaluation Versus All Available Options

A critical distinction between NDM and CRDM exists in terms of the number of options considered and the manner in which they are evaluated. NDM relies on the consideration of the singular evaluation of options (serial processing), and at times the concurrent consideration of a few options, using both intuition and analytical deliberation. The CRDM model stipulates the concurrent consideration of all available options in a completely analytical fashion without any use of intuitive faculties. An early study of decision making in naturalistic environments by Klein, Calderwood, and Clinton-Cirocco (1988) found that novices and experts in high-risk, time-pressured contexts were "roughly equally likely to deliberate about options" (p. iv); experts relied approximately equally on serial and concurrent processing and novices relied exclusively on concurrent processing. The important distinction here lies in what they deliberated about rather than how many options were considered. Experts thought more about situational aspects of the decision problem, created novel solutions, used more imagery in their process, and spent more time thinking about future contingencies. Novices, on the other hand, deliberated more about how to implement the decision options and their timing. These professionals indicated a "strong preference or initial impulse to act in a given way, and deliberation involved momentarily considering whether this choice was workable in the given situation" (p. 24). Participants in this study considered no more than two options 97 percent of the time; this contradicts the exhaustive consideration of all available options that is stipulated by CRDM.

Demystifying Intuition

Intuition is a critical component of macrocognition. However, CRDM ignores intuition or devalues it as being too mystical to be used. "Intuition is nothing more and nothing less than recognition. The situation has provided a cue: This cue has given the expert access to information stored in memory, and information provides the answer" (Simon, 1992). This definition aligns well with Evans' (2008) conceptualization of type 1 (intuitive) processes as automatic, involuntary, and effortless. Intuition in a profession differs from guessing, however. Kahneman and Klein (2009) stipulate several conditions that must be met in order for a reliance on intuition to be genuinely skilled under the RPD model. The decision-making environment must be sufficiently regular and provide valid cues, and the outdoor leader must have sufficient time to learn those cues.

The activities and natural environments in which outdoor leaders operate often do provide regular and valid cues. For example, one can assimilate reasonably quickly the technical, social, environmental, and programmatic cues associated with "rock climbing site," "high-ropes course," or "class 2 rapid." Apprenticing and mentorship in such environments should guide the time the novice interacts and practices with these cues and environments, and should the truly novel happen—as

it does at times—the supervisor is there to help the developing outdoor leader make meaning out of the situation (e.g., a Vygotskian zone of proximal development).

Evans (2010) provides us with a structural model of the interplay between intuition and reflection that he describes as default–interventionist. The "rapid type 1 (intuitive) process provides a quick default solution to a problem, which may either be accepted or intervened upon with explicit type 2 reasoning. When such intervention occurs, the default intuition may (or may not) be overridden" (p. 314). Evans cites neural-imaging evidence that suggests that the brain "appears to detect conflict when intuitive and reflective processes would deliver different judgments and social-neuroscience research would suggest that distinct neural systems are responsible for implicit and explicit social judgments and that [intuitive processes] are inhibited when [reflective processes] take control."

Clearly, novice outdoor leaders do not have the depth of experience to have as well-developed mental models, prototypes, and other cognitive structures as experts in the field. Novices take longer to arrive at a conclusion and ponder more elements of a situation and may be more analytical in their deliberation. Novice outdoor leaders do not completely lack prior knowledge; the term for that is "naïvety" (Shanteau, 1992, p. 255). As well, in many areas of task performance, experts do no better than novices in making decisions (Shanteau, 1992). These include tasks with dynamic stimuli; decisions about behavior; and situations in which experts disagree on stimuli, problems are less predictable, few errors are expected, tasks are unique, feedback is unavailable, only subjective analysis is possible, the problem cannot be broken down, and decision aids are rare (p. 259). It is also possible to have all the experience in the world and never rise to the level of expert. Novice outdoor leaders need to gain experience within a structure that best enables them to develop mental models, perceptual skills, sense of typicality, routines, and declarative knowledge in the environment in which they will be used professionally. Regardless of where one is on the path to expertise, the same cognitive structures support us all.

Beyond Decision Making to Education

The macrocognitive approach also closely aligns with the experiential learning models (e.g., Kolb, 1984) that practitioners in the field rely on. The action–reflection interactions that these models imply are meant to be situated in authentic environments and involve the whole person as a learner as well as the complex contexts in which they occur. So, what should decision-making training for outdoor leaders look like from a macrocognitive philosophy? I have written before (Galloway, 2002) that training for naturalistic settings should include the task features commonly found therein: ill-structured problems, heavy workload, time stress and high stakes, and multiple players and organizational norms, as recommended by Means and colleagues (1993). But beyond this statement that training should be as realistic and authentic as possible, what other implications exist for developing judgment in outdoor leaders? Crandall, Klein, and Hoffman (2006) recommend that the cognitive landscape be taken into account in that cognition is goal-directed behavior and that individuals use their prior knowledge differently across the range of experience. The features of the situation itself, the nature of the challenge, and the tools available are vital considerations, as are the team members who share in the task and the organizational constraints that are in play at the time.

Beare and Lynch (2005) make a very convincing argument for using NDM rather than CRDM in training outdoor leaders. They suggest using methods such as simulation, reflection, apprenticeships, decision aids (e.g., mnemonics), and storytelling to reinforce the "mental simulation, pattern recognition, and mental organization of experience-based knowledge" (p. 216) required for the selection of the most viable option in outdoor leader judgment as outlined by Klein and colleagues' (2003) RPD model. This suggestion is in direct opposition to the mechanistic analysis of all possible options and a cost-benefit analysis embodied by the CRDM.

In addition to these instructional techniques, we can use think-aloud protocols (Ericsson and Simon, 1993) to make the trainer's thought process available to the student. We can use the premortem technique (Klein, 2009, p. 63), in which students are asked to imagine that the event has already occurred and that their problem-solving strategy has failed and are then asked to list all the reasons it could have failed. I have used both these methods to very good effect in training rock climbers. In fact, I have discovered that the most revealing question to ask an outdoor leader-in-training is, "What's wrong with this climbing anchor?" Before posing this critical question, I use think-aloud in every step of the process, from appropriate site selection to the placement of each piece of gear to the final

weighting of the entire construction. I have gone through the premortem process while thinking aloud as well and through this process made my tacit knowledge and mental models available to the student. Using these techniques routinely, I am able to see whether the students understand.

Facilitation of reflection while in realistic situations also supports this model. Teachable moments are a beautiful example of dual-process cognition being used as both a decision-making tool and a pedagogical device. Paul Petzoldt described this mechanism as the grasshopper method, in which an educator recognizes a situation that has bearing on the curriculum or program and takes a moment to anchor the situation in the minds of the students so that all have this point of reference for later discussion (Wagstaff and Cashel, 2001). To me, the interesting question is what brings to the instructor's mind the opportunity to grasshopper and how they determine its merit. It has been my experience that these opportunities arise from intuition, but consideration of them—their relevance to the journey, their potential educational impact, and so on—occurs with reflection. This also aligns with Klein and colleagues' (2003) pattern matching and mental simulation.

The reason the grasshopper method is so powerful is that we cannot know to a substantive degree what our students know and where their experience has taken them. We can test, we can generalize, and we can assume, but we have not walked in their shoes and we cannot be sure what experiences they draw on. The grasshopper method isolates a shared moment in time and space in which we as instructors can frame a known contextual situation for students as a point of reference and use that situation to integrate an important—and known—pattern into their developing understanding (e.g., mental models). We may encourage them to generalize from the situation and in turn point out others like it. If we dispense with considering only the rational side and embrace intuition as well, the grasshopper method allows us to ask in that moment questions such as "what are your instincts telling you now?" and "how do you feel about the situation?" and bring those implicit influences into the light, where they can be engaged and critiqued in a professional context as acceptable or unacceptable intuitive judgments. Keep in mind that experts are just as susceptible to poor intuition as novices when their assessment of the situation is flawed.

If I were to try to faithfully apply CRDM in any of these contexts, each student would be required to break down the situation in terms of its components and objectively analyze the strengths and weaknesses of each piece in turn by a preset criteria, generate lists of cost–benefit relationships for a range of possible applications for the situation, and then determine which would be best suited to the context. CRDM requires these steps each time it is used, and this process would take an inordinate amount of time to complete, even when the best choice is obvious to all. The outcome is also significantly different. In using CRDM I would be able to see the student's analytical ability to determine the optimal anchor without time pressure or risk of loss, but I would not be able to observe their naturally existing cognitive process and interact with them in an educative fashion. There would be no place for discussion of how the situation feels to the student, what their gut is telling them, or even that they have an intuition to follow, which CRDM is meant to ignore. Teachable moments could stretch to hours, and attempting such a discussion midway up a multipitch route one-on-one would be untenable or dangerous, potentially moreso with a larger group of beginning climbers at ground level.

I concede the point that these techniques are used currently and with good effect; however, my assertion is that we are using them for the wrong reasons. Rational decision-making models are unrelated to these techniques—there is no place for a gut feeling within the CRDM framework. In this regard, we as a profession have built our house on a weak foundation. It is our professional responsibility to renovate our collective understanding when advances are made. We have no difficulty embracing the latest technology to ensure the safety of our students, so why should we hesitate to examine the theoretical underpinnings of how and why we train outdoor leaders to use that gear with their students?

Conclusion

The development of more experienced professionals is far more rich and contextual than that of novices in the same profession. However, little evidence exists that novices use an entirely different process than experts—they simply have less to go on. Judgment is not an entity unto itself; it is contextual and an inherent cognitive function and it is linked to multiple facets of professional performance. Whereas CRDM attempts to decontextualize and consider many options in order to provide optimum decisions, NDM and the other macrocognitive functions strive to adopt, adapt, and

succeed in the midst of the actual context, which in the case of outdoor leadership usually involves time stress and high stakes. CRDM does offer an interesting method for dispassionate discussion of the events of a day, and this is well illustrated by its incorporation into the Wilderness Education Association curriculum (Drury et al., 2005, p. 156). However, this curriculum and others like it do not present a coherent and realistic model of decision making and, in my view, should not be taught to any outdoor instructors, regardless of their level of expertise, as a method of making decisions. Rather, it offers a powerful method of review of and reflection on decisions that have already been made with the purpose of considering the multifaceted and evolving nature of professional action in the field.

The more I read on the topic of decision making, the more I come to believe that it is not a separate cognitive function, although we treat it as such. Perhaps it is nothing more or less than human thought and experience in action. If so, we should focus our efforts on developing that ability rather than attempting to study or teach artificial notions of choice or judgment. McCammon (2001) succinctly observes that "it's probably not possible to teach people how to make decisions, because they already do it pretty well. . . . Learning to make better decisions, however, is a different matter, one that can be addressed by applying current knowledge of how people learn" (p. 29).

References

Beare, M., & Lynch, P. (2005). Learning decision making for the outdoors: A naturalistic perspective. In T.J. Dickson, T. Gray, & B. Hayllar (Eds.), *Outdoor and experiential learning: Views from the top* (pp. 210-220). Dunedin, New Zealand: Otago University Press.

Boyes, M.A., & O'Hare, D. (2003). Between safety and risk: A model for outdoor adventure decision making. *Journal of Adventure Education and Outdoor Learning, 3*(1), 63-76.

Cacciabue, P.C., & Hollnagel, E. (1995). Simulation of cognition: Applications. In J.M. Hoc, P.C. Cacciabue, & E. Hollnagel (Eds.), *Expertise and technology: Issues in cognition and human–computer cooperation* (pp. 55-74). Hillsdale, NJ: LEA.

Crandall, B., Klein, G., & Hoffman, R.R. (2006). *Working minds: A practitioner's guide to cognitive task analysis.* Cambridge, MA: MIT Press.

de Groot, A.D. (1946/1978). *Thought and choice in chess.* 1st ed. New York: Mouton.

de Groot, M. (1970). *Optimal statistical decisions.* New York: McGraw-Hill.

Drury, J.K., Bonney, B.F., Berman, D., & Wagstaff, M.C. (2005). *The backcountry classroom: Lessons, tools and activities for teaching outdoor leaders.* 2nd ed. Helena, MT: Globe Pequot.

Endsley, M.R. (1995). Toward a theory of situation awareness in dynamic systems. *Human Factors, 37,* 32-64.

Ericsson, K., & Simon, H. (1993). *Protocol analysis: Verbal reports as data.* 2nd ed. Boston: MIT Press.

Evans, J. (2008). Dual-processing accounts of reasoning, judgment, and social cognition. *Annual Review of Psychology, 59,* 255-278.

Evans, J. (2010). Intuition and reasoning: A dual process perspective. *Psychological Inquiry, 21,* 313-326.

Galloway, S.P. (2002). Theoretical cognitive differences in expert and novice outdoor leader decision making: Implications for training and development. *Journal of Adventure Education and Outdoor Learning, 1*(3), 19-28.

Galloway, S.P. (2007). Experience and medical decision making in outdoor leaders. *Journal of Experiential Education, 30*(2), 99-116.

Kahneman, D., & Klein, G. (2009). Conditions for intuitive expertise: A failure to disagree. *American Psychologist, 64*(6), 515-526.

Klein, G. (1998). *Source of power: How people make decisions.* Cambridge, MA: MIT Press.

Klein, G. (2009). *Streetlights and shadows: Searching for the keys to adaptive decision making.* Cambridge, MA: MIT Press.

Klein, G.A., Calderwood, R., & Clinton-Cirocco, A. (1988). *Rapid decision making on the fire ground* (Technical Report No. DTIC No. AD-A199492, www.dtic.mil). Alexandria, VA: U.S. Army Research Institute.

Klein, G., Ross, K.G., Moon, B.M., Klein, D.M., Hoffman, R.R., & Hollnagel, E. (2003). Macrocognition. *IEEE Intelligent Systems,* May/June, 81-85.

Kolb, D. (1984). *Experiential learning: Experience as the source of learning and development.* Englewood Cliffs, NJ: Prentice-Hall.

Martin, B., Schmid, D., & Parker, M. (2009). An exploration of judgment and decision making among novice outdoor leaders: A dual process approach. *Journal of Outdoor Recreation, Education and Leadership, 1*(1), 38-54.

McCammon, I. (2001). Decision making for wilderness leaders: Strategies, traps, and teaching methods. In *Proceedings of the Wilderness Risk Managers Conference* (pp. 16-29). Lander, WY: National Outdoor Leadership School.

Means, B., Salas, E., Crandall, B., & Jacobs, O. (1993). Training decision makers for the real world. Decision making in action: Models and methods. In G.A. Klein, J. Orasanu, R. Calderwood, & C.E. Zsambok (Eds.), *Decision making in action: Models and methods* (pp. 306-326). Westport, CT: Ablex.

Mitten, D. (2002). An analysis of outdoor leaders' ethics guiding decisions. In M. Bialeschki, K. Henderson, A. Young, & R. Andrejewski (Eds.), *Research in outdoor education, volume 6.* Bradford Woods, IN: Coalition for Education in the Outdoors.

Seaman, J., & Coppens, A.D. (2006). Repertoire of practice: Reconceptualising instructor competency in contemporary adventure education. *Journal of Adventure Education & Outdoor Learning, 6*(1), 25-37.

Shanteau, J. (1992). Competence in experts: The role of task characteristics. *Organizational Behaviour and Human Decision Processes, 53,* 252-266.

Simon, H. (1957). A behavioral model of rational choice. In *Models of man: Social and rational; Mathematical essays on rational human behavior in a social setting.* New York: Wiley.

Simon, H.A. (1992). What is an explanation of behavior? *Psychological Science, 3,* 150-161.

Tozer, M., Fazey, I., & Fazey, J. (2007). Recognizing and developing adaptive expertise within outdoor and expedition leaders. *Journal of Adventure Education and Outdoor Learning, 7*(1), 55-75.

Wagstaff, M., & Cashel, C. (2001). Paul Petzoldt's perspective: The final 20 years. *Journal of Experiential Education, 24*(3), 160-165.

Zakay, D., & Wooler, S. (1984). Time pressure, training, and decision effectiveness. *Ergonomics, 27,* 273-284.

Controversial Issue 19

Is it possible to effectively accomplish the goals of outdoor education through online programming?

ichard Louv's (2005) best-selling book *Last Child in the Woods: Saving Our Children From Nature-Deficit Disorder* drew attention to a growing chasm between children and the natural world. Louv attributed this divide to the growing prevalence of technology in society, specifically television, video games, computers, and the Internet. Louv's analysis helped inspire the creation of the No Child Left Inside Coalition as well as the No Child Left Inside Act of 2008, which was introduced by Representative John Sarbanes. This bill was passed by the House but was never voted on by the Senate, so it was reintroduced to Congress in the summer of 2011 by Representative Sarbanes, Senator Jack Reed, and Senator Mark Kirk. The bill was still in review as of January 2012 in both the House and Senate.

Professionals in the field of outdoor education have used Louv's book to draw attention to the vital role that interpretive and environmental education programs, camps, and traditional adventure programs can play in promoting the goals of the No Child Left Inside initiative, and professionals in the field of outdoor education have been positioning themselves to fulfill this role. Interestingly, as the adventure program industry has positioned itself to help resolve the growing disconnect between children and nature, many have also begun to deliver educational programming using the very technology that has contributed to the problem. Counterintuitive as it may seem, we are witnessing the emergence of online outdoor education programs in primary, secondary, and postsecondary schools around the world.

This raises the question, Is it possible to effectively accomplish the goals of outdoor education through online programming? Bruce Martin argues that online adventure programming offers an exciting new forum through which to achieve the goals of adventure programming. He argues that broadening our understanding of the nature of the practice of outdoor education as well as the nature of adventure experience can help us to provide access to millions of individuals who may otherwise not have an opportunity to engage in adventure programming. He also argues that online adventure programming can enable practitioners to engage students in more expansive realms of inquiry than they could through more traditional adventure programs.

Amy Shellman, Eddie Hill, and Ron Ramsing, on the other hand, argue that the online option is antithetical to the nature of adventure programming. In light of the role of the instructor in the learning process and the current limitations of online programming, they argue that such programming falls short when it comes to accomplishing the goals of outdoor education. In particular, they argue that participants cannot effectively experience through online adventure programming key characteristics of the educational process in outdoor education, including small-group experiential learning activities facilitated by skilled instructors in authentic settings and the educational attributes often emphasized in outdoor education.

Reference

Louv, R. (2005). *Last child in the woods: Saving our children from nature-deficit disorder*. Chapel Hill, NC: Algonquin Books.

Is it possible to effectively accomplish the goals of outdoor education through online programming?

YES Virtual Adventures: New Frontiers in Adventure Education

Bruce Martin, PhD, associate professor of recreation and sport pedagogy, Ohio University, Athens, Ohio, United States

Determining whether it is possible to effectively accomplish the goals of outdoor education through online programming depends on how one defines outdoor education and what one considers the goals of outdoor education to be. Based on conventional definitions of outdoor education (e.g., Gilbertson et al., 2006; Martin et al., 2006; Priest, 1999; Priest and Gass, 2005), the idea of conducting online programming to achieve the goals of outdoor education may seem counterintuitive. Indeed, in light of Louv's (2005) compelling indictment of technology as one of the chief sources of what he terms "nature-deficit disorder" in today's youths, the idea of attempting to accomplish the goals of outdoor education through online programming may seem oxymoronic.

However, when framing the nature and goals of outdoor education in less parochial, more holistic terms than conventional definitions allow, online programming presents an exciting new forum through which to accomplish the goals of outdoor education. In fact, online adventure programs can help expand the reach of the adventure programming industry to millions of individuals who otherwise would not have an opportunity to engage in adventure programming. My point is not to suggest that online adventure programming should supplant traditional adventure programming or to suggest that online adventure programs are necessarily more effective than traditional adventure programs. My point is that online adventure programming is a medium that can complement more traditional adventure programs in achieving the goals of outdoor education. Online adventure programming can be used to expand the scope and the effectiveness of traditional adventure programming.

I base my argument on current research that indicates that online educational programs can be an effective medium through which to fulfill the goals of outdoor education. I also base my argument on a challenge to reconsider our basic notion of adventure experience and to include virtual adventure in our thinking. Doing so opens an expansive new domain in which adventure programming can enrich the lives of individuals and the cultures in which they live. I use the terms "outdoor education" and "adventure education" interchangeably throughout this argument.

A Framework for Online Adventure Education

More than one in four students in higher education partake in online learning, and enrollment in online courses has grown nearly 18 percent annually since 2003. Little doubt exists that information technology has greatly influenced education in America (Allen and Seaman, 2010). According to Allen and Seaman (2010), 73.6 percent of public institutions indicate that this medium is critical to their long-term strategy. A variety of pedagogical strategies for use of online learning exist, but hybrid or blended approaches appear to be more beneficial for promoting student learning outcomes. The hybrid model of online learning, in which face-to-face instruction is complemented by content delivered via the Internet, has been shown to enhance critical-thinking skills by providing learners with more exposure to content via multiple formats as well as additional time for reflection and, therefore, more in-depth response to discussions with peers or feedback on specific assignments (Buzzetto-More and Sweat-Guy, 2006; Gorsky and Blau, 2009; McFarlin, 2008). A natural advantage of online learning is that learners have flexibility and are less likely to be tied to formal meeting times. This flexibility perhaps provides the learner with opportunities for greater engagement and learning on their own terms (Buzzetto-More and Sweat-Guy, 2006).

Aaron Doering (2006) developed a framework for online programming that he termed the adventure learning framework. Doering (2006) defines adventure learning as "a hybrid online educational environment that provides students with opportunities to explore real-world issues through authentic learning experiences within collaborative online learning environments" (p. 200). Although this definition betrays a limited appreciation of the broader historical and philosophical scope of the practice of adventure education, Doering offers a good example of the way in which the principles of adventure education can be applied through online programming. Specifically, Doering's (2006) adventure learning framework is based on seven principles:

1. a researched curriculum grounded in problem-solving;
2. collaboration and interaction opportunities among students, experts, peers, and content;
3. the use of the Internet for delivery of the curriculum learning environment;
4. the enhancement of curriculum with media and text from the field in a timely manner;
5. learning opportunities synched with adventure learning curriculum;
6. pedagogical guidelines of the curriculum and online learning environment; and
7. education that is adventure based. (p. 200)

The first two and the last of these principles are highly consistent with the principles of adventure education. Adventure education in general is grounded in problem-solving and problem-based learning. This approach is one of the hallmarks of experiential learning and outdoor education (Hunt, 1999; Rapparlie, 2009; Wurdinger, 1997; Wurdinger and Priest, 1999). Problem-based learning is rooted in John Dewey's (1916, 1938) theory of inquiry. In fact, understood in terms of Dewey's ideas on the role of thinking in the process of inquiry, little separation exists between the process of inquiry and the nature of adventure. As Dewey (1916) notes:

> It also follows that all thinking involves risk. Certainty cannot be guaranteed in advance. The invasion of the unknown is of the nature of adventure; we cannot be sure in advance. The conclusions of thinking, till confirmed by the event are, accordingly, more or less tentative or hypothetical. (p. 148)

The process of inquiry is centered on rendering indeterminate situations determinate. Or, as Hunt (1999) notes, "Inquiry is a disciplined response to a situation that is indeterminate and which demands intellectual resolution" (p. 121).

Another hallmark of adventure education is its emphasis on interpersonal growth and development through the facilitation of group cohesion and effectiveness (Priest, 1999; Priest and Gass, 2005). Though interactions in virtual domains differ from interactions in more conventional life situations, the principle of collaboration and interaction in Doering's adventure learning framework provides a basis for students to engage in the process of interpersonal growth and development that is emphasized in more traditional adventure education programs. Collaboration and interaction in the adventure learning framework occur both within the physical classroom and online in "collaboration zones" (Doering, 2006, p. 203). Many kinds of interaction and collaboration occur within these contexts. Students interact with teachers and the subject matter in both the physical and online classrooms. Teachers use online resources to assist students in the problem-solving tasks through which lessons are framed. They also help guide students in interacting and collaborating with experts and content online and provide the needed scaffolding for successful online interactions in "moderated chat environments" (Doering, 2006, p. 205). Furthermore, teachers are able to take advantage of opportunities to interact with content experts through online collaboration; these opportunities might not exist without this technology. Doering (2006) notes that "students work with each other in the classroom, but more importantly, with students throughout the world within the chat and collaboration zone environments" (pp. 205-206). Finally, Doering (2006) notes:

> Adventure learning is based upon creating opportunities for students to collaborate and reflect within the online learning environment in order to encourage transformative learning. Transformative learning requires all learners to work together through social negotiation—discussing, solving, and reflecting, and reflecting on the problem to be solved. Social negotiation can arise at high levels with an adventure learning approach as individuals who are goal-directed are working together to solve a common task within a common place—a collaboration zone. (p. 207)

The remaining principles account for the use of varying forms of technology through which to engage in adventure experience and considerations for structuring curricula to ensure that instructors effectively facilitate student learning based on these experiences.

Numerous studies have documented the effectiveness of Doering's (2006) adventure learning framework (Doering, Miller, and Veletsianos, 2008; Doering and Veletsianos, 2008; Koseoglu and Doering, 2011; Miller, Veletsianos, and Doering, 2008; Moos and Honkomp, 2011). Two examples of such adventure learning programs are the Arctic Transect 2004 and the GoNorth! series delivered through the University of Minnesota. Describing these programs, Doering, Miller, and Veletsianos (2008) state, "In all of these programs, adventurers and educators dogsled throughout the Arctic location of study/exploration as learners around the world collaborate and learn about the region of travel and the supportive content-based curriculum" (p. 252).

Moos and Honkomp (2011) conducted a study to assess the effectiveness of Doering's (2006) adventure learning framework in increasing student motivation and learning outcomes in a suburban Minnesota middle school. In August of 2009, a group of seventh and eighth graders learned about social studies as they followed their geography teacher's adventures in Africa. Their teacher, Christian Gilbertson, spent several days involved in a service learning project to assist orphaned children, two days on safari, and seven days climbing Mt. Kilimanjaro. Gilbertson used multiple forms of technology to remain connected with his students during his expeditions. He sent daily lessons to his students via e-mail. He updated students on his whereabouts by using a Satellite Pour l'Observation de la Terre (SPOT) satellite transponder to enter into Google Maps the geographical coordinates of his field position. He sent his students periodic updates via voice recordings using a satellite phone. As Moos and Honkomp (2011) note, "This equipment allowed for the creation of an adventure learning environment that contained content aligned to Minnesota's seventh and eighth grade geography and earth science standards" (p. 234). After returning from his expedition, Gilbertson posted this content on a website designed to document adventure learning expeditions and used this content in subsequent geography lessons. The study's findings indicate that students' motivation levels and levels of learning significantly increased as a result of participating in this adventure learning experience.

Another online program of this sort is the JASON Project. Named for the mythological Greek explorer, the project was founded in 1989 by Robert Ballard, the oceanographer and explorer who discovered the shipwreck RMS Titanic. After discovering the shipwreck, Ballard received thousands of letters from school children wanting to join his next expedition. To feed the curiosity and passion for exploration and discovery that had been sparked in these children, Ballard founded the JASON Project to connect "students with scientists and researchers in real and near-real time, virtually and physically, to provide mentored, authentic, and enriching science learning experiences" (The JASON Project, 2011). The JASON Project has developed a wide variety of curricula in partnership with agencies such as the National Oceanic and Atmospheric Administration, the National Aeronautic and Space Administration, and the National Geographic Society to promote education through exploration. These curricula include the following:

- *Mysteries of Earth and Mars*, which focuses on the big questions that scientists face concerning the nature and history of these planets;

- *Online Expedition: Humpback Whales*, an online-only program in which students study the relationship between humpback whale singing and whales' social interactions off the coast of Maui; and

- *Rain Forests: A Wet and Wild Adventure*, a hybrid distance learning program that gives students an opportunity to explore the Peruvian Amazon rainforest through two weeks of live broadcasting from the rainforest, among other activities.

Since it was founded in 1989, the JASON Project has connected more than 10 million students and teachers with remote reaches of the world through online exploration and discovery.

Virtual Adventures in Health and Fitness

One day, I went to my neighbor's house to retrieve my daughters from a play date. When I entered the house, I found my daughters and their friends excitedly jumping up and down, swaying their bodies left and right, ducking, and dodging as they navigated a raft down a raging river. They were playing the video game Kinect Adventures. Kinect is the first immersive video game device to allow players to engage in a game without using handheld controllers. Players' involvement in the game is based on their own physical movements. The room was filled with screams, groans, laughter, and fun. My daughters were engaged in an environment that blended the physical and the virtual, that involved physical challenges that required a certain level of mastery and competence to overcome, and that required cooperation with their playmates to succeed at the game. Although one might question the transformative value of such an experience, it is clear that the game produced positive outcomes for my daughters and their friends. The game provided them an opportunity to engage in an experience that was socially rich and that required a high level of physical activity, both of which are aligned with traditional outcomes of physical education and adventure education.

Hayes and Silberman (2007) argue that video gaming is an untapped resource in the field of physical education. They argue that video games have great potential for increasing students' motivation and ability to engage in sport and other movement-based activities. Excessive game play has been associated with childhood obesity (Green and Reese, 2006); however, a number of studies have shown positive benefits associated with newer forms of gaming technology, called exergames. Papastergiou (2009) conducted a review of the scientific literature on the use of exergames in health and physical education and found that the literature identifies numerous benefits: increased motivation for exercise, increased participation in physical activity, improved fitness levels, improved body weight, improved understanding of physiological concepts and movement principles, enhanced motor skills, and improved teamwork through multiplayer games. Fogel and colleagues (2010) evaluated the effects of exergaming in a physical education classroom and found that exergames increased the amount of time that students engaged in physical activity and provided greater opportunities to engage in physical activity compared with traditional physical education programming.

Other studies have documented the general benefits of exergaming. Griffiths (2010) reports that the immersive and disassociative aspects of online gaming can provide therapeutic benefits and that online gaming can provide general psychological benefits by helping to boost individual self-esteem. A number of additional studies have documented positive health benefits associated with exergaming for general populations (e.g., Anderson-Hanley and Arciero, 2011; Irwin et al., 2011; Pfeiffer et al., 2011; Wollersheim et al., 2010).

The issue of health and wellness has long been a concern in adventure programming. The Scouting movement emerged in large part to address public health concerns that were prevalent in Britain in the early 20th century. Outward Bound emerged in large part to address similar concerns in Britain during the mid-20th century. Promoting health and wellness are foundations of both Scouting and Outward Bound. To address these same concerns, Project Adventure has developed a number of programs in the United States in recent years, including programs that incorporate adventure activities into physical education curricula. Project Adventure's approach is outlined in *Adventure Curriculum for Physical Education* (Panicucci et al., 2003). Given the positive benefits that online gaming can yield, why not include adventure-based online gaming (or exergaming) in the mix of strategies and approaches that we can use to promote increased levels of physical activity in children?

Many in the adventure programming industry would challenge the authenticity of virtual adventure experiences. However, in an autoethnographic account of the nature of experience, Karen Fox (2008) notes, "People engaged in video games actually go through physiological changes related to fear, excitement, and anger even though they never 'really' encounter the events" (p. 40). She notes further, "If these are also experiences, a relatively well-articulated theoretical and scholarly rationale is essential to support a particular *type* of experience for the field of experiential education" (p. 40). I contend that virtual experiences are authentic experiences and that these experiences can yield transformative educational benefits. Twining (2009), for example, notes, "Open virtual worlds like Second Life virtual world offer opportunities for people to have radically different 'lived experiences' of educational systems and thus seem to be the ideal vehicle for exploring alternative models of education" (p. 498). These spaces, according to Twining, encourage playfulness and testing of boundaries among visitors to those spaces.

Ironically, Ryan Geiss, a computer programmer and engineer who was instrumental in helping Microsoft develop the motion-recognition system that enables players to engage in controller-free video gaming, considers himself somewhat of a luddite. In an interview about his contributions to the development of the Kinect device, Geiss states, "I like to hike and camp. I don't even own an Xbox" (Feran, 2011). Geiss' interest in computer programming has never been based on a passion for gaming; rather, it has been based on the creativity involved in developing computer graphics and music visualization. Before working for Microsoft on the Kinect game system, Geiss gained recognition in the industry for his work in developing three-dimensional music visualizers. Although his professional life is devoted to computer programming, Geiss expresses an interest in something larger. He states, "Every time I go out hiking, I'm looking at trees and mountains, and thinking how I can create them on a computer. Nature is so interesting and complex—I don't want to replace it. It's just fun to replicate it" (Feran, 2011).

Conclusion

L.B. Sharp, who studied under John Dewey at Columbia University in New York in the late 1920s and who is thought to be the first to implement and experiment with Dewey's educational philosophy in the outdoors (Carlson, 2009), once famously wrote, "That which ought and can best be taught inside the schoolrooms should there be taught, and that which can best be learned through experience dealing directly with native materials and life situations outside the school should there be learned" (Sharp, 1943, p. 363). Sharp penned these sentiments nearly 70 years ago, just as televisions began to appear in the living rooms of households around America and throughout much of the developed world. He likely could not have conceived of a domain in which authentic learning experiences could be had through representational forms of media such as avatars and in virtual domains such as collaboration zones (Doering, 2006). As Bredo (1994) notes, at the turn of the 20th century, Dewey was attempting to reconcile the old and the new in his educational writings. Bredo (1994) writes:

> When Dewey was writing, around the turn of the century, the United States was rapidly changing from a largely rural and agrarian society to a largely urban and industrial one. This involved significant moral and intellectual dislocation, with many people clinging to old beliefs despite changed conditions, while others focused on new possibilities that were inconsistent with older beliefs and mores. (p. 24)

We are presently experiencing similar disjunctions as society continues to change and progress. One of the areas of contemporary life in which this is most evident is in the development of new information technologies that have begun to redefine (and promise to continue redefining) the very nature of human experience and culture. The ramifications of these changes will permeate all areas of human existence, including how we experience nature and engage in adventurous experience. The most profound discoveries of our day—indeed, some of the most profound discoveries in human history—have been facilitated by the very technologies and representational forms of media that we are discussing. The recent discovery of Earthlike planets in the habitable zones of other solar systems and the search for evidence of life beyond that which exists here on Earth are but two significant examples. The technological developments that have created the virtual forms and symbolic representations of the world and the universe around us have greatly enhanced adventure experience today.

Just as Sharp could not have conceived of the virtual domains in which we now operate, it is difficult for us to imagine the potential evolution of information technology and the nature of human experience in our future. Films like James Cameron's *Avatar* inspire the imagination, and the tenacity of engineers like Ryan Geiss in pushing technological development gives confidence that the nature of human experience and interaction is likely to continue changing dramatically in the years to come. We stand to benefit greatly by embracing these changes rather than remaining grounded solely in purist traditions in adventure programming. As such, the following addendum should be added to Sharp's (1943) maxim: That which can best be learned through digital media and in virtual domains dealing with symbolic representations of native materials and life situations should thus be learned.

References

Allen, E., & Seaman, J. (2010). *Learning on demand: Online education in the United States, 2009.* Needham, MA: Sloan Consortium.

Anderson-Hanley, C., & Arciero, P.J. (2011). Seniors cybercycling for cognitive health. *Journal of Sport and Exercise Physiology,* Supplement, S20-S22. (Abstr.)

Bredo, E. (1994). Reconstructing educational psychology: Situated cognition and Deweyian pragmatism. *Educational Psychologist, 29*(1), 23-35.

Buzzetto-More, N., & Sweat-Guy, R. (2006). Incorporating the hybrid learning model into minority education at a historically black university. *Journal of Information Technology Education, 5,* 153-164.

Carlson, J. (2009). *Never finished . . . just begun: A narrative history of L.B. Sharp and outdoor education.* Edina, MN: Beaver's Pond Press Inc.

Dewey, J. (1916). *Democracy and education.* New York: Free Press.

Dewey, J. (1938). *Logic: The theory of inquiry*. New York: Holt, Rinehart, and Winston.

Doering, A. (2006). Adventure learning: Transformative hybrid online education. *Distance Education, 27*(2), 197-215.

Doering, A., Miller, C., & Veletsianos, G. (2008). Adventure learning: Educational, social, and technological affordances for collaborative hybrid distance education. *Quarterly Review of Distance Education, 9*(3), 249-265.

Doering, A., & Veletsianos, G. (2008). Hybrid online education: Identifying integration models using adventure learning. *Journal of Research on Technology in Education, 41*(1), 23-41.

Feran, T. (2011). Homegrown genius. *The Columbus Dispatch,* February 20, D1.

Fogel, V.A., Miltenberger, R.G., Graves, R., & Koehler, S. (2010). The effects of exergaming on physical activity among inactive children in a physical education classroom. *Journal of Applied Behavior Analysis, 43*(4), 591-600.

Fox, K. (2008). Rethinking experience: What do we mean by this word "experience"? *Journal of Experiential Education, 31*(1), 36-54.

Gilbertson, K., Bates, T., McLaughlin, T., & Ewert, A. (2006). *Outdoor education: Methods and strategies*. Champaign, IL: Human Kinetics.

Gorsky, P., & Blau, I. (2009). Online teaching effectiveness: A tale of two instructors. *International Review of Research in Open and Distance Learning, 10*(3), 1-27.

Green, G., & Reese, S.A. (2006). Childhood obesity: A growing phenomenon for physical educators. *Education, 127*(1), 121-124.

Griffiths, M. (2010). Online video gaming: What should educational psychologists know? *Educational Psychology in Practice, 26*(1), 35-40.

Hayes, E., & Silberman, L. (2007). Incorporating video games into physical education. *Journal of Physical Education, Recreation and Dance, 78*(3), 18-24.

Hunt, J.S. (1999). Philosophy of adventure education. In J.C. Miles & S. Priest (Eds.), *Adventure programming* (pp. 115-122). State College, PA: Venture.

Irwin, B.C., Feltz, D.L., Kerr, N.L., & Schimpke, S. (2011). Virtual partners: Harnessing group dynamics to boost motivation to exercise. *Journal of Sport and Exercise Physiology,* Supplement, S20-S22. (Abstr.)

The JASON Project. (2011). What is JASON? www.jason.org/public/WhatIs/JASON.aspx [December 28, 2011].

Koseoglu, S., & Doering, A. (2011). Understanding complex ecologies: An investigation of student experiences in adventure learning programs. *Distance Education, 32*(3), 339-355.

Louv, R. (2005). *Last child in the woods: Saving our children from nature-deficit disorder*. Chapel Hill, NC: Algonquin Books.

Martin, B., Cashel, C., Wagstaff, M., & Breunig, M. (2006). *Outdoor leadership: Theory and practice*. Champaign, IL: Human Kinetics.

McFarlin, B.K. (2008). Hybrid lecture-online format increases student grades in an undergraduate exercise physiology course at a large urban university. *Advances in Physiology Education, 32*, 86-91.

Miller, C., Veletsianos, G., & Doering, A. (2008). Curriculum at forty below: A phenomenological inquiry of an educator/explorer's experience with adventure learning in the arctic. *Distance Education, 29*(3), 253-267.

Moos, D.C., & Honkomp, B. (2011). Adventure learning: Motivating students in a Minnesota middle school. *Journal of Research on Technology in Education, 43*(3), 231-252.

Panicucci, J., Constable, N., Hunt, L., Kohut, A., & Rheingold, A. (2003). *Adventure curriculum for physical education*. Beverly, MA: Project Adventure Inc.

Papastergiou, M. (2009). Exploring the potential of computer and video games for health and physical education: A literature review. *Computers and Education, 53*(3), 603-622.

Pfeiffer, K.A., Peng, W., Winn, B., & Sutton, D. (2011). Developing a theory-based video game to increase intrinsic motivation to exercise. *Journal of Sport and Exercise Physiology,* Supplement, S20-S22. (Abstr.)

Priest, S. (1999). The semantics of adventure programming. In J.C. Miles & S. Priest (Eds.), *Adventure programming* (pp. 111-114). State College, PA: Venture.

Priest, S., & Gass, M.A. (2005). *Effective leadership in adventure programming*. 2nd ed. Champaign, IL: Human Kinetics.

Rapparlie, L.E. (2009). How do we learn? An exploration of John Dewey's pattern of inquiry. In B. Stremba & C.A. Bisson (Eds.), *Teaching adventure education theory: Best practices* (pp. 128-134). Champaign, IL: Human Kinetics.

Sharp, L.B. (1943). Outside the classroom. *The Educational Forum, 7*(4), 361-368.

Twining, P. (2009). Exploring the educational potential of virtual worlds—Some reflections from the SPP. *British Journal of Educational Technology, 40*(3), 496-514.

Wollersheim, D., Merkes, M., Shields, N., Liamputtong, P., Wallis, L., Reynolds, F., & Koh, L. (2010). Physical and psychosocial effects of Wii video game use among older women. *International Journal of Emerging Technologies and Society, 8*(2), 85-98.

Wurdinger, S. (1997). *Philosophical issues in adventure education*. 3rd ed. Dubuque, IA: Kendall/Hunt.

Wurdinger, S.D., & Priest, S. (1999). Integrating theory and application in experiential learning. In J.C. Miles & S. Priest (Eds.), *Adventure programming* (pp. 187-192). State College, PA: Venture.

Is it possible to effectively accomplish the goals of outdoor education through online programming?

NO Keeping the Outdoors in Outdoor Education: The Conundrum of Online Education

Amy Shellman, PhD, assistant professor of recreation, parks, and leisure studies, SUNY Cortland, Cortland, New York, United States

Eddie Hill, PhD, assistant professor of recreation and tourism studies, Old Dominion University, Norfolk, Virginia, United States

Ron Ramsing, PhD, associate professor of recreation administration, Western Kentucky University, Bowling Green, Kentucky, United States

"That which ought and can best be taught inside the schoolrooms should there be taught, and that which can best be learned through experience dealing directly with native materials and life situations outside the school should there be learned."

—Sharp, 1943, p. 363

Outdoor education has existed arguably since the dawn of humankind, when our ancestors learned which plants were safe to eat, what hunting grounds were most fruitful, and where they might best quench their thirst. Although outdoor education today takes many forms and aims to achieve myriad outcomes, it seems almost antithetical to conceive of outdoor education as a process of virtual programming. Considering the goals of outdoor education, the role of the instructor in the learning process, and the current limitations of online programming, our stance is that online programming falls short when it comes to accomplishing the goals of outdoor education. In particular, online programming cannot effectively transmit the small-group experiential learning activities facilitated by skilled instructors in an authentic setting, educational attributes that are often emphasized in outdoor education.

Broadly defined by Donaldson and Donaldson (1958), outdoor education is "education in, about, and for the out of doors" (p. 63). Hence, outdoor education may include using the natural world as a venue for learning any number of subjects (e.g., ecological relationships), developing physical skills relevant to the outdoor environment (e.g., kayaking), or developing an appreciation of and value for the natural environment (e.g., environmental stewardship). Given this definition, it stands to reason that one may teach outdoor education using a variety of means in any number of settings. We argue that although one may be able to teach a variety of topics and subjects online, outdoor education is best taught using face-to-face, direct contact between participants, instructor, and, of course, the outdoors. The argument we present here is from the perspective of three faculty members in higher education who have significant personal experience as field staff for a number of outdoor education programs, including Outward Bound, private industry, and university-based programs. We argue that online programming is not an effective means to accomplish the goals of outdoor education for three main reasons:

1. outdoor education aims to connect people with the outdoors whereas online programming perpetuates a disconnect between nature and individuals that has, in part, contributed to a host of societal problems;

2. online programming is inconsistent with the general principles and practices underlying outdoor adventure programming; and

3. it is impossible to replicate through online programming the authentic communities that are characteristic of outdoor adventure programs.

Goals and Means of Outdoor Education

A 1971 report by the Council on Outdoor Education and Camping of the American Association for

Health, Physical Education, and Recreation (as cited in Smith, 1972) describes several educational goals and means of attaining those goals in the outdoors (for a sampling of these, see table 19.1). In addition to these, other goals of outdoor education include appreciation for and understanding of the natural world, developing healthy personal and social attitudes and values, and influencing the way participants think, feel, and behave. One may argue that many of these goals can be met through online education, and perhaps to some extent they can. However, the question remains as to how effective online programming can be in achieving such goals.

Priest (1986) describes six characteristics of outdoor education: 1) it is a method of learning, 2) it is experiential, 3) it occurs primarily outdoors, 4) it is holistic and requires the use of all senses, 5) it is based on interdisciplinary curricula, and 6) it is about relationships involving people and natural resources. More recently, Gilbertson and colleagues (2006) describe outdoor education as "a method of teaching and learning that emphasizes direct, multisensory experiences and uses an integrated approach to learning by involving the natural, community, and individual environments" (p. 5). In examining such descriptions of outdoor education, it seems quite difficult to emulate in a meaningful way interaction between participants and the use of multiple senses in virtual learning environments.

Many of the current practices and models of outdoor education have evolved from the Outward Bound program model. A key component of the Outward Bound process as described by Walsh and Golins (1976) is the social situation cocreated by the learner and the instructors. Furthermore, looking at the history of Outward Bound (for a detailed history of Outward Bound see Miner and Boldt, 2002) as well as current practices, it is difficult to imagine that one could achieve similar outcomes (e.g., character development, leadership, self-efficacy, resilience, and so on) through online programming. It is safe to say that one could not as effectively achieve through online learning the intangible outcomes (e.g., empowerment, sense of achievement, sense of community) of an outdoor education program. One is hard pressed to argue that it is possible to replicate online the feelings and learning associated with getting lost and needing to figure out where the group is because they failed to keep track of their field bearing. The virtual world presents essentially no real-life consequences, no real need to overcome adversity. Can one learn map and compass lessons through online programming? Sure. But would one achieve the experience and associated life-lesson outcomes as effectively as one would by using a map and compass in the field? No. Moreover, a recent study of Outward Bound participants found that group debriefs and the presence of supportive others contributed to

Table 19.1   Goals and Means of Outdoor Education

General educational goal: to . . .	Means in the outdoors: through . . .
develop the full potential of the individual	optimum exposure to and involvement with the natural environment
develop knowledge, skills, attitudes, and appreciations for the use of leisure time	exposure to outdoor interests and instruction in outdoor sports and component skills
promote the development of social relations and individual responsibility	group living experiences, particularly in resident outdoor education
promote the development of civic responsibility	active participation and problem-solving situations in the community, improvement of the physical environment, and development of good human relationships
promote the development of aesthetic interests and appreciations	participation in positive experiences in the natural environment that contribute to creative expression of talent
help individuals become more self-reliant and secure	adventuresome and challenging outdoor pursuits and skills that require initiative and active participation in solving problems related to comfort, safety, and survival
provide opportunities for individuals to strengthen their self-concept	achieving success and accomplishments in activities that are meaningful to the learner

participant development and were significantly correlated with outcome measures of empowerment and resilience (Shellman, 2009). In the same study, participants articulated the empowering effects of overcoming challenges in helping them realize they could accomplish more than they initially thought possible. This supports the position that outdoor education is better suited than online programming for live teaching in situ. These are just a few examples of how online outdoor education falls short of achieving the goals that nature's classroom can so effectively accomplish.

Technology: Not the Solution, But Part of the Problem

Richard Louv's (2005) national bestseller, *Last Child in the Woods*, drew much attention to outdoor education. Louv appeared on *Oprah*, *The Today Show*, and numerous other venues to bring attention to a very compelling and important message: Although not a clinical diagnosis, children's lack of exposure to nature and learning about the natural environment is contributing to nature-deficit disorder, a term coined by Louv to describe the negative effects (e.g., decreased physical activity, obesity, attention disorders) of children's increasing disconnect with nature. The premise of his argument is that too much time inside connected to electronic media (e.g., the Internet, television, video games, and so on) is negatively affecting development, and that the outdoor environment can help young people learn and flourish.

In crafting a convincing argument for getting young people outside and away from electronics, Louv references numerous studies that demonstrate the salutogenic effects of natural environments on human health, including emotional, psychological, and physical well-being (e.g., increased creativity, decreased stress, improved balance and agility, and so on). He also presents several compelling reasons for the increasing disconnect between children and nature; among them is technology. Today, young people have ready access to all kinds of attractive (and distracting) electronic entertainment, including computers, cell phones, iPods, and video games. Alarmingly, but perhaps not surprisingly, when Louv asked one boy where he preferred to play, the child responded, " I like to play indoors better, cause that's where all the electrical outlets are" (Louv, 2005, p. 10). The pull of technology appears to be even stronger for college students, who seem to be continuously attached to some electronic device, be it their cell phone, computer, or iPod. In light

of this, if the goal is to educate students about the outdoors, an online course in outdoor education seems especially oxymoronic and would serve to further alienate students from the outdoors. Hence, although in some instances online programming may be an effective means of education, one cannot achieve most of the more powerful lessons and goals of outdoor education when devoid of interaction with the natural environment.

Authentic Experience or Virtual Reality?

As information technology advances, the role of the educator continues to evolve. Although all educators share similar responsibilities (e.g., sharing expectations, crafting outcomes, creating learning environments, creating authentic and meaningful assignments) regardless of how the content is delivered, the role of the educator is critical for enhancing learning. One can argue that assignments posted online can require students to visit an outdoor site or engage in some other type of outdoor experience. However, an important contributor to the process, the educator, is largely absent from the equation once the directions have been posted. "The instructor-to-student and instructor-to-group interaction is so central to the learning experience" that a whole book was written on the role of the instructor in the Outward Bound process (Kalisch, 1979, p. 3).

Moreover, students and teachers relate differently, and better, when the outdoors becomes the classroom (Hammerman, Hammerman, and Hammerman, 2001). Seeing teachers in regular clothes hiking through a bog or laying in a sleeping bag stargazing as a member of a dream circle can help students begin to view teachers as more like them, which can enhance rapport in other learning situations. Such environments also allow teachers to see students in a different light. Many of us can probably recall a story about a student who, despite struggling in a traditional classroom environment, blossomed in the outdoors—excited, curious, and interested in a new learning environment—and seeing this, the teacher responded accordingly and gained a new perspective on the student. These experiences shared between educator and student are simply not possible through online programming, where students interface with teachers through the sterile medium of electronic stimuli and pixilated screens.

Kilpatrick (1927) argues that the most beneficial of all school activities occur when students and teachers work alongside one another to solve problems. Kilpatrick suggests that learning demands actual experience in a social situation in order to facilitate application. Such facilitated application, according to Dewey (1938), is critical for learning experiences to be meaningful. In accordance with Dewey, considered by many to be the father of experiential education, in order for an experience to be educative, the teacher is responsible for planning, organizing, and structuring the learning experience. Although teachers can do this to some degree through online programming, such a medium does not allow the teacher to observe the students firsthand, nor does it allow for any direct experience and interaction between teacher and learner in the environment.

Given the challenge of limited face-to-face interaction with peers that is inherent in online learning, one is hard pressed to argue that online programming is equivalent to an authentic experience in a face-to-face setting accompanied by a skilled outdoor educator. Although Gorsky and Blau (2009) found that the creation of a social presence in the online community aided in developing personal and purposeful relationships between educators and learners, this presence is a secondary and indirect experience and is not an adequate substitute for direct interaction. In the virtual world, it is impossible for a teacher to directly observe a student's level of comfort with the natural world. It is impossible for students to smell the delicious vanilla–butterscotch scent of a Jeffrey pine or experience the tongue-numbing sensation of licking the underside of a banana slug. It is impossible for the teacher to observe how students respond when their peers give them critical feedback on their performance. It is impossible to tell whether students are engaged in the learning task at all. Nor does the virtual world allow the teacher to take advantage of spontaneous opportunities for learning, or teachable moments (e.g., a bald eagle soaring overhead), that frequently present themselves when teacher and students interact directly in the natural environment.

Virtual environments may provide direction and prompt students to engage in an experience, but they lack the authenticity that is perceived as crucial to education (Dewey, 1938). If the goal of education is to provide students with meaningful learning experiences, it rests with the educator to find or create and facilitate such meaningful experiences (Coates, 2010). Although the Internet may be an efficient means of transmitting information to students, it is not an effective mode of providing learning experiences that meaningfully fulfill the goals of outdoor education. When teachers

are present with students, they are better able to guide students through reflective learning activities and assist them in applying information and hence are more likely to facilitate meaningful learning experiences.

What Is Diminished or Lost in the Virtual World?

To illustrate the importance of direct interaction in effectively achieving the goals of outdoor education, we present a long-standing outdoor education program in the recreation, parks, and leisure studies (RPLS) department at SUNY Cortland. One course, the outdoor education practicum (OEP), is required of all RPLS students regardless of major. OEP is a 13-day wilderness experience held in Adirondack State Park. This experience, reported by many to be life changing, has its roots in traditional outdoor education. The sense of community and accomplishment described by participants would be impossible to match through an online experience. In fact, in alumni surveys, many list OEP as the most powerful and meaningful experience of their student career at SUNY Cortland. It would be almost counterintuitive as educators to shift all outdoor education to a distance-learning model and steal this powerful, transformative experience from students for the sake of efficiency.

Researchers have explored sense of place and group cohesion during the OEP experience (e.g., Todd et al., 2008), and although results indicate that sense of place was not significantly correlated to sense of community, the evidence was overwhelmingly positive that the OEP experience built a sense of community among students. It would border on the ridiculous to state that a 13-day outdoor education program through online programming builds a sense of community of students as effectively as having them experience group living and learning out in the field in all the elements. Online learning certainly has its place in education. However, in terms of personal and group development, it lacks the authenticity that field-based programming can provide.

Much has been written on sense of community, place attachment, and belongingness within wilderness settings (e.g., Manning, 2010). Social scientists have even provided theoretical frameworks in which to ground sense of community (e.g., McMillan and Chavis, 1986). Sarason (1974) proposes that sense of community is less about physical space and more about a sense of relatedness to others. This type of impact also comes from taking student groups into outdoor settings, or at least taking them to nonfamiliar places where they are no longer comfortable. Luckner and Nadler (1997) indicate that disequilibrium must occur for this change to take place. For the student to experience personal growth, a trained facilitator is often needed to foster this experience and safely lead the student through a growth zone. This art of facilitation is delicate and requires continuous and often immediate feedback during the outdoor pursuit. Such a process would be extremely challenging, if not impossible, to implement through online programming.

Despite some of the potential advantages associated with online programming, this mode of instruction is not as effective in achieving the goals of outdoor education as are more traditional, field-based approaches. Ultimately, to be effective, learning needs to be remembered. We tend to remember those events and experiences in our lives that are out of the ordinary, that tap our senses and our emotions, and that we share with others. Achieving this requires real-time instruction that incorporates field experiences. If we recall some of our most significant learning experiences, how many of us would count among them any that entailed sitting in front of our computer screen flipping through a PowerPoint lecture, posting a response on an online discussion board, or listening to a podcast? Our guess is not many.

Conclusion

Much of society is moving to a digital world, but that does not mean we should sacrifice teaching outdoor education in its most effective way. Teaching via online programming would diminish the value and richness many of us have gained throughout our years as outdoor education students. A recent article in *USA Today* (Swartz, 2011) reports that overuse of social media networks (e.g., Flickr, Twitter, Facebook, and so on) has been linked to an increase in mistakes and a loss of productivity in the workplace. Such findings blame the overstimulation on the abundance and need to be in many virtual places at once. In addition, advocating for the use of online programming to achieve the goals of outdoor education adds to the national concern of distancing our youth from nature, resulting in what Louv (2005) coined nature-deficit disorder, a current problem that could only grow if outdoor education is to go online.

Outdoor education has a rich tradition that is the foundation for many secondary and tertiary education programs in the United States. Many of us can likely recall powerful outdoor education experiences that may be the very reason we chose to pursue a profession in, or related to, outdoor education. Perhaps it was a college class, an Outward Bound course, or a teacher who showed us the power of the outdoors and what can happen when people and the outdoors come together. It could have been a majestic mountain view, working with a group on a challenge course element, the refreshing scent of a Fraser fir, reaching the summit of our first mountain, or seeing wildlife in its natural environment. Would it not be a disservice to all if the next generation of students has only computer-screen images of such experiences?

References

Coates, T. (2010). *Crossroads and decisions: Where do we go from here?* Julian Smith Award Lecture, AAPHERD Convention, Indianapolis, IN. www.aahperd.org/aapar/people/councils/loader.cfm?csModule=security/getfile&pageid=62889 [December 21, 2010].

Dewey, J. (1938). *Experience and education.* New York: Touchstone.

Donaldson, G.W., & Donaldson, L.E. (1958). Outdoor education: A definition. *Journal of Physical Education, Recreation and Dance, 29*(5), 63.

Gilbertson, K., Bates, T., McLaughlin, T., & Ewert, A. (2006). *Outdoor education: Methods and strategies.* Champaign, IL: Human Kinetics.

Gorsky, P., & Blau, I. (2009). Online teaching effectiveness: A tale of two instructors. *International Review of Research in Open and Distance Learning, 10*(3), 1-27.

Hammerman, D.R., Hammerman, W.M., & Hammerman, E.L. (2001). *Teaching in the outdoors.* 5th ed. Danville, IL: Interstate Publishing.

Kalisch, K.R. (1979). *The role of the instructor in the Outward Bound educational process.* Kearney, NE: Morris.

Kilpatrick, W.H. (1927). *Education for a changing civilization.* New York: Macmillan.

Louv, R. (2005). *Last child in the woods: Saving our children from nature-deficit disorder.* Chapel Hill, NC: Algonquin Books of Chapel Hill.

Luckner, J., & Nadler, R. (1997). *Processing the experience: Strategies to enhance and generalize learning.* Dubuque, IA: Kendall/Hunt.

Manning, R. (2010). *Studies in outdoor recreation: Search and research for satisfaction.* 3rd ed. Corvallis, OR: Oregon State University Press.

McMillan, D., & Chavis, D. (1986). Sense of community: A definition and theory. *Journal of Social Psychology, 16,* 6-23.

Miner, J.L., & Boldt, J.R. (2002). *Outward Bound USA: Crew not passengers.* Seattle: The Mountaineers.

Priest, S. (1986). Redefining outdoor education: A matter of many relationships. *Journal of Environmental Education, 17*(3), 13-15.

Sarason, S.B. (1974). *The psychological sense of community: Perspectives for community psychology.* San Francisco: Jossey-Bass.

Sharp, L.B. (1943). Outside the classroom. *The Educational Forum, 7*(4), 361-368.

Shellman, A. (2009). *Empowerment and resilience: A multi-method approach to understanding processes and outcomes of adventure education experiences.* Unpublished doctoral dissertation. Bloomington, IN: Indiana University.

Smith, J. (1972). *Outdoor education.* Upper Saddle River, NJ: Prentice-Hall.

Swartz, J. (2011, February 1). Social media users grapple with information overload. *USA Today.* www.usatoday.com/tech/news/2011-02-01-tech-overload_N.htm [December 28, 2011].

Todd, S., Young, A., Anderson, L., O'Connell, T., & Breunig, M. (2008). Sense of place in outdoor pursuits trip groups. In D. Klenosky & C.C. Fisher (Eds.), *Proceedings of the 2008 Northeastern Recreation Research Symposium* (pp. 172-180). Bolton Landing, NY: U.S. Department of Agriculture, Forest Service, Northern Research Station.

Walsh, V., & Golins, G. (1976). *The exploration of the Outward Bound process.* Denver: Colorado Outward Bound School.

Controversial Issue 20

Is outcomes-based research currently more important than critical research for the field of adventure programming?

All types of research can be conducted when there are no constraints on resources. However, in many Western countries in recent years, research funding has become more contestable and research providers have been increasingly pressured to conduct particular types of research. Lather (2006), for example, notes that within educational research there has been a "resurgent positivism and governmental imposition of experimental design as the gold standard in research methods" (p. 35). This resurgence of the experimental design sits within a context of increasing budget cuts in institutions of higher education in many countries. Adventure program research is not immune to the shifts in what counts as excellent research, nor are adventure programs exempt from decreasing budgets. Despite this new political reality, some have called to move away from positivistic approaches and toward research that is grounded in critical theory and that focuses on the situatedness of a particular adventure program experience (Rea, 2008).

This context produces tension between competing adventure program research approaches, and questions of research priorities arise. For example, is it better to seek funding for research that aims to find out whether an adventure program produces desired results, or is it more important to fund research that questions the fundamental propositions on which all adventure programming rests? Responses to these questions inevitably involve ethical, epistemological, political, and pragmatic perspectives.

In teaching for research in adventure programming, it is important to look not just at research methods but at the broader political landscape in which research occurs. This includes questions concerning the types of research currently being supported via funding bodies and the implications that this support has for what we know about adventure programs and how we think about our practices in the field and in research. Given that we do not have unlimited resources to do all the research many of us would like to do, how are decisions about research priorities made in the field of adventure programming and who should make these decisions? Are there implications for the field of adventure programming if, in our research, we eschew methods of research favored by major funding organizations and government policies?

The following argument considers this dilemma by addressing the question, Is outcomes-based research currently more important than critical research for the field of adventure programming? Robyn Zink argues that outcomes-based research is essential in providing evidence that adventure programs achieve intended results. Outcomes-based research is also essential in identifying the effective elements of programs and thus provides a basis for promoting best practices in the industry. These two functions help both in program development and in securing and retaining funding for programs.

Pip Lynch, on the other hand, argues that an urgent need exists for critical research from which new theory building in adventure programming can develop. The new theory and the critical research behind it both inform a more coherent, robust basis for adventure programming practices. Critical research, moreover, is important in questioning the assumptions on which the practices of adventure programming are based and helps to reveal how these assumptions support or limit the purported objectives of practice. Lynch also argues that critical research opens windows to future possibilities and the contributions that adventure programming can make to some of the significant challenges in the modern world. This argument addresses questions such as where limited adventure programming research resources should go, the sorts of knowledge that are produced by different types of research, and how that knowledge can be used in adventure program practice.

References

Lather, P. (2006). Paradigm proliferation as a good thing to think with: Teaching research in education as a wild profusion. *International Journal of Qualitative Studies in Education, 19*(1), 35-57.

Rea, T. (2008). Methodologies in outdoor education research: Approaches from an alternate discourse. *Journal of Adventure Education and Outdoor Learning, 8*(1), 43-53.

Is outcomes-based research currently more important than critical research for the field of adventure programming?

YES Outcomes-Based Research Produces Key Evidence Supporting Adventure Programming

Robyn Zink, PhD, MA, independent researcher, Zink Research, Dunedin, New Zealand

We have probably all heard people proclaim, and maybe have even said ourselves, that we know adventure programs work. After all, we have seen the difference a program can make to the participants. But how do we know this and where is the evidence that supports this assumption? Most of us, rightly, do not find it acceptable when politicians, policy makers, or industry leaders say, "Trust us—we know what we're doing!" Yet we expect parents to do exactly that when they hand their children over to us. We also expect funding bodies to trust us when they hand over money from what is an ever-shrinking pot of funding for educational programs.

Along with this increased competition for funding, policy makers and governments are looking more and more to make decisions on evidence-based research (Babbie, 2007). Lather (2006) observes that within education research, governments are turning to evidence-based research that is grounded in an experimental design. "Experimental design" refers to a biomedical model of research in which changes are measured in reference to a control group. The experimental design can produce evidence of how an outcome is achieved as well as what the outcome of an intervention is; the latter is particularly pertinent to establishing and communicating the effectiveness of adventure programming in the current political and funding climate. That is, evidence is being sought in response to the question, "Is this program producing the intended result or outcome?" The type of research that produces such evidence is known as outcomes-based research.

At the same time, some adventure programming researchers call to move away from research focused on impacts and outcomes toward research that looks at the situatedness and particularities of individual programs and participants (Rea, 2006, 2008). These competing calls, in an environment of decreasing resources, inevitably create tensions about the sorts of research that should have pri-

ority. Responses to this tension involve political and pragmatic questions of how research can best serve the needs of the adventure programming field. In addressing this issue, I focus on the role that outcomes-based research has in producing key evidence to support adventure programming.

In making the case for outcomes-based research, I describe this sort of research and discuss two significant benefits of undertaking it: program improvements, and the ability to justify the existence of and need for adventure programming in the current political climate. I then discuss some of the challenges of undertaking high-quality outcomes-based research in adventure programming. Lynch argues that an urgent need exists for critical research (see page 309); however, conducting this type of research at this time is perilous. These perils include the limited evidence of critical research delivering on its promise for change, the inability to make comparisons and links across a variety of contexts, and the lack of clarity in the terminology used. I conclude my discussion of this issue by arguing that researchers need to be able to respond to the current political climate because research has to reflect and meet the needs of that climate to get recognition and gain funding for adventure programs.

What Is Outcomes-Based Research?

At its most basic level, outcomes-based research tells us the difference a particular experience makes. Outcomes-based research is concerned with measuring this difference. The key objective in this research is to establish the effectiveness of a particular intervention and to help "practitioners make decisions about *how* to practice . . ." (Ewert and Sibthorp, 2009, p. 377, italics in the original). Good-quality outcomes-based research allows one to make meaningful comparisons between programs, thus helping practitioners make decisions about what to do based on evidence from the whole field of adventure programming, not just from their own program. Good-quality outcomes-based research will garner respect in the scientific world (Sibthorp, 2000) and will enhance the standing of adventure programming as a credible field.

Stronach (2008) states that outcomes-based research is not necessarily associated with a discipline base such as philosophy, economics, or psychology. It refers to "a research purpose rather than a specific method" (Babbie, 2007, p. 349). It is about finding out whether something has occurred and what caused any change that did occur. Outcomes-based research is about looking at what *is* rather than what *should be* (Babbie, 2007).

Measurement is at the heart of outcomes-based research. Sibthorp (2000) states, "Measurement involves the numerical description and differentiation of things and allows communication about and comparisons between concepts that could otherwise become confusing" (p. 102). One of the challenges of measurement is deciding what to measure and how to measure it. To be credible, "researchers must take measurement quite seriously in evaluation research, carefully determining all the variables to be measured and getting appropriate measures for each" (Babbie, 2007, p. 355). Researchers must pay careful attention to issues of validity and reliability and to developing shared definitions of variables to be measured (Sibthorp, 2000). They must also be cognizant of the inherently political nature of determining what is to be measured and how it is to be measured (Babbie, 2007). The view that science and research are neutral has long disappeared (Punch, 1998). Decisions about what to measure and how to measure something are shaped by the larger social and political context in which research is located (Taylor and Balloch, 2005). After all, the findings from a research project can make the difference between a program continuing to exist and program funding being cut.

Why We Need Credible Outcomes-Based Research in Adventure Programming

The outcomes that have received the most attention in adventure program research to date are largely associated with personal and social development (see, for example, Gassner and Russell, 2008; Gilles and Speelman, 2008; Hans, 2000; McKenzie, 2000). Hattie and colleagues (1997) also identified outcomes of adventure programs associated with academic improvement and an increased sense of adventure. Two key justifications exist for high-quality outcomes-based research in adventure programming today. The first is that we need to know what we can achieve in our programs. The second is that the current political and economic climate demands that we support our claims with evidence.

Using Outcomes-Based Research to Promote Evidence-Based Practice

In a discussion about educational research, Feuer (2006) argues that the aim of research seeking evidence of outcomes is the continual improvement of teaching and learning. Shooter (2010) notes that it is now standard practice in many adventure programs to document the outcomes of those programs. I later discuss some of the challenges of ascertaining whether a desired outcome has been achieved.

One pressing problem with regard to examining adventure programs is bringing together disparate research to paint a coherent picture of what adventure programs achieve and how they achieve these outcomes. Both Pinch (2009) and Sibthorp (2009) argue that we need to evaluate programs to examine what we do, not to validate what we do. Good-quality outcomes-based research that continues to build on existing studies helps to fill current gaps in understanding (Shooter, 2010). Ewert and Sibthorp (2009), Nichols (2000), and Russell and Sibthorp (2004), for example, have suggested various models around which to build research so that individual research projects contribute to a comprehensive understanding of program outcomes and enable rigorous comparison of results across studies. Building a more comprehensive picture of adventure programming through outcomes-based research also facilitates communication with others in the field, including policy makers and funding agencies.

Improving the teaching and learning that occurs in adventure programs is only one reason, albeit a very important one, for having sound and rigorous research that tells us what adventure programming does. Adventure programs are not unique in the claims they make about outcomes. For example, many arts-based, service learning, and sports programs make similar claims. Research must help us understand how the processes and outcomes of adventure programming address contemporary social and educational issues. Indeed, Lather (2006) goes so far as to state that this is our warrant to conduct research in the first place.

Adventure programs are comparatively expensive to run because of the high student-to-staff ratios and equipment and travel costs. They also have an inherent risk factor that is absent from many other programs that purport to achieve similar outcomes. Some studies indicate that organizations are turning away from the provision of adventure programs because of the financial and legal ramifications of offering risky programs (Lugg and Martin, 2001; Zink and Boyes, 2006). Unless we have evidence of how adventure programs address contemporary issues and how they are uniquely positioned to achieve these outcomes, we should not be surprised that funders turn to other programs that make similar claims and that do not have the added cost and complexity of working in a risky environment (Pinch, 2009).

Good-quality outcomes-based research provides a foundation for programmers and policy makers to argue how adventure programs can contribute to addressing many of the educational and social problems of the day (Feuer, 2006). Although the sorts of research being undertaken have proliferated and there have been ongoing calls to use a greater range of research methodologies, it is unclear whether this proliferation has led to greater clarity in understanding what adventure programs can achieve or how they work. Rist (1998) makes a similar point and suggests that greater complexity in the research landscape has left policy makers less able to understand the relevant issues and, consequently, how best to proceed in identifying the educational and social issues that adventure programming can address. I argue that program providers are no more able to deal with the complexity of the research landscape than are policy makers. We need to ask ourselves which paradigm has contributed the most to adventure programming practice with regard both to understanding how outcomes are achieved and to our ability to communicate those outcomes to each other and to the wider world.

Establishing the Relevance of Adventure Programming in the Current Political Climate

Another equally compelling justification exists for outcomes-based research in the field of adventure programming today. Research is coming under increasing scrutiny within universities and from government agencies, which ultimately fund research (Babbie, 2007). The legislative and policy changes that promote scientifically based research in education in many countries are well documented (Denzin, 2008; Lather, 2006; St. Pierre, 2006; Stronach, 2008; Torrance, 2008).

Researchers in the area of adventure programming need to be cognizant of the political and policy climate irrespective of their ontological or epistemological stance regarding research. This has become particularly important given the increasing calls within the field for more critical research that looks at understanding the experiences of particular participants within specific programs (e.g., Allison and Pomeroy, 2000; Rea, 2006, 2008).

Torrance (2008) argues that research and policy must work together. Researchers must be able to talk to people who develop and set policy. This means that the policy makers must see the research as relevant. Because outcomes-based research, particularly quantitative research, fits the expectations of policy makers very neatly, we researchers need to know how statistics work and what they do (Lather, 2006). Both researchers and practitioners need to understand how outcomes-based research can help to improve and deliver quality adventure programs that achieve desired outcomes. To conduct research that does not, in some way, respond to the political climate may mean that researchers find they do not have a place at the negotiation table when it comes to decisions about what programs and research work will get funded. Sibthorp (2009) found that if he wanted research funding, he had to do research that funders were interested in supporting.

St. Pierre (2006) makes the point that the stakes are high when it comes to choosing the type of research to undertake. The quality and veracity of research are increasingly being measured through the criteria of the biomedical experimental research design. Quality-assessment frameworks are being used more widely to measure more detail of the delivery of education (Denzin, 2008). For example, in 2004 the Institute of Education Science in the United States argued that the dominance of qualitative research in education was "a clear sign of the mismatch between the focus of the practice community and the current research community" (Lather, 2006, p. 45). The solution the Institute of Education Science proposed is greater training in psychometrics and statistical analysis for doctoral students if future research in education is going to contribute to solving the problems we face. If adventure program researchers are unable to do likewise, adventure programming is in danger of not even making it on the list of possible educational or intervention options to be supported and funded.

As researchers, we need to be able to identify and address the professional needs and knowledge gaps in the field. Currently, discussion about research training in our field is limited. Given the methodological challenges of conducting high-caliber outcomes-based research (discussed later), better research training in outcomes-based methods can only enhance our understanding of adventure programs. This area deserves attention. How well are research students placed to respond to the gaps in the field and the demands of the current political and funding climate? Producing good-quality outcomes-based research demands high-level research skills because adventure programming interventions are inherently complex (Sibthorp, 2000).

Challenges to Conducting Sound Outcomes-Based Research in Adventure Programming

Outcomes-based research can be threatening because it is about finding out whether something is there or whether a particular intervention makes a desired difference (Babbie, 2007). Findings from this type of research can challenge cherished beliefs and assumptions about what adventure programming can achieve. In two seminal works, Hattie and colleagues (1997) and McKenzie (2000) undertook meta-analyses of adventure programming research. In both cases they found that research in the field was largely informed by a desire to identify and quantify the outcomes that programs achieved. Although they brought together significant bodies of research in their respective studies, their ability to make comparisons or draw conclusions across the studies they reviewed was limited due to the methodological weaknesses inherent in many of the studies. Little consistency existed among the methods used, and many were so poorly designed that Hattie and colleagues (1997) state that they read more like promotional material than research and often ignored any contrary evidence. In a recent meta-analysis of research measuring the effectiveness of challenge ropes courses, Gilles and Speelman (2008) comment that they were often unable to judge the quality of a piece of research because not enough information was provided about how data were collected and analyzed.

Priest and Gass (2005) point out that the experimental model is difficult to implement in adventure programming research for a number of reasons. Identifying a control group is often problematic, particularly for programs that target specific populations and have an educational or therapeutic intent. Small groups are a normal part of adventure programs; this creates challenges when using statistical models to draw conclusions about outcomes. Many programs are custom designed for a specific group, so no two programs are exactly alike. We work with the added challenge that the majority of programs take place in outdoor settings and the environmental conditions constantly change; this can have a significant effect on activities and outcomes (Bocarro and Richards, 1998). Researchers must be as rigorous as possible in the design, analysis, and reporting of research so that we can draw the most credible conclusions from data across studies with a degree of confidence.

The aim of outcomes-based research is to improve practice and to communicate clearly to practitioners and to policy makers what happens. That is, the aim is to make a positive difference in the "real world" (Babbie, 2007). A tendency exists within critical research to assume that it is better positioned to achieve the ideals of social justice as it works to unmask the myriad ways in which power is held and wielded. Critical research has itself been criticized for falling far short of the ideal of bringing about change that will empower and liberate those who are disadvantaged (see, for example, Sicilia-Camacho and Fernandez-Balboa, 2009). As Denzin (2008) notes, nothing about any form of research is inherently good or bad. What is problematic are sweeping generalizations that direct attention away from the various purposes to which any research method can be used. Critical research can be complicit in supporting the status quo, whereas outcomes-based research can bring about social change that is advantageous to marginalized groups.

One aim of good-quality outcomes-based research is to find ways to make meaningful comparisons between programs so that the utility of various interventions can be assessed. Critical research, on the other hand, is focused on the particular; that is, on the details of a specific program and the individuals within that program (Rea, 2006, 2008). A significant limitation of much of critical research is that the studies produced are "small-scale, disconnected, non-cumulative studies that do not provide convincing explanations of educational phenomena or how best to develop teaching and learning" (Torrance, 2008, pp. 55-56). A focus on the particular provides little scope for practitioners and policy makers to make decisions about how best to achieve desired outcomes across a range of contexts. A focus on the particular in research is a disservice to adventure programming at this time given that significant gaps still exist in our understanding of what adventure programs can achieve and how to best realize these outcomes. Although things may be unique to each situation, it is also clear that some things are "reliably produced given certain environmental factors" (Protevi, 2009, p. 22).

To make meaningful comparisons between programs, researchers have to very carefully define the terms used (Babbie, 2007; Sibthorp, 2000). Maxwell (2008) states that the experimental method might more regularly force us to argue clearly and define the terms we use carefully rather than remain vague or obfuscate the discussion with complex and technical language that so often characterizes critical research. As noted earlier, this is an inherently political process. It underscores the need for excellent research training so students can engage in the work of clearly defining terms used and understand "both the politics of evaluation practice and the political role attributed to evaluation" (Taylor and Balloch, 2005, p. 1). As long as researchers clearly identify and define the environmental factors they are focusing on, outcomes-based research can make a significant contribution to understanding what is reliably produced given a certain set of circumstances. This, in turn, gives practitioners and policy makers confidence that the interventions they use are based on credible evidence rather than on a whim or ideology (Feuer, 2006).

Conclusion

Without a doubt, a great need exists for good-quality research that documents adventure program outcomes and how these outcomes are achieved to enhance the quality of programs we offer. We need to be able to clearly argue why adventure programming matters, and to do that we need to have effective research on the outcomes of our programs. Unless we can clearly state what the outcomes of adventure programs are and how our programs achieve these outcomes, we do not have a strong foundation to improve our practices or to argue for the ongoing existence of these programs.

Different types of research produce different ways of thinking and acting around a phenomenon. The debate about the sorts of knowledge produced through different research paradigms is ongoing and vigorous. Outcomes-based research sets out to establish what is going on in a program. But decisions about the type of research to undertake are also political and pragmatic. Students, researchers, and program directors need to understand these political and pragmatic tensions and locate their

work within these tensions (Lather, 2006). The current political climate demands work that provides evidence of purported outcomes. Researchers need to be able to conduct research that responds to this climate.

Eschewing outcomes-based research in favor of critical work could have serious negative consequences for adventure programs and research on these programs at this time. Given the significant gaps in what we know about the impact of adventure programming practices, outcomes-based research is vital in understanding what we do in programming and how we can improve our practice. Given the current political and policy climate in which audit and accountability culture dominates, we need to undertake research that responds to that climate and enables discussions with policy makers and funders about the veracity and value of the programs and research we are advocating for. At the present time, outcomes-based research is more important than critical research to the adventure programming field.

References

Allison, P., & Pomeroy, E. (2000). How shall we "know"? Epistemological concerns in research in experiential education. *The Journal of Experiential Education, 23*(2), 91-98.

Babbie, E. (2007). *The practice of social research.* 11th ed. Belmont, CA: Thomson Higher Education.

Bocarro, J., & Richards, A. (1998). Experiential research at risk: The challenge of shifting traditional research paradigms. *Journal of Experiential Education, 21*(2), 102-107.

Denzin, N.K. (2008). The new paradigm dialogs and qualitative inquiry. *International Journal of Qualitative Studies in Education, 21*(4), 315-325.

Ewert, A., & Sibthorp, J. (2009). Creating outcomes through experiential education: The challenge of confounding variables. *Journal of Experiential Education, 31*(3), 376-389.

Feuer, M.J. (2006). Response to Bettie St. Pierre's "Scientifically based research in education: Epistemology and ethics." *Adult Education Quarterly, 56*(4), 267-272.

Gassner, M.E., & Russell, K.C. (2008). Relative impact of course components at Outward Bound Singapore: A retrospective study of long-term outcomes. *Journal of Adventure Education and Outdoor Learning, 8*(2), 133-156.

Gilles, H.L., & Speelman, E. (2008). Are challenge (ropes) courses an effective tool? A meta-analysis. *Journal of Experiential Education, 31*(2), 111-135.

Hans, T.A. (2000). A meta-analysis of the effects of adventure programming on locus of control. *Journal of Contemporary Psychotherapy, 30*(1), 33-60.

Hattie, J., Marsh, J.W., Neill, J.T., & Richards, G.E. (1997). Adventure education and Outward Bound: Out-of-class experiences that make a lasting difference. *Review of Educational Research, 67*(1), 43-87.

Lather, P. (2006). Paradigm proliferation as a good thing to think with: Teaching research in education as a wild profusion. *International Journal of Qualitative Studies in Education, 19*(1), 35-57.

Lugg, A., & Martin, P. (2001). The nature and scope of outdoor education in Victorian schools. *Australian Journal of Outdoor Education, 5*(2), 42-48.

Maxwell, J.A. (2008). The value of realist understanding of causality for qualitative research. In N.K. Denzin & M.D. Giardina (Eds.), *Qualitative inquiry and the politics of evidence* (pp. 163-181). Thousand Oaks, CA: Sage.

McKenzie, M.D. (2000). How are adventure education program outcomes achieved? A review of the literature. *Australian Journal of Outdoor Education, 5*(1), 19-27.

Nichols, G. (2000). A research agenda for adventure education. *Australian Journal of Outdoor Education, 4*(2), 22-31.

Pinch, K.J. (2009). The importance of evaluation research. *Journal of Experiential Education, 31*(3), 390-394.

Priest, S., & Gass, M.A. (2005). *Effective leadership in adventure programming*. 2nd ed. Champaign, IL: Human Kinetics.

Protevi, J. (2009). *Political affect: Connecting the social and the somatic*. Minneapolis: University of Minnesota Press.

Punch, M. (1998). Politics and ethics in qualitative research. In N.K. Denzin & Y.S. Lincoln (Eds.), *The landscape of qualitative research: Theories and issues* (pp. 156-184). Thousand Oaks, CA: Sage.

Rea, T. (2006). "It's not as if we're teaching them . . .": Reflective thinking in the outdoor classroom. *Journal of Adventure Education and Outdoor Learning, 6*(2), 121-134.

Rea, T. (2008). Methodologies in outdoor education research: Approaches from an alternate discourse. *Journal of Adventure Education and Outdoor Learning, 8*(1), 43-53.

Rist, R.C. (1998). Influencing the policy process with qualitative research. In N.K. Denzin & Y.S. Lincoln (Eds.), *Collecting and interpreting qualitative materials* (pp. 400-424). Thousand Oaks, CA: Sage.

Russell, A., & Sibthorp, J. (2004). Hierarchical data structures in adventure education and therapy. *Journal of Experiential Education, 27*(2), 176-190.

Shooter, W. (2010). A closer look at the 'inner workings' of adventure education: Building evidence-based best practice. *Journal of Experiential Education, 32*(3), 290-294.

Sibthorp, J. (2000). Measuring weather . . . and adventure education: Exploring the instruments of adventure education research. *Journal of Experiential Education, 23*(2), 99-107.

Sibthorp, J. (2009). Making a difference with experiential education research: Quality and focus. *Journal of Experiential Education, 31*(3), 456-459.

Sicilia-Camacho, A., & Fernandez-Balboa, J.M. (2009). Reflecting on the moral basis of critical pedagogy in PETE: Toward a Foucauldian perspective on ethics and care of the self. *Sport, Education and Society, 14*(4), 443-463.

St. Pierre, E.A. (2006). Scientifically based research in education: Epistemology and ethics. *Adult Education Quarterly, 56*(4), 239-266.

Stronach, I. (2008). On promoting rigor in educational research: The example of the UK's research assessment exercise. In N.K. Denzin & M.D. Giardina (Eds.), *Qualitative inquiry and the politics of evidence* (pp. 80-96). Walnut Creek, CA: Left Coast Press.

Taylor, D., & Balloch, S. (2005). The politics of evaluation: An overview. In D. Taylor & S. Balloch (Eds.), *The politics of evaluation: Participation and policy implementation* (pp. 1-17). Bristol, U.K.: The Policy Press.

Torrance, H. (2008). Building confidence in qualitative research: Engaging the demands of policy. In N.K. Denzin & M.D. Giardina (Eds.), *Qualitative inquiry and the politics of evidence* (pp. 55-79). Walnut Creek, CA: Left Coast Press.

Zink, R., & Boyes, M. (2006). The nature and scope of outdoor education in New Zealand schools. *Australian Journal of Outdoor Education, 10*(1), 11-21.

Is outcomes-based research currently more important than critical research for the field of adventure programming?

Critical Research Produces a Robust Knowledge Base for Adventure Programming

Pip Lynch, PhD, MEd, professor of friluftsliv (outdoor life), Norwegian School of Sport Sciences, Oslo, Norway

In times of financial stringency in outdoor programming, critical research is essential. Financial pressure is felt more keenly in educational organizations and programs that have more tenuous links to mainstream curricula or less robust theoretical and philosophical foundations. Arguably, adventure programming falls into both these categories. As I illustrate in this argument, recent research literature takes to task many of the fundamental assumptions in adventure programming research and practice and exposes in them deep flaws that undermine any conclusions drawn from outcomes-based research. Therefore, an urgent need exists for critical research as a basis for new theories that inform a more coherent, robust foundation for adventure programming practices and, consequentially, outcomes-based research.

The critiques of adventure programming are so strident that they threaten the integrity of the field as a whole. Only by clarifying its foundational concepts and ideas can the field continue to claim a place in the wider human enterprise of education. Securing such a place goes hand in hand with securing funding for ongoing research and field practice.

What Is Critical Research?

Rather than accepting the social world as it appears to be and then describing and measuring it, critical social science takes a skeptical stance and questions not only the way things appear to be but also how knowledge about them is created and what other possibilities might exist. It refuses to accept that human society is governed by immutable laws and it seeks to expose the "ambiguities, misrepresentations, distortions and even falsehoods among . . . competing explanations for particular social phenomena" (Willis, 1999, p. 98).

The outdoors, for example, is not as straightforward as it seems, according to critical researchers. In adventure programming, the outdoors is usually understood as natural physical environments, at best unmodified by humans. Natural environments make up the backdrop to outdoor programming; they tend to be universalized (e.g., as wilderness) so that the details of ecology, geography, and climate are ignored. Yet, as several authors (e.g., Brookes, 2002; Stewart, 2004) point out, many different forms of outdoors exist even in one region of one country, and each potentially affects the types of experiences, and therefore education, possible. To take a universalized understanding of outdoors and apply it to adventure programming is to promote a particular view of the world for a particular purpose. Noting that aspects of outdoor programming also occur in indoor locations, such as climbing walls, training pools, and even classrooms, Zink and Burrows (2008) suggest that the view promoted by a universalized outdoors is that of a simplified place, unlike the cluttered complexities of everyday, urban life, and that this view works to produce particular sorts of knowledge through adventure programming. I come back to this point shortly.

Critical social science is informed by the work of critical social theorists who target totalizing theories (e.g., Marxist theory of class relations) as problematic (Kincheloe and McLaren, 1994). In totalizing theories, one understands social relations and activity through relatively fixed directions of power and influence (e.g., the wealthy oppress the poor). In education, totalizing theories tend to view school and schooling as (in one reading) institutions of social reproduction (Kincheloe and McLaren, 1994). By contrast, critical theorists have unmasked the myriad ways in which actors of all backgrounds hold and wield power, suggesting complex networks of social interaction incorporating linear (e.g., class) interactions, among many others. That is, critical theorists dispute the usefulness of singular, all-encompassing views of the way society works and instead stress the multiple ways in which individuals and social groups hold, withhold, use, abuse, enact, and act on power and influence. In education, critical theorists view schools and educational programs as sites of possibility rather than inevitability; sites that may hold rich possibilities for individual empowerment just as they may also hold possibilities for suppression, oppression, ambivalence, none of these, or all of these. In adventure programming, for example, participants may use the novelty of adventure activities as opportunities to experience, and experiment with, relative freedom from the constraints of their usual social contexts (e.g., expectations of school or family).

However, as Lynch and Moore (2004) observe, adventure programming can also reinforce and inculcate capitalist and materialist ideologies, for example, through use of the latest equipment and focus on work-oriented values such as teamwork and leadership. Conversely, they argue, it might also provide individual participants with possibilities for subverting capitalism and constructing new ways of understanding their lives. Similarly, Martin (2004) argues that outdoor adventure can be an important tool for connecting individuals with natural environments.

Critical theory takes many forms, and deep disagreements exist between some of its proponents. Nonetheless, critical theorists, following the work of Jurgen Habermas, agree that knowledge is shaped by the interests it serves. For Habermas, human values, judgments, and interests (politics) give rise to the "possible modes of thought through which reality may be constituted and acted upon" (Carr and Kemmis, 1986, p. 134). To expose modes of thought, critical theorists analyze language and discourses (lines of argument). Language, culture, and identity are central concerns and characterize the data of critical researchers. Competing lines of argument vie for the supremacy of the knowledge they produce. Knowledge, then, is never stable and should not be considered truth; it is always contingent on the social and personal histories through which it was produced.

We now return to Zink and Burrows' (2008) critique of the meaning of "outdoors" in adventure programming. These authors argue that many outdoor researchers and practitioners have accepted a common language in which the outdoors is a straightforward, uncomplicated place where human encounters can occur in natural, straightforward ways. Thinking of the outdoors as uncomplicated has produced similar thinking about the activity that occurs there. Thus, outdoor adventure program participants reveal their natural selves, engage in more authentic interactions with one another, and

are able to understand their real selves much more clearly than is possible in other (complicated) contexts. The problem for the adventure programming field in this is that the assumption of individual naturalness through the outdoors obscures other possibilities (such as the way many contemporary adventure programming practices assume a norm of white, middle-class affluence) that are then not available as possible program characteristics, processes, or outcomes.

Thinking about outdoors as natural "invokes the assumption of a universalised nature" that is divorced from "social differences such as class, race and gender . . ." (Smith, 1996, p. 41). It supports practices of programming that treat all environments similarly, that overlook human impacts and technologies (e.g., resource use, high-tech equipment), and that are distinct and distant from participants' everyday lives (Beard, 2003). Thinking about outdoors as socially constructed and contested, an unstable concept with multiple definitions produced through multiple social and personal histories, leaves open possibilities for outdoor programming to be socially transformative. Critical social science research seeks to be socially active, to inform and empower social actors (people) so that their understandings of their situations enable them to develop wider ranges of responses in their own interests. In adventure programming, this might mean using the opportunities that adventure activity provides to engage participants in exploring and understanding their experiences of gender, age, ethnicity, sexuality, economic status, and religion and, by doing so, empowering them to transform their lived realities. Going further, critical adventure programming might work at a community level, over an extended period of time, to support individuals (such as at-risk youths) in negotiating new roles for themselves (Deane, Harre, and Moore, 2009; Warren, 2002).

What Can Critical Research in Adventure Programming Do?

Critical research can expose assumptions. It can expose actual networks of influence, activity, and interest, including those of the researchers themselves. It can illuminate the ways in which these interests, activities, and influences bear on particular problems. The knowledge generated can enable social actors (e.g., people involved in the problem) to develop new ways of thinking about and responding to the problem, thus potentially transforming their lives and, ultimately, society. Critical researchers in adventure programming have tackled a wide range of issues, some of which are gender (e.g., Humberstone, 1986, 2000; Kiewa, 2001; Warren, 1996), place (e.g., Wattchow and Brown, 2011), sexuality (e.g., Dignan, 2002), and facilitation (e.g., Stan, 2009) and other topics mentioned elsewhere in this issue.

Early critical education research in the United Kingdom, for example, took to task assumptions about the influence of class on student learning and life chances. Paul Willis' *Learning to Labour* (1977, 1979) illustrates the ways in which working-class schoolboys subverted educationalists' attempts to "rescue" them from following their parents into physical labor. He showed that the boys were not simply inert social objects on which the forces of social reproduction played; rather, they actively produced their own destinies by resisting the interventions intended to improve their life situations. Indeed, they actively projected affinity to class and cynicism toward schooling as a vehicle for social mobility. In a similar vein, adventure programming is not just an exercise in applying an intervention (the program) to subjects (participants) in order to divert them from a life considered less successful. Participants actively create meaning from their outdoor experiences (Davidson, 2001), and they do so in relation to the possibilities offered by their particular social context. Stidder and Haasner (2007) report Jewish and Arab children as young as 10 years old engaging in these processes in their description of cross-cultural reconciliation through adventure education. Leberman (2007) reports that women prisoners have used adventure programs to generate new expectations for their lives while in prison and postrelease. Loynes (2010) argues that "narrative enquiry helps educators to understand the particular meaning of experiences to individuals" (p. 144). He reports that, through telling and retelling their personal stories, marginalized young adults in learner-centered residential adventure programs can construct new ways of living their lives. Story telling gives them "identities, voice and power giving them the potential to support transformative trajectories in their future life paths" (p. 143). Further, Zink's (2005) work, following the critical theorist Michel Foucault, shows how outdoor education students position themselves in relation to teachers and to activities by enacting information gleaned from their social world. The students, she observed, understood that they would gain enhanced confidence from participating in challenging activities. Further, they understood

that their role as students was to report *expected* outcomes (such as enhanced confidence) from their experiences. Zink (2005) states, "students have to take care in the ways they express the meanings they construct for these to count as learning within the discourses of outdoor education" (pp. 17-18).

Focusing on language can expose networks of influence. Critical social research asks whose interests are served by use of particular words and names (such as "adventure") in particular contexts. Put another way, they seek to expose the work such terms perform in the social sphere in which they are used. In an example drawn from the sociology of race, McLaren (1997) notes that critical researchers have shown how meanings associated with the terms "negro" and "black" have been used for different purposes at different times in the United States (and, it should be noted, elsewhere). In the 1960s, "negro" signified natural and unchanging difference to the dominant white culture and was used to justify institutional racism. More recently, "black" has been taken as a signifier of crime and social dysfunction, thus potentially working against those who identify with their ethnic heritage and experience by legitimate means (McLaren, 1997). Ethnicity, race, and culture have received very little attention by adventure programming researchers and are ripe for extensive investigation. The few existing studies point out that it is sometimes the absence of words and terms relating to ethnicity that illuminates the dominant white, Anglo Saxon network of influence in this field in many Western, English-speaking nations. Wattchow (2004) notes the almost complete absence of indigenous Maori "voices" during a paddling expedition to the South Island of New Zealand. In contrast, Hamilton (2003) exposes the use of terms and stereotypical images relating to indigenous North Americans in Ontario summer camps as another way that the interests of nonindigenous camp stakeholders are maintained relative to those of the indigenous population. Lowan (2009), however, deliberately emphasizes indigenous terms in a report on research into indigenous perspectives on place in outdoor programming; in doing so, he challenges the dominance of nonindigenous networks of influence and fosters the interests of people in those networks.

Another example examines the language of danger in adventure programming as a means by which to promote the interests of some groups over others. Brookes' (1997) reading of adventure programming texts and newsletters from one commercial emergency-response organization illuminates various ways that one can understand the need for first aid qualifications. In one reading, first aid qualifications enable outdoor practitioners working with groups to operate as singular, heroic field leaders who come to the aid of their injured, passive, and helpless participants. In another reading, advanced first aid qualifications equip professional, highly trained paramedics to swoop in from outside the group to effect rescue and retrieval. Less apparent in the first aid discourses is the possibility of a community of skilled participants who can look after one another's needs and perhaps even organize their activity in such as way as to reduce the potential for physical injury (i.e., "low" adventure rather than "high" adventure).

Critical research illuminates and problematizes uncontested assumptions, including those that are inherent in some outcomes-based research. Program evaluations that aim to measure learning outcomes from challenge activities, for example, tend to take for granted the well-promoted centrality of risk to the process of learning (see, for example, Miles and Priest, 1999; Mortlock, 1984; Priest and Gass, 2005; Wurdinger, 1997), but the relationship between risk and learning is neither clear nor uncontested (Brown and Fraser, 2009; Wolfe and Samdahl, 2005). Wolfe and Samdahl (2005) question whether even the best instructors can manage risk situations so that all learners experience optimal challenge for their particular learning needs. This would require the instructor to intuit what level and type of risk learners perceive, to moderate the activity and environment accordingly, and to do so simultaneously for all learners. In adventure activities, high levels of instructor control required to manage risk inevitably reduce possibilities for participants to manage risk themselves, thus reducing the potential learning from exposure to risk. Studies have not empirically examined what learning is going on in instructor-managed situations, but Brown and Fraser (2009) argue that it is likely to

> provide learners with a "do" or "not do" binary. Either they take the risk (and hopefully succeed) or do not (and are found wanting). Little in the way of growth and learning opportunities are afforded in such artificial situations that in effect, do not require significant decision-making by the learner, and thus no ownership of consequences. (p. 70)

Without ownership of consequences, little or no learning takes place. Risk in adventure programming is "presented all too often as a central 'good'

for all learners at all times" (Brown and Fraser, 2009, p. 69), but this assumption does not hold up well under close scrutiny. As examples, survivors of domestic violence or immigrant refugees from war-torn nations may not benefit from exposure to risk activities; rather, they may be further traumatized. Similarly, individuals who relish risk, such as delinquent youths and corporate financiers, may not have much to learn from risk in challenging outdoor activities and further encouragement to take risks may ultimately harm them and others (Wolfe and Samdahl, 2005). These are not arguments refuting *any* role for risk in outdoor learning, but rather are arguments for more nuanced, fine-tuned understandings of that role with respect to the particular contexts in which adventure programming operates.

Experience is a central tenet of adventure programming, yet critical research contests it, too (Bell, 1993; Fox, 2008). Roberts (2008) offers three variations of experience. He uses the term "variations as opposed to stages or traditions" (Roberts, 2008, p. 31) in order to avoid suggesting an unwarranted permanence or continuity.

The first variation is Dewey's "interactive experience" in which "the past and present interact to create a future, and the meaning of such interaction is directly correlative to the connections we make in the process" (p. 21). This variation values social action for democracy and is expressed in familiar ways through outdoor programs that emphasize group processes, cooperation, and teamwork.

The second variation emphasizes personal, sensory, and spiritual experience. In this phenomenological approach, "an individual ought to have direct experience that is transformative [and] thus set apart as a qualitatively better way of knowing and acting" (p. 25). Programs focusing on engagement with the natural world, solo components of programs, and journeys to very novel, exotic locations are expressions of this meaning of experience.

Roberts' third variation springs from critical theory, in which experience is viewed politically as a means by which individuals can engage with and potentially alter the injustices in their lives (injustices perpetrated by them as well as injustices visited upon them). To date, few if any adventure programs appear to operate with this variation of experience, yet they offer great potential for advancing the cause of social justice. It should be apparent at this point that experience is not a simple concept, nor is it the same for everyone. Research into adventure program experiences can be complicated, convoluted, multifaceted, and messy but nonetheless is essential for understanding what goes on in adventure programs.

Critical Adventure Programming Research in the Current Political Climate

Critical research is neither superior nor inferior to other forms of research, but it is arguably more important than other forms of research to adventure programming at the present time. At present, a trend exists in some Western nations (especially the United States, United Kingdom, Australia, and New Zealand) toward prioritizing experimental education research and evaluating the effectiveness of education programs, including adventure programs. This trend is an understandable response to governmental demands for evidence-based funding in the face of public criticism of expenditure (Lather, 2006). However, as the preceding discussion shows, effectiveness studies and outcomes-based research focus on end products of assumed processes. Assumptions about what is meant by "adventure" and "outdoors," about what constitutes experience and how students can speak about experience, and about the role of risk all undermine any claims outcomes-based research can make about the effects of adventure programming on individuals and groups. In a climate of reducing financial support, then, it is better to spend precious research money on research that can uncover meanings buried within adventure programming activity than to spend it studying estimations of reality that are known to be flawed.

Further, at this stage in the development of adventure programming, critical research is essential for its ability to inform transformation of the field. In an era when the social, political, and environmental costs of human activity need urgent attention, adventure programming risks relegation to the scrap heap of anachronism, a relic of a time when individualism, materialism, and unbridled consumption reigned supreme. There is now greater expectation on educators that their programs will engage with current problems and help forge a more sustainable future in which people coexist with greater understanding and tolerance of one another and with greater understanding and care for other living organisms. If adventure programming is to respond to this expectation, researchers and practitioners must find ways to engage with particular environments and the particular needs of individual participants. The field of adventure programming can no longer afford to assume that generalized learners will have generalized experiences in generalized outdoor environments from which standardized outcomes result. The specific outcomes that result depend on the particular circumstances of the program. These details urgently need to be explored, and critical research is the way to do it.

Finally, critical research produces not just new knowledge but also new tools to think with. It is important to develop these tools so that adventure programming research can continue to mature. Lather's (2006) concern is that a narrow definition of what constitutes good and valuable education research works to constrain thinking about what education is, what it can achieve, and how it can operate. Outcomes-based research may be directly useful in policy contexts but does not make for either good policy or good research (Lather, 2004). Outcomes-based research might find that adventure programs enhance self-concept (Hattie et al., 1997), for example, but it does not go further. Critical research can provide nuanced understandings of what "self" means to participants and thereby stimulate new thinking about how the self is portrayed, constructed, expressed, and possibly transformed during adventure programs.

Conclusion

Critical research is essential to the development of emerging fields of research such as adventure programming. It is particularly important in times of financial stringency, when every dollar spent must contribute to advancing sound knowledge relevant to the field. Critical research questions the taken-for-granted ideas on which much outcomes-based research rests. Among these untested ideas are those of a universal outdoors and a universal environment, both devoid of locally relevant detail. There are also untested assumptions that participants' life histories and demographic characteristics are irrelevant to their experiences with adventure programming, that experience is neither person- nor context-specific, and that participants are largely passive recipients of program interventions. By testing these and other assumptions and teasing out the multiple, nuanced meanings associated with adventure programming, critical research provides the essential service of strengthening the foundation for subsequent outcomes-based studies. More importantly, critical research illuminates the political dimensions of knowledge production in adventure program research and practice. This enables researchers and practitioners to understand the context within which adventure programming occurs and to respond to whatever challenges it presents.

References

Beard, C. (2003). The circle and the square: Nature and artificial environments. In B. Humberstone, H. Brown, & K. Richards (Eds.), *Whose journeys? The outdoors and adventure as social and cultural phenomena. Critical explorations or relations between individuals, 'others', and the environment* (pp. 187-198). Penrith, U.K.: The Institute for Outdoor Learning.

Bell, M. (1993). What constitutes experience? Rethinking theoretical assumptions. *Journal of Experiential Education, 16*(1), 19-24.

Brookes, A. (1997). You'll be in constant danger, and loving it. In T. Gray & B. Hayllar (Eds.), *Catalysts for change. Papers from the 10th National Outdoor Education Conference* (pp. 43-49). Sydney, Australia: The Outdoor Professionals/AOEC/University of Wollongong/University of Technology Sydney.

Brookes, A. (2002). Lost in the Australian bush: Outdoor education as curriculum. *Journal of Curriculum Studies, 34*(4), 405-425.

Brown, M., & Fraser, D. (2009). Re-evaluation risk and exploring educational alternatives. *Journal of Adventure Education and Outdoor Learning, 9*(1), 61-77.

Carr, W., & Kemmis, S. (1986). *Becoming critical. Education, knowledge and action research*. London: Falmer Press.

Davidson, L. (2001). Qualitative research and making meaning from adventure: A case study of boys' experiences of outdoor education at school. *Journal of Adventure Education and Outdoor Learning, 1*(2), 11-20.

Deane, K.L., Harre, N., & Moore, J. (2009). *Individual growth in a community-based youth development program*. Paper presented at the 117th Annual Convention of the American Psychological Association, Toronto, Ontario, Canada.

Dignan, A. (2002). Outdoor education and the reinforcement of heterosexuality. *Australian Journal of Outdoor Education, 6*(2), 77-80.

Fox, K. (2008). Rethinking experience: What do we mean by this word 'experience'? *Journal of Experiential Education, 31*(1), 36-54.

Hamilton, T. (2003). The representation and appropriation of indigenous cultures at Ontario summer camps. *The Ontario Journal of Outdoor Education, 15*(1), 9-15.

Hattie, J., Marsh, H.W., Neill, J.T., & Richards, G.E. (1997). Adventure education and Outward Bound: Out-of-class experiences that make a lasting difference. *Review of Educational Research, 67*(1), 43-87.

Humberstone, B. (1986). Learning for a change: A study of gender and schooling in outdoor education. In J. Evans (Ed.), *Physical education, sport and schooling—Studies in the sociology of physical education* (pp. 195-215). Lewes, U.K.: Falmer Press.

Humberstone, B. (2000). *Her outdoors: Risk, challenge and adventure in gendered open spaces*. Monograph 66. Brighton, U.K.: Leisure Studies Association.

Kiewa, J. (2001). Stepping around things: Gender relationships in climbing. *Australian Journal of Outdoor Education, 5*(2), 4-12.

Kincheloe, J.L., & McLaren, P.L. (1994). Rethinking critical theory and qualitative research. In N.K. Denzin & Y.S. Lincoln (Eds.), *Handbook of qualitative research* (pp. 138-157). London: Sage.

Lather, P. (2004). Scientific research in education: A critical perspective. *British Educational Research Journal, 30*(6), 759-772.

Lather, P. (2006). Paradigm proliferation as a good thing to think with: Teaching research in education as a wild profusion. *International Journal of Qualitative Studies in Education, 19*(1), 35-57.

Leberman, S. (2007). Voices behind the walls: Female offenders and experiential learning. *Journal of Adventure Education and Outdoor Learning, 7*(2), 113-129.

Lowan, G. (2009). Exploring place from an Aboriginal perspective: Considerations for outdoor and environmental education. *Canadian Journal of Environmental Education, 14*, 42-58.

Loynes, C. (2010). Journeys of transition: The role of narrative within the Stoneleigh Project. *Journal of Adventure Education and Outdoor Leadership, 10*(2), 127-145.

Lynch, P., & Moore, K. (2004). Adventures in paradox. *Australian Journal of Outdoor Education, 8*(2), 3-12.

Martin, P. (2004). Outdoor adventure in promoting relationships with nature. *Australian Journal of Outdoor Education, 8*(1), 20-28.

McLaren, P. (1997). Multiculturalism and postmodern critique: Toward a pedagogy of resistance and transformation. In A.H. Halsey, H. Lauder, P. Brown, & A.S. Wells (Eds.), *Education: Culture, economy and society* (pp. 520-540). Ney York: Oxford University Press.

Miles, J.C., & Priest, S. (Eds.). (1999). *Adventure programming*. State College, PA: Venture.

Mortlock, C. (1984). *The adventure alternative*. Milnthorpe, U.K.: Cicerone Press.

Priest, S., & Gass, M.A. (2005). *Effective leadership in adventure programming*. 2nd ed. Champaign, IL: Human Kinetics.

Roberts, J. (2008). From experience to neo-experiential education: Variations on a theme. *Journal of Experiential Education, 31*(1), 19-35.

Smith, N. (1996). The production of nature. In G. Robertson, M. Mash, L. Tickner, J. Bird, B. Curtis, & T. Putnam (Eds.), *FutureNatural: Nature, science, culture* (pp. 35-54). London: Routledge.

Stan, I. (2009). Recontextualising the role of the facilitator in group interaction in the outdoor classroom.

Journal of Adventure Education and Outdoor Learning, 9(1), 23-43.

Stewart, A. (2004). Decolonising encounters with the Murray River: Building place responsive outdoor education. *Australian Journal of Outdoor Education, 8*(2), 46-55.

Stidder, G., & Haasner, A. (2007). Developing outdoor and adventurous activities for co-existence and reconciliation in Israel: An Anglo-German approach. *Journal of Adventure Education and Outdoor Learning, 7*(2), 131-140.

Warren, K. (1996). Women's outdoor adventures: Myth and reality. In K. Warren (Ed.), *Women's voices in experiential education*. Dubuque, IA: Kendall/Hunt.

Warren, K. (2002). Preparing the next generation: Social justice in outdoor leadership education and training. *The Journal of Experiential Education, 25*(1), 231-238.

Wattchow, B. (2004). Many voices speak the river: Education in an adventure-river-landscape. *Educational Insights, 9*(1). www.ccfi.educ.ubc.ca/publication/insights/v09n01/articles/wattchow.html [September 15, 2010].

Wattchow, B., & Brown, M. (2011). *A pedagogy of place. Outdoor education for a changing world*. Melbourne, Australia: Monash University Press.

Willis, E. (1999). *The sociological quest. An introduction to the study of social life*. 3rd ed. St Leonards, New South Wales, Australia: Allen and Unwin.

Willis, P. (1977). *Learning to labour: How working class kids get working class jobs*. Farnborough, U.K.: Saxon House.

Willis, P. (1979). *Learning to labour*. Aldershot, U.K.: Gator.

Wolfe, B.D., & Samdahl, D.M. (2005). Challenging assumptions: Examining fundamental beliefs that shape challenge course programming and research. *Journal of Experiential Education, 28*(1), 25-43.

Wurdinger, S.D. (1997). *Philosophical issues in adventure education*. 3rd ed. Dubuque, IA: Kendall/Hunt.

Zink, R. (2005). Maybe what they say is what they experience: Taking students' words seriously. *Australian Journal of Outdoor Education, 9*(2), 14-20.

Zink, R., & Burrows, L. (2008). "Is what you see what you get?" The production of knowledge in-between the indoors and the outdoors in outdoor education. *Physical Education and Sport Pedagogy, 13*(3), 251-265.

About the Editors

Bruce Martin, PhD, is an associate professor in the department of recreation and sport pedagogy at Ohio University in Athens, Ohio. Before joining the faculty at Ohio University, he taught at the University of Northern Colorado and Sheldon Jackson College in Sitka, Alaska.

Martin's teaching and research interests are focused on the practice of outdoor leadership and adventure programming. At Ohio University, Martin teaches courses that help students develop the knowledge, skills, and dispositions required for effective professional practice in the fields of outdoor leadership and adventure programming. He is an author of the text *Outdoor Leadership: Theory and Practice* (Human Kinetics, 2006) and has authored numerous publications related to the practice of outdoor leadership and adventure programming.

Martin has more than 20 years of experience as an outdoor and adventure programming professional. He has worked as a camp counselor, professional river guide, and Outward Bound instructor. He is a member of the Association for Experiential Education (AEE), the Wilderness Education Association (WEA), the American Canoe Association (ACA), and Leave No Trace Center for Outdoor Ethics (LNT). He currently holds ACA certifications as a level 4 river kayak instructor trainer and level 4 coastal kayak instructor. He is a certifying instructor for the WEA and LNT master educator instructor program.

Martin earned his PhD in social foundations of education from the University of Virginia. He earned two master's degrees, one in experiential education from Minnesota State University at Mankato and another in human dimensions of natural resources from Colorado State University at Fort Collins. He earned his bachelor's degree in history from Virginia Commonwealth University.

In his free time, Martin enjoys helping his daughters develop an appreciation for the wild outdoors. He also enjoys recreational boating and reading. Martin resides in Athens, Ohio.

Mark Wagstaff, EdD, is a professor in the department of recreation, parks, and tourism at Radford University in Radford, Virginia, where he coordinates the outdoor recreation concentration. He is a coauthor of *Outdoor Leadership: Theory and Practice* (Human Kinetics, 2006); *Backcountry Classroom: Lessons, Tools and Activities for Teaching Outdoor Leaders* (Globe Pequot Press, 2005); and *Technical Skills for Adventure Programming* (Human Kinetics, 2009).

In addition to teaching adventure programming at the college level since 1997, Wagstaff has experience as a professional river guide, North Carolina Outward Bound School field instructor, and Wilderness Education Association instructor. He is a member of the Association for Experiential Education, Wilderness Education Association, American Canoe Association, and Leave No Trace Center for Outdoor Ethics. He is also a certifying instructor for the WEA and LNT master educator instructor program.

Wagstaff received his bachelor's and master's degrees in recreation from North Carolina State University. He earned his doctorate in education from Oklahoma State University, where he also coordinated the campus outdoor recreation program.

Wagstaff resides in Christiansburg, Virginia. He enjoys whitewater canoeing, fly fishing, and upland bird hunting.

You'll find other outstanding
recreation resources at
www.HumanKinetics.com

In the U.S. call 1.800.747.4457
Australia 08 8372 0999
Canada. 1.800.465.7301
Europe . . . . . +44 (0) 113 255 5665
New Zealand 0800 222 062

HUMAN KINETICS
The Information Leader in Physical Activity & Health
P.O. Box 5076 • Champaign, IL 61825-5076